0°
30°E
90°E
120°E
150°E
ARCTIC OCEAN
Arctic Circle
NORWAY
SWEDEN
FINLAND
ESTONIA
LATVIA
LITHUANIA
BELARUS
RUSSIA
UNITED KINGDOM
DENMARK
RUS.
IRELAND
NETH.
BELG.
GER.
POLAND
CZ. REP.
UKRAINE
MOLDOVA
AUS.
SLOV.
HUNG.
FRANCE
SWITZ.
SLO.
CRO.
ROM.
GEORGIA
BOS. & HERZ.
SERB.
BUL.
F.Y.R.O.M.
ARMENIA
PORTUGAL
SPAIN
ITALY
ALB.
GREECE
TURKEY
AZERBAIJAN
KAZAKHSTAN
UZBEKISTAN
TURKMENISTAN
KYRGYZSTAN
TAJIKISTAN
MONGOLIA
N. KOREA
S. KOREA
JAPAN
CHINA
MOROCCO
TUNISIA
MALTA
CYPRUS
LEB.
ISRAEL
SYRIA
IRAQ
IRAN
AFGHANISTAN
KUWAIT
BAHRAIN
QATAR
JORDAN
PAKISTAN
NEPAL
BHUTAN
30°N
ALGERIA
LIBYA
EGYPT
SAUDI ARABIA
WESTERN SAHARA
MAURITANIA
Tropic of Cancer
TAIWAN
INDIA
BURMA
LAOS
UNITED ARAB EMIRATES
OMAN
YEMEN
PACIFIC OCEAN
MALI
NIGER
CHAD
SUDAN
ERITREA
DJIBOUTI
BANGLADESH
THAILAND
VIETNAM
PHILIPPINES
CAMBODIA
1.
2.
3.
4.
5.
6.
7.
8.
9.
10.
11.
12.
NIGERIA
C.A.R.
ETHIOPIA
SOMALIA
SRI LANKA
BRUNEI
MALAYSIA
PALAU
EQUATORIAL GUINEA
SÃO TOMÉ AND PRÍNCIPE
GABON
CONGO
ZAIRE
UGANDA
KENYA
SINGAPORE
Equator
NAURU
0°
RWANDA
BURUNDI
MALDIVES
SUMATRA
INDONESIA
PAPUA NEW GUINEA
Cabinda (ANGOLA)
TANZANIA
SEYCHELLES
DIEGO GARCIA
JAVA
TIMOR
SOLOMON IS.
ANGOLA
MALAWI
ZAMBIA
MOZAMBIQUE
INDIAN OCEAN
MADAGASCAR
NAMIBIA
ZIMBABWE
BOTSWANA
Tropic of Capricorn
MAURITIUS
AUSTRALIA
SOUTH AFRICA
SWAZILAND
LESOTHO
30°S
1. SENEGAL
2. GAMBIA
3. GUINEA BISSAU
4. GUINEA
5. SIERRA LEONE
6. LIBERIA
7. CÔTE D'IVOIRE
8. GHANA
9. TOGO
10. BENIN
11. BURKINA FASO
12. CAMEROON
60°S
Antarctic Circle

Cultural Anthropology

A GLOBAL PERSPECTIVE FOURTH EDITION

RAYMOND SCUPIN

Lindenwood University

PRENTICE HALL
Upper Saddle River, New Jersey 07458

Library of Congress Cataloging-in-Publication Data

Scupin, Raymond.
    Cultural anthropology: a global perspective / Raymond Scupin. —
      4th ed.
      p.   cm.
    Includes bibliographical references and index.
    ISBN 0-13-082576-X
      1. Ethnology.   I. Title.
   GN316.S39   2000
   306—dc21   99-38544
                                      CIP

Editorial Director: Charlyce Jones Owen
Editor-in-Chief: Nancy Roberts
Managing Editor: Sharon Chambliss
AVP, Director of Production and Manufacturing: Barbara Kittle
Production Liaison: Fran Russello
Project Manager: Marianne Hutchinson (Pine Tree
   Composition, Inc.)
Manufacturing Manager: Nick Sklitsis
Prepress and Manufacturing Buyer: Ben Smith
Creative Design Director: Leslie Osher
Interior and Cover Design: Thomas Nery
Cover Art: David Buffington/PhotoDisk, Inc.
Director, Image Resource Center: Melinda Reo
Manager, Rights and Permissions: Kay Dellosa
Image Specialist: Beth Boyd
Photo Researcher: Teri Stratford
Art Director: Nancy Wells
Line Art Coordinator: Guy Ruggiero
Electronic Art Creation: ElectraGraphics
Marketing Manager: Christopher DeJohn
Copy Editing: Kathryn Beck
Proofreading: Pine Tree Composition, Inc.

This book was set in 10/12 Garamond Light by
Pine Tree Composition, Inc., and was printed
and bound by Courier Companies, Inc.
The cover was printed by Phoenix Color Corp.

Printed in the United States of America
10 9 8 7 6 5 4 3 2

ISBN 0-13-082576-X

Prentice-Hall International (UK) Limited, *London*
Prentice-Hall of Australia Pty. Limited, *Sydney*
Prentice-Hall Canada Inc., *Toronto*
Prentice-Hall Hispanoamericana, S.A., *Mexico*
Prentice-Hall of India Private Limited, *New Delhi*
Prentice-Hall of Japan, Inc., *Tokyo*
Prentice-Hall Asia Pte. Ltd., *Singapore*
Editora Prentice-Hall do Brasil, Ltda., *Rio de Janeiro*

Brief Contents

PART I

BASIC CONCEPTS IN ANTHROPOLOGY

1 Introduction to Anthropology   1
2 Human Evolution   20

PART II

BASIC CONCEPTS OF CULTURE AND SOCIETY

3 Culture   37
4 The Process of Enculturation   62
5 Language   90
6 Anthropological Explanations   118
7 Analyzing Sociocultural Systems   133

PART III

PRESTATE SOCIETIES

8 Band Societies   160
9 Tribes   183
10 Chiefdoms   214

PART IV

STATE SOCIETIES

11 Agricultural States   234
12 Industrial States   255

PART V

CONSEQUENCES OF GLOBALIZATION

13 Globalization and Aboriginal Peoples   284
14 Globalization in Latin America, Africa,
   and the Caribbean   310
15 Globalization in the Middle East
   and Asia   340

PART VI

ANTHROPOLOGY AND THE GLOBAL FUTURE

16 Contemporary Global Trends   369
17 Applied Anthropology   394

Contents

Boxes   xv

Preface   xvii

About the Author   xxiii

PART I

BASIC CONCEPTS IN ANTHROPOLOGY

1 Introduction to Anthropology   1

Anthropology: The Four Subfields   3
Physical Anthropology   4
Archaeology   6
Linguistic Anthropology   8
Ethnology   10
Holistic Anthropology, Interdisciplinary
  Research, and the Global Perspective   10
Applied Anthropology   12
Anthropology and Science   12
The Scientific Method   13
Limits of Science   14
Anthropology and the Humanities   15
Why Study Anthropology?   16
Critical Thinking and Global Awareness   16
Summary   17
Study Questions   18
Key Terms   18
Internet Exercises   18
Suggested Readings   19

2 Human Evolution   20

Theories of Evolution   21
Origin Myths   21
The Darwinian Revolution   22
Principles of Inheritance   23
The Evolution of Life   23
Hominid Evolution   24
Australopithecus   24
Homo habilis   25
Homo erectus   25

Archaic Homo sapiens   26
Modern Homo sapiens   27
Modern *Homo sapiens* Culture:
  The Upper Paleolithic   28
Tools   28
Variation in the Upper Paleolithic
  Technologies   29
Upper Paleolithic Subsistence and Social
  Organization   29
The Upper Paleolithic in Europe   30
Migration of Upper Paleolithic Humans   31
Human Variation   32
Skin Color   32
Summary   34
Study Questions   35
Key Terms   35
Internet Exercises   35
Suggested Readings   36

PART II

BASIC CONCEPTS OF CULTURE AND SOCIETY

3 Culture   37

The Characteristics of Culture   38
Culture Is Learned   39
Symbols and Symbolic Learning   39
Culture Is Shared   41
The Components of Culture   41
Values   44
Beliefs   44
Norms   45
Ideal versus Real Culture   48
Cultural Diversity   48
Food and Adaptation   49
Dress Codes and Symbolism   50
Race, Racism, and Culture   51
Racism in Western Society   51
Critiques of Scientific Racism   53
Race and Intelligence   53
The Cultural and Social Significance of Race   55
Ethnicity   55

Ethnicity: Two Anthropological Perspectives 56
Cultural Universals 58
Summary 59
Study Questions 60
Key Terms 60
Internet Exercises 61
Suggested Readings 61

4 The Process of Enculturation **62**

Biology versus Culture 64
Instincts and Human Nature 64
Human Beings as Animals 64
Instincts in Animals 65
Instincts and Learned Behaviors 65
Do Humans Possess Instincts? 66
Drives 66
Culture versus Instinct 66
Enculturation: Culture and Personality 67
Early Studies of Enculturation 67
Childhood Training 70
Psychoanalytic Approaches in Anthropology 73
Sigmund Freud 73
Understanding Incest Avoidance and the
  Incest Taboo 76
Biological Explanations of Incest Avoidance 76
Marital Alliance and the Incest Taboo 77
Childhood Familiarity Hypothesis 77
Incest Avoidance: Interactionist Perspectives 78
Enculturation and the Sex Drive 78
Codes of Sexual Behavior 78
Homosexual Behavior 79
Enculturation and Cognition 80
Structuralism 80
Jean Piaget 80
Evolutionary Psychology 82
Enculturation and Emotions 83
Culture and Mental Illness 84
What Is Abnormal? 84
Culture-Specific Disorders 85
The Limits of Enculturation 86
Unique Biological Tendencies 86
Individual Variation 86
Summary 87
Study Questions 88
Key Terms 88
Internet Exercises 88
Suggested Readings 88

5 Language **90**

Nonhuman Communication 92
Teaching Apes to Sign 92
Ape Sign Language Reexamined 92

Ethological Research on Ape Communication 93
Animal Communication and Human Language 94
Productivity 94
Displacement 94
Arbitrariness 94
Combining Sounds to Produce Meanings 95
The Evolution of Language 95
The Anatomy of Language 95
The Structure of Language 97
Phonology 97
Syntax 98
Semantics 99
Language Acquisition 100
Chomsky on Language Acquisition 100
Language, Thought, and Culture 106
The Sapir–Whorf Hypothesis 106
Historical Linguistics 108
The Family-Tree Model 108
Assessing Language Change 110
Sociolinguistics 110
Dialectal Differences in Spoken Language 110
Honorifics in Language 111
Greeting Behaviors 111
Nonverbal Communication 113
Kinesics 113
Proxemics 114
Summary 115
Study Questions 116
Key Terms 116
Internet Exercises 116
Suggested Readings 117

6 Anthropological Explanations **118**

Nineteenth-Century Evolutionism 119
Unilineal Evolution: Tylor 120
Unilineal Evolution: Morgan 120
Unilineal Evolution: A Critique 121
Diffusionism 121
British Diffusionism 121
German Diffusionism 121
The Limitations and Strengths of Diffusionism 121
Historical Particularism 122
Boas versus the Unilineal Evolutionists 122
Functionalism: British Anthropology 123
Structural Functionalism:
  Radcliffe-Brown 123
Psychological Functionalism: Malinowski 123
The Limitations of Functionalism 124
Twentieth-Century Evolutionism 124
Steward and Cultural Ecology 125
The Strengths of Neoevolutionism 125
Criticisms of Cultural Ecology 126
Cultural Materialism 126
Marxist Anthropology 127

Evaluation of Marxist Anthropology 127
Sociobiology 128
  A Case Study: Sexual Behavior 128
  Inclusive Fitness and Kin Selection 128
  Sociobiology: A Critique 129
Symbolic Anthropology 129
  Criticisms of Symbolic Anthropology 130
Materialism versus Culturalism 130
Summary 130
Study Questions 131
Key Terms 132
Internet Exercises 132
Suggested Readings 132

7 Analyzing Sociocultural Systems **133**

Ethnological Fieldwork 134
  Ethnological Research and Strategies 135
  Ethics in Anthropological Research 140
  Analysis of Ethnological Data 140
Variables Studied by Ethnologists 141
Subsistence and the Physical Environment 141
  Modern Cultural Ecology 141
  Biomes 142
  Subsistence Patterns and Environments 142
Demography 142
  Fertility, Mortality, and Migration 142
  Population and Environment 144
  Population and Culture 145
Technology 145
  Anthropological Explanations of Technology 145
Economy 146
  The Formalist Approach 146
  The Substantivist Approach 146
  Modern Economic Anthropology 146
Social Structure 147
  Components of Social Structure 147
  The Family 148
  Marriage 148
  Gender 148
  Age 150
Political Organization 151
  Types of Political Systems 152
  Decision Making in a Political System 152
  Warfare and Feuds 152
  Law and Social Control 153
Religion 154
  Myths 154
  Rituals 155
  Religious Specialists 155
  Religious Movements 156
Cross-Cultural Research 156
Summary 157
Study Questions 157

Key Terms 158
Internet Exercises 158
Suggested Readings 159

PART III

PRESTATE SOCIETIES

8 Band Societies **160**

Modern Foraging Environments
  and Subsistence 162
  Deserts 162
  Tropical Rain Forests 163
  Arctic Regions 164
  Mobility and Subsistence 165
  Optimal Foraging Theory 165
Foragers and Demographic Conditions 165
  Fissioning 166
  Infanticide 166
  Fertility Rates 166
Technology in Foraging Societies 167
Economics in Foraging Societies 167
  Reciprocity 168
  Collective Ownership of Property 169
  The Original Affluent Society? 169
  The Affluence Hypothesis Challenged 170
Social Organization in Foraging Societies 170
  Marriage and Kinship 171
  Gender 173
  Age 174
Political Organization in Foraging Societies 176
  Characteristics of Leadership 176
  Warfare and Violence 177
  Conflict Resolution 178
Religion in Foraging Societies 178
  The Dreamtime 178
  Eskimo Religion 179
  Art, Music, and Religion 179
Summary 181
Study Questions 181
Key Terms 182
Internet Exercises 182
Suggested Readings 182

9 Tribes **183**

Environment and Subsistence
  for Horticulturalists 185
  Amazon Horticulturalists: The Yanomamö 186
  New Guinea Horticulturalists: The Tsembaga 187
  *Horticulturalists in Woodland Forest
    Areas: The Iroquois* 187

x   Contents

Environment and Subsistence for Pastoralists   187
  East African Cattle Complex   188
Demographics and Settlement   188
Technology   189
  Horticultural Technology   189
  Pastoralist Technology   190
Economics   190
  Money   190
  Property Ownership   191
Social Organization   191
  Families   191
  Descent Groups   192
  Functions of Descent Groups   194
  Marriage   194
  Gender   198
  Age   200
Political Organization   202
  Sodalities   202
  How Leaders Are Chosen   202
  Pastoralist Tribal Politics   203
  Explaining Tribal Warfare   204
  Law and Conflict Resolution   205
Religion   208
  Animism and Shamanism in South America   208
  Witchcraft and Sorcery   208
  Familistic Religion   209
Art and Music   210
  Musical Traditions   210
Summary   211
Study Questions   211
Key Terms   212
Internet Exercises   212
Suggested Readings   212

10 Chiefdoms   **214**

Enviornment, Subsistence, and Demography   216
  Pacific Island Chiefdoms   216
  African Chiefdoms   216
  Native American Chiefdoms   217
  Demography   218
Technology   219
  Housing   219
Political Economy   220
  Food Storage   220
  Property Ownership   220
  The Evolution of Chiefdoms   220
  Economic Exchange   221
Social Organization   225
  Rank and Sumptuary Rules   225
  Marriage   227
  General Social Principles   227
  Gender   228
  Age   228

Slavery   228
Law and Religion   229
  Law   229
  Religion   229
  A Case Study: Law and Religion in Polynesia   229
  Shamanism   230
  Human Sacrifice   230
Art, Architecture, and Music   230
  Music   231
Summary   232
Study Questions   232
Key Terms   233
Internet Exercises   233
Suggested Readings   233

PART IV

STATE SOCIETIES

11 Agricultural States   **234**

Demography   236
Technology   237
  Agricultural Innovations   237
  The Diffusion of Technology   238
Political Economy   239
  The Division of Labor   239
  Property Rights   239
  The Command Economy versus the Entrepreneur   240
  The Peasantry   240
  Trade and Monetary Exchange   241
Social Organization   242
  Kinship and Status   242
  Marriage   243
  Gender, Subsistence, and Status   244
Social Stratification   245
  The Caste System   245
  Racial and Ethnic Stratification   246
Law   246
  Mediation and Self-Help   247
Warfare   247
Religion   249
  Ecclesiastical Religions   249
  Universalistic Religions   249
  Divine Rulers, Priests, and Religious Texts   249
The Collapse of State Societies   249
  Reasons for Collapse   250
  Evaluating Theories   252
Summary   252
Study Questions   253
Key Terms   254

Internet Exercises   254
Suggested Readings   254

12 Industrial States   255

The Commercial, Scientific,
   and Industrial Revolution   257
   Modernization   258
Environment and Energy Use   258
Demographic Change   259
   The Demographic Transition   259
   Urbanization   259
Technology and Economic Change   260
   Technology and Work   260
   The Division of Labor   260
   Economic Exchange   261
   Perspectives on Market Economies   262
   The Evolution of Economic Organizations   266
Social Structure   267
   Kinship   267
   Family   267
   Marriage   268
   Gender   269
   Age   271
Social Stratification   272
   The British Class System   272
   Class in the United States   273
   Class in Japan and the Former Soviet Union   273
   Ethnic and Racial Stratification   274
Political Organization   275
   Political Organization in Socialist States   275
   Industrialism and State Bureaucracy   277
Law   278
   Japanese Law   278
Warfare and Industrial Technology   278
Religion   279
   Religion in Socialist States   280
   Religion in Japan   281
Summary   281
Study Questions   282
Key Terms   282
Internet Exercises   282
Suggested Readings   283

PART V

CONSEQUENCES OF GLOBALIZATION

13 Globalization and Aboriginal Peoples   284

Globalization: Theoretical Approaches   285
   Modernization Theory   285

First, Second, and Third Worlds   286
Dependency Theory   288
World-Systems Theory   289
Anthropological Analysis and Globalization   291
Globalization and Prestate Societies   292
Vanishing Foragers   292
   The Ju/'hoansi Foragers   292
   The Dobe Ju/'hoansi   293
   The Mbuti Pygmies   293
   The Ik   294
   The Siriono   295
Tribes in Transition   295
   North American Horticulturalists   295
   South American Horticulturalists   297
   Pastoralist Tribes   298
Chiefdoms in Transition   299
Forms of Resistance in Native Societies   301
   Revitalization Among Native Americans   301
   Melanesia and New Guinea: The Cargo Cults   302
   A Hawaiian Religious Renaissance   304
A Lost Opportunity   305
   A Case Study: Native American Knowledge   306
   Preserving Indigenous Societies   306
Summary   308
Study Questions   308
Key Terms   309
Internet Exercises   309
Suggested Readings   309

**14 Globalization in Latin America,
   Africa, and the Caribbean   310**

Globalization and Colonialism in Latin
   America, Africa, and the Caribbean   312
   Latin America   312
   Africa   312
   The Caribbean   314
Consequences of Globalization
   and Colonialism   315
   Demographic Change   315
   Economic Change   316
   Religious Change   317
Political Changes: Independence
   and Nationalist Movements   322
   Explaining Revolution   324
Uneven Development in Latin America,
   Africa, and the Caribbean   325
   Peripheral Societies   325
   Semiperipheral Societies   326
Ethnological Studies of the Peasantry in Latin
   America, Africa, and the Caribbean   328
   African Peasants: A Unique Phenomenon?   328
Social Structure in Latin America, Africa,
   and the Caribbean   329

Latin American Social Relationships   329
African Social Relationships   330
Patterns of Ethnicity in Latin America, Africa,
   and the Caribbean   331
   Ethnicity in Latin America   331
   Ethnicity in Africa   332
   Ethnicity in the Caribbean   334
Urban Anthropology   336
Summary   337
Study Questions   338
Key Terms   338
Internet Exercises   339
Suggested Readings   339

15 Globalization in the Middle East and Asia   340

Colonialism and Globalization in the Middle
   East and Asia   342
   The Middle East   342
Asia   344
Consequences of Colonialism for the Middle
   East and Asia   345
   Demographic Change   345
   Economic Changes   346
   Religious Change   346
   *Political Change: Independence
   and Nationalism*   347
   Revolutionary Movements in Asia   348
Uneven Development in the Middle East
   and Asia   349
   Oil and the Middle East   349
   Withdrawal from the Global Economy   350
Ethnological Studies of the Societies in the
   Middle East and Asia   351
   A Middle Eastern Village in Transition   351
   Middle Eastern Family, Marriage, and Gender   352
   *Social Structure, Family, and Gender
   in India and Southern Asia*   355
   Family and Gender in China   358
Ethnic Tensions in the Middle East and Asia   359
Islamic Revitalization   362
   A Case Study: The Islamic Revolution in Iran   362
   The Islamic Revolution   363
   Islamic Revitalization in Afghanistan   364
Summary   366
Study Questions   367
Key Terms   368
Internet Exercises   368
Suggested Readings   368

PART VI

ANTHROPOLOGY AND THE GLOBAL FUTURE

16 Contemporary Global Trends   369

Environmental Trends   370
   Mechanized Agriculture and Pollution   371
   Air Pollution   371
Population Trends   371
   The Demographic-Transition Model Applied   372
Technological Change   375
   Energy-Consumption Patterns   375
   Loss of Biodiversity   375
Pessimists versus Optimists
   on Global Issues   376
   The Doomsday Model   376
   The Optimists: The Logic-of-Growth Model   376
   *The Pessimists and the Optimists:
   An Assessment*   377
   The Sustainability Model   380
Economic Trends   380
   Multinational Corporations   380
   Case Study: The Potlatch Corporation   381
   Emerging Economic Trends   382
Political Trends   387
Ethnic Trends   387
Religion and Secularization   390
The Role of Anthropology   391
Summary   392
Study Questions   392
Key Terms   393
Suggested Readings   393

17 Applied Anthropology   394

The Role of Applied Anthropologists
   in Planned Change   395
   The Informant Role   396
   The Facilitator Role   396
   The Analyst Role   397
   The Representative Role   397
   The Future of Applied Anthropology   398
Medical Anthropology   398
Applied Anthropology and Substance Abuse   401
Applied Archaeology: Cultural Resource
   Management   402
   Preserving the Past   403

Cultural Relativism and Human Rights   404
  Relativism Reconsidered   404
  A Resolution to the Problem of Relativism   405
  The Problem of Intervention   406
  Universal Human Rights   406
  The Role of Applied Anthropology   406
Summary   408
Study Questions   408
Key Terms   409

Internet Exercises   409
Suggested Readings   409

Glossary   **411**

References   **420**

Photo Credits   **438**

Index   **439**

Boxes

◎ ANTHROPOLOGISTS AT WORK

C. Loring Brace: Physical Anthropologist   6
Patty Jo Watson: Archaeologist   8
Bambi B. Schieffelin: Linguistic Anthropologist   9
Napoleon Chagnon: Ethnologist   11
The Japanese Corporation: An Anthropological
   Contribution from Harumi Befu   276
Eric Wolf: A Global Anthropologist   291
Kristin Norget: Research in Mexico   320
Susan Brownell: Ethnography in China   360
David Edwards: Ethnography in Afghanistan   365
John McCreery: Applying Anthropology
   in Japan   399

◎ CRITICAL PERSPECTIVES

Key National Symbols   42
The Anthropology of the "Self"   74

Postmodernism and the Future
   of Ethnological Research   138
Human Aggression: Biological or Cultural?   206
Aztec Warfare: A Puzzling Case   248
The Downfall of the Moche   250
Graduation: A Rite of Passage in U.S. Society   280
The Sacred Cow   356

◎ APPLYING ANTHROPOLOGY

Basic versus Applied Research   13
Clyde Snow: Forensic Anthropologist   33
Multiculturalism in U.S. Society   46
Saving Languages   102
Studying Industrial Corporations   264
Marketing Products of the Rain Forest   307
Famines and Food Problems in Africa   334
World Migration and Refugees   388

Preface

EDUCATIONAL GOALS AND ORIENTATION OF THIS TEXT

We all recognize that the world is getting smaller. Instantaneous global communications, trade among far-flung nations, geopolitical events affecting countries and hemispheres, and the ease of international travel are bringing people and cultures into more intimate contact with one another than ever before, forcing this generation of students to become more knowledgeable about societies other than their own. With that in mind, this textbook is grounded in the belief that an enhanced global awareness is essential for people preparing to take their place in the fast-paced, increasingly interconnected world of the twenty-first century. We know that anthropology is ideally suited to introduce students to a global perspective. All the subfields in anthropology have a broad focus on humanity; this helps liberate students from a narrow, parochial view and enables them to see and understand the full sweep of the human condition.

The anthropological perspective, which stresses critical-thinking processes, the evaluation of competing hypotheses, and the skills to generalize from specific data and assumptions, contributes significantly to a well-rounded education. This text engages readers in the varied intellectual activities underlying the anthropological approach by delving into both classic and recent research in the fields that make up anthropology.

Its emphasis on cultural anthropology notwithstanding, this text reflects a strong commitment to anthropology's traditional holistic and integrative approach. It spells out how the four basic subfields of anthropology—physical anthropology, archaeology, linguistics, and ethnology—together yield a comprehensive understanding of humanity. Because the subfields tend to overlap, insights from all of these subfields are woven together to reveal the holistic fabric of a particular society or the threads uniting all of humanity.

An interdisciplinary outlook also resonates throughout this book. All contemporary anthropologists draw on the findings of biologists, paleontologists, geologists, economists, historians, psychologists, sociologists, political scientists, religious studies specialists, philosophers, and researchers in other fields whose work sheds light on anthropological inquiry. In probing various anthropological topics, this text often refers to research conducted in these other fields. In addition to enlarging the scope and reach of the text, exploring interactions between anthropology and other fields sparks the critical imagination that brings the learning process to life.

The comparative approach, another traditional cornerstone of the anthropological perspective, is spotlighted in this text as well. When anthropologists assess fossil evidence, artifacts, languages, or cultural beliefs and values, they weigh comparative evidence, while acknowledging the unique elements of each society and culture. This text casts an inquiring eye on materials from numerous geographical regions and historical eras to enrich student understanding.

A diachronic approach also characterizes this book. In evaluating human evolution, prehistoric events, language divergence, or developments in social structure, anthropologists must rely on models that reflect changes through time, so this diachronic orientation suffuses the text.

TWO UNIFYING THEMES OF THIS TEXT

The thematic architecture of this textbook is to introduce students to the diversity of human societies and cultural patterns the world over and the similarities that make all humans fundamentally alike. To achieve these parallel goals, we pay as much attention to universal human characteristics as we do particular cultural characteristics of local regions.

Another overarching theme is to point out the growing interconnectedness of humans throughout the world and the positive and negative consequences of this reality. Contacts and interactions among people in different societies have occurred throughout history. However, modern advances in communication and transportation have accelerated the process of globalization in recent decades. One goal of this text is to call on anthropological studies of various societies to discover how people are responding to the process of globalization.

ORGANIZATION OF THE BOOK

In this fourth edition, the arrangement and treatment of topics differ from that of other texts. In Part I, we introduce the basic concepts within the four fields of anthropology. Chapter 1 introduces the field of anthropology and explains how it relates to the sciences and humanities. This lead-in chapter also examines how anthropologists use the scientific method. Chapter 2 presents basic evolutionary concepts, focusing on the most recent findings in paleoanthropology and archaeology with regard to human evolution.

In Part II, Chapters 3, 4, 5, 6, and 7 reinforce one another. Chapter 3 examines the concept of culture as it is understood in anthropology. Beginning with the notions of material and nonmaterial culture, this chapter goes on to cite examples of cultural diversity found throughout the world. Here we also stress cultural universals and similarities that unify all of humanity.

In this edition, we also integrate the discussion of the concept of culture with the process of enculturation in order to bridge Chapters 3 on culture with Chapter 4 on the enculturation process. To refine our discussion of culture and enculturation we develop some new materials on recent research in cognitive anthropology.

In Chapter 4, we emphasize how anthropologists bridge the gap between biology and culture as they gain a greater understanding of enculturation and personality development in unfamiliar societies? To answer this question, we turn to the classic studies conducted by Ruth Benedict and

Margaret Mead as well as the most recent research in psychoanalytic anthropology, childhood training in societies around the world, incest, sexuality, cognition, emotions, and the cross-cultural research on personality disorders.

In addition, in Chapter 4 on the enculturation process we have a discussion of the new controversial field of evolutionary psychology. Many psychological anthropologists have been attempting to incorporate the findings from this new field into their hypotheses.

Chapter 5, on language, dovetails with the previous chapter in several key ways. We have refined our discussion of the differences between ape communication and human language. New conclusions have been reached recently in the laboratory research and primatological fieldwork on ape communication as compared with human languages. Following up on these studies, we have revised our section on Chomsky's transformational model, and other related anthropological findings that suggest interactive relationships between biology and culture. We have expanded our discussion of the Sapir–Whorf hypothesis. Other research findings in linguistic anthropology, including historical linguistics, complements material in the emerging field of sociolinguistics, introducing students to the most recent developments in the field.

Theory—classic and contemporary—frames Chapter 6, which offers a critical evaluation of the strengths and weaknesses of each theoretical paradigm. This chapter also amplifies the earlier treatment of the material-nonmaterial aspects of culture by comparing theories highlighting material culture with those placing greater emphasis on nonmaterial, symbolic culture.

Beginning with Chapter 7, this text presents a much different organizational scheme compared with that of other texts. Instead of structuring the book according to specific topics in anthropology, such as subsistence, economy, family, kinship, political organization, and religion, this text organizes the material based on levels of societal organization and regional topics.

In this fourth edition of *Cultural Anthropology: A Global Perspective,* Chapter 7 walks students through the methods, research strategies, and some ethical dilemmas that confront ethnological researchers. Then readers learn about the major variables ethnologists analyze to gain insight into different types of societies: environment and subsistence, demography, technology, economy, social structure, family, kinship, gender, age, political systems, law, and religion. With this background students are ready to understand subsequent chapters.

Chapter 7 also presents the multidimensional approach, which most contemporary anthropologists use to analyze the elements of society and culture. Rather than grounding an understanding of society and culture in a single factor, this orientation taps into both material and nonmaterial aspects of culture to holistically view the full spectrum of society and to produce a balanced treatment of key issues that are aspects of anthropological analysis.

In Part III (Chapters 8, 9, and 10) the text reports the major anthropological findings related to prestate societies (bands, tribes, and chiefdoms). Because these classifications have been open to interpretation among anthropologists, these labels are used with extreme caution. Even though many anthropologists either shun these terms or seriously question their utility in describing complex, changing societies, we believe that these classifications give students who are first exposed to the discipline a good grasp of the fundamentals of prestate societies.

In Part IV, Chapters 11 and 12 move on to agricultural and industrial state societies, whose key characteristics emerge in the interconnections among variables such as political economy and social stratification. Chapter 11 features the basic elements of agricultural societies as revealed by archaeologists, historians, and anthropologists. Chapter 12 opens with a new look at the Industrial Revolution and the process of modernization, segueing into comparative research conducted in England, Western Europe, the United States, the former Soviet Union, and Japan to illustrate the dynamics of industrial states.

Sound pedagogical logic underlies this approach. Instead of presenting important anthropological research on demography, gender, economy, kinship, ethnicity, political systems, and religion as single chapters (usually corresponding to single lectures), this organizational scheme spotlights how these variables permeate the entire spectrum of human experience in different types of societies.

While the single-chapter format tends to marginalize these topics, this text's approach—based on different levels of societal organization—allows students to focus on the interconnections between the political economy and gender, age, family, kinship, religion, demography, technology, environment, and other variables. As a result, students gain a holistic understanding of human societies.

Organizing material according to levels of societal organization in no way implies or endorses a simplistic, unilineal view of sociocultural evolution. In fact, the ladderlike evolutionary perspective on society comes in for criticism throughout the text. While recognizing the inherent weaknesses of using classifications such as "tribes" and "chiefdoms"—including the parallel tendencies to lump diverse societies into narrow categories and to create artificial boundaries among societies—we believe that these groupings nonetheless serve the valuable purpose of introducing beginning students to the sweeping concepts that make anthropology distinctive. Generalizations about tribes and chiefdoms help students unfamiliar with anthropology's underpinnings to absorb basic concepts and data; the complexities and theoretical controversies within the discipline can always be addressed in more specialized advanced courses.

In Part V, we have made some significant changes that we believe will make the text more user friendly and easily digestible for students. First, in Chapter 13 we include a discussion of modernization theory with a critique of the terminology of First, Second, Third, and Fourth Worlds as being too simplistic to apply to what anthropological data demonstrates. This Cold War terminology is outdated from today's standpoint, especially based on ethnographic data regarding the complex levels of development and diversity found in the so-called Third World—and the Second World, the formerly industrial socialist societies that have mostly dissipated.

In Chapter 13, we delve into the theoretical paradigms that anthropologists have modified to understand the interrelationships among various societies of the world. Modernization, dependency, and world-systems theories (and criticisms of them) are introduced to develop the global perspective. We emphasize that societies cannot be understood as independent, isolated units. This global perspective informs all the subsequent chapters, reinforcing a sense of global awareness among students.

Chapter 13 also considers the problems generated by contact between the industrial states and prestate aboriginal societies. It goes on to address a number of salient questions raised by these contacts: How are these prestate societies becoming absorbed into global economic and political networks? How are prestate peoples responding to this situation? And, what are anthropologists doing to enhance the coping strategies of these native peoples?

Another significant change that we adopt in this fourth edition is the development of two new chapters, Chapters 14 and 15, which focus on Latin America, Africa, and the Caribbean (Chapter 14) and the Middle East and Asia (Chapter 15). These two chapters emphasize the globalization taking place in all these regions and reveal what some anthropologists are finding in their local studies related to the overall trend of globalization. We emphasize how all of these cultural regions are becoming more interconnected. These chapters document the evolving interrelationships between Western countries and these non-Western regions by drawing on historical research. In addition to probing classic ethnographic research, contemporary issues in each region are placed within a broad historical context, offering readers finely honed diachronic insights into social and political developments in each of these non-Western areas.

In Part V, Chapter 16 concludes this section by highlighting contemporary global trends that are changing our world. Anthropological research is brought to bear on environmental, demographic, economic, political, ethnic, and religious trends shaking the foundations of many societies. Among the topics addressed in this context are global warming, the Green Revolution, the increasing consumption of nonrenewal energy by industrial societies, the impact of multinational corporations, the demise of socialist regimes, and the rise of new ethnic and religious movements.

Chapter 17 sheds light on the fifth subfield of anthropology: applied anthropology. Here we consider key issues in applied anthropology, including social impact assessment research, medical anthropology, cultural resource management, and recent research aimed at solving practical problems in societies the world over. One of the goals of this chapter is to introduce students to new career possibilities in the field of anthropology.

FEATURES OF THIS TEXT

BOXES

In Critical Perspectives boxes, designed to stimulate independent reasoning and judgment, students take the role of anthropologist by engaging in active, critical analysis of specific problems and issues that arise in anthropological research. A successful holdover from the first edition, these Critical Perspectives boxes encourage students to use rigorous standards of evidence when evaluating assumptions and hypotheses regarding scientific and philosophical issues that have no easy answers. By probing beneath the surface of various assumptions and hypotheses in these exercises, students stand to discover the excitement and challenge of anthropological investigation.

Anthropologists at Work boxes, profiling prominent anthropologists, humanize many of the issues covered in the chapters. These boxes—another carryover from the first edition—go behind the scenes to trace the personal and professional development of some of today's leading anthropologists.

Finally, a number of Applying Anthropology boxes, a carryover from the previous edition, show students how research in anthropology can help solve practical problems confronting contemporary societies. Students often ask, What relevance does anthropology have to the problems we face in our generation? These Applying Anthropology boxes answer the relevance question head on. For example, one box notes that anthropologists unearth research data to help ease tensions in multicultural relations in U.S. society. Another box describes how linguistic anthropologists work with indigenous peoples to preserve their languages as the indigenous peoples adjust to the modern world. The concluding chapter of the text ties together many of these Applying Anthropology boxes by placing in perspective the full panoply of issues addressed in applied anthropology.

PEDAGOGICAL AIDS

For sound pedagogical reasons, we have retained some features to this fourth edition of *Cultural Anthropology: A Global Perspective*. Each chapter opens with profound questions that will help guide students to the most important issues addressed in the chapter. And, each chapter ends with Study Questions that address issues covered in the chapter that students can use to help comprehend the material in the chapter.

In addition, each chapter ends with a list of Key Terms that will help students focus on important concepts introduced in the chapter. Finally, the fourth edition includes a new feature, Internet Exercises, which are designed to help students use the World Wide Web to explore various topics and issues addressed in the chapters.

SUPPLEMENTS

This carefully prepared supplements package is intended to give the instructor the resources needed to teach the course and the student the tools needed to successfully complete the course.

Instructor's Resource Manual   This essential instructor's tool includes chapter overviews, chapter objectives, lecture and discussion topics, classroom activities, research and writing topics, and additional print and non-print resources.

Test Item File   This carefully prepared manual includes over 1,300 questions in multiple-choice and true/false formats. All test questions are page-referenced to the text.

Prentice Hall Custom Test   Prentice Hall's testing software program permits instructors to edit any or all items in the Test Item File and add their own questions. Other special features of this program, which is available for Windows and Macintosh, include random generation of an item set, creation of alternative versions of the same test, scrambling question sequence, and test preview before printing.

Prentice Hall Anthropology Power-Point Slide Presentation   Version II—Created by Roger J. Eich of Hawkeye Community College, this Power-Point slide set combines graphics and text in a colorful format to help convey anthropological principles in a new and exciting way. Created in PowerPoint, an easy-to-use, widely available software program, this set contains over 300 content slides.

Videos   A selection of high-quality award-wining videos from the Filmmakers Library collection is available upon adoption. Please see your Prentice Hall sales representative for more information.

Transparency Acetates   Taken from graphs, diagrams, and tables in this text and other sources, over 50 full-color transparencies offer an effective means of amplifying lecture topics.

The New York Times/Prentice Hall *Themes of the Times*   *The New York Times* and Prentice Hall are sponsoring *Themes of the Times,* a program designed to enhance student access to current information relevant to the classroom. Through this program, the core subject matter provided in the text is supplemented by a collection of timely articles from one of the world's most distinguished newspapers, *The New York Times.* These articles demonstrate the vital, ongoing connection between what is learned in the classroom and what is happening in the world around us. To enjoy a wealth of information provided by *The New York Times* daily, a reduced subscription rate is available. For information, call toll-free: 1-800-631-1222.

Prentice Hall and *The New York Times* are proud to co-sponsor *Themes of the Times.* We hope it will make the reading of both textbooks and newspapers a more dynamic, involving process.

Study Guide   Designed to reinforce information in the text, the study guide includes chapter outlines and summaries, key concepts, critical thinking questions, student self-tests, and suggested readings.

Companion Website   In tandem with the text, students can now take full advantage of the World Wide Web to enrich their study of cultural anthropology through the Scupin Website. This resource correlates the text with related material available on the Internet. Features of the Website include chapter objectives, study questions, as well as links to interesting material and information from other sites on the Web that can reinforce and enhance the content of each chapter. *Address:* **www.prenhall.com/scupin.**

Anthropology on the Internet 1999–2000   This brief guide introduces students to the origin and innovations behind the Internet and provides clear strategies for navigating the complexity of the Internet and World Wide Web. Exercises within and at the end of the chapters allow students to practice searching for the myriad of resources available to the student of anthropology. This 96-page supplementary book is free to students when shrink-wrapped as a package with *Cultural Anthropology, 4/E.*

ACKNOWLEDGMENTS

A textbook like this one requires the enormous effort of many people. I would like to thank the following reviewers for their valuable comments on the various editions of this textbook.

Susan Abbott-Jamieson, University of Kentucky; Kelly D. Alley, Auburn University; Barbara Gallatin Anderson, Southern Methodist University; Robert Bee, University of Connecticut; Harumi Befu, Stanford University; John E. Blank, Cleveland State University; Barry Bogin, University of Michigan–Dearborn; Donald E. Brown, University of California–Santa Barbara; Robert Carmack, SUNY–Albany; A. H. Peter Castro, Syracuse University; Miriam S. Chaiken, Indiana University of Pennsylvania; Gail W. Cromack, Onondaga Community College; James Duvall, Contra Costa College; Allen S. Ehrlich, Eastern Michigan University; Michele Ruth Gamburd, Portland State University; Josef Gamper, Monterey Peninsula College; Alan Goodman, Hampshire College; Leonard Greenfield, Temple University; Joan Gross, Oregon State University; Raymond Hames, University of Nebraska; W. Penn Handwerker, Humboldt State University; Elvin Hatch, University of California–Santa Barbara; Richard D. Harris, University of Portland; Robert W. Hefner, Boston University; Benita J. Howell, University of Tennessee–Knoxville; Arian Ishaya, DeAnza Community College; Norris Johnson, University of North Carolina–Chapel Hill; Rita S. Kipp, Kenyon College; Nancy B. Leis, Central Michigan University; William Leons, University of Toledo; James Lett, Indian River Community College; Kenneth E. Lewis, Michigan State University; Ann P. McElroy, SUNY–Buffalo; Robert R. McIrvin, University of North Carolina–Greensboro; Nancy P. McKee, Washington State University; Ester Maring, Southern Illinois University–Carbondale; Barry H. Michie, Kansas State University; David Minderhout, Bloomsburg University; Katherine Moore, Bentley College; Robert Moorman, Miami-Dade Community College–North; James Myers, CSU–Chico; Tim O'Meara, Melbourne University; John W. Page, Kirkland, Washington; Curt Peterson, Elgin Community College; Leonard Plotnicov, University of Pittsburgh; Tab Rasmussen, Washington University–St. Louis; James L. Ross, University of Akron; Susan D. Russell, Northern Illinois University; Paul Rutledge, University of Missouri–St. Louis; Michael Salovesh, Northern Illinois University; L. Schell, SUNY–Albany; Edwin S. Segal, University of Louisville; David H. Spain, University of Washington; John Townsend, Syracuse University; Robert B. Townsend, College of Lake County; Trudy Turner, University of Wisconsin at Milwaukee; Stephen A. Tyler, Rice University; Virginia J. Vitzthum, University of California–Riverside; Alaka Wali, University of Maryland; Ronald K. Wetherington, Southern Methodist University; Aubrey Williams, University of Maryland, and Larry Zimmerman, University of South Dakota. I also extend thanks to all colleagues who sent me photos and information for use in the biography boxes.

I am grateful for the unwavering support given to this project by Prentice Hall. Without the moral support and encouragement of acquisitions editor Nancy Roberts and managing editor Sharon Chambliss, I would have never been able to complete it. My thanks to development editor Robert Weiss, who took an often unwieldy manuscript and transformed it into an effective teaching instrument for the first edition of the text. Susanna Lesan, the development editor for the second edition, provided many useful insights and helped clarify numerous issues that might have confused students.

My production editor, Marianne Hutchinson, devoted an inordinate amount of time to points of detail and organization and did much to help me meet my deadlines. I also thank photo researcher Teri Stratford for help in selecting exceptional illustrations to supplement the written text. My warmest appreciation goes to my wife, Susan, whose emotional support and patience throughout the duration of the first, second, third, and now fourth editions of this text, made this work possible.

Anyone with comments, suggestions, or recommendations regarding this text is welcome to send an e-mail (internet) message to the following address: scupin@lindenwood.edu.

Raymond Scupin

About the Author

Raymond Scupin is professor of anthropology at Lindenwood University. He received his B.A. degree in history and Asian Studies, with a minor in anthropology, from the University of California–Los Angeles. He completed his M.A. and Ph.D. degrees in anthropology at the University of California–Santa Barbara. Dr. Scupin is truly a four-field anthropologist. During graduate school, Dr. Scupin did archaeological and ethnohistorical research on Native Americans in the Santa Barbara region. He did extensive ethnographic fieldwork in Thailand with a focus on understanding the ethnic and religious movements among the Muslim minority. In addition, he taught linguistics and conducted linguistic research while based at a Thai university.

Dr. Scupin has been teaching undergraduate courses in anthropology for over twenty years at a variety of academic institutions, including community colleges, research universities, and a four-year liberal arts university. Thus, he has taught a very broad spectrum of undergraduate students. Through his teaching experience, Dr. Scupin was prompted to write this textbook, which would allow a wide range of undergraduate students to understand the holistic and global perspectives of the four-field approach in anthropology.

Dr. Scupin has published many studies based on his ethnological research in Thailand. He recently returned to Thailand and other countries of Southeast Asia to update his ethnographic data. He is a member of many professional associations, including the American Anthropological Association, the Asian Studies Association, and the Council of Thai Studies.

Introduction
to Anthropology

CHAPTER OUTLINE

Anthropology: The Four Subfields
Physical Anthropology / Archaeology / Linguistic Anthropology / Ethnology

Holistic Anthropology, Interdisciplinary Research, and the Global Perspective

Applied Anthropology

Anthropology and Science
The Scientific Method / Limits of Science

Anthropology and the Humanities

Why Study Anthropology?
Critical Thinking and Global Awareness

CHAPTER QUESTIONS

- What is unique about the field of anthropology as compared with other disciplines?
- How does the field of anthropology bridge the sciences and the humanities?
- Why should any student study anthropology?

ANTHROPOLOGIST MORTON FRIED ONCE POINTED out the similarities among space travel, science fiction, and the field of anthropology (1977). He noted that when Neil Armstrong became the first human to set foot on the moon, in July 1969, his step constituted first contact. To space travelers and science fiction writers, first contact refers to the first meeting between humans and extraterrestrial beings. To anthropologists, the phrase refers to initial encounters between peoples of different societies. For thousands of years, peoples throughout the world have had first contacts with each other. Perhaps in the future, through further exploration in space, there may be initial encounters between humans and creatures from other worlds.

Imagine the year 2100, when space travelers from earth have these first contacts with extraterrestrials in far-off galaxies. Undoubtedly, the travelers from Earth will want to grasp the nature of these beings. Because the extraterrestrial beings will certainly differ physically from humans, the space travelers will attempt to investigate their physical characteristics. For this investigation they will examine the environmental conditions of the distant planet to determine how these creatures originated and why they developed specific physical traits. They will also look closely at physical variations within the extraterrestrial population.

Beyond individual physical characteristics of the extraterrestrial beings, the space explorers will wonder how the extraterrestrial society has developed. So they will try to study the technology and other aspects of the foreign society that would indicate patterns of change over time. In the year 2100, space scientists may be able to conduct this analysis with sophisticated equipment and methods that allow them to examine the layers of the newly discovered planet's crust to locate different inventions, buildings, or art forms that have emerged in specific time periods.

One of the first problems the space travelers will almost surely encounter is communicating with the extraterrestrials. They will need to determine the form of communication used by these creatures and attempt to distinguish patterns of sounds or other methods used to transmit information. The

Neil Armstrong on the moon.

the same way that future space travelers would investigate the lifestyles of extraterrestrials. Anthropologists have developed specialized procedures over the past hundred years to conduct their investigations. There are two major goals of anthropology: to understand the uniqueness and diversity of human behavior and human societies around the world and to discover the fundamental similarities that link human beings the world over—both in the past and the present. To accomplish these goals, anthropologists undertake systematic case studies of people living in particular locations, in the past and present, and use comparative techniques to assess the similarities and differences among societies.

Using these goals as a springboard, anthropology has forged distinctive objectives and propelled research that has broadened our understanding of humanity, from the beginnings of human societies to the present. This chapter introduces the distinctive approaches used in anthropology to achieve these goals.

space travelers may discover that different forms of communication are used in different places on the planet, prompting the human visitors to compare these disparate communication patterns to understand the different language groupings found on the planet.

The space scientists could also gain an understanding of the extraterrestrials by living in their communities and observing their behavior. In addition to recording these behaviors as accurately as possible, the space travelers might have to participate in the extraterrestrials' rituals and daily activities to gain an insider's perspective.

The space travelers would strive to determine in what ways these extraterrestrials resemble and differ from human beings on Earth. Drawing on all of their findings, they would compare the extraterrestrials' physical characteristics, the development of their society over time, their forms of communication, and their overall behavior and thought with that of humans.

As we will see in this chapter, the field of anthropology seeks to understand humanity in much

Anthropology: The Four Subfields

The word *anthropology* stems from the Greek words *anthropo,* meaning "human beings" or "humankind," and *logia,* translated as "knowledge of" or "the study of." Thus, we can define **anthropology** as the systematic study of humankind. This definition in itself, however, does not distinguish anthropology from other disciplines. After all, historians, psychologists, economists, sociologists, and scholars in many other fields systematically study humankind in one way or another. Anthropology stands apart because it combines four subdisciplines, or subfields, that bridge the natural sciences, the social sciences, and the humanities. These four subdisciplines—physical anthropology, archaeology, linguistic anthropology, and ethnology—give anthropologists a broad approach to the study of humanity the world over, both past and present. Figure 1.1 shows these subfields and the various specializations that make up each one. A discussion of these subdisciplines and some of the key specializations in each follows.

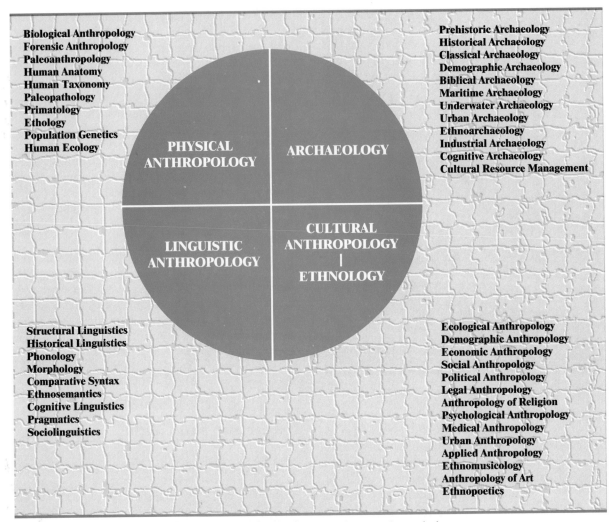

Biological Anthropology
Forensic Anthropology
Paleoanthropology
Human Anatomy
Human Taxonomy
Paleopathology
Primatology
Ethology
Population Genetics
Human Ecology

Prehistoric Archaeology
Historical Archaeology
Classical Archaeology
Demographic Archaeology
Biblical Archaeology
Maritime Archaeology
Underwater Archaeology
Urban Archaeology
Ethnoarchaeology
Industrial Archaeology
Cognitive Archaeology
Cultural Resource Management

PHYSICAL ANTHROPOLOGY

ARCHAEOLOGY

LINGUISTIC ANTHROPOLOGY

CULTURAL ANTHROPOLOGY | ETHNOLOGY

Structural Linguistics
Historical Linguistics
Phonology
Morphology
Comparative Syntax
Ethnosemantics
Cognitive Linguistics
Pragmatics
Sociolinguistics

Ecological Anthropology
Demographic Anthropology
Economic Anthropology
Social Anthropology
Political Anthropology
Legal Anthropology
Anthropology of Religion
Psychological Anthropology
Medical Anthropology
Urban Anthropology
Applied Anthropology
Ethnomusicology
Anthropology of Art
Ethnopoetics

Figure 1.1   This figure shows the four core subfields of anthropology. It also includes some of the various specializations that have developed within each of the subfields, which you will be introduced to in this text. Many of these specializations overlap with one another in the actual studies carried out by anthropologists.

PHYSICAL ANTHROPOLOGY

Physical anthropology is the branch of anthropology most closely related to the natural sciences. Physical anthropologists conduct research in two major areas: human evolution and human variation. The majority of physical anthropologists focus their studies on human evolution. Some investigate **fossils,** the preserved remains of bones and living materials from earlier periods, to reconstruct the evolution and ways of life of our early human ancestors. The study of human evolution through analysis of fossils is called **paleoanthropology** (the prefix *paleo* means "old" or "prehistoric"). Paleoanthropologists use a variety of sophisticated scientific techniques to date, classify, and compare fossil bones to determine the links between modern humans and their biological ancestors.

Other physical anthropologists explore human evolution through **primatology,** the study of primates. **Primates** are mammals that belong to the same overall biological classification as humans and therefore share similar physical characteristics

Although anthropologists study the distinctive features of different cultures, they also recognize the fundamental similarities among people throughout the world.

and a close evolutionary relationship with us. Many primatologists observe primates such as chimpanzees, gorillas, gibbons, and orangutans in their natural habitats to ascertain the similarities and differences between these other primates and humans.

Still other physical anthropologists focus their research on the range of physical variation within and among different human populations. These physical anthropologists study human variation by measuring physical characteristics such as body size, by comparing blood types, or by examining differences in skin color or hair texture. Noting how disparate physical characteristics have enabled these populations to adapt to different geographical environments, these physical anthropologists shed light on how human populations have developed.

ANTHROPOLOGISTS AT WORK

C. Loring Brace: Physical Anthropologist

C. Loring Brace was an undergraduate at Williams College where he pursued a major in geology, with a strong dose of biology. His family roots go back to early migrants from southern England who settled in Massachusetts and Connecticut, one of whom helped bring Charles Darwin's ideas to the attention of the U.S. public. After being drafted into the military from graduate school to serve in the Korean War, Brace returned to graduate school in the mid-1950s at Harvard University to focus on the field of physical anthropology, or paleoanthropology. He worked under all the leading evolutionary biologists and anthropologists of that time. In the summer of 1959 Brace had the opportunity to work at a French Paleolithic site with one of

his teachers from Harvard, Hallam L. Movius. This field experience taught him that excavation was an extremely important element in paleoanthropology; however, he recognized that the skeletal data and artifacts had to be synthesized carefully to tell a coherent story about human evolution.

After this fieldwork experience, Brace traveled and visited prehistoric skeletal collections in Monaco, Italy, Switzerland, Paris, Croatia, and London to study the chronological sequence of human evolution. He initiated a new way of understanding the phase of the famous prehistoric Neanderthal discovered throughout Europe. He posited the hypothesis that Neanderthals are the same species as modern Homo Sapiens. Through his research efforts and

C. Loring Brace.

publications, the name of Neanderthal was eventually changed to *Homo sapiens neanderthalensis.* Brace has studied carefully the evolution of teeth in the various types of ancient fossils of the past. He developed the hypothesis that the cultural innovation of cooking for Neanderthals was important in the reduction in the size of their teeth. This was a unique hypothesis combining both cultural and

ARCHAEOLOGY

Through **archaeology,** the branch of anthropology that seeks out and examines the artifacts of past societies, we can learn much about the lifestyles, history, and evolution of those societies. **Artifacts,** the material products of former societies, provide tangible clues to the lifestyle of an extinct society. Some archaeological sites reveal spectacular jewelry like that found by the movie character Indiana Jones, or the treasures of a pharaoh's tomb. Most artifacts are not so glamorous, however. For example, archaeologists often spend hours sorting through ancient garbage, or **middens,** to figure out how members of an early society ate their meals, what tools they used in their household and other work, and what lifeways gave meaning to their lives.

Some archaeologists investigate past societies that did not have written documents. Known as prehistoric archaeologists, these researchers study the artifacts of groups such as Native Americans to understand how these people lived. Other archaeologists, called classical archaeologists, conduct research on ancient civilizations such as in Egypt, Greece, and Rome, in collaboration with historians. Historical archaeologists also work with historians in investigating the artifacts of societies of the more recent past. For example, many historical archaeologists are probing the remains of plantations in the southern United States to gain an understanding of the lifestyles of slaves and slave owners during the nineteenth century.

In a novel approach, still other archaeologists have turned their attention to the more recent past.

physical evolution. He continued to pursue the ideas of linking cultural artifacts with physical evolution such as the use of dinnerware and its effects on the evolution of jaws and teeth. With careful analysis he has been able to propose many useful hypotheses that have been subjected to testing by other physical anthropologists.

Brace began teaching and building a physical anthropology component of the anthropology department at UC Santa Barbara in the early 1960s. From Santa Barbara he moved to the University of Michigan, where he has become the curator of the Physical Anthropology Unit in the Museum of Anthropology. He has an extensive fossil collection from all over the world, which he continues to analyze to develop fruitful hy-

potheses. He has traveled all over the world to do research in his chosen field. Brace's students include many of the leading physical anthropologists today such as Dean D. Falk, Carol J. Lauer, Frank Spencer, and Robert Hinton.

One of the most important issues in which Loring Brace has been involved is the study of race within anthropology. He has criticized the American cultural tendency to classify different peoples into distinctive racial categories, which has had negative effects on society and the field of physical anthropology. He collaborated with the senior physical anthropologist Ashley Montagu, who wrote the definitive treatise on the myth of race, entitled *Man's Most Dangerous Myth: the Fallacy of Race*. This book was first published

in 1942 during the Nazi period and represented the first systematic attempt to debunk the racialistic thinking of scientists and lay people on this subject. A new 1997 edition of Montagu's critical work has just been published. Brace wrote the foreword to this edition, emphasizing the importance of anthropological research in this area. C. Loring Brace has been working on a new book called *Race Is A Four Letter Word*, which criticizes the racialistic thinking of many social scientists. Known as a maverick to many of his colleagues, Brace continues to stimulate new ideas and hypotheses in the field of physical anthropology.

For example, in 1972 William L. Rathje began a study of modern garbage as an assignment for the students in his introductory anthropology class. Even he was surprised at the number of people who took an interest in the findings. A careful study of garbage reveals insights about modern society that cannot be ferreted out in any other way. Whereas questionnaires and interviews depend on the cooperation and interpretation of respondents, garbage provides a physical record of actual human activity. Rathje's "garbage project" is still in progress and, combined with information from respondents, offers an unusual look at patterns of waste management, consumption, and alcohol use in contemporary U.S. society (Rathje & Ritenbaugh, 1984).

Despite the popular image of archaeology as an adventurous, even romantic pursuit, it usually con-

sists of methodical, rigorous, painstaking scientific research. Typically, the research begins with a field survey of a particular region, or site, where the archaeologist looks for surface artifacts or other clues to past habitation. If the archaeologist gathers enough evidence in the field survey, a small test excavation—or several test excavations—are conducted to examine the site. Depending on the results of these tests, the archaeologist may launch a full-scale dig at the site. In the excavations, broken fragments of pottery, stone, glass, and other materials are collected. These artifacts are then classified and analyzed in a laboratory setting. It may take months or even years to fully classify and analyze the results of an excavation.

Only after intensive analysis do archaeologists cautiously interpret the data they have collected

ANTHROPOLOGISTS AT WORK

Patty Jo Watson: Archaeologist

After two years of studies in zoology at Iowa State College, Patty Jo Watson changed course and decided to pursue graduate study in archaeology at the University of Chicago. Working with Robert Braidwood, Watson became adept at using precise scientific methods to assess artifacts left behind by past societies. Early in her career, Watson participated in the excavation of a prehistoric society in the Middle East. Later, after marrying philosopher and geologist Richard (Red) Watson, professor of philosophy at Washington University in St. Louis, who introduced her to cave exploration, she focused her energies on investigating the prehistory of caves.

Watson took a keen interest in Native American cave explorers in Kentucky, especially in the Mammoth Cave system, the longest network of caves in the world, with approximately three hundred and fifty miles of interconnected passageways. The system includes

Salts Cave, Colossal Cave, Unknown Cave, Crystal Cave, and many others. For more than twenty years, Watson and her colleagues have surveyed, mapped, and explored the prehistoric artifacts of the Mammoth Cave system. They uncovered evidence that Native American cavers, thought to be purely hunter-gatherers, actually cultivated plants to supplement their diet of game animals and wild plants. This discovery has yielded major insights concerning the development of agriculture in native North American societies.

Watson, the Edward Mallinckrodt Distinguished University Professor of Anthropology at Washington University, and two of her colleagues have written two major books on the philosophy of archaeology: Explanation in Archaeology: An Explicitly Scientific Approach (1971) and Archaeological Explanation: The Scientific Method in Archaeology (1984). As

Patty Jo Watson.

a result of her contributions to cave archaeology and the prehistory of Native American culture made over a thirty-five-year career, Watson was inducted into the National Academy of Sciences, an honor the New York Times described as "second only to the Nobel Prize." She is one of a small number of American women selected for membership in this prestigious organization.

and begin to generalize about the conditions of a past society. Unlike the glorified adventures of fictional archaeologists, the real-world field of archaeology thrives on the intellectually challenging adventure of careful, systematic, scientific research that enlarges our understanding of past societies.

LINGUISTIC ANTHROPOLOGY

Linguistics, the study of language, has a long history that dovetails with the discipline of philosophy but is also one of the integral subfields of anthro-

pology. Linguistic anthropology focuses on the relationship between language and culture, how language is used within society, and how the human brain acquires and uses language. As do other types of anthropologists, linguistic anthropologists seek to discover the ways in which languages are different from each other as well as how they are similar to one another. Two wide-ranging areas of research in linguistic anthropology are structural linguistics and historical linguistics.

Structural linguistics explores how language works. Structural linguists compare grammatical

ANTHROPOLOGISTS AT WORK

Bambi B. Schieffelin: Linguistic Anthropologist

As an undergraduate at Columbia University, Bambi Schieffelin was drawn to two fields: anthropology and comparative literature. After spending a summer on a field trip to rural Bolivia and a year in the southern highlands of Papua New Guinea, Schieffelin decided to pursue a doctorate in anthropology, with a specialty in linguistic anthropology. She combined the fields of developmental psychology, linguistics, and anthropology, which prepared her for fieldwork among the Kaluli people in Papua New Guinea. After completing her Ph.D. degree, Schieffelin spent a year teaching at the University of California at Berkeley and also teaching linguistics at Stanford University. Since 1986 she has been teaching at New York University in the department of anthropology.

Schieffelin's work focuses on language use and socialization. She studies how language is learned and acquired by children, and how it is used in various social contexts. She has collaborated with Elinor Ochs to develop innovative approaches to understanding how language use is influenced by socialization. Together they have edited several volumes, including *Language Socialization across Cultures* (1987). In addition, Schieffelin has developed these topics in her own book, *The Give and Take of Everyday Life: Language Socialization of Kaluli Children* (1990).

Through their research on children's language socialization, Schi-effelin and Ochs contributed to a cross-cultural understanding of this process. Until the early 1970s, most of the theories on language and socialization had been drawn from psychological research on middle-class Americans. Schieffelin and Ochs focused instead on language and socialization among many different societies. They emphasized the importance of cultural practices in shaping verbal activities. For example, prior to their research, it was assumed that "baby talk" was the same all over the world. They found, however, that "baby talk" is not universal and is linked to ideas that people have about children.

In her ethnographic research, Schieffelin tape records and transcribes everyday social interactions in different speech communities. She has carried out research in Papua New Guinea since 1967, focusing not only on language socialization, but on language change and the introduction of literacy into a nonliterate society. In addition to this work in a relatively traditional society, Schieffelin has worked in a number of urban speech communities in the United States, where linguistic diversity is apparent on every street corner. Her research in Philadelphia among Sino-Vietnamese focused on language socialization and literacy, and her studies of Haitians in New York analyzed language socialization and code switching practices.

As a linguistic anthropologist Schieffelin tries to integrate two

Bambi Schieffelin.

perspectives. First, she focuses on how the study of language use can lead to insights into how culture is transmitted from generation to generation in everyday social interactions. Second, she analyzes the ways in which language expresses social relationships and cultural meanings across different social and political contexts. Her work represents the most current developments in linguistic anthropology today.

Linguistic anthropologists have broadened their vision of places in which to investigate language use—including legal, medical, scientific, educational, and political arenas—as these contexts are critical to understanding how power is produced and distributed. They are also studying all varieties of literacy, including television and radio, providing new perspectives on these new forms of global communication.

patterns or other linguistic elements to learn how contemporary languages mirror and differ from one another. Structural linguistics has also uncovered some intriguing relationships between language and thought patterns among different groups of people. Do people who speak different languages with different grammatical structures think and perceive the world differently from each other? Do native Chinese speakers think or view the world and life experiences differently from native English speakers? These are some of the questions that structural linguists attempt to answer.

Linguistic anthropologists also examine the connections between language and social behavior in different cultures. This specialty is called **sociolinguistics.** Sociolinguists are interested both in how language is used to define social groups and how belonging to particular groups leads to specialized kinds of language use. In Thailand, for example, there are thirteen forms of the pronoun *I:* One form is used with equals, other forms come into play with people of higher status, and some forms are used when males address females (Scupin, 1989).

Another area of research which has interested linguistic anthropologists is **historical linguistics.** Historical linguistics concentrates on the comparison and classification of different languages to discern the historical links among languages. By examining and analyzing grammatical structures and sounds of languages, researchers are able to discover rules for how languages change over time, as well as which languages are related to one another historically. This type of historical linguistic research is particularly useful in tracing the migration routes of various societies through time, confirming archaeological and paleoanthropological data gathered independently. For example, through historical linguistic research, anthropologists have corroborated the Siberian origins of many Native American populations.

ETHNOLOGY

Ethnology, more popularly known as **cultural anthropology,** is the subfield of anthropology that examines various contemporary societies throughout the world. Ethnologists do research in all parts of the world, from the tropical rainforests of Zaire and Brazil to the arctic regions of Canada, from the deserts of the Middle East to the urban areas of China. Until recently, most ethnologists conducted research on non-Western or remote cultures in Africa, Asia, the Middle East, Latin America, and the Pacific Islands, and on the Native American populations in the United States. Today, however, many anthropologists have turned to research on their own cultures to gain a better understanding of its institutions and cultural values.

Cultural anthropologists or ethnologists (sometimes the terms *sociocultural anthropologist* or *ethnographer* are used interchangeably with *cultural anthropologist* or *ethnologist*) use a unique research strategy in conducting their fieldwork in different settings. This research strategy is referred to as **participant observation,** which involves learning the language and culture of the group being studied by participating in the group's daily activities. Through this intensive participation, the ethnologist becomes deeply familiar with the group and can understand and explain the society and culture of the group as an insider. We discuss the methods and techniques of ethnologists at greater length in Chapter 7.

The results of the fieldwork of the ethnologist or cultural anthropologist are written up as an **ethnography,** a description of a society. A typical ethnography reports on the environmental setting, economic patterns, social organization, political system, and religious rituals and beliefs of the society under study. This description of a society is based on what anthropologists call ethnographic data. The gathering of ethnographic data in a systematic manner is the specific research goal of the ethnologist or cultural anthropologist.

Holistic Anthropology, Interdisciplinary Research, and the Global Perspective

Most anthropologists are trained in all four subfields of anthropology. Because of all the research being done in these different fields, however—more than three hundred journals and hundreds of books are published every year dealing with anthropological research—no one individual can keep abreast of all the developments across the discipline's full spectrum. Consequently, anthropol-

ANTHROPOLOGISTS AT WORK

Napoleon Chagnon: Ethnologist

Napoleon Chagnon was born in Port Austin, Michigan, in 1938. As a physics major at the University of Michigan, he chose to take a few anthropology courses to fulfill some of his liberal arts requirements. These courses so captivated him that he changed his major and ultimately earned B.A., M.A., and Ph.D. degrees in anthropology at Michigan. After completing his Ph.D. in 1966, he joined the Department of Human Genetics at the University of Michigan Medical School and participated in a multidisciplinary study of the Yanomamö Indians of Venezuela and Brazil.

Chagnon has returned to do fieldwork among the Yanomamö almost every year since 1966, enabling him to conduct a long-term, systematic study of change within this population. Chagnon's ethnographic studies, and the many excellent educational films that he and colleague Timothy Asch have produced, have made the Yanomamö well-known around the world.

Chagnon's description of his first fieldwork experience with the Yanomamö demonstrates how "culture shock" can affect ethnologists who encounter a society radically different from their own. He describes his initial experience with the Yanomamö after a long voyage up the Orinoco River, arriving at a riverbank near the village:

> I looked up and gasped when I saw a dozen burly, naked, sweaty, hideous men staring at us down the shafts of their arrows! Immense wads of green tobacco were stuck between their lower teeth and lips, making them look even more hideous, and strands of dark green slime dripped or hung from their nostrils—so long that they clung to their [chests] or drizzled down their chins. (1983:10) [The dark green slime was the remains of a hallucinogenic drug that the Yanomamö had taken.]

Eventually Chagnon adjusted to his new environment and conducted a thorough, systematic ethnographic study. In a book

Ethnologist Napoleon Chagnon, who studied the Yanomamö Indians of South America.

about his fieldwork, *Studying the Yanomamö* (1974), he describes both his analytical techniques and his immersion into Yanomamö society.

Over time, Chagnon became personally involved in the lives of the Yanomamö. His deep personal ties with the Yanomamö prompted him to help them grapple with problems stemming from their confrontation with new, external pressures (see Chapter 13). Chagnon has spearheaded an international effort to aid the Yanomamö in their adjustment to the modern world.

---

ogists usually specialize in one of the four subfields. Nevertheless, most anthropologists are firmly committed to a **holistic** approach to understanding humankind—a broad, comprehensive account that draws on all four subfields under the umbrella of anthropology. This holistic approach involves the analysis of both biological and cultural phenomena. In other words, anthropologists study the physical characteristics of humans, including their genetic endowment, as well as their social

and cultural environments. Through collaborative studies among the various specialists in the four subfields, anthropologists can ask more broadly framed questions about humanity.

Anthropology does not limit itself to its own four subfields to realize its research agenda. Although it stands as a distinct discipline, anthropology has strong links to other social sciences. Cultural anthropology or ethnology, for instance, is closely related to sociology. In the past, cultural anthropologists examined the traditional societies of the world, whereas sociologists focused on modern societies. Today cultural anthropologists and sociologists explore many of the same societies using similar research approaches. For example, both rely on statistical and nonstatistical data whenever appropriate in their studies of different types of societies.

As we shall discover in later chapters, ethnology also overlaps with the fields of psychology, economics, and political science. Ethnologists draw on psychology when they assess the behavior of people in other societies. Psychological questions bearing on perception, learning, and motivation all figure in ethnographic fieldwork. Additionally, ethnologists probe the economic and political behavior and thought of people in various societies, using these data for comparative purposes.

Finally, anthropology dovetails considerably with the field of history, which, like anthropology, encompasses a broad range of events. Every human event that has ever taken place in the world is a potential topic for both historians and anthropologists. Historians describe and explain human events that have occurred throughout the world; anthropologists place their biological, archaeological, linguistic, and ethnographic data in the context of these historical developments.

Through the four subfields and the interdisciplinary approach, anthropologists have emphasized a global perspective. The global perspective enables anthropologists to consider the biological, environmental, psychological, economic, historical, social, and cultural conditions of humans at all times and in all places. Anthropologists do not limit themselves to understanding a particular society or set of societies but rather attempt to go beyond specific or local conditions and demonstrate the interconnections among societies throughout the world. This global perspective is used throughout this text to show how anthropologists place their findings in the interconnecting worldwide community of humanity.

Applied Anthropology

Although the four major subfields of anthropology (physical anthropology, archaeology, linguistic anthropology, and ethnology) are well established, a fifth major subfield has in recent years come to be recognized. **Applied anthropology** is the use of data gathered from the other subfields of anthropology in an effort to offer practical solutions to problems within a society. These problems may be environmental, technological, economic, social, political, or cultural. Many anthropologists are at work attempting to solve different types of problems through the use of anthropological data, as is discussed in the box on page 13.

Anthropology and Science

Most of the knowledge anthropologists acquire through their research is scientific, as opposed to knowledge based on common sense or religious beliefs. Commonsense knowledge is rooted in experience and folk traditions maintained by members of a society—the kind of information that "everyone is supposed to know." Commonsense knowledge includes assumptions about putting on warm clothing in cold weather and bringing an umbrella if it is going to rain, for example. People who do not accept these assumptions are said to lack common sense. Yet ethnographic and cross-cultural research in anthropology has demonstrated that commonsense knowledge is not as common as we might think. This research indicates that as humans, we are not born with commonsense knowledge. Commonsense knowledge tends to vary both among different societies and among different groups within the same society.

Anthropologist Clifford Geertz gives an example of how commonsense knowledge about gender differs from society to society. Every so often an individual is born with both male and female genitalia. Called *hermaphrodites,* these individuals are viewed with horror by most Americans, and American parents of these infants almost always agree to have them undergo surgery immediately after birth to correct this abnormality. The Navajo Indians, by contrast, view hermaphrodites with wonder and awe and treat them as gifted leaders. In still another perspective, Geertz describes the Pokot tribal people of East Africa, who do not look upon this genetic anomaly as an abnormality at all and consider these people normal (Geertz, 1983).

APPLYING ANTHROPOLOGY

Basic versus Applied Research

The four basic subfields of anthropology—physical anthropology, archaeology, linguistic anthropology, and ethnology—are all devoted to the examination of the "big" questions. These "big" questions concern the origins of humankind, the essential elements of human nature, the development of civilizations, the nature and diversity of human languages, and the similarities and differences among our cultural values, institutions, and practices around the world. These "big" questions involve anthropologists in basic research, research that is directed toward gaining knowledge about humanity for its own sake. Most anthropologists associated with colleges and universities are involved in this type of *basic research*.

Another type of research, however, is becoming increasingly important in anthropology. *Applied research* is study directed toward gaining knowledge that can be utilized in an effort to meet a recognized need or solve a particular problem for humanity. Applied research in anthropology involves the use of research methods and skills developed in basic research to solve human problems and fulfill the needs of various societies.

Chapter 17 will be devoted to a more in-depth look at applied anthropology. In addition, throughout the text a number of boxes entitled "Applying Anthropology" will introduce you to this new and rapidly developing subfield of anthropology. You will see how anthropologists apply their skills to deal with recent problems in the growth of multiculturalism within U.S. society or how applied research is helping native peoples conserve their indigenous languages to solve practical problems in their communities. You will be introduced to applied anthropologists who help communities preserve their cultural heritage, help corporations better understand international business, help government agencies understand the impact of programs or development projects, and help resolve global problems such as the settlement of refugees. You will learn that the subfield of applied anthropology is increasing in popularity because of the growing opportunities for solving practical problems at both the local and global levels. As we explore these endeavors, you will understand the intricate connections emerging between the basic and applied research areas within anthropology.

American commonsense views about gender differ radically from those of the Navajo and the Pokot. As we can see, commonsense notions may vary from or even contradict one another from society to society, and sometimes even within a society.

Religion and faith constitute another source of human knowledge. Religious beliefs and faith are most often derived from sacred texts, like the Bible, but they are also based on intuitions, dreams, visions, and extrasensory perceptions. Most Christians have faith that Jesus Christ is the son of God, whereas Buddhists, Muslims, and Jews ground their religious beliefs in other traditions. Religious beliefs are cast in highly personal terms and, like commonsense knowledge, span a wide and diverse range.

THE SCIENTIFIC METHOD

In contrast to commonsense knowledge and religious faith, scientific knowledge is not based on traditional wisdom or revelations. The source of scientific knowledge, called the **scientific method,** is a logical system used to evaluate data derived from systematic observation. Anthropologists rely on the scientific method to investigate both the natural and the social worlds because the approach allows them to make certain claims about knowledge and to verify these claims with systematic, logical reasoning. Through critical thinking, logical reasoning, and skeptical thought, anthropologists strive to suspend their judgment about any claim for knowledge until it has been publicly verified.

Testability and verifiability lie at the core of the scientific method. If a scientific proposition is not testable, it cannot be considered for inclusion in the body of scientific knowledge. There are two ways of developing testable propositions: the inductive method and the deductive method. In the **inductive method,** the scientist first makes observations and collects data (see Figure 1.2). Most of the data collected are classified as variables. A **variable** is any data that changes from case to case. For example, different races, heights, and people's age and sex all constitute variables. These data are then classified by the scientist according to their similarities and differences. The scientist then develops a hypothesis about the data. A **hypothesis** is a testable proposition concerning the relationship between particular sets of variables in the collected data. The practice of testing hypotheses is the major focus of the scientific method, as communities of scientists test each other's hypotheses to confirm or refute them. If a hypothesis is found to be valid, it may be woven together with other hypotheses into a general theory. **Theories** are interconnected hypotheses that offer general explanations for natural or social phenomena. The systematic evaluation of hypotheses and theories enables scientists to state their conclusions with a certainty that cannot be applied to commonsense or religious knowledge.

The **deductive method** of scientific research begins with a general theory from which scientists develop a hypothesis to be tested. Initial hypotheses are sometimes referred to as "guesstimates" because they may be based merely on guesswork by the scientist. These hypotheses are rigorously tested through experimentation and replications. The testing and retesting of hypotheses is the most significant characteristic of the scientific method, ensuring the reliability of scientific claims. As we will see in this text, numerous hypotheses have been developed to provide explanations and generalizations regarding human activity in the past and the present. Through the scientific evaluation of hypotheses advanced by independent researchers or teams of an-

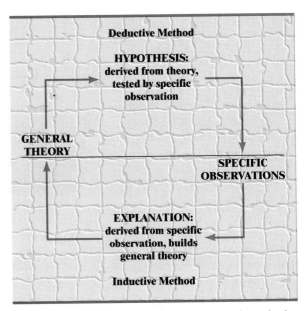

Figure 1.2   Deductive and inductive research methods.

thropologists, we have gained a more profound understanding of the human condition.

LIMITS OF SCIENCE

Despite the thoroughness and verification that characterize the scientific method, scientific explanations of reality have certain limitations. The scientific method as described above is to some extent an ideal within the anthropological community. In actuality, scientific practice is a much more complex and difficult process. Ideally, anthropologists strive for objective knowledge, knowledge that is beyond their personal beliefs, values, or biases. Like all people, however, anthropologists have their personal beliefs, values, and biases, which are known collectively as subjective knowledge. In addition, anthropologists in a particular field share **paradigms,** sets of beliefs, assumptions, techniques, ideals, and research strategies that shape their observations and conclusions (Lett, 1987). Ideally, when a certain paradigm can no longer explain observed data, anthropologists should abandon or modify it to conform to their new knowledge. In practice, the opposite frequently occurs: anthropologists sometimes cling to outdated paradigms, even in the face of clearly contradictory evidence, thereby misinterpreting data and formulating inaccurate hypotheses. Then, at some point, when the evidence becomes overwhelming, new paradigms may be substituted for the outdated ones (Kuhn, 1970). In later chapters we will examine the major paradigms in anthropology.

The point here is not that scientific progress in anthropology is impossible. Through the testing of hypotheses, anthropology has produced vast amounts of objective, verifiable knowledge. Empirical evidence can be verified publicly by many people, weeding out contradictory, subjective knowledge and increasing the body of objective knowledge. Poor hypotheses are rejected and replaced by better explanations. This process makes the scientific method much more effective than other means of acquiring knowledge.

Some critics have suggested that the limitations inherent in scientific inquiry make it unsuitable for the study of humankind. They argue that human conduct is so complex and unpredictable that hypothesis testing, the core of the scientific method, is not a worthwhile endeavor in the social sciences. In response, social scientists point out that all physical and natural phenomena are complex and unpredictable, yet physicists and other scientists persist in testing hypotheses. Other critics assert that human behavior can never be measured precisely, making scientific statements about human conduct or societies improbable. However, the same criticism can be directed at the methods of astrophysicists who figure the size of black holes in space through mathematical calculations. Although astrophysicists can rarely set up controlled conditions in laboratories to measure these phenomena accurately, they still formulate hypotheses based on high-level abstract mathematical computations.

Nevertheless, anthropologists and other social scientists run up against very real limitations in the use of the scientific method in their disciplines. This is especially the case within cultural anthropology or ethnology, where the anthropologist is attempting to examine cultural phenomena. The myriad forms of human behavior and culture grow from complex roots, and sorting out the causes and effects of human activity challenges the most insightful among us. In addition, the problems of trying to replicate the results of research within different societies around the world present formidable challenges for the anthropologist (Roscoe, 1995). In general, the four fields of anthropology

do not attempt to spell out "final truths." As a rule, anthropological knowledge rarely deals with such ultimate truths. Like other scientists, most anthropologists view these limitations as a challenge rather than a frustrating dilemma.

Anthropology and the Humanities

In addition to its interconnections with the natural and social sciences, the discipline of anthropology is also aligned with the humanistic fields of inquiry. This is particularly true with respect to the field of ethnology, as these researchers are involved in the study of different contemporary cultures. When participating in the life and experience of people in various societies ethnologists must confront a multitude of different behaviors and values that may have to be translated and interpreted. The archaeologist also confronts this type of problem when studying past cultures and civilizations from different regions of the world. Similar issues confront the linguistic anthropologist as they translate and understand various languages. Many anthropologists explore the creative cultural dimensions of humanity, such as myth, folklore, poetry, art, music, and mythology. *Ethnopoetics,* for example, is the study of poetry and how it relates to the experiences of people in different societies. For example, a provocative study of the poetry of a nomadic tribe of Bedouins in the Middle East has yielded new insights into the concepts of honor and shame in these societies (Abu-Lughod, 1987). Another related field, *ethnomusicology,* is devoted to the study of musical traditions in various societies throughout the world. Ethnomusicologists record and analyze music and the traditions that give rise to these musical expressions, exploring similarities and differences in musical performance and composition. Other anthropologists study the art of particular societies, such as pottery styles among Native American groups.

Studies of fine art conducted by anthropologists have contributed to a more richly hued, global portrait of humankind. Artistic traditions spring up in all societies, and anthropologists have shed light on the music, myths, poetry, literature, and art of

Ethnomusicologists study the musical traditions of different societies. This photo shows Japanese females playing the string instrument called the koto.

non-Western and other remote peoples. As a result, we now have a keener appreciation of the diverse creative abilities exhibited by humans throughout the world. As anthropologists analyze these humanistic and artistic traditions, they broaden our understanding of the economic, social, political, and religious conditions that prevail within these societies.

Why Study Anthropology?

Many students today question the practical benefits of their educational experience. Hence, you might ask, why study anthropology? First, anthropology contributes to a general liberal arts education, which helps students develop intellectually and

personally, as well as professionally. Numerous studies indicate that a well-rounded education contributes to a person's success in any chosen career, and because of its broad interdisciplinary nature, anthropology is especially well suited to this purpose.

CRITICAL THINKING AND GLOBAL AWARENESS

In the context of a liberal arts education, anthropology and anthropological research cultivate critical-thinking skills. As we noted earlier, the scientific method relies on constant evaluation of and critical thinking about data collected in the field. Also, by being exposed to the cultures and lifestyles of unfamiliar societies, students may adopt a more critical and analytical stance toward conditions in their own society. Critical-thinking skills enhance the reasoning abilities of students wherever life takes them.

Anthropology also creates an expanding global awareness and an appreciation for cultures other than our own. In this age of rapid communication, worldwide travel, and increasing economic interconnections, young people preparing for careers in the twenty-first century must recognize and show sensitivity toward the cultural differences that exist among peoples, while understanding the fundamental similarities that make us all distinctly human. In this age of cultural diversity and increasing internationalization, sustaining this dual perception—of underlying similar human characteristics and outward cultural differences—has both practical and moral benefits. Nationalistic, ethnic, and racial bigotry are rife today in many parts of the world, yet our continuing survival and happiness depend on greater mutual understanding. Anthropology promotes a cross-cultural perspective that allows us to see ourselves as part of one human family in the midst of tremendous diversity. Our society needs citizens not just of some local region or group but also, and more importantly, as citizens of a complex interlocking world. We need

world citizens who can work in an inescapably multicultural and multinational world to work cooperatively to solve our most pressing problems of bigotry, poverty, and violence.

In addition, an anthropology course gives students a chance to delve into a discipline whose roots lie in both science and the humanities. As we have seen, anthropology brings to bear rigorous scientific methods and models in examining the causes of human evolution, behavior, and social relationships. But anthropologists also seek a humanistic understanding of other societies in all their rich cultural complexity. Anthropology casts a wide net, seeking an understanding of ancient and contemporary peoples, biological and societal developments, and human diversity and similarities throughout the world.

Viewing life from the anthropological perspective, students will also gain a greater understanding of their personal lives in the context of a long period of human evolution and development. In learning about behavior patterns and cultural values in distant societies, students question and acquire new insights into their own behavior. Thus, anthropology nurtures personal enlightenment and self-awareness, one of the fundamental goals of education.

SUMMARY

Anthropology consists of four subfields: physical anthropology, archaeology, linguistic anthropology, and ethnology (cultural anthropology). Each of these subfields uses distinctive methods for examining humanity in the past and in all areas of the world today. Physical anthropologists investigate human evolution and the physical variation of human populations across many geographical regions. Archaeologists study the past by analyzing artifacts, or material remains, of past societies. Linguistic anthropologists focus their studies on languages, seeking out historical relationships among languages, pursuing clues to the evolution of particular languages, and comparing one language with another to determine differences and similarities.

Ethnologists conduct fieldwork in various societies to examine people's lifestyles. They describe these societies in written studies, called ethnographies, that highlight behavior and thought patterns characteristic of the people studied. In examining societies ethnologists use systematic research methods and strategies, primarily participant observation, which involves participating in the daily activities of the people they are studying.

Anthropologists draw on the scientific method to investigate humanity while recognizing the limitations of science in grasping the subtleties of human affairs. Yet anthropology is also a humanistic discipline that focuses on such cultural elements as art, music, and religion. By bridging science and the humanities, anthropology enables us to look at humanity's biological and cultural heritage with a broad perspective.

For students, anthropology creates a global awareness and a deep appreciation of humanity past and present. By evaluating anthropological data, students develop critical-thinking skills. And, the process of anthropological inquiry—exploring other cultures and comparing them to one's own—sheds light on one's personal situation as a human being in a particular time and place.

STUDY QUESTIONS

1. As an anthropologist on a starship in the twenty-first century, you are a specialist in "first contact" situations. Briefly describe your goals and methods.

2. As an anthropologist you find out about the existence of a group of humans in the Amazon rainforest that has never been contacted. How would you use the four subfields of anthropology to investigate this human community?

3. How do anthropologists utilize the scientific method in their studies? What are the limitations of the scientific method in anthropological studies?

4. You are talking with a friend who asks, "Why would anyone want to study anthropology? What practical benefits may be gained from taking a course in anthropology?" How would you answer your friend?

5. What is the holistic approach and how is it related to anthropology, the four subfields, and other disciplines?

KEY TERMS

anthropology
applied anthropology
archaeology
artifacts
cultural anthropology
deductive method
ethnography
ethnology
fossils

historical linguistics
holistic
hypothesis
inductive method
linguistics
middens
paleoanthropology
paradigms
participant observation

primates
primatology
scientific method
sociolinguistics
structural linguistics
theories
variable

INTERNET EXERCISES

1. Peruse **http://www.wsu.edu:8001/vcwsu/commons/to...ure/culture-definitions/geertz-text.html.** How do the twelve definitions of culture presented by Clyde Kluckhohn compare to the field of anthropology explained in this book?

2. After reading the section of Chapter 1 about archaeology, look at the following website: **http://www.ibm.com/sfasp/arch.htm.** Read the section titled "The Adventure of The Ancient 3-D Jigsaw Puzzle." How does modern high technology help archaeologists do their jobs?

⊚ SUGGESTED READINGS

AGAR, MICHAEL H. 1980. *The Professional Stranger: An Informal Introduction to Ethnography*. New York: Academic Press. This excellent introduction to how ethnologists prepare for fieldwork also presents an insightful autobiographical account of fieldwork conducted in various locations across the United States.

BARFIELD, THOMAS (Ed.) 1997. *The Dictionary of Anthropology*. Oxford: Blackwell Publishers Ltd. This is a useful source for looking up any of the topics addressed within cultural anthropology. It contains the most current references for most of the research areas within cultural anthropology.

BOYD, ROBERT, AND JOAN B. SILK. 1997. *How Humans Evolved*. New York: W. W. Norton. One of a number of introductory textbooks in physical anthropology. Various sections deal with the fossil record, genetics, primates, and human evolutionary trends.

CHAGNON, NAPOLEON A. 1974. *Studying the Yanomamö*. New York: Holt, Rinehart and Winston. A renowned anthropologist's thorough introduction to ethnological fieldwork. It includes many classic examples of "culture shock" experienced by ethnologists in the course of fieldwork.

FAGAN, BRIAN M. 1988. *Archaeology: A Brief Introduction*. Glenview, IL: Scott, Foresman. A concise introduction to the field of archaeology. The sophisticated techniques and procedures used by contemporary archaeologists are highlighted.

HICKERSON, NANCY P. 1980. *Linguistic Anthropology*. New York: Holt, Rinehart and Winston. A succinct examination of anthropological linguistics, focusing on the most important topics in this subfield of anthropology.

LEVINSON, DAVID, AND MELVIN EMBER (Eds.) 1996. *Encyclopedia of Cultural Anthropology* (4 vols). New York: Henry Holt and Company. This four-volume encyclopedia has extensive essays on the most important research topics within cultural anthropology written by the leading researchers in the discipline.

PEACOCK, JAMES L. 1986. *The Anthropological Lens: Harsh Light, Soft Focus*. Cambridge: Cambridge University Press. In this well-written work, James Peacock introduces the importance of anthropology as a discipline that deepens our understanding of humanity. He demonstrates how the study of anthropology contributes toward more self-understanding.

POWDERMAKER, HORTENSE. 1966. *Stranger and Friend: The Way of an Anthropologist*. New York: Norton. A classic autobiographical account chronicling ethnological fieldwork in Africa and the United States. The unique problems and challenges confronting a female ethnologist are addressed in this volume.

Human Evolution

CHAPTER OUTLINE

Theories of Evolution
Origin Myths / The Darwinian Revolution / Principles of Inheritance / The Evolution of Life

Hominid Evolution
Australopithecus / Homo habilis / Homo erectus / Archaic Homo sapiens / Modern Homo sapiens

Modern Homo sapiens Culture: The Upper Paleolithic
Tools / Variation in Upper Paleolithic Technologies / Upper Paleolithic Subsistence and Social Organization / The Upper Paleolithic in Europe / Migration of Upper Paleolithic Humans

Human Variation
Skin Color

CHAPTER QUESTIONS

- How does evolutionary theory differ from origin myths?

- What is natural selection?

- What are the earliest forms of hominids, and what makes them different from other primates?

- How does Homo habilis differ from the Australopithecines?

- How do anthropologists explain the migration of Homo erectus out of Africa?

- What are the cultural characteristics of Homo erectus?

- What are the physical and cultural characteristics of the Neanderthals of Europe?

- What are the two different models of evolutionary development of modern humans?

- What are the cultural features of the Upper Paleolithic?

- What factors of natural selection are thought to have been responsible for differences of skin color in modern humans?

Theories of Evolution

THE MOST PROFOUND HUMAN QUESTIONS ARE THE ones that perplex us the most. Who are we? Why are we here? Where did we come from? What is our place in the universe? What is the purpose of our lives? What happens after death? These questions have been shared by all peoples throughout history. Most cultures have developed sophisticated ideas and myths to provide answers to these fundamental questions. **Cosmologies** are conceptual frameworks that present the universe (the cosmos) as an orderly system and include answers to those basic questions about the place of humankind in the universe.

ORIGIN MYTHS

Traditionally, these questions have been the basis for origin myths, usually considered the most sacred of all cosmological conceptions. *Origin myths* account for the ways in which supernatural beings or forces formed the earth and people. They are transmitted from generation to generation through ritual, education, laws, art, and cultural performances such as dance and music. They are highly symbolic and are expressed in a language rich with various levels of meaning.

Many origin myths deal with the origin of humans in the context of the origin of the universe. For example, the Navajo Indians traditionally believed that Holy People, supernatural and sacred, lived below ground in twelve lower worlds. A massive underground flood forced the Holy People to crawl through a hollow reed to the surface of the earth, where they created the universe. A deity named Changing Woman gave birth to the Hero Twins, called Monster Slayer and Child of the Waters. Mortals, called Earth Surface People, emerged, and First Man and First Woman were formed from the ears of white and yellow corn.

Another cosmological tradition, found in India, teaches that life resulted from the opening of a cosmic egg, which is the source of all life. In China, in the religious tradition of Taoism, male and female principles known as *yin* and *yang* are the spiritual and material sources for the origins of humans and other living forms. *Yin* is considered the passive, negative, feminine force or principle in the universe, the source of cold and darkness; *yang* is the active, positive, masculine force or principle, the source of heat and light. Taoists believe that the interaction of these two opposite principles brought forth the universe and all living forms out of chaos.

Western Origin Myths   In the Western tradition, the ancient Greeks had various mythological explanations for the origin of humans. One early view was that Prometheus fashioned humans out of water and earth. Another had Zeus ordering Pyrrha, the inventor of fire, to throw stones behind his back; these stones became men and women. Later Greek cosmological views were more scientifically based. Thales of Miletus (c. 636–546 B.C.) argued that life originated in the sea and that humans initially were fishlike, eventually moving onto dry land and evolving into mammals. A few hundred years later, Aristotle (384–322 B.C.) suggested an early theory of creation through evolution. Based on comparative physiology and anatomy, his argument stated that life had evolved from simple lower forms, such as single-celled amoebas, to complex higher forms, such as humans.

The most important cosmological tradition affecting Western views of creation stems from the Book of Genesis in the Bible. This Judaic tradition describes how God created the cosmos. It begins with "In the beginning God created the heaven and the earth," emphasizing that the Creation took six days, during which light, heaven, earth, vegetation, sun, moon, stars, birds, fish, animals, and humans originated. In Genesis the creator is given a name, Yahweh, and is responsible for creating man, Adam, from "dust" and placing him in the Garden of Eden. Adam names the animals and birds. Woman, Eve, is created from Adam's rib. Later, as Christianity spread throughout Europe, the biblical cosmology became the dominant origin myth in the Western world.

THE DARWINIAN REVOLUTION

In the Western world following the medieval period (c. A.D. 1450), scientific discoveries began to influence conceptions about humanity's relationship to the rest of the universe. Copernicus and Galileo presented the novel idea that the earth is just one of many planets revolving around the sun, rather than the center of the universe, as had traditionally been believed. As this idea became accepted, humans could no longer view themselves and their planet as the center of the universe. This shift in cosmological thinking set the stage for entirely new views of humanity's links to the rest of the natural world.

New developments in the geological sciences began to expand radically the scientific estimates of the age of the earth. These and other scientific discoveries in astronomy, biology, chemistry, mathematics, and other disciplines dramatically transformed Western thought.

Darwin, Wallace, and Natural Selection   Two individuals affected strongly by this scientific revolution were Charles Darwin and Alfred Wallace, nineteenth-century British *naturalists* (a term used at that time to refer to biologists). These biologists contributed significantly to the growth of scientific knowledge through their ideas on evolution. **Evolution** refers to the process of change within species over time. Evolutionary theory holds that existing species of plants and animals have emerged over millions of years from simple organisms. Before the mid-1800s, a few thinkers had suggested evolutionary theories, but because of a lack of understanding of how old the earth really was and the absence of a reasonable explanation for the evolutionary process, most people could not accept them.

Working independently, Darwin and Wallace made observations of living species around the world. Impressed by the diversity of living species, they developed an explanation of the basic mechanism of evolution. This mechanism is known as **natural selection.**

In 1831, Darwin began a five-year voyage around the world on a British ship, the HMS Beagle. During this journey he collected numerous species of plants and animals from many different environments. Meanwhile, Wallace was observing different species of plants and animals on the islands off Malaysia. Although both Darwin and Wallace arrived at the theory of natural selection simultaneously and independently, Darwin went on to present a thorough and completely documented statement of the theory in his book *On the Origin of Species*, published in 1859.

In their theory of natural selection, Darwin and Wallace emphasized the enormous variation that exists in all plant and animal species. They also noted that individuals in a species reproduce at a rate that cannot be supported by the environment; thus, their offspring must compete for food to survive. Those born with variations or traits that make them better able to compete are the ones that survive and pass on their traits to their offspring. Darwin and Wallace called this process natural selection because nature, or the demands of the environment, actually determines which individuals (or which traits) survive. This process, repeated countless times over millions of years, is the means by which species evolve or develop over time.

Examples of Natural Selection   One problem Darwin faced in writing *On the Origin of Species* was a lack of well-documented examples of natural selection at work. Most major changes in nature take place over a period of thousands or millions of years; only when animals or plants are exposed to rapid, fundamental changes in their environment can we actually observe natural selection in action.

A classic case of natural selection, known as *industrial melanism,* was occurring in the industrial areas of England during Darwin's lifetime, although he was unaware of it. During the 1850s, populations of English moths showed variations in color—some were light, others were dark. The lighter-colored moths were more common. After this period, however, the darker-colored variety became more common. The reason for this was a change in the environment, as black soot from industrial pollution gradually covered the trees. The light-colored moths, being highly visible against the blackened trees, were eaten by birds. In contrast, the dark-colored moths had an adaptive advantage because they were concealed against the background of the dark-colored trees; hence, this

population survived and reproduced in greater numbers. This process of natural selection has been confirmed experimentally with the release of light-colored and dark-colored moths in urban areas (Bishop, Cook, & Muggleton, 1978).

Natural selection is currently viewed as a major guiding force in the evolution of living species. It enabled Darwin to explain the mechanisms of biological evolution, and it remains a powerful explanation for the development of living species of plants and animals today.

PRINCIPLES OF INHERITANCE

Darwin contributed to the modern understanding of biological evolution by thoroughly documenting the variation of living forms and by identifying the process of natural selection. But Darwin did not understand how individuals pass on traits to their offspring. This discovery, and the study of heredity, was left to the experiments of an Austrian monk, Gregor Mendel (1822–1884). During the 1860s Mendel began a series of breeding experiments with pea plants. The results of these experiments revolutionized biological thought. Although his findings were not recognized until the twentieth century, they have shaped our basic understanding of inheritance. Through his experiments Mendel established the new science of **genetics,** a field of biology that deals with the inheritance of different characteristics.

From the work of Mendel and other biologists, we now know that traits are determined by genes. A **gene** is a discrete unit of hereditary information that determines specific physical characteristics of organisms. It is estimated that a human being inherits more than 100,000 genes that specify various physical characteristics. Most sexually reproducing plants and animals have two genes for every physical trait, one inherited from each parent.

THE EVOLUTION OF LIFE

Modern scientific findings indicate that the universe as we know it began to develop between 10 billion and 20 billion years ago. Approximately 4.6 billion years ago, the sun and the earth developed, and about a billion years later the first forms of life appeared in the sea. Through the process of natural selection, living forms that developed adaptive characteristics survived and reproduced. Geological forces and environmental alterations bringing about both gradual and rapid changes led to the evolution of new forms of life. Plants, fish, amphibians, reptiles, and eventually mammals evolved over millions of years of environmental change.

About 67 million years ago diverse groups of mammals known as **primates** began to evolve in different areas of the world. Primates include *prosimians,* such as lemurs, tarsiers, and lorises; and *anthropoids,* such as monkeys, apes, and humans. Primate evolution followed general trends, resulting in complex traits such as increased brain size compared with body size, improved vision, longer periods of offspring dependence on their mothers, a complex social life, and enhanced learning abilities. The most successful primates have been humans, who today exist in most environments. The human primate, with its upright posture, large brain, and increased learning capacities, has been able to adapt to many types of environments through culture, as we will discuss in Chapter 3.

Hominid Evolution

Anthropologists have been evaluating hypotheses regarding hominid evolution for the past hundred years (see Figure 2.1). **Hominids,** a family of primates that includes the direct ancestors of humans, share certain subtle features in their teeth, jaws, and brain. However, by far the major characteristic that identifies them as a distinct group is the structural anatomy needed for bipedalism, the ability to walk fully erect on two legs. **Bipedalism** is not a characteristic of modern apes, such as chimpanzees and gorillas, who can stand upright but do most of their walking on four limbs. The first hominids date to about 5.6 to 5.8 million years ago in Africa and belong to what has been referred to as *Ardipithecus ramidus.* The fossil evidence for these particular creatures is extremely fragmentary, but they do indicate that these creatures were fully bipedal. However, fossil evidence is abundant for the hominids known as *Australopithecus.*

AUSTRALOPITHECUS

Fossil evidence for several species of australopithecines has been discovered in Africa. The most complete early known form of this genus, found in

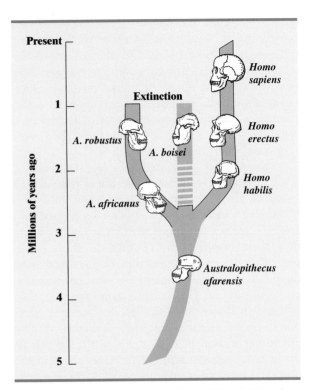

Figure 2.1   Different interpretations of hominid evolution. Various theories have placed *Australopithecus africanus* in a position ancestral to *Homo,* or to both *Homo* and later australopithecines. The robust australopithecines are placed on their own side branch. In 1979 Johanson and White named a new species, *A. afarensis,* which they placed at the base of the hominid family tree leading to both the australopithecines and *Homo. A. africanus* was then moved to a side branch leading to the robust australopithecines. Other interpretations are also being evaluated. Some researchers have suggested that the split between the *Homo* and *Australopithecus* lines occurred more than 4 million years ago.

the Afar region of Ethiopia, is known as *Australopithecus afarensis.* It was discovered in 1974 by a joint American-French team of paleoanthropologists led by Donald Johanson. The best-known *A. afarensis* individual is popularly known as "Lucy" (named after the Beatles' song "Lucy in the Sky with Diamonds"). Forty percent of the skeleton of this individual was preserved, allowing paleoanthropologists to determine its precise physical characteristics. "Lucy" is a female Australopithecus with features such as a small cranium, or skull—440 cubic centimeters (cc), compared with a capacity

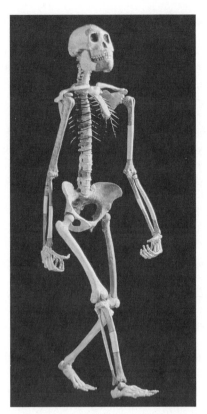

Skeletal remains of Australopithecus afarensis *recovered by Donald Johanson at Hadar, Ethiopia, in 1974. Informally known as "Lucy," the find is unique because of its age and completeness.*

of 1,000 to 1,800 cc for modern humans—indicating a small brain and large teeth. Lucy's skull resembles that of a modern chimpanzee; however, below the neck the anatomy of the spine, pelvis, hips, thigh bones, and feet has characteristics of a fully bipedal creature. Lucy was fairly small, weighing approximately 75 pounds, and was about 3.5 to 4 feet tall.

Other australopithecines from later periods have been discovered in both southern and eastern Africa: *Australopithecus africanus* and larger types of australopithecines classified as *Australopithecus robustus*. Based on the fossil evidence, many paleoanthropologists hypothesize that *A. afarensis,* which dates from 3.5 million years ago, gave rise to the later forms of australopithecines between 3 million and 2 million years ago (Shipman, 1986a). However, future discoveries may extend the human lineage farther back in time.

HOMO HABILIS

East African sites continued to produce fossil hominids throughout the 1960s and 1970s. These fossils, classified as *Homo habilis,* have an average-sized skull, 640 cc, indicating a much larger brain than that of the australopithecines. *H. habilis* dates from between 2.2 million and 1.6 million years ago; it therefore coexisted with later species of australopithecines. This is what would be expected in an evolutionary perspective.

Oldowan Technology   At several sites in eastern and southern Africa, archaeologists have discovered early stone tools known as *chopper tools* or *hammer stones.* These tools have jagged cutting edges that were used to break off chips of stone to form flakes. Called *Oldowan tools,* these tools could be used for cutting the hides of animals and whittling wood for making wooden spears or digging sticks. Archaeologists are not sure whether the Oldowan tools are associated with australopithecines or *Homo habilis.*

The importance of the discovery of the Oldowan tools is that the tools suggest early hominids had the intellectual capacity to fashion stone tools to develop a more effective means of subsistence. This innovation indicates an increased brain size, which led in turn to new forms of complex learning. The Oldowan technology marks the beginnings of what is known as the Lower Paleolithic stage of hominid evolution, or the Old Stone Age.

HOMO ERECTUS

The next stage of hominid evolution is associated with fossils discovered both inside and outside Africa. In China, Java (a major island in Indonesia), the Middle East, Europe, and Africa, paleoanthropologists have investigated fossil remains of a hominid population known as *Homo erectus.* These finds date to between 1.65 million and 300,000 years ago.

Anatomically, *H. erectus* fossils represent a major new stage of hominid evolution, especially with respect to brain size. The cranial capacity of *H. erectus* ranges between 775 and 1,225 cc, placing the skull size of some of these individuals within the range of that of modern humans (Campbell, 1987). This evidence indicates that most of the growth in brain size occurred in the frontal lobes, an area associated with intellectual skills (Wolpoff, 1980). The populations of *H. erectus* differed from modern humans in that they had a low, sloping forehead and thick, massive jaws with large teeth. From the neck down, their skeletal features are similar to those of modern humans, but their bones are much heavier, indicating a very powerful musculature. Yet their skeletal features fall within the range of modern human populations.

Migration of *Homo erectus* Given that the early hominids lived in Africa, the question arises of how *H. erectus* became so widely dispersed throughout the world. The major hypothesis is that as populations increased, a certain percentage migrated into new territories by a process known as budding (Campbell, 1987). Through this process, a few individuals would split from an original group and form a new, autonomous group in a more favorable territory. If each budding group moved 15 miles in each generation (25 years), then *H. erectus* could have migrated from Africa to Europe in 5,000 years and to China in 15,000 years.

As these populations migrated across continents, they encountered different climates and environments. This movement occurred during a period known geologically as the *Pleistocene epoch,* which marked the later stage in what we popularly call the *Ice Age.* During this time, huge masses of ice, called *glaciers,* spread over the northern continents, producing colder climates in the temperate zones such as Europe and northern Asia and increases in rainfall in the tropical areas, creating grasslands and new lakes. *H. erectus* populations had to adapt to a wide variety of climatic and environmental conditions whether they remained in the tropics, as many did, or migrated to new areas of the world.

Fire *Homo erectus* probably could not have survived in the colder climates without the use of fire. The use of fire to cook food added an important element to the diet. Cooking food made it more digestable and safer to consume. In addition, fires could be used to keep predators away, enabling *H. erectus* to survive more effectively. It is unclear whether *H. erectus* knew how to make fire (fire begun by lightning or forest fires could have been kept lit), but there is no question that fire was controlled.

Acheulian Technology An abundance of stone tools associated with *H. erectus* indicates a remarkable evolution in technology. This new technology, called *Acheulian,* shows a definite continuation and refinement of the Oldowan technology. The Oldowan technology involved making tools by flaking off pieces of stone to be used as cutters, choppers, and hammer stones. The Acheulian techniques were much more sophisticated, using bone or antler to strike off flakes from both sides of a prepared core of stone. The Acheulian techniques enabled *H. erectus* to make implements such as clevers, hand axes, and scrapers.

The tools produced through this technology made *H. erectus* efficient hunters, able to kill large game animals such as bear, deer, and elephant, as well as smaller game. Thus, the Acheulian technology made possible a more effective means of subsistence, which required both cooperative and intellectual efforts. Most paleoanthropologists suggest that improvements in language and modes of communication probably began to evolve with the *H. erectus* lifestyle. Undoubtedly, the increase in brain size, especially in the frontal lobes, indicates a capacity for more complex learning. The ability to communicate aided cooperation in activities such as hunting and improvements in technological development. The *H. erectus* stage of hominid evolution represents a very complex adaptation to the conditions of the Pleistocene epoch.

ARCHAIC *HOMO SAPIENS*

The fossil evidence for the next major stage of hominid evolution—archaic *Homo sapiens*—is dated from about 300,000 to 40,000 years ago. Archaic *Homo sapiens* were widespread throughout Europe (including England), Africa, Asia, and the Middle East. The best-known example is the Neanderthal, the hominid population that lived in Europe about 100,000 to 35,000 years ago.

Physically, all archaic *H. sapiens* populations shared some general characteristics, although variations existed from region to region. The skeletal evidence suggests that they were short, about 5 feet tall, but powerfully built. The hands and feet were wider and thicker than those of modern humans. The skull and face were broad, with a larger jaw, larger teeth, and extremely prominent brow ridges. The Neanderthal physique has become the model for the stereotype of "cave men" frequently portrayed in cartoons and other popular entertainment.

This image of a brutish prehistoric creature is misleading. The skull of the Neanderthal was large, ranging from 1,200 cc to 2,000 cc, and could accommodate a brain as large as, or even larger than, that of a modern human. Moreover, recent studies of the Neanderthal skull indicate that the structure of the brain was essentially the same as that of modern humans, suggesting similar intellectual capacities.

Neanderthal Technology   The stone tool industry associated with Neanderthal populations is called the *Mousterian tradition,* named after a rock shelter at Le Moustier, France, where it was first described. It shows a remarkable variability compared with earlier technologies. Mousterian implements could have been used for cutting, leather working, piercing, food processing, woodworking, hunting, and producing weapons (Binford & Binford, 1966; Bordes, 1968). Neanderthals also must have been capable of making some type of clothing, or else they would not have been able to survive the cold European climate. In addition, archeologists have discovered evidence of the extensive occupation of caves and rock shelters, as well as open-air sites that may have been temporary camps occupied during the summer months. Archaeological evidence includes the remains of charcoal deposits and charred bones, indicating that, like earlier *H. erectus,* Neanderthals used fire not only for warmth but also for cooking and perhaps for protection against dangerous animals.

The remains discovered at the Neanderthal sites suggest that, like populations of archaic *H. sapiens* in other areas, Neanderthals were efficient hunters. They hunted both small and large game, including such extinct creatures as European elephants, giant elk, bison, and huge bears weighing up to 1,500 pounds. These bears, related to the Alaskan brown bear, are known as "cave bears" and were formidable prey for Neanderthal hunters.

Neanderthal Rituals and Beliefs   The evidence surrounding cave bear kills has led some archaeologists to suggest that Neanderthals conducted religious activities. In a cave in Switzerland, archaeologists found stone-lined rectangular pits containing more than twenty cave bear skulls and covered by an enormous flat stone. The site appears to be some sort of shrine. Similar findings at other locations have led some archaeologists to view these complexes as evidence of a Neanderthal cave bear cult.

Intentional burial of their dead is another indication of religious beliefs among Neanderthals. These were the first hominids, as far as we know, to do this. Burial sites, perhaps even family cemeteries, have been found in different locations. Significantly, the deceased were buried along with tools or food offerings. For example, a burial site known as Shanidar, discovered in the Zagros Mountains of Iraq, contained the remains of four individuals, one of whom appears to have been surrounded by a bed of flowers, as deduced from an analysis of fossilized pollen.

These burial sites and cave bear findings provide indirect evidence for religious beliefs and perhaps for a belief in an afterlife. Although some archaeologists have questioned whether the Neanderthals did actually maintain a cave bear cult (Chase & Dibble, 1987), the evidence for spiritual beliefs is suggestive. Modern human populations that perform burials inevitably believe in an afterlife.

MODERN *HOMO SAPIENS*

Anatomically modern *Homo sapiens* populations appeared widely about 40,000 years ago. Between 40,000 and 10,000 years ago, these populations migrated to places all over the globe, adapting both physically and culturally to conditions in different regions.

Physically, these modern *Homo sapiens* populations were much the same as modern humans. These fossilized skeletons do not have the heavy, thick bones, large teeth, and prominent brow ridges associated with the Neanderthals and other archaic forms. The high, vaulted shape of the skull is modern, and the dimensions are similar to those of modern-day humans. From the cold climates of northern Asia to the deserts of Africa, groups of *H. sapiens* shared similar characteristics as part of one species. However, like populations today, these early groups developed different physical traits, such as body size and facial features, as a result of local environmental conditions and selective pressures.

The Evolution of Modern *Homo sapiens* Although paleoanthropologists generally agree that *H. erectus* evolved into *H. sapiens*, they disagree about how, where, and when this transition took place. Early interpretations were based on limited information and often emphasized the uniqueness of individual finds. Recent researchers have offered a number of different theories (Howells, 1976; Stringer & Andrews, 1988; Mellars, 1989). These can be described by two general models representing opposing perspectives: the *multiregional evolutionary model* and the *replacement model.*

The *multiregional evolutionary model* suggests that the gradual evolution of *H. erectus* into modern *H. sapiens* took place in different regions of the Old World. Evolutionary processes affected genetic variation in local *H. erectus* populations, creating regional variation. In this context *H. sapiens* traits first appeared in certain areas, but widespread sharing of genes between populations prevented the evolution of distinct species. The emergence of modern *H. sapiens* was, therefore, a widespread phenomenon, though different regional populations continued to exhibit distinctive features.

The replacement model suggests that modern *H. sapiens* evolved in one area of the world (Africa) and migrated to other regions, where the species replaced earlier *H. sapiens* such as Neanderthal. Thus, this hypothesis proposes that modern *H. sapiens* populations are all descended from a common ancestral group; consequently, the diversity among modern humans is marginally small.

This replacement hypothesis has been referred to as the "Eve hypothesis" in the media, because it suggests that there is a direct genetic link between a woman or a group of women in Africa about 200,000 years ago and modern *H. sapiens*. Anthropologists have been evaluating both fossil and genetic evidence to determine which of these two competing models is more valid in explaining the emergence of modern *H. sapiens*.

Modern *Homo sapiens* Culture: The Upper Paleolithic

In general, the material artifacts associated with modern *H. sapiens* populations become increasingly complex. Throughout Africa, the Middle East, Asia, the Americas, and Australia, complicated and elaborate technologies and other culturally decorative artifacts are found in abundance. This period is called the *Upper Paleolithic:* the term *Paleolithic* refers to "Old Stone Age," whereas *Upper* indicates the later stages of this period. The Upper Paleolithic dates between the time period of 40,000 and 10,000 years ago, approximately.

The technological and social innovations of the Upper Paleolithic represent a creative explosion in technology. Innovation of this magnitude required a highly developed capacity for the accumulation and transmission of knowledge, likely indicating that the inhabitants had developed efficient subsistence strategies that allowed free time for experimentation and innovation.

TOOLS

These different traditions encompass a tremendous amount of variation in stone tool types. The most important technological shift in stone tool production involved the making of *blades:* long, narrow flakes that could be used to produce many types of knives, harpoons, and spear points. Among the most striking examples of Upper Paleolithic percussion flaking are *Solutrean projectiles,* dated to 20,000 years ago. These implements, often several inches long, probably functioned as spear points. Yet the flaking is so delicate and the points so sharp that it is difficult to imagine them fastened to the end of a spear. It has, in fact, been suggested that they were made as works of art, not tools for everyday use.

In addition, specialized stone tools, including *borers,* or drills, and *burins,* chisel-like tools for working bone or ivory, were produced. Tools such as these would have aided in the manufacture of the bone, antler, and ivory artifacts that become increasingly common during the Upper Paleolithic. A particularly important piece of equipment that appeared during this time period is the *spear-thrower,* a piece of wood or ivory that increased the power of the hunter's arm. The increased leverage provided by the spear-thrower enabled Upper Paleolithic hunters to hurl projectiles much faster than they could otherwise.

Another category of artifact that became common is the **composite tool,** an implement fashioned from several different materials. An example of a composite tool is the harpoon, which might consist of a wooden shaft that is slotted for the insertion of sharp stone flakes. Also discovered at Upper Paleolithic sites were needles for sewing clothing, and fibers for making rope, nets, trapping equipment, and many other artifacts.

Shelters   Upper Paleolithic sites have also produced numerous indications of shelters, some of which were quite elaborate, in many parts of the world. Some of the more spectacular were found at a 15,000-year-old site at Mezhirich in the Ukraine. This site contained five shelters constructed of bones from mammoths, an extinct species of elephant (Gladkih et al., 1984). The mammoth's jaws were used as the base, and the ribs, tusks, and other bones were used for the sides. The interiors contained work areas, hearths, and accumulations of artifacts, suggesting that they were inhabited for long periods. Storage pits were located in areas between the structures. It is estimated that the settlement may have been occupied by fifty people.

VARIATION IN UPPER PALEOLITHIC TECHNOLOGIES

Variations in tools found in different regions suggest that early humans had developed specialized technologies suited to particular environments. These variations also reflect the fact that different regions contained different forms of stone from which tools could be manufactured. In addition, regional differences may also reflect variations in culture, ethnicity, and individual expression. Archaeologist James Sackett, who has studied the classic Middle and Upper Paleolithic finds of France, notes that even tools that may have served the same function exhibit a great deal of variation (1982). Many Upper Paleolithic artisans made their stone tools in distinctive styles that varied from region to region. Today we often associate distinctive dress, decoration, and housing with different ethnic groups. To archaeologists, expressions of ethnic identity preserved in material remains are extremely important. Frequently we refer to archaeological cultures, which are defined on the basis of the distinctive artifacts they left behind. Stone tools may provide the first indications of ethnic and cultural divisions in human populations.

Expressive elements are also seen in other Upper Paleolithic artifacts. In comparison with the Middle Paleolithic, there are more nonutilitarian objects, including items for personal adornment (White, 1982). Some of these artifacts were obtained from distant sources, providing evidence of the development of trade networks.

UPPER PALEOLITHIC SUBSISTENCE AND SOCIAL ORGANIZATION

Middle and Upper Paleolithic societies employed many of the same subsistence strategies as had Lower Paleolithic groups. The Upper Paleolithic technology indicates that early *H. sapiens* were efficient hunters. Many sites contain large heaps of

Reconstruction of an Upper Paleolithic dwelling constructed with mammoth bones.

bones of mammoths and other animals. In addition, piles of animal bones have been found at the bottoms of high cliffs. These finds suggest that *H. sapiens* hunters had stampeded the animals off cliffs to be killed and butchered by hunters waiting below. Archaeologists have also found remains of traps used by Upper Paleolithic hunters to snare animals.

Upper Paleolithic people also gathered plants to supplement their food resources. Plants were probably used for both nutritional and medicinal purposes. However, the generally small size of Upper Paleolithic living areas and the limited amount of plant remains recovered from archaeological sites provide only an incomplete view of diet during that period.

Social Organization One way to develop hypotheses about the lifestyle and social organization of prehistoric people is to study the social organization of contemporary groups with similar subsistence strategies (Price & Brown, 1985). Anthropologists recognize, however, the limitations of this approach. Present-day hunters and gatherers occupy marginal areas such as the dry desert regions of southern Africa. In contrast, Paleolithic foraging populations resided in all types of environments, many of which were rich in food resources. Most likely these abundant food resources enabled Paleolithic foragers to gather adequate food supplies without expending excessive amounts of energy.

Contemporary foraging societies, with their relatively small groups, low population density, highly nomadic subsistence strategies, and loosely defined territorial boundaries, have social organizations that serve to tie *kin* (related individuals) together and foster unity within and among groups. In the past, these flexible social relationships may have enabled foragers to overcome ecological and organizational problems.

Whether ethnographic data on the social organization of "modern" foragers can instruct us on the type of social systems Paleolithic foragers had is as yet an open question. Some archaeological studies suggest that the size of domestic groups of Paleolithic societies corresponds to that of contemporary foragers (Pfeiffer, 1985; Campbell, 1987), but other anthropologists suggest that ethnographic models underestimate the diversity of prehistoric

hunting and gathering adaptations. They also point out that modern hunter-gatherer societies may have been greatly modified through recent encounters with the outside world. We shall return to this topic in Chapter 8.

THE UPPER PALEOLITHIC IN EUROPE

Changes seen in the Upper Paleolithic period in Europe are indicative of developments in much of the world. The best-known people of the Upper Paleolithic in Europe are the Cro-Magnon. The name *Cro-Magnon* comes from a site in Dordogne, France, dated at about 25,000 years ago. The fragmentary remains of five or six individuals recovered from a rock shelter in 1868 provided the first evidence for what was initially identified as the Cro-Magnon. The Cro-Magnon remains are typified by the skull of the "Old Man," which belonged to an adult male less than 50 years of age. The skull is high and vaulted, with a cranial capacity of approximately 1,600 cc. Other skulls in the collection display a combination of archaic and modern traits. Some have heavy bones and developed brow ridges, suggesting similarities with Neanderthals.

The finds at Cro-Magnon are *not* associated with any particular race. Skeletal remains bearing many similar features have been found in other parts of western Europe and North Africa, as have tool remains comparable to those found at Cro-Magnon. The different Cro-Magnon sites contain artifacts that demonstrate an elaborate technology, far superior to that of previous societies.

Cro-Magnon Culture About 17,000 years ago, some Cro-Magnon groups became specialists in procuring game from migrating herds of reindeer. These groups established summer camps, perhaps with lightweight tents, built on rises that provided a good view of the herds. In the winter the groups would relocate in smaller groupings back in the warmth and shelter of the caves. Another critical element of Cro-Magnon technology was the ability to start a fire whenever one was needed. Cro-Magnons used materials such as iron pyrite to make sparks to ignite dry tinder. Archaeological evidence for this mastery of fire is widespread, ranging from Belgium to the heartland of Russia. Hearths are found in caves and sometimes in open-air sites with remnants of shel-

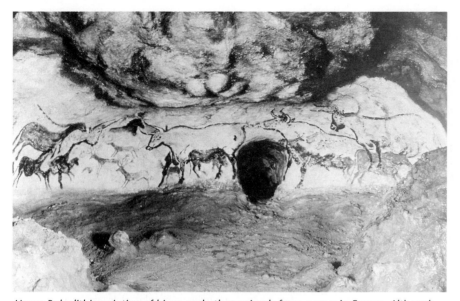

Upper Paleolithic painting of bison and other animals from a cave in France. Although interpretations of the meanings vary, paintings such as these convey the changing nature of the Paleolithic.

ters. Many of these sites contained charred wood and large quantities of bone ash, indicating that Cro-Magnons used fire for cooking as well as for heat.

In addition to their other technological accomplishments, the Upper Paleolithic peoples of Europe produced an impressive array of artistic creations. Thousands of bone, ivory, and stone sculptures of anatomically elaborate figures, including some known as the "Venus fertility goddesses," are found throughout Europe. Mural paintings found in the caves of Spain and France, such as those of the Lascaux Caves, are magnificent abstract and naturalistic paintings of animals and sometimes of humans dressed in the hides of animals. These murals might have been intended to celebrate a successful hunt or to ensure a better future. That some murals are located deep within underground caves may indicate that this art held profound spiritual and religious significance for its creators. What could be a more awe-inspiring site for a religious celebration or initiation ceremony than a dark underground chamber with beautiful paintings? On the other hand, some art may in essence be "art for art's sake," painted solely for enjoyment (Halverson, 1987).

MIGRATION OF UPPER PALEOLITHIC HUMANS

Upper Paleolithic hunters and gatherers developed specialized technologies that helped them to adapt to different environments in ways their precursors could not have. The remarkable abilities of *H. sapiens* to exploit such a wide variety of environments enabled these peoples to increase their populations, leading to modern human habitation of all parts of the globe. During the Upper Paleolithic, modern *H. sapiens* migrated throughout the world, including North and South America and Australia, continents that had previously been unoccupied by hominids.

The movement of modern *H. sapiens* populations into new areas was aided by changes in world climatic conditions during the past 100,000 years. This period encompasses the latter part of the Pleistocene, or Ice Age, when climatic conditions were much cooler and moister than they are now. Northern Europe, Asia, and North America were covered by glaciers, which were extensions of the polar ice caps. The vast amount of water frozen in these glaciers lowered world sea levels by hundreds of feet, exposing vast tracks of land,

Clovis spear points found at various sites in North America. First described at a site near Clovis, New Mexico, these spear points are characteristic of North American Paleo-Indian cultures.

known as *continental shelves*, that were previously (and are currently) beneath the sea. Many world areas that are today surrounded by water were at that time connected to other areas.

Upper Paleolithic Hunters in America   Archaeologists believe that the first humans came to the Western Hemisphere from Siberia over what is now the Bering Strait into the area of modern Alaska. Following herds of large game animals, these people migrated southward into North and South America. Today, the Bering Strait is a frigid body of water connecting the Pacific and Arctic oceans. Between 75,000 and 11,500 years ago, however, the glaciers and lower sea levels transformed this region on several occasions into a land mass more than 1,000 miles wide known as *Beringia* (Hopkins, 1982). Beringia served as a natural land bridge connecting Asia with North America. However, some archaeologists think that some of these early migrants may have sailed down the coast of the Americas along the ice formations along the Pacific ocean.

The Asian origin of Native Americans is supported by several lines of evidence, including physical similarities such as blood type and tooth shape between Asian and American Indian populations. In addition, studies of the languages spoken in both areas indicate a common origin.

But although most anthropologists agree that Native Americans migrated from Asia, they do not

agree on when this migration occurred; the estimates run from 30,000 to 12,000 years ago.

Human Variation

As we have seen, modern *H. sapiens* populations migrated throughout the world, adjusting to different environmental conditions. As different populations settled in different environments, they developed certain variations in physical characteristics as a result of natural selection and other evolutionary processes. Although *H. sapiens* is one species, some physical differences exist among groups. Variations occur with respect to body size, eye color, hair texture and color, shape of lips and nose, blood type, and eyelid form. In certain cases these characteristics are related to the types of selective pressures that existed in a particular environment; in other cases they are simply the result of physical isolation in certain areas during past eras.

SKIN COLOR

An obvious physical trait that varies in humans is skin pigmentation. Skin pigmentation became the primary basis for classifying different populations into different "races." In general use, the term *race* refers to the physical characteristics of a population that are based on common descent. Anthropologists have been attempting to classify and measure physical characteristics of differing populations for more than two centuries. One eighteenth-century approach placed all peoples in one of four racial categories: Europeans (white), Americans (red), Asiatics (yellow), and Africans (black). These early attempts to classify humans by skin color led to stereotypes regarding different human populations.

Modern classifications, which are based on more scientific knowledge of genetics, evolution, and geography, sometimes include hundreds of racial categories (Garn, 1971). However, many modern anthropologists believe that any system of racial classification is too rigid and inflexible to deal with the actual dynamics of population movement, genetic change, intermarriage, and other conditions affecting the physical characteristics of a population (Templeton, 1998).

APPLYING ANTHROPOLOGY

Clyde Snow: Forensic Anthropologist

The investigation of fossilized skeletal materials and human variation in the past and among living human populations has opened the way to many practical applications. For example, a specialty known as *forensic anthropology*, the identification of human skeletal remains for legal purposes, has emerged as an applied discipline within physical anthropology. Forensic anthropologists, trained to recognize subtle anatomical differences in human skeletal fragments, often assist police in solving homicides and missing-persons cases.

Clyde Collins Snow obtained a master's degree in zoology from Texas Tech University and planned to pursue a Ph.D. in physiology, but his career plans were interrupted by military service. While stationed at Lackland Air Force Base near San Antonio, he was introduced to the field of archaeology and became fascinated with the ancient artifacts discovered in the surrounding area.

After leaving the military, Snow attended the University of Arizona, where his zoological training and archaeology interests led him to a Ph.D. in physical anthropology. He became skilled at identifying old bones and artifacts. With his doctoral degree completed, he joined the Federal Aviation Administration as a consulting forensic anthropologist,

providing technical assistance in the identification of victims of aircraft accidents. Snow also lent his expertise to the design of safety equipment to prevent injuries in aircraft accidents.

As word of Snow's extraordinary skill in forensic anthropology spread, he was called to consult on and provide expert testimony in many criminal cases. His testimony was crucial at the sensational murder trial of John Wayne Gacy, accused of murdering more than thirty teenagers in the Chicago area. Snow also collaborated with experts in the reinvestigation of President John F. Kennedy's assassination. These experts built a full-scale model of Kennedy's head to determine whether Lee Harvey Oswald could have inflicted all of Kennedy's wounds. They did not uncover any scientific evidence to contradict the Warren Commission's conclusion that Oswald was the sole assassin.

Most recently Snow and his team have been recognized for their contributions to human rights issues. Snow served as a consultant to the Argentine government's National Commission on Disappeared Persons in its efforts to determine the fate of thousands of Argentines who were abducted and murdered by military death squads between 1976 and 1983, when the country was under the rule of a military

Dr. Clyde Snow.

dictatorship. As a result of his investigations, Snow was asked to testify as an expert witness in the trial of the nine *junta* members who ruled Argentina during the period of military repression. He also assisted people in locating their dead relatives.

Snow stresses that in his human rights investigative work he is functioning as an expert, not necessarily as an advocate. He must maintain an objective standpoint in interpreting his findings. The evidence he finds may then be presented by lawyers (as advocates) in the interests of justice.

Dr. Snow's human rights work is supported by various agencies such as the American Association of Advanced Sciences, the Ford Foundation, the J. Roderick MacArthur Foundation, Amnesty International, Physicians for Human Rights, and Human Rights Watch.

Variations in skin pigmentation among humans reflect adaptations to Paleolithic environments with different amounts and intensities of sunlight.

In general, however, it does appear that a dark pigmentation provides protection from ultraviolet radiation, which can cause sunburn, sunstroke, and skin cancers such as melanoma. Originally, as *H. sapiens* evolved in the tropical zones near the equator, a darker skin pigmentation most likely proved adaptive. But later, as populations moved into more temperate regions with less sunlight, other selective pressures produced lighter skin pigmentations. For example, in cold climates, dark-skinned individuals are at greater risk for frostbite than lighter-skinned individuals. In the cold climate of Korea during the Korean War, African American soldiers were over four times more likely to get frostbite than European-American soldiers. These observations, along with other data from a variety of studies, indicate that in colder northern climates darker skin is more prone to cold injury than lighter skin (Relethford, 1997).

It must be emphasized that these physical variations among *H. sapiens* populations are only "skin deep." In fact, geneticists believe that only about 4 genes out of more than 100,000 code for skin color. Racial theories claiming the supposed superiority of certain groups over others have no scientific basis. Except for general similarities in color and body size, individuals in any given population differ widely from one another in respect to longevity, vitality, athletic ability, intelligence, and other personal characteristics. All populations throughout the world produce individuals who differ widely in their physical and mental abilities. Racism or ethnic prejudice based on the belief in the superiority or inferiority of a particular group is unjustifiable, not only morally but also scientifically.

⊚ SUMMARY

All peoples have explanations for the origins of the universe and humankind. Following the scientific revolution in the West, various developments in the natural sciences led to what is known as the Darwinian revolution. Charles Darwin and Alfred Wallace developed separately the model of natural selection to explain the origins and development of life. Later developments in the field of genetics, along with the ideas of natural selection, are used by modern scientists to explain the evolution of life.

Paleoanthropologists have been investigating hominid evolution throughout the twentieth century. A number of early species known as Australopithecines existed in Africa at least 4 million years ago. These creatures were fully bipedal. Other later hominids, referred to as *Homo habilis,* discovered in Africa, are associated with toolmaking.

Later hominids known as *Homo erectus* were dispersed across several continents, including Africa, Europe, and Asia. *H. erectus* had a large brain and is associated with a sophisticated technology that includes the use of fire. The fossil record indicates that by 200,000 years ago populations of hominids known as archaic *Homo sapiens* inhabited different regions of the world. One example of archaic *Homo sapiens* is referred to as Neanderthal. Neanderthal is associated with a refined material culture that includes various types of stone tools, fire, clothing, and perhaps religious rituals and beliefs.

Anatomically modern *H. sapiens* date from about 40,000 years ago. The technology of modern *H. sapiens* is referred to as the Upper Paleolithic. Many different types of specialized tools were developed in different environments in the Upper Paleolithic. In addition, cave paintings, sculpture, and engravings are associated with this period.

Paleoanthropologists and geneticists are trying to determine the evolutionary relationships of archaic and anatomically modern *H. sapiens*. One of the most recent hypotheses is based on genetic data from modern females that indicates an ancestral line in Africa dating to about 200,000 years ago. Many leading scientists have questioned the basic tenets of this genetic model. Much more research needs to be done on this important question.

As modern humans adjusted to different environments, natural selection continued to play a role in determining physical characteristics. For example, variations in skin pigmentation reflect adaptions to environments with different amounts and intensities of sunlight. However, modern scientific evidence demonstrates that skin color does not correspond to any difference in the mental capacities of any population.

STUDY QUESTIONS

1. Your parents have phoned you to find out how things are going at college (translation: "Do you need money?") and what you are studying. You tell them that you are learning about early hominids, the australopithecines, *Homo habilis,* and *Homo erectus.* Your mother and father say, "I just can't believe that we came from chimpanzees!" How do you answer them?

2. What is natural selection and how does it work? Give an example of natural selection in action.

3. Where were the earliest hominids found? Describe the hominid "Lucy."

4. Discuss the emergence of the species *Homo erectus.* Where are these fossils found? How old are they?

5. Discuss the differences between the Neanderthals and modern *Homo sapiens.*

6. Describe the specific changes that characterized the evolution of technology from the Oldowan through the Acheulian, Mousterian, and Upper Paleolithic periods.

7. Contrast the multiregional evolutionary model with the replacement model.

8. Is skin color related to any environmental factors? Discuss whether different skin colors are more adaptive in different environments.

9. Should contemporary models of human evolution be classified as origin myths? Why or why not?

KEY TERMS

bipedalism	evolution	hominids
composite tool	gene	natural selection
cosmologies	genetics	primates

INTERNET EXERCISES

1. After reading the section on human evolution in Chapter 2, look at the Skull Module website of the California State University, Chico, anthropology department: **http://www.csuchico.edu/ anth/Module/skull.html.** Explore the site. How can anthropology students use this site? How does this site relate to the chapter? Does it help in understanding the anatomy of the skull described in the chapter? Why or why not?

2. Read the section of Chapter 2 on hominid evolution. Explore the website **http://www.cruzio.com/~cscp/index.htm.** How does the fossil skull on the first page compare to a modern human skull (compare to the skull used in the first Internet Exercise of this chapter)? What type of skull is it? What is the evidence for human evolution in China?

SUGGESTED READINGS

DARWIN, C. R. [1859] 1975. *On the Origin of Species by Means of Natural Selection; or, The Preservation of the Favored Races in the Struggle for Life*. New York: Cambridge University Press. A readily obtainable reprint of one of the most important books of all time. This long essay by Darwin is still of great significance to modern readers.

GOULD, STEPHEN JAY. 1989. *Wonderful Life: The Burgess Shale and the Nature of History*. New York: Norton. This fascinating work by North America's most famous biologist and paleontologist presents the current thinking on evolutionary processes. Gould's earlier books, based on essays from the magazine *Natural History*, including "An Urchin in the Storm," "Ever Since Darwin," "The Panda's Thumb," "The Flamingo's Smile," "Bully for Brontasaurus," and "Dinosaurs in a Haystack," are also suggested reading for anyone who seeks to understand the most important issues in modern evolutionary thought. For a very readable book examining the limitations of different attempts to relate race and intelligence, see Gould's *The Mismeasure of Man*, 1996 (New York: Norton, 1996).

JOHANSON, DONALD C., AND MAITLAND A. EDEY. 1981. *Lucy: The Beginnings of Humankind*. New York: Simon & Schuster. An exciting, firsthand account of Johanson's discovery of Lucy (*Australopithecus afarensis*) in Hadar, Ethiopia, and the role of this discovery in restructuring interpretations of human origins. The book also includes an excellent overview of the history and development of the field of paleoanthropology.

LEWIN, ROGER. 1987. *Bones of Contention: Controversies in the Search for Human Origins*. New York: Simon & Schuster. A highly readable account of the intriguing debates among paleoanthropologists and how biases sometimes shape the scientific interpretations of human evolution.

————1993. *Human Evolution: An Illustrated Introduction*, 3rd ed. Boston: Blackwell. A brief but excellent illustrated overview of the major questions that paleoanthropologists and archaeologists have been investigating in their most recent research.

SPROUL, BARBARA. 1979. *Primal Myths: Creating the World*. New York: Harper & Row. A superb collection of origin myths found throughout the world. It demonstrates the range of the human creative imagination for constructing cosmologies.

3

Culture

CHAPTER OUTLINE

The Characteristics of Culture

Culture Is Learned
  Symbols and Symbolic Learning

Culture Is Shared

The Components of Culture
  Values / Beliefs / Norms / Ideal versus Real Culture

Cultural Diversity
  Food and Adaptation / Dress Codes and Symbolism

Race, Racism, and Culture
  Racism in Western Society / Critiques of Scientific Racism / Race and Intelligence / The Cultural and Social Significance of Race / Ethnicity / Ethnicity: Two Anthropological Perspectives

Cultural Universals

CHAPTER QUESTIONS

- What are the basic characteristics of the term culture as discussed by anthropologists?

- What are the basic components of culture?

- How does culture lead to both differences and similarities among people in widely separated societies?

- What are the differences between race and ethnicity?

The Characteristics of Culture

CULTURE IS A FUNDAMENTAL CONCEPT WITHIN THE discipline of anthropology. In everyday use, most people in this country use the word culture to refer to "high culture"—Shakespeare's works, Beethoven's symphonies, Michelangelo's sculptures, gourmet cooking, imported wines, and so on. Anthropologists, however, use the term in a much broader sense to refer to all of the learned and shared ideas and products of a society. E. B. Tylor, the first professional anthropologist, proposed a definition of culture that includes all of human experience:

> *Culture . . . is that complex whole which includes knowledge, belief, arts, morals, law, custom, and any other capabilities and habits acquired by man as a member of society. (1871)*

This view suggests that culture includes tools, weapons, fire, agriculture, animal domestication, metallurgy, writing, the steam engine, glasses, airplanes, computers, penicillin, nuclear power, rock-and-roll, video games, designer jeans, religion, political systems, subsistence patterns, science, sports, and social organizations. In Tylor's view, culture includes all aspects of human activity from the fine arts to popular entertainment, from everyday behavior to the development of sophisticated technology. It contains the plans, rules, techniques, designs, and policies for living.

This nineteenth-century definition of culture has some terminology that would not be acceptable to modern anthropologists. For example, it relies on the word *man* to refer to what we currently would refer to as *humanity*. Most anthropologists today would accept a broad conception of **culture** as a shared way of life that includes values, beliefs, and norms transmitted within a particular society from generation to generation.

Notice that this definition includes the term *society*. In general terms, **society** refers to a particular group of animals within a specific territory. In particular, it refers to the patterns of relationships among the animals within this definite territory. Whereas "culture" is unique to human beings, other types of animals may live in groups or societies. Biologists often refer to certain types of insects, herd animals, and social animals such as monkeys and apes as living in societies.

In the past, anthropologists attempted to make a simple distinction between culture and society. Society was said to consist of the patterns of relationships among people within a specified territory, and culture was viewed as the byproducts of those relationships. This view of society as distinguishable from culture was derived from ethnographic studies of small-scale societies. In such societies, people within a specific territory usually share a common culture. However, in most countries where modern anthropologists conduct ethnographic research, the societies are extremely complex and consist of distinctive groups that maintain different cultural traditions. Thus, this simple distinction between society and culture is too artificial for modern anthropologists.

Many anthropologists have adopted the hybrid term sociocultural system—a combination of the terms society (or social) and culture—to refer to what used to be called "society" or "culture." As will be seen in later chapters, many anthropologists use the term sociocultural system as the basic conceptual framework for analyzing ethnographic research.

Culture is Learned

The unique capacity for culture in the human species depends on learning. We do not inherit our culture through our genes in the way we inherit our physical characteristics, as we discussed in Chapter 2. Instead, we obtain our culture through the process of enculturation. **Enculturation** is the process of social interaction through which people learn and acquire their culture. We will study this process in more detail in the next chapter. Humans acquire their culture both consciously, through formal learning, and unconsciously, through informal interaction. Anthropologists distinguish among several types of learning. One type is known as **situational learning,** or trial-and-error learning, in which an organism adjusts its behavior on the basis of direct experience. In other words, a stimulus is presented in the environment, and the animal responds and receives reinforcement or feedback from the response, either

in the form of a reward (pleasure) or punishment (pain). Psychologists refer to this type of learning as *conditioning.*

Humans and many other animals, even single-celled organisms, learn situationally and modify their behavior in different situations. For example, dogs can learn a variety of tricks through rewards such as treats given after the completion of the trick. In some cases, human behavior can be modified through conditioning. Overeating, gambling, and smoking can sometimes be reduced through psychological techniques involving rewarding new forms of behavior.

Another form of learning, called **social learning,** occurs when one organism observes another organism respond to a stimulus and then adds that response to its own collection of behaviors. Thus, the organism need not have the direct experience; it can observe how others behave and then imitate or avoid these behaviors. Obviously, humans learn by observing classmates, teachers, parents, friends, and the media. Other social animals also learn in this manner. For example, wolves learn hunting strategies by observing pack members. Similarly, chimpanzees observe other chimps fashioning twigs with which to hunt termites and then imitate these behaviors.

SYMBOLS AND SYMBOLIC LEARNING

The form of learning that is uniquely human and that provides the basis for the capacity for culture is known as **symbolic learning.** Symbolic learning is based on our linguistic capacity and ability to use and understand **symbols,** arbitrary meaningful units or models we use to represent reality. Symbols are the conceptual devices that we use to communicate abstract ideas to one another. We communicate these symbols to one another through language. For example, children can learn to distinguish and name coins such as pennies, nickels, and quarters and use this money as a symbolic medium of exchange. The linguistic capacity that we are born with gives us the unique ability to make and use symbolic distinctions.

Humans learn most of their behaviors and concepts through symbolic learning. We do not have to depend on situational learning or observations of others to perceive and understand the world and one another. We have the uniquely human

A pigeon being conditioned to behave in a specific manner. This is an example of situational learning.

A teacher using a chalkboard to communicate ideas—an example of symbolic learning.

This photo shows a chimpanzee using a tool, a crumpled leaf as a sponge for drinking water. The chimp learned this behavior by observing other chimps—an example of social learning.

ability to abstract the essence of complex events and patterns, creating images through symbols and bestowing meaning on them.

Through the ability to symbolize, humans can learn and create meanings and transmit these meanings to one another effectively. Parents do not have to depend on direct experience to teach children. As children mature they can learn abstract rules and concepts involving symbolic communication. When we study mathematics, we learn to manipulate abstract symbols. As you read this text-

book, you are learning new ideas based on symbols transmitted to you through English words in ink on a page. Symbolic learning has almost infinite possibilities in terms of absorbing and using information in creative ways. Most of our learning as humans is based on this symbolic-learning process.

Symbols and Signs   Symbols are arbitrary units of meaning, in contrast to **signs,** which are directly associated with concrete physical items or activities. Many nonhuman animals can learn signs. For example, a dog can learn to associate the ringing of a bell (a physical activity) with drinking water. Hence, both humans and other animals can learn signs and apply them to different sorts of activities or to concrete items.

Symbols are different from signs in that they are not associated with any direct, concrete item or physical activity; they are much more abstract. A symbol's meaning is not always obvious. However, many symbols are powerful and often unconscious stimuli of behaviors or emotional states. For example, the designs and colors of the flags of different countries represent symbolic associations with abstract ideas and concepts. In some flags the color red may refer to blood, whereas in others it may symbolize revolution. In many countries, the desecration of the national flag, itself a symbol, is considered a crime. When the symbols associated with particular abstract ideas and concepts that are related to the national destiny of a society are violated, powerful emotions may be aroused.

The ability of symbolization, creating symbols and bestowing meaning on them, enhances our learning capacities as humans in comparison with other types of animals. Anthropologist Leslie White maintained that the most distinctive feature of being human is the ability to create symbols:

> *It is impossible for a dog, horse, or even an ape, to have any understanding of the meaning of the sign of the cross to a Christian, or of the fact that black (white among the Chinese) is the color of mourning. No chimpanzee or laboratory rat can appreciate the difference between Holy water and distilled water, or grasp the meaning of Tuesday, 3, or sin. (1971: 23–24)*

Symbols and Culture The human capacity for culture is based on our linguistic and cognitive ability to symbolize. Culture is transmitted from generation to generation through symbolic learning and language. (In Chapter 5 we will discuss the relationship between language and culture.) Through the transmission of culture, we learn how to subsist, how to socialize, how to govern our society, and what gods to worship. Culture is the historical accumulation of symbolic knowledge that is shared by a society. This symbolic knowledge is transmitted through learning, and it can change rapidly from parents to children and from one generation to the next. Generally, however, people in societies go to great lengths to conserve their culture and symbolic traditions. The persistence of cultural and symbolic traditions is as widespread as cultural change.

Culture is Shared

Culture consists of the shared practices and understandings within a society. To some degree culture is based on shared meanings that are to some extent "public" and thus beyond the mind of any individual (Geertz, 1973). Culture exists before the birth of an individual into the society, and it will continue (in some form) beyond the death of any particular individual. These publicly shared meanings provide designs or recipes for surviving and

contributing to the society. On the other hand culture is also within the mind of individuals. For example, we mentioned that children learn the symbolic meanings of money in coins of different denominations and bills. The children figure out the meanings of money by observing practices and learning the various symbols that are public. However, the child is not just a passive assimilator of that cultural knowledge. Cognitive anthropologists such as Roy D'Andrade and Naomi Quinn emphasize *schemas,* or cultural models that are internalized by individuals and have an influence on decision making and behavior. In their view, culture is acquired by and modeled as schemas within individual minds and can motivate, shape, and transform the symbols and meanings (Quinn and Holland, 1987; D'Andrade, 1989).

It is apparent that cultural understandings are not shared equally by all members of a society. Even in small-scale societies, culture is shared differently by males and females or by young and old. Some individuals in these societies have a great deal of knowledge regarding agriculture, medical practices, or religious beliefs; those beliefs and that knowledge are not equally distributed. In our complex industrialized society, culture consists of a tremendous amount of information and knowledge regarding technology and other aspects of society. Different people learn different aspects of culture, such as repairing cars or television sets, understanding nuclear physics or federal tax regulations, or composing music. Hence, to some extent culture varies from person to person, from subgroup to subgroup, from region to region, from age group to age group, and from gender to gender. Yet, despite this variation, common cultural understandings allow members of society to adapt, to communicate, and to interact with one another. Without these common understandings, a society could not exist.

The Components of Culture

At the beginning of the chapter we defined culture as a shared way of life. Within this broad definition, anthropologists have tried to isolate the key elements that constitute culture. Two of the most basic components are material and nonmaterial culture.

CRITICAL PERSPECTIVES

Key National Symbols

Societies throughout the world have drawn upon important key cultural symbols as a means of distinguishing their community from others. Some of these cultural symbols are secular or nonreligious in meaning, whereas others have religious connotations. Anthropologist Victor Turner (1967) described symbols as "multivocal," suggesting that they have multiple meanings for people within a society. He also said that symbols have the characteristic of "condensation," having the ability to unify many things and actions into a single formation.

National symbols such as flags have the potential for expressing deep-felt emotions in condensed forms. Flags, with their great public visibility, have been an extremely important symbolic medium of political communication throughout the centuries. In U.S. society, the flag is a key secular symbol reflecting deeply felt community ties. A number of legal battles have been waged over the so-called desecration of the U.S. flag. For example, members of the Jehovah's Witnesses religious sect refuse on principle to salute the flag, for which they have been prosecuted. Political protesters, such as those opposed to the Vietnam War in the 1960s, have tried to dramatize their cause by burning the flag or otherwise defacing it. In the late 1980s the issue found its way to the Supreme Court, which ruled that a pro-

tester who had burned the flag at the 1988 Republican National Convention was merely expressing free speech. The Court later ruled that a law protecting the flag from desecration was unconstitutional. This issue remains controversial for many U.S. citizens. There is a political movement to amend the Constitution to protect the flag.

Various religious symbols have produced fundamental meanings and metaphors for many countries throughout the world. For example, the symbols associated with the Virgin Mary in Roman Catholicism have developed into national symbols of unity for some countries.

In Mexico, the symbolism associated with the Virgin of Guadalupe has served to unify different ethnic communities (Wolf, 1958; Kurtz, 1982; Ingham, 1986). After Spain had colonized the indigenous Indian communities of Mexico beginning in the sixteenth century, many of the Indians, such as the Aztecs, were converted to Roman Catholicism. According to Mexican tradition, the Virgin Mary appeared before a Christianized Indian, Juan Diego, in 1531, in the form of a brown-skinned Indian woman.

Tepeyac, the place where the apparition occurred, was the sacred site of an Aztec fertility goddess, Tonantzin, known as Our Lady Mother. Aztec cosmology contained many notions regarding

the virgin births of deities. For example, Huitzilopochtli, the deity believed to have led the Aztecs to their home in Tenochtitlan, had been miraculously conceived by the Aztec mother goddess. Thus, Aztec religious conceptions regarding Tonantzin somewhat paralleled Catholic teachings about Mary.

During the Virgin's appearance, she commanded Juan Diego to inform the bishop of Mexico that a shrine should be built at the spot. The Shrine of the Virgin of Guadalupe is today a huge church, or basilica. Over the altar, Juan Diego's cloak hangs embossed with the image of a young, dark-skinned woman wearing an open crown and flowing gown standing on a half-

A portrait of the Madonna. Murillo, Bartolomeo Esteban. "The Immaculate Conception of Escorial." Museo del Prado, Madrid, Spain. Scala/Art Resource. N.Y.

moon that symbolizes the Immaculate Conception.

The Virgin of Guadalupe became a potent symbol that has endured throughout generations, assuming different meanings for different social groups. To the Indians of Mexico, the Virgin embodies both Tonantzin and the newer Catholic beliefs and aspirations concerning eternal salvation. To the mestizos, people with mixed Spanish and Indian ancestry, she represents the supernatural mother who gave them a place in both the indigenous and colonial worlds. To Mexicans in general, the Virgin represents the symbolic resolution of the many conflicts and problems that resulted from violent encounters between the Europeans and the local population (Kurtz, 1982). The Guadalupe shrine has become one of the most important pilgrimage sites in Mexico.

The Virgin Mary has also played an important symbolic role in a European country that has undergone major political and social transformations. Until recently Poland was a socialist country under the indirect control of the former Soviet Union. Beginning in the 1980s, however, the Polish people, who were organized through a union-based political party known as Solidarity, began to challenge the Communist Party that ruled Poland. During Communist Party rule in Poland, religious symbolism and Roman Catholicism, deeply rooted in Polish history, were to some

degree repressed by the government. One of the most important symbols of Polish Catholicism is a famous picture of the Virgin Mary in a Paulite monastery. According to Polish tradition, the picture, known as the Black Madonna of Czestochowa, was painted by St. Luke the Evangelist, one of the authors of the Christian New Testament, on a piece of Cypress wood from the table used by Mary. After the picture was placed in the monastery, where it was revered by many Polish Catholics, a party of robbers raided the monastery for treasures in 1430 and slashed the image of the Madonna with a sword. Although painstakingly restored, the picture still bears the scars of that destruction, with sword slashes on the cheek of the Black Madonna.

As Poland was divided among different countries such as Sweden, Germany, Turkey, and Russia during various periods, the image of the Black Madonna served as a symbol of Polish religious and national unity. It became one of the most important pilgrimage sites for Polish Catholicism. Millions of pilgrims from Poland and other European countries made their way to the Czestochowa shrine every year to take part in various religious rites. When the Solidarity movement in Poland challenged the Communist Party during the 1980s, leaders such as Lech Walesa wore an image of the Black Madonna on their suit lapels. Pope John Paul II visited the

Black Madonna shrine and placed a Golden Rose there to help resuscitate religiosity in Poland. Thus, the Black Madonna image served to unify Polish Catholics in their struggle against the antireligious stance of the Communist authorities.

National symbols, whether religious or secular, have played extremely important roles in mobilizing people and countries in times of transition and struggle. These national symbols reflect the deep feelings that tie peoples together in what some scholars have referred to as "imagined communities" (Anderson, 1983). Regardless of whether these communities are imagined or not, such symbols are key aspects of culture that are likely to be retained by societies worldwide in the twenty-first century.

Points to Ponder

1. What kinds of feelings and emotions do you have when you hear your national anthem played as you watch your flag?

2. Can you think of any other examples of national symbols that have played a role in world history or politics?

3. Are there any disadvantages of national symbols that have influenced various societies?

4. Could international symbols be developed that would draw all of humanity together?

Material culture consists of the physical products of human society (ranging from weapons to clothing styles), whereas **nonmaterial culture** refers to the intangible products of human society (values, beliefs, and norms). As was discussed previously, the earliest traces of material culture are stone tools associated with *Homo habilis.* These consist of a collection of very simple choppers, scrapers, and flakes. Modern material culture consists of all the physical objects that a contemporary society produces or retains from the past, such as tools, streets, buildings, homes, toys, medicines, and automobiles. Ethnologists investigate the material culture of the societies they study, and they also examine the relationship between the material culture and the nonmaterial culture: the values, beliefs, and norms that represent the patterned ways of thinking and acting within a society. Archaeologists, meanwhile, are primarily concerned with interpreting past societies by studying their material remains.

VALUES

Values are the standards by which members of a society define what is good or bad, holy or unholy, beautiful or ugly. They are assumptions that are widely shared within the society. Values are a central aspect of the nonmaterial culture of a society and are important because they influence the behavior of the members of a society. The predominant values in the United States include individual achievement and success, efficiency, progress, material comfort, equality, freedom, science, rationality, nationalism, and democracy, along with many other assumptions (Williams, 1970; Bellah et al., 1985). Although these values might seem normal to Americans, they are not accepted values in all societies. For instance, just as American society tends to emphasize individualism and self-reliance, other societies, such as Japan, stress cooperation and community interest instead.

BELIEFS

Beliefs held by the members of a society are another aspect of nonmaterial culture. **Beliefs** are cultural conventions that concern true or false assumptions, specific descriptions of the nature of the universe and humanity's place in it. Values are generalized notions of what is good and bad; be-

liefs are more specific and, in form at least, have more content. "Education is good" is a fundamental value in American society, whereas "grading is the best way to evaluate students" is a belief that reflects assumptions about the most appropriate way to determine educational achievement.

Most people in a given society assume that their beliefs are rational and firmly grounded in common sense. As we saw in Chapter 1, however, commonsense beliefs may not necessarily be scientifically valid. For example, our commonsense understandings may lead us to conclude that the earth is flat and stationary. When we look around us, the plane of the earth looks flat, and we don't feel as if the earth is rotating around the sun. Yet our commonsense beliefs about these notions are contradicted by the knowledge gained by the scientific method.

Many anthropologists refer to the worldview of a particular society. A **worldview** consists of various beliefs about the nature of reality and provides people with a more or less consistent orientation toward the world. Worldviews help people interpret and understand the reality surrounding them. In some societies such as the traditional Azande of East Africa or the Navajo Indians of the Southwest region of the United States, witchcraft is believed to cause illnesses in some unfortunate individuals. In other societies, such as that of Canada, illness is diagnosed by medical doctors using the scientific method, and the causes of illness are attributed to viruses, bacteria, or other material forces.

Some beliefs may be combined into an **ideology.** An ideology consists of cultural symbols and beliefs that reflect and support the interests of specific groups within society (Yengoyan, 1986). Particular groups promote ideologies for their own ends as a means of maintaining and justifying economic and political authority. Different economic and political systems—capitalism, socialism, communism, democratic institutions, and totalitarian governments—are based on differing ideologies. For example, capitalist societies maintain that individuals should be rewarded monetarily based on their own self-interest. In contrast, socialist societies emphasize the well-being of the community or society over individual self-interest.

In some societies, especially complex societies with many different groups, an ideology may produce **cultural hegemony,** the ideological control

Many women in Islamic countries wear the "chador," a garment that is worn over regular clothing. Patterns of dress vary widely throughout the world.

by one dominant group over beliefs and values. For example, one dominant ethnic group may impose its cultural beliefs on subordinate groups. In the United States, the dominant ethnic group in the eighteenth and nineteenth centuries, white Anglo-Saxon Protestants, was able to impose its language, cultural beliefs, and practices on Native Americans in U.S. society. In many areas of the world, minority groups were often forced to accept the ideologies of the economically and politically dominant groups.

NORMS

Norms—a society's rules of right and wrong behavior—are another aspect of nonmaterial culture. Norms are shared rules or guidelines that define how people "ought" to behave under certain circumstances. Norms are generally connected to the values, beliefs, worldviews, and ideologies of a so-

ciety. For example, we have seen that in American culture individualism is a basic value that is reflected in the prevailing worldview. Not surprisingly, then, American society has many norms based on the notion of individual initiative and responsibility. Individuals are admonished to work for their own self-interest and not to become a burden to their families or community. Older Americans, if self-sufficient, are not supposed to live with their children. Likewise, self-sufficient young adults beyond a certain age are not supposed to live with their parents. These norms that reflect the value of individualism contrast with the norms existing in many other societies. In many agricultural societies it would be immoral to allow aging parents to live outside the family. In these societies the family is a moral community that should not be separated. Rather than individualism, these norms emphasize communal responsibility within the family unit. Some anthropologists use the term **ethos** to refer to the socially acceptable norms within a society (Geertz, 1973).

Folkways Norms guiding ordinary usages and conventions of everyday life are known as **folkways.** Members of a society frequently conform to folkways so readily that they are hardly aware these norms exist. For example, if a Chinese anthropologist were to ask an American why Americans eat with knives and forks, why Americans allow dating between single men and women without chaperones, or why American schoolchildren are not allowed to help one another on exams, he or she might get vague and uninformative answers, such as "Because that's the way it is done," or "It's the custom," or even "I don't know." Ethnologists are accustomed to receiving these kinds of answers from the members of the society they are studying. These folkway norms or standards of etiquette are so embedded in the society that they are not noticeable unless they are openly violated.

Folkways help ensure that social life proceeds smoothly by providing guidelines for an individual's behavior and expectations of other people's behavior. At the same time, folkways allow for some flexibility. Although most people conform to folkways most of the time, folkways are sometimes violated, but these violations are not severely punished. Thus, in American society people who eat with chopsticks rather than with a knife and fork

APPLYING ANTHROPOLOGY

Multiculturalism in U.S. Society

Since the nineteenth century, the population of the United States has become more ethnically and culturally diverse. During the past forty years there has been a significant growth in the population of peoples of non-European ancestry. A decline in the birthrate of the majority of the white population of European descent coupled with new trends in immigration and higher birth rates of ethnic minorities are changing the ethnic landscape of U.S. society.

As indicated by Figure 3.1, recent immigration from Europe to the United States represents a tiny fraction compared with that of immigration from Latin America and Asia. The ethnic diversity of non-European immigrants to the United States is remarkable. Among the Asians are Filipinos, Koreans, Chinese, Japanese, Vietnamese, Laotians, Cambodians, Thais, Indians, and Pakistanis. From Latin America are Central Americans from El Salvador, Guatemala, and Mexico, and people from other countries of South America. And, from the Middle East and Africa have come Palestinians, Iraqis, Iranians, Lebanese, Syrians, Israelis, Nigerians, and Egyptians. The majority of these immigrants have come to the United States seeking economic opportunities, political freedom, and improved social conditions.

The population of the United States is approximately 270 million. Ethnic minorities are increasing their proportion of this population very rapidly. There are significant numbers of African Americans in every major urban center in the United States. The African American population is about 34 million, or 12 percent of the total population. The Hispanic American population, which in-

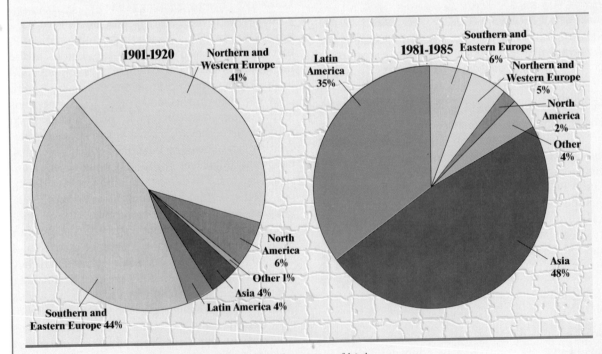

Figure 3.1   Legal immigrants admitted to the U.S. by region of birth.

Source: Leon F. Bauvier and Robert W. Gardner. "Immigration to the U.S.: The Unfinished Story." Population Bulletin, 40(4). Washington, D.C. Population Reference Bureau, Inc., 1986 and U.S. Census Bureau, Statistical Abstract of the United States: 1998. Reprinted with permission.

cludes Mexican Americans, Puerto Ricans, Cuban Americans, and other peoples from Latin America, has grown to 25 million. The population of Native Americans is approaching 2 million. The Asian American population has doubled in the past ten years to more than 7 million people.

As of the year 2000, approximately 46 percent of the population of California is of Hispanic, Asian, and African descent. In San Francisco County, the approximate figure is 65 percent, most of whom are of Asian heritage. In Los Angeles, the ethnic minority population accounts for approximately 60 percent of the total population, most of whom are of Hispanic descent. Similar demographic changes are evident across the country in major metropolitan areas. The United States has truly become a multicultural society.

As a response to this multiculturalism, federal, state, and local governments in the United States have encouraged the development of programs to prepare people to live in this new type of society. For example, at least twenty-two states have developed guidelines to implement a multicultural approach within their educational systems. These guidelines have resulted in changes in curriculum and the content of textbooks to attempt to fairly portray the ethnic and cultural groups that compose the country's multicultural heritage.

Some anthropologists have become involved in trying to solve some of the problems that have resulted from these new ethnic and demographic trends. These applied anthropologists have been using knowledge from different cultures to educate people in different types of institutions in the United States. For example, applied anthropologists have been providing intercultural-training workshops in schools, hospitals, police departments, businesses, and other community settings in areas where different ethnic groups are involved with one another. These anthropologists are using their ethnographic knowledge about different cultures of the world to help people from different ethnic and religious backgrounds understand one another.

For example, the author of this textbook was called upon to help direct an intercultural workshop for a police department in a rural area of Missouri that had recently experienced the immigration of ethnic minorities from urban areas. The police department had had no experience in dealing with African Americans and Hispanic Americans. The workshop was intended to provide some help in overcoming some of the problems that had developed between the police department and the new ethnic communities. The workshop included an introduction to what anthropologists have discovered regarding prejudice and discrimination on a worldwide basis, and how some societies have resolved these problems. It also provided cultural background about ethnic minorities in the United States and demonstrated examples of communication and value differences that sometimes create conflict between ethnic groups.

Applied anthropologists have been working with educators and education researchers in a number of areas regarding multiculturalism in U.S. society. They have helped contribute to curriculum development projects aimed at multicultural education and have also provided cultural background information to help educators adapt their teaching to the specific needs of ethnic minority children.

However, many applied anthropologists have become aware of some inherent problems with these multicultural education programs. In some cases cultural ideas can be applied in an overzealous manner by educators. Anthropologist Jacquetta Hill-Burnett discovered that teachers would sometimes use cultural information regarding Puerto Rican Americans to stereotype children in the classroom (1978). Another researcher found a similar tendency in teachers of Eskimo and Indian children in Alaska (Kleinfeld, 1975). Thus, anthropologists have to provide cultural information for use in the multicultural settings in U.S. society but must also be extremely cautious about providing broad generalizations about cultural differences that can be used as the basis of ethnic stereotypes. One of the major lessons that anthropology has to teach is that despite being part of an ethnic or cultural group, individuals differ from one another.

or who do not keep their lawns neatly mowed are not considered immoral or depraved, nor are they treated as criminals.

Mores   Mores (pronounced "MOR-ays") are much stronger norms than are folkways. Members of society believe that their mores are crucial for the maintenance of a decent and orderly way of life. People who violate mores are usually severely punished, though punishment for the violation of mores varies from society to society. It may take the form of ostracism, vicious gossip, public ridicule, exile, losing one's job, physical beating, imprisonment, commitment to a mental asylum, or even execution.

For example, in some Islamic societies such as Iran and Saudi Arabia, the manner in which a woman dresses in public is considered morally significant. If a woman violates the dress code in these societies, she may be arrested and imprisoned. As we shall see later in the text, in hunting-and-gathering societies, individuals who do not share goods or resources with others are often punished by gossip, ridicule, and occasionally ostracism.

Not all norms can be neatly categorized as either folkways or mores. Distinguishing between the two is especially difficult when dealing with societies other than our own. In reality, norms fall at various points on a continuum, depending on the particular circumstances and the society under consideration. The prohibition of public nudity may be a strong norm in some societies, but it may be only a folkway or pattern of etiquette in another society. Even within a society, rules of etiquette may come to have moral significance. For example, as already discussed, the proper form of dress for women in some societies is not just a matter of etiquette but has moral or religious connotations.

Values, beliefs, norms, and worldviews are used by many social scientists when referring to nonmaterial culture. However, not all anthropologists agree with concise, clear-cut distinctions among these terms. The terms are used only to help us understand the complex symbolic aspects of nonmaterial culture.

IDEAL VERSUS REAL CULTURE

When discussing values, beliefs, and norms, ethnologists often distinguish between ideal culture and real culture. **Ideal culture** consists of what people say they do or should do, whereas **real culture** refers to their actual behaviors. Ethnologists have discovered that the ideal culture frequently contrasts with people's actual behavior. For instance, a foreign anthropologist may learn that Americans cherish the value of equal opportunity, yet in observing Americans, the anthropologist might encounter many cases in which people from different economic, class, racial, ethnic, and religious backgrounds are treated in a highly unequal manner. In later chapters, we will discuss how some societies are structured around kinship ties and principles of lineage such as patrilineal and matrilineal descent. Anthropologists often discover, however, that these kinship and descent principles are violated by the actual practices of people (Kuper, 1988). Thus, in all societies anthropologists find that there are differences between the ideal and real cultural practices of individuals.

Cultural Diversity

Throughout history, humans have expressed an interest in cultural diversity. Different values, norms, beliefs, and practices have been recognized by peoples everywhere. Whenever different societies have come into contact with one another, people have compared and contrasted their respective cultural traditions. Societies often differentiated themselves from one another based on these variant cultural patterns. For example, one of the first Western historians, Herodotus, a Greek scholar of the fifth century B.C., wrote about the different forms of behavior and belief in societies such as Egypt. He described how the Egyptians behaved and thought differently from the Greeks.

Writings on the diversity of cultures have often been based on ethnocentric attitudes. **Ethnocentrism** is the practice of judging another society by the values and standards of one's own society. To some degree, ethnocentrism is a universal phenomenon. As humans learn the basic values, beliefs, and norms of their society, they tend to think of their own culture as preferable, ranking other cultures as less desirable. In fact, members of a society become so committed to particular cultural traditions that they cannot conceive of any other way of life. They often view other cultural traditions as strange, alien, inferior, crazy, or immoral.

The study of cultural diversity became one of the principal objectives of anthropology as it developed as a profession in the nineteenth century. But like earlier writers, nineteenth-century anthropologists often reinforced ethnocentric beliefs about other societies (see Chapter 6). In the twentieth century, however, anthropologists began to recognize that ethnocentrism prevents ethnologists from viewing other cultures in a scientific manner.

To combat the problem of ethnocentrism, twentieth-century anthropologists developed the concept of cultural relativism. **Cultural relativism** is the view that cultural traditions must be understood within the context of a particular society's solutions to problems and opportunities. Because cultural traditions represent unique adaptations and symbolic systems for different societies, these traditions must be understood as objectively as possible. Cultural relativism offered anthropologists a means of investigating other societies without imposing ethnocentric assumptions.

Although cultural relativism provides a sound methodological basis for ethnographic research, it may involve some serious ethical problems. For example, many ethnologists have found themselves in societies in which cultural practices produce physical harm for people. How does the ethnologist refrain from making a value judgment about such cultural practices as infanticide or geronticide (the killing of elderly people)? This issue is an ever-present problem for ethnologists and deserves careful thought. The moral problems raised by cultural relativism are discussed in Chapter 17.

FOOD AND ADAPTATION

To understand the difference between human biological and cultural behaviors, we may simply observe the variety of ways in which different societies satisfy a basic biological drive such as hunger. Although humans are omnivorous animals with the ability to digest many types of plants and animals for nutrition, there are many differences in eating behaviors and food preferences throughout the world.

American culture labels animals as either edible or inedible. Most Americans would be repulsed by the thought of eating insects and insect larvae, but many societies consider these to be delicacies. American culture also distinguishes between "pets," which are not eaten, and "farm animals" such as chickens, cows, and pigs, which can be eaten. In the United States, horses are considered pets, and there are no industries for raising them for human consumption. Yet horse meat is a regular part of the Continental European diet. The French, Belgians, Dutch, Germans, Italians, Poles, and Russians consume significant quantities of horse meat each year (Harris, 1985).

Anthropologist Marvin Harris has shown that cultural dietary preferences frequently have an adaptive significance (1974, 1977, 1985). For example, the religious traditions of Judaism and Islam forbid the eating of pork. In Judaism since the time of the ancient Israelites, pigs have been viewed as abominable animals not suited for human consumption. Yet pigs have been a primary source of protein and fat throughout China and Europe. In some societies in the Pacific Islands pigs are so highly regarded they are treated as members of the family (but they are also eaten). Because so many societies show no aversion to the consumption of pork, Harris has tried to explain the prohibitions in Judaism and Islam. The best-known explanations are that the pig is an unclean animal and that it carries diseases such as trichinosis, which is caused by a type of tapeworm. Harris, however, considers these explanations to be unsatisfactory. Regarding cleanliness, Harris acknowledges that because pigs cannot sweat, in hot, dry climates such as the Middle East they wallow in their excrement to keep cool. He points out, however, that other animals, such as goats and chickens, can also be dirty, but they are eaten. Similarly with disease, Harris notes that many other animals, such as cows, which are widely consumed, also carry diseases.

Harris explains the pig taboo with reference to the ecological conditions of the Middle East. He maintains that the restrictions represented a cultural innovation that helped the societies of this region to adapt. About 1200 B.C., the ancient Israelites had settled in a woodland area that had not been cultivated. As they rapidly cut down trees to convert areas to irrigated agricultural land, they also severely restricted areas suitable for raising pigs on natural forage. Eventually pigs had to be fed grains as supplements, which made them extremely costly and direct competitors with humans. Moreover, they required artificial shade and moisture to keep cool. In addition, pigs were not useful for pulling plows or producing milk, hides, or wool for clothing.

According to Harris, despite the increasing costs associated with pig raising, people were still tempted to raise them for nutritional reasons. He hypothesizes that the pig taboo was established through religious authorities and texts to inhibit this practice. Therefore, the pig was redefined as an unclean animal. Neighbors of the ancient Israelites, such as the Egyptians, began to share the abhorrence of the pig. The pig taboo was later incorporated into the Islamic religious text, the Qur'an, so that today both Muslims and Jews are forbidden to eat pork.

Thus, in Harris's hypothesis, in the hot, dry regions of the world where pigs were poorly adapted and extremely costly to raise, the meat of the pig came to be forbidden. In contrast, in the cooler, wetter areas of the world that are more appropriate for pig raising, pig taboos were unknown.

DRESS CODES AND SYMBOLISM

Although some cultural differences may relate to the environmental adaptations of societies, much cultural diversity is a consequence of symbolic creations. Symbols provide the basis of meaningful shared beliefs and worldviews within a society. Because of our inherent cultural capacity, we tend to be meaning-seeking creatures. In addition to the satisfaction of biological needs, we have needs for meaning and significance in our personal and social lives.

The importance of symbols as a source of cultural diversity can be seen in the dress codes and hairstyles of different societies. In most situations, the symbolism of clothing and hairstyles communicates different messages ranging from political beliefs to identification with specific ethnic or religious groups. The tartan of a Scottish clan, the Mao jacket of a Chinese revolutionary, the black leather jacket and long hair of a motorcycle gang member in the United States, and the veil of an Islamic woman in Saudi Arabia provide a symbolic vocabulary that creates cultural diversity.

Many examples of clothing styles could be used to illustrate how symbols contribute to cultural diversity. Consider, for instance, changing dress codes in the United States. During the 1960s, many young people wore jeans, sandals, and beads to symbolize their rebellion against what they conceived as the conformist inclinations of American society. By the 1980s, many of the same people were wearing "power suits" as they sought to advance up the corporate ladder.

An example of how hairstyles can create meaningful symbolic codes can be seen in a group known as the Rastafarians (sometimes known as Rastas or Rastaman) of Jamaica. The majority of the people of Jamaica are of African descent. During the eighteenth and nineteenth centuries, they were brought to Jamaica by European slave traders to work on plantations. The Rastafarians are a specific religious group within Jamaica who believe that Haile Selassie (1892–1975), the former emperor of Ethiopia, whose original name was Ras Tafari, was the black Messiah who appeared in the flesh for the redemption of all blacks exiled in the world of white oppression. Rastafarian religion fuses Old Testament teachings, Christian mysticism, and Afro-Jamaican religious beliefs. The Rastafarian movement originated as a consequence of harsh economic, political, and living conditions in the slums of Jamaica.

In the 1950s, during the early phase of the Rastafarian movement, some male members began to grow their hair in "locks" or "dreadlocks" to symbolize their religious and political commitments. This hairstyle became well known in Western society through reggae music and Rasta musicians such as the late Bob Marley. Rastafarians derive the symbolism of the dreadlock hairstyle of the Rastafarians from the Bible. They view the unshaven man as the natural man and invoke Samson as one of the most important figures in the Bible. Dreadlocks also reflect a dominant symbol within the Rastafarian movement, the lion, which is associated with Haile Selassie, one of whose titles was the "Conquering Lion of Judah." To simulate the spirit of the lion, some Rastas do not cut their hair, sometimes growing their locks 20 inches or more.

In addition, the dreadlock hairstyle has a deeper symbolic significance in Jamaican society, where hair was often referred to as an index of racial and social inequality. Fine, silky hair was considered "good," whereas woolly, kinky hair was frowned on (Barrett, 1977). The white person with fine, silky hair was considered higher on the social ladder than was the typical African descendant in Jamaica. Thus, the Rastafarian hairstyle was a defiant symbol of resistance to the cultural values and norms of Jamaican society.

The late Bob Marley, a Rastafarian musician.

The cultural symbolism of the Rastafarian dreadlocks and long beards represents savagery, wildness, danger, disorder, and degeneration. It sends the message that Rastafarians are outside of Jamaican society. Dreadlocks are viewed by many Jamaicans as unkempt, dangerous, and dirty. Yet to the Rastafarians, dreadlocks symbolize power, liberation, and defiance. Through their hairstyle they announce to society that they do not accept the values, beliefs, and norms of the majority of the people.

Thus, to a great extent, culture consists of a network of symbolic codes that enhance values, beliefs, worldviews, and ideologies within a society. Humans go to great lengths to create symbols that provide meaning for individuals and groups. These symbolic meanings are a powerful source of cultural diversity.

Race, Racism, and Culture

As we saw in Chapter 2 physical characteristics such as skin pigmentation, nose shape, and hair texture have prompted people throughout history to classify humans into different "races." The earliest recordings of racial classifications go back to the ancient Egyptians, Israelites, and Greeks. Later attempts to employ racial classifications based on "scientific criteria" have foundered because they were too rigid to account for the tremendous variation within different so-called "races." The majority of anthropologists today find dividing different populations into distinctive racial categories or classifications problematic. Clearly bounded racially distinct populations are not found in the real world. However, it cannot be denied that humans in both the past and present have used various racial classifications to categorize people, and develop stereotypes about the behavior and mental abilities of different "racial categories." These categories have often been used throughout human history as the basis and justification of **racism,** the belief that some races are superior to other races. Racism can often result in discrimination and hostile acts towards different peoples and societies.

RACISM IN WESTERN SOCIETY

The belief that some "races" are superior to others has a deep history in Western society. The conceptual idea that one's racial and physical characteristics are linked to mental abilities and behaviors was inherent within ancient Greek society. Philosophers such as Plato (427–347 B.C.) argued that there were different "essences" for different types of people. According to Plato people were born with different types of souls, which gave them particular dispositions or *essences.* For example, he claimed that certain categories of people had the essence—or were suited to be—rulers, soldiers, farmers, or slaves. Another Greek, Hippocrates (460–377 B.C.), the well-known medical specialist of ancient Greek society, developed a "humoral-environmental" essentialist theory to classify various peoples throughout the world. According to Hippocrates there were four elements that constituted the universe: fire, air, earth, and water. These four elements were transformed into *humors,* or essences, that were present in all forms of life. One of the primary humors in humans was the type of blood inherited, which contained different distributions of the four elements, which produced varying personality and behavioral dispositions among populations. Hippocrates maintained that the different populations of humanity had different essences and temperaments. For example, he claimed that the people of Asian descent were "gentle, well-fed, courageous," and could endure suffering. However, Asian people would not develop industrious habits because pleasure dominated their lives.

This type of classification based on the idea of inherited blood, essences, and humors continued to influence many people during the medieval period in Western society and resulted in simplified stereotypes of behavior and temperaments of people around the world. In the medieval period it was accepted that there was a Great Chain of Being, which posited natural essential categories based on a hierarchy established by God and nature. Eventually, racial groupings based on blood, essences, and humors were placed within this hierarchy, with the white European race at the top, and other "colored" peoples of the world below the white Europeans. By correlating physical characteristics with cultural differences, classification systems such as these assumed erroneously that populations that shared certain physical traits, especially skin color, also exhibited similar patterns of behavior. These beliefs gave rise to many popular misconceptions and generalizations concerning the values, traditions, and behaviors of non-Western peoples.

Later, after the period of the 1500s in European society when explorers began to have contact with many peoples and cultures outside of Europe, various forms of *scientific racism* began to replace the earlier medieval conceptions. And, the prior conceptual frameworks based on blood and humors influenced these models of scientific racism. As Europeans began to discover civilizations and cultures in the Americas, Africa, the Middle East, and Asia, they associated the skin color of many of the people in these non-Western societies with certain forms of essences, behavior, and mental developments. Europeans measured these civilizations in comparison with their own, and designated them as savage and barbaric when compared with their own. And, since many of these people had a different skin color, they began to assume that the level of these civilizations had something to do with the skin color, essence, or race of these populations.

For example, in one of the earliest scientific efforts to organize human variation into racial categories, the Swedish scientist Carolus Linnaeus constructed a taxonomy in 1758 that divided *H. sapiens* into four races based on skin color: Europeans (white), North American Indians (red), Asiatics (yellow), and Africans (black). Yet, his classification of humans was influenced by ancient and medieval theories and various ideas about European superiority. For example, he classified the American Indians with reddish skin as choleric and with a need to be regulated by customs. Africans with black skin were relaxed, indolent, negligent, and governed by caprice. In contrast, Europeans with white skin were described as gentle, acute, inventive, and governed by laws.

Eventually, these scientific racist beliefs were used to rationalize slavery and the political oppression of various groups around the world. These so-called scientific racist views were used to promote the African slave trade and colonization and imperialism throughout the world. Following Darwin's publications on human evolution, many writers based allegedly "scientific" racist philosophies on misinterpretations of his theory. In nineteenth-century England, thinkers such as Herbert Spencer and Francis Galton believed that social evolution worked by allowing superior members of society to rise to the top while inferior ones sank to the bottom. These views reinforced the false belief that particular groups of people, or races, had quantifiably different intellectual capacities.

In 1853 similar ideas coalesced into a four volume scientific treatise by the French aristocrat Joseph Arthur de Gobineau entitled *Essai sur l'inegalité des races humaines (The Inequality of the Races of Humanity)*. In this work, Gobineau described the whole of human history as a struggle among the various "races" of humanity. He argued that each race had its own, either high or low, intellectual capacity and that there were stronger and weaker races. Gobineau promoted the conquest of so-called weaker races by allegedly stronger ones. He opens the book with the statement that everything great, noble, and fruitful in the works of humanity springs from the Aryan family, the so-called super-race. The Aryans spread out to create first the Hindu civilization, then the Egyptian, Assyrian, Greek, Chinese, Roman, German, Mexican, and Peruvian civilizations (Banton, 1998, Montagu, 1997). Gobineau argued that these civilizations declined because of "racial mixing." These so-called scientific views of racism were later taken up by writers such as Houston Stewart Chamberlain in twentieth-century Europe, whose writings, in turn, influenced Adolph Hitler. Gobineau's ideas were the philosophical progenitors of Hitler's *Mein Kampf,* which promoted the notions of racial superiority and inferiority. In the 1930s, the Nazi scientific racist ideology, based on the presumed superiority of a pure "Aryan race," was used to justify the annihilation of millions of Jews and other "non-Aryan" peoples such as Slavs and Gypsies in Europe.

CRITIQUES OF SCIENTIFIC RACISM

Within the field of anthropology a number of scholars were subjecting these scientific racist beliefs to rigorous testing and evaluation. In the United States an anthropologist, Franz Boas (1858–1943), who had immigrated from Germany, was leading a concerted effort to assess these scientific racist ideas. Boas and his students took precise assessments of the physical characteristics of different populations including cranial capacity and brain size. His research began to challenge the scientific racist views. The research demonstrated conclusively that brain size and cranial capacities of modern humans differ widely within all so-called races. This anthropological research resulted in findings that conclusively showed that there were no so-called superior or inferior races. Boas's research also confirmed that there was no direct link between race, brain size, cranial capacity, and intelligence levels. This pioneering research initiated a program of further research among the four fields of anthropology that continues to challenge scientific racist beliefs wherever they appear. This research has demonstrated time and time again that racist beliefs have no basis in fact: human groups never fit into such neat categories. For example, many Jewish people living in Europe during the Holocaust possessed the same physical features as those associated with the so-called Aryans. The physical anthropologists of Nazi ideology who advocated Aryan racist ideology found it difficult to define precisely which physical characteristics supposedly distinguished one "race" from another (Schafft, 1999). Presently, a number of groups such as the Pioneer Fund persist in supporting research that purports to demonstrate scientifically that races differ in mental abilities and intelligence.

RACE AND INTELLIGENCE

Intelligence is the capacity to process and evaluate information for problem solving. It can be contrasted with *knowledge*—the storage and recall of learned information. Heredity undoubtedly plays a role in intelligence: this is confirmed by the fact that the intelligence of genetically related individuals (for example, parents and their biological children) displays the closest correlation. Yet other factors also come into play. In no area of study have the varying effects of genes, environment, and culture been more confused than in the interpretation of intelligence. Most scientists agree that intelligence varies among individuals. Yet it has been difficult to measure intelligence objectively because tests inevitably reflect the beliefs and values of a particular cultural group. Nevertheless, a number of devices have been developed to measure intelligence, most prominent among them the *intelligence quotient* (IQ) test, invented by French psychologist Alfred Binet in 1905. Binet's test was brought to the United States and modified to become the Stanford-Binet test. The inventors warned that the test was only valid when the children tested came from similar environments; yet the IQ test is widely used today for tracking students in the U.S. educational system, sparking controversy among educators and social scientists alike. In a controversial book called *The Bell Curve: Intelligence and Class Structure in American Life* (1994), Richard Herrnstein and Charles Murray argue that research supports the conclusion that race is related to intelligence. Utilizing a bell-curve statistical distribution, they place the intelligence quotient (IQ) of people with European ancestry at 100. People of East Asian ancestry exceed that standard slightly, averaging 103; people of African descent fall below that standard, with an average IQ of 90. Their findings imply that IQ scores are related to genetic differences among races.

A number of scientists have noted the faulty reasoning and flawed methods used by Herrnstein and Murray, and others who have attributed IQ differences between African Americans and European Americans, or other so-called racial groupings. If there were truly differences in IQ between African Americans and European Americans—accurately reflected, genetically determined differences in intelligence between these two groups—then African Americans with more European ancestry ought to have higher IQ scores than those with less European ancestry. In a major IQ study of hundreds of African Americans that was based on blood testing to determine European ancestry, Scarr and Weinberg (1978) found no significant correlation between IQ scores and the degree of European admixture. More recent studies of ethnic groups around the world demonstrate that most of the documented racial differences in intelligence are a result of environmental factors (Sowell, 1994, 1995).

Scholars have tracked IQ scores for various racial and ethnic categories from the early years of the twentieth century. For example, early immigrants to the United States from European nations such as Poland, Italy, and Greece, as well as from Asian countries including China and Japan, scored ten to fifteen points below longtime U.S. citizens. However, people in these same ethnic categories today—Asian Americans, Polish Americans, Italian Americans, or Greek Americans—have IQ scores that are average or above average. Among Italian Americans, for example, average IQ rose by almost ten points in fifty years; within Polish and Chinese Americans, the rise was almost twenty points. It is obvious that as immigrants settled in the United States, their new cultural and environmental surroundings affected them in ways that improved their performance on IQ tests.

Among African Americans, Northerners have historically scored higher than Southerners on IQ tests, by about ten points. Moreover, the IQ scores of African Americans who migrated from the South to the North after 1940 rose the same way they did among immigrants from abroad. Other studies indicate that middle-class African Americans score higher on IQ tests than do lower-class white Americans. These test scores indicate that cultural patterns matter. African Americans are no less intelligent than other groups, but, carrying a legacy of disadvantage, many contend with a cultural environment that discourages self-confidence and achievement. Most anthropological research on this topic indicates that when differences in socioeconomic status and other factors were controlled for, the difference between African Americans and European Americans was insignificant. In Japan, a group of people known as the *burakumin,* who exhibit no major physical differences between themselves and other Japanese people but who have been subject to prejudice and discrimination for centuries in their society, tend to score lower on IQ tests than other Japanese (Molnar, 1983, 1997). This indicates the strong influence of socioeconomic factors in measuring IQ tests. Additional studies show that educational enrichment programs boost IQ scores (Loehlin, Lindzey, & Spuhler, 1975; Molnar, 1983, 1992). Much research has determined that IQ scores increase within every generation of every population by three to five points, indicating the profound influence of social and educational conditions on IQ scores. The other major criticism of Herrnstein and Murray and like-minded theorists is that they reify the concept of race as if races were based on clear-cut and distinct genetic groups, ignoring the enormous variation within these so-called races.

Most psychologists agree that intelligence is not a readily definable characteristic like height or hair color. Psychologists view intelligence as a general capacity for "goal-directed adaptive behavior"—that is, behavior based on learning from experience, problem solving, and reasoning (Myers, 1998). Though this definition of intelligence would be acceptable to most social scientists, we now recognize that some people are talented in mathematics, others in writing, and still others in aesthetic pursuits such as music, art, and dance. Because abilities vary from individual to individual, psychologists such as Howard Gardner question the view of intelligence as a single factor in human makeup. Based on cross-cultural research, Gardner (1983) has concluded that intelligence does *not* constitute a single characteristic but rather amounts to a mix of many differing faculties. According to Gardner, each of us has distinct aptitudes for making music, for spatially analyzing the visual world, for mastering athletic skills, and for understanding ourselves and others—a type of social intelligence. Not surprisingly, Gardner concludes that no single test can possibly measure what he refers to as these "multiple intelligences."

The vast majority of anthropologists and other scientists concur with Gardner's findings that intelligence spans a wide and diverse range. The IQ test ranks people according to their performance of various cognitive tasks, especially those that relate to scholastic or academic problem solving. Yet it cannot predict how successfully a person will adapt to specific environmental situations or even handle a particular job. Throughout the world people draw on various forms of intelligence to perform inventive and creative tasks, ranging from music composition to the development of efficient hunting strategies. Before we call someone "intelligent," we have to know what qualities and abilities are important in that person's environment. Different sorts of cognitive abilities lead to success in a hunting and gathering society, an agricultural society, or an industrial society.

THE CULTURAL AND SOCIAL SIGNIFICANCE OF RACE

Even though race does not have the biological foundations it is assumed to have in common sense, not only is the concept of race very important in the United States, but it is found to resonate in many societies. For example, in Puerto Rico, an island colonized by the Spanish, and later by the U.S., racial classifications are used to categorize different people by skin color. Puerto Ricans use *blanco* to refer to whites, *preito* to refer to blacks, and *trigueno* to refer to tan-skinned people. In Brazil, a complex racial classification exists that uses different criteria with which to categorize people than in the U.S. They do not see or define races in the same way as people in the U.S. An individual categorized as "black" in the U.S. might be categorized as "white" in Brazil (Harris, 1964).

Since the nineteenth century in the United States there is what has been termed the **hypodescent concept** of racial classification. This means that in cases of racial mixture the offspring of the parents has the race of the parent with the lowest racial status. Since black Americans were considered to be a lower "race" a person is considered black if he or she has a black ancestor anywhere in their family history. This is known as the **one-drop rule** of racial classification because it is based on the myth that one drop of "black blood" is sufficient to determine racial blackness. Thus, Americans with both white and black ancestry are usually classified as black and often encouraged to identify as black in personal and social contexts. In contrast, a person is classified as white if he or she has no black ancestry anywhere in their family history. This means that in order to be white, a person has to prove a negative, the absence of black ancestors. Other racial categories such as *mulatto* (half black and half white), *quadroon* (one-quarter black and three-quarters white), and *octoroon* (one-eighth black and seven-eighths white) were developed to go along with this one-drop rule. Until the 1950s in Louisiana, it was illegal for a doctor to give a blood transfusion from a black person to a white person. Despite the fact that this notion of the one-drop rule is mythical and is based on false notions of "racial essences," these ideas still persist in some circles.

In contrast to the one-drop rule, in the U.S. Native American Indians are treated differently. Because Native Americans have entitlements based on legislation, the U.S. federal government has sometimes imposed *blood quanta* rules of at least 50 percent ancestry from a particular tribe in order to be classified as a Native American Indian. This has created considerable confusion both legally and socially for many Native American peoples. The one-drop rule and *blood quanta* tests emphasize that the mythical ideas of racial essences are deeply embedded within the folk wisdom and culture of U.S. society. Similar folk conceptions are held about race in other societies. In Northern Ireland, both Protestants and Catholics say that they can identify members of the other group based on physical differences, despite their obvious physical similarities. Anthropologists have long recognized that although these folk conceptions of race are obviously based on arbitrary categories, they have a profound social and cultural significance in many societies.

ETHNICITY

One of the basic misconceptions in early Western racist and later scientific racist views was the confusion of race and culture. Purported racial characteristics such as skin color, nose shape, or other traits were associated with particular 'essences' that determined behavior and cultural attributes. However, one of the basic findings based on the research of Franz Boas and later anthropologists is that the physical characteristics of a particular group of people are not associated with any particular behavior or culture or language. In other words, one's language or culture is not inherited through biological transmission or genetics. One acquires his or her language and culture through *enculturation,* by learning the various language, symbols, values, norms, and beliefs in the environments one is exposed. Since the 1960s anthropologists have used the term *ethnicity* or *ethnic group* to refer to an individual's cultural heritage, which is separable from one's physical characteristics. **Ethnicity** is a shared cultural heritage. An **ethnic group** is a collectivity of people who believe they share a common history, culture, or ancestry. Thus, one's ethnicity is not innately determined by biology or purported racial characteristics. Despite early classifications of the European "race" or the English, German, French, Italian, or Polish "races," these differences among Europeans were not based on physical differences, but rather on linguistic and cultural variation. Likewise, there is no African race; rather, Africa is a continent where thousands of different ethnic groups that vary from region to region reside. The variations among the Chinese, Japanese, and Koreans are not based on racial differences but on ethnic differences.

ETHNICITY: TWO ANTHROPOLOGICAL PERSPECTIVES

Ethnic unrest and tension are prevalent in today's world. Newspapers and television news are rife with stories about ethnic violence among the peoples of the former Soviet Union, Africa, Sri Lanka, India, Ireland, the Middle East, and the United States. Anthropologists have been systematically examining ethnicity since the 1960s. Members of ethnic groups often share cultural traits such as language, religion, dress, and food. Today, most complex societies are plural societies that contain many ethnic groups. Anthropologists have analyzed ethnicity with two differing models known as the *circumstantialist* model and the *primordialist* model.

The Circumstantialist Model The **circumstantialist model** emphasizes the situational (or circumstantial) nature of ethnicity. Anthropologists such as Frederick Barth (1969) noted the fluidity of ethnic relations in different types of plural soci-

eties. Although ethnic groups maintain boundaries such as language to mark their identity, people shift their language and ethnic identity in different types of social interaction. For example, in the United States, people of German descent may refer to themselves as "German Americans" to distinguish themselves from "Irish Americans" or "Italian Americans." Should they happen to be among Europeans, however, these same people might refer to themselves simply as "Americans." The circumstantialist model explains how people draw on their ethnic identity for specific economic, social, and political purposes. For example, in adapting to certain economic niches in a multiethnic society, a group might emphasize its shared ethnic identity as a means of enhancing cooperation with other members of the group. In migrating to different areas of the world migrants often use ethnic ties as a means of social adjustment when they migrate to new areas. Groups may pursue political interests through ethnic allegiances. In numerous situations, people may manipulate ethnic traditions and symbols to their advantage.

Many anthropologists in the 1960s believed that ethnic identities are so fluid and situational that they will eventually disappear. Multiethnic or plural societies, including the United States, have implemented policies based on the goal of **assimilation,** the absorption of different ethnic groups into one ethnicity. Educational institutions encouraged the teaching of a national language and history and promoted specific cultural practices and values to eliminate ethnic identities and meld minorities into one culture. U.S. government and educational policies encouraged the development of English-language skills and the abandonment of traditional ethnic differences. This is an example of *cultural hegemony,* or the imposition of one set of norms, values, beliefs, language, and symbolism onto other ethnic groups. For example, Native American Indians and Hispanic Americans were sometimes forced to abandon their language and culture to adapt to U.S. society. In the U.S., ethnic identity was assumed to be dysfunctional in the organization of a modern society. As we will see later in this text, many other societies throughout the world have also been engaged in assimilation and cultural hegemonic policies.

This circumstantialist view of ethnicity also asserts that ethnicity will be displayed to a different degree by various ethnic groups. Ethnic traits will vary from one historical time to another, and group identity may shift from one generation to another. Ethnic groups are not stable collective entities. They may appear and vanish within a generation or less than a generation. Ethnic groups will come into being during different historical periods. **Ethnogenesis** refers to the origins of an ethnic group. Ethnogenesis has taken place throughout the world in many different historical circumstances. For example, a small ethnic group in U.S. society known as the Amish first originated in Switzerland during the sixteenth century. The Amish are a group of Anabaptists who split off from the mainstream of their religion during the Protestant Reformation. After ethnogenesis, the Amish began to define themselves as different from other Anabaptists, Protestants, and Catholics, and they subsequently faced a great deal of persecution from the religious authorities (Kraybill and Olshan, 1994). Eventually, the Amish fled to the United States in the 1700s settling first in Lancaster, Pennsylvania. From there, they have grown in size, and live in 20 different states in the U.S. The Amish population is about 100,000. There are no longer any Amish in Europe. Ethnogenesis is an ongoing process for many people throughout the world.

The Primordialist Model Despite the attempts at assimilation and cultural hegemonic policies, ethnicity remains a driving force in world affairs. The **primordialist model** maintains that ethnic affiliation persists because it is fundamental to a person's identity. This model emphasizes that conceptions of common descent, language, and religious attachments become deeply rooted through enculturation. In this view, as people are enculturated into a particular ethnic group, they form deep emotional attachments to that group. These emotional sentiments are sometimes evident through *ethnic boundary markers,* which distinguish one ethnic group from another. For example, the Amish, described above, have maintained very strong ethnic boundary markers in U.S. society despite assimilation and cultural hegemonic policies. They emphasize their ethnic difference through language by speaking a German dialect among themselves. The Amish dress in a traditional manner similar to the

An Amish family.

cultural codes of the 1600s. Men wear hats and long beards, and women wear long hair, which is always covered by a hat in public. Based on their interpretation of the Bible, the Amish strive to maintain a conservative traditional way of life that does not allow the adoption of modern technology such as electricity, automobiles, or television. They do not allow their children to be educated beyond the eighth grade so that they are not exposed to modern U.S. culture. The Amish have a deeply emotional attachment to their ethnicity and culture. Other ethnic groups in U.S. society have similar primordial sentiments regarding their ethnic traditions and culture.

Anthropologists have begun to recognize that both the circumstantialist and primordialist views can be combined to account for ethnic interaction in a society. Ethnicity is deeply ingrained, but it is also subject to change; sociocultural and historical conditions determine which tendency prevails. For example, when an ethnic group lives together in a distinct region, ethnic persistence tends to predominate. In contrast, when ethnic groups are dispersed throughout a territory, as in a plural society, ethnic cohesiveness is reduced, and interethnic communication is more common. As we will see in later chapters, anthropological research in various areas of the world have led to insights regarding ethnic relations.

Cultural Universals

As previously discussed, early anthropologists emphasized cultural diversity in their research and writings. Some anthropologists, however, began to recognize that humans throughout the world share some fundamental behavioral characteristics. George Murdock, an anthropologist who devoted himself to cross-cultural analysis, compiled a lengthy list of cultural universals from hundreds of societies. **Cultural universals** are essential behavioral characteristics of societies, and they are found all over the world. Murdock's list of cultural universals can be seen in Table 3.1; it includes such basics as language, cooking, family, folklore, games, community organizations, decorative art, education, ethics, myths, food taboos, numbers, personal names, magic, religion, puberty customs, toolmaking, and sexual restrictions. Although the specific

content and practices of these universals may vary from society to society, the fact that these cultural universals exist underlies the essential reality that modern humans are of one biological family and one species.

In a recent book entitled *Human Universals* (1991), anthropologist Donald E. Brown suggests that in their quest for describing cultural diversity, many anthropologists have overlooked basic similarities in human behavior and culture. This led to stereotypes and distortions about people in other societies; they were viewed as "exotic," "inscrutable," and "alien."

Following in Murdock's footsteps, Brown describes many human universals. In one imaginative chapter Brown creates a group of people he refers to as the "Universal People," who have all of the traits of any people in any society throughout the world. The Universal People have language with a complex grammar to communicate and think abstractly; kinship terms and categories for distinguishing relatives and age groupings; gender terms for male and female; facial expressions to show basic emotions; a concept of the self as subject and object; tools, shelter, and fire; patterns for childbirth and training; families and political groupings; conflict; etiquette; morality, religious beliefs, and worldviews; and dance, music, art, and other aesthetic standards. Brown's depiction of the Universal People clearly suggests that many behaviors and other aspects of human behavior result from certain problems that all societies face to maintain their physical and social survival. For a society to survive it must have mechanisms to care for children, adapt to the physical environment, produce and distribute goods and services, maintain order, and provide explanations of the natural and social environment. In addition, many universal behaviors result from fundamental biological characteristics common to all people.

Anthropologists have discovered that culture can be both diverse and universal. The challenge for anthropology is to understand the basis of both this diversity and universality. To paraphrase a saying of the late anthropologist Clyde Kluckhohn: Every human is like all other humans, some other humans, and no other human. The major objective of cultural anthropology is to investigate the validity of this statement.

Table 3.1   A List of Some Cultural Universals Described by Murdock

age grading	faith healing	joking	pregnancy usages
athletics	family	kin groups	property rights
bodily adornments	feasting	kin terminology	propitiation of supernatural beings
calendar	fire making	language	puberty customs
community organization	folklore	magic	religious rituals
cooking	food taboos	marriage	residence rules
cooperative labor	funeral rites	mealtimes	sexual restrictions
cosmology	games	medicine	soul concepts
courtship	gestures	modesty	status differentiation
dancing	gift giving	mourning	tool making
decorative art	greetings	music	trade
division of labor	hair styles	mythology	visiting
dream interpretation	hospitality	numerals	weaning
education	housing	obstetrics	weather control
ethics	hygiene	personal names	
ethnobotany	incest taboos	population policy	
etiquette	inheritance rules	postnatal care	

Source: Adapted from George Peter Murdock, "The Common Denominator of Cultures." Republished with permission of the Columbia University Press, 562 W. 113th St., New York, NY 10025. *The Science of Man in the World Crisis* (table), edited by Ralph Linten, 1945. Reproduced by permission of the publisher via Copyright Clearance Center.

 SUMMARY

Culture is a key concept in anthropology. Culture is the learned, shared way of life that is transmitted from generation to generation in a society. Humans learn through direct experience (situational learning), observation (social learning), and symbols (symbolic learning). Symbols are arbitrary meanings that vary from society to society. Many anthropologists view symbolic learning as the major distinction between human and nonhuman animals.

Culture includes material and nonmaterial components. The material aspect of culture consists of tools, clothing, shelter, armaments, and other innovations that enable humans to adapt to their environments. The nonmaterial components of culture are values, beliefs, norms, worldviews, and ideologies.

Different societies maintain different cultural and symbolic structures, creating the great variety and diversity of norms, values, worldviews, and behaviors. Ethnologists have discovered that cultural items ranging from dress to technology to sexual practices to dietary habits are enormously diverse. Race and culture were misunderstood for

many centuries in Western society. As Europeans explored the world, they confused the culture and behavior of different peoples with superficial physical traits such as skin color. Eventually, this led to distortions within early scientific classifications of races of humans. In addition, scientific racist beliefs began to dominate Western society, resulting in tragic human events such as the Holocaust under Nazi Germany. Anthropologists have been engaged in criticizing scientific racist beliefs in the past and the present with sound evidence and rigorous examination of indicators such as IQ tests. Despite the useless scientific enterprise of classifying races throughout the world, societies continue to use folk taxonomies of race to distinguish different people. These folk taxonomies have profound social and cultural meaning for societies around the world.

Another confusion that developed within Western societies and other areas of the world is the identification of race with culture. Anthropologists have used the term ethnic group or ethnicity to distinguish ethnicity from race and are actively engaged in studying ethnic relations in different regions of the world.

Anthropologists also recognize that many patterns of human behavior are universal. The universal distribution of certain cultural traits suggests

Murdock

that humans everywhere have similar biological requirements and tendencies that influence behavior. Thus, anthropologists have been engaged in exploring both the diversity and similarity of human cultures throughout the world.

STUDY QUESTIONS

1. How do anthropologists differentiate culture from nonhuman animal behavior?

2. As a college student, you have probably heard quite a bit about "cultural diversity" or "multiculturalism" and the changing demographics in the United States. What is multiculturalism? Why is it important to understand this concept? Are there any dangers in implementing multicultural education programs?

3. Using an anthropological perspective, explain the statement, "You are what you eat."

4. After reading the section on dress codes and symbolism, pick another example of dress codes and hairstyles and explain what they symbolize to the individuals involved.

5. How did Westerners misunderstand the difference between race and culture?

6. Can you distinguish ethnic groups from each other in your own society? How do you make that distinction?

7. If you were to create the "Universal People" (see page 58), how would they behave and organize themselves, what would they believe, and how might they act? After you have constructed these imaginary people, read Donald E. Brown's chapter on "Universal People" (in *Human Universals,* 1991) for comparison.

8. Interpret the statement, "Every human is like all other humans, some other humans, and no other human."

KEY TERMS

assimilation	ethnogenesis	primordialist model
beliefs	ethos	racism
circumstantialist model	folkways	real culture
cultural hegemony	hypodescent concept	signs
cultural relativism	ideal culture	situational learning
cultural universals	ideology	social learning
culture	material culture	society
enculturation	mores	symbolic learning
ethnic group	nonmaterial culture	symbols
ethnicity	norms	values
ethnocentrism	one-drop rule	worldview

INTERNET EXERCISES

1. Refer to **http://www.indiana.edu/~iupress/ fall96/wiredu.html.** What does Kwasi Wiredu feel is the basis for cultural universals? Why? What is the connection between cultural particularities and cultural universals? What makes intercultural communication possible?

2. What is the premise of relativism as portrayed by the following website: **http://www.wsu. edu:8001vcwsu/commons/topicsculture/ culture-definitions/shweder.html?** How does this compare to the textbook section on the components of culture?

 SUGGESTED READINGS

ANGELINO, E., ed. 1999. *Annual Editions: Anthropology 99/00.* Guilford, CT: Dushkin. A good selection of brief essays by many anthropologists, introducing material based on ethnographic findings from other societies.

BARASH, DAVID. 1981. *The Whisperings Within: Evolution and the Origin of Human Nature.* New York: Penguin Books; and BARASH, DAVID. 1986. *The Hare and the Tortoise: Culture, Biology, and Human Nature.* New York: Penguin Books. Two popular books by a zoologist-psychologist who relies on the interactionist approach to understand human behavior and culture.

BARRETT, RICHARD A. 1984. *Culture and Conduct,* 2d ed. Belmont, CA: Wadsworth. A concise text that presents both the adaptive and symbolic aspects of culture studied by anthropologists.

BELLAH, ROBERT N., ET AL. 1986. *Habits of the Heart: Individualism and Commitment in American Life.* New York: Harper & Row. An analysis of American culture, emphasizing the conflict in values between a deeply rooted individualism and a sense of community interests.

ERIKSEN, THOMAS HYLLAND. 1993. *Ethnicity & Nationalism: Anthropological Perspectives.* London: Pluto Press. This text is an overview of ethnicity and the study of ethnicity through an anthropological viewpoint. It contains many ethnographic examples of ethnic change and ethnic persistence in different regions of the world.

GEERTZ, CLIFFORD. 1973. *The Interpretation of Cultures.* New York: Basic Books. A selection of essays by one of the most prominent contemporary anthropologists, who emphasizes a symbolic approach to the analysis of culture.

MONTAGU, ASHLEY. 1997. *Man's Most Dangerous Myth: The Fallacy of Race,* 6th ed. Walnut Creek: CA: Altamira Press. This book is the classic statement by a trained physical anthropologist regarding the abuse of racial classification and the problems these classifications have created in the world. The first edition was published in 1942 at the height of the Nazi period. It represented the most fundamental attack of Nazi racialistic theories by American anthropologists. The most recent edition critiques the fallacies of the IQ studies that show supposed correlations between race and IQ.

The Process
of Enculturation

CHAPTER OUTLINE

Biology versus Culture

Instincts and Human Nature
Human Beings as Animals / Instincts in Animals / Instincts and Learned Behaviors / Do Humans Possess Instincts? / Drives / Culture versus Instinct

Enculturation: Culture and Personality
Early Studies of Enculturation / Childhood Training

Psychoanalytic Approaches in Anthropology
Sigmund Freud / Modern Psychoanalytic Anthropology

Understanding Incest Avoidance and the Incest Taboo
Biological Explanations of Incest Avoidance / Marital Alliance and the Incest Taboo / Childhood Familiarity Hypothesis / Incest Avoidance: Interactionist Perspectives

Enculturation and the Sex Drive
Codes of Sexual Behavior / Homosexual Behavior

Enculturation and Cognition
Structuralism / Jean Piaget

Evolutionary Psychology

Enculturation and Emotions

Culture and Mental Illness
What Is Abnormal? / Culture-Specific Disorders

The Limits of Enculturation
Unique Biological Tendencies / Individual Variation

CHAPTER QUESTIONS

- What is the relationship between individuals and culture as studied by psychological anthropologists?

- How does nonhuman animal behavior differ from human behavior?

- How have anthropologists studied enculturation and its relationship to personality formation, sexual behavior, cognition, emotions, and mental disorders?

- In what way are the studies of enculturation limited?

IN THE PREVIOUS CHAPTER, WE EXPLORED THE concept of culture as it reflects the differences and similarities in human behavior and thought around the world. This chapter focuses on how anthropologists study the relationship between the individual and culture, or the process of enculturation. Anthropologists who focus on the process of enculturation are known as **psychological anthropologists.** Recall from Chapter 3 that *enculturation* is the process of social interaction through which people learn their culture. Unlike psychologists, who tend to study people within the psychologists' own societies, psychological anthropologists observe people and the process of enculturation in many different types of societies. Their research findings are then used as the basis of cross-cultural studies to determine how and why behavior, thoughts, and feelings differ and are similar from society to society.

Psychological anthropologists study the development of personality characteristics and individual behaviors in a given society and how they are influenced by enculturation. In their studies, anthropologists need to question basic assumptions regarding human nature. Is human nature primarily of biological influences or of cultural factors? In order to study this question psychological anthropologists focus on the enculturation process and precisely how these processes influence personality characteristics, sexual behavior, thinking and cognition, emotional development, and particular abnormal behaviors in different societies. This chapter considers some of the major research by psychological anthropologists on the process of enculturation.

Biology versus Culture

Before we explore the specific aspects of psychological anthropology, we need to consider some questions. One fundamental concept that anthropologists reflect on is what is frequently referred to as "human nature." Two questions immediately arise when discussing this concept: If there are basic similarities or universal patterns of human behavior, does that mean that human nature is biologically transmitted through heredity? If this is the case, to what extent can culture or learning change human nature to produce variation in behavior within different societies? These questions have led to a controversy in anthropology, with some anthropologists emphasizing biological influences on human behavior and others emphasizing the social or cultural influences that affect behavior.

Today, however, most anthropologists realize that neither of these influences exists in absolute, pure form. Modern anthropologists are therefore adopting an *interactionist perspective,* which combines the effects of biology and culture, to explain human behavior. Anthropologists recognize that human behavior depends on both our biological endowment and what we learn from our society or culture. What interactionists care about is the strength of the biologically based and learned factors in any behavior.

Instincts and Human Nature

Another fundamental question addressed by anthropologists is to what extent human nature is similar to that of other animals. For example, according to the traditional view of humans, the human body is "animal-like" or "machine-like," and the human mind is separate from the body. For many Westerners this image of humans was used to distinguish humans from other types of animals.

HUMAN BEINGS AS ANIMALS

What do we mean when we say that humans are animal-like? This statement can create misunderstandings because of the different meanings we give to the word animal. On the one hand, we distinguish animals scientifically from plants and minerals. This system of classification places humans in the animal category. On the other hand, animal is sometimes used in a derogatory or pejorative sense. For example, in one of the earliest uses of the word in written English, Shakespeare wrote:

> *His intellect is not replenished, hee is onely an animal, onely sensible in the duller parts* (Love's Labour's Lost, *IV. ii).*

This is the negative meaning of the term that we associate with films such as *Animal House,* referring to "uncivilized," "irrational," "unthinking," and "brutish" behaviors. In attempting to understand humans fully, anthropologists emphasize only the scientific meaning of the word *animal.* Anthropologists maintain that humans are partly like all animals, partly like certain types of animals, and partly like no other animal.

Because they are part of the animal kingdom, humans share certain characteristics with all animals. We have to consume certain amounts of carbohydrates, proteins, and minerals to survive, just as other animals do. We cannot photosynthesize and process our own foods from within as plants do. In addition, we share certain characteristics with particular types of animals. For example, like other mammals we have body hair, and human mothers have the capacity to suckle their offspring with milk produced after birth. Similarly, like other primates, such as chimpanzees and gorillas, we have stereoscopic, color vision; we have nails instead of claws; we are extremely sociable; and our infants experience a long period of dependence on adults.

Despite these similarities with other animals, humans are unquestionably the most complex, intelligent, and resourceful creatures on the planet. Humans have spread and adapted to every continent, becoming the most widely dispersed animal on the earth. We have been the most creative species in respect to our abilities to adjust to different conditions, ranging from tropical rainforests to deserts to rural agricultural areas to urban environments. Anthropologists have asked the question, What gives the human species its tremendous flexibility in adjusting to these different environments?

INSTINCTS IN ANIMALS

One way of answering this question is to compare the fundamental behaviors of human and nonhuman animals. Many animals inherit instincts that allow them to take advantage of the specific conditions of their environment. **Instincts** are fixed, complex, genetically based, unlearned, species-specific behaviors that promote the survival of different species. Instinctive behaviors occur widely within the animal kingdom. For example, certain species of birds migrate during the winter season. Temperature changes or differences in ultraviolet radiation from the sun trigger biochemically based, inborn hormonal reactions that act on neurological mechanisms, stimulating all normal individuals within a particular species of bird to fly in a certain direction. This behavior enables the birds to find sufficient feeding grounds for survival during the winter season.

A weaver finch building a nest—an example of instinctive behavior.

Another example of these species-specific instincts is the nest-building behavior of certain bird populations. In an experiment, scientists isolated as many as five generations of weaver finches and did not supply them with nest-building materials. (Weaver finches are small, brightly colored, seed-eating birds that construct complicated nests with side entrances.) When the scientists released the sixth generation of birds, however, these birds automatically built nests identical to those of their ancestors.

Bears hibernating, salmon swimming upstream to lay eggs during a specific season, spiders spinning perfect webs, and infant turtles and alligators walking unaided toward the water after hatching from eggs are other examples of instinctive behaviors. These behaviors can be thought of as a kind of innate knowledge with which these animals are born. This does not mean that nonhuman animals do not learn complex behaviors, however. In fact, many of them do learn many types of behaviors, but some of their behaviors are rigid and genetically based.

INSTINCTS AND LEARNED BEHAVIORS

The fact that some animal behaviors are instinctive does not mean that environment has nothing to do with these behaviors. Although some animal behavior is near-perfect when it first appears, typically the development of most animal behavior involves a continuous interaction between the organism and the environment.

For example, song learning by birds varies from species to species. Some species do not need to be exposed to the specific vocalizations to reproduce them in near-perfect form. A particular species of dove sings a species-specific type of "coo" in perfect form even when reared with other species of doves. In contrast, parrots can learn to imitate any song they hear. But generally, many other birds, such as chaffinches, need to be exposed to the adult song during their early months to acquire the specific vocalization for their particular species (Hinde & Stevenson-Hinde, 1987).

Most ethologists agree that complex instincts in different types of animals can be classified as exhibiting a more open or closed genetic program. Closed types of instincts remain fairly stable, even when environmental conditions change, whereas open types respond more sensitively to changing circumstances. In the cases just described, the song patterns of the dove represent a closed instinct, whereas the parrot's song imitations are an open instinct.

DO HUMANS POSSESS INSTINCTS?

Because humans are part of the animal kingdom, the question arises, Do we have any instinctive behaviors? This question is difficult to answer because we use the word *instinct* in different contexts. Sometimes we refer to athletes as having the right kind of instincts in going toward the basket or goal line. Upon further reflection, however, it is obvious that basketball or football players who respond in an automatic way to a play situation do so only after practicing for long hours and developing the coordination and skillful moves necessary for competitive sports. Because athletic skills are learned, they are not comparable to the instinctive behaviors of animals. We also use the term to refer to some intuitive processes. For example, we have all heard about relying on our instincts in making difficult decisions. Again, surely, these instincts are not something with which we are born but are based on our experiences and memories.

Obviously, these meanings of the word *instinct* do not compare with the scientific meaning. Do humans, then, have any closed instincts like those of other nonhuman animals? Do we have any automatic, biologically controlled behaviors? Because of the wide range of behaviors shown by humans, most anthropologists and other social scientists agree that humans do not have any closed instincts.

We do have some genetically determined behaviors called simple reflexes, or involuntary responses, such as being startled by a loud noise, blinking our eyes, breathing, or throwing out our arms when we lose our balance. These reflexive behaviors are automatic responses to environmental conditions, and we do them unconsciously. But these are not comparable to the complex behaviors related to the closed instincts of some other species. Some scientists, however, including some anthropologists who refer to themselves as "evolutionary psychologists," believe that humans also have some genetically prepared behaviors that have enabled us to adapt to varying conditions in our evolutionary history. Yet the evolutionary psychologists see the prepared behaviors as unlike the closed instincts of some other animals, because they can be shaped by environmental conditions. We discuss the views of evolutionary psychologists further in a subsequent section.

DRIVES

We also have basic, inborn **drives**—biological urges such as hunger, thirst, and sex—that need satisfaction. These drives are important for the survival of the species. Yet, again, these drives are not comparable to the closed instincts of nonhuman animals. We are not programmed to satisfy these in a rigid, mechanical manner. Rather, the ways in which we satisfy them are learned through experience. We do not automatically build a spider's web to capture our food; we have to learn to find food in ways that vary widely in many different types of environments. And, unlike some other animals, we may choose to override rather than to satisfy these drives. For example, people can ignore the hunger drive by going on hunger strikes as a political protest.

If we do not have closed instincts, what do we have that makes us so successful and creative? The answer is that we have the capacity for flexibility in creating conditions and providing solutions for human survival. Many animals have a *closed biogram,* a genetically closed behavioral complex that is related to their specific environment. For example, certain species of birds in temperate regions migrate from north to south in the winter season. In contrast, humans have an *open biogram,* an extremely flexible genetic program that is shaped by learning experiences.

CULTURE VERSUS INSTINCT

In addition to open biograms, our unprecedented success in adapting to different conditions reflects the influence of human culture. Our capacity for culture, an inherent aspect of the human mind, has enabled us to modify our behaviors and to shape and adjust to our natural environment. The capacity for culture is genetically programmed through the human brain and nervous system. Culture has replaced the closed instincts of nonhuman animals. But culture is not transmitted biologically through genetic programming. Instead, it is learned through the enculturation process and is passed on from generation to generation. Culture frees us from relying on the slow process of natural selection to adapt to specific environments.

Genes (see Chapter 2) do not specifically encode for narrowly defined types of human behavior. We are not genetically programmed to build shelters in a certain manner, to devise patterns of economic distribution, to get married, to vote for a president, to carry out a revolution, or to believe in a particular religion. These are learned behaviors based on enculturation processes that make up the economic, social, political, and religious practices and concepts of a particular society. Without culture, we would not be able to adjust to the tremendous range of environments throughout the world. We would not be able to adapt to Arctic conditions, hunt animals and collect plants, herd cattle, plant crops, or drive a car. The development of the human mind, with the capacity for culture, represents the greatest revolutionary breakthrough in the evolution of life.

Enculturation: Culture and Personality

Enculturation is a lifelong process, and it links the individual, the society, and the culture. Immediately after they are born, people begin to absorb through unconscious and conscious learning—situational, social, and symbolic—the etiquette, mores, values, beliefs, and practices of their society. Enculturation is therefore the process through which culture is transmitted from generation to generation.

Enculturation is a vital foundation of our humanity. Virtually helpless at birth, an infant needs care and is completely dependent on others for survival. Through the interaction of enculturation with biologically based predispositions, a person acquires his or her **personality,** the fairly stable patterns of thought, feeling, and action associated with a specific person. Personality includes several components: the cognitive, emotional, and behavioral. The cognitive component of personality consists of thought patterns, memory, belief, perception, and other intellectual capacities. The emotional component includes emotions such as love,

hate, envy, jealousy, sympathy, anger, and pride. The behavioral component consists of the skills, aptitudes, competence, and other abilities or potentials that are developed throughout the course of a person's life.

EARLY STUDIES OF ENCULTURATION

During the 1930s and 1940s, a number of anthropologists began to research enculturation to learn about the influence of culture on personality development. At this time, some social scientists suggested that biology and race are the most influential determinants of human behavior (see Chapter 3). In Germany, for example, social scientists who were members of the Nazi party promoted the idea that because of biological characteristics some races are superior to others in respect to behavior and thought. Cultural anthropologists in the United States began to challenge this view of biological or racial determinism through research on enculturation (Degler, 1991). In particular, two women anthropologists, Ruth Benedict and Margaret Mead, became pioneers in early psychological anthropology. They published extensively and became prominent in this area of research. Both of these anthropologists maintained that each society and culture has a unique history. After studying processes such as child rearing and enculturation, they proposed that every culture is characterized by a dominant personality type. Culture, they argued, is essentially "personality writ large." The field studies they did became the basis of what was then called culture-and-personality theory.

Benedict and Culture Types   One classic example of the application of culture-and-personality theory is Benedict's analysis of the Plains and Pueblo Native American societies. In an essay titled "Psychological Types in the Cultures of the Southwest" (1928) and in a classic book, *Patterns of Culture* (1934), Benedict classified Pueblo societies as having an *Apollonian* (named for the Greek god Apollo) culture. The cultural ethos stressed gentleness, cooperation, harmony, tranquility, and peacefulness. According to Benedict, these values explain why members of Pueblo societies were "moderate." The Pueblo rarely indulged in violence, and they avoided the use of drugs and alcohol to transcend their senses.

Ruth Benedict portrayed the Plains Indians such as those in this 1890 photo as "Dionysian," or excessive in their behavior.

In contrast, Benedict characterized the Plains societies as *Dionysian* (after the Greek god Dionysius). The values and ethos of the Plains groups were almost the direct opposite of those of the Pueblo. The Plains Indians were involved in warfare and violence, and their ritual behavior included the use of drugs, alcohol, fasting, and bodily self-torture to induce religious ecstasy. Benedict extended her analysis to such groups as the Kwakiutl Native American peoples and the Dobu of Melanesia. She referred to the Kwakiutl as "megalomaniacs" and the Dobuans as "paranoid," fearing and hating one another. In each case, she claimed that the group's values and ethos had created a distinctive cultural personality. In Benedict's analysis, the culture of a particular society can be studied by studying the personality of its bearers. The patterning or configuration of a particular culture is simply reflected in an individual's personality.

Mead in Samoa Mead was one of the most influential contributors to the field of culture and personality. Although most of her ethnographic reports focused on fairly isolated, small-scale societies located in the Pacific Islands, she addressed issues that concerned U.S. society, particularly adolescence, child care, and relationships between males and females. At the age of 23, Mead went to the Pacific island of Samoa to study adolescent development. In the United States and other societies, adolescence was usually identified with emotional conflict and rebellion against parental authority.

Her mentor, Franz Boas (see Chapter 3), wanted her to investigate this aspect of life in Samoa to determine whether this pattern of adolescent devel-

Margaret Mead with Samoan girl.

opment is universal. The central research question that Mead was to investigate was whether adolescent problems are the products of physiological changes occurring at puberty or the result of cultural factors.

Mead resided in Samoa for nine months and interviewed fifty Samoan girls in three villages. She concluded that, in contrast to U.S. society, adolescence in Samoa was not characterized by problems between the young and the old. She attributed the difference between the two societies to different sets of values, which produce different cultural personalities. In her book *Coming of Age in Samoa* (1928), she argued that Samoan society emphasized group harmony and cooperation. These values arose, according to Mead, from Samoan child-rearing practices. Samoan children were raised in family units that included many adults. Therefore, youngsters did not develop strong emotional ties to any one adult. Consequently, she argued, emotional bonds were relatively shallow.

For this reason, Mead continued, Samoan society was more casual than U.S. society. Children openly learned about sexuality, and adolescents freely engaged in premarital sex. In addition, Mead contended that Samoan society shared a common set of values and standards. Therefore, Samoan children were not exposed to conflicting values and political and religious beliefs, as were U.S. adolescents. For these reasons, Mead concluded, Samoan children experienced a much easier transition from adolescence into adulthood than did their counterparts in the United States.

The Culture-and-Personality School: An Evaluation The anthropological school represented by Mead and Benedict stimulated more careful research regarding personality and culture. Much of the data provided by these early psychological anthropologists was important in understanding the enculturation process. As a result of these early studies, we now have a better understanding of personality formation, thought, behavior, and emotional development within different human societies.

Despite these accomplishments, the culture-and-personality school has been criticized on many fronts. One major shortcoming cited is the practice of characterizing an entire society in terms of one dominant personality. Culture-and-personality the-

orists assumed that all members of a given society share the same cultural knowledge. In fact, culture and knowledge are distributed differently and unequally within society. Some people have a knowledge of values, beliefs, and ideologies that others do not have. Thus, defining an entire society as a single personality creates cultural stereotypes rather than a realistic portrait of a people. Benedict, for example, neglected much data that suggested that both the Plains and Pueblo societies exhibited Apollonian and Dionysian behaviors.

The culture-and-personality school has also been criticized for focusing entirely on the nonmaterial aspects of culture. Theorists such as Benedict went so far as to argue that cultural values are completely autonomous from material conditions (Hatch, 1973). Therefore, they did not include such factors as technology or the physical environment in their explanations of human behavior. Again using Benedict as an example, the fact that traditional Plains Indians were primarily bison-hunting groups whereas the Pueblo peoples were agriculturalists in a semiarid desert was not included in her analysis, yet this fact was obviously important in their societies.

A final criticism of the culture-and-personality theorists is their tendency to attribute human behavior entirely to cultural factors. Of course, their emphasis on cultural determinants rather than biological determinants reflects the attempt to criticize the biological and racialistic determinism prevalent during that period. However, in their descriptions they tended to dismiss any biological basis of behavior. This extreme culturalist perspective has since come under attack by a number of critics, most notably Australian anthropologist Derek Freeman.

The Freeman–Mead Controversy In 1983 Freeman attracted a great deal of attention when he published a controversial book titled *Margaret Mead and Samoa: The Making and Unmaking of an Anthropological Myth*. Having conducted fieldwork in Samoa intermittently since 1940, Freeman concluded that Mead's findings were largely erroneous. Whereas Mead had portrayed the Samoan people as lacking strong passions, aggression, warfare, a sense of sin or guilt, rape, suicide, and other behaviors associated with intense emotions, Freeman claimed to find all of these behaviors.

Freeman challenged Mead by asserting that strong emotional ties did exist between parents and children in Samoan society. He also challenged Mead's conclusions concerning casual attitudes toward sexuality. Pointing out that Samoa had converted to Christianity during the 1830s, Freeman asserted that most Samoans had puritanical views toward sexuality. He found that virginity for girls was highly valued, casual sexual liaisons were prohibited, and adultery was severely punished. Government records indicated that the incidence of rape in Samoa (proportionate to population size) was twice as high as that in the United States.

Freeman also rejected Mead's claims for an easy transition from adolescence to adulthood. He noted that adolescents were severely punished by their parents for any transgressions. He presented charts illustrating that offenses and delinquent behaviors among Samoans peaked at the age of 16, especially for males. Thus, Freeman concluded that adolescents in Samoa go through a period of deviance and rebellion against their elders in the same way that other adolescents around the world do. Freeman asserted that hormonal changes as well as cultural influences have consequences for adolescent behavior everywhere. Samoan adolescents are not much different from adolescents elsewhere.

How could two anthropologists studying the same people arrive at such radically different conclusions? Freeman insisted that Mead's fieldwork was marked by many methodological shortcomings. He pointed out, for example, that Mead had studied the Samoan language for only six weeks prior to her fieldwork. Thus, her language skills were too limited for her to communicate accurately with the Samoans. Moreover, instead of residing with a Samoan family, she lived with an American family and conducted interviews intermittently from her household. Because she was a young female, she was not invited to important ceremonies. Of the fifty females she interviewed, half were not past puberty and therefore could not serve as models of the transition from adolescence to adulthood.

Freeman argued that the major reason for Mead's misinterpretation of Samoan society was her extreme reliance on the model of cultural determinism of theorists such as Benedict. Thus, Mead's portrayal of Samoa as a society without adolescent problems supported the claims of her close colleagues at that time, who maintained that biology has little influence on behavior. In contrast, Freeman emphasized an interactionist approach, which focuses on both biological and cultural influences. He argued that the biological changes that accompany adolescence inevitably affect adolescent behavior.

The Freeman–Mead debate remains a major controversy in anthropology. Supporters of Mead point out that Freeman studied Samoa years—and even decades—after Mead did. Because societies are not static, it is possible that Samoan values and lifestyles had changed by the time of Freeman's work. Freeman has a new book, *Margaret Mead and the Heretic: The Making and Unmaking of an Anthropological Myth* (1996), in which he emphasizes how Mead was strongly influenced by the ideas of cultural determinism. He indicates that Mead overlooked any type of biological influences on behavior. However, others note that Mead did not discount biology entirely; she merely rejected the extreme biological deterministic views of their time (Shankman, 1998). The Freeman–Mead controversy serves as an excellent example of how anthropologists have been struggling to develop interactionist accounts of human behavior.

CHILDHOOD TRAINING

Despite limitations of early research on enculturation and culture and personality, pioneering women anthropologists such as Margaret Mead, Ruth Benedict, and others were the first to systematically examine the effects of childhood training on personality development. Male ethnographers had not paid much attention to this subject. This innovative research has resulted in a much-improved understanding of the techniques of childhood training and enculturation throughout the world. Since then, a number of studies of childhood training by psychological anthropologists have contributed to this area of research.

The Six Cultures Project An important outgrowth of the research of psychological anthropologists such as Mead, Benedict, and others was the attempt to systematize the studies of enculturation and childhood training. In the 1950s a number of psychological anthropologists planned an extensive study of child rearing in six different societies.

Six pairs of ethnographers, most of them husband–wife teams, organized field studies of six communities. The communities were the Gusii of eastern Africa, the Rajputs of northern India, the Taira of Okinawa, the Mixtecan Indians of Mexico, the Tarong of the Philippines, and Orchard Town, a small New England community. The results of these ethnographic studies were published in three major books, *Six Cultures* (1963), *Mothers of Six Cultures* (1964), and *Children of Six Cultures* (1974).

These studies revealed the diversity of enculturation patterns regarding child rearing in different regions. Rather than relying on psychological testing, these ethnographers used intensive direct observation of child behavior in natural settings. They observed child behavior in different activities: at home during play, in gardens at work, and in school during learning. They collected statistical data on the variability of behavior in different categories to make sure they had a reliable portrait of the children's behavior. The studies indicate the way in which personality is shaped by both conscious training and unconscious enculturation processes.

Some of the generalizations that resulted from the six cultures study are that the behavior of the Mixtecan Indians, the Tarong, and the Orchard Town children was less aggressive than that of the Taira, Rajputs, and Gusii children. The latter three groups exhibited more aggressive-authoritarian behavior and less sociable-intimate behavior than the former group. For example, among the Gusii and Rajputs there were many more assaults, homicides, and litigation than in the other groups. The factors that influenced this difference in behavior appear to be household and family organization. In the Mixtecan, Tarong, and Orchard Town families, both husbands and wives have joint responsibilities for authority, they usually eat and sleep together, and they provide models of behavior for their children. In these societies the children were less dependent, more self-sufficient, and less prone to violence. The other three societies were based on male-dominated families that tended to enforce vigorous authority over the children. These children were more dependent, more submissive, and less responsible, and they took little initiative in solving their own problems (Whiting & Whiting, 1975).

Some critics have suggested that the Six Cultures Project was limited because the categories and procedures used to compare different modes of child rearing and institutions seem arbitrary. Others have suggested that the conclusions of the Six Cultures Project are not very surprising, in that age, gender, setting, and type of sociocultural system can all be shown to influence children's behavior. However, aside from the joint publications that resulted from the Six Cultures Project, the individual ethnographic reports from the different societies rank among the best studies in the field of childhood training and enculturation. They have provided models for many of the ongoing ethnographic research projects on this subject in the present.

Japanese Childhood Training Some contemporary ethnographic research projects focus on the type of childhood training and enculturation that influences the learning of basic concepts of a particular culture. One study, conducted by Joy Hendry (1992), focused on how children in Japan become enculturated. According to the Western stereotype, Japanese society is characterized as "collectivistic" rather than "individualistic." A related stereotype is that Japanese society is a

A Japanese mother with her baby.

"consensus," or "conformist," society, with everyone submitting to the norms of the group. Hendry's ethnographic research on whether these stereotypes are correct focused on how children learn their initial concepts of Japanese culture and adjust to group behaviors.

Hendry found that small children are extremely important in Japanese culture. Babies are afforded every possible individual attention. For example, many highly educated mothers gave up their careers to dedicate themselves to full-time nurturing once a child was born. The child is to be kept in a secure, harmonious household. A tiny child is often strapped to a mother's back or front while the mother works, shops, and performs daily routines. Also, an adult will lie down with a child at bedtime until he or she falls asleep. Although it would appear that the child is totally indulged, the child learns a great many routine tasks such as eating, washing, dressing, and toilet training through repetition until the child can do these tasks on his or her own.

During this early phase of enculturation the child learns two basic cultural concepts: *uchi,* or "inside of the house, including the people inside," and *soto,* the outside world. Human beings are categorized by these concepts, and various behaviors in a Japanese household, such as removing shoes before entering the house, reinforce the inside/outside dichotomy. *Uchi* is associated with safety, security, and cleanliness. *Soto* is where danger may lurk; big dogs, strangers, or even demons and ghosts may also be outside. For the first few years of their lives children play with siblings, cousins, and gradually with close neighbors. They are allowed to play in the immediate neighborhood from as early as 2 years of age if it is a safe environment. According to Hendry the child begins to build up a new set of "inside" personal relations with neighbors who live nearby.

At the age of 4 or 5, the child is introduced to group life with outsiders in a kindergarten or day nursery. At first the children cry for awhile and refuse to join in, but eventually they become involved with the new group of fellow kindergartners, and this becomes a new *uchi* group for them. They learn to cooperate with one another in the group and begin to develop an identity appropriate for group life. However, Hendry emphasizes that the children do not lose their individuality.

Each child is treated as an individual by the teacher, who obtains a great deal of background knowledge about the child. (Parents fill out forms regarding their child's strengths and weaknesses, likes and dislikes, their siblings, and other details.) In addition, teachers visit the child's home at least once during the academic year. Thus, along with learning to cooperate with their new *uchi* group, these children also become familiar with their own individuality and the individual characteristics of their peers. When engaging in group activities, whether in games, sports, learning activities, or other responsibilities, the children teach each other personal skills and abilities so that the entire group will benefit.

Hendry concluded that even though Japanese children learn to participate in many group-oriented activities, they do not completely lose their sense of individuality. Although Japanese society does not emphasize individualism in the same way U.S. society does, with connotations of self-assertion and individual rights, Japanese children develop their own sense of self in respect to their individual talents and abilities.

Two-Way Enculturation   One of the conclusions based on the new types of psychological anthropology studies such as Joy Hendry's is that children are not just passive recipients in the enculturation process. Instead, they are active contributors to the meaning and outcome of interactions with other members of society. As an example, in another ethnographic study, Bambi Schieffelin analyzed how Kaluli children in Papua New Guinea learn to decipher particular concepts and relationships for different social settings (1990). The Kaluli children learn about the relationship *ade,* which involves requests between brothers and sisters based on appeal. *Ade* behavior is a unique relationship between older sisters and younger brothers encouraged by mothers in early childhood. The younger brothers are socialized to appeal to an older sister for goods, services, and attention. The older sister "feels sorry for" her younger brother and shares food and nurtures him affectionately. Later as children become older they may use *ade* as a device to get something from someone or when they want to gain sympathy from someone. In other words they learn to use the *ade* relationship in various contexts in which there are expectations of nurturing, sharing, and giving out feelings of compassion (Schieffelin, 1990). Thus Kaluli children learn the content and meaning of this *ade* relationship in the course of specific interactions with other people as they grow older. They learn to apply this cultural concept in many different social contexts with people outside the family. Caregivers may give verbal instruction and enforce other norms of the culture, but the contributions of the children themselves in this process are extremely important.

This new perspective in psychological anthropology moves away from a "one-way" conception of enculturation, which tended to emphasize children as passive recipients of culture. Modern psychological anthropologists emphasize a "two-way" conception that focuses on the interactive relationships between child and caregiver, child and siblings, child and peers, or child and outsiders. The child is viewed as an active agent in this new conception of enculturation. Children learn to design appropriate responses to specific social situations and contexts as they are exposed to them. Psychological anthropologists are contributing to a better understanding of how children acquire cultural knowledge through exposure and active participation in everyday social interaction.

Psychoanalytic Approaches in Anthropology

SIGMUND FREUD

A number of psychological anthropologists have been influenced by the concepts and ideas of Sigmund Freud, the founder of psychoanalysis and psychiatry. Freud (1856–1939), a Viennese physician trained in the natural sciences, viewed human behavior as a reflection of innate emotional factors. His theory of human behavior emphasizes the importance of emotions in the development of an individual's personality. He tried to demonstrate that a great deal of emotional life is unconscious; that is, people are often unaware of the real reasons for their feelings and actions. Freud postulated that the personality is made up of three sectors: the *id, ego,* and *superego.*

Freud believed that all humans are born with unconscious, innate drives for sex and aggression. These unconscious desires are part of the *id.* Ac-

cording to Freud, these drives promote the seeking of immediate pleasure and the avoidance of pain. The id represents the basic needs of humans, needs that exist in the unconscious.

Freud maintained that the id is rooted in the biological organism and is present at birth: The newborn is basically a bundle of needs. He thought that the sexual and aggressive drives are often frustrated by society. This frustration often results in what Freud termed repression, wherein the energy based on these sexual and aggressive drives of the id is redirected into socially approved forms of expression. Eventually, the second part of the personality, the ego, becomes differentiated from the id. The *ego* represents the conscious attempt to balance the innate pleasure-seeking drives of the human organism with the demands and realities of the society. The ego is the "conscious" part of the personality and is sometimes referred to as the "reality part" of the personality.

Finally, the human personality develops the *superego,* which is the presence of culture within the individual. The superego is based on the internalized values and norms of society, which create the individual's conscience. The superego develops first in response to parental demands, but gradually the child learns that he or she has to respond to the society and culture at large. For example, Freud hypothesized that all male children are driven by an unconscious desire to have an affectionate and sexual relationship with their mother. This unconscious desire leads to hostility toward their natural father, the authority figure within the family. Freud called this the Oedipus complex. This desire is frustrated by the morality and norms of society, the superego, and the enculturation process. These emotional feelings become repressed, and the mature ego of the individual emerges to intervene between these desires and the dictates of society.

Freud's hypotheses were highly controversial in his own lifetime and remain so today. Although his theories are based on limited examples from his European medical and psychoanalytic practice, he extended his conclusions to include all of humanity. Freud's conceptions regarding enculturation have been modified by some modern anthropologists who study the role of childhood experiences in the formation of personality. However, his theories of emotional development and the role of the

CRITICAL PERSPECTIVES

The Anthropology of the "Self"

One topic that is currently inspiring a great deal of cross-cultural research is the issue of the individual, or the concept of the "person" within society. More specifically, many anthropologists are addressing the question, Do people in different societies view themselves as "individuals," "selves," or "persons" who are separate from their social group? If not, can we assume that people in these societies are "self-motivated" or "self-interested" in pursuing various goals? We usually make this assumption to explain our own behaviors and those of other people in our own society. Can we use this assumption to explain the behavior of people in other societies?

In the West, we tend to regard people as individuals who feel free to pursue their self-interests, to marry or not to marry, and to do what they want with their private property. Individualism is stressed through cultural beliefs and ideologies that serve as a basis for our economic, social, political, legal, and religious institutions. But is this sense of individualism a "natural" condition, or is it a byproduct of our distinctive social and historical development? One way of answering this question is through cross-cultural research. If we find that other people do not think in these terms, then we can assume that our thoughts about the self, mind, and individual are conditioned by our historical and cultural circumstances.

One early theorist who influenced modern anthropological research on these questions was Marcel Mauss, a French sociologist who argued that the concept of the "self" or "person" as separate from the "role" and "status" within society arose in relationship to modern capitalist society (1985 [1938]). Relying on the ethnographic research of anthropologists such as Franz Boas, he theorized that the concept of the individual person had developed uniquely in the West through the evolution of Roman law, Christian ideas of morality, and modern philosophical thought.

For example, according to Mauss, during the medieval period in Europe it would have been unheard of to think of an individual as completely separate from the larger social group. Medieval Christianity portrayed the individual as merely an element in God's creation, which was referred to as the "great chain of being." All elements in the universe were

---

unconscious in personality represent significant contributions to anthropological research on enculturation.

MODERN PSYCHOANALYTIC ANTHROPOLOGY

One of the most prominent contemporary anthropologists who uses a neo-Freudian approach in understanding human behavior is Melford Spiro. During his career, Spiro, a prodigious fieldworker, has done ethnographic research on the Ojibwa Indians, the Ifaluk people of Micronesia, the Israelis, and Burmese Buddhists. In all of his fieldwork he states that his principal objective has been to illu-minate "the universal through an examination of the particular" (Spiro, 1971).

Spiro maintains that human behavior cannot be adequately explained solely by environmental circumstances. He adopts some of Freud's concepts to explain universal phenomena such as aggression, sexuality, competition, and cooperation within society. In some of his early studies of the Ifaluk, he underscored the relationship among basic needs, cultural beliefs, and societal demands. For example, Spiro analyzed the Ifaluk belief in malevolent ghosts as a means of reducing interpersonal aggression and stimulating cooperation. Thus, according to Spiro (1952), the belief in harmful ghosts, an aspect of the superego that influences personality development, inhibits the expression of innate aggressive desires of the id.

arranged in a hierarchy from God to angels, humans, animals, trees, rocks, and other inorganic materials. All of these elements had a distinct value, depending on their distance from God. To modern Westerners, these views appear strange and outmoded. However, according to some anthropologists, our view of ourselves as independent from groups and environments may be just as strange.

Influenced by Mauss, French anthropologist Louis Dumont (1970) argued that modern Western notions of individualism differ from those of other societies such as India. In his book *Homo Hierarchicus*, he contrasted Western individualism with Indian Hindu conceptions that value social hierarchy. He pointed out that Hindu philosophy treats individuals as members of caste groups, which are linked to one another in a social hierarchy. Thus, from the Hindu vantage point, individuals cannot be thought of as separate from their social environment.

Francis Hsu, a Chinese American anthropologist, maintained that the Chinese concept of self is radically different from that of the West (1981). Hsu argued that whereas individualism permeates all U.S. values and institutions, in China the individual is inclined to be socially and psychologically dependent on others. He contrasted the individual-centeredness of American society with the situation-centeredness of Chinese society. He concluded that the individual in China is strongly encouraged to conform to familistic and group norms.

Hsu argued that the situation-centeredness of Chinese society is partly responsible for its lack of economic and political development. In contrast, he believed that the individualism of American society has encouraged capitalist enterprise and democratic institutions. However, he also believed that the American concern for self and individualism has led to rampant materialism and consumerism and a lack of concern for the overall good of society.

Points to Ponder

1. To what extent are your views of yourself as a distinct individual influenced by prevailing social norms?

2. Do you think that people throughout the world hold similar views? Why or why not?

3. Do you agree with Hsu's analysis of the benefits and shortcomings of widespread individualism?

4. What would be the advantages and disadvantages of a system that emphasizes the overall society rather than the individual?

Spiro's most recent work (1982) is a restudy of a classic ethnographic study by Bronislaw Malinowski of the Trobriand Islands. Malinowski did his study in the 1920s, a time in which Freud's ideas were becoming popular. Malinowski discovered that in Trobriand society, the natural, or biological, father plays a minor role in the family. The mother's brother is the principal authority within the Trobriand family. Malinowski reported that tension exists between the male children and their maternal uncle, rather than between natural father and son. From this data, Malinowski claimed that the Trobrianders do not have the Oedipus complex. In other words, he challenged Freud's claims about the universal occurrence of this phenomenon.

Relying on Malinowski's data on Trobriand society, Spiro concluded that Malinowski ignored much evidence bearing on the relationships within the Trobriand family. One problem was that Malinowski focused on adolescent males, whereas Freud maintained that the Oedipus complex develops during the infantile stage of development. Furthermore, as Spiro indicated, Malinowski overlooked the continuing sexual relationship between the biological father and mother. Spiro suggested that this does create sexual jealousy and tension between a son and his natural father. From his neo-Freudian psychoanalytic perspective, Spiro hypothesized that Trobriand male children develop an Oedipus complex just as do all male children throughout the world.

Spiro's psychoanalytic view does not represent the only view of enculturation in anthropology. Yet his use of psychoanalytic models in combination with ethnographic field methods to offer comprehensive hypotheses on the relationship among society, culture, and personality formation has been significant. Anthropologists inspired by the Freudian approach attempt to study the relationship among the unconscious thoughts, emotions, and motives of humans. In some cases they collaborate with psychiatrists to study dreams, symbols, fantasy life, interrelations among family members, and sexual relations (Paul, 1989; Herdt & Stoller, 1990).

Understanding Incest Avoidance and the Incest Taboo

One of the topics addressed by psychological anthropologists is incest. During their studies of interrelationships among family members and sexual relations in various societies, psychological anthropologists have noted the widespread avoidance of incestuous behavior. They have developed various hypotheses to understand what are referred to as incest avoidance and the incest taboo. Freud offered a mythical explanation for the origins of the incest taboo in his book *Totem and Taboo* (1913). In this book Freud proposed that the incest taboo is a result of the Oedipus complex and the rivalry between fathers and sons. According to Freud, in the earliest family the sons rebelled against their fathers, resulting in what he referred to as "Primal Patricide." Having killed their fathers, the sons felt a sense of guilt, so they developed the incest taboo prohibiting sexual relations within the family.

Although anthropologists no longer take Freud's myth of the Primal Horde seriously, a recent book by Robert Paul, *Moses and Civilization: The Meaning Behind Freud's Myth* (1996) indicates that Freud was struggling to understand the relationships between fathers and sons, and men and women, and the family in modern Western civilization. There is no question that Freud's notions have had an enormous influence on thinking about the problems of incest avoidance and the incest taboo. Anthropologists have been studying these issues regarding incest and the family for a long period of time, and have developed a number of different hypotheses to explain the worldwide prevalence of the incest taboo.

Incest involves sexual relations or marriage between certain relatives. Incest avoidance refers to the shunning of sexual relations and marriage between certain relatives. **Incest avoidance** is a universal phenomenon (Brown, 1991). The **incest taboo** is based on strong cultural norms that prohibit sexual relations or marriage between certain relatives. Although incest avoidance is found universally, incest taboos are not. Anthropologists find that some societies view incest with disgust and revulsion; these societies have strong prohibitions or taboos against incest. Yet in other societies, people view incest as such an incredulous and even laughable behavior that no taboo is called for (Van den Berghe, 1979).

Marriage and sex between parent and child or brother and sister are forbidden in almost all societies, although certain exceptions do exist. Ancient Egyptians, Hawaiians, and Incas institutionalized incestuous brother-sister marriages within their ruling classes. This phenomenon is known as *royal incest*. The purpose of these practices was to maintain the ruling families' economic wealth and political power. For most people in most societies, however, marriages within the immediate family are forbidden.

BIOLOGICAL EXPLANATIONS OF INCEST AVOIDANCE

One ancient and widely held view of incest avoidance is that inbreeding within the immediate family causes genetic defects. This view is connected with the observation that abnormal or defective negative traits that are carried within the family would be accentuated by inbreeding.

The problem here is that inbreeding itself does not cause harmful genes to exist; it only perpetuates these genes within the immediate family. Little evidence exists suggesting that in Hawaiian, Egyptian, or Incan cultures, incestuous marriages resulted in any harmful, long-term genetic consequences. Populations apparently can be highly inbred for many generations and survive quite well. Thus, anthropologists must seek alternative explanations of the universality of incest avoidance.

MARITAL ALLIANCE AND THE INCEST TABOO

Rather than focus on biological tendencies, some anthropologists have concentrated on the social consequences of inbreeding. In an early explanation, E. B. Tylor (1889) hypothesized that incest taboos originated as a means to create alliances among different small-scale societies. Marriages outside of one's group create kinship alliances that encourage cooperation and improve chances for survival. Tylor coined the phrase "Marry out or be killed out" to summarize his argument that if people did not create these social alliances, dire consequences would follow, including warfare among the different groups. More recently, anthropologists Leslie White and Claude Levi-Strauss have presented variations of this functionalist hypothesis (White, 1959; Levi-Strauss, 1969). The problem with these hypotheses is that they explain the origins of marrying outside of one's group rather than incest taboos (Van den Berghe, 1980).

Another type of explanation was proposed by Malinowski, who viewed the incest taboo as a mechanism that functions to sustain the family as an institution (1927). Malinowski argued that brother-sister, father-daughter, or mother-son marriages or sexual relations would generate status-role conflict and rivalry within the family, leading to dysfunctions and possible dissolution. The incest taboo thus serves to reduce family friction and conflict and to maintain harmony within the family. Obviously, this view is closest to the traditional Freudian perspective on the incest taboo.

CHILDHOOD FAMILIARITY HYPOTHESIS

Another explanation of the origin and perpetuation of incest avoidance is known as the childhood familiarity hypothesis, which proposes that siblings raised together in the family do not become erotically involved or sexually attracted to one another because of a biological tendency. Children living in close association with one another, however, would develop mutual sexual aversion and avoid incest.

These Israeli children are eating lunch on a kibbutz. Anthropologists find that children who are raised together on a kibbutz usually do not marry one another.

A number of psychological anthropological studies appear to support this hypothesis. Arthur Wolf studied a marriage pattern in Taiwan called "minor marriage" (known locally as *sim-pua marriage*), in which a very young girl was adopted into the family of her future husband. The boy and the future bride were then raised in a sibling type of relationship. The purpose of this system was to allow the girl to adjust to her new family through a long association with her husband's kin. Wolf (1970) interviewed many people who were involved in these arranged relationships and found that most of them were dissatisfied both sexually and romantically with their spouses. Both males and females were inclined to have extramarital relations, and divorce rates were higher than normal. These conclusions appear to support the childhood familiarity hypothesis.

Another study, conducted in Israel, also presented evidence to support this hypothesis. When European Jews first settled in what was then known as Palestine, in the early twentieth century, they established collectives known as *kibbutzim.* Within these *kibbutzim,* children were separated from the family into peer groups of six to eight to be raised and socialized together. Children in these peer-group settings had sibling-like relationships with one another.

To examine the childhood familiarity hypothesis, Israeli anthropologist Yonina Talmon (1964) studied the second generation of three *kibbutzim*. She discovered that there were no married couples who had known each other from peer groups in the *kibbutzim*. Although as small children these individuals may have shown a sexual interest in members of the opposite sex within their peer groups, this interest diminished after maturity. A later comprehensive study of 211 *kibbutzim* by anthropologist Joseph Shepher (1983) found that of 2,769 married couples, only 14 marriages were from the ranks of the peer groups. Moreover, every one of these 14 marriages had been dissolved through separation or divorce.

INCEST AVOIDANCE: INTERACTIONIST PERSPECTIVES

Today, most anthropologists agree that incest avoidance likely occurs for a variety of reasons. From an evolutionary perspective, the rule of marrying outside one's family would help to create alliances. It would also induce greater genetic diversity, thereby enhancing the adaptation and survival of different populations. In an extensive cross-cultural analysis of mating systems, Melvin Ember (1975) hypothesized that populations expanding as a result of agricultural developments began to notice the spread of (not the creation of) harmful genes as a result of inbreeding and therefore created incest prohibitions. And, additionally, as Malinowski had suggested, incest avoidance would support family roles and functions.

The fact that incest does occur, coupled with the existence of institutionalized incestuous marriage practices in the royal families of some societies, indicates that incest avoidance cannot be reduced to a biological instinct. Humans are not biologically programmed to avoid incest in any mechanistic fashion. The most comprehensive explanation of incest has to take into account generalized biological tendencies along with sociocultural factors.

In a new refinement of the childhood familiarity hypothesis, Paul Roscoe (1994) offers an interactionist explanation of incest avoidance. He suggests that relatives who are raised in close association with one another develop strong emotional bonds, or "kinship amity," culturally based values

that lead to a sense of mutual support and intense feelings of affection. In contrast, sexual arousal and sexual relations are connected to some degree with aggressive impulses, which have a physiological and neurological basis. Thus, sexual-aggressive impulses are depressed between close kin, who have developed kinship amity. In addition, according to Roscoe's hypothesis, kinship amity can be extended to distant kin through enculturation, resulting in an incest taboo that prohibits sex between more distant relatives. Interactionist explanations such as Roscoe's, combining both biological and cultural factors, are producing insightful hypotheses regarding incest avoidance.

Enculturation and the Sex Drive

Human sexuality is a subject that connects the biological and cultural aspects of the individual and society. The sex drive, sexual maturation, and sexual activity have different meanings for individuals depending on societal and cultural context. What are considered "normal" or "abnormal" or "deviant" patterns of sexuality differ from one society to another.

Anthropologists have studied enculturation and its consequences for sexual practices in varying societies. Like our biological drive of hunger, sex is a natural biological drive or urge for humans universally. However, this drive is channeled into certain directions through the process of enculturation.

CODES OF SEXUAL BEHAVIOR

Societies differ with respect to how permissive or restrictive their codes or norms regarding sexuality are. Some societies approve of premarital and extramarital sexual relations, whereas others strictly segregate males from females to prohibit such relations. In some societies sexual activity begins very early for both males and females to prepare for marriage. For example, with the Lepcha of Sikkim (a small kingdom north of India in the Himalayan mountains), girls have their first sexual experience before puberty. In Lepcha society, sexual activity is considered as much a necessity as food or drink—and like food or drink, it for the most part does not matter from whom one receives it, though one is naturally grateful to those who provide it (Lindholm and Lindholm, 1980). The Lepcha have a great deal of sexual freedom and appear to have very little sexual jealousy.

The antithesis of this permissive pattern of sexuality is found in some Arab societies of the Middle East. In Saudi Arabia girls and women are strictly segregated from boys and men. Young girls begin wearing a cloak and veil at the age of puberty. Saudi Arabian society prohibits the mixing of males and females and to this end provides separate institutions for education, work, and other public facilities. In Saudi society a family's honor is judged by its control over the sexuality of its daughters. Brides are expected to be virgins, and to guarantee this, families prevent daughters from interacting with boys. Sexual segregation and the dress code are strongly enforced by religious police in Saudi society.

Other highly restrictive attitudes and patterns of sexuality are found in societies such as the Inis Beag Islanders of Ireland, studied by anthropologist John Messenger (1971). Sex is never discussed openly at home or near children. Parents give no sexual instruction to children. Messenger reported that the Inis Beag people lack basic knowledge regarding sexual matters. For example, there seems to be a general ignorance of the ability of females to have orgasms, any expression of male or female sexuality is considered deviant, and it is believed that sexual activity weakens men. Females and males are separated from an early age. Dancing is permitted, but there is no touching or contact between males and females. Dirty jokes and nudity are strongly frowned upon. Messenger reports that there is little evidence of any premarital sex, or any sexual foreplay between married people. Generally people marry very late in age, and there is a high percentage of celibate males in the population.

HOMOSEXUAL BEHAVIOR

In exploring sexuality in other societies psychological anthropologists have examined homosexuality by using a comparative, cross-cultural approach. Homosexuality in ancient societies such as that of the Greeks and Romans was a well-accepted pattern of behavior. Many societies have had institutionalized cultural roles for people who are not classified as either male or female. In the country of Oman, anthropologist Unni Wikan (1991) describes individuals known as *xaniths,* who are transsexuals and represent a third gender. In some islands of Southeast Asia such as Bali and Java, third-gender individuals are not only accepted but have important roles to play in the society (Brown, 1976). In some Native American societies, particular males wore female clothing and devoted themselves to offering sexual services to male warriors. These individuals were referred to as *berdaches* and were regarded as different from both males and females. These homosexuals also provided resources and took care of other subsistence activities for their neighbors and relatives in the society (Callender & Kochems, 1983).

Anthropologist Serena Nanda (1990) has done an extensive ethnographic study of the *hijras* of India, who are viewed as neither man nor woman. They are born as males but undergo an operation in which their genitals are surgically removed. This operation transforms them, not into females (because they cannot give birth), but into *hijras,* a third gender. The *hijras* are followers of a particular Hindu deity and earn their living by performing at various types of religious ceremonies. They dress like females and to some extent exaggerate feminine behavior, but they also indulge in certain male-only behaviors such as smoking a hookah (water pipe) and cigarettes. Within the cultural context of Indian society, the *hijras* are considered neither deviant nor unnatural, but rather simply an additional form of gender.

Anthropologists have described a variety of male homosexual practices among the highland societies of Papua New Guinea. Among peoples such as the Etoro and the Sambia, male homosexuality is incorporated into initiation rituals. In these societies there appear to be no distinctions among heterosexual, homosexual, or bisexual individuals. Gilbert Herdt (1987) describes how prepubescent Sambian males are initiated into male secret societies and engage in strictly homosexual activities with the older males of these societies. They are obligated to perform regular oral intercourse on the older males and believe that obtaining the gift of semen from their seniors will enable them to become strong, vigorous warriors. These boys are forbidden to engage in any heterosexual relationships for about ten years. Following this lengthy period, they marry and from that time onward take up heterosexual relationships with their wives.

United States society has gone through different cycles of restrictiveness and permissiveness regarding cultural norms influencing sexual practices (D'Emilio, 1988). In the early history of the United States, Puritan norms equated sexuality with sinful behavior. Later, in the nineteenth century, American society reinforced restrictive Puritan attitudes. But in the 1920s a more liberal, permissive era of sexual attitudes developed. The 1950s proved to be once again a more restrictive period, but this was followed by the sexual revolution of the 1960s. U.S. society is extremely complex, and many different norms and attitudes are represented in respect to sexuality. The restrictive legacy of Puritanism still exists within some groups, as evidenced by the various legal statutes that have emerged in some states regarding homosexual practices. The attempt to regulate sexual behavior by government is a U.S. practice that has been abandoned by most other Western governments.

Enculturation and Cognition

Psychological anthropologists have been exploring thinking processes, or cognition, among different peoples in various societies. One assumption held widely by nineteenth-century and early twentieth-century social scientists was that people in small-scale or so-called primitive societies have different forms of cognition from people in civilized societies. This assumption was challenged by a number of anthropologists, who focused on cognitive development from a cross-cultural perspective.

STRUCTURALISM

Following World War II, French anthropologist Claude Levi-Strauss founded a field of study known as structuralism. The primary goal of structuralism is to investigate the thought processes of the human mind in a universal context; consequently, it is a field that overlaps with psychological anthropology. Structuralists are interested in the unconscious and conscious patterns of human thinking. In one of his first major books, *The Savage Mind* (1966), Levi-Strauss discussed how peoples living in small-scale societies use the same unconscious thinking and reasoning processes that peoples in large-scale, complex societies do. He proposed that there is a universal logical form in human thought and cognition around the world.

Drawing on the field of linguistics, Levi-Strauss argued that thinking is based on "binary oppositions." In other words, humans classify the natural and social world into polar types (binary oppositions) as a stage of reasoning. For example, foods are classified as raw versus cooked, or hot versus cold. From these binary contrasts, coherent patterns of thought are developed. Levi-Strauss focused on such diverse phenomena as kinship, mythology, cuisine, and table manners to discover the hidden structural logic underlying these diverse cultural ideas and practices. Even though the rules and norms that structure these ideas and practices may appear arbitrary, Levi-Strauss believed that a "deep universal structure" underlies these cultural phenomena. Thus, this universal structure of the mind produces similar thinking and cognition throughout the world.

JEAN PIAGET

Jean Piaget (1896–1980), a Swiss psychologist, spent more than a half-century studying the ways in which children think, perceive, and learn. His research has influenced the anthropological perspective on cognition and enculturation. Piaget focused not only on what children learn but also on how they understand the world. He identified four major stages of cognitive development: sensorimotor, preoperational, concrete-operational, and formal-operational. Piaget hypothesized that these stages reflect biological maturation as well as enculturation. As each child progresses through these stages, he or she acquires more information and begins to organize and perceive reality in new and different ways.

Piaget's Four Stages of Human Development
The first stage of human development in Piaget's scheme is the *sensorimotor stage,* in which a child experiences the world only through the senses in terms of physical contact. In this stage, which corresponds to approximately the first two years of life, the infant explores the world through touching, sucking, listening, and other direct contact. According to Piaget, at this first stage children may imitate the sounds of others, but they do not have the capacity to use symbols.

Psychological anthropologists are studying the cognitive development of children everywhere in the world.

The second stage, the *preoperational stage,* refers to the level of cognitive development in which symbols—including language—are first used. During this stage, roughly ages 2 to 7, children begin to experience the world abstractly. This symbolic learning enables children to conceive of something without having direct contact with it. Children gain the ability to distinguish among their ideas of the world, dreams, fantasies, and objective reality. Yet at this second stage, children do not use symbols as adults do. They learn to attach meanings and names to objects in their specific environment, but they do not conceptualize the world in general terms.

In the third stage, the *concrete-operational stage,* children between ages 7 and 11 begin to use logic, connecting events in terms of cause and effect, and they learn to manipulate symbols in a more sophisticated manner. At this stage children are also able to put themselves in the position of another person and perceive a situation from another's point of view. This allows them to engage in complex activities such as games that involve a number of participants (such as most team sports).

The fourth stage, known as the *formal-operational stage,* is the level of cognitive development characterized by highly abstract concepts and formal reasoning processes. At about age 12, children develop the capacity to think of themselves and the world in highly abstract terms rather than only in terms of concrete situations. They can envision alternatives to reality by proposing differing hypotheses for evaluation. In this final stage of cognitive development, which continues throughout adult life, children begin to use reasoning processes and abstract symbols to interpret and understand the world.

Piaget suggested that certain innate categories regulate and order our experience of the world. Although he was certainly aware that the learning of values, norms, and beliefs is not the same from society to society, he believed that humans everywhere progress in the same sequence through the various stages described above. He also recognized that the precise age at which each stage of cognitive development is reached varies from individual to individual, depending on innate mental capacities and the nature of the enculturation experience.

Applying Piaget's Four Stages   A number of anthropologists have been influenced by Piaget's model of enculturation and cognitive development. British anthropologist Maurice Bloch (1977, 1985) has suggested that many cultural universals are the result of biopsychological factors shared by all humans that interact with the practical conditions of the world. For example, Bloch postulated that all humans have innate capabilities to perceive time and space in the same way. Time and space are fundamental concepts that enable humans to adapt to the practical conditions of the world. These practical conditions include changes in seasons, climatic and environmental characteristics, and the overall effects of natural aging processes. In Bloch's view, people can learn to conceptualize time and space in radically different ways, depending on religious beliefs and worldviews. For example, in the Hindu tradition, people perceive time cyclically in relationship to the creation and destruction of the universe that takes place over millions of years. In the Judeo-Christian tradition, people perceive time in a more linear fashion from the time of creation to the present. However, in both the Hindu and Judeo-Christian cultures, in everyday, practical circumstances, people perceive time both cyclically and linearly in relationship to the cycle of seasonal changes or the life cycle of an individual through biological aging.

Other anthropologists have been testing Piaget's theories throughout the world to determine whether his stages are indeed universal. For example, researchers studying African infants have discovered that the sensorimotor stage is identical in both African and European babies (Dasen, 1977). One noted psychological anthropologist, Michael Cole, has surveyed the field of cross-cultural Piagetian-based studies and concluded that the basic thinking processes are similar among all humans everywhere. All people use similar patterns of logic and develop an understanding of cause and effect relationships. People everywhere develop classification systems through similar processes of abstraction and generalization. The differences among cultural groups lie in the content of the values, beliefs, and norms of society (Cole & Scribner, 1974).

Evolutionary Psychology

A recent development that attempts to emphasize the interaction of nature (biology) and nurture (learning and culture) in understanding and explaining enculturation, human cognition, and human behavior is the field known as *evolutionary psychology*. This field includes anthropologists such as John Tooby, Daniel Sperber, Donald Symons, Mark Flinn, and a number of psychologists, including Leda Cosmides and Paul Rozin. **Evolutionary psychology** is a field that draws on ethnographic research, psychological experiments, and evolutionary theory to demonstrate how the human brain developed and how it influences thinking processes and behavior. They begin with the understanding of the effects of evolution during the long period of the Paleolithic that caused the emergence of a specific form of human brain. Evolutionary psychologists suggest that the mind and culture coevolved. They believe that natural selective forces must have shaped the mind and behavior. Consequently, since natural selective forces are

highly specific, they hypothesize that the human brain is divided into specialized modules, or independent units, which contain various functions that enabled our ancestral humans to adapt to Paleolithic conditions. These specific modules within the brain predispose humans to perceive, think, and behave in certain ways to allow for adaptation. In other words, there are genetically induced "evolved predispositions" that have consequences for human perception, thinking, emotions, and behavior today. For example, in the next chapter we review the research indicating that the human brain has a language learning module enabling children to learn their language without learning the specific complex rules of grammar for communication.

Aside from the language learning module, evolutionary psychologists, in a book entitled *The Adapted Mind* (1992), edited by John Tooby and B. Cosmides, have hypothesized that modules in the brain enable humans to understand intuitively the workings of nature, including motion, force, and how plants and animals function. The authors refer to psychological research that demonstrates how infants distinguish objects that move around like balls from living organisms, such as people and animals, that are self-propelled.

In addition, as is discussed in the next chapter, many anthropologists have documented that people tend to use similar characteristics to classify plants and animals, despite living in very different environments. These anthropologists theorize that innate, specialized modules in the human brain help develop an intuitive understanding of biology and physics. Just as children learn their language without learning the formal grammatical rules, humans can perceive, organize, and understand basic biological and physical principles without learning formal scientific views.

Evolutionary psychologists further contend that the mind uses different rules to process different types of information. For example, they suggest there are innate modules that help interpret and predict other people's behavior and modules enabling humans to understand basic emotions such as happiness, sadness, anger, jealousy, and love. In addition, these specialized modules influence male-female relationships, mate choice, and cooperation or competition among individuals.

In *The Adapted Mind,* anthropologist Jerome Barkow asks why people like to watch soap operas and answers that the human mind is designed by evolution to be interested in the social lives of others—rivals, mates, relatives, offspring, and acquaintances. To be successful in life requires a knowledge of many different phenomena and social situations, evolutionary psychologists argue, and innate predispositions influence how we sense, interpret, think, perceive, communicate, and imagine to adapt and survive in the world.

Evolutionary psychologists tend to emphasize the commonalities and similarities in culture and behavior found among people in different parts of the world. Thus, they are interested in the types of human universals described by anthropologist Donald Brown (see Chapter 3). Although evolutionary psychologists do not ignore learning or culture, they hypothesize that innate modules or mechanisms in the brain make learning and enculturation happen.

Many evolutionary psychologists believe that some of the evolved predispositions that are inherited may not be as adaptive today as they were during the time of the Paleolithic. For example, humans during that period had to worry more about danger from wild animals and about getting enough salt and sugar to eat for survival, but such evolved predispositions may not help humans adapt to modern society.

Evolutionary psychology has been criticized by some anthropologists for not emphasizing the richness and complexity of culture. However, the field is in its infancy and will most likely grow to offer another interactionist perspective on human thought and behavior.

Enculturation and Emotions

One significant question asked by psychological anthropologists is to what degree enculturation influences emotions. Obviously, different language groups have different terms for emotions, but do the feelings of anger, happiness, grief, and jealousy vary from society to society? Do some societies have unique emotions? Or are all human emotions the same throughout the world?

Psychological anthropologists have been conducting research on the topic of emotions since the early research of Benedict and Mead. As discussed earlier in the chapter, Benedict and Mead argued that each culture is unique and that people in these societies have different personalities and, consequently, different types of emotions. These different emotions are a result of the unique kind of enculturation that has shaped the individual's personality. In their view, the enculturation process is predominant in creating varying emotions among different societies. In other words, culture determines not only how people think and behave but also how they feel emotionally.

In contrast, other early psychological anthropologists focused on universal biological processes that produce similar emotional developments and feelings in people throughout the world. According to this perspective, emotions are seen as instinctive behaviors that stimulate physiological processes involving hormones and other chemicals in the brain. In other words, if an individual feels "anger," this automatically raises his or her blood pressure and stimulates specific muscle movements. In this view, emotional developments are part of the biology of humans universally, and thus emotions are experienced the same everywhere.

More recently, anthropologists have emphasized an interactionist approach, taking both biology and culture into account in their studies of emotions. A study conducted by Karl Heider (1991) focused on three different ethnic groups in the country of Indonesia. The three groups are the Minangkabau in West Sumatra, the Minangkabau Indonesians, and the Javanese. Heider systematically described the vocabulary of emotions that each of these groups use to classify their feelings of sadness, anger, happiness, fear, surprise, love, contempt, shame, and disgust, along with other feelings. Through intensive interviews and observations, Heider proceeded to determine whether the vocabulary of emotions is directly related to specific emotional behaviors.

Following his ethnographic study, Heider concluded that four of the emotions—sadness, anger, happiness, and surprise—tend to be what he classifies as basic, cross-cultural emotions. In other words, these emotions appear to be universally understood and stable across cultures. Other emotions, however, such as love, fear, and disgust, appear to vary among these societies. For example, love among the Minangkabau and Minangkabau Indonesians is mixed with the feeling of pity and is close to sadness. Fear is also mixed with guilt, and feelings of disgust are difficult to translate across cultural boundaries. Heider emphasizes that his study is preliminary and needs much more analysis and reanalysis; nevertheless, it is an interesting use of the interactionist approach to the study of emotions.

In *Thinking through Cultures: Expeditions in Cultural Psychology* (1991), psychological anthropologist Richard Shweder emphasizes that ethnographic research on emotions has demonstrated the existence of both universals and culturally specific aspects of emotional functioning among people in different societies. He uses a piano keyboard as an example to discuss emotional development in children. Children have something like an emotional keyboard, with each key being a separate emotion: disgust, interest, distress, anger, fear, contempt, shame, shyness, guilt, and so forth. A key is struck whenever a situation such as loss, frustration, or novelty develops. All children recognize and can discriminate among basic emotions by a young age. However, as adults, the tunes that get played on the keyboard vary with experience. Some keys do not get struck at all, whereas others are played extensively.

Shweder concludes, "It is ludicrous to imagine that the emotional functioning of people in different cultures is basically the same. It is just as ludicrous to imagine that each culture's emotional life is unique" (1991: 252). Anthropologists recognize that an interactionist approach that takes into account human universals and cultural variation is necessary to comprehend the enculturation process and emotional development.

Culture and Mental Illness

Another area of interest for psychological anthropology is the study of mental illness in different societies. The major concerns of these studies revolve around two questions: Is there a universal concept of "normal" and "abnormal" behavior? and Do mental illnesses differ in their symptoms or patterns in different societies? These questions serve as the basis for many ethnographic projects in different societies.

WHAT IS ABNORMAL?

In the early twentieth century, one of the assumptions within the fields of psychiatry and psychology was that mental illness and abnormal behavior are universal. In other words, depression, schizophrenia, psychoses, and other mental disorders are essentially the same for all humans. For example, in the field of psychiatry, particular types of mental disorders were classified by specific symptoms. Thus, a psychosis was classified as a type of mental disturbance characterized by personality disorganization, disturbed emotional responses, and a loss of contact with reality. A neurosis was characterized as a nonpsychotic disorder marked by considerable anxiety for individuals, especially when they are involved in social interaction.

These classifications of mental illness were challenged by psychological anthropologists such as Benedict in the 1930s. Benedict argued that all criteria of abnormality reflect the particular culture of the individual and must be understood within the context of that culture. In her classic book *Patterns of Culture* (1934), Benedict remarked:

> It does not matter what kind of "abnormality" we choose for illustration, those which indicate extreme instability, or those which are more in the nature of character traits like sadism or delusions of grandeur or of persecution, there are well described cultures in which these abnormals function with ease and with honor and apparently without danger of difficulty to the society. ([1934] 1959: 263)

In other words, Benedict questioned whether any type of absolute standards of "normalcy" as defined by Western preoccupations and categories were satisfactory criteria for mental health. Benedict described a situation in which an individual heard very loud voices, was plagued by dreams of falling off cliffs, and feared being devoured by swarms of yellow jackets. This individual went into a trance state, lay rigid on the ground, and shortly thereafter recovered and danced for three nights in a row. Although in Western society this individual would be treated as "abnormal," Benedict suggested that this behavior and thought was not unusual in some societies. The individual described was a form of medicine man or woman and was not only accorded respect but enjoyed tremendous prestige within the particular Native American tribe to which he or she belonged.

Ethnographic descriptions such as these demonstrate the difficulties of classifying mental illness across cultural boundaries. When the concept of abnormality is applied cross-culturally it becomes an extremely vague concept. Behavior that is considered deviant in one society may represent a culturally acceptable form of behavior in another. The fields of modern psychiatry and psychology have been attempting to revise their classification of mental illnesses and often work with anthropologists on joint research projects to refine understandings of psychological disorders.

CULTURE-SPECIFIC DISORDERS

A number of ethnographic studies have focused on mental disorders that are unique to certain cultural settings. These culture-specific disorders include *latah, amok, windigo,* and *pibloktoq. Latah* has been described as a mental disorder in areas of Southeast and East Asia. In Southeast Asia *latah* appears as a type of hysteria or fear reaction that afflicts women who become easily startled, resulting in compulsively imitating behaviors or shouting repetitive phrases that they have heard (*echolalia*). Sometimes this disorder is triggered by the word *snake* or by tickling. In the East Asian area of Mongolia, however, David Aberle (1961) described a form of *latah* that affects men. These men may be startled suddenly and put their hands into a fire, jump into a river, or begin to scream obscenities wildly.

Amok is a culture-specific disorder that is described in Malaysia, Indonesia, and parts of the Philippines. It is a disorder of middle-aged males following a period of withdrawal marked by brooding over a perceived insult. During this period, in which the individual loses contact with reality, he may suffer from stress and sleep deprivation, and consume large quantities of alcohol. Then a wild outburst marked by rage occurs, with the individual attempting a violent series of murderous attacks. The man may pick up a weapon such as a machete and attack any person or animal in his path. These aggressive, homicidal attacks will be followed by prolonged exhaustion and amnesia (Bourguignon, 1979). *Amok* appears to be a culturally sanctioned form of violent behavior viewed as an appropriate response to a specific situation in these Southeast Asian regions. (The

Malay term *amok* has entered the English language, referring to wild, aggressive behavior, as in someone "running amok.")

Another culture-specific disorder, formerly found among the males of the Chippewa, Cree, and Montagnais-Naskapi Indians in Canada, is referred to as the *windigo psychosis*. It is described as a disorder in which the affected individual becomes deeply depressed and begins to believe that he has been possessed or bewitched by the spirit of a *windigo,* a cannibal giant with a heart or entrails of ice. The individual may have symptoms of nausea, anorexia, and insomnia and may see other humans being transformed into beavers or other animals. As these hallucinations occur, the individual begins to have an overwhelming desire to kill and eat these humans (Barnouw, 1985). This insatiable craving for human flesh has resulted in documented cases of homicide and cannibalism among some of these people (Marano, 1982; Barnouw, 1985).

The disorder *pibloktoq,* also referred to as Arctic hysteria, is found among Eskimo adults in Greenland and other Arctic regions. It may affect both men and women, but has been described more frequently among women. The subject is initially irritable or withdrawn, then becomes violently emotional. The victim may scream as if terrified, tear off her clothes, run out into the snow, jump into fire, throw things around, and begin to "speak in tongues." After this period of excitement, the woman sometimes has convulsive seizures and then may fall asleep. On awakening she may be perfectly calm and have no memory of the incident. *Pibloktoq* usually has a high frequency in the winter, and a number of persons living in a small community may be afflicted with it during the cold months (Wallace, 1972). Thus, it may be a more extreme form of what Americans sometimes call "cabin fever."

A number of explanations have been put forth to explain these culture-specific mental disorders. For example, the *windigo* disorder has been attributed to the experience of starvation and famine conditions that can occur in the wintertime. Anthony Wallace (1972) suggests that a lack of calcium in the diet of Eskimos may partially explain the occurrence of *pibloktoq*. In both of these areas the drastic annual variation in daylight may be partially responsible for these behavioral and emotional disturbances (Bourguignon, 1979).

Some critics believe that these culture-specific disorders may be just different expressions of certain illnesses such as paranoid schizophrenia or other types of psychoses. Persecution ideas, hysteria, panic disorders, and other bizarre behaviors occur in all societies to one degree or another. There is a substantial body of evidence from various sources that certain types of depression and schizophrenia are caused by biochemical disorders that are genetically inherited (McMahon & McMahon, 1983). International surveys by the World Health Organization have examined disorders such as schizophrenia around the world and have found some basic similarities in the symptom profiles (Marsella, 1979). Psychological anthropologists have found, however, that the cultural beliefs and worldviews, family communication patterns, early childhood training, and particular life stresses of certain societies influence the content of these mental disorders. The delusions, hallucinations, and other symptoms that occur with these disorders reflect wide-ranging cultural variations throughout the world. Psychological anthropologists are beginning to combine biological explanations with cultural variables to arrive at more comprehensive, interactionist explanations of mental illness and personality disorders.

The Limits of Enculturation

When we consider enculturation or socialization, we are confronted with this question: Are humans only robots who respond rigidly to the demands of their innate drives and the norms of their culture? If our behavior depends so much on the enculturation process, what becomes of human concepts such as freedom and free will? Do people in our society or other societies have any personal choice over their behavior, or is all behavior and thought shaped by innate drives and the norms of these societies?

UNIQUE BIOLOGICAL TENDENCIES

In actuality, although enculturation plays a major role in producing personality and behavioral strategies within society, there are a number of reasons why enculturation is not completely determinative.

First, people are born with different innate *tendencies* (not instincts) for responding to the environment in a variety of ways. Our individual behavior is partially a result of our biological constitution, which influences our hormones, metabolism, and other aspects of our physiology. All societies have people who differ with respect to temperament because of these innate tendencies. Enculturation cannot produce people who respond only to environmental or cultural pressures in a uniform manner.

INDIVIDUAL VARIATION

Second, enculturation is never a completely uniform process. The experiences of past enculturation are blended in unique ways by each individual. Even in the most isolated, small-scale societies, young people behave differently from their parents. Furthermore, not all people in a particular society are socialized or enculturated in exactly the same manner. The vast amounts of information transmitted through enculturation often lead to variations in what children are taught in different families and institutions.

In addition, norms do not dictate behavior in any rigid manner. People in any society are always confronted with contradictory norms, and society is always changing, affecting the process of enculturation. Enculturation rarely provides people with a precise blueprint for the behavioral responses needed in the many situations they face.

Thus, enculturation is an imprecise process. People may internalize the general program for behavior—a series of ideal norms, rules, and cultural guidelines for action—but how these general principles apply in any specific set of concrete circumstances is difficult or impossible to specify. In some cases, people obey social and cultural rules completely, whereas in others they violate or ignore them. Enculturation provides the historically developed cultural forms through which the members of society share meanings and symbols and relate to one another. But in reality, people maneuver within these cultural forms, choosing their actions to fulfill both their own needs and the demands of their society.

SUMMARY

Psychological anthropologists attempt to understand similarities and differences in behavior, thought, and feelings among societies by focusing on the relationship between the individual and culture, or the process of enculturation. One question that psychological anthropologists focus on is the degree to which human behavior is influenced by biological tendencies versus learning. Today, most anthropologists have adopted an interactionist approach that emphasizes both biology and culture as influences on enculturation and human behavior.

Another related question is whether humans, as part of the animal kingdom, have instincts—genetically programmed behaviors—that nonhuman animals have. Many nonhuman animals have closed instincts that rigidly structure their behavior patterns, allowing for survival and adaptation in specific environmental conditions. These closed instincts have been selected by environmental factors over millions of years of evolution.

It does not appear that humans have closed instincts. Instead, humans have the unique capacity for culture, which enables them to modify and shape their behavior to adapt to different environmental conditions. Without enculturation, humans are unable to think, behave, and develop emotionally in order to function in society.

The early studies of enculturation, called culture-and-personality studies, focused on culture as if it were an integrated type of personality. These early studies by pioneers such as Ruth Benedict and Margaret Mead provided some important data regarding enculturation processes, but they often exaggerated the significance of cultural determinants of human behavior. However, these efforts led to a more systematic examination of enculturation and childhood training. These studies have refined our understanding of childhood training in many different types of societies.

The theories of Sigmund Freud have had an influence on psychological anthropology. His model of enculturation and personality development has been used by a number of psychological anthropologists to investigate human behavior. In some cases, anthropologists collaborate with psychoanalysts to study dreams, sexual fantasies, family relations, and topics such as incest. Incest, incest avoidance, and the incest taboo have been studied thoroughly within anthropology, leading to insightful explanations for these phenomena.

Enculturation's relationship to sexual practices and norms has been a topic of research in psychological anthropology. A wide variation of sexual practices and norms in different parts of the world have been described. These practices and norms, including widely distributed patterns of homosexual behavior and acceptance of a third gender beyond male and female, indicate how enculturation influences the sex drive in human communities.

The relationship between enculturation and cognition has been a field of study within psychological anthropology. Structuralist anthropology, developed by Claude Levi-Strauss, focuses on the relationship between culture and thought processes. Levi-Strauss hypothesized that the human mind is structured to produce underlying patterns of thinking that are universally based.

Psychologist Jean Piaget's studies on the development of cognitive processes have also influenced psychological anthropology. Many researchers are actively engaged in testing Piaget's stage model of cognitive development in different societies. Evolutionary psychologists have hypothesized that humans have some genetically prepared predispositions that have a wide-ranging influence on enculturation, cognition, and human behavior. Their research, though controversial, has been a leading example of interactionist research in psychological anthropology.

Emotional development is another area of study in psychological anthropology. Researchers are trying to understand how emotions such as sadness, happiness, fear, anger, and contempt are similar and different from one society to another. Their findings indicate that there are both universal and specific cultural variations with respect to emotional development in different societies.

Psychological anthropologists have been exploring different forms of mental disorders in various societies. This type of research has led anthropology to challenge some of the typical classifications used in Western psychiatry and psychology to define mental disorders.

STUDY QUESTIONS

1. Discuss the differences between closed and open instincts. In your opinion, do humans have instincts?

2. What are some of the methods of enculturation used in your society? Give an example of how your own personality has been affected by enculturation.

3. Can anthropologists classify various cultures by identifying certain personality characteristics found among certain individuals, as did Ruth Benedict? Discuss the limitations of this approach.

4. Are emotional expressions universal? To what extent are human emotions such as anger or jealousy similar or different around the world?

5. Describe a pattern of human behavior that you believe to be "normal" for your society but that might be considered "abnormal" in another society.

 KEY TERMS

drives	incest avoidance	personality
evolutionary psychology	incest taboo	psychological anthropologists
incest	instincts	

 INTERNET EXERCISES

1. Explore **http://www.indiana.edu/~wanthro/ URBAN.htm.** Look at section 3.1 on early urban sociology. How do the concepts of Gemeinschaft and Gesellschaft relate to the concept of enculturation?

2. Play Lacan's Imaginary Prisoner Game at **http:// www.uta.edu/huma/enculturation/1 2/hein emann/index.html.** Now that you have played this game, how does it create enculturation? Compare your ideas to the text definition of enculturation.

 SUGGESTED READINGS

BARNOUW, VICTOR. 1985. *Culture and Personality*. Homewood, IL: Dorsey Press. An excellent account of the whole field of psychological anthropology. It includes many of the classic studies as well as an evaluation of the overall field and data collected by psychological anthropologists.

BOURGUIGNON, ERIKA. 1979. *Psychological Anthropology: An Introduction to Human Nature and Cultural Differences*. New York: Holt, Rinehart and Winston. This book is another thorough introduction to the field of psychological anthropology. Bourguignon includes discussion of the classics and takes up topics such as the studies of altered states of consciousness and mental illness.

SHORE, BRADD. 1996. *Culture in Mind: Cognition, Culture, and the Problem of Meaning*. New York: Oxford University Press. A recently published book that criticizes many of the early approaches to combining culture and psychology in explaining human thought and behavior. Shore advocates a psychological anthropology approach that draws on recent trends in cognitive science and structuralism.

SHWEDER, RICHARD. 1991. *Thinking through Cultures: Expeditions in Cultural Psychology*. Cambridge, MA: Harvard University Press. A state-of-the-art introduction to major questions addressed by psychological anthropologists. This book includes many findings by psychologists and how those findings bear on anthropological studies.

WHITE, GEOFFREY M., and JOHN KIRKPATRICK, eds. 1985. *Person, Self, and Experience: Exploring Pacific Ethnopsychologies*. Berkeley: University of California Press. This anthology contains a series of essays by psychological anthropologists who focus on the Pacific Islands. They describe how enculturation influences emotions, cognition, and behavior in various ways throughout the Pacific region. These researchers tend to emphasize the cultural perspective, viewing psychological development as primarily induced by cultural processes.

Language

CHAPTER OUTLINE

Nonhuman Communication
Teaching Apes to Sign / Ape Sign Language Reexamined / Ethological Research on Ape Communication

Animal Communication and Human Language
Productivity / Displacement / Arbitrariness / Combining Sounds to Produce Meanings

The Evolution of Language
The Anatomy of Language

The Structure of Language
Phonology / Syntax / Semantics

Language Acquisition
Chomsky on Language Acquisition

Language, Thought, and Culture
The Sapir–Whorf Hypothesis

Historical Linguistics
The Family-Tree Model / Assessing Language Change

Sociolinguistics
Dialectal Differences in Spoken Language / Honorifics in Language / Greeting Behaviors

Nonverbal Communication
Kinesics / Proxemics

CHAPTER QUESTIONS

- What is it that makes human languages unique in comparison with nonhuman animal communication?

- What does the research indicate about nonhuman animal communication?

- What do anthropologists conclude about the evolution of language?

- How do linguistic anthropologists study language?

- What have anthropologists learned about how children acquire their languages?

- What is the relationship between language and culture?

- How do anthropologists study the history of languages?

- What does the field of sociolinguistics tell us about language use?

- What other forms of communication do humans use aside from language?

IN CHAPTER 4 WE DISCUSSED HOW THE CAPACITY FOR culture enables humans to learn symbolically and to transmit symbols from generation to generation. **Language** is a system of symbols with standard meanings. Through language, members of a society are able to communicate with one another. It is an integral aspect of culture. Language allows humans to communicate with one another about what they are experiencing at any given moment, what they have experienced in the past, and what they are planning for the future. Like culture, the language of any particular individual exists before the birth of the individual and is publicly shared by the members of a society. People born in the United States are exposed to an English-speaking language community, whereas people in Russia learn the Russian language. These languages provide the context for symbolic understanding within these different societies. In this sense, language, as part of culture, transcends the individual. Without language, humans would have difficulty transmitting culture. Without culture, humans would lose their unique "humanity."

When linguists refer to language they usually mean spoken language. Yet spoken language is only one form of communication. **Communication** is the act of transferring information to others. As we will discover in this chapter, many nonhuman animals have basic communication skills. We will also discover that humans communicate with one another in ways other than through language.

91

Nonhuman Communication

TEACHING APES TO SIGN

Psychologists and other scientists have conducted a considerable amount of research on animal communication. Some of the most interesting and controversial research on animal communication has been done on chimpanzees and gorillas, animals that are close physiologically and developmentally to humans. In 1966 psychologists Allen and Beatrice Gardner adopted a female chimpanzee named Washoe and began teaching her the American Sign Language (ASL, or Ameslan), a nonvocal form of communication used by the deaf. After several years, Washoe was able to master hundreds of signs. This was truly a remarkable feat for a chimpanzee, and it challenged the traditional assumption that only humans have the capacity for using symbols (Gardner & Gardner, 1969).

At the Yerkes Regional Primate Research Center at Emory University in Atlanta, Georgia, in the 1970s a chimpanzee named Lana was taught to communicate through a color-coded computer keyboard. Researchers concluded that Lana was able to use and combine signs in the computer language. For example, she referred to a cucumber as a "green banana" and to an orange as an "apple that is orange" (Rumbaugh, 1977). Primatologist Roger Fouts, who took over Washoe and three other survivors of the Gardners' project, found that these chimps could produce category words for certain types of foods: Celery was "pipe food"; watermelon was "candy drink"; and radish, a food first tasted by Washoe, was "hurt cry food" (Fouts & Budd, 1979).

In a widely publicized study of the 1970s, Francine Patterson taught Koko, a female gorilla, to use 170 ASL words. Koko was billed as the world's first "talking" gorilla (Patterson & Linden, 1981; Patterson & Cohn, 1978). At the age of 4 she was given an intelligence test based on the Stanford-Binet Intelligence Scale and scored an 85, only slightly below the score of an average human child. Patterson contends that Koko even told stories about her violent capture in Africa. In addition, according to Patterson, Koko demostrated the capacity to lie, deceive, swear, joke, and combine signs in new and creative ways.

APE SIGN LANGUAGE REEXAMINED

These studies of language use by apes have challenged traditional ideas regarding the gap between humans and other types of animals. They are not, however, without their critics. One source of criticism is based on work done at Columbia University by psychologist Herbert Terrace (1986). Terrace began examining the previous ape language studies by training a chimpanzee named Nim Chimpsky. Videotapes of the learning sessions were used to observe carefully the cues that may have been emitted by the trainers. Terrace also viewed the videotapes of the other studies on chimpanzee communication.

Terrace's conclusions challenged the earlier studies. Videotape analysis revealed that Nim rarely initiated signing behaviors, signing only in response to gestures given by the instructors, and that 50 percent of his signs were simply imitative. Unlike humans, Nim did not learn the two-way nature of conversation. Nim also never signed without expecting some reward. In addition, Nim's phrases were random combinations of signs. And, Nim never signed to another chimpanzee who knew ASL unless a teacher coached him. Finally, the videotapes of the other projects showed that prompters gave unconscious signals through their body gestures to the chimpanzees.

Terrace's overall conclusions indicate that chimpanzees are highly intelligent animals who can learn many signs. They cannot, however, understand syntax, the set of grammatical rules govern-

Researcher Joyce Butler showing Nim the chimpanzee the sign for drink.

ing the way words combine to form sentences. An English-speaking child can systematically place a noun before a verb followed by an object without difficulty. A chimpanzee cannot use these types of grammatical rules to structure sentences. Terrace concludes that although chimpanzees have remarkable intellectual capacities and excellent memories, they do not have the syntactical abilities of humans to form sentences.

Terrace's work has not ended the ape language debate. In her book *Ape Language: From Conditioned Response to Symbol* (1986), Sue Savage-Rumbaugh reports on a 10-year-old chimpanzee named Kanzi who, she believes, communicates at the level of a 2-year-old child. Kanzi has learned to communicate with lexigrams, geometric word-symbols that act as substitutes for human speech. Two hundred and fifty lexigrams are displayed on a large keyboard. At the age of 2 1/2, Kanzi spontaneously reached for the keyboard and pointed to the lexigram for chase, and ran away. Savage-Rumbaugh observed him repeatedly touch the lexigram for chase and scamper off. By age 6, Kanzi had mastered a vocabulary of ninety symbols.

In addition, Savage-Rumbaugh notes that Kanzi indicated that he understood spoken English words. She observed Kanzi listening to spoken words like a human child does. The preliminary research indicates that Kanzi could understand English words, even when produced by a speech synthesizer. Another astonishing revelation reported by Savage-Rumbaugh is that Kanzi appeared to have a crude command of syntax. He seemed to be able to use word order to convey meaning. On his own initiative Kanzi requested activities in the order he desired them. For example, if he wanted to be chased and play-bitten, he first pressed the lexigram for chase, then bite. Savage-Rumbaugh reports that Kanzi could understand some 650 sentences.

These more recent research results are impressive, but whether they indicate that apes can use true language remains unclear. Most anthropologists have concluded that apes show the ability to manipulate linguistic symbols when the symbols are hand gestures or plastic symbols. That they cannot transmit language beyond the level of a 2-year-old human child does not mean that they are failed humans. Chimps are perfectly good at

being chimps. It would appear that humans have much different sorts of linguistic capacities.

ETHOLOGICAL RESEARCH ON APE COMMUNICATION

In addition to laboratory research on animal communication, a number of studies have been done by **ethologists,** scientists who study the behavior of animals in their natural setting. Ethologists find that many types of animals have *call systems*—certain sounds or vocalizations that produce specific meanings—that are used to communicate for adaptive purposes. Animals such as prairie dogs, chickens, various types of monkeys, and chimpanzees have call systems.

In an ethological study of gorillas in central Africa, George Schaller isolated twenty-two vocalizations used by these primates. This compares with twenty vocalizations used by howler monkeys, thirty used by Japanese macaque monkeys, and nine used by gibbons (Schaller, 1976). Like these other vocalizations, the gorilla sounds are associated with specific behaviors or emotional states, such as restful feeding states, sexual behavior, playing, anger, and warnings of approaching threats. Infant gorillas also emit certain sounds when their mothers venture off. Schaller admits that some of the vocalizations were not accompanied by any specific type of behavior or stimulus.

Chimpanzee Communication: Jane Goodall

The most impressive long-term investigation of chimpanzees in their natural environment is being carried out by Jane Goodall, a primatologist who has been studying the chimpanzees of the Gombe Game Reserve in Africa since 1960. Goodall has gathered a great deal of information on the vocalizations used by these chimps. Her observations have shown that the chimpanzees use a great variety of calls, which are tied directly to emotional states such as fear, annoyance, and sexual excitement. She concludes that "the production of a sound in the absence of the appropriate emotional state seems to be an almost impossible task for the chimpanzee" (Goodall, 1986: 125).

Goodall found that the chimps use "intraparty calls," communication within the group, and "distance calls," communication to other groups.

Intraparty calls include pant-grunts directed to a higher-ranking individual within the group as a token of respect, and barks, whimpers, squeaks, screams, coughs, and other sounds directed toward other chimps in the immediate group. Distance calls serve a wider range of functions, including drawing attention to local food sources, announcing the precise location of individuals in the home territory, and, in times of distress, bringing help from distant allies. Further research is needed to discover whether the chimps use these vocalizations to distinguish among different types of foods and dangers in the environment.

Animal Communication and Human Language

Both laboratory and field studies of animal communication offer fascinating insights into the question of what distinguishes human communication from animal communication. Many Western philosophers have identified speech as the major distinction between humans and other animals. Modern studies on animal communication, however, suggest that the language gap separating humans from other animals is not as wide as it once appeared. At the same time, these studies also indicate that fundamental differences exist between animal communication and human languages. The question is not whether animals can communicate, because we know that almost every animal can. The real question is, How does animal communication differ from human communication? In searching for an answer to this question, linguistic anthropologists have identified a number of distinctive characteristics of human languages. The four most important features are productivity, displacement, arbitrariness, and combining sounds (Hockett & Ascher, 1964).

PRODUCTIVITY

Human languages are inherently flexible and creative. Users of human languages, even small children, can create sentences never heard before by anyone. There are no limits to our capability to produce messages that refer to the past, present, or future. In contrast, animal communication systems in natural settings are rigid and fixed. The sounds

of animal communications do not vary and cannot be modified. The offspring of chimpanzees will always use the same pattern of vocalization as the parents. In contrast, the highly flexible nature of human languages allows for efficient and creative uses of symbolic communication. William von Humboldt, a nineteenth-century linguist, used the phrase "the infinite use of finite media" to suggest the idea of linguistic productivity (von Humboldt, 1836/1972; Pinker, 1994).

DISPLACEMENT

It is clear from field studies, and to some extent from laboratory studies, that the meaning of a sound or vocalization of a nonhuman animal is closely tied to a specific type of stimulus. For example, the chimpanzee's vocalization is associated with a particular emotional state and stimulus. Thus, a growl or scream as a warning to the group cannot be made in the absence of some perceived threat. Similarly, animals such as parrots and mynah birds can learn to imitate a wide variety of words, but they cannot substitute or displace one word for another. In contrast, the meanings of sounds in human languages can refer to people, things, or events that are not present, a feature called *displacement*.

This capacity for displacement enables humans to communicate with one another using highly abstract concepts. Humans can express their objectives in reference to the past, present, and future. They can discuss spiritual or hypothetical phenomena that do not exist concretely. They can discuss their past history through myth or specific genealogical relations. Humans can refer to what will happen after death through myth or theological concepts such as heaven or spiritual enlightenment. Displacement allows humans to plan for the future through the use of foresight. Obviously this linguistic ability for displacement is interrelated with the general symbolic capacities that are shared by humanity, providing the basis of culture as discussed in Chapter 3. Symbolic capacities allow humans to manipulate abstract concepts to develop complex beliefs and worldviews.

ARBITRARINESS

The arbitrariness of sounds in a communication system is another distinctive feature of human languages. Words seldom have any necessary connection with the concrete objects or abstract symbols they represent. In English we say *one, two,* and *three* to refer to the numbers, whereas the Chinese say *yi, er,* and *san.* Neither language has the "correct" word for the numbers, because there is no correct word. *Ouch* is pronounced *ay* in Spanish, and *ishkatak* in the Nootkan Indian language. A German shepherd dog does not have any difficulty understanding the bark of a French poodle. An English speaker, however, will have trouble understanding a Chinese speaker.

COMBINING SOUNDS TO PRODUCE MEANINGS

We have mentioned that various animals have sounds that indicate different meanings in specific contexts. Human languages also have units of sound that can be correlated with units of meaning. Every human language has between twelve and sixty of these sound units, called *phonemes.* A **phoneme** is a unit of sound that distinguishes meaning in a particular language. For example, in English the difference between *dime* and *dine* is distinguished by the sound difference or phonemic difference between /m/ and /n/. English has forty-five phonemes, Italian has twenty-seven, and Hawaiian has thirteen (Farb, 1974). Nonhuman animals cannot combine their sound units to communicate new meanings; one vocalization is given to indicate a specific response. In contrast, in human languages the same sounds can be combined and recombined to form different meanings. For example, the Hawaiian language, with only thirteen sound units, has almost three thousand words consisting of different combinations of three sounds, and more than 5 million words formed by combinations of six sounds. Phonemes that may have no meaning can be combined and recombined to form literally as many meaningful units as humans need or want. Primates and other animals do not have this ability.

Having defined these distinctive features of human language, we can discern fundamental differences between human and animal communication. However, some researchers working with chimpanzees in laboratories are still not willing to label human languages as "true languages," as distinguished from "animal communication systems." They criticize what they refer to as the "anthro-pocentric" view of language—the view that takes human language as its standard. Because chimpanzees do not have the physical ability to form the sounds made by humans, it may be unfair to compare their language strictly in terms of vocal communication.

The Evolution of Language

Throughout the centuries, linguists, philosophers, and physical anthropologists have developed theories concerning the origins of human language. One early theory, known as the "bowwow" theory, maintains that language arose when humans imitated the sounds of nature by the use of onomatopoeic words, such as "cock-a-doodle-do," or "sneeze," or "mumble." Another theory argues that language evolved as humans detected the natural sounds of objects in nature. Known as the "ding-dong" theory, this argument assumed that a relationship exists between a word and its meaning because nature gives off a harmonic ring. For example, all of nature, including rocks, streams, plants, and animals, were thought to emit a ringing sound that could be detected by humans. Supposedly the harmonic ring of a rock sounded like *rock.* Both theories have been discredited, replaced by other hypotheses concerning the evolution of language.

THE ANATOMY OF LANGUAGE

As discussed earlier in the text, the evolution of hominids was accompanied by increases in brain size. The expansion of the hominid brain reflects the increasing size of the cerebral cortex, the part related to all of the higher functions of the brain, such as memory and, most likely, symbolic and cultural capacities. Although many capacities of the human brain, including memory, learning, and other functions, are not completely understood by modern science, we do know that the cerebral cortex contains the billions of nerve cells needed for receiving, storing, and processing information.

The Human Brain and Speech Other centers of the brain play important roles in the human capacity for language. The human brain is divided into two hemispheres. Although neither hemisphere is dominant, and both play important roles in all functions, most human linguistic skills are more closely identified with one hemisphere. In general, the left hemisphere controls specialized functions related to linguistic abilities, and the right hemisphere is related to spatial orientation and proportion. One area of the brain that is located in the left hemisphere and that especially influences human language abilities is known as *Broca's area;* it is associated with the production of sound or pronunciation and with grammatical abilities.

Another area related to linguistic abilities is *Wernicke's area,* also located in the left hemisphere of the brain. Wernicke's area is associated with the ability to understand the meanings of words and sentences, or the semantics of language. This center of the brain is important for listening and reading.

Human Anatomy and Speech Other anatomical and physiological features contribute to human language abilities. No animal other than the human being has the anatomy for sustaining speech production. Human vocal organs form an irregular tube connecting the lungs, windpipe, and the larynx, the voice box containing the vocal cords. Another vocal organ is the *pharynx,* the part of the vocal tract between the back of the tongue and the larynx extending into the nasal cavity. The *larynx* serves to hold air in the lungs and to control its release. These vocal organs work in conjunction with our tongue, lips, and nose to produce speech. The lungs force air through the pharynx, which changes shape to control the column of air. The nasal cavity, lips, and tongue can constrict or stop the flow of air at any point, enabling us to make vowel or consonant sounds. The organs involved in producing speech are illustrated in Figure 5.1.

The major difference between the anatomical structure of chimpanzees and that of modern humans in relation to speech is the enlargement of the vocal tract and the location of the pharynx cavity above the voice box in humans. Although enlargement of the vocal tract makes breathing more difficult, increases the risk of death from choking, and crowds the teeth, which can lead to impacted wisdom teeth, the advantages of having language must have outweighed the disadvantages caused by the change in anatomy. Nonhuman primates such as chimps cannot speak: Their vocal mecha-

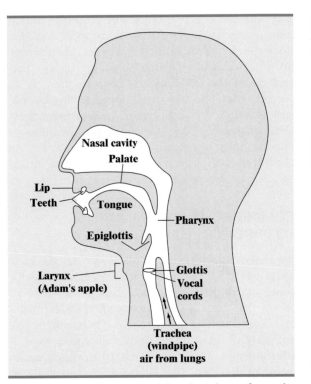

Figure 5.1 An illustration of the physiology of speech making, which is unique to humans.

nisms do not permit it, and their tongues cannot make sounds that can be used for speech production.

Could Early Hominids Speak? Some physical anthropologists are using complex computer programs to compare the anatomy of primates, early hominids, and modern humans. Through this method, Philip Lieberman and Jeffrey Laitman have proposed a hypothesis regarding the evolution of language. They suggest that australopithecines did not have the vocal tract needed to produce the range of vowels found in human language. They also conclude that Neanderthals, archaic *Homo sapiens,* could not produce vowels such as *a, i,* and *u,* thus limiting their linguistic abilities (Laitman, 1984; Lieberman, 1984). However, if Neanderthals could produce and combine phonemes into meaningful units, they may have had language. But most researchers conclude that language as we know it appeared only within the last 100,000 years or so and is associated with the development of the vocal tract and other characteristics of modern *Homo sapiens.*

This analysis has given rise to a popular hypothesis regarding the evolution of language. The hypothesis suggests that australopithecines probably communicated through sign communication, vocal calls, and gestures. These communication abilities developed gradually with the evolution of *H. habilis, H. erectus,* and archaic *H. sapiens.* Eventually, these developments led to the increased symbolizing power of language that is associated with modern humans. Without more evidence, however, these hypotheses remain controversial.

Whatever the precise determinants of the evolution of language, it is difficult to identify the critical stage in the evolution from a simple, sign-based communication system to a more advanced symbolic form of language. It is, however, recognized that this capacity broadly expanded human capabilities for adaptation and creativity. The capacity for language was probably the last major step in our biological evolution. Since that time, human history has been dominated by cultural rather than biological evolution. This cultural evolution and the subsequent developments in adaptation and creativity could not have occurred before an adequate language ability.

The Structure of Language

Linguistic anthropologists compare the structure of different languages. To do so, they study the sounds of a language, phonology; the words of a language, morphology; the sentence structure of a language, syntax; and meaning, semantics. More than six thousand languages have existed throughout history, all of which have contained these four components, although the components vary considerably from one language to another.

PHONOLOGY

Phonology is the study of the sounds made in speech. The sounds, or **phones,** of languages differ from one another. To study phonetic differences among languages, linguists have developed the International Phonetic Alphabet (IPA), which consists of eighty-one symbols. Each sound is used somewhere in the world, although no single language contains all of them. Each language has its own phonetic system consisting of all the sounds of its speakers. As we have already seen, human languages, which have only a limited number of sounds, can combine these sounds to produce complex meanings.

Units of Sound   Linguists attempt to describe a phonetic system by isolating what are called minimal pairs: words that resemble one another but contain one distinctive sound difference. For example, the difference between the *d* and *t* in English words such as *dime* and *time* or *den* and *ten* is contrasted by one sound difference; it is a *minimal pair.* This minimal-pair difference between /d/ and /t/ represents a contrast in meaning, or a *phonemic difference.* (As discussed earlier, a *phoneme* is a unit of sound that distinguishes meaning in a particular language. Thus the sound difference between /d/ and /t/ will indicate a difference in meaning in a word that is spoken.)

When linguistic anthropologists analyze the sounds of a language, they distinguish between the phonetic and phonemic differences. The *phonetic* sound patterns are due to variations in the location of the tongue and lips, the length of time a sound is held, and the stress, pitch, and tone of the sound. The phonemic differences are derived from the patterns of the sounds that create the contrasts in meaning. Many Asian languages such as Chinese and Thai are *tonal*—that is, a word's meaning is affected by the tones (contrasting pitches) of the sounds that make up the word. Put another way, the tones of the language have phonemic value. To an English speaker's ear, a Chinese or Thai speaker sounds musical. For example, in Thai *may* can mean "new," "to burn," or "silk," depending on the tone used.

Pueblo Indians use many nasalized sounds to produce phonemic differences. Arabs use the back of the tongue and the throat muscles, whereas Spanish speakers use the tip of the tongue. The !Kung of southern Africa have a unique manner of producing phonemic differences. They use a sharp intake of air to make clicks that shape meaning for them. Their language also requires more use of the lips to produce smacks than most other languages. The !Kung language has been referred to as a "clicking language."

Most people are unaware of the complex physiological and mental processes required for producing phonetic and phonemic contrasts within their native tongue. Only through extensive phonetic and phonological analysis by linguists and anthropologists is this component of language understood.

Morphology   To study the words of human languages, anthropologists isolate the **morphemes,** the smallest units of a language that convey meaning. The study of morphemes is called **morphology.** Morphemes may be short, only a single phoneme; or they may be a combination of phonemes. They are the minimal building blocks of meaning and cannot be reduced further. *Bound morphemes* are those morphemes that cannot stand alone, such as suffixes and prefixes. For example, in English *s* is a bound morpheme that indicates the plural, and the prefix *un-* is a bound morpheme meaning "not." *Free morphemes,* in contrast, are independent units of meaning; they can stand alone, for example, as nouns, verbs, adjectives, or adverbs. Words such as *boy, girl, happy,* and *close* are free morphemes.

In any language, morphemes are limited in number, and languages differ in how these morphemes are used and combined. In contrast to many languages, English has complex rules governing the formation of plurals of certain words (for example, *geese, mice, children,* and *shrimp*). Some languages, such as Chinese, generally use one morpheme for each word. Other languages, such as the Eskimo language, combine a large number of affixes to form words.

SYNTAX

The **syntax** of a language is the rules for the way phrases and sentences are made up out of words. For example, these rules determine whether a subject comes before or after a verb, or whether an object follows a verb. Linguistic anthropologist Joseph Greenberg (1990) has classified languages based on word order within sentences—that is, the location of the subject (S), the verb (V), and the object (O). He demonstrates that these components occur in six possible orders: VSO, SVO, SOV, VOS, OSV, and OVS. But, in fact, what Greenberg finds in his cross-linguistic comparison is that usually just three patterns of word order occur: VSO, SVO, SOV.

Although most languages permit variation in syntax to allow for emphasis in expression, Green-

berg's hypothesis suggests that some innate universal capacities may influence word order. For example, the expression for the English sentence "The boy drank the water" can be found in all languages. Notice the variations in syntactical order among six different languages:

```
              S       V         O
English: the bóy dránk the wáter
              S          V      O
Russian: mál'c̆ik vy´pil vódu
              V       S        O
Arabic: s̆áraba lwáladu lma-?a
              S        V       O
Hausa: ya-ro- yás̆a- ruwa-
              S         V       O
Thai: dègchaaj dyym nàam
              S          O       V
Quechua: wámbra yakúta upiárqan
```
(Hausa is a West African language. Quechua is a language of the ancient Incas and their modern descendants.)

A man teaching a young girl to write with Chinese characters, each of which represents a word.

SEMANTICS

Semantics is the study of the meaning of symbols, words, phrases, and sentences of a language. The field of semantics has led to important developments in linguistic anthropology. A specialty has developed to account for the meaning of concepts and terms with respect to time, space, color, and other aspects of the environment. This specialty, sometimes referred to as *ethnosemantics,* or *cognitive anthropology,* focuses on the meaning of language as it relates to beliefs, concepts, and patterns of thought in different societies.

Kinship Terms The goal of ethnosemantics is to understand the meanings of words, phrases, sentences, and how members of other societies use language to organize things, events, and behaviors. For example, this type of analysis has been applied to kinship terminologies of many societies. It became increasingly clear to many anthropologists that they could not understand the kinship terms of other societies by simply translating them into English. English terms such as *mother, father, brother, brother-in-law, cousin, aunt,* and *uncle* treat kinship differently from the kinship terms of other societies.

Some groups classify their kin with very precise terms for individuals, no matter how distantly they are related. English kin terms are fairly precise and distinct with respect to genealogical relatedness, yet English does not specify every kin relationship precisely. For example, English speakers do not distinguish between maternal and paternal uncles or aunts. Chinese kinship terminology, on the other hand, includes different terms for one's mother's brother and one's father's brother. There are separate terms for every sibling as well as for different cousins. This is an example of a highly descriptive kinship terminology. Other forms of kinship terminologies are highly generalized. In the Hawaiian kinship system, there is no specific term to parallel the English term *father.* Instead, the Hawaiians use one general term to classify their father and all male relatives in their father's generation. Some kinship terminologies, such as those of the Iroquois Indians, are intermediate between the descriptive and the generalized forms. The Iroquois have one single term for one's father and father's brother but two separate terms for one's mother and one's mother's brother. As we shall see later in the text, these kinship terminologies often reflect basic social organization and the way people trace their descent in the family.

Classifying Reality Anthropologists also use the ethnosemantic approach to study how different societies understand and classify such everyday objects as animals, plants, diseases, and foods. Ethnosemantic research on color terms has led to some intriguing hypotheses regarding human psychology and human nature. Languages vary with respect to how many basic words are used in classifying colors. For example, in English we have separate terms for the colors green and blue. In contrast, in Tzeltal (a Mayan language) a single term is used for both colors.

One early hypothesis in anthropological linguistics was that because colors are classified with different terms in different areas, the peoples of these societies perceive the color spectrum in arbitrary ways. This view assumes that the specific language spoken in a society organizes people's objective experiences and perceptions in ways unique to that language. This perspective is usually referred to as a form of **linguistic relativism,** the theory that language molds habits of cognition and perception. In this view, different languages actually point speakers toward different views of reality. Thus, there is nothing inherent in the color spectrum or human perception that would lead people to classify colors in any designated manner. People "cut up reality" in any way they please, and the words used to describe colors are arbitrary.

A Case of Linguistic Universals: Classifying Colors Anthropologists Brent Berlin and Paul Kay have been studying the basic color terms of different societies since the 1960s. They analyzed the color-naming practices of informants from ninety-eight globally distributed language groups and found that societies differ dramatically in the number of basic color terms they possess—from two in some New Guinea tribes to eleven in English. They showed, however, that despite this difference, all color terms used by diverse societies follow a systematic pattern (1969).

A language with only two color terms will divide the color spectrum between white and black. If a language contains three terms, the spectrum will be black, red, and white. A language with four terms will have black, red, white, and either green, yellow, or blue. A language with six terms will have black, white, red, yellow, green, and blue. Language systems add basic color terms in a systematic progression until a maximum of eleven terms is reached.

Berlin and Kay suggest that this pattern indicates an evolutionary sequence common to all languages. Red is adopted after white and black. In general, a language does not adopt a term for brown unless it already has six color terms. English, most Western European languages, Russian, Japanese, and several others add four color terms—gray, pink, orange, and purple—after brown is classified. Berlin and Kay correlate the evolution of color terms with the evolution of society. Societies with only two color terms have a simple level of technology, whereas societies with eleven basic color terms have a complex technology.

The evidence from Berlin and Kay's study suggests that color naming is not at all arbitrary. If color terms were selected randomly, there would be thousands of possible color systems. In fact, there are only thirty-three possible color-naming systems. This study demonstrates the existence of *linguistic universals,* language features found universally.

In a more recent ethnosemantic study, James Boster concluded that, as with colors, people from different societies classify birds in similar ways. Boster (1987) found that the South American Jivaro Indian population classified species of native birds in a manner corresponding to the way scientists classify these birds. To discover whether this pattern of classification was random, Boster had University of Kentucky students with no scientific training and no familiarity with South American birds classify these birds. The students did so with the exact criteria used by both the Jivaro Indians and the Western scientists.

These findings offer a strong critique of linguistic relativism. If reality were inherently unorganized and could be perceived in any way, then color naming and animal and plant classification would be completely arbitrary. The results of this research support the notion that people the world over share certain cognitive abilities, and language is as likely to reflect human cognition as it is to shape it. It suggests that evolution selected certain fundamental visual-processing abilities for humans everywhere (Lakoff,

1987). Thus, ethnosemantic research has been fruitful in providing interactionist models of the ways in which humans everywhere classify, understand, and interpret their natural and social environment.

Language Acquisition

Although human infants are born with the ability to speak a language, they are not born preprogrammed to speak a particular language such as English. Just as infants are exposed to enculturation to absorb and learn about their culture, they must be exposed to the phonemes, morphemes, syntax, and semantics of the language within their culture. Linguistic anthropologists have examined this process, drawing on different hypotheses regarding language acquisition.

The empiricist philosopher John Locke (1632–1704) suggested that the human mind at birth is like a blank tablet, a *tabula rasa,* and that infants learn language through habit formation. This hypothesis was further developed by behavioral psychologists such as B. F. Skinner, who maintained that infants learn language through conditioned responses and feedback from their environment. An infant might babble a sound that resembles an acceptable word like Daddy and would then be rewarded for that response. Thus rewarded, the child would use the word Daddy in certain contexts. According to Skinner, children learn their entire language through this type of social conditioning.

The Enlightenment French philosopher René Descartes (1596–1650) advocated a contrasting view of language learning. He argued that innate ideas or structures in the human mind provide the basis for learning language. Until the late 1950s, most linguists and anthropologists working on language assumed that Locke's model, and by extension Skinner's was correct. However, by about 1960 evidence began to accumulate that suggested that, in fact, humans come into the world especially equipped not only to learn language, but to learn any human language.

CHOMSKY ON LANGUAGE ACQUISITION

The most influential modern proponent of Descartes's hypothesis is linguist Noam Chomsky. Chomsky is interested in how people learn grammar, the

Noam Chomsky.

set of rules that determine how sentences are constructed to produce meaningful statements. Most people cannot actually state the rules of their grammar, but they do use the rules to form understandable sentences. For example, in English we can transform the active sentence "Bill loves Mary" into a passive sentence, "Mary is loved by Bill." This change requires much grammatical knowledge, but most English speakers carry out this operation without thinking about it. According to Chomsky, all children learn these complex rules readily and do not seem to have difficulty producing meaningful statements, even when they have not been exposed to linguistic data that illustrates the rules in question. Furthermore, children are able to both produce and understand sentences they have never heard before. All this would be impossible, Chomsky claims, if learning language depended on trial and error learning and reinforcement as Skinner had thought. In other words, Chomsky suggests that we are born with a brain prewired to enable us to acquire language easily; Chomsky often refers to this prewiring as universal grammar.

Universal grammar serves as a template, or model, against which a child matches and sorts out the patterns of morphemes and phonemes and the subtle distinctions that are needed to communicate in any language. According to Chomsky, a behavioristic understanding of language learning is too simplistic to account for the creativity and productivity of any human language. In his view, the universal structure of the human mind enables the child to acquire language and produce sentences never heard before.

Another important contribution of Chomsky's is the realization that human languages, despite their apparently great diversity, are really more alike than they are different. Anthropologists had previously assumed that languages could vary infinitely, and there was no limit to what could be found in a human language. Chomsky and the researchers that followed him, in contrast, have catalogued many basic, underlying ways in which all languages are really the same. In this view, a hypothetical Martian linguist visiting Earth would probably decide that all humans speak dialects of Human Language. Note that this is somewhat parallel to the search for cultural universals described in chapter three.

Chomsky's model is referred to as a *generative grammar approach*. This implies that the speakers of languages generate sentences from a *deep, or underlying, structure,* and that these are mapped onto a surface structure, the sentence as it is actually spoken, by way of a relatively small set of rules which specify things like basic word order, the pronunciation of words, and so on, that are specific to particular languages. For example, in English we might say "Bill loves Mary," with subject plus verb plus object (SVO) word order, whereas in Japanese the order of verb and object would be reversed as "Bill Mary loves" (*Bill wa Mary o aishiteimasu*). The underlying or deep structure, in which there is a subject (Bill), an object (Mary), and a verb expressing "love" is the same for both languages.

Chomsky's model also helps explain the semantic relationship between paired sentences such as "Bill loves Mary" and "Mary is loved by Bill" which have different surface features, but for which the deep structure is essentially the same. Chomsky thinks that children learn complex transformational rules that transform elements within the deep structure into the surface structure of spoken sentences (see Figure 5.2).

APPLYING ANTHROPOLOGY

Saving Languages

There are more than four thousand languages distributed throughout a population of about 5.5 billion people in the world. As many linguistic anthropologists have noted, however, tens of thousands of languages have become extinct through the years. In Western Europe, hundreds of languages disappeared with the expansion of agricultural empires that imposed their languages on conquered peoples. For example, during the expansion of the Roman Empire for approximately a thousand years, many tribal languages disappeared as they were replaced by Latin. Currently, only forty-five native languages still exist in Western Europe.

When Columbus discovered the Americas, more than two thousand languages existed among different Native American peoples. Yet even in pre-Columbian America, before A.D. 1500, native languages were displaced by the expansion of peoples such as the Aztecs and Incas in Central and South America. As the Spanish and British empires expanded into these regions, the indigenous languages began to disappear even more rapidly. A similar process has been ongoing throughout Asia, Africa, and the Middle East.

The majority of people in the world speak one of the "large" groups of languages, such as Mandarin Chinese (with more than 1 billion speakers), Spanish, or English. Most of the more than four thousand languages that exist

are spoken in small-scale societies that have an average of five thousand people or so. For example, Papua New Guinea alone has perhaps as many as a thousand different languages distributed among various ethnic groups (Diamond, 1993). Other islands in countries such as Indonesia may have as many as four hundred different languages. Yet, in all of the areas of the Pacific and Asia, the "larger" languages are beginning to replace the "small" ones.

Some linguists estimate that if the present rate of the disappearance of languages remains constant, within a century or two our four thousand languages could be reduced to just a few hundred. For example, as young people in the Pacific Islands begin to move from rural to urban regions they usually abandon their traditional language and learn a majority tongue to be able to take advantage of educational and economic opportunities. As the media, including television, radio, and newspapers, opt for a majority language, more people will elect to abandon their native languages. These are global processes that have resulted in linguistic homogeneity and the loss of traditional languages.

In North America and Alaska there are some two hundred languages ranging from Inuit and Yupik among the native Alaskans to Navajo, Hopi, Choctaw, Creek, Seminole, Chickasaw, and Cherokee in other areas. However, most of these languages are now on the

verge of extinction. As Europeans began to expand and control North America and Alaska, they forced Native American children to speak the English language as a means of "civilizing" them. In many cases, Native American children were removed from their families and were forbidden to speak their native languages. In addition, most Native American peoples have had to learn English to adjust to circumstances in an English-language-dominated society. Thus, very few of the Native American languages are actively spoken.

Some people say that this process of global and linguistic homogenization, and the loss of traditional languages, is a positive development. As people begin to speak a common language, communication is increased, leading to improvements in societies that formerly could not unify through language. For example, in India, hundreds of languages existed before the British colonized the area. As the educated class in India (a small minority) began to learn and speak English, this helped provide a means of unifying India as a country. Many people say that for the purpose of developing commerce and political relationships, the abandonment of native languages is a good thing. Many businesspeople and politicians argue that multiple languages inhibit economic and political progress, and the elites of many countries have directly encouraged language loss.

A number of linguistic anthropologists, however, disagree with these policies. They may agree that people ought to have some common language to understand one another, to conduct business, and to have common political goals. But, they argue that this does not have to mean eliminating minority languages—it only requires that people become bilingual or multilingual. In most societies throughout the world, including Western Europe, people routinely learn two or more languages as children. The United States and Japan are exceptional in being monolingual societies.

Linguistic anthropologists find from their studies that people who are forced to abandon their native languages and cultures begin to lose their self-esteem. Bilingualism would permit these people to retain their own language while simultaneously learning the majority language to be able to share in a common national culture.

The U.S. government is beginning to realize that bilingualism has a positive influence on community development among minority populations such as Native Americans. Recently, a number of educational programs have been funded under the U.S. Bilingual Education Act. This act encourages the development of English-speaking skills; however, it also offers instruction in the native languages. During the 1980s there were more than twenty Title VII projects serving Native American students from sixteen different language backgrounds.

Through these government-sponsored programs, linguistic anthropologists have been actively engaged in both research and language-renewal activities among the Native American population (Leap, 1988). These activities have led many younger Native Americans to become interested in studying their traditional languages, which may lead to improvements in classroom learning and inhibit high dropout rates among young students.

Anthropologist Russell Bernard has promoted the value of maintaining the native languages of people through the use of microcomputers (1992). Microcomputers can be used by anthropologists to help develop writing systems and literature for native languages. Through this computer technol-ogy, anthropologists can help native peoples to produce literature in their own languages for future generations. Bernard emphasizes that this will enable all of humanity to profit from the ideas of these people. Bernard was able to establish a center in Mexico where the Indian population could learn to use computers to write in their native languages. Sixty Indian people have learned to write directly in languages such as Mixtec, Zapotec, Chatino, Amuzgo, Chinantec, and Mazataec. These native authors will use these texts to teach adults and children of their home regions to read. Projects such as these represent opportunities for anthropologists to apply their knowledge in solving important problems in U.S. society and beyond.

Anthropologists are assisting people such as these Crow Indian children in learning and thus saving their native languages.

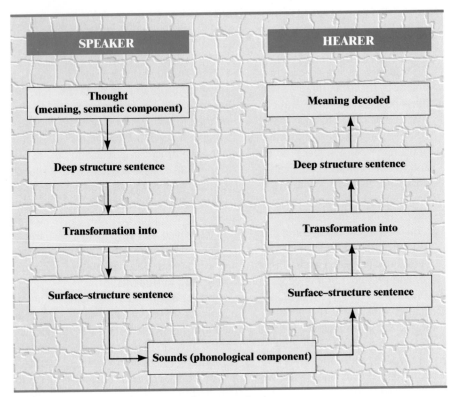

Figure 5.2 Noam Chomsky's transformational rules.

Chomsky proposes a *critical stage,* somewhere between the ages of 1 and 3, at which language learning takes place for children. If children are not exposed to language during that period, they may never be able to learn it. Chomsky believes that the human brain contains genetically programmed blueprints or modules for language learning. Consequently, most children learn complicated linguistic rules automatically and easily.

Creole Languages One source of evidence for Chomsky's model of innate universal grammar is research on specific types of languages known as *creole* and *pidgin* languages. Linguist Derek Bickerton has compared these two types of languages from different areas of the world. Pidgin and creole develop from cross-cultural contact between speakers of mutually unintelligible languages. A pidgin language emerges when people combine terms from at least two different languages and develop a simple grammatical structure to communicate with one another. For example, in the New Guinea highlands, where many different languages were spoken, a pidgin language developed between the indigenous peoples and the Westerners.

In some cases, the children of the pidgin speakers begin to speak a creole language. The vocabulary of the creole language is similar to that of the pidgin, but the grammar is much more complex. There are more than a hundred known creole languages. Among them are the creole languages developed between African slaves and Europeans, leading to languages such as Haitian Creole. A Hawaiian creole language emerged after contact between English-speaking Westerners and native Hawaiians.

What is remarkable, according to Bickerton, is that all these languages share similar grammatical patterns, despite the lack of contact among these diverse peoples. For example, Hawaiian Creole uses the English word *walk* in a very different manner from standard English. The phrase *bin walk* means "had walked"; *stay walk* is continuing action, as in "I am walking" or "I was walking"; and *I bin stay walk* means "I had been walking." Although this phrasing might sound unusual to a person from England or the United States, it does conform to a clear set of grammatical rules. Very similar tense systems are found in all other creole languages, whatever their vocabularies or geographic origins.

Bickerton suggests that the development of creole languages may parallel the evolution of early human languages. Because of an innate universal grammatical component of the human mind, languages emerged in uniform ways. The prehistoric languages would have had structures similar to that of the creole languages. As languages developed in various types of environments with different characteristics, people evolved different vocabularies and sentence structures. Yet when societies are uprooted by cultural contact, the innate rules for ordering language remain intact. Bickerton's thesis suggests that humans do have some sort of universal linguistic acquisition device, as hypothesized by Chomsky (Bickerton, 1985).

Ebonics As a Creole Language   A number of linguists have been doing research on Ebonics, a distinctive variety of American English spoken by some African Americans. The term *Ebonics* is derived from the words *ebony* and *phonics* meaning "black sounds" (Rickford, 1997). Ebonics is also known as Black English Vernacular (BEV), Black English (BE), African American Vernacular English (AAVE) and African American English (AAE). The majority of African Americans do not speak Ebonics; however, it is commonly spoken among working-class and, in particular, among adolescent African Americans. Linguistic anthropologists have suggested that Ebonics may have emerged as a creole language under the conditions of slavery in the United States. As slaves from Africa, captured from different areas and speaking an enormous variety of languages, were placed together on plantations in the American South, they developed a pidgin to communicate. From this pidgin, the children may have created a systematic syntax and grammar, as they were at the critical stage of language learning. Just as Jamaican or Haitian creole emerged in the Caribbean under the conditions of slavery, a variety of creoles may have evolved in the United States. One form of an early creole still exists among African Americans off the coast of South Carolina and Georgia on the Sea Islands. This creole is known as Gullah. Other forms of creole

speech may have been introduced by the large numbers of slaves coming from Jamaica or Barbados into the American South, or could have emerged within early communities of slaves within the United States. Ebonics may very well be a product of this early creolization.

Linguist John Rickford notes that Ebonics is not just the use of slang. There are some slang terms in Ebonics such as *chillin* (relaxing) or *homey* (close friend), but there is a systematic grammar and pronunciation within the language. There are standard usages of sentences within Ebonics such as *He runnin* ("He is running") or *He be running*, ("He is usually running") or *He BIN runnin* ("He has been running for a long time and still is)." Other rules such as dropping consonants at the end of words such as *tes(t)* and *han(d)* are evident within Ebonics. Rickford emphasizes that Ebonics is not just a lazy form of English. Ebonics is no more lazy English than Italian is a lazy form of Latin. These are different languages with systematically ordered grammar and pronunciation usages.

A controversy regarding Ebonics developed in Oakland, California, when the school board announced that they were going to recognize Ebonics as a separate language. The school board was committed to teaching American Standard English to the African American students. However, because of the prejudices and misunderstandings regarding Ebonics as "a lazy form of English," the school board set off a controversy all over the United States. Linguistic anthropologist Ronald Kephart has commented on this Ebonics controversy based on his extensive research on the study of Creoles in the Caribbean (Monaghan, Hinton, and Kephart, 1997). Kephart studied creole English on the island of Carriacou and Grenada. He did research on young students who were reading in the creole language as well as learning standard forms of English. The children who read in the creole language were able to learn the standard forms of English more readily, and they enjoyed the process. Kephart suggests that the recognition of Ebonics by the school board in Oakland would help children learn American Standard English. These children would appreciate the fact that the language they brought with them into the school was to be respected as another form of English, and they would develop more positive attitudes about themselves, and not be treated as "illiterate" or "lazy" children. This would help promote more effective learning strategies and enable the students to master American Standard English in a more humane manner.

It appears that language acquisition depends on both biological readiness and learning. The ability to speak seems to be biologically programmed, whereas a specific language is learned from the society the child grows up in. Children who are not exposed to language during their "critical period" may not be able to learn to use language properly. Research such as Chomsky's provides for further advances in an interactionist approach to test hypotheses regarding language, biology, mind, and thought.

Language, Thought, and Culture

In the early part of the twentieth century, Edward Sapir and Benjamin Whorf carried out studies of language and culture. Sapir was a prodigious fieldworker who described many Native American languages and provided the basis for the comparative method in anthropological linguistics. Whorf, an insurance inspector by profession and a linguist and anthropologist by calling, conducted comparative research on a wide variety of languages. Sapir and Whorf's research led their students to formulate a highly controversial hypothesis that differs dramatically from the theories of Chomsky and the ethnosemanticists.

THE SAPIR–WHORF HYPOTHESIS

The **Sapir–Whorf hypothesis** assumes that a close relationship exists between language and culture and that language defines experiences for us. In other words, although humans everywhere have approximately the same set of physical organs for perceiving reality—eyes to see, ears to hear, noses to smell—the human nervous system is bombarded with sensations of all kinds, intensities, and durations. These sensations do not all reach our consciousness. Rather, humans have a filtering device that classifies reality. This filtering device, according to the Sapir–Whorf hypothesis, is language. In this view, language, in effect, provides us with a special pair of glasses that heighten certain percep-

tions and dim others, determining what we perceive as reality.

A Case Study: The Hopi Language   To understand this hypothesis we should look at some examples given by Whorf. Whorf compared the grammar of English with that of the Native American Hopi language of the southwestern part of the United States. He found that the verb forms indicating tense differ in these two languages. English contains past, present, and future verb forms; the Hopi language does not.

In English we can say, "I came home," "I am coming home," or "I will come home." The Hopi do not have the verb corresponding to the use of come (Whorf, 1956). From this type of example, Whorf inferred that Hopi and English speakers think about time in fundamentally different ways: English speakers conceptualize time in a measurable, linear form, speaking of a length of time or a point in time. We say that time is short, long, or great. We can save time, squander it, or spend it.

To the Hopi, in contrast, time is connected to the cycles of nature. Because they were farmers, their lives revolved around the different seasons for planting and harvesting. The Hopi, Whorf argued, did not see time as a motion upon space (that is, as time passing) but as a getting later of everything that has ever been done. Whorf concluded that the Hopi did not share the Western emphasis on history, calendars, and clocks. From evidence such as this, Sapir and Whorf developed their hypothesis that the language of a speaker provides a grid, or structure, that categorizes space, time, and other aspects of reality into a worldview. The Sapir–Whorf hypothesis is thus an example of linguistic relativism because it maintains that the world is experienced differently among different language communities.

Universals of Time Expression   Anthropological linguist Ekkehart Malotki (1983) investigated the Sapir–Whorf hypothesis by reexamining the Hopi language. His research, based on many interviews with Hopi speakers, showed that in fact the Hopi calculate time in units very similar to those of native English speakers. He concluded that Whorf had exaggerated the extent to which language determines people's perceptions of time and demonstrated that the Hopi make linguistic distinctions between the past and the present based on tense

Hopi Indians preparing for their traditional butterfly dance. The Hopi language has been the subject of controversy within linguistic anthropology.

form. In the Hopi language tense is distinguished between future and nonfuture, instead of between past and present.

In a recent book, anthropologist Hoyt Alverson (1994) investigates four different unrelated languages to determine how time is conceptualized. Alverson studies the metaphors and symbolic usages of time in the Mandarin language of the Chinese, the Hindi language of India, the Sesotho language of Africa, and English. He looks at 150 different linguistic usages of time from native speakers and shows that each language uses essentially the same types of metaphors and categories to express time. For example, time is always conceptualized as partible and divisible, and it can be expressed as either linear or circular. This study, along with Malotki's, suggests that all humans share a common cognitive framework when conceptualizing time. These findings, undoubtedly, have implications for humanity's genetic heritage, a universal cognitive evolution, and a common identity as a species.

Although these studies appear to have refuted the Sapir–Whorf hypothesis, most linguistic anthropologists agree that a relationship exists between language and thought. Rather than assert that language determines thought, they maintain that language in-

fluences the speaker's thinking and worldview. Some experts refer to this approach as a "weak" version of the linguistic relativity hypothesis.

At the same time, some contemporary researchers have looked for ways to reformulate the Sapir–Whorf hypothesis in the form of a more precise, testable hypothesis about the relationship between language, thought, and behavior. For example, John Lucy (1992) compared speakers of English and Yucatec Mayan to see if their languages led them to perform differently on tasks involving remembering and sorting objects. As predicted from the grammar of the languages, English speakers appeared to attend more closely to the number and also to the shape of the objects, while Mayan speakers paid less attention to number and more attention to the material from which the objects were made.

It is also true that specific languages contain the vocabulary needed to cope in particular environments. The need for a specific vocabulary in a society does not necessarily mean that language determines our perception of reality. After all, when a need to express some unlabeled phenomenon arises, speakers easily manufacture new words. English-speaking skiers, like Eskimos, distinguish among several types of snow, speaking of *powder, corn,* and so on.

Language may also influence social perception. For example, many women in English-speaking societies have long objected to the use of *man, men,* or *mankind* to refer to humanity, and *he* to refer to any person, male or female. They argue that the use of these masculine terms reinforces the idea that humanity is male and women are outsiders, the "second sex." Other gender-biased language occurs when words such as *lady* and *girl* are used in a demeaning manner to refer to women. In addition, the tradition of addressing females by the title Mrs. or Miss also reflects gender bias in English-speaking countries.

To help explain this, another linguistic anthropologist, M. J. Hardman-de-Bautista (1978), has formulated the notion of *linguistic postulates,* distinctions that are made obligatorily in language and that also reflect distinctions central to culture. For example, in English, biological sex is marked on the third-person singular pronouns (*she, he*). This distinction between female and male permeates English speaking culture in important ways—for example, in how children are socialized into appropriate behavior ("be a nice little girl; act like a lady; be a man," etc.). In the Aymara language of Peru and Bolivia, in contrast, the third-person pronoun is not marked for sex or number, so that Aymara *jupa* means "she/he/they." Instead, for Aymara, the relevant contrast is human versus nonhuman, and *jupa* cannot be used to refer to an animal, such as a dog or llama; instead, a different pronoun must be used. Aymara children are not taught to behave like "nice girls" or "good boys" but rather to behave "like human beings, not like animals."

To remedy gender biases, some people have tried to change their linguistic habits. They have adopted terms such as humankind, person, and Ms. Terms such as policeman and fireman have been changed to police officer and firefighter. The adoption of more neutral ways of expressing gender may affect perceptions of gender relations in these societies.

Historical Linguistics

Historical linguistics is the study of language change and the historical relationships among different languages. The research in historical linguistics tries to discover what kinds of changes occur in languages and why. Research on this subject began in the late eighteenth century when Sir William Jones, a British legal scholar, suggested that the linguistic similarities of Sanskrit, an ancient Indian tongue, to ancient Greek, Latin, German, and English indicate that all these languages were descended from a common ancestral language. It was discovered that all these languages are part of one family, the Indo-European family, and share certain words and grammar. For example, the English word *three* is *trayas* in Sanskrit, *tres* in Latin, *treis* in Greek, and *drei* in German (see Table 5.1). The similarity in Indo-European languages led some early anthropologists to conclude that all current languages could be traced to a single language family.

THE FAMILY-TREE MODEL

Modern historical linguists agree that they probably can never reconstruct the original language, but they still may be able to reach far back into history to reconstruct an early **protolanguage,** a parent language for many ancient and modern languages. Many linguists hold the view that all languages change in a regular, recognizable way and that similarities among languages are due to a historical relationship among these languages. In other words, people living in adjacent areas of the world would tend to share similar phonological, syntactical, and semantic features of their languages. For example, the Romance languages of French, Spanish, Portuguese, Italian, and Romanian developed from Latin because of the historic relationship with one another through the influence of the Roman Empire. This view is known as the *family-tree theory* of language change (see Figure 5.3).

Most recently, historical linguists have been working with archaeologists to reconstruct the Proto-Indo-European language. They have found that the Indo-European languages did spread within distinctive regions for certain societies. British archaeologist Colin Renfrew (1989) hypothesizes that the spread of the Indo-European languages was linked to the spread of a particular technology and material culture. He suggests that the Indo-European languages spread throughout Europe from an original homeland in Anatolia, today part of Turkey, as early cultures adopted in-

Table 5.1   Comparative Word Chart of Indo-European Languages

English	Sanskrit	Latin	Greek	German	Old English
To bear	Bhar	Ferre	Fero	Gebären	Beran
Father	Pitar	Pater	Patir	Vater	Fæder
Mother	Matar	Mater	Mitir	Mutter	Modor
Brother	Bhratar	Frater	Frater	Bruder	Brodor
Three	Trayas	Tres	Treis	Drei	Brie
Hundred	Sata	Centum	Ekaton	Hundert	Hund
Night	Nisitha	Noctis	Nikta	Nacht	Niht
Red	Rudhira	Ruber	Erithros	Rot	Read
Foot	Pàda	Pedis	Podos	Fuss	Fot
Fish	Piska	Piscis	Ikhthis	Fisch	Fisc
Goose	Hamsa	Anser	Khin	Gans	Gos
What	Kwo	Quod	Ti	Was	Hwæt
Where	Kva	Quo	Pou	Wo	Hwær

Source: Table from *The Way of Language: An Introduction* by Fred West, copyright ©1975 by Harcourt, Inc., reproduced by permission of the publisher.

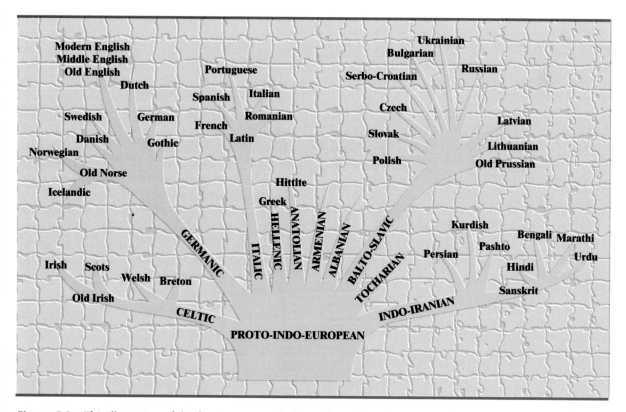

Figure 5.3 This illustration of the family-tree model shows the relationships among the various Indo-European languages.

tensive agriculture. Similarly, English is currently promoted throughout the world as the language of television, computers, and other features of Western technology.

ASSESSING LANGUAGE CHANGE

To reconstruct a family tree of languages, the linguist compares the phonological (sounds) and morphological (words) characteristics of different languages. Linguistic anthropologist Morris Swadesh (1964) developed a systematic method of assessing historical language change. His goal was to date the separation of languages from one another using a statistical technique known as *glottochronology* (from the Greek *glotta,* meaning "tongue," and *chronos,* meaning "time"). Swadesh reasoned that the vocabulary of a language would remain stable at some times but would change rapidly at others. Words for plants, animals, or technology would change quickly if the speakers migrated or came into contact with other groups. Swadesh thought, however, that a core vocabulary (words for pronouns and numbers, or for the body, earth, wood, and stone) would remain immune to cultural change. He thought that if we could measure the rate of retention of this core vocabulary, then we could measure the separation of one language from another.

By comparing core vocabularies from different languages, linguists found that on the average, 19 percent of this core vocabulary would change in a language in approximately 1,000 years. In other words, about 81 percent of the core vocabulary would be retained. From this formula, linguistic anthropologists have reconstructed languages and produced "family trees" of languages from around the world.

Through the study of language change, linguistic anthropologists have put to rest the idea that all current languages in the world can be traced to a single language family. Language change has been swift in some circumstances and gradual in others. *Multiple borrowings,* or the spread of vocabulary and grammar throughout the world, have affected most languages. Two linguistic researchers emphasize that many of the world's languages, including Russian, French, and English, have in their past development undergone radical change through *language mixing* (Thomason & Kaufman, 1988). In

this book the researchers claim that in the same way that many creole languages have emerged (discussed earlier in the chapter), other languages have developed through intensive culture contact. Instead of development of language from one source, there apparently are different centers and regions of language change.

Sociolinguistics

Linguistic anthropologists have researched the use of language in different social contexts, a field known as *sociolinguistics.* The sociolinguist takes the speech community as the framework for understanding the variation of speech in different social contexts. The speech community is a social unit within which speakers share various ways of speaking. For example, in American society certain patterns of English syntax and pronunciation are acceptable in specific contexts (American Standard English), whereas others are considered unacceptable. An American child may sometimes learn nonstandard words in the family environment, and, if the family considers them cute, the child may continue to use them. Eventually, however, the child moves out of the family into the larger speech community, encountering speech habits that differ from the home. If the child uses those words in school or with others, he or she will be reprimanded or laughed at.

Through a process of enculturation and socialization into the speech community, the child learns the language used in a variety of social contexts. Language plays a prominent role in the process of enculturation. American children learn the regional pronunciation and grammatical usages within their speech community.

DIALECTAL DIFFERENCES IN SPOKEN LANGUAGE

A speech community may consist of subgroups that share specific linguistic usages within a larger common language family. If the linguistic usages of these subgroups are different but mutually intelligible, their language variations are called dialects. **Dialects** are linguistic differences in pronunciation, vocabulary, or syntax that may differ within a single language. For example, dialectal differences in American Standard English exist within the Northeast, Midwest, South, and Southwest. In the southern United States, one might hear such grammatical items as "It wan't (or weren't) me," or pronunciation characteristics such as *Miz* for *Mrs.* and the frequent loss of *r* except before vowels: *foah* for *four, heah* for *hear,* and *sulfuh* for *sulfur* (West, 1975).

Certain dialects of English are looked on as more prestigious than others, reflecting educational, class, ethnic, race, and regional differences. When viewing language as a global phenomenon, however, all languages are dialects that have emerged in different locales and regions of the world. In actuality the English language is not one standard language but consists of many different dialects. To say that British English is more "correct" than American Standard English simply because England is the homeland of English does not make sense to a linguist. The forms of English spoken in England, Australia, Canada, the United States, India, South Africa, or the West Indies have distinctive differences in pronunciation and vocabulary. The same generalization can be applied to many languages and dialects.

Some linguists studying speech communities in the United States have concluded that specific regional dialects are gradually disappearing. As people move from one region to another for jobs and education, and as television and movies influence speech patterns, Americans are beginning to sound more alike (West, 1975). Through similar changes, many of the same processes are influencing different dialects and languages the world over.

HONORIFICS IN LANGUAGE

Sociolinguists have found that a number of languages contain honorific forms that determine the use of grammar, syntax, and other word usage. *Honorific forms of language* are used to express differences in social levels among speakers and are common in societies that maintain social inequality and hierarchy. Honorific forms can apply to the interaction between males and females, kin and nonkin, and higher- and lower-status individuals. For example, in many of the Pacific Island societies such as Hawaii, a completely separate honorific vocabulary was used when addressing a person who was part of the royal family. People of lower rank were not allowed to use these forms of language among themselves.

In the Thai language, a number of different types of honorific pronouns are used in various social contexts. Factors such as age, social rank, gender, education, officialdom, and royal title influence which pronouns are used. For example, the first-person pronoun *I* for a male is *phom,* a polite form of address between equals. The pronoun for *I* shifts to *kraphom* if a male is addressing a higher-ranking government official or a Buddhist monk. It shifts to *klaawkramom* when a male is addressing the prince of the royal family. All together there are thirteen different forms of the pronoun *I*. Similar differences exist for the other pronouns in Thai to express deference, politeness, and respect (Palakornkul, 1972; Scupin, 1989).

In the Japanese and Korean languages, honorific forms require speakers to distinguish among several different verb forms and address terms that indicate deference, politeness, or everyday speech. Different speech levels reflect age, gender, social position, and outgroupness (the degree to which a person is considered outside a particular social group) (Martin, 1964). Specifically, the Japanese distinguish between *tatemae* and *honne* in all of their linguistic expressions: *Tatemae* is a very polite form of expression used with strangers; *honne* is the expression of "real" feelings and can be used only with close friends and family.

GREETING BEHAVIORS

The exchange of greetings is the most ordinary, everyday use of language and gesture found universally. Yet sociolinguistic studies indicate that these routine greeting behaviors are considerably complex and produce different meanings in various social and cultural contexts. In many contexts English speakers in the United States greet one another with the word *Hi* or *Hello*. (The word *hello* originated from the English phrase *healthy be thou*.) Members of U.S. society also greet one another with questions such as "How are you?" or "How's it going?" or "What do you know?" In most contexts these questions are not considered serious questions, and these exchanges of greetings are accompanied by a wave or a nod, a smile, or other gesture of recognition. They are familiar phrases that are used as exchanges in greetings. These greetings require little thought and seem almost mechanical.

Among Muslim populations around the world the typical greeting between two males is the shaking of hands accompanied by the Arab utterance *As-salam ale-kum,* "May the peace of [Allah] be with you." This is the phrase used by Muslims even in non-Arabic speaking societies. The Qur'an, the sacred religious text of Muslims, has an explicit injunction regarding this mode of greeting for the male Muslim community (Caton, 1986). A similar greeting of *Scholem aleicham,* "May peace be with you," is found among the Jewish populace throughout the world. In some Southeast Asian societies such as Vietnam the typical greeting translates into English as "Have you eaten rice?"

All of the above greetings express a concern for another person's well-being. Although the English and Vietnamese greetings appear to be concerned with the physical condition of the person, whereas the Arab and Jewish phrases have a more spiritual connotation, they all essentially serve the same social purpose: They enable humans to interact in harmonious ways.

Yet there is a great deal more social information contained in these brief greeting exchanges than appears on the surface. For example, an English-speaking U.S. person can usually identify the different types of social contexts for the following greeting exchanges:

1. "Hi, Mr. Thomas!
   "Hello, Johnny. How are you?"
2. "Good morning, Monica."
   "Good morning, sir."
3. "Sarah! How are you? You look great!"
   "Bill! It's so good to see you!"
4. "Good evening, Congressman."
   "Hello there. Nice to see you."

In greeting 1. the speakers are an adult and child; in 2. there is a difference in status, and the speakers may be an employee and employer; in 3. these speakers are close acquaintances; in 4. the second speaker does not remember or know the other person very well (Hickerson, 1980).

The author of this text did a systematic sociolinguistic study of greeting behaviors found among different ethnic and religious groups in Thailand (Scupin, 1989). Precise cultural norms determine

Ethiopian Jewish males greeting each other. In many societies, males often greet each other with a kiss on the cheek.

the forms of greetings given to people of different status levels and ethnic groups. The traditional greeting of Thai Buddhists on meeting one another is expressed by each raising both hands, palm to palm, and lightly touching the body between the face and chest. Simultaneously, the person utters a polite verbal phrase. This salutation, known as the *waaj,* (pronounced "why"), varies in different social contexts. The person who is inferior in social status (determined by age and social class) initiates the *waaj,* and the higher the hands are raised, the greater the deference and politeness expressed. For example, a young child will *waaj* a superior by placing the fingertips above the eyebrows, whereas a superior returning a *waaj* will raise the fingertips only to the chest. A superior seldom performs a *waaj* when greeting someone of an inferior status. Other ethnic and religious groups such as the Muslims in Thailand use the *waaj* in formal interactions with Thai Buddhists, but among themselves they use the traditional Muslim greeting described previously.

Another form of Thai greeting found among Buddhists includes the kraab, which involves kneeling down and bowing to the floor in conjunction with the *waaj* in expressing respect to a superior political or religious official. The *kraab* is used to greet a high-ranking member of the royal family, a Buddhist monk, respected officials, and, traditionally, one's parents (Anuman-Rajadhon, 1961). These deferential forms of greetings are found in other societies that maintain social hierarchies based on royal authority, political, or religious principles.

Though greeting behaviors differ from one society to another, anthropologists find that all peoples throughout the world have a means to greet one another to establish a basis for social interaction and demonstrate their concern for one another's welfare.

Nonverbal Communication

In interacting with other people, we use nonverbal cues as well as speech. As with language, nonverbal communication varies in human populations, in contrast to the nonverbal communication of nonhuman animals. Dogs, cats, and other animals have

no difficulty communicating with one another in nonverbal ways. Human nonverbal communication, however, is extremely varied. It is often said that humans are the only creatures who can misunderstand one another.

KINESICS

Some anthropological linguists study gestures and other forms of body language. The study of **kinesics** is concerned with body motion and gestures used in nonverbal communication. Researchers estimate that humans use more than 250,000 facial expressions. Many of these expressions have different meanings in different circumstances. For example, the smile indicates pleasure, happiness, or friendliness in all parts of the world. Yet in certain contexts, a smile may signify an insult (Birdwhistle, 1970). Thus, the movement of the head, eyes, eyebrows, and hands or the posture of the body may be associated with specific symbolic meanings that are culturally defined.

Many types of nonverbal communication differ from society to society. Americans point to things with their fingers, whereas other peoples point with only their eyes, their chin, or their head. Shaking our head up and down means "yes" and from side to side means "no," but in parts of India, Greece, and Turkey the opposite is true. An "A-OK" sign in the United States or England means "you are all right," but it means "you are worth zero" in France or Belgium, and it is a very vulgar sign in Greece and Turkey (Ekman et al., 1984). Pointing to your head means "he or she is smart" in the United States, whereas it means "stupid" in Europe. The "V" sign of the 1960s meant "peace"; in contrast, in World War II England it meant "victory." In Greece it is an insult. Obviously humans can easily misunderstand each other because of the specific cultural meanings of nonverbal gestures.

Despite all these differences, however, research has revealed certain universal features associated with some facial expressions. For example, research by psychologist Paul Ekman and his colleagues suggests that there are some basic uniformities regarding certain facial expressions. Peoples from various societies recognize facial expressions indicating emotional states such as happiness, grief, disgust, fear, surprise, and anger. Ekman studied peoples re-

Some human facial expressions are based on universally recognized emotions.

cently contacted by Western society, such as the Fore people of Papua New Guinea (Ekman, 1973). When shown photos of facial expressions, the Fore had no difficulty determining the basic emotions that were being expressed. This research overlaps with the psychological anthropology studies of emotions discussed in the previous chapter. Ekman has concluded that some universal emotional expressions are evident in certain facial displays of humans throughout the world.

PROXEMICS

Another nonverbal aspect of communication involves the use of space. **Proxemics** is the study of how people in different societies perceive and use space. Studies by Edward T. Hall (1981) indicate

that no universal rules apply to the use of space. In American society, people maintain a different "personal space" in different situations. We communicate with our intimate acquaintances at a range of about 18 inches; however, with nonintimates our space expands according to how well we know the person. In some other societies people communicate at very close distances irrespective of the relationship among them.

Nonverbal communication is an important aspect of social interaction. Obvious gestural movements, such as bowing in Japan and shaking hands in the United States, may have a deep symbolic significance in certain contexts. The study of nonverbal communication will enrich our understanding of human behavior and might even improve communication among different societies.

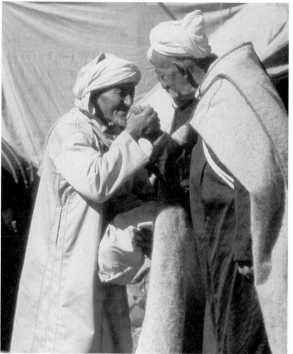

When communicating, Arab males stand at a closer distance to each other than do U.S. males.

⟳ SUMMARY

Language is a vital component of human cultural knowledge. It is the most important means of expressing and transmitting symbols and culture from one person to another. Language is the major means of communication for humans. A great deal of laboratory and field research is shedding light on how the closest related species to humans, the apes, can learn sophisticated sign communication.

Linguists have focused on some specific criteria that distinguish human languages from animal communication. All human languages have certain features such as productivity, displacement, arbitrariness, and combining sounds that set them apart from animal communication systems.

Linguistic anthropologists study the structure of language by studying sound patterns (phonology), the meaning of words (morphology), and how these meaningful units are put together in phrases and sentences (syntax). They also focus on the meaning (semantics) of different terms used to classify reality. Although there are many differ-

ences in how people in various societies use terms to describe kinship relations and physical phenomena, linguistic anthropologists have found some universals, such as the way people classify basic color terms. This suggests that humans have common biological capacities that determine how they perceive certain aspects of reality.

Linguistic anthropologists are interested in how language is acquired as an aspect of the enculturation process. The behaviorist model suggests that language is learned through positive and negative conditioning. In contrast, linguist Noam Chomsky suggests that all humans use an innate, or genetically encoded, capability for learning complicated syntax and grammar. Chomsky's model has led to research on languages such as creole languages.

Another topic explored in linguistic anthropology is the relationship among language, thought, and culture. An early hypothesis, known as the Sapir–Whorf hypothesis, suggested that language acts as a filter for the classification and perception of reality. This is known as linguistic relativism.

In reexamining the Sapir–Whorf hypothesis, anthropologists have concluded that the hypothesis exaggerates the extent to which language determines the perception of time, space, and other aspects of reality. Most modern anthropologists do not accept an extreme form of linguistic relativism as proposed by Sapir and Whorf's students.

Historical linguistics is the study of how languages are related to one another and how they have diverged from one another. Linguistic anthropologists have examined the historical relationships among languages. This research has helped understand the process of language change.

Sociolinguistics focuses on the relationship between language and society. Sociolinguists exam-

ine social interactions and the ways in which people use certain linguistic expressions that reflect the dialect patterns of their speech community. Researchers have found that many languages have nuances in linguistic usage such as greeting patterns or speech differences that vary according to age, gender, and status.

The study of nonverbal communication is also a rich field for linguistic anthropology. Although much nonverbal communication varies around the world, some forms can be understood universally. Anthropologists focus on the use of body language (kinesics) and the use of space (proxemics) to understand better how people supplement their spoken-language skills with nonverbal communication.

STUDY QUESTIONS

1. Suppose you are studying chimp communication. What are the limitations that you will have in teaching the chimps a human language?

2. Give some examples of unique human linguistic abilities.

3. Provide some examples of phonemes, morphemes, syntax, and semantic aspects of language.

4. Do you agree with Skinner's or Chomsky's view of language learning? Why?

5. Can you think of any ways in which language influences culture, or vice-versa?

6. What types of body language or gestures are universally understood?

KEY TERMS

communication	morphemes	protolanguage
dialects	morphology	proxemics
ethologists	phoneme	Sapir–Whorf hypothesis
kinesics	phones	semantics
language	phonology	syntax
linguistic relativism		

INTERNET EXERCISES

1. Refer to the Ethnologue website found at **http://www.sil.org/ethnologue/ethnologue. html.** Click on the Geographic Distribution of Living Languages link under Contents. How many living languages are there? Why do you think that there is such an unequal distribution of languages? What historical and geographical factors may have led to this modern distribution?

2. As you explore the Ethnologue site at **http://www.sil.org/ethnologue/top100.html,** list the languages with which you are unfamiliar. Next, click on the three letter code for English [ENG]. How many countries speak English? Why so many?

SUGGESTED READINGS

CAVILLI-SFORZA, LUIGI LUCA, AND FRANCESCO CAVILLI-SFORZA. 1995. *The Great Human Diasporas: The History and Evolution*. New York: Addison-Wesley Publishing. A broad overview of the migrations of peoples and languages since the beginnings of humankind. This book combines genetic research and biology with historical linguistics to examine human migrations up to the present.

CHOMSKY, NOAM. 1968. *Language and Mind*. New York: Harcourt, Brace & World. One of the primary texts by this innovative thinker, who changed the direction of linguistic research. This text is a highly philosophical critique of behaviorist approaches to understanding language.

CLARK, VIRGINIA P., PAUL A. ESCHHOLZ, AND ALFRED F. ROSA, eds. 1981. *Language: Introductory Readings,* 3d ed. New York: St. Martin's Press. A comprehensive collection of useful contemporary essays based on research by linguists in many fields.

FARB, PETER. 1975. *Word Play: What Happens When People Talk*. New York: Bantam Books. A highly entertaining book on language by the late Peter Farb, a writer by profession and an anthropologist and linguist by avocation.

HYMES, DELL, ed. 1964. *Language in Culture and Society: A Reader in Linguistics and Anthropology*. New York: Harper & Row. The standard anthology of essays containing classic articles in the field of linguistic anthropology.

PINKER, STEVEN. 1994. *The Language Instinct: How the Mind Creates Language*. New York: HarperCollins Press. A highly readable account of the latest research in linguistic research.

TRUDGILL, PETER. 1983. *Sociolinguistics: An Introduction to Language and Society*. New York: Penguin Books. A popular introduction to the field of sociolinguistics by a British linguist.

WEST, FRED. 1975. *The Way of Language: An Introduction*. New York: Harcourt Brace Jovanovich. A concise introduction to linguistics for the general reader. It covers all of the major topics that linguists study, ranging from the evolution of language to sociolinguistics.

Anthropological
Explanations

CHAPTER OUTLINE

Nineteenth-Century Evolutionism
Unilineal Evolution: Tylor / Unilineal Evolution: Morgan / Unilineal Evolution: A Critique

Diffusionism
British Diffusionism / German Diffusionism / The Limitations and Strengths of Diffusionism

Historical Particularism
Boas versus the Unilineal Evolutionists

Functionalism: British Anthropology
Structural Functionalism: Radcliffe-Brown / Psychological Functionalism: Malinowski / The Limitations of Functionalism

Twentieth-Century Evolutionism
Steward and Cultural Ecology / The Strengths of Neoevolutionism / Criticisms of Cultural Ecology

Cultural Materialism

Marxist Anthropology
Evaluation of Marxist Anthropology

Sociobiology
A Case Study: Sexual Behavior / Inclusive Fitness and Kin Selection / Sociobiology: A Critique

Symbolic Anthropology
Criticisms of Symbolic Anthropology

Materialism versus Culturalism

CHAPTER QUESTIONS

- What are the basic differences between the nineteenth-century and twentieth-century theoretical approaches in anthropology?

- What are the basic strengths and weaknesses of the various theories in anthropology?

IN CHAPTER 1 WE DISCUSSED THE SCIENTIFIC method and its application to anthropology. In that discussion we noted how anthropologists collect and classify data and then develop and test hypotheses. In the physical sciences scientists use these hypotheses to formulate theories from which they make predictions about natural phenomena. Chemists can rely on precise mathematical laws to help them deduce and predict what will happen when two chemical elements interact with one another. Physicists can predict from laws of gravity and motion what will happen when a spherical object is dropped from a building at a certain speed. These types of predictions allow engineers to produce aircraft that use certain fuels and withstand certain physical pressures, enabling them to fly long distances.

Although anthropology relies on the scientific method, its major objective is to provide explanations of human society and behavior. Human behavior is extremely complicated. The product of many different, interacting variables, it can seldom, if ever, be predicted. Anthropologists cannot predict the outcome of interactions between two individuals or among small groups, let alone among large groups at the societal level. Consequently, anthropology as a discipline does not have any specific theories and laws that can be used to predict human action or thought. For the most part, anthropologists restrict their efforts to testing hypotheses and improving their explanations of human society and behavior.

Nineteenth-Century Evolutionism

Modern anthropology emerged from the intellectual atmosphere of the Enlightenment, an eighteenth-century philosophical movement that stressed social progress based on human reason, and Darwin's theory of evolution. The first professional anthropologist—that is, an individual appointed to an academic position of anthropology—was a nineteenth-century British scholar, Edward B. Tylor. In 1871 Tylor published a major work titled *Primitive Culture*. At that time, Great Britain was involved in imperialistic expansion all over the world. Tylor thus had access to descriptions of non-Western societies through his contacts with travelers, explorers, missionaries, traders, and government officials. He combined these descriptions with nineteenth-century philosophy and Charles Darwin's ideas to develop a theory of societal evolution.

UNILINEAL EVOLUTION: TYLOR

The major question addressed by early anthropologists was, Why are societies at similar or different levels of evolution and development? Tylor tried to answer that question through an explanation known as unilineal evolution. **Unilineal evolution** is the view that societies evolve in a single direction toward complexity, progress, and civilization. Tylor's basic argument was that because all humans are bestowed with innate rational faculties, they are continuously improving their societies. Through this process of evolution societies move toward "progress" and "civilization."

In arriving at this conclusion, Tylor used accounts from Western observers to compare certain cultural elements from different societies, including technology, family, economy, political organization, art, religion, and philosophy. He then organized this evidence into categories or stages ranging from what he termed "savagery" to "barbarism" to "civilization," categories reflecting the unilineal evolutionary views of the nineteenth century. Theorists assumed that hunter-gatherers and other non-Western societies were living at a lower level of existence than were the "civilized" societies of Europe. This was an ethnocentric view of societal development based on the belief that Western society is the center of the civilized world and that non-Western societies are inherently inferior.

Tylor and other nineteenth-century thinkers also claimed that "primitives" would eventually evolve through the stages of barbarism to become civilized like British gentlemen and ladies. However, Tylor believed that these societies would need some assistance from the civilized world to reach this stage.

UNILINEAL EVOLUTION: MORGAN

Another nineteenth-century anthropologist who developed a unilineal scheme of evolution was an American, Lewis Henry Morgan (1818–1881). Mor-

gan was a lawyer and banker who became fascinated with Native American societies. He gathered information on the customs, language, and other aspects of the culture of the Iroquois of upstate New York. Eventually, under the auspices of the Smithsonian Institution, he distributed questionnaires to missionaries and travelers to collect information about many other non-Western societies.

Morgan and Kinship Theories   Morgan was particularly interested in kinship terms used in different parts of the world. He observed that the Iroquois kinship terms were very different from those of English, Latin, Greek, and other European societies. He also noticed that these kinship terms were similar to those of the Ojibwa Indians, a group living in the midwestern United States. This led him to explore the relationship between the Iroquois and other peoples. Using the aforementioned questionnaires, he requested specific information on kinship terms from people all over the world.

From this data, Morgan began to conceive of the evolution of the family in a worldwide sense. He speculated that humans originally lived in "primitive hordes," in which sexual behavior was not regulated and individuals didn't know who their fathers were. He based this assumption on the discovery that certain peoples, such as Hawaiians, use one general term to classify their father and all male relatives in their father's generation. He postulated that brother-sister marriage then developed, followed by group marriage, and eventually a matriarchal family structure in which women held economic and political power. Morgan believed that the final stage of the evolution of the family began when males took control of the economy and politics, instituting a patriarchal system.

In addition to exploring the evolution of the family, Morgan, like Tylor, surveyed technological, economic, political, and religious conditions throughout the world. He compiled this evidence in his book *Ancient Society* ([1877] 1964), which presented his overall scheme of the evolution of society. Paralleling Tylor's views, Morgan believed in a hierarchy of evolutionary development from "savagery" to "civilization."

According to Morgan, one crucial distinction between civilized society and earlier societies is private property. He described the "savage" societies as "communistic," in contrast to "civilized" societies, whose institutions are based on private property.

UNILINEAL EVOLUTION: A CRITIQUE

Although these nineteenth-century thinkers shared the view that humanity was progressing through various stages of development, their views were ethnocentric, contradictory, and speculative and their evidence secondhand, based on the accounts of biased Europeans. The unilineal scheme of evolution was much too simplistic to account for the development of different societies.

In general, the unilineal evolutionists relied on nineteenth-century racist views of human development and misunderstandings of biological evolution to explain societal differences. For example, both Morgan and Tylor believed that people in various societies have different levels of intelligence. They believed that the people in so-called savage societies have less intelligence than those in "civilized societies." This view of intelligence is no longer accepted by the scientific community. Nevertheless, despite their inadequate theories and speculations regarding the evolution of society, these early anthropologists provided the first systematic methods for thinking about and explaining the similarities and diversity of human societies.

Diffusionism

Another school of thought that used the comparative method to explain why different societies are at different levels of development was diffusionism. **Diffusionism,** which developed in the early part of the twentieth century, maintains that societal change occurs when societies borrow cultural traits from one another. Cultural knowledge regarding technology, economic ideas, religious views, or art forms spreads, or diffuses, from one society to another. There were two major schools of diffusionism: the British version associated with G. Elliot Smith and William J. Perry, and the German version associated with Father Wilhelm Schmidt.

BRITISH DIFFUSIONISM

The British school of diffusionism derived its theory from research on ancient Egypt. Smith and Perry were specialists in Egyptian culture and had carried out research in Egyptology for a number of years. From this experience they concluded that all aspects of civilizations, from technology to religion, originated in Egypt and diffused to other cultural areas. To explain the fact that some cultures no longer had cultural traits from Egypt, they resorted to an ethnocentric view, maintaining that some cultures had simply become "degenerate." That is, in contrast to the civilized world, the lesser developed peoples had simply forgotten the original ideas borrowed from Egypt.

GERMAN DIFFUSIONISM

The German school of diffusionism differed somewhat from that of the British. Schmidt and his followers argued that *several* early centers of civilization had existed and that from these early centers cultural traits diffused outward in circles to other regions and peoples. In German this view is referred to as the *Kulturkreise* (culture circles) school of thought. In explaining why some primitive societies did not have the characteristics of civilization, the German school, like the British diffusionists, argued that these peoples had simply degenerated. Thus, diffusionist views, like the unilineal evolutionary views, represent ethnocentric perspectives of human societies outside the mainstream of Western civilization.

THE LIMITATIONS AND STRENGTHS OF DIFFUSIONISM

Early diffusionist views were based on erroneous assumptions regarding humankind's innovative capacities. Like the unilineal theorists, they maintained racist assumptions about the inherent inferiority of different non-Western peoples. The diffusionists assumed that some people were not sufficiently innovative to develop their own cultural traits.

Another limitation of the diffusionist approach is its assumption that cultural traits in the same geographical vicinity will inevitably spread from one society to another. Anthropologists find that diffusion is not an inevitable process. Societies can adjoin one another without exchanging cultural traits. For example, as we saw in Chapter 3 generations of Amish people in the United States have deliberately maintained their traditional ways despite being part of a nation in which modern technology is predominant.

However, diffusionism as a means of understanding societal development does have some validity. For example, diffusionism helps explain the emergence of the classical civilizations of Egypt, Greece, Phoenicia, and Rome. These peoples maintained continuous contact through trade and travel, borrowing many cultural traits from one another, such as writing systems.

Historical Particularism

An early twentieth-century movement that developed in response to the unilineal evolutionary theory was led by the U.S. anthropologist Franz Boas, whom we discussed in Chapter 3. This movement proposed an alternative answer to why societal similarities and differences exist. Boas was educated in Germany as a natural scientist. Eventually he conducted fieldwork among the Eskimo in northern Canada, and a Native American people known as the Kwakiutl, who lived on the Northwest Coast. He later solidified his position as the nation's foremost leader in anthropology at Columbia University in New York, where he trained many pioneers in the field until his retirement in 1937. Boas had a tremendous impact on the development of anthropology in the United States and internationally.

BOAS VERSUS THE UNILINEAL EVOLUTIONISTS

Boas became a vigorous opponent of the unilineal evolutionists. He criticized their attempts to propose stages of evolution through which all societies evolve. He also criticized their use of the comparative method and the haphazard manner in which they organized the data to fit their theories of evolutionary stages. He maintained that these nineteenth-century schemes of evolution were based on insufficient empirical evidence. Boas called for an end to "armchair anthropology," in which scholars took data from travelers, traders, and missionaries and plugged these data into a speculative model of evolution. He proposed that all anthropologists do rigorous, scientifically based fieldwork to collect basic ethnographic data.

Portrait of Franz Boas.

Boas's fieldwork experience and his intellectual training in Germany led him to conclude that each society has its own unique historical development. This theory, known as **historical particularism,** maintains that each society must be understood as a product of its own history. This view led Boas to adopt the notion of *cultural relativism,* the belief that each society should be understood in terms of its own cultural practices and values (see Chapter 3). One aspect of this view is that no society evolved higher or lower than another. Thus, we cannot rank any particular society above another in terms of degree of savagery, barbarity, or civility. Boas called for an end to the use of these derogatory, ethnocentric terms.

The Boasian view became the dominant theoretical trend in anthropology during the first half of the twentieth century. Anthropologists began to do ethnological fieldwork in different societies to gather sound empirical evidence. Boas instituted the participant-observer method as a basic research strategy of ethnographic fieldwork (see Chapter 1). This strategy enabled ethnologists to gather valid empirical data to explain human behavior. Boas also encouraged his students to develop their linguistic skills so that they could learn the languages of the peoples they studied.

Boas worked in all four subfields of anthropology: physical anthropology, archaeology, ethnology, and linguistics. As we saw in Chapter 3, some of his most important work involved taking precise assessments of the physical characteristics, including brain size and cranial capacity, of people in different societies. Boas was one of the first scientists in the United States to demonstrate that brain size and cranial capacities of modern humans are not linked directly to intelligence. His research indicated that brain size and cranial capacity differ widely within all races. Boas's findings challenged the racist assumptions put forward by the unilineal evolutionists. They also repudiated the type of racism that characterized black-white relations in the United States, as well as Nazi theories of racial superiority.

A direct outgrowth of the Boasian approach was the emergence of *culture-and-personality theory* in American anthropology. Boas trained two particularly noteworthy students, Ruth Benedict and Margaret Mead, pioneering anthropologists whose research is described in Chapter 4. The anthropological school represented by Benedict and Mead led to the development of more careful research regarding personality and culture. The methods used in this field have been refined and tested by many anthropologists (Barnouw, 1985). As a result, we now have a better understanding of enculturation and personality formation in human societies.

Functionalism: British Anthropology

At approximately the same time that Boas and his U.S. students were questioning the claims of the unilineal evolutionists, British anthropologists were developing their own criticisms through the school of thought known as functionalism. **Functionalism** is the view that society consists of institutions that serve vital purposes for people. Instead of focusing on the origins and evolution of society, as the unilineal theorists did, the British functionalists explored the relationships among different institutions and how these institutions function to serve society or the individual. The question of whether these institutions serve the interests of society at large or the interests of the individual person divided the school of functionalism into two camps, each associated with a prominent figure in British anthropology: A. R. Radcliffe-Brown and Bronislaw Malinowski.

STRUCTURAL FUNCTIONALISM: RADCLIFFE-BROWN

The type of functionalism associated with Radcliffe-Brown is sometimes referred to as *structural functionalism*. Radcliffe-Brown had done research in Africa and on the Andaman Islands in southeastern Asia. He focused on the structure of society as reflected in the differing institutions that function to perpetuate the survival of society. He argued that a society's economic, social, political, and religious institutions serve to integrate the society as a whole. For example, he studied the social institutions that function to enhance group solidarity in small-scale societies. In some of his studies he emphasized how males had to marry outside their particular group into another group. Once the male marries, he establishes an important relationship with his wife's kin. Because he is an outsider, he has to show extreme respect to his new in-laws, so that he does not produce hostility. He may also establish a "joking relationship" with them, whereby hostility is reduced by playful teasing. Radcliffe-Brown suggested that all norms for specific behaviors and obligations among different people in kinship relationships promote order and stability. Thus, to Radcliffe-Brown, these social institutions serve society's needs.

PSYCHOLOGICAL FUNCTIONALISM: MALINOWSKI

Malinowski's functionalism differed from that of Radcliffe-Brown in that it focused on how society functions to serve the *individual's* interests or needs. This view is known as *psychological functionalism*. Malinowski did his major ethnographic study in the Trobriand Islands off the coast of Papua New Guinea. He tried to demonstrate how individuals use cultural norms to satisfy certain needs.

Malinowski's analysis of magic among the Trobriand islanders illustrates his psychological functionalism. He observed that when the islanders

Bronislaw Malinowski.

went fishing in enclosed lagoons where fishing was reliable and safe, they depended on their technical knowledge and skill alone. When they went fishing on the open sea, however, which was more dangerous and highly unpredictable, they employed extensive magical beliefs and techniques. Thus, Malinowski argued that the use of magic arises in situations in which humans have no control over circumstances, such as weather conditions. Magical techniques are used to reduce internal anxieties and tensions for these individuals. In addition to magic, the Trobrianders have an elaborate system of beliefs concerning death, the afterlife, sickness, and health. These beliefs aid in serving the needs of individuals as they adapt to the circumstances and exigencies of life. In other words, the individual has needs, both physiological and psychological, and cultural institutions, customs, and traditions exist to satisfy them.

THE LIMITATIONS OF FUNCTIONALISM

Like the other early developments in anthropology, functionalism has its theoretical weaknesses. It fails to explain why societies are different or similar. Why do some societies have different types of institutions when similar ones might be able to fill the same function? This weakness arose from the tendency of functionalists to ignore historical proc-

esses. They were not concerned with the historical development of differing institutions but rather focused exclusively on how these institutions serve society and the individual. They could not explain, for example, why British society experienced rapid technological change whereas other societies did not, when all of these societies had similar needs.

Functionalists were also unable to explain social and cultural change very well, because they tended to view societies as static and unchanging. They could not explain why if all institutions perform a particular function these institutions would need to change.

Functionalism as a school of thought has influenced a great deal of research in anthropology, however. By focusing on the detailed, specific functions of institutions within existing societies, it encouraged the collection of valuable ethnographic data. As with Boas in U.S. anthropology, Radcliffe-Brown and Malinowski moved their field beyond the speculative theories of the "armchair anthropologists."

Twentieth-Century Evolutionism

After World War II some anthropologists renewed their interest in evolutionary explanations of societal and cultural phenomena. Up until that time most anthropologists had devoted themselves to criticizing the unilineal evolutionists. But some anthropologists, led by Leslie White of the University of Michigan, suggested a new twentieth-century perspective on the evolution of society, which is sometimes referred to as *neoevolutionism.*

White treated societies, or *sociocultural systems,* as entities that evolved in relation to the amount of energy captured and used by each member of society. This energy is directed toward the production of resources for their survival. In White's words, "Culture evolves as the amount of energy harnessed per capita per year is increased, or as the efficiency of the instrumental means of putting the energy to work is increased" ([1949] 1971: 368). In other words, the degree of societal development is measured by the amount of energy harnessed by these sociocultural systems. The greater the energy, the more highly evolved the sociocultural system.

White's hypothesis of cultural evolution explained the differences in levels of societal development by examining differences in technology and energy production. For example, he hypothesized that small-scale hunting-and-gathering societies had not developed complex sociocultural systems because they depended primarily on human energy for production. Because of a limited energy source for producing resources, their societies were simple, meager, and undeveloped. But following the agricultural revolution and the capture of energy through the domestication of plants and animals, sociocultural systems changed dramatically. The agricultural revolution represented an efficient use of human energy in harnessing new energy reserves, such as using draft animals to pull plows. In turn, these technological changes led to the emergence of cities, complex states, powerful political and religious elites, and new ideologies.

According to White, tracing the modern industrial age, as fossil-fuel technology developed, new forms of energy such as coal, oil, and natural gas were used, and sociocultural changes accelerated. Up until the Industrial Revolution, the changes in agricultural societies had been gradual, taking several thousand years. In contrast, the Industrial Revolution has taken less than two hundred years to produce widespread global transformations. Because White focused on sociocultural change on the global level rather than on particular societies, his approach has been called *general evolution*.

STEWARD AND CULTURAL ECOLOGY

At about the same period of time, anthropologist Julian Steward turned his attention to the evolution of society. Steward was instrumental in establishing the field of *cultural ecology*. Also called *ecological anthropology,* cultural ecology stresses the interrelationship among the natural conditions in the environment—rainfall, temperature, soils—and technology, social organization, and attitudes within a particular sociocultural system. Steward focused on how specific sociocultural systems adapt to environmental conditions.

Steward's cultural-ecology framework divides sociocultural systems into two different spheres: the culture core and secondary features. The *culture core* consists of those elements most closely related to subsistence—the environment, technol-

ogy, and economic arrangements. The other characteristics, such as social organization, politics, and religion, constitute secondary features of society. Because Steward investigated the detailed characteristics of different environments, his approach is referred to as *specific evolution,* as opposed to White's general evolution. One of his most illustrative case studies involved the Shoshone Indians of the Great Basin of the western United States.

A Case Study: The Shoshone The Shoshone were hunter-gatherer groups whose society revolved around gathering seeds, pine nuts, roots, and berries, and hunting rabbits and antelopes. Steward discovered that these subsistence activities had definite effects on the organization of Shoshone kinship groups. Like all hunter-gatherer societies, the Shoshone were nomadic, moving from one location to another based on the availability of food. The Shoshone lived in a hot and dry desert environment that supported meager supplies of plants and animals. These people were forced to live in small, elementary family units and travel frequently in search of food. For a few months in the winter, however, they could live in larger social groups among interrelated family units because of the supply of pine nuts in the mountains. Thus, the environment and the availability of resources had a definite influence on the form of social organization during different seasons for these hunter-gatherer societies.

Through cases like this Steward demonstrated how environmental influences (part of the culture core) affect the cultural developments in a sociocultural system. Steward used this approach to examine the agricultural civilizations of South America, Mesoamerica, the Near East, and the Far East. He found remarkable parallels in the evolution of these different civilizations. They all had irrigation systems, specialized occupations, centralized governments, and formalized state religions. Steward emphasized that many of these parallels were the result of similar environmental conditions, such as river valleys and alluvial plains that offered opportunities for the emergence of agricultural civilizations.

THE STRENGTHS OF NEOEVOLUTIONISM

The twentieth-century evolutionists differed from the nineteenth-century evolutionists in several ways. First, they did not assume a unilineal direction of society through formalized stages such as savagery, barbarism, and civilization. Second, they were not ethnocentrically biased or racist when it came to understanding why different societies are at various levels of development. They abandoned crude terms such as "savagery" and explored environment, technology, and energy resources in assessing levels of sociocultural development. Third, they did not assume that sociocultural evolution toward complexity (or "civilization") is always equated with "progress," as did the nineteenth-century theorists. The neoevolutionists held that some aspects of small-scale societies are in fact better than those of complex societies. For example, in some respects family and social relationships tend to be more stable in small-scale societies than in large, complex societies.

Cultural ecology has become an extremely sophisticated area of research. It has been influenced by developments in biological ecology and theories derived from mathematics, computer modeling, and related sciences. Cultural ecologists do careful research on energy expenditures, use of resources, exchanges of nutrients, population, and interrelations among these factors and with cultural values. As we will see in later chapters, the research findings of ecological anthropology help to explain sociocultural similarities and differences.

CRITICISMS OF CULTURAL ECOLOGY

A number of anthropologists have criticized the cultural-ecology approach for a variety of reasons. Some critics claim that in emphasizing the role of the environment, cultural ecologists do not take into account historical or political factors (Geertz, 1963a; Friedman, 1974; Keesing, 1981; Hefner, 1983). Thus, for example, cultural ecologists can explain how Shoshone culture represents an adaptation to a desert environment, but they cannot explain how or why the Shoshone came to reside in an environment with scarce resources. An explanation of this kind would require detailed historical research examining local and global political factors.

Another criticism is that cultural ecology reduces human behavior to simple adaptations to the external environment. Because of the emphasis on adaptation, cultural ecologists tend to view every cultural element as the best of all possible solutions to the problems of subsistence and energy re-

quirements. In fact, many sociocultural adaptations may involve compromises at the time that turn out later to be maladaptations.

For example, a number of cultural ecologists have used their models to explain the development of warfare in different societies. Some hypothesize that warfare is associated with land ownership, population size, and resource shortages (Vayda, 1961; Sweet, 1965; Meggitt, 1977). As populations expand in areas with scarce resources, societies resort to warfare to secure additional resources and thereby restore stability to the sociocultural system. Critics suggest that this explanation ignores various historical, political, and cultural factors that contribute to warfare, such as conflicting political or religious ideologies. Furthermore, they suggest that this is an extreme form of adaptationism. In most cases, warfare is definitely maladaptive.

Cultural Materialism

The theoretical view known as cultural materialism was developed by anthropologist Marvin Harris as a direct extension of twentieth-century evolutionism and cultural ecology. **Cultural materialism** is the research strategy that focuses on technology, environment, and economic factors as key determinants in sociocultural evolution. Cultural materialists divide all sociocultural systems into *infrastructure, structure,* and *superstructure.* The infrastructure includes the technology and the practices used for expanding or limiting the production of basic resources such as food, clothing, and shelter. The structure consists of the domestic economy (family structure, domestic division of labor, age and gender roles) and the political economy (political organization, class, castes, police, military). The superstructure includes philosophy, art, music, religion, ideas, literature, advertising, sports, games, science, and values.

According to cultural-materialist theory, the infrastructure largely determines the structure and superstructure of sociocultural systems. As the infrastructure changes, the structure and superstructure may change accordingly. Technology, energy, and environmental factors are crucial to the development of all aspects of society. All societies must devise ways to obtain food and shelter, and they must possess an adequate technology and energy to provide for the survival and continuity of the population. Although cultural materialists do not deny that superstructural and structural components of society may influence cultural evolution, they see infrastructural factors as being far more important. This theoretical perspective represents an extension of the foundations laid down by White and Steward.

Marxist Anthropology

Another major theoretical perspective in anthropology stems directly from the writings of Karl Marx (1818–1883). Though most of Marx's writings focus on capitalist societies, he also produced a broad evolutionary scheme of societal development throughout the world. Basing some of his notions on Lewis Henry Morgan's evolutionary thought, Marx theorized that society had evolved through various stages: the tribal, the Asiatic, the feudal, and, finally, the capitalist stage. Having advanced this far, these societies would then proceed to the socialist and communist stages.

An Indian farmer working his fields. Marx believed that societies evolved through stages such as the Asiatic, in which the land was cultivated by peasant farmers.

Marx's approach is a form of materialism because it emphasizes how the systems of producing material goods shape all of society. Marx argued that the mode of production in material life determines the general character of the social, political, and spiritual processes of life ([1859] 1959).

Unlike the functionalist anthropologists, who focused on the maintenance of order and stability in society, Marx believed that society is in a state of constant change as a result of class struggles and conflicts among groups within society. Writing at the time of early industrialization and capitalism in Europe, he viewed these developments as causes of exploitation, inequality in wealth and power, and class struggle.

According to Marx, the industrial mode of production had divided society into classes of capitalists, those who own the means of production (the factories), and the proletariat (the workers), those who sell their labor to the owners as a commodity. The capitalist class exploits the labor of workers to produce a surplus for their own profits. This exploitation leads to harsh working conditions and extremely low wages for the proletariat class. This social arrangement sets the stage for a class struggle between these opposing segments of society. Marx suggested that all the major social and cultural transformations since the Industrial Revolution could be seen as a result of this class conflict.

EVALUATION OF MARXIST ANTHROPOLOGY

It must be emphasized that current Marxist anthropologists do not accept the unilineal model of evolution suggested by Marx. For example, most Marxist anthropologists recognize that Marx's prediction regarding the evolution of socialist and communist stages of society from the capitalist stage is wrong. Historically, socialist and communist revolutions occurred in the former Soviet Union and China, which were by no means industrial-capitalist societies. The industrial societies that Marx had focused on, such as Great Britain and Germany, did not develop into what Marx conceived of as socialist or communist societies.

Nevertheless, modern Marxist anthropologists view as valid Marx's analytical approach to understanding societal development and some of the inherent problems of capitalist society. His critical perspective on the institutions of society, modes of production, and the results of group conflict has inspired many fruitful hypotheses regarding social and cultural evolution and development.

Sociobiology

During the 1970s, a new and influential theory known as sociobiology emerged. **Sociobiology** is the systematic study of the biological basis of social behavior, including the development of culture. Sociobiologists begin with the Darwinian assumption of *natural selection,* that some genetic characteristics survive over others on the basis of how well they contribute to survival and reproductive success. Sociobiologists are not concerned with how specific genes may lead to specific forms of cultural behavior; rather, they are interested in general strategies of behavior. This includes sexual reproductive strategies and caring for children and other kin, and how these strategies may be influenced by biological factors. According to this approach, these biological factors are based on innate predispositions that influence human behavior.

A CASE STUDY: SEXUAL BEHAVIOR

One important premise of sociobiology is that the survival and perpetuation of our own genes is the overall goal of our behavior. In light of this, consider, for example, how sociobiologists explain sexual reproductive strategies. According to sociobiologists, nature has assigned females and males very different parts to play in the reproductive process. Whereas males release millions of sperm in a single ejaculation, women produce only a relatively few eggs, perhaps four hundred over a lifetime, and women are pregnant for nine months and cannot become pregnant again for a period of time. Thus, in principle at least, males are biologically capable of fathering thousands of offspring, whereas females are able to bear a much smaller number of children.

From these biological givens, sociobiologists attempt to explain cultural practices and values related to sexuality. Consider, for example, the "double standard" in our society, that is, the pattern by which males are generally more free to engage in sexual activity than are females. Sociobiologists view this cul-

Sociobiologists maintain that traditional families that tend to be polygamous, with males having more than one wife, are based on natural reproductive strategies.

tural pattern as a result of the general biological strategies of reproduction of males and females. Males may reproduce their genes most efficiently through a strategy of sexual promiscuity, but this strategy does not serve the reproductive interests of females. Each pregnancy demands great amounts of energy expenditure. Thus, the efficient female strategy is to choose carefully a male whose qualities will contribute to her child's ability to survive and reproduce most successfully (Symons, 1979).

In this type of analysis, sociobiologists do not view the sexual behavior of males and females as the result of fixed, unchanging instincts. Rather, they consider sexual behaviors to be general behavioral tendencies that can be modified or even neutralized by certain learning experiences. Yet sociobiologists maintain that through evolution these behavioral tendencies will promote certain types of cultural values and practices.

INCLUSIVE FITNESS AND KIN SELECTION

Because our close relatives share many of the same genes that we do, sociobiologists hypothesize that it is in our reproductive interest to see those genes also survive. *Inclusive fitness* is the assumption that living organisms, including humans, maximize their own reproductive fitness through their offspring, in addition to the reproductive success of those who share similar genes. Thus, one would assist others who have a similar genetic heritage in maximizing their fitness. A related concept, kin selection, maintains that people tend to favor and promote the reproductive success of their close relatives by performing altruistic actions in their interest. For example, according to sociobiologists, the prevalence of *nepotism*, favoring one's own kin over others in economic, social, and political pursuits, reflects the general strategy of kin selection.

Sociobiologists do not argue that male and female reproductive strategies, kin selection, and inclusive fitness behaviors are conscious processes, just that in the course of evolution people who did not practice these behaviors have been gradually eliminated. Thus, over a long period of evolution certain innate predispositions survived. According to sociobiologists, these innate predispositions influence a wide variety of human behaviors, including economic behavior, kinship relations, aggression, the presence or absence of warfare in small-scale societies, and male-female relationships.

SOCIOBIOLOGY: A CRITIQUE

Sociobiology is a relatively new approach to understanding culture, and many anthropologists remain skeptical of its value. Anthropologist Marshall Sahlins (1976) views this approach as an abuse of evolutionary theory in explaining cultural phenomena. Focusing on kin selection, he cites cases in which human kinship systems are organized by cultural rather than by precise biological categories. For example, he notes that in some societies there are kinship categories for "brothers," "aunts," "uncles," and so on, that have little relationship to actual genealogical relationships. Sahlins concludes that human kinship is not always organized according to degree of genetic relatedness, as sociobiology predicts, and he dismisses sociobiology as a valid theory.

Sociobiologists have responded to such critiques generally by emphasizing that their hypotheses are tentative and need to be evaluated and tested through empirical research. They argue that to dismiss the entire field of sociobiology through examples of ethnographic data that do not appear to

support the theory is extreme. Furthermore, sociobiologists doubt that biological forces will ever be shown to "determine" human behavior and that human behavior is always a result of both biological and cultural factors. Still, they hypothesize that some biological tendencies may make some cultural patterns easier to learn than others.

Symbolic Anthropology

Another theoretical orientation in anthropology is **symbolic anthropology,** the study of culture through the interpretation of the meaning of the symbols, values, and beliefs of a society. This school of thought focuses on the symbolic rather than the material aspects of culture. Symbolic anthropologists suggest that many cultural symbols cannot be readily reduced to the material conditions and adaptive mechanisms of a society, as proposed by cultural materialists. Rather than viewing values, beliefs, and worldviews as a reflection only of environmental, technological, or economic conditions, symbolic anthropologists argue that these cultural symbols may be completely autonomous from material factors.

From this standpoint, symbolic anthropologists argue that human behavior cannot be explained through the use of the scientific method. The goal of their research is instead to interpret the meaning of symbols within the worldviews of a particular society. Recall that in Chapter 3 we discussed the hairstyles of people in different societies. The symbolic anthropologist tries to discern how such symbols help people produce meaning for themselves. A particular hairstyle may become a symbolic metaphor, communicating messages.

The methodology of symbolic anthropology focuses on the collection of data—especially data reflecting the point of view of the members of the society studied—on kinship, economy, ritual, myth, and values. Symbolic anthropologists describe this type of data collection as producing a thick description, the attempt to interpret the relationships among different symbols within a society. To do this they must interpret the meanings of the symbolic concepts and metaphors from the point of view of the people in a specific society. The aim of the symbolic anthropologist is to make other people's values, beliefs, and worldviews meaningful and intelligible.

CRITICISMS OF SYMBOLIC ANTHROPOLOGY

A number of criticisms have been directed at symbolic anthropology. One major charge is that symbolic anthropologists focus exclusively on cultural symbols at the expense of other variables that may influence human thought and behavior. Symbolic anthropologists may therefore neglect the conditions and processes that lead to the making of culture (Fox, 1985; Roseberry, 1982). For example, economic and political power may be important factors in the development of cultural values and norms. Dominant groups may be responsible for the emergence of cultural hegemony in a society. Critics emphasize that culture cannot be treated as an autonomous phenomenon separate from historical, political, and economic processes and conditions that affect a society.

Another criticism is that symbolic anthropology substitutes one form of determinism for another. Instead of emphasizing technological or economic variables, symbolic anthropologists stress the meaning of cultural symbols. Despite their rejection of causal explanations, they have been accused of reducing explanations of society and human activity to the "meanings" of cultural symbols.

Materialism versus Culturalism

One major division in anthropology is between those anthropologists who prefer materialist explanations of society and those who prefer culturalist explanations. *Materialists* focus on technological, environmental, biological, and economic factors to explain human behavior and society. This group, which includes the cultural materialists, some Marxist anthropologists, and sociobiologists, views many aspects of culture as having a material purpose. *Culturalists,* including the structuralists and many psychological anthropologists, discussed in Chapter 4, and symbolic anthropologists, focus on the symbolic aspect of culture. Their aim is to study the meaning of symbols in a society. To the culturalists, symbols and culture may not have a material purpose at all but rather establish meaningfulness for the people in a society.

Anthropologist Richard Barrett (1984) notes that the difference between the materialist and culturalist approaches is related to the nature of society and human existence itself. As Barrett emphasizes, every society must confront the problem of adjusting to the practical circumstances of life. People need food, shelter, clothing, and the necessary technology and energy for survival. This is the material component of culture; it is related to survival. There is also the nonmaterial aspect of culture: norms, values, beliefs, ideologies, and symbols. These cultural norms and symbols have emotional significance. Symbols may not be related at all to the practical circumstances of life; instead, they may indicate some aesthetic or moral values that are not related to the material conditions of society.

Thus, the distinction between the material and nonmaterial aspects of culture has led to different approaches to the analysis of human behavior and society. In later chapters we will learn how anthropologists have employed these approaches in explaining and interpreting human affairs.

 S U M M A R Y

The first professional anthropologists, notably E. B. Tylor and Lewis Henry Morgan, proposed a theory known as *unilineal evolution* to explain the differences and similarities in societal evolution. The unilineal evolutionists maintained that societies evolve in one direction from a stage of savagery through one of civilization. In the early twentieth century, another theory proposed *diffusionism* as the best explanation of the differences and similarities among societies. The British diffusionists argued that all civilization emanated from Egypt, whereas the German diffusionists maintained that there were several original centers of civilization. Although modern anthropologists consider these early views as being of limited value, diffusionism remains important in anthropological thought.

Another early twentieth-century theory, *historical particularism,* was developed in the United States from the ideas of Franz Boas. Boas criticized the unilineal view that societies could be ranked and compared with one another. Instead, he argued that each society is a unique product of its historical circumstances.

At about the same time, *functionalism* developed in British anthropology. Anthropologists such as A. R. Radcliffe-Brown and Bronislaw Malinowski focused on cultural institutions as serving societal or individual needs. Although functionalist explanations proved limited in explaining such matters as cultural change, they did provide valuable ethnographic data.

Following World War II, some anthropologists turned to new evolutionary theories. Anthropologists such as Leslie White and Julian Steward began to analyze how environment, technology, and energy requirements led to the evolution of societies. This *neoevolutionism* avoided the ethnocentric ideas of nineteenth-century unilineal evolution.

As an outgrowth of neoevolutionism, a school of thought known as *cultural materialism* developed through the writings of Marvin Harris. Harris systematized the analysis of sociocultural systems and maintained that the key determinant of socio-cultural evolution is the infrastructure, including technology, environment, and material conditions.

Another anthropological school of thought evolved from the writings of Karl Marx. In the 1970s, a number of anthropologists applied Marxist ideas about the mode of production to the analysis of preindustrial and industrial societies. Marxist anthropologists introduced a global view of societal evolution.

Sociobiology is the study of the biological tendencies that influence social behavior. Sociobiologists rely on concepts of inclusive fitness and kin selection to demonstrate that some forms of human behavior are conditioned by innate predispositions. They propose that certain patterns of behavior such as sexuality, aggression, warfare, and kinship relations are affected by innate tendencies. Although they agree that cultural factors play a definite role in human behavior, they argue that we cannot explain human behavior without considering the role of biology.

Symbolic anthropology focuses on the study of cultural beliefs, worldviews, and ethos of society. Symbolic anthropologists treat cultural traditions as texts that need to be interpreted by the ethnographer. Symbolic anthropology represents a means of analyzing cultural traditions without reducing them to material conditions.

 ## STUDY QUESTIONS

1. Discuss the principal differences between nineteenth-century models of unilineal evolution and twentieth-century neoevolutionary theories. Who were the principal proponents of each?

2. What are some of the weaknesses of the theory that there was only one source for the development of all civilizations?

3. Define historical particularism. Do you think that this approach can be used along with investigations of cultural evolution? Why or why not?

4. Compare and contrast the perspectives of the neoevolutionists, cultural ecologists, cultural materialists, and Marxists. Are these theoretical views similar in any way, or are they mutually exclusive and contradictory?

5. What are some of the criticisms that have been leveled against the cultural ecological approach?

Do you think these criticisms are valid? If so, how would you modify the cultural ecological perspective to take into account the criticism?

6. Discuss the principal effects that the writings of Karl Marx have had on anthropological theory. Do you think that Marxist anthropology is the same as communist anthropology? Why or why not?

7. Comment on this quote: "The sociobiological perspective is simply incorrect because genes do not determine all of cultural behavior. We do not have genes for being good or bad, for war or peace, or for classifying the world in set ways."

8. Compare and contrast the perspective of the symbolic anthropologists with the Marxists' and cultural materialists' perspectives.

KEY TERMS

cultural materialism	historical particularism	symbolic anthropology
diffusionism	sociobiology	unilineal evolution
functionalism		

 INTERNET EXERCISES

1. Look through the website **http://www.indi-ana.edu/~wanthro/theory.htm.** Click on Ann Reed and Applied Anthropology. How does the field of applied anthropology utilize anthropological theory as presented throughout this chapter? Can applied anthropology exist without knowledge of theory, or is applied anthropology the application of theory to various situations?

SUGGESTED READINGS

CHAGNON, N. A., AND W. IRONS, eds. 1979. *Evolutionary Biology and Human Social Behavior*. North Scituate, MA: Duxbury Press. A collection of papers by anthropologists who use sociobiology in their analysis of human behavior.

HARRIS, MARVIN. 1968. *The Rise of Anthropological Theory*. New York: Thomas Y. Crowell. A thorough account of the history of anthropological thought from the perspective of a cultural materialist.

————. 1979. *Cultural Materialism: The Struggle for a Science of Culture*. New York: Random House. A presentation of the cultural-materialist theory in comparison with contending approaches. Harris tries to show the superiority of this theory when compared with structuralism, Marxist anthropology, sociobiology, and other perspectives.

————. 1999. *Theories of Culture in Postmodern Times*. Walnut Creek, CA: Altamira Press. This book represents Marvin Harris's most recent defense of cultural materialism in the midst of postmodernist critiques of theories in anthropology.

HATCH, ELVIN. 1973. *Theories of Man and Culture*. New York: Columbia University Press. A comprehensive summary of anthropological theories from the nineteenth century to the modern era. This book compares and contrasts the major theorists such as Tylor, Boas, Benedict, Malinowski, White, and Steward.

LAYTON, ROBERT. 1997. *An Introduction to Theory in Anthropology*. Cambridge: Cambridge University Press. A recent treatment of theory within anthropology from a British perspective drawing on a great deal of ethnographic material to illustrate particular orientations.

LETT, JAMES. 1987. *The Human Enterprise: A Critical Introduction to Anthropological Theory*. Boulder, CO.: Westview Press. A critical introduction to the basic theories in anthropology using a scientific and materialist focus.

MCGEE, JON R., AND RICHARD L. WARMS. 1996. *Anthropological Theory: An Introductory History*. Mountain View, CA: Mayfield. A thorough anthology of the writings of the leading anthropologists from all the various schools of thought, with extensive footnotes and documentation emphasizing the strengths and weaknesses of various views.

MANNERS, R. A., AND D. KAPLAN, eds. 1968. *Theory in Anthropology: A Sourcebook*. Chicago: Aldine. An anthology of readings consisting of different theoretical perspectives held by anthropologists.

TERRAY, EMMANUEL. 1972. *Marxism and "Primitive" Societies: Two Studies*. New York: Monthly Review Press. The application of neo-Marxist ideas to the analysis of small-scale societies. This book illustrates the development of Marxist anthropology in the 1970s.

Analyzing Sociocultural Systems

CHAPTER OUTLINE

Ethnological Fieldwork
Ethnological Research and Strategies / Ethics in Anthropological Research / Analysis of Ethnological Data

Variables Studied by Ethnologists

Subsistence and the Physical Environment
Modern Cultural Ecology / Biomes / Subsistence Patterns and Environments

Demography
Fertility, Mortality, and Migration / Population and Environment / Population and Culture

Technology
Anthropological Explanations of Technology

Economy
The Formalist Approach / The Substantivist Approach / Modern Economic Anthropology

Social Structure
Components of Social Structure / The Family / Marriage / Gender / Age

Political Organization
Types of Political Systems / Decision Making in a Political System / Warfare and Feuds / Law and Social Control

Religion
Myths / Rituals / Religious Specialists / Religious Movements

Cross-Cultural Research

CHAPTER QUESTIONS

- How do ethnologists study society and culture?

- What are the various concepts and variables that ethnologists rely on to do their fieldwork?

- What are the strengths and limitations of the cross-cultural approach?

IN CHAPTER 6 WE SURVEYED A NUMBER OF THEORET- ical perspectives that cultural anthropologists use to explain human behavior and cultural differences and similarities. As we discussed in Chapter 3, at times anthropologists use the term *sociocultural system* in analyzing their data. Sociocultural systems are made up of different variables, such as environmental, demographic, technological, economic, social-organizational (social structure, family, marriage, age, gender relations), political, and religious variables. Anthropologists use the holistic approach to analyze sociocultural systems, which means showing how all of these variables influence one another.

In later chapters, we examine types of sociocultural systems to illustrate the interconnection of these variables. This chapter presents a broad overview of the basic variables that anthropologists investigate when explaining the similarities and differences in societies. Various concepts and terms used by anthropologists to examine variables are also introduced. This will prepare you to evaluate the results of ethnological findings discussed in later chapters.

Ethnological Fieldwork

In Chapter 1 we introduced the subfield of anthropology known as ethnology or cultural anthropology. This subfield focuses on the study of contemporary societies all over the world. To prepare for ethnological fieldwork, the anthropologist must be well grounded in the different theoretical perspectives of anthropology that were discussed in Chapter 6. This background knowledge is especially important for developing a research design for the fieldwork. A *research design* is the formulation of a strategy to examine a particular topic and specifies the appropriate methods for gathering the richest possible data. The research design must take into account the types of data that will be collected and how those data relate to existing anthropological knowledge. Within the research design the ethnologist has to specify what types of methods will be used for the investigation. Typically, the ethnologist develops the research design, which is then reviewed by other anthropologists, who recommend it for funding by various government or private research foundations.

Before going into the field for direct research, the ethnologist analyzes available *archival data*, including photos; films; missionary reports; business and government surveys; musical recordings; journalistic accounts; diaries; court documents; medical records; birth, death, marriage, and tax records; and landholding documents. These data help place the communities to be studied in a broad context. Historical materials in the archives help the ethnologist to evaluate the usefulness of the observations and interviews he or she will document. Archival data can enrich the sources of information that fieldworkers obtain once they get to the field.

ETHNOLOGICAL RESEARCH AND STRATEGIES

After receiving funding and obtaining the proper research clearances from the country in which the subjects of the research are located, the ethnologist takes up residence in that society to explore the institutions and values of that society. This is the basis of the participant observation method, which involves learning the language and culture of the group being studied and participating in its daily activities. Language skills are the most important asset that an ethnologist has in the field.

One of the major means of learning about culture and behavior is through direct observation, sometimes referred to as *naturalistic observation*. Naturalistic observation consists of making accurate descriptions of the physical locale and daily activities of the people in the society. This may involve creating maps or at least being able to read maps to place the society's physical location in perspective. It may also involve more intensive investigation into soil conditions, rates of precipitation, surveys of crops and livestock, and other environmental factors. Naturalistic observation also involves accurate and reliable records of the ethnologist's direct observations of human social interaction and behavior.

Some ethnologists use what is called *time-allocation analysis* to record how much time the people within the society spend in various activities: work, leisure, recreation, religious ceremonies, and so on. For example, Allen Johnson (1975)

did a systematic time-allocation study of the Machiguenga Indians, who live in the Andes Mountains in Peru. He found that men worked 4.6 hours per day and women worked 4.2 hours per day in the production and preparation of food. Women spent 2.1 hours and men spent 1.4 hours per day in craft production. Men were involved for 1.6 hours per day in trade and wage work, and women did housework and child care activities for 1.1 hours. The total amount of labor time allocated for this work was 7.6 for men and 7.4 for women. This type of time-allocation study can be useful in assessing how different societies use their time in various activities.

Key Informants Usually the ethnologist learns about the society through trusted *key informants*, who give the ethnologist insight into the culture's patterns (Powdermaker, 1966; Wax, 1971; Agar, 1980). These informants become the initial source of information and help the ethnologist identify major sources of data. Long-term collaboration with key informants is an integral part of quality ethnological research.

The ethnologist tries to choose key informants who have a deep knowledge of the community. These informants are usually "native ethnologists" who are interested in their own society. They may serve as tutors or guides, answering general questions or identifying topics that could be of interest to the ethnologist. They often help the ethnologist establish rapport with the people in the community. In many situations, the people may not understand why the ethnologist is interested in their society. The key informant can help explain the ethnologist's role. In some cases, the key informant may become involved in interviewing other people in the community to assist the ethnologist in collecting data. The relationship between the key informant and the ethnologist is a close personal and professional one that usually produces lifelong friendship and collaboration.

Interviews Ethnologists use a number of *unstructured interviews*, which may involve open-ended conversations with informants, to gain insights into a culture. These unstructured interviews may include the collecting of life histories, narratives, myths, and tales. Through these interviews, the ethnologist may also find out information on dispute settlements, legal transactions, political

Ethnologist Richard Lee interviewing the !Kung San.

conflicts, and religious and public events. Unstructured interviewing sometimes involves on-the-spot questioning of informants.

The strength of this type of interviewing is that it gives informants tremendous freedom of expression in attempting to explain their culture (Bernard et al., 1986). The informant is not confined to answering a specific question that is designed by the ethnologist. The informant may, for example, elaborate on connections between certain beliefs and political power in the community. Fredrik Barth (1975) discovered through his informant among the Baktaman people of New Guinea that when young males go through their initiation ceremonies they are introduced to the secret lore and sacred knowledge of the males who are in authority. Thus, cultural beliefs are transmitted along with political authority. Without his informant's help, Barth might not have paid attention to this relationship between belief and the transmission of authority.

Following this unstructured interviewing, the ethnologist focuses on specific topics of interest related to the research project. The ethnologist then begins to develop *structured interviews*. Structured interviews systematically ask the same question of every individual in a given sample. The ethnologist must phrase the questions in a meaningful and

sensitive manner, a task that requires a knowledge of both the language and the lifestyle of the people being studied.

By asking the same type of question to every individual in a given sample, the ethnologist is able to obtain more accurate data. If the ethnologist receives uniform answers to a particular question, then the data are more likely to be reliable. If a great deal of variation in responses is evident, then the data will be more unreliable or may indicate a complex issue with many facets. The structured interview helps assess the validity of the collected data. By asking people the same type of question, the ethnologist attempts to gain more quality control over his or her findings. This type of data quality control must be a constant aspect of the ethnologist's research strategy.

To develop an effective questionnaire, the ethnologist must collaborate with her or his informants. This is tedious and difficult methodological work, but it is necessary if the ethnologist is to understand the workings of the society.

If the society is large, the ethnologist must distribute the questionnaire schedule to a **random sample** of the society. A random sample is a representative sample of people of different ages, genders, economic and political status, and other characteristics within the society. In a random sample, all of the individuals in the society have an equal chance of being selected for the survey. If the ethnologist draws information from only one sector of the population—for example, males or young people—the data may be biased. This shortcoming would limit the ability of the ethnologist to develop a well-rounded portrait of the society.

Quantitative and Qualitative Data Through the structured interviews, the ethnologist gathers basic **quantitative data:** census materials, dietary information, income and household-composition data, and other data that can be expressed as numbers. This information can be used as a database for developing a description of the variations in economic, social, political, and other patterns in the society. For example, dietary information can inform the ethnologist about the basic health and nutritional problems that the society may have. Quantitative data provide background for the ethnologist's direct and participant observations and further open-ended interviews with the individuals in the society.

The data achieved through participant observation and interviewing is **qualitative data,** the nonstatistical information that tends to be the most important aspect of ethnological research. Qualitative data include descriptions of social organization, political activities, religious beliefs, and so on. For example, as we discussed in Chapter 3, the religious beliefs of some societies have influenced their cultural preferences for various foods. Islamic and Jewish cultural traditions prohibit the eating of pork, whereas orthodox Hindus encourage meatless, vegetarian diets. This type of qualitative data about a society helps the ethnologist interpret the quantitative data. Ordinarily, both quantitative and qualitative data are integral to ethnological research.

Ethnologists have a number of different methods for recording qualitative data. The best-known method is *field notes*, which are the systematic recording of observations or interviews into a field notebook. Ethnologists should have some training in how to take useful field notes and how to manage them for more effective coding and recording of data. An increasing number of ethnologists now use the computer as a means of constructing databases to manage their field notes. They select appropriate categories for classifying the data. For ex-

ample, an ethnologist may have specific categories for kinship terms, religious taboos, terms for plants, animals, colors, and foods, and so on. These data can then easily be retrieved for analysis. Some ethnologists rely on tape recorders for interviews, though they recognize the problems such devices present for producing valid accounts. Most ethnological fieldworkers utilize photography to record and help document their findings. Ethnologists must use extreme caution when using these technologies, however, for in some cultures people are very sensitive about being recorded or photographed.

Today, many anthropologists use video cameras when gathering primary data. Video recording is one of the most exciting recent developments in anthropology and has stimulated a new area of anthropological research known as *visual anthropology*. The visual documentation of economic, social, political, and ritual behavior sometimes reveals intricate patterns of interaction in a society, interactions that cannot otherwise be described thoroughly. One drawback to video recording, however, is that people who know they are being filmed frequently behave differently from the way they would normally. This may distort the ethnologist's conclusions. On the other hand, the video can be used to present playbacks to informants for comments on the recorded behaviors. William Rittenberg, who did studies of Buddhist rituals in villages in central Thailand, often played back his video recordings of rituals to members of the community. The informants, including the Buddhist monks, would view the recordings and offer more elaborate explanations of the meanings of the ritual. These strategies frequently help the ethnologist gain a more comprehensive understanding of the culture.

Culture Shock Ethnological fieldwork can be a very demanding task. Ethnologists sometimes experience **culture shock,** a severe psychological reaction that results from adjusting to the realities of a society radically different from one's own. An ethnologist raised in the United States who may have to eat unfamiliar foods such as reptiles or insects, reside in uncomfortable huts in a rainforest, or observe practices such as cannibalism or infanticide could experience culture shock. Of course, the actual degree of culture shock may vary de-

CRITICAL PERSPECTIVES

Postmodernism and the Future of Ethnological Research

Although ethnographic fieldwork has long been a fundamental aspect of anthropology, one current school is challenging basic ethnographic assumptions and methodologies. This group, known as *postmodernist anthropologists,* includes such figures as James Clifford, George Marcus, and Michael Fischer. The postmodernists suggest that traditional ethnographic research is based on a number of unsound assumptions. One such assumption is that the ethnographer is a detached, scientifically objective observer who is not influenced by the premises and biases of her or his own society.

Clifford characterizes one of the models maintained by ethnographers such as Malinowski as that of the "scientific participant-observer" (1983). In his ethnographies, Malinowski eliminated any reference to himself and recorded data that was then written as the documentation of an "objective scientist." Malinowski produced his descriptions as if he did not have any involvement with the Trobriand people. It was as if he were some sort of computing machine without feelings, biases, or emotions, who was simply recording everything about native life.

According to postmodernist critics, ethnographies such as those compiled by Malinowski were intended as a type of scientific study in which the subjects behaved and the ethnographer simply recorded this behavior. From this standpoint, the post-

modernists complain that the ethnographers assume they have a thoroughly scientific and objective view of reality, whereas the native view is highly subjective, based on traditional worldviews and cosmologies.

Another type of inquiry criticized by the postmodernists is the interpretive model used by symbolic anthropologists such as Clifford Geertz (Clifford, 1983). In contrast with the "objective" model, the interpretive model focuses on the understanding of symbols from the point of view of the members of the society. It assumes that the people in a particular society have a better understanding than others of their own concepts, and the interpretive anthropologist must try to reconstruct these understandings so that others can also understand the meanings of these symbols.

For example, in Clifford Geertz's description of a cockfight in Balinese society, the gambling and the cockfight are viewed as a text that has meaning for the participants (1973). Geertz suggests that the meaning of the cockfight reflects the status rivalries among the Balinese men. He refers to the cockfight as a "status bloodbath." Geertz views the cockfight in relation to the competition among various groups and factions within the Balinese community. The interpretation offered by Geertz suggests that the natives provide cultural meaning for themselves

through the activities associated with the cockfight.

The postmodernists critique this type of interpretive ethnology because it is also written as if the ethnologist disappears from the setting through empathy with the subjects. In other words, the people themselves are not described as offering their own interpretations but instead the ethnologist is looking over their shoulders and reading the cultural meanings and texts of their society and interpreting them.

Postmodernists and Contemporary Research

One of the basic reasons for the postmodernist critiques is that the situation for ethnographic studies has changed substantially. Until recently, most subjects of ethnographic studies were illiterate peoples adjusting to the impact of the West. But as more people throughout the world become educated and familiar with the field of anthropology, Western ethnographers can no longer claim to be the sole authorities regarding anthropological knowledge. Many people in Latin America, Africa, the Middle East, and Asia can and do speak and write about their own cultures (some have even become anthropologists), and they are disseminating knowledge about their own societies. The world is no longer dependent on Western anthropologists to gather ethnographic data.

Indigenous people are beginning to represent themselves and their societies to the world.

Postmodernists have recommended that ethnographers today adopt a different way of researching and writing. Instead of trying to distance themselves from their subjects, ethnographers should present themselves in dialogue with their subjects. Clifford (1983) argues that an ethnography should consist of many voices from the native population, rather than just a dialogue between the ethnographer and one of his or her informants.

Reaction to this postmodernist critique has varied within the discipline. On the one hand, some ethnographers have charged the postmodernists with characterizing traditional ethnographic methodologies unjustly. Many ethnographers, they contend, were engaged in a form of dialogue with their informants and other members of the societies being studied.

On the other hand, the postmodernist debate has stirred many anthropologists to rethink their roles. Currently, more ethnographers are writing about their actual interactions and relationships with the people they study. The data and personal reflection method is no longer pushed into the background but instead is presented as a vital ingredient of the ethnography.

In the 1980s, a number of ethnographies appeared that reflected the postmodernist emphasis on interaction between ethnographers and their subjects. Some of these new ethnographies are based on the life histories of people within the studied population.

Following two periods of fieldwork among the !Kung San, hunters and gatherers of the Kalahari Desert in southwest Africa, the late Marjorie Shostak completed a life history of Nisa, a !Kung woman (1981). Shostak interviewed numerous !Kung women to gain a sense of their lives. She focused on the life history of Nisa, who discussed her family, her sex life, marriage, pregnancies, her experiences with !Kung men, and growing older. Shostak cautioned that Nisa does not represent a "typical" !Kung female because her life experiences are unique (as are all individuals in any society). In addition, Shostak exercised extreme care in discussing with Nisa the material that would go into the book to ensure a faithful representation of Nisa's life.

If we look back over years of ethnographic research, we find many accounts in which anthropologists were scrupulous in their representation of people in other societies. To this extent the postmodernist critics have exaggerated the past mistakes of ethnographers. However, the postmodernists have alerted ethnographers to some unexamined assumptions concerning their work. Today, most anthropologists do not claim a completely "objective" viewpoint. Anthropologists generally want to maintain empathy with the people they study, yet they usually attempt some critical detachment as well. Otherwise, they could easily become merely the voices and spokespersons of specific political interests and leaders in a community (Errington & Gewertz, 1987).

Collaborative fieldwork, with teams of ethnographers and informants working together to understand a society, is most likely the future direction for ethnographic study. The image of a solitary ethnographer such as Malinowski or Margaret Mead isolated on a Pacific island is outmoded (Salzman, 1989). Collaborative research will lead to more systematic data collection and will offer opportunities to examine hypotheses of both ethnographers and subjects from a variety of perspectives.

Points to Ponder

1. Do you think that cultural anthropologists can do research on other societies in an "objective" manner?

2. Do you believe that anthropologists should strive toward objectivity in their research?

3. How does an anthropologist compare to a news reporter in trying to gain an objective or neutral stance?

4. If you were an anthropologist, how would you try to do objective research?

5. Would you be able to shed your own biases and ethnocentric attitudes in conducting your research?

pending on the differences and similarities between the society studied and the anthropologist's own society. The symptoms may range from mild irritation to surprise or disgust.

Usually after the ethnologist learns the norms, beliefs, and practices of the community, the psychological disorientation of culture shock begins to diminish. Part of the challenge for anthropologists is adjusting to a different society and gaining a much better perspective on one's own society. In addition, the adjustment process enables an ethnologist to understand herself or himself better.

ETHICS IN ANTHROPOLOGICAL RESEARCH

Ethnologists must not only be trained in appropriate research and analytical techniques, they must also abide by the ethical guidelines of their discipline. In many instances, ethnologists conduct research on politically powerless groups dominated by more powerful groups. When ethnologists engage in participant observation, they usually become familiar with information that might, if made public, become harmful to the community or to individuals in the community. For example, when researching isolated or rural communities, ethnologists might come across certain economic or political behavior or information that could be used by government authorities. This might include the specific sources of income for people in the community or whether they participate in political opposition to the government. Whenever possible, ethnologists attempt to keep such information confidential so as not to compromise their informants or other sources of data.

Most ethnographic reports do not include the real identities of informants or other people. Ethnologists usually ensure their informants anonymity, if at all possible, so that these individuals will not be investigated by their governments. Sometimes ethnologists use pseudonyms (fictional names) to make identification difficult. Ethnologists also attempt to be frank and open with the population under study about the aims of the research. At times this is difficult because the community does not understand the role of the ethnologist (Kurin, 1980; Chagnon, 1997). Out of courtesy, the ethnologist should give the community a reasonable account of what he or she wants to do.

In general, ethnologists do not accept research funding for projects that are supposed to be clandestine or secretive. Although this type of research has been conducted by some anthropologists in the past (especially during World War II), contemporary anthropologists have adopted a code of ethics that reflects their grave reservations about undercover research.

ANALYSIS OF ETHNOLOGICAL DATA

The results of ethnological research are documented in a descriptive monograph referred to as an *ethnography.* In writing the ethnographic description, the ethnologist must be extremely cautious. The accumulated field notes, photos, perhaps video or tape recordings, and quantitative data from survey sources must all be carefully managed to reduce bias, distortion, and error. The ethnologist must analyze these data, making sure to cross-check the conclusions from a variety of sources, including informants, censuses, observations, and archival materials. In addition, the ethnologist should plainly distinguish the views of the people being studied from his or her interpretation of those views.

Independent and Dependent Variables Culture, society, and human behavior are not just a random array of occurrences that develop without rhyme or reason; they are the result of interacting variables that influence the human condition. Anthropologists frequently find that different variables interact, and this interaction of two variables is called a **correlation.** For example, a particular society may experience both population increases and a high incidence of warfare. This does not necessarily mean that the population growth *causes* the warfare, or vice versa; it simply means that both conditions exist within the society. To determine whether a causal relationship exists between these variables would require further investigation, including, in many cases, comparisons with other societies. Further research may indicate that the relationship between population and warfare is a spurious correlation, that is, two variables occur together, but each is caused by some third variable.

Alternatively, research may indicate that in a certain society the rate of population growth does influence the frequency of warfare. In such cases the anthropologist might hypothesize that population increases cause the high incidence of warfare. This hypothesis could then be tested and evaluated by other anthropologists.

In determining cause-and-effect relationships, anthropologists distinguish between independent and dependent variables. An **independent variable** is the causal variable that produces an effect on another variable, the **dependent variable.** In the previous example, population growth would be the independent variable because it determines the incidence of warfare, which is the dependent variable.

In actuality, this example of determining causal relationships is far too simplistic. Anthropologists recognize that no aspect of culture and society can be completely explained by any single cause or independent variable. They rely instead on hypotheses that are *multidimensional,* in which many variables interact with one another. This multidimensional approach must be kept in mind when considering the specific variables explored by ethnologists in their study of different societies. The multidimensional approach is linked with the holistic perspective in anthropology, that is, the attempt to demonstrate how sociocultural systems must be understood through the interconnections among variables.

Variables Studied by Ethnologists

The major variables of sociocultural systems include subsistence and the physical environment, demography, technology, the economy, social structure (including family and marriage, and gender and age relations), political organization, and religion. Although this is not a complete list of the specific variables studied by ethnologists, it provides the general framework for understanding different societies. An explanation of these variables follows to help you understand the discussions of different types of societies considered in the rest of the book.

Subsistence and the Physical Environment

Living organisms, both plant and animal, do not live or evolve in a vacuum. The evolution and survival of a particular species is closely related to the type of physical environment in which it is located. The speed of a jackal or an arctic fox has evolved in relationship to the predators and prey found in East Africa or the Arctic. The physical characteristics of the orchid plant make it highly suitable for surviving in a tropical environment. The environment affects the organism directly and, as Charles Darwin noted, affects the passing on of certain adaptive characteristics that enable these life forms to survive and reproduce in their particular surroundings.

Biologists use the term *adaptation* to refer to the process in which an organism adjusts successfully to a specific environment. Most organisms adapt to the environment through the physical traits that they inherit. Humans, however, adapt to their specific environments primarily through culture. By any measure, humans have been the most successful living forms in terms of adapting to different environments. Humans occupy an extraordinary range of environments from the tropics to the Arctic and have developed cultural solutions to the various problems that have arisen in these different regions. Anthropologists have been studying these adaptive strategies and cultural solutions to explain both the similarities and differences among societies.

MODERN CULTURAL ECOLOGY

The term *ecology* was coined by German biologist Ernest Haeckel in the nineteenth century from two Greek words that mean "the study of the home." **Ecology** is the study of living organisms in relationship to their environment. Here we are defining *environment* broadly to include both the physical characteristics and the forms of life found in a particular region. In biology, ecological studies focus on how plant and animal populations survive and reproduce in specific environmental niches. An **environmental niche** refers to the locale that contains various plants, animals, and other ecological conditions to which a species must adjust.

As noted in Chapter 6, there is a school of thought known as **cultural ecology,** the systematic study of the relationships between the environment and society. Anthropologists recognize that humans can adjust in extremely creative ways to different environments. Nevertheless, humans, like other organisms, are connected to the environment in a number of ways. Just as the environment has an impact on human behavior and society, humans have a major impact on their environment. Modern cultural ecologists examine these dynamic interrelationships as a means of understanding different societies.

BIOMES

In their studies of different environments, cultural ecologists use the concept of a biome. A **biome** is an area distinguished by a particular climate and certain types of plants and animals. Biomes may be classified by certain attributes, such as mean rainfall, temperature, soil conditions, and vegetation, that support certain forms of animal life (Campbell, 1983). Cultural ecologists investigate the relationship between specific biomes and human sociocultural systems. Some of the different biomes that will be encountered in this text are listed in Table 7.1.

SUBSISTENCE PATTERNS AND ENVIRONMENTS

In U.S. society, when we have the urge to satisfy our hunger drive we have many options: We can go to a local fast-food restaurant, place money into a machine to select our choice of food, or obtain food for cooking from a grocery store. Other societies have different means of obtaining their food supplies. Ethnologists study **subsistence patterns,** the means by which people in various societies obtain their food supplies. As we will see in later chapters, the amount of sunlight, the type of soil, forests, rainfall, and mineral deposits all have an effect on the type of subsistence pattern a particular society develops. The specific biome and environmental conditions may limit the development of certain types of subsistence patterns. For example, arctic conditions are not conducive to agricultural activities, nor are arid regions suitable for rice production. These are the obvious limitations of biomes and environmental conditions on subsistence patterns.

The earliest type of subsistence pattern, known as *foraging,* or *hunting–gathering,* goes back to perhaps 2 million years ago. This pattern of subsistence, along with others such as *horticulture, pastoralism,*

various types of *intensive agriculture,* and developments in *agribusiness* in industrial societies, is introduced in subsequent chapters. As we will see, these subsistence patterns are not only influenced by the environment but also directly affect the environment. In other words, as humans transform their subsistence pattern to adapt to the environment, the environment is also transformed to varying degrees depending on the type of subsistence pattern developed. The interaction between subsistence pattern and environment has become an extremely important topic in anthropology and has a direct bearing on how human–environmental relationships may be modified in the future.

Demography

Demography is the study of population and its relationship to society. Demographers study changes in the size, composition, and distribution of human populations. They also study the consequences of population increases and decreases on human societies. *Demographic anthropology* has become an important specialty in anthropology.

Much of the research in demographic anthropology is concerned with the quantitative description of population. Demographic anthropologists design censuses and surveys to collect population statistics on the size, age and sex composition, and increasing or decreasing growth of population of a society. After collecting these data, demographic anthropologists focus on three major variables in a population: fertility, mortality, and migration.

FERTILITY, MORTALITY, AND MIGRATION

To measure **fertility,** the number of births in a society, demographic anthropologists use the **crude birthrate,** that is, the number of live births in a given year for every thousand people in a population. They also measure **mortality,** the incidence of death in a society's population, by using the **crude death rate,** that is, the number of deaths in a given year for every thousand people. In measuring **migration rate,** the movement of people into and out of a specified territory, demographic anthropologists determine the number of *in-migrants,* people moving into the territory, and the number of *out-migrants,* people moving out of the territory. They

Table 7.1 A Listing of the Various Biomes Discussed in the Text, Along with Their Major Characteristics

Biome	Principal Locations	Precipitation Range (mm/year)	Temperature Range (hr °C) (daily maximum and minimum)	Soils
Tropical rainforest	Central America (Atlantic coast) Amazon basin Brazilian coast West African coast Congo basin Malaya East Indies Philippines New Guinea N. E. Australia Pacific islands	1,270–12,700 Equitorial type: frequent torrential thunderstorms Tradewind type: steady, almost daily rains No dry period	Little annual variation Max. 29–35 Min. 18–27 No cold period	Mainly reddish laterites
Tropical savanna	Central America (Pacific coast) Orinoco basin Brazil, S. of Amazon basin N. central Africa East Africa S. central Africa Madagascar India S. E. Asia Northern Australia	250–1900 Warm-season thunderstorms Almost no rain in cool season Long dry period during low sun	Considerable annual variation; no really cold period *Rainy season (high sun)* Max. 24–32 Min. 18–27 *Dry season (low sun)* Max. 21–32 Min. 13–18 *Dry season (higher sun)* Max. 29–40 Min. 21–27	Some laterites; considerable variety
Temperate grasslands	Central North America Eastern Europe Central and western Asia Argentina New Zealand	300–2000 Evenly distributed through the year or with a peak in summer Snow in winter	*Winter* Max. -18–29 Min. -28–10 *Summer* Max. 21–49 Min. -1–15	Black prairie soils Chestnut and brown soils Almost all have a lime layer
Temperate deciduous forest	Eastern N. America Western Europe Eastern Asia	630–2300 Evenly distributed through year Droughts rare Some snow	*Winter* Max. -12–21 Min. -29–7 *Summer* Max. 24–38 Min. 15–27	Gray-brown podzolic Red and yellow podzolic
Northern coniferous forest	Northern N. America Northern Europe Northern Asia	400–1000 Evenly distributed Much snow	*Winter* Max. -37– -1 Min. -54– -9 *Summer* Max. 10–21 Min. 7–13	True podzols Bog soils Some permafrost at depth, in places
Arctic tundra	Northern N. America Greenland Northern Eurasia	250–750 Considerable snow	*Winter* Max. -37– -7 Min. -57– -8 *Summer* Max. 2–15 Min. -1–7	Rocky or boggy Mush pattened ground Permafrost

Source: Adapted from W. D. Billings, *Plants, Man, and the Ecosystem,* 2d ed. (Belmont, CA: Wadsworth, 1970). Reprinted by permission of the publisher.

Fertility trends are studied by anthropologists to determine how different populations are growing or declining.

then use these numbers to calculate the **net migration,** which indicates the general movement of the population in and out of the territory.

To assess overall population change, demographic anthropologists subtract the crude death rate from the crude birthrate to arrive at the *natural growth rate* of a population. The natural growth rate is usually the major indicator of population change in a society. By adding the rate of migration, these anthropologists are able to calculate total population change.

Rates of fertility, mortality, and migration are also influenced by a number of other variables. Fecundity, the potential number of children that women in the society are capable of bearing, has an influence on fertility rates. Physically, a woman could bear a child every year during the period she is capable of conception. **Fecundity** varies, however, according to the age of females at puberty and menopause, nutrition, workload, and other conditions in the societies and individuals being studied.

Life expectancy is the number of years an average person can expect to live. A particularly important component of the life expectancy rate in a society is the **infant mortality rate,** the number of babies per thousand births in any year who die before reaching the age of 1. When the infant mortality rate is high, the life expectancy—a statistical

average—decreases. Disease, nutrition, sanitation, warfare, the general standard of living, and medical care are some of the factors that influence mortality, life expectancy, and infant mortality rates.

Migration is related to a number of different factors. In many instances, migration is involuntary. For example, the Cajun people of Louisiana are descendants of French people who were forced out of Canada by the British in the 1700s. Migration can also be voluntary. This type of movement is influenced by what demographers refer to as *push–pull factors. Push factors* are those that lead people to leave specific territories; examples are poverty and political instability. *Pull factors,* such as economic opportunity and political freedom, are powerful incentives for people to move to other societies.

POPULATION AND ENVIRONMENT

Demographic anthropologists study the relationship between environments (specific biomes) and population. One variable they investigate is **carrying capacity,** the maximum population that a specific environment can support. This concept refers to the environment's potential energy and food resources that can be used to support a certain number of people. Some environments contain food and energy resources that allow for substantial population increases, whereas other environments contain only limited resources.

For example, in the past, desert and arctic biomes had carrying capacities that severely limited population increases. In contrast, various river valley regions containing water and fertile soils permitted opportunities for greater population size. As we will see in later chapters, the development of mechanized agriculture, fertilizers, and synthetic pesticides increases the carrying capacity for many different environments.

POPULATION AND CULTURE

Demographic anthropologists examine not only the relationship between environment and population but also cultural values and practices that affect fertility, mortality, and migration rates. In some societies, religious beliefs encourage high birthrates. In others, political authorities institute programs to increase or decrease population growth. One recent area of anthropological research involves gathering data and developing hypotheses on decisions concerning the "costs and benefits" of having children and the consequences of these individual decisions on fertility. Anthropologists also investigate strategies of population regulation, such as birth control techniques. These topics and others constituting some of the research in demographic anthropology are introduced in later chapters.

Technology

The term *technology* is derived from the Greek word *techne,* which refers to art or skill. When we hear this term we usually think of tools, machines, clothing, shelter, and other such objects. As defined by modern anthropologists, however, **technology** consists of all the human techniques and methods of reaching a specific subsistence goal or of modifying or controlling the natural environment. Technology is cultural in that it includes methods for manipulating the environment. But technology is also the products of those methods which are important in changing the environments in which humans live, work, and interact. Thus, technology consists not merely of physical tools but also of cultural knowledge that humans can apply in specific ways. In societies in which peo-

ple use technologies such as bows and arrows, canoes, plows, penicillin, or computers, the cultural knowledge needed to construct, design, and use these materials is extremely important.

To sustain life, human societies need to produce and allocate goods and services to provide food, clothing, shelter, tools, and transportation. **Goods** are elements of material culture produced from raw materials in the natural environment, ranging from the basic commodities for survival to luxury items. The commodities for survival may include axes and plows for clearing land and cultivating crops. Luxury commodities include items such as jewelry, decorative art, and musical instruments. **Services** are elements of nonmaterial culture in the form of specialized skills that benefit others, such as giving spiritual comfort or providing medical care. Goods and services are valued because they satisfy various human needs. To produce these goods and services, societies must have suitable technologies.

ANTHROPOLOGICAL EXPLANATIONS OF TECHNOLOGY

As stated in Chapter 6, nineteenth-century theorists like E. B. Tylor and Lewis Morgan constructed a unilineal scheme of technological evolution in which societies progressed from the simple, small-scale technology of the "savages" to the more complex technology of modern civilizations. In the twentieth century, these simplistic views of technological evolution were rejected through detailed ethnographic research. Anthropologists such as Leslie White, Julian Steward, and the cultural materialists came to view technology as one of the primary factors of cultural evolution. White defined technology as an energy-capturing system made up of energy, tools, and products—that is, all the material means with which energy is harnessed, transformed, and expended (1959). The cultural materialists view technology as a basic and primary source of sociocultural change. They argue that we cannot explain different technological developments in society with reference to "values." Instead, technology must be viewed as a method designed to cope with a particular environment. Therefore, variations in environment, or habitat, could account for the differences between, say, the Eskimo and the Australian Aborigine societies.

White's views on technology, as well as the views of other cultural materialists, have been criticized as a form of "technological determinism." Although the cultural materialists see sociological, ideological, or emotional factors as conditioning or limiting the use or development of technology, these factors exert little influence on sociocultural systems compared to technology's dominant role. Anthropologists are currently evaluating this cultural materialist hypothesis to determine whether technology is a primary variable in societal development or whether a number of factors work in conjunction with technology to condition societal developments and evolution.

Economy

Like other animals, humans require food and shelter. In addition, humans have special needs for other goods and services ranging from color televisions, designer jeans, and jewelry to medical care, hunting skills, and spiritual guidance. As we have seen, these goods and services are produced through technology. The **economy** of a society consists of the social relationships that organize the production, distribution, and exchange of goods and services. *Production* is the organized system for the creation of goods and services. *Distribution* is the process of handing out, or allocating, the goods and services to members of society. *Exchange* is the process whereby members of society transfer goods and services among one another.

Anthropologists have found that the economy is closely connected with the environment, subsistence base, demographic conditions, technology, and division of labor of the society. The **division of labor** consists of specialized economic roles (occupations) and activities. In small-scale societies, the division of labor is typically simple, and in large-scale societies it is extremely complex. In the twentieth century, ethnographic descriptions of different types of societies have generated two perspectives on economic systems: the *formalist* and *substantivist* approaches.

THE FORMALIST APPROACH

The formalist view maintains that all economic systems are fundamentally similar and can be compared with one another. Formalists assume that all people act to maximize their individual gains. In other words, all humans have a psychological inclination to calculate carefully their self-interest. Formalists hypothesize that people do not always choose the cheapest and most efficient strategies to carry out their economic decisions, but they do tend to look for the best "rational" strategy for economic decision making.

Formalists hold that the best method for studying any economy is to employ the same general theories developed by economists. Formalists collect quantitative data and interpret these data by using sophisticated mathematical models developed by economists. They focus on such economic variables as production and consumption patterns, supply and demand, exchange, and investment decisions. One classic formalist study, by anthropologist Sol Tax (1953), focused on economic decision making in Guatemalan Indian communities. Tax analyzed the economic transactions in the traditional markets of these communities. He concluded that although the economy was undeveloped, the people made the same types of economic decisions as people in the developed world. Tax referred to these Indians as "penny capitalists."

THE SUBSTANTIVIST APPROACH

The substantivist approach draws its supporting hypotheses from twentieth-century ethnographic studies. Substantivists maintain that the ways of allocating goods and services in small-scale societies differ fundamentally from those of large-scale Western economic systems. Thus, the social institutions found in small-scale societies or larger agricultural societies produce economic systems that are fundamentally different from the market economies of Western societies. According to substantivists, preindustrial economies are not driven by the motive of individual material gain or profit, as are industrial economies. They argue that the economy is embedded in the sociocultural system, including the kinship systems, values, beliefs, and norms of the society.

MODERN ECONOMIC ANTHROPOLOGY

Most anthropologists today do not identify exclusively with the formalist or the substantivist perspective; instead, they recognize the contributions of both perspectives to our knowledge of economic systems (Wilk, 1996). Modern anthropologists investigate the different patterns of production, ownership, distribution, and exchange in relationship to ecological, demographic, and cultural factors. They collect quantitative economic data along with more qualitative cultural data to explain the workings of economic systems. In later chapters we will discuss the empirical data gathered by anthropologists about different types of economic systems.

Social Structure

All inorganic and organic things, from planets to living cells, have a structure; that is, they consist of interrelated parts in a particular arrangement. Buildings, snowflakes, amoebas, and the human body all have a certain structure. A book has a certain structure consisting of rectangular printed pages, binding, and a cover. All books have a similar structure, although the characteristics of different books can vary significantly.

Anthropologists use the image of structure when they analyze different societies. Societies are not just random, chaotic collections of people who interact with one another. Rather, social interaction in any society takes place in regular patterns. As we discussed in Chapter 4, through the process of enculturation, people learn the norms, values, and behavioral patterns of their society. In the absence of social patterns, people would find social life highly confusing. Anthropologists refer to this pattern of relationships in society as the **social structure.** Social structure provides the framework for all human societies.

COMPONENTS OF SOCIAL STRUCTURE

One of the most important components of social structure is status. A **status** is a recognized position that a person occupies in society. A person's status determines where he or she fits in society in relationship to everyone else. A status may be based on or accompanied by wealth, power, prestige, or a combination of all of these. Thus, the different statuses in a society are related to the division of labor, the political system, and other cultural variables.

All societies recognize both ascribed and achieved statuses. An **ascribed status** is one that is attached to a person from birth or that a person assumes involuntarily later in life. The most prevalent ascribed statuses are based on family and kinship relations (for example, daughter or son), sex (male or female), and age. In addition, in some societies ascribed statuses are based on one's race or ethnicity. For example, as we will see in a later chapter, skin color was used to designate ascribed status differences in South Africa under the system of *apartheid.* In contrast, an **achieved status** is one based at least in part on a person's specific actions. Examples of achieved statuses in the United States are one's profession and level of education.

Closely related to status is the concept of social roles. A **role** is a set of expected behavior patterns, obligations, and norms attached to a particular status. The distinction between status and role is a simple one: You "occupy" a certain status, but you "play" a role (Linton, 1936). For example, as a student you occupy a certain status that differs from that of your teacher, administrators, and other staff. As you occupy that status you perform by attending lectures, taking notes, participating in class, and studying for examinations. This concept of role is derived from the theater and refers to the parts played by actors on the stage. If you are a husband, mother, son, daughter, teacher, lawyer, judge, male, or female, you are expected to behave in certain ways because of the norms associated with that particular status.

As mentioned, a society's social statuses usually correspond to wealth, power, and prestige. Anthropologists find that all societies have inequality in statuses, which are arranged in a hierarchy. This inequality of statuses is known as **social stratification.** The degree of social stratification varies from one society to another depending on technological, economic, and political variables. Small-scale societies tend to be less stratified—that is, they have fewer categories of status and fewer degrees of difference regarding wealth, power, and prestige—than large-scale societies.

Anthropologists find that in some societies wealth, power, and prestige are linked with ownership of land or the number of animals acquired. In our society, high status is strongly correlated with the amount of wages or salary a person receives or how much property in the form of stocks or other paper assets is held. Exploring the causes of differing patterns of social stratification and how this stratification relates to other facets of society is an important objective of an ethnological study.

The social structure of any society has several major components that anthropologists look at when analyzing a society. These components are discussed in the following sections on family, marriage, gender, and age.

THE FAMILY

In a comprehensive cross-cultural study, George Murdock (1945) found that almost all societies recognize the family. Anthropologists define the **family** as a social group of two or more people related by blood, marriage, or adoption who live or reside together for an extended period, sharing economic resources and caring for their young. Anthropologists differentiate between the *family of orientation,* the family into which people are born and receive basic enculturation, and the *family of procreation,* the family within which people have or adopt children of their own (Murdock, 1949). The family is a social unit within a much wider group of relatives, or *kin.*

Although variations exist in types and forms, Murdock found that the family is a universal aspect of social organization. The reason for the universality of the family appears to be that it performs certain basic functions that serve human needs. The primary function of the family is the nurturing and enculturation of children. The basic norms, values, knowledge, and worldview of the culture are transmitted to children through the family.

Another function of the family is the regulation of sexual activity. Every culture places some restrictions on sexual behavior. Sexual intercourse is the basis of human reproduction and inheritance; it is also a matter of considerable social importance. Regulating sexual behavior is therefore essential to the proper functioning of a society. The family prohibits sexual relations within the immediate family through the incest taboos as discussed in Chapter 4.

Families also serve to protect and support their members physically, emotionally, and often economically from birth to death. In all societies people need warmth, food, shelter, and care. Families provide a social environment in which these needs can be met. Additionally, humans have emotional needs for affection and intimacy that are most easily fulfilled within the family.

The two major types of families found throughout the world are the *nuclear* and *extended families.* A typical **nuclear family** is composed of two parents and their immediate biological offspring or adopted children. George Murdock believed that the nuclear family is a universal feature of all societies (1949). However, as will be seen in later chapters, the nuclear family is not the principal kinship unit in all societies. In many societies the predominant form is the **extended family,** which is composed of parents, children, and other kin relations bound together as a social unit.

MARRIAGE

In most societies the family is a product of **marriage,** a social bond sanctioned by society between two or more people that involves economic cooperation and culturally approved sexual activity. Two general patterns of marriage exist: **endogamy,** which is marriage between people of the same social group or category, and **exogamy,** marriage between people of different social groups and categories.

A marriage may include two or more partners. **Monogamy** generally involves one spouse of each sex in the marriage. Though this is the most familiar form of marriage in Western industrial societies, it is not the only type of marriage practiced in the world. Many societies practice some form of **polygamy,** marriage involving a spouse of one sex and two or more spouses of the opposite sex. There are two forms of polygamy: **polygyny,** marriage between one husband and two or more wives, and **polyandry,** marriage between one wife and two or more husbands. Although the majority of the world's population currently practice monogamy, polygyny is a common form of marriage and is associated with 80 percent of human societies (many of which have relatively small populations) (Murdock, 1981a, b). Polyandry is the rarest form of marriage, occurring in only 0.5 percent of all societies. As we will see, anthropologists have developed hypotheses regarding why certain forms of marriage develop within particular sociocultural systems.

GENDER

Gender relationships are another important component of the social structure of a society. When anthropologists discuss relationships between males and females in a society, they distinguish between

A wedding ceremony in the United States. Anthropologists study the marital relationships of people and how those ceremonies relate to other aspects of society.

sex and *gender*. **Sex** refers to the biological and anatomical differences between males and females. These differences include the primary sexual characteristics—the sex organs—and secondary sexual characteristics, such as breasts and wider hips for females and more muscular development of the upper torso and extensive body hair for males. Note that these are general tendencies, to which many exceptions exist. That is, many males are smaller and lighter and have less body hair than many females. Nevertheless, in general, males and females are universally distinguished by physiological and anatomical differences.

In contrast to sex, **gender** is based on a cultural rather than biological distinction. Gender refers to the specific human traits attached to each sex by a society. As members of a particular society, males and females occupy certain statuses such as son, daughter, husband, wife, father, and mother. In assuming the *gender roles* that correspond to these different status positions, males are socialized to be "masculine," and females are socialized to be "feminine." Anthropologists find that definitions of *masculine* and *feminine* vary among different societies.

Gender and Enculturation One major issue regarding gender is the degree to which enculturation influences male and female behavior. To study this issue, anthropologists focus on the values, beliefs, and worldviews that may influence gender roles. They also observe the types of activities associated with young boys and girls. In many societies, boys and girls play different games as an aspect of enculturation. For example, in U.S. society, boys are traditionally encouraged to participate in aggressive, competitive team sports, whereas girls are usually not encouraged to do so. Cultural values and beliefs that affect gender roles are found in other societies as well.

Gender and the Division of Labor A basic component of the division of labor in most societies is the assigning of different tasks to males and females. In studying this phenomenon, anthropologists focus on the issue of whether physical differences between males and females are responsible for these different roles. To address this issue, they ask a number of questions. Is there a universal division of labor based on sex? Does physical strength have anything to do with the work patterns associated with gender? Do child care and pregnancy determine or influence economic specialization for females? To what degree do values and beliefs ascribed to masculine or feminine behavior affect work assignments?

Gender and Status   Another important issue investigated by anthropologists is the social and political status of males and females in society. As noted in Chapter 6, some early anthropologists such as Lewis Morgan believed that females at first had a higher social and political status than males, but through time that pattern was reversed. Anthropologists currently focus on how the status of males and females is related to biology, the division of labor, kinship relations, political systems, and values and beliefs.

Although sex characteristics are biologically determined, gender roles vary in accordance with the technological, economic, and sociocultural conditions of particular types of societies. In later chapters we explore some recent studies by anthropologists who have broadened our understanding of the variation of gender roles among a wide range of societies.

AGE

Like kinship and gender, age is a universal principle used to prescribe social status in sociocultural systems. The biological processes of aging are an inevitable aspect of human life; from birth to death our bodies are constantly changing. Definite biological changes occur for humans in their movement from infancy to childhood to adolescence to adulthood and to old age. Hormonal and other physiological changes lead to maturation and the onset of the aging process. For example, as we approach old age our sensory abilities begin to change. Taste, eyesight, touch, smell, and hearing begin to diminish. Gray hair and wrinkles appear, and we experience a loss of height and weight and an overall decline in strength and vitality. Although these physical changes vary greatly from individual to individual and to some extent are influenced by societal and environmental factors, these processes are universal.

The biology of aging, however, is only one dimension of how age is related to the social structure of any specific culture. The human life cycle is the basis of social statuses and roles that have both a physical and a cultural dimension. The cultural meanings of these categories in the life cycle vary among different societies, as do the criteria people use to define age-related statuses. The definitions of the statuses and roles for specific ages have wide-ranging implications for those in these status positions.

Age and Enculturation   As people move through the different phases of the human life cycle, they continually experience the process of enculturation. Because of the existence of different norms, values, and worldviews, people in various societies may be treated differently at each phase of the life cycle. For example, the period of enculturation during childhood varies among societies. In the United States and other industrialized societies, childhood is associated with an extensive educational experience that continues for many years. In many preindustrial societies, however, childhood is a relatively short period of time, and children assume adult status and responsibilities at a fairly young age.

Another factor influenced by aging in a society is how individuals are viewed at different ages. How is "old age" defined? For example, in many societies old age is not defined strictly in terms of the passage of time. More frequently, old age is defined in respect to changes in social status, work patterns, family status, or reproductive potential (Cowgill, 1986). These factors influence how people are valued at different ages in a society.

Age and the Division of Labor   Another societal factor that is influenced by the aging process is the economic role assumed by a person at different stages of the life cycle. Children everywhere are exposed to the technological skills they will need to survive in their environment. As they mature, they assume specific positions in the division of labor. Just as male and female roles differ, the roles for the young and old differ. For example, in some preindustrial societies, older people occupy central roles, whereas in others they play no important role at all. In industrial societies, the elderly generally do not occupy important occupational roles.

Age and Status   Age is one of the key determinants of social status. People are usually assigned a particular status associated with a phase of the life cycle. The result is **age stratification,** the unequal allocation of wealth, power, and prestige among people of different ages. Anthropologists find that age stratification varies in accordance with the level of technological development. For example, in many preindustrial societies, the elderly have a relatively high social status, whereas in most industrial societies the elderly experience a loss of status.

One of the most common ways of allocating the status of people at different ages is through age grades. **Age grades** are statuses defined by age, through which a person moves as he or she ages. For example, the age grades in most industrial societies correspond to the periods of infancy, preschool, kindergarten, elementary school, intermediate school, high school, young adulthood, middle age, young old, and old old (Cowgill, 1986). Each of these grades conveys a particular social status.

Age Status and Rites of Passage Anthropologists have done considerable research on the **rites of passage,** rituals associated with the life cycle and the movement of people between different age–status levels. Almost all cultures have rites of passage to demarcate these different stages of the life cycle. Arnold Van Gennep (1960), a Belgian anthropologist, wrote a classic study of different rites of passage throughout the world. He noted similarities among various rites connected with birth, puberty, marriage, and funerals. According to Van Gennep, these rites of passage are characterized by three interconnected stages: separation, marginality, and aggregation.

The first phase, *separation,* transforms people from one age status to another. In this phase, people leave behind the symbols, roles, and norms associated with the former position. The second phase, referred to as *marginality,* places people in a state of transition or a temporary period of ambiguity. This stage often involves separating individuals from the larger society to undergo traditional ordeals or indoctrination. The final phase is *aggregation,* or *incorporation,* when individuals assume their new status.

The best-known examples of these rites of passage are various religious rituals associated with adolescence, such as the confirmation rituals associated with Catholicism and the bar mitzvah rituals in Judaism. In later chapters we encounter examples of different rites of passage. The importance of these rites as an aspect of aging, status, and enculturation are explored there.

Political Organization

In the early twentieth century, German sociologist Max Weber introduced definitions of political power and authority that have since been adopted by anthropologists. Weber defined **political power** as the ability to achieve personal ends despite opposition. In this sense, political power can be based on physical or psychological coercion. Weber perceived this type of political power as *illegitimate,* in that it is unacceptable to most members of a society. According to Weber, the most effective and enduring form of political power is based on **authority,** power generally perceived by members of society as *legitimate* rather than coercive.

A brief example will illustrate the difference between illegitimate and legitimate power. If a large country invades and conquers a smaller one, the occupied people generally will not consider their new rulers to be legitimate. Thus, the rulers must rely on coercion to enforce their laws and to collect payments in the form of taxes or tributes. In contrast, most U.S. citizens voluntarily comply with the tax laws. Although they may complain, they

Anthropologists study the relationship between age and status. Elderly Japanese tend to have a higher status in their society than elderly Americans.

perceive their government as representing legitimate authority. Although physical coercion and force might be used to arrest some people who refuse to pay their taxes, in the majority of cases such actions are not necessary.

TYPES OF POLITICAL SYSTEMS

The general categories used by anthropologists to describe political systems are band, tribe, chiefdom, and state. A **band** is the least complex—and most likely the oldest—form of political system. It is the most common form among hunter-gatherer societies. Political institutions in band societies are based on close kinship relations within a fairly small group of people. **Tribes** are more complex societies with political institutions that unite larger groupings of people into a political system. Tribes do not have centralized, formal political institutions, but they do have **sodalities,** groups based on kinship, age, or gender that provide for political organization. For example, in some tribal societies of Papua New Guinea, secret male societies function as political institutions.

Chiefdom political systems are more complex than tribal societies in that they are formalized and centralized. Chiefdoms establish centralized, legitimate authority over many communities through a variety of complex economic, social, and religious institutions. Despite their size and complexity, however, chiefdoms are still fundamentally organized by kinship principles. Although chiefdoms have different levels of status and political authority, the people within these levels are related to one another through kinship ties. Eric Wolf (1982) has classified bands, tribes, and chiefdoms as *kin-ordered societies.*

States are political systems with centralized bureaucratic institutions to establish power and authority over large populations in distinctive territories. State systems are not based on kinship. State bureaucracies govern society on behalf of ruling authorities through procedures that plan, direct, and coordinate highly complex political processes. State political systems range from the early bureaucratic political units of agricultural societies such as Egypt and China to the modern industrial societies of the United States, Japan, the former Soviet Union, and European nations.

These various types of societies are discussed in later chapters. Nevertheless, it must be emphasized here that this classification does not represent a single scheme of political evolution for the entire world. The archaeological and ethnological data demonstrate again and again that a stage-by-stage development or evolution from band to tribe to chiefdom to state did not occur in all areas. These classifications are to be used only as categories to organize the vast amounts of data accumulated by anthropologists. As with all models, the boundaries separating the various categories are somewhat arbitrary.

DECISION MAKING IN A POLITICAL SYSTEM

An important topic in the study of a society is the day-to-day, individual decision making and competition for power and authority. In studying this topic, anthropologists may focus on fields or arenas within a society. A *field* is an area in which political interaction and competition take place. It may involve a part of a society, or it may extend beyond the boundaries of a society. For example, a field could be a whole tribe, a chiefdom, a state, or several of these units. A political *arena* is a more local, specific area in which individual actors or small groups compete for power and authority. An arena may be made up of factions, elites, or political parties in a society.

WARFARE AND FEUDS

The study of politics includes political conflicts within and among societies. Two major forms of conflicts are warfare and feuds. Anthropologists define **warfare** as armed combat among territorial or political communities. They distinguish between *internal warfare,* which involves political communities within the same society or culture, and *external warfare,* which occurs among different societal groups. A **feud** is a type of armed combat occurring within a political community and usually involves one kin group taking revenge against another kin group (Otterbein, 1974). Anthropologists examine the different biological, environmental, demographic, economic, social, political, and other cultural variables that influence warfare and feuds.

LAW AND SOCIAL CONTROL

Another aspect of political anthropology is the study of law and social control. As discussed in Chapter 3, one aspect of nonmaterial culture is the normative dimension, or *ethos*. All societies maintain an ethos that encourages certain behaviors and prohibits others. This ethos, along with the society's values, makes up the moral code that shapes human behavior. The particular ethos of a society represents an attempt to establish social control through various internal and external mechanisms. The internal mechanisms of social control are built into the enculturation process itself. Through enculturation, people learn the specific norms regarding society's expectations. Thereafter, those who violate these norms frequently experience emotional and cognitive discomfort in the form of guilt. Thus, internalized norms can shape and influence people's behavior even in the absence of constraints from other people.

Despite these internal mechanisms, however, individuals frequently violate norms. For a variety of reasons, enculturation does not bring about perfect social control in a society. Hence, in addition to internal mechanisms, societies use external mechanisms to enforce norms. External mechanisms take the form of *sanctions:* rewards (positive sanctions) for appropriate behaviors, and punishments (negative sanctions) for inappropriate behaviors.

Societies vary with respect to both the nature of their moral code and the types of external sanctions used to enforce the moral code. What one societal group considers deviant or unethical may be acceptable to another group. Divorce is an acceptable solution for severe marital conflicts in the United States. In Italy and Ireland, however, despite recent legislation that allows divorce, many still view it as an unethical pattern of behavior.

In large, complex social groups, sanctions are usually highly formalized. Rewards can take the form of public awards, parades, educational or professional degrees, and banquets. Negative sanctions include fines, imprisonment, expulsion, and sometimes death. In small-scale societies, sanctions tend to be informal. Examples of positive sanctions are smiles, handshakes, pats on the back, hugs, and compliments. Negative sanctions include restricted access to certain goods and services, gossip, frowns, impolite treatment, and ostracism.

Law as Formalized Norms and Sanctions   Anthropologists define laws as clearly defined norms, violations of which are punished through the application of formal sanctions by ruling authorities. In the 1960s, ethnologist Leonard Pospisil

Complex societies rely on organized police or military force to demonstrate political authority.

attempted to distinguish law from other social norms, based on his research among the Kapuakan tribe of New Guinea. He specified four criteria that must be present for a norm to be considered a law: (1) authority, (2) intention of universal application, (3) obligation, and (4) sanction (1967). To institutionalize legal decisions, a society must have members who possess recognized authority and can therefore intervene to settle disputes. These authorities must be able to enforce a verdict by either persuasion or force. Their verdicts must have universal application; that is, these decisions must be applied in the same manner if a similar situation arises in the future. This distinguishes legal decisions from those based purely on political expediency.

Obligation refers to the status relationships among the people involved in the conflict. If status relationships are unequal, the rights, duties, and obligations of the different parties can vary. Legal decisions must attempt to define the rights and obligations of everyone involved and to restore or create an equitable resolution of the conflict. Finally, punitive sanctions must be applied to carry out the legal decision.

Religion

As we saw in Chapter 2, archaeologists have discovered evidence of religious beliefs and practices associated with archaic *Homo sapiens* that date back to 100,000 years ago. Religion appears to be a cultural universal, although specific beliefs and practices vary significantly from one society to another. For example, some religions are based on the worship of an all-knowing, all-powerful supreme being, whereas others have many deities, and some have no deities at all.

Humans learn their religious traditions through the process of enculturation. Religious convictions are therefore shaped by the historical and social situations in which a person lives. For example, a person enculturated in ancient Greece would most likely have believed in many deities, among whom Zeus was the most powerful.

In studying the anthropology of religion, a critical point must be understood: Anthropologists are not concerned with the "truth" or "falsity" of any particular religious belief. Being based on the sci-

entific method, anthropology is not competent or able to investigate supernatural or metaphysical questions that go beyond empirical data. Rather, anthropological research on religion focuses on the relationship of doctrines, beliefs, and other religious questions to other aspects of society. The major question posed by anthropologists is, How do religious beliefs affect, relate to, and reflect the sociocultural conditions and concerns of a group of people?

Contemporary anthropological perspectives on religion encompass a number of approaches. Clifford Geertz (1973: 90) offered a sophisticated definition of religion:

> *A religion is a system of symbols which acts to establish powerful, pervasive, and long-lasting moods and motivations in men by formulating conceptions of a general order of existence and clothing these conceptions with such an aura of factuality that the moods and motivations seem uniquely realistic.*

Let us examine this definition more closely. Central to any religion is a "system of symbols" that includes all sacred objects, ranging from Christian crucifixes, native American 'medicine pouches,' and Buddhist relics to sacred myths such as Genesis or the Ramayana of Hinduism. These symbols produce "moods," such as happiness and sadness, and "motivations" that provide direction or ethical goals in a person's life. Hence, religious symbols enhance particular feelings and dispositions, creating an intense sense of awe in individuals. This sense of awe is induced through the use of sacred symbols in rituals and other religious performances to create an atmosphere of mystery going beyond everyday experience. But religious symbols also create and reaffirm a worldview by "formulating conceptions of a general order of existence." This worldview provides meaning or purpose to life and the universe. A religious worldview helps people discern the meaning of pain and suffering in the world. Sacred myths help people make sense of the world and also explain and justify cultural values and social rules.

MYTHS

The study of the religious worldview includes the analysis of myths. **Myths** consist of a people's assumed knowledge about the universe and the natural and supernatural worlds, and humanity's place

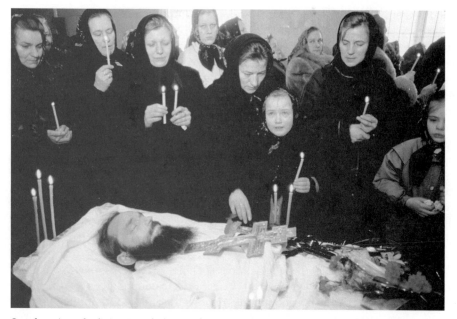

One function of religion is to help people cope with major events and crises, such as death.

in these worlds. In Chapter 2, we presented some basic myths or *cosmologies* regarding the creation of the universe. All societies have such sacred myths. Anthropologists focus on a number of questions regarding myths: Why do myths of a particular type exist in different societies? What is the relationship between myths and other aspects of sociocultural systems? Are myths distortions of historical events? What are the functions of myths?

RITUALS

The final portion of Geertz's definition—that these systems of symbols act to clothe those conceptions in "such an aura of factuality that the moods and motivations seem uniquely realistic"—attempts to deal with the question often asked about religious belief: How do humans come to believe in ideas about spirits, souls, revelations, and many unsupportable or untestable conceptions? Geertz's answer to this question is that religious rituals in which humans participate create an "aura of factuality." It is through ritual that deeper realities are reached. Religion is nonempirical and nonrational in its search for truth. It is not based on conclusions from scientific experience but is "prior" to experience. Religious truth is not "inductive," providing evidence for metaphysical explanations. It

symbolically and abstractly evokes the ultimate concerns of humans. Through ritual activities these symbolic and abstract nonempirical truths are given meaning.

Religious **rituals** consist of repetitive behaviors that communicate sacred symbols to members of society. Examples of religious rituals are the Catholic Mass, Jewish Passover rites, and the Native American sweat lodge rites, which include prayer, meditation, and other spiritual communication. Anthropologist Edmund Leach (1966) emphasized that religious rituals communicate these sacred symbols and information in a condensed manner. He noted that the verbal part of a ritual is not separable from the behavioral part and that rituals can have different symbolic meanings for people in a society. In other words, religious rituals convey a unique, personal, psychological experience for every individual who participates.

RELIGIOUS SPECIALISTS

One important area of research in the anthropology of religion is the study of religious specialists in different societies. Every society has certain individuals who possess specialized, sacred knowledge. Such individuals officiate over rituals and interpret myths. The type of religious specialist varies with the form of sociocultural system. **Shamans** are part-time religious practitioners who are believed to have contact with supernatural beings and powers. They do not have a formalized official status as religious practitioners in their respective societies. Aside from their religious functions, they participate in the same subsistence activities and functions as anyone else in their society. Anthropologists also use terms such as *native healer, medicine man,* and *medicine woman* to refer to these practitioners.

The terms **priest** and **priestess** refer to full-time religious specialists who serve in an official capacity as the custodians of sacred knowledge. In contrast to shamans, priests and priestesses are usually trained through formal educational processes to maintain religious traditions and rituals. Priests and priestesses are usually associated with more complex sociocultural systems.

RELIGIOUS MOVEMENTS

Another topic of interest in the anthropology of religion is the analysis of religious movements. In early approaches of the social sciences, religion was viewed simply as an outcome of certain economic or political conditions in society. It was assumed that as society developed modern economic and political institutions, religious traditions would disappear. Religion was viewed as a peripheral element that served only to conserve society as a static system. Today, however, some anthropologists have begun to analyze religious beliefs and worldviews as major variables that induce societal change. For example, ethnologists studying Islamic fundamentalist movements have concluded that in the Middle East, religion is a major force for social change. These new modes of understanding religious traditions are analyzed in subsequent chapters.

Cross-Cultural Research

This chapter has focused on the analysis of variables and their interconnections within specific societies. Although the primary objective of ethnological research is to improve our understanding of a particular sociocultural system, another aim is to provide a basis for comparing different societies and to offer general explanations for human be-

havior. Specific ethnographies provide the necessary data for this type of cross-cultural research. Cross-cultural research is frequently used by anthropologists to explore the various conditions that influence the development of societies throughout the world.

Cross-cultural research has been an ongoing project in anthropology for the past hundred years or so. Recently, a great deal of ethnographic data has been computerized in the Human Relations Area Files, commonly known as the HRAF. The HRAF contains descriptive ethnographic data on more than 300 societies. Initiated by George P. Murdock of Yale University, it is made up of original ethnographic descriptions classified for cross-cultural research purposes. Murdock incorporated data on 862 societies in his *Ethnographic Atlas* (1981) and on 563 societies that cover the major geographic regions of the world in his *Atlas of World Cultures* (1981). These ethnographic databases enable scholars to retrieve information quickly and can be used for statistical and computerized cross-cultural research. These databases are extremely valuable sources for assessing the differences and similarities among cultures.

Cross-cultural studies allow anthropologists to make distinctions between behaviors that are culture specific and those that are universal. These distinctions help anthropologists provide general explanations for human behavior. In doing so, these studies help fulfill the major goals of anthropological research.

Cross-cultural methods have some limitations, however. One major weakness is that some ethnologists in the past may not have taken historical circumstances into account when describing the particular conditions in a society. This may have led to a static, unchanging portrait of the society studied. For example, the description of the economic practices of people in Africa, Asia, or the Pacific Islands may not make sense outside of a specific historical context. These societies had historical relationships with other societies outside of their own cultural boundaries, and these relationships resulted in changes in the particular economic practices observed by the ethnologist. In later chapters of this text we explore why ethnologists must understand the historical context of different societies that they study so that they can fully comprehend the behavior being observed.

Another problem with cross-cultural studies lies with faulty ethnographic reporting, which can produce unreliable data, contributing in turn to a distorted image of the society being studied. Consequently, anthropologists approach cross-cultural research with caution. Contemporary anthropologists who use these data must review the work of their predecessors who gathered the basic information to assess its validity. Through careful examination of the original data in the HRAF and other cross-cultural databases, modern anthropologists will make further progress toward formulating sound generalizations regarding the cultures of humankind.

 ## SUMMARY

Ethnologists conduct fieldwork in different societies to examine people's lifestyles. They describe societies in written studies called ethnographies, which focus on behavior and thought among the people studied. Ethnologists must use systematic research methods and strategies in their examination of society. Their basic research method is participant observation, which involves participating in the activities of the people they are studying.

In their analyses of sociocultural systems, anthropologists investigate cause-and-effect relationships among different variables. They use a multidimensional approach, examining the interaction among many variables to provide explanations for the similarities and differences among societies.

Anthropologists explore the interaction between the environment and subsistence practices. They examine the biomes of different regions to determine the influence of environment on societal development. They investigate fertility, mortality, and migration to detect changes in demographic conditions. They also investigate the relationship between cultural values and population.

Technological and economic variables are assessed in the analysis of society and culture. The technology and economy of a society produce distinctive differences in the division of labor. Anthropologists find that technology and economic conditions are also influenced by cultural values and norms.

Another area of research is social structure, including the family, marriage, kinship, gender, and age. These components of social structure are related to the division of labor and other cultural conditions.

Different types of political organizations and legal systems are explored by anthropologists. Through detailed ethnological research and cross-cultural comparisons, anthropologists have found that specific types of political and legal systems have been influenced by various societal conditions. To analyze different forms of political systems, anthropologists classify societies into bands, tribes, chiefdoms, and states.

The anthropology of religion is devoted to the examination of diverse religious beliefs and worldviews. Myths, rituals, religious specialists, and religious movements are explored in relationship to other aspects of society.

Much ethnographic data has been coded for computer use in cross-cultural studies. These cross-cultural studies can be employed to develop general explanations regarding human behavior in specific societies and across cultural boundaries.

STUDY QUESTIONS

1. What are some of the things that an ethnologist has to do to prepare herself or himself for fieldwork?

2. What are some of the research goals of demographic anthropologists as they relate to fieldwork? Why is a demographic perspective important in anthropological research?

3. Do you think that technology is the primary, basic source of sociocultural change? Do values play any role in sociocultural change?

4. The formalist and substantivist approaches to understanding an economic system are decidedly different. Are these approaches mutually exclusive, or could they be used together to examine the economic system of a society? Explain.

5. What are the basic components or patterns of family and marriage from an anthropological view?

6. Have you ever gone through a rite of passage? If so, what was it? Have you experienced more than one? Pick one rite of passage that you have experienced and describe it in terms of Van Gennep's stages of separation, marginality, and incorporation (aggregation).

7. What is the difference between legitimate and illegitimate political power? Give an example of each.

8. Review Clifford Geertz's definition of religion. What do you think are the strengths or weaknesses of his definition?

9. What are the benefits and limitations of conducting cross-cultural research?

KEY TERMS

achieved status
age grades
age stratification
ascribed status
authority
band
biome
carrying capacity
chiefdom
correlation
crude birthrate
crude death rate
cultural ecology
culture shock
demography
dependent variable
division of labor
ecology
economy
endogamy
environmental niche

exogamy
extended family
family
fecundity
fertility
feud
gender
goods
independent variable
infant mortality rate
life expectancy
marriage
migration rate
monogamy
mortality
myths
net migration
nuclear family
political power
polyandry
polygamy

polygyny
priest
priestess
qualitative data
quantitative data
random sample
rites of passage
rituals
role
services
sex
shamans
social stratification
social structure
sodalities
states
status
subsistence patterns
technology
tribes
warfare

INTERNET EXERCISES

1. Discover the life of a Vietnamese gang member in Los Angeles by visiting **http://cwis.usc.edu/dept/elab/buidoi/vietgangs.html.** Click on Introduction to the Project and read the description. What do you feel is the premise of this web-site? What is the value of visual anthropology to ethnology?

2. Ethical issues in anthropology are often at the forefront of research. While looking at the web-

site **http://www.ameranthassn.org/sp23.htm,** read the introduction by Joan Cassell and Sue-Ellen Jacobs. How do they think case studies improve anthropological practice? Why are ethical considerations important to anthropological research? How do the views on ethics on this website compare to those in the chapter?

 ## SUGGESTED READINGS

BOHANNON, PAUL, ed. 1967. *Law and Warfare: Studies in the Anthropology of Conflict*. Garden City, NY: Natural History Press. A classic introduction to the field of legal anthropology. This series of readings includes descriptive data and hypotheses regarding how anthropologists ought to examine law in different societies.

CAMPBELL, BERNARD. 1983. *Human Ecology: The Story of Our Place in Nature from Prehistory to the Present*. New York: Aldine. A concise introduction to anthropological research in the field of cultural ecology.

COHEN, RONALD, AND JOHN MIDDLETON, eds. 1967. *Comparative Political Systems: Studies in the Politics of Preindustrial Societies*. Garden City, NY: Natural History Press. A collection of readings based on research from the field of political anthropology. It consists of detailed ethnological analyses of political systems in various regions of the world.

DALTON, GEORGE, ed. 1976. *Tribal and Peasant Economies: Readings in Economic Anthropology*. Austin: University of Texas Press. An anthology introducing the field of economic anthropology in a nontechnical manner. The essays in this collection illustrate the most important debates in economic anthropology, including the formalist versus substantivist debate.

GRABURN, NELSON, ed. 1971. *Readings in Kinship and Social Structure*. New York: Harper & Row. A collection of fifty-nine essays covering the field of social anthropology from 1860 to the modern period. The readings represent some of the best-known anthropological writings regarding family, marriage, and kinship.

LEHMANN, ARTHUR C., AND JAMES E. MYERS, eds. 1997. *Magic, Witchcraft, and Religion: An Anthropological Study of the Supernatural,* 4th ed. Mountain View, CA: Mayfield. An anthology containing a good selection of both classic and contemporary essays dealing with the anthropology of religion. The emphasis of the text is on the nonliterate religious traditions.

OSWALT, WENDELL. 1976. *An Anthropological Analysis of Food-Getting Technology*. New York: Wiley. A unique overview of the various types of technologies used in preindustrial societies.

SCUPIN, RAYMOND (Ed.) 2000. *Religion and Culture: An Anthropological Focus*. Upper Saddle River, NJ: Prentice Hall. This textbook is a reader containing original essays by various anthropologists on all of the indigenous and major religious traditions throughout the world.

Band Societies

CHAPTER OUTLINE

Modern Foraging Environments and Subsistence
Deserts / Tropical Rain Forests / Arctic Regions / Mobility and Subsistence / Optimal Foraging Theory

Foragers and Demographic Conditions
Fissioning / Infanticide / Fertility Rates

Technology in Foraging Societies

Economics in Foraging Societies
Reciprocity / Collective Ownership of Property / The Original Affluent Society?

Social Organization in Foraging Societies
Marriage and Kinship / Gender / Age

Political Organization in Foraging Societies
Characteristics of Leadership / Warfare and Violence / Conflict Resolution

Religion in Foraging Societies
The Dreamtime / Eskimo Religion / Art, Music, and Religion

CHAPTER QUESTIONS

- How are the environments of the modern foraging or band societies different from those of the Paleolithic?

- What are the distinguishing features of the population, economy, social life, political systems, and religious traditions of band societies?

AS DISCUSSED PREVIOUSLY, EARLY SOCIETIES DID not produce their own food but instead survived by hunting and gathering, or foraging. A **hunter-gatherer,** or **foraging,** society is a society whose subsistence is based on the hunting of animals and gathering of vegetation. The basic economic, social, and political unit of hunter-gatherer societies is the **band.**

Food production as a subsistence pattern developed relatively recently, about 12,000 to 10,000 years ago. Thus, for almost 99 percent of humanity's life span, humans lived as foragers. This lifestyle has been the most enduring and persistent adaptation humans have ever achieved. Therefore, band societies have been the basic type of sociocultural system for perhaps as long as 1 million years. Hence, the study of the foraging way of life has been of particular interest to anthropologists as a means of understanding Paleolithic lifestyles; consequently, anthropologists have studied numerous contemporary hunting-and-gathering societies. Early ethnologists thought that these studies could help provide models for understanding Paleolithic societies.

Unlike some of their nineteenth-century predecessors, however, modern anthropologists do not assume that contemporary hunting-and-gathering societies are representative of this type of society at early stages of human evolution. Paleolithic hunting-and-gathering societies existed in nearly all the major biomes of the world, whereas modern band societies of this type exist only in limited, **marginal environments,** those that are not suitable for intensive agriculture. Therefore, contemporary hunters and gatherers are modern peoples who have adapted to extreme environmental conditions.

In addition, as will be emphasized in Chapter 13, all of these modern hunter-gatherer societies have been altered by surrounding societies. For example, hunter-gatherers in Southeast Asia and Africa have carried on continuous economic exchanges with nearby agricultural societies for centuries. More recently, industrial societies have dramatically affected these hunting-and-gathering societies. Many of the hunter-gatherers have been forced by modern nation-states to relocate and adjust to areas not suitable to their traditional subsistence practices. For reasons such as these, studies of modern hunting-gathering societies do not offer precise comparative data for evaluating Paleolithic societies.

You will notice that in this chapter we refer to hunter-gatherers in both the past and present tenses. As a result of contacts with other peoples, many traditional practices and institutions of band societies have been transformed. The past tense is used to describe these traditional phenomena. Those traditions that have managed to persist into the present are discussed in the present tense.

Modern Foraging Environments and Subsistence

During the last 10,000 years, foraging societies have grown fewer and fewer and are now restricted to marginal environments. Deserts, tropical rain forests, and arctic areas are considered marginal environments, because until recently too much labor and capital were needed to irrigate deserts, plant crops in the Arctic, or slash down

tropical forests for agriculture. Consequently, those few foraging or hunter-gatherer societies that adjusted to these marginal environments managed to exist in relative isolation from surrounding groups. Figure 8.1 shows the locations of the major hunter-gatherer societies.

DESERTS

Various cultural-ecological studies have been done with foragers surviving in desert environments. One long-term study focuses on the !Kung San or Ju/'hoansi of the Kalahari Desert in southwestern Africa. The San occupied the southern Africa for thousands of years along with another, biologically related population known popularly as the Hottentots, or Khoi. Archaeologist John Yellen (1985) located prehistoric sites in the Kalahari that have been dated to well over 11,000 years ago. This evidence suggests that the !Kung San had been residing in this region before agriculture spread to the surrounding region.

Most historians and archaeologists agree that the processes of migration and culture contact with

Figure 8.1   Hunter-gatherer societites discussed in this chapter.

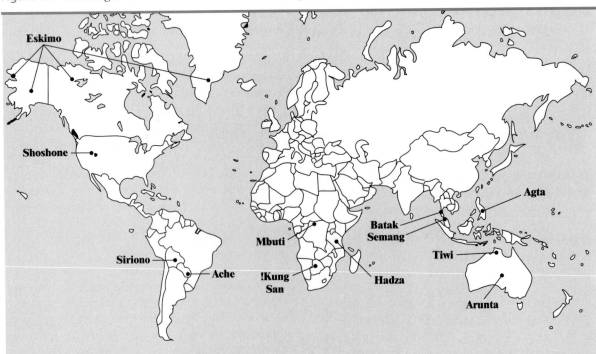

Ju/'hoansi of the Kalahari.

surrounding societies have affected the !Kung San, and the "modern" !Kung San do not represent a pure remnant of Paleolithic society. The frequency of interaction of San accelerated with European expansion and settlements throughout southern Africa in the eighteenth century (see Chapter 13). Presently, the population of the Ju/'hoansi or San is estimated at around 100,000 people.

Richard Lee, who studied the Ju/'hoansi or San from the 1960s through the 1990s, gives a comprehensive picture of their food-gathering and dietary practices. At the time he studied them, between 60 and 80 percent of the San diet consisted of nuts, roots, fruit, melons, and berries, which were gathered by the women. Meat from hunting was less common, providing only 20 to 30 percent of the diet. To procure this diet, the San did not need to expend enormous amounts of time and energy. In fact, Lee estimated that San adults spent between two and three days each week finding food. Women often were able to gather enough in one or two days to feed their families for a week, leaving time for resting, visiting, embroidering, and entertaining visitors. Males spent much of their leisure time in ritual activities, including curing ceremonies (Lee, 1972b, 1979, 1993).

Other foraging societies existed in various arid and semiarid desert biomes, an example being the Great Basin Shoshone, a Native American group discussed in Chapter 6. Shoshone males hunted and trapped game, and Shoshone females gathered seeds, insects, and assorted vegetation. Both males and females harvested wild pinyon nuts, which the women mixed with seeds and insects and ground into flour for cooking.

Many of the Australian Aborigines were hunter-gatherers living in deserts that made up one-third of the continent. One group, known as the Arunta, lived in the interior desert region. They subsisted on the various species of animals and plants found in their habitat. Women and children gathered seeds, roots, snails, insects, reptiles, burrowing rodents, and eggs of birds and reptiles. Arunta males specialized in hunting larger game such as the kangaroo, the wallaby, the large, ostrichlike emu, and smaller birds and animals. Ethnographic studies indicate that Aborigines spent four to five hours per day per person in gathering food (Sahlins, 1972).

TROPICAL RAIN FORESTS

Foragers have also adapted to the marginal environments of tropical rain forests. In the central African country of Zaire, a group of foragers known as the Mbuti Pygmies resides in the luxuriant Ituri Rain Forest. The first evidence of the Mbuti peoples comes from early Egyptian accounts of an expedition into the Ituri Forest. From other archaeological data, it appears that the Mbuti have inhabited this region for at least 5,000 years. Colin

Turnbull (1983), who did ethnological research among the Mbuti in the 1960s, suggests that there was no dramatic change in Mbuti culture until about 450 years ago, after Europeans came to Africa.

The division of labor among the Mbuti resembles that of other hunting-and-gathering groups. Males hunt elephants, buffalo, wild pigs, and other game, and females gather vegetation. The entire group, however, is involved in the hunting endeavor. Mbuti males set up nets to capture the game, after which they stand guard with spears. Youths with bows and arrows stand farther back from the nets to shoot any game that escapes, while women and children form semicircles to drive the game into the nets. More independent hunting is done by older males and youths, who may wander off to shoot monkeys and birds.

Another hunting-gathering people, known as the Semang, inhabit the tropical forests of the Malaysian and Thai peninsula. They live in the foothills and lower slopes of dense rain forests that have exceptionally heavy precipitation. Although in the past the Semang may have hunted large game such as elephants and buffalo, they abandoned large-game hunting when they took up the blowgun instead of the bow and arrow (Keyes,

1977). Today, Semang males fish and hunt small game. However, Semang subsistence depends primarily on the gathering of wild fruits and vegetables including yams, berries, nuts, and shoots collected by females.

ARCTIC REGIONS

Survival in arctic conditions has inspired considerable creative adjustments by groups of foragers popularly known as the Eskimo. The Eskimo refer to themselves as the Inuit. Early Eskimo culture has been dated to at least 2500 B.C. Some Eskimo live in northwestern Alaska near the Bering Sea, and others live in the arctic regions of northern Canada, extending eastward all the way to Greenland. The northwestern Alaska Eskimo hunt sea mammals such as bowhead whales, seals, and walruses. Interior groups such as the Netsilik in central Canada, who were studied by ethnologist Asen Balikci, hunt caribou, musk oxen, an occasional polar bear, seals, and birds. They also fish in nearby bays.

Because vegetation historically was scarce in arctic regions, it was a prized food. After killing the caribou, male hunters ate the animal's stomach so as to obtain the valued undigested vegetation. Although their diet consisted primarily of meat, the

Inuit hunters in Alaska.

Eskimo generally satisfied their basic nutritional requirements of carbohydrate, protein, and vitamins from eating berries, green roots, and fish and fish oil. They preferred cooked foods, but boiling food over fires fueled by blubber oil was slow and expensive; consequently, the Eskimo ate most of their food raw.

The division of labor among the Eskimo was unlike that of most other foraging societies, because of the scarcity of vegetation. Women were not specialized collectors. However, during the summer season males and females gathered larvae, caribou flies, maggots, and deer droppings that contained vegetation.

MOBILITY AND SUBSISTENCE

No matter what their particular environment, all hunters and gatherers share one characteristic: mobility. As food and other resources become scarce in one site, the groups have to move on to another. The Mbuti Pygmies, for example, reside in certain areas during the rainy season and other areas during other seasons, depending on the supply of game (Turnbull, 1983). The San moved frequently in the pursuit of resources. During the winter dry season, they congregated in large groupings around several watering holes, but during the rainy season the groups dispersed into small units. The San moved when subsistence required (Lee, 1969). Most Eskimo groups also have to move during different seasons to pursue game and other resources. For example, the northwestern Alaska Eskimos move from the coastal areas into the interior regions during the summer seasons to hunt herds of caribou.

These nomadic behaviors are not arbitrary or spontaneous. Rather, they are carefully planned to minimize labor while providing vital resources. These patterns of mobility represent an admirable appreciation and intimate knowledge of the environment in which these foragers reside.

OPTIMAL FORAGING THEORY

One of the ways in which anthropologists attempt to study the subsistence and foraging practices of hunter-gatherers is referred to as optimal foraging theory. Optimal foraging theory is used to try to predict what potential foods the foragers should exploit, if they are to make the most efficient use

of time and energy. It is also used to predict what foods would be avoided because exploiting them would take up time and energy that could be used more efficiently for procuring other foods. It assesses the immediate costs and benefits of utlizing different subsistence strategies.

One of the most extensive uses of optimal foraging theory was used by Kristin Hawkes, Kimberly Hill, and James O'Connell, a team of anthropologists who studied the Ache hunter-gatherers of the tropical rain forests of Paraguay in South America (1982). These anthropologists found that the optimal foraging theory tended to predict the types of foods procured by the Ache. They started by having the Ache rank the kinds and types of foods that they foraged. Then, the anthropologists carefully observed what foods were actually procured. For example, they observed that the Ache picked oranges rather than killing monkeys most of the time. Though oranges give a lower yield in calories than monkeys, the processing time was much shorter for oranges than monkeys. The anthropologists calculated that the average return from Ache hunting was 1,115 kilocalories per hour per person. But when they picked oranges the individual's average return rose to 4,438 kilocalories per hour. Therefore, oranges were a much more profitable and efficient food to exploit. The Ache told the anthropologists that monkeys were not worth hunting because they were not fat enough. However, when they came across a monkey, they would kill it for food. The Ache tended to make the kinds of decisions one would expect according to optimal foraging calculations. This study, along with other optimal foraging studies, demonstrates that hunter-gatherers make very efficient use of their environment for subsistence purposes.

Foragers and Demographic Conditions

As we have seen, modern foragers live in marginal environments and travel from location to location. The requirement of mobility to procure resources has had a major effect on demographic conditions in these societies. Unlike food producers, hunters and gatherers must depend on the naturally occurring food resources in their territories. These food resources determine and limit excessive population growth. Generally, the population densities of foragers as measured in relation to the carrying capacity of their environments are extremely low.

Demographic studies such as those done by ethnologists Richard Lee (1972a) and Nancy Howell (1979) on the Ju/'hoansi or San have enabled anthropologists to make certain generalizations concerning demographic conditions among modern foragers. Population size among the San was carefully controlled in a number of ways. According to Lee (1979), the San knew how many people could be supported in specific territories and how many people were needed to provide sufficient resources. Having too many people leads to shortages of resources, whereas having too few people leads to ineffective foraging strategies.

FISSIONING

One of the most important means of limiting population growth for foragers is fissioning. **Fissioning** is the movement of people from one group to another when the population begins to increase and food or other material resources become scarce. Resource scarcity creates population pressure in the form of hardships and problems that emerge as the biome's resources become overtaxed. In such cases, the typical response is for a portion of the population to migrate to other geographic regions. Fissioning was most likely the primary means of population control for Paleolithic foragers and to some extent explains the worldwide expansion of the human species.

Fissioning is practiced by modern foragers to a limited extent. Its success depends on the presence of unoccupied land into which the excess population can expand. In situations where an increasing population is surrounded by other populations and fissioning is not possible, conflict between groups becomes likely, although sometimes fusion, or groups combining with one another, occurs (Hammel & Howell, 1987).

INFANTICIDE

Another means of population control in some foraging societies is **infanticide,** the deliberate abandonment or killing of infants, usually immediately after birth. Infanticide has been well documented

in foraging societies. Joseph Birdsell (1968) hypothesized that infanticide is a means of spacing children. Because a woman can carry only one child in her arms at a time as a nomadic gatherer, there is a need to space childbirth. Typically, childbirth was spaced at intervals of four years.

Most cases of infanticide in these foraging societies appear to be decisions made by individuals in response to famine conditions or to anticipated food and material scarcities (Harris & Ross, 1987). Infanticide in some of these societies is also associated with the birth of twins (supporting two children might be difficult or impossible) and with genetically abnormal infants.

FERTILITY RATES

Other lines of demographic research investigate the relatively slow rate of population growth for foraging societies. Some anthropologists are testing demographic hypotheses on the relationship among nutrition, physiological stress, breast-feeding, and rates of fertility (Howell, 1979; Lee, 1979). The purpose of these studies is to determine whether biological factors rather than cultural practices such as infanticide may induce low fertility rates and thus slow population growth for foragers.

For example, Nancy Howell's research on the San indicates that a low caloric diet and the high energetic rate needed for female foraging activities may postpone the occurrence of menarche, the onset of menstruation at puberty, which does not appear in San females until a mean age of 16.6 years (Howell, 1979), compared with 12.9 years in the United States (Barnouw, 1985). The low body weight of San females, whose average weight is 90 pounds, also influences the late onset of menarche. This slower rate of maturation may be related to the low fertility of the San.

Other studies have suggested that breast-feeding contributes to low fertility rates. Breast-feeding stimulates the production of prolactin, a hormone that inhibits pregnancy. San women breast-feed their infants for three to four years. Considering the workload and general ecological conditions San women must deal with, this prolonged nursing may produce a natural, optimal birth interval, or spacing of children (Blurton Jones, 1986, 1987).

This factor, along with sexual abstinence, abortion, infanticide, and delayed marriage, may be evidence of early forms of fertility control in prehistoric foraging societies.

Technology in Foraging Societies

In Chapter 2, we discussed the evolution of technology during the Paleolithic period. The crude stone tools of the Lower Paleolithic gave way to the more sophisticated stone tool complex of the Upper Paleolithic. As humans migrated across the continents, technology became specialized, enabling populations to adjust to different types of environments.

Until recently, anthropologists believed that many modern hunter-gatherers had limited technologies. Nineteenth-century anthropologists thought that these limited technologies reflected a simplicity of mind and lack of skill. Modern anthropologists, in contrast, regard these technologies as highly functional in particular ecological conditions. More important, technology does not refer just to tools or artifacts; it also includes the cultural knowledge that has to be maintained by the society. All foraging peoples have an extensive knowledge of their environmental conditions and of the appropriate means of solving technological problems in these environments.

Desert foragers such as the Ju/'hoansi or San use small bows and arrows and spears. Australian Aborigines did not have the bow and arrow, but they used the well-known boomerang (which did not return to the thrower), spears, and spear-throwers for hunting in desert areas. In tropical rain forests, foragers make traps, snares, and sometimes nets such as those used by the Mbuti. The Mbuti also make fire-hardened wooden spears and arrow tips for hunting. Some foraging groups, like the Semang, use the blowgun for hunting game. Most of the desert and rain forest foragers use natural poisons to make their hunting more efficient. In some cases, the foragers take various types of poisons from plants and place the poisons in streams to kill fish. In other cases they put poison on the tips of their arrows to kill game.

As we have seen, fruit and vegetable gathering is at least as important as hunting in foraging societies. In the desert and tropical rain forest, the implements for gathering are uncomplicated. The cultural knowledge needed for gathering, however, is profound. The people need to know where to find the plants, when to find them during different seasons, which plants are edible, what plants are scarce or plentiful, and so on. In most cases, gathering food is the responsibility of women and children. The typical tool is a simple sharpened stick for digging up tubers or getting honey out of hives. Sometimes these foragers also use net bags, bark, wooden bowls, or other natural objects to carry nuts, seeds, water, or fruit. For example, San women used large ostrich eggs to hold and carry water.

An extremely complex foraging technology was created by the Eskimo to procure animal food resources. The classic Eskimo technology has evolved over the past 3,000 years and includes equipment made from bone, stone, skin, wood, and ice. *Umiaks* (large boats) and *kayaks* (canoes) are used for whaling, sealing, and transportation. Eskimo technology also includes dogsleds, lances, fish spears, bows and arrows, harpoons with detachable points, traps, fish hooks, and soapstone lamps used with whale and seal oil for heating and cooking. Unlike the desert and rain forest foragers who wear very little clothing, the Eskimo people have developed sophisticated techniques for curing hides from caribou and seals to make boots, parkas, and other necessary arctic gear.

Economics in Foraging Societies

Despite the vast differences in physical environment, subsistence, and technology, most foraging societies have similar economic systems. The major form of economic system identified with these societies is called the **reciprocal economic system** (Sahlins, 1972). A reciprocal economic system is based on exchanges among family groups as a means of distributing goods and services throughout the society. The basic principle underlying this system is **reciprocity,** the widespread sharing of goods and services in a society. One reason for this system of reciprocal exchange is that the consumption of food and other resources is usually immediate, because there is very little storage capacity for any surplus. Thus, it makes sense to share what cannot be used anyway.

RECIPROCITY

The many descriptions of economic transactions and exchanges in foraging societies have led Marshall Sahlins to distinguish three types of reciprocity: generalized, balanced, and negative (1965, 1972).

Generalized Reciprocity   This form of exchange is based on the assumptions that an immediate return is not expected and that the value of the exchanges will balance out in the long run. The value of the return is not specified, and no running account of repayment of transactions is calculated. Although **generalized reciprocity** exists in all societies—for example, in the United States when parents pay for their offsprings' food, clothing, and shelter—in foraging societies these transactions form the basis of the economic system.

Anthropologists used to refer to generalized reciprocity as a gift, to distinguish it from trade or barter. Neither altruism nor charity, however, accurately describes these transactions. Rather, these exchanges are based on socially recognized family and kinship statuses. Because such behaviors are expected, gratitude or recognition is usually not required. In fact, in this form of reciprocity it might be impolite or insulting to indicate that a return is expected. For example, among the San and Eskimo foragers, a "thank-you" for food or other services is interpreted as an insult (Freuchen, 1961; Lee, 1969). Generosity is required in these small-scale societies to reduce envy and social tensions, promote effective cooperation, distribute resources and services, and create obligations.

Examples of generalized reciprocity occur among foragers like the San, Mbuti, and Eskimo. Aside from food, which is shared with everyone in the group, the San have a generalized exchange system known as *hxaro,* which not only circulates goods but also—and *primarily*—solidifies social relationships by creating mutual obligations among related kin (Lee, 1993). The *hxaro* system involves exchanging goods ranging from weapons to jewelry. Constant circulation of these material goods not only enhances and maintains kin ties through mutual obligations but also inhibits the accumulation of wealth by any individuals in the society. This enables these societies to remain **egalitarian,** which refers to societies that have very small differences in wealth among individuals. There are no rich or poor in these types of societies.

Balanced Reciprocity   A more direct type of reciprocal exchange with an explicit expectation of immediate return is **balanced reciprocity.** This form of reciprocity is more utilitarian and more like trade and barter than is generalized reciprocity. The material aspect of the exchange is as important as the social aspect. People involved in these transactions calculate the value of the exchanges, which are expected to be equivalent. If an equal return is not given, the original donor may not continue the exchange relationship. Balanced reciprocity is usually found in contexts of more distant kinship relations. Because most exchanges and transactions in modern foraging societies take place among close kin, balanced reciprocity is practiced less frequently than is generalized reciprocity.

Negative Reciprocity   Sahlins (1972) defined negative reciprocity as the attempt to get something for nothing. **Negative reciprocity** means no reciprocity at all. It may involve bargaining, haggling, gambling, cheating, theft, or the outright seizure of goods. In general, negative reciprocity is least common in small-scale foraging societies, in which kinship relations predominate.

Exchange and Altruism   In foraging societies, where reciprocity reigns, people may appear to outsiders as naturally generous, altruistic, and magnanimous. But as Lee noted in reference to the economy of the !Kung or Ju/'hoansi:

> *If I had to point to one single feature that makes this way of life possible, I would focus on* sharing. *Each Ju is not an island unto himself or herself; each is part of a collective. It is a small, rudimentary collective, and at times a fragile one, but it is a collective nonetheless. What I mean is that the living group pools the resources that are brought into camp so that everyone receives an equitable share. The !Kung and people like them don't do this out of nobility of soul or because they are made of better stuff than we are. In fact, they often gripe about sharing. They do it because it works*

for them and it enhances their survival. Without this core of sharing, life for the Ju/'hoansi would be harder and infinitely less pleasant (1993:60).

It appears that these hunting and gathering peoples are no more noble than other people. Rather, the conditions of their existence have led them to develop economic practices that enable them to survive in their particular habitat.

COLLECTIVE OWNERSHIP OF PROPERTY

In the nineteenth century, Lewis Morgan proposed that early economic systems associated with small-scale societies were *communistic*. In his book *Ancient Society* ([1877] 1964), Morgan claimed that during the early stages of cultural evolution, the productive technology and economic resources were shared by everyone in the society. Today, Morgan's views appear too simplistic to account for the vast range of economic systems found in small-scale societies.

Ethnological data indicate that hunting-and-gathering societies have differing forms of property relations, which reflect their particular ecological conditions. Among some groups such as the Ju/'hoansi or San, the Eskimo, and the Western Shoshone, where resources are widely distributed, ethnologists report that there are no exclusive rights to territory. Though specific families may be identified with a local camp area, territorial boundaries are extremely flexible, and exclusive ownership of resources within a territory is not well defined. For example, among the San, waterholes were frequently said to be owned by individual families. Yet few restrictions are placed against other families or groups in using these resources. Many foraging groups may have rights of temporary use or rights to claim resources if needed but not "once-and-for-all" rights that exist in modern capitalist societies (Bloch, 1983).

However, in other foraging societies such as that of the Owens Valley Paiute Indians, who resided near the edge of the Great Basin region in the American West, exclusive rights to territory were well defined and defended against outsiders. The Paiute were heavily dependent on pinyon nuts, which were concentrated in one area and were a more predictable source of food than game animals. Specific territorial ties and exclusive rights to land carrying these resources became important for

bands and families. The defense of these resources was economically beneficial to the Paiute. In a comparison of territorial rights among different hunter-gatherers, anthropologists Rada Dyson-Hudson and Eric Smith (1978) found that the greater the predictability and concentration of resources within a particular region, the more pronounced were the conceptions of private ownership and exclusive rights to territory among foragers.

Other forms of private property in foraging societies are associated with individuals—pets, ornaments, clothing, and items of technology like bows, knives, scrapers, and blowguns. Such items are usually regarded as a form of private personal property over which the person who owns them has certain rights.

THE ORIGINAL AFFLUENT SOCIETY?

Until recently, the traditional picture of foraging societies was that of people with limited technologies who were at the mercy of a harsh environment. It seemed that in these dire environmental circumstances people had to work constantly to survive. In the 1960s, however, anthropologists began to draw on ethnographic studies to produce a much different image of hunter-gatherer societies. Modern ethnologists gathered basic data on the types of production systems that hunter-gatherers use, the amount of time they spend in production and subsistence, the role of mobility in their adaptation, and how long they live.

The ethnographic data reported in Lee and De-Vore's work indicate that contemporary foraging societies usually have an adequate and reliable food base. Lee (1972a, b, 1979, 1984, 1993), for example, has argued that the !Kung diet was nutritionally adequate. The data also indicate that these foragers expended minimal labor to provide for their basic physical needs. Finally, the life expectancy in these societies turns out to be much greater than was once thought. These findings have led some anthropologists to refer to foragers as "original affluent societies" or "leisured societies" (Sahlins, 1972).

Sahlins, for example, argued that the worldview of foragers differs radically from that of capitalist societies. He suggested that the sharing-oriented economy of people such as the !Kung demonstrates that the forager's needs are few and are easily satisfied by a relatively meager amount of labor time. In Sahlins's view, foragers do not value the accumulation of material goods in the same way that people in modern capitalist societies do.

It is obvious that for populations that have to maintain a nomadic lifestyle, the accumulation of resources would be unproductive. Material possessions would be burdensome when trekking across the ice of the Arctic or through the dense rain forests. Without a way to store large quantities of food, it would be irrational to accumulate food resources only to have them spoil.

Further evidence of the affluence of foragers is drawn from the demographic conditions for these groups. For example, Lee argued that the composition of the Ju/'hoansi or San population demonstrates that these people were not on the edge of starvation. Ten percent of the individuals surveyed by Lee were over 60 years of age, "a proportion that compares favorably to the percentage of elderly in industrialized populations" (Lee, 1968: 36). The blind, senile, or disabled continued to be supported by the !Kung. The system of reciprocal exchanges thus ensures the survival of these individuals.

THE AFFLUENCE HYPOTHESIS CHALLENGED

Some recent anthropological research, however, has challenged the notion of the original affluent societies. Although the San and similar groups may spend only a few hours each day and a few days each week bringing in basic food resources, they must also spend time making tools, weapons, and clothing; processing and cooking food; planning for future foraging activities; solving disputes; healing the sick; and raising children (Konner, 1982). In other words, we can view the San and other foragers as affluent only if we restrict our definition of work to the actual quest for food.

The study of the Ache, foragers who live in the rain forest of eastern Paraguay, mentioned above, illustrates the shortcomings of the affluence hypothesis. The team of ethnologists analyzed Ache subsistence activities (Hill et al., 1985). They discovered that Ache males spend forty to fifty hours a week in the quest for special kinds of food. Time-allocation studies such as these challenge the notion that all foragers spend minimal time in pursuit of food resources.

Furthermore, recent medical research has challenged Lee's arguments that the San diet is nutritionally sound. Although the diet is well balanced in respect to carbohydrates, proteins, and fats, the overall caloric intake of the San appears to be inadequate. The small physical size of the San may be due to the fact that mothers usually have not supplemented nursing with additional food intake for infants over 6 months old. Moreover, the entire San population has suffered from seasonal food shortages and starvation (Konner, 1982).

This recent research on the Ju/'hoansi or San does not totally refute the overall hypothesis regarding the original affluent societies. In general, it appears that in some cases, especially in the tropical rain forest, groups like the Mbuti and the Semang have an abundance of vegetables and fruits. In contrast, groups such as the Shoshone or the Ache have to expend much more time in securing basic resources. When there is a ready presence of resources, relative affluence is possible. But when these items are absent or less plentiful, subsistence becomes much more demanding.

Another factor that influences the relative affluence of foraging societies is the ability to keep resources over a period of time. Although most of these societies did not store food, groups such as the Eskimo had limited storage capacities. Some Eskimo groups dug holes beneath the permafrost so that they could store meat. The storage of meat, berries, and greens enabled the Eskimo to maintain a certain amount of affluence even in winter. They thus had a steady, reliable source of meat and vegetation as a base for subsistence activities.

Social Organization in Foraging Societies

The fundamental social organization in foraging societies is based on family, marriage, kinship, gender, and age. The two basic elements of social organization for foraging populations are the nuclear family and the band. The nuclear family is the small family unit associated with procreation: parents and offspring. The nuclear family appears to be most adaptive for hunting-gathering societies because of the flexibility needed for the location and easy distribution and exchange of food resources, and the other exigencies of hunting (Fox, 1967; Pasternak, 1976).

The most common type of band is made up of a related cluster of nuclear families ranging in size from twenty to one hundred individuals. At times, in societies such as the desert-dwelling Shoshone Indians, the bands may break up into nuclear families to locate food and other resources. Under other circumstances, several families may cooperate in hunting and other foraging activities. In some instances, bands may contain up to four or five (sometimes more) **extended families,** in which married children and their offspring reside with their parents. These multifamily bands provide the webs of kinship for foraging societies, enabling them to cooperate in subsistence and economic exchanges.

The specific number of people in a band depends on the carrying capacity of the natural environment. Most foraging groups had a range of twenty to one hundred people. Foragers in the desert, arctic, and the tropical rain forest all lived in small multifamily bands residing in separate territories. Typically, band organization is extremely flexible, with members leaving and joining bands as circumstances demand. Personal conflicts and shortages of resources may encourage people to move into or out of bands. In some cases, when food or water resources are scarce, whole bands may move into the territories of other bands.

MARRIAGE AND KINSHIP

Although a number of foraging groups practice polygyny, the most common type of marriage found in foraging societies is monogamy. Marriages are an important means of cementing social relationships. In some cases, betrothals are arranged while the future spouses are still young children. Typically, the girl is much younger than the male. For example, Ju/'hoansi or San girls are often married between the ages of 12 and 14, whereas males may be 18 to 25 years old or older.

Though these marital arrangements are regular features of foraging societies, it does not mean they are easily accepted by the couple. A San woman expressed herself on her first marriage:

When I married my husband Tsau [/Twa continued], I didn't fight too hard, but I cried a lot when I was taken to sleep in his hut. When the elders went away I listened carefully for their sleeping. Then, when my husband fell asleep and I heard his breathing, I very quietly sat up and eased my blanket away from his and stole away and slept by myself out in the bush.

In the morning the people came to Tsau's hut and asked, "Where is your wife?" He looked around and said, "I don't know where my wife has gone off to." Then they picked up my tracks and tracked me to where I was sitting out in the bush. They brought me back to my husband. They told me that this was the man they had given to me and that he wouldn't hurt me.

After that we just lived together all right. At first when we slept under the same blanket our bodies did not touch, but then after a while I slept at his front. Other girls don't like their husbands and keep struggling away until the husbands give up on them and their parents take them back. (Lee, 1993:83)

Marriage Rules   Marital arrangements in foraging societies are intended to enhance economic, social, and political interdependence among bands and to foster appropriate band alliances. To do this, rules are established to determine who may marry whom. Many of these rules concern marriages among cousins. A common marriage rule found in foraging societies is referred to as *cross-cousin marriage.* A **cross cousin** is the offspring of one's father's sister or one's mother's brother. In effect, a cross-cousin marriage means that a male marries a female who is his father's sister's daughter or his mother's brother's daughter.

In addition, foraging societies frequently have rules of residence that specify where the married couple must reside. Most band societies practice patrilocal residence, in which the newly married couple resides with the husband's father. Thus, if a man marries a woman from a different band, she must join her husband's band. In such societies, the patrilocal residence rule and cross-cousin marriage combine to create a system called *restricted marital exchange,* in which two groups exchange women (Levi-Strauss, 1969). The purpose of this system is to foster group solidarity by encouraging kinship alliances.

The kinship diagram illustrated in Figure 8.2 gives a visual model of the social structure in some foraging societies. In the diagram, Ego is used as a point of reference, and kinship relationships are

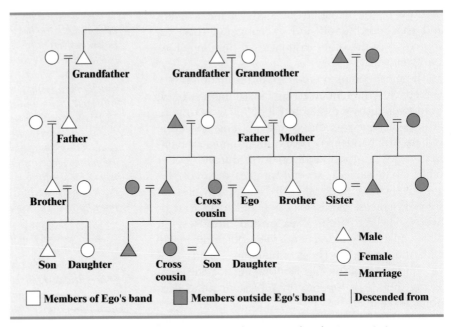

Figure 8.2 Kinship and marriage patterns in hunting-and-gathering societies.

traced from Ego's offspring, parents, grandparents, and other relatives. Note that Ego has married his father's sister's daughter (his cross cousin on his father's side). Because of the rule of patrilocal residence, Ego's father's sister had to move to another band with her husband. Therefore Ego is marrying outside his own band.

Like Ego, Ego's wife's brother has married a woman outside his band. In keeping with the cross-cousin rule, their daughter has married Ego's son. Ego's daughter will eventually marry someone from another band. Through the rules of cross-cousin marriage and patrilocal residence, this restricted exchange develops strong networks of interfamily and interband kinship relations. These kin networks widen over the generations, expanding economic, social, and political relationships.

Brideservice Some foraging societies practice *brideservice,* in which a male resides for a specified amount of time with his wife's parents' band. The rule of residence that requires a man to reside with his wife's parents is called **matrilocal residence.** Among the Ju/'hoansi or San, brideservice can last eight to ten years, and the husband and wife don't return to the husband's father's band for residence (the patrilocal rule) until after several children are born (Lee, 1993). The husband will help his wife's band in their subsistence activities, which helps consolidate both economic and social ties between the two bands. Another reason the San practice brideservice is that females are not sexually mature at the time of their marriage. San girls who marry before their menarche are not expected to have sexual intercourse with their husband. Thus, the brideservice period coincides with female maturation. But brideservice also functions to reinforce the kinship and reciprocal ties between bands.

Other Marital Patterns among Foragers Not all foraging societies conform to the marital patterns just described. For example, Eskimo marriage involved no preferred rules regarding cousin marriage or rituals and ceremonies sanctioning the new couple's relationship. The man and woman simply began residing with each other. To some extent, the Eskimo viewed this marriage arrangement as a pragmatic and utilitarian relationship for economic and reproductive purposes (Balikci, 1970).

Another aspect of Eskimo marriage is the well-known tradition of *wife exchange.* In some cases, males established partnerships with other males that include having sexual intercourse with each other's wives. Usually it is clear that both the men and the women involved make decisions about this. However, ethnologist Ansen Balikci records cases wherein wives were threatened and intimidated if they did not want to participate (1970). One of the most important aspects of wife exchange was the interregional social networks established among these families. In addition, the children produced from these exchanges were considered siblings. This further enhanced the development of kinship obligations and reciprocity.

Divorce In most cases, divorce is easily accomplished in hunting-and-gathering societies. For example, !Kung divorces, which are most frequently initiated by the wife, are simple matters characterized by cordiality and cooperation. The divorced couple may even live next to one another with their new spouses. Because there are no rigid rules or complex kinship relations beyond the nuclear family to complicate divorce proceedings, the dissolution of a San marriage is a relatively easy process (Lee, 1993).

Divorce was also frequent and easily obtained among the Eskimo (Balikci, 1970). As with the San, one reason for this was the lack of formal social groups beyond the nuclear family. Another reason was the absence of strict rules governing marriage and postmarital residence. Significantly, divorce did not necessarily lead to the cutting of kin ties. Even if an Eskimo couple separated, and this happened for nearly 100 percent of the marriages studied, the kin ties endured (Burch, 1970). Sometimes the couple reunited, and the children of first and second marriages became a newly blended family. Thus, divorce frequently extended kin ties, an important aspect of sociocultural adaptation in severe arctic conditions.

GENDER

Gender as an aspect of social structure in foraging societies is an extremely important area of ethnological research. The interrelationships among gender, subsistence, and economic and political patterns have been investigated by ethnologists.

Gender and the Division of Labor Considerable ethnological research has demonstrated that gender roles in foraging societies are strongly related to the basic division of labor. Prior to recent ethnological research on foraging societies, anthropolo-

Ju/'hoansi women carrying their children while gathering vegetation and roots.

gists believed that male subsistence activities, especially hunting and fishing, provided most of the food resources. However, as we have seen, in some of the foraging societies such as the Ju/'hoansi or San, the Semang, and Mbuti, women are economically dominant, because gathering and collecting vegetation is the primary means of securing food (Martin & Voorhies, 1975; Dahlberg, 1981). One comprehensive cross-cultural analysis, however, which is based on all of the available evidence for foraging societies in the past and present and is contained in the *Ethnographic Atlas,* indicates that males have typically obtained most of the nutritional foods through hunting and fishing (Ember, 1978).

Biological Explanations of the Division of Labor One question posed by modern ethnologists is: Why is the division of labor in foraging societies so strongly related to gender roles? There are several possible answers to this question. The first is that males hunt and women gather because males are stronger and have more endurance in the pursuit of large game. Another possibility is that because women bear and nurse children, they lack the freedom of mobility necessary to hunt (Friedl, 1975). A third answer is that gathering, especially near a base camp, is a relatively safe activity that entails no potential dangers for women who are either pregnant or caring for children (Brown, 1970b).

There is evidence for and against each of these theories. We have seen, for example, that in some foraging societies men and women are involved in both hunting and gathering. In addition, women often perform tasks that require strength and stamina, such as carrying food, children, water, and firewood—thus, gathering resources is not a sedentary or leisurely activity. Based on this evidence, anthropologist Linda Marie Fedigan (1986) has proposed that heavy work and child-care activities may not be mutually exclusive, as was previously thought.

Many research questions pertaining to gender roles and subsistence among foragers remain for future anthropologists. Much of the recent evidence suggests that gender roles and subsistence activities are not as rigid as formerly thought. Among the Batak foragers of the rain forests of Malaysia and the Agta in the Philippines, both men and women perform virtually every subsistence task (Estioko-Griffin & Griffin, 1978; Endicott, 1988). The same pattern is demonstrated by the Tiwi of Australia and the Hadza foragers of East Africa (Goodale, 1971; Woodburn, 1982). In these cases, it appears that the subsistence strategies for both males and females are open, and behavior is flexible.

Female Status   Closely related to gender roles and subsistence is the question of the social status of women. Empirical data suggest that gender relations tend to be more *egalitarian*—men and women having equal status—in foraging societies than in other societies (Friedl, 1975; Martin & Voorhies, 1975; Endicott, 1988). This may reflect the substantial contributions women make in gathering food.

Richard Lee notes, for example, that as a result of their important role in economic activities, San women participate equally with men in political decision making (1981). San women are treated respectfully, and there is little evidence of male domination or the maltreatment of females. A similar generalization could be applied to the Mbuti and Semang, as well as to most of the other foragers.

This hypothesis suggests, however, that in societies in which female contributions to the food supply are less critical or less valued, female status

is lower. For example, among some of the Eskimo and other northern foraging groups for whom hunting was the only subsistence activity, females do not gather much in the way of resources for the family. Consequently, those societies tended to be more **patriarchal,** or male dominated, in political and economic matters (Friedl, 1975; Martin & Voorhies, 1975).

Clearly, equality between males and females in foraging societies is not universal. In some groups such as the San and Agta, women have more equality, whereas in others such as the Eskimo, females have a lower status. Even in the most egalitarian groups, males tend to have some inherent cultural advantages. In addition, males are more likely to become the political and spiritual leaders in foraging societies. When considering gender relations in a broad, cross-cultural perspective, however, foragers tend to have much more equality than do most other societies.

AGE

Like kinship and gender, age is used in virtually all foraging societies as a basis for assigning individuals their particular status in the social hierarchy. Patterns of age stratification and hierarchy vary considerably from society to society, depending on environmental and cultural conditions. Age is also a primary aspect of the division of labor in foraging societies.

Children and Rites of Passage   The period of childhood among foragers is a time of playful activity and excitement. But it is also a time when children learn their basic subsistence activities, economic responsibilities, and political roles. In his studies of the Mbuti Pygmies, Turnbull (1961, 1983) has provided us with a thorough account of childhood in a foraging society.

At the age of 3, the Mbuti child enters the *bopi,* a tiny camp about a hundred yards away from the main camp, which might be considered a playground. Older children and adults do not enter the *bopi.* Within the *bopi,* all the children are part of an age grade and are equal to one another and remain so throughout the rest of their lives. It is the area in which children become enculturated and learn the importance of age, kinship, and gender, and the activities associated with these statuses.

Within the *bopi* are noncompetitive play activities for boys and girls. Many of these activities reinforce the rules of hunting and gathering. The elders bring the children out of the bopi to show them how to use nets to hunt animals. Children also play house to learn how to take care of their households later in life.

Before the age of puberty, boys and girls quit going into the *bopi* and join the main camp with older youths. When they reach puberty, Mbuti males and females have separate, informal rites of passage. The puberty ritual, known as the *Elima* for Mbuti females, occurs at the first menstruation, which is an occasion for great rejoicing because it is a sign that the girl is ready for marriage and motherhood. For a month the girl resides in a special hut with her agemates, and they are watched over by an older female. The girl learns the special songs of the *Elima* and occasionally appears in front of the hut while young men sit outside to admire the girls. At this time, the females sing the *Elima* songs and the boys sing in response in a form of flirtation. Through their participation in the *Elima* ritual, the Mbuti males demonstrate their readiness for adulthood and marriage.

The Roles of the Elderly   In foraging societies, old age tends to be defined less in terms of chronology and more in terms of some change in social status related to involvement in subsistence or work patterns, or becoming grandparents (Glascock, 1981). In all societies, however, the onset of old age is partially defined in terms of the average life span. The general demographic and ethnological data on foraging societies indicate that definitions of "old age" vary from 45 to 75 years old.

An early study of aging hypothesized that in hunting-and-gathering societies, older people wield little power and have low status (Simmons, 1945). This argument was based on the assumption that, because foraging societies had few material goods that older people controlled and could use as leverage with the younger generation, old age represented a loss of status. This hypothesis suggested that the status of older people is correlated with subsistence and economic activities. As foraging people age and decline in strength and energy, their subsistence contribution may be limited, thereby diminishing their status.

Most of the ethnological data, however, do not support this hypothesis. In an early account of for-

agers in the Andaman Islands off the coast of India, for example, A. R. Radcliffe-Brown (1922/1964) described the reverence and honor given to older males. Among the Mbuti Pygmies, age is a key factor in determining status, and the elders make the most important economic and political decisions for the group. Despite the fact that young people sometimes openly ridicule older people, the elders are able to dominate Pygmy society because of their cultural knowledge (Turnbull, 1983).

Anthropologists who have studied the Ju/'hoansi or San point out that though there was little material security at old age, the elderly were not abandoned and have a relatively high status (Thomas, 1959; Lee, 1984). Despite the fact that older people do not play a predominant productive role in subsistence activities, they are able to remain secure because of close kinship ties. Through reciprocal exchanges within the economic system of these foraging societies, older people are able to maintain a relatively secure existence.

Anthropologists find that older people in foraging societies generally have a higher status than do younger people. Because of their accumulated knowledge, which is needed for subsistence activities, political decision making, and intellectual and spiritual guidance, older people tend to be respected and are treated with a great deal of deference. Human memory serves as the libraries of these societies and is important for the preservation of culture and the transmission of knowledge. Cultural and historical traditions are memorized and handed down from generation to generation. Control of information is one important basis of esteem for the elderly in nonliterate societies.

In general, the evidence indicates that only in cases of extreme deprivation are the elderly in foraging societies maltreated. In their investigation of the treatment of the elderly in a wide variety of foraging societies, researchers concluded that practices directed against the elderly, such as abandonment, exposure, and killing, occur only under severe environmental circumstances, in which the elderly are viewed as burdens rather than assets (Glascock & Feinman, 1981). These practices have been documented for groups ranging from the Eskimo to the Siriono, but these cases appear to be exceptional. In most foraging societies, the young have moral obligations to take care of the elderly.

Child Care Activities   Turnbull (1983) has remarked that one of the significant universal roles of elderly grandparents is babysitting. While the parents in foraging societies are involved in subsistence chores like hunting and collecting, grandparents often are engaged in child-care activities. Among the San and the Mbuti, elderly grandparents care for small children while the children's mothers are away on gathering activities. The elderly teach the grandchildren the skills, norms, and values of the society. Reflecting on the Mbuti Pygmy elders, who spend time in storytelling and reciting myths and legends, Turnbull indicates that this role is the primary function of the Mbuti elderly in the maintenance of culture. In most foraging societies, this is the typical pattern for relationships between the young and the old.

Political Organization in Foraging Societies

Just as the band is the fundamental element of social organization in most hunting-and-gathering societies, it is also the basic political unit. As we saw in the discussion of social organization, bands are tied together through kinship and marriage, creating reciprocal economic and social relationships throughout the community. Each band, however, is politically independent of the others and has its own internal leadership. Most of the leaders in the bands are males, but females also take on some important leadership roles. Leaders are chosen because of their skills in hunting, food collecting, communication, decision making, or other personal abilities.

Political leaders generally do not control the group's economic resources or exercise political power as they do in other societies, and there is little, if any, social stratification between political leaders and others in the band. In other words, band societies are highly egalitarian, with no fundamental differences between those with and those without wealth or political power. Thus, leaders of bands must lead by persuasion and personal influence rather than by coercion or withholding resources. Leaders do not maintain a military or police force and thus have no definitive authority.

In a recent extensive cross-cultural study of the political processes of hunting-gathering societies,

Christopher Boehm (1993) developed an imaginative hypothesis to explain the lack of political power and domination in these egalitarian societies. Boehm suggested that there is a pattern of "reverse dominance" in these societies, which keeps anyone from becoming coercive or politically dominating the group in any manner. Reverse dominance ensures that the whole group will have control over anybody who tries to assert political power or authority over them. Reverse dominance is practiced through criticism and ridicule, disobedience, strong disapproval, execution of offenders or extremely aggressive males, deposing leaders, or outright desertion (an entire group leaving a particularly dominant leader). Boehm finds that reverse dominance and related political processes are widespread in band societies, reinforcing patterns of egalitarianism. In a related hypothesis, Peter Gardner (1991) suggests that foraging societies tend to have strong cultural values that emphasize individual autonomy. Like Boehm, Gardner suggests that hunter-gatherers dislike being dominated and disdain conforming to norms that restrict their individual freedom. From reviewing many cases of band societies, Gardner indicates that the cultural values promoting individual autonomy enable these people to sustain their egalitarian way of life while promoting flexibility in their behavior, a distinguishing feature of foraging societies.

CHARACTERISTICS OF LEADERSHIP

In most cases, leadership in hunting-and-gathering societies is not sought out by individuals, because there are few benefits or advantages in becoming a leader. Leaders do not accrue power or economic resources in these egalitarian societies. They do, however, have a tremendous responsibility for the management of the band. In a classic essay in political anthropology, Claude Levi-Strauss (1944) described the band leader of the Nambikuara of South America as entirely responsible for selecting the territories for procuring game; ordering and organizing hunting, fishing, and collecting activities; and determining the conduct of the band in relation to other groups in the region. Yet Levi-Strauss emphasized the consensual aspect of this leadership pattern. The leader has no coercive power and must continuously display skill in building consensus within the band to provide political order.

A quote from a San leader sums up the pattern of leadership among hunter-gatherer societies: "All you get is the blame if things go wrong." Morton Fried (1967) notes a remark frequently heard from band leaders: "If this is done it will be good." These remarks indicate the lack of authority that leaders of bands have in these societies. Levi-Strauss (1944), however, states that some people in all societies desire the nonmaterial benefits such as prestige that can be gained through assuming leadership responsibilities. Therefore, despite the lack of political power or material benefits, foraging leaders may be motivated by other cultural concerns.

Another characteristic of band political leadership is that it is transient; leaders of bands do not hold permanent positions or offices. This informal leadership pattern adds to the weakness of centralized political authority in band societies. Informal leadership is somewhat situational in that it varies according to circumstances—the band will call on the appropriate type of leader when dealing with a specific type of activity. In some bands, for example, certain individuals may be good at solving disputes within the band or between bands. These individuals may be chosen to deal with such problems when they arise. In general, then, band leadership is diffuse and decentralized.

This minimal pattern of leadership also involves an informal type of political succession. Most hunting-and-gathering societies have no definitive rules for passing leadership from one individual to another. Rather, leadership is based on personal characteristics. It may also be based on supernatural powers that the individual is believed to possess. When an individual dies, his or her influence and authority also die. This lack of rules for succession emphasizes the decentralization of political power and authority in band societies.

WARFARE AND VIOLENCE

Contemporary foraging societies generally engage in very limited warfare. Carol Ember's (1978) cross-cultural research indicates that 64 percent of the worldwide sample of foraging societies engaged in warfare at least once every two years. Most of the ethnographic evidence, however, suggests that warfare among foragers took the form of sporadic violence rather than continual fighting. Because al-

most the entire population was engaged in the day-to-day hunting and collecting of food, no long-term fighting could be sustained. Also, the lack of centralized political institutions to implement large-scale military mobilization inhibits the development of intense or frequent warfare. No standing armies with specialized warriors can be organized for continual warfare.

A classic case of "restrained" warfare among foraging populations was provided by the Tiwi of Australia (Hart, Pilling, & Goodale, 1988). War parties of thirty men from two different bands, each armed with spears and wearing white paint symbolizing anger and hostility, met in an adjoining territory. The dispute had originated because some of the males from one band had apparently seduced females from the opposing band. In addition, the senior males of one of the bands had not delivered on their promise to bestow daughters to the other band—a deliberate violation of the norms of reciprocal marital exchange.

Both sides first exchanged insults and then agreed to meet with one another on the following day to renew old acquaintances and to socialize. On the third day, the duel resumed, with males throwing spears in all directions, resulting in a chaotic episode in which some people, including spectators, were wounded. Most of the battle, however, involved violent talk and verbal, rather than physical, abuse. Although variations on this type of warfare exist among the Tiwi, warfare generally did not result in great bloodshed.

Richard Lee described conflict among the Ju/'hoansi or San, which involves fights and homicides. Lee (1984) found twenty-two cases of homicide by males and other periodic violence, usually related to internal disputes over women. As Eric Wolf (1987: 130) comments: "Clearly the !Kung are not the 'Harmless People' that some have thought them to be: They fight and sometimes injure other individual !Kung."

Anthropologist Bruce Knauft (1988) has summarized several generalizations concerning violence in foraging societies. First, these societies lack a competitive male-status hierarchy; in fact, there is a strong tendency to discourage this type of interpersonal competition. Status competition among males is a major source of violent conflict in other types of societies. Second, in contrast to many other societies, public displays of interpersonal violence are not culturally valued among foragers. Instead, these societies seek to minimize animosities. Finally, because of the emphasis on sharing food and other resources, rights to property are not restricted. All of these factors serve to reduce the amount of violence in these societies.

CONFLICT RESOLUTION

Because of the lack of formal government institutions and political authority, social control in foraging societies is based on informal sanctions. One basic mode of conflict resolution that occurs frequently among groups such as the Ju/'hoansi or San is for the people involved to move to another band. Thus, the flexibility of band organization itself is an effective means of reducing conflict. Furthermore, the economic and social reciprocities and the frequent exchanges among bands also serve to reduce conflicts. These reciprocal ties create mutual obligations and interdependencies that promote cooperative relationships.

Nevertheless, violations of norms do lead to more structured or more ritualized means of conflict resolution in foraging societies. Among the Mbuti, for example, age groups play specific roles in the conflict resolution process. Children play an essential role in resolving conflicts involving misbehavior such as laziness, quarreling, or selfishness. Children ridicule people who engage in these behaviors, even if these people are adults. Young children excel at this form of ridicule, which usually is sufficient to resolve the conflict.

When these measures do not succeed, the elders in the group assert their authority. They try to evaluate the dispute carefully and show why things went wrong. If necessary they walk to the center of the camp and criticize individuals by name, although they frequently use humor to soften their criticism. Through this process, elders reinforce the norms and values of Mbuti society (Turnbull, 1983).

The Eskimo Song Duel Another example of dispute resolution is the Eskimo song duel. The song duel was often used to resolve conflicts between males over a particular female. Because Eskimo society lacks specific rules of marriage, males would sometimes accuse others of wife stealing. In these types of conflicts, the two males encountered each other in front of a large public meeting. They then insulted each other through improvised songs, and the crowd resolved the conflict by selecting a winner. With the declaration of a winner, the dispute was resolved without the use of any formal court system or coercion (Hoebel, 1954).

Religion in Foraging Societies

The religions associated with modern foragers are based on oral traditions referred to by Mircea Eliade (1959) as "cosmic religions." Cosmic religions are intimately associated with nature: The natural cycle of seasons; inorganic matter such as rocks, water, and mountains; and other features of the natural environment are invested with sacred significance. Spirit and matter are inseparable. In addition, cosmic religions are not identified with any particular historical events or individuals, as are the "literate" religious traditions of Judaism, Islam, Christianity, Buddhism, and Hinduism.

The sacredness of the natural environment is sometimes expressed in a form of **animism,** the belief that spirits reside within all inorganic and organic substances. Yet, as applied to the metaphysical conceptions in the Ju/'hoansi or San, the Australian Aborigine, or Mbuti cultural systems, the label animism appears too simplistic. Concepts of a god or gods are found in combination with animistic beliefs.

THE DREAMTIME

An illuminating example of a cosmic religion among foragers is the Australian Aborigine notion of *dreamtime* (Stanner, 1958). The dreamtime exists in the "other world," the world associated with the time of creation, where a person goes in dreams and visions and after death. It is believed that at the time of creation the ancestors deposited souls of all living forms near watering holes, and eventually these souls or spirits were embedded in all matter, from rocks and water to trees and humans. The unification of all substance and spirit was a by-product of the work of these ancestral beings. All of these spirits come to the world from the dreamtime; the birth of the universe is like a fall from the dreamtime.

The Aborigines believe that the ancestral beings still exist in the dreamtime, where they act as intermediaries between that world and the profane, everyday world of human affairs. The ancestral beings intervene in life, controlling plant, animal, and human life, and death. This fundamental belief provides explanations for pain, joy, chaos, and order in human life. The dreamtime is a fundamental and complex conception that embraces the creative past and has particular significance for the present and future.

According to Aborigine conceptions, life without the dreamtime is extremely unfilling. The invisible side of life can become visible through rituals, ceremonies, myths, art, and dreams. Aborigines believe that through these activities they can communicate with their ancestral beings. This belief is reflected in Aborigine rites of passage. In initiation ceremonies it is believed that the individual moves farther and farther back into the dreamtime. In puberty rituals, which for males included circumcision, subincision (the cutting of the penis lengthwise to the urethra), and other bloodletting actions, the individual is dramatically moved from one status to another through contact with the dreamtime. The rite of passage at death moves the individual into the invisibility of the dreamtime.

The dreamtime also conveys certain notions of morality. According to Aborigine traditions, the ancestral beings originally lived like other humans and had the capacity for being both moral and immoral, both good and evil (Stanner, 1958, 1978). The immoral behavior of the dreamtime beings is highlighted to accentuate what is proper and moral in human affairs. Thus, this religion creates a moral order that functions to sustain social control in the physical world. Although the dreamtime ancestors do not directly punish human wrongdoers, they have provided a blueprint for proper behavior with respect to obligations, reciprocities, and social behavior in general.

ESKIMO RELIGION

The Eskimo maintain a religious belief system that involves curers or healers who control and manipulate the supernatural world. In contrast to some of the "literate" religious traditions, Eskimo religion does not assume the existence of an omnipotent supreme being. The Eskimo do believe that every living creature possesses a soul or spirit that is reincarnated after death. They believe that the

souls of deceased individuals remain in the vicinity of the living. The Eskimo do not maintain a belief in an afterworld, or heaven, in which these souls congregate after death. Rather, they believe that these souls remain close to the natural world. The spirits of animals allow themselves to be hunted and are constantly reincarnated in other animal forms to be hunted again to ensure the Eskimo way of life.

Within these general conceptions of spirituality the Eskimo believe in soul loss, in which a person's soul is taken from the body as a result of unforeseen circumstances. Soul loss causes mental and physical illness for the individual. It is often believed that the soul has been stolen by another spirit. The Eskimo cope with these situations through *shamanism*.

Two different forms of shamanism are found in Eskimo culture. One form is hereditary, passed on through either parent. The more common variety involves people who receive shamanistic powers through direct contact with the supernatural, usually through dreams, visions, or hallucinations.

People usually go through an extensive training period before they can begin practicing as a shaman. Eskimo shamans learn various relaxation techniques to induce trance states. They also learn methods of healing, curing, and exorcism. These techniques are used to produce group emotional experiences so as to enhance spiritual growth. In many cases, the shamanistic performances work effectively in curing illnesses or resolving emotional problems. Undoubtedly, in certain instances the Eskimo beliefs and cultural conceptions surrounding shamanism trigger certain states of mind that produce positive psychological and even physical consequences such as overcoming illness and injuries.

ART, MUSIC, AND RELIGION

The art of foraging societies is intimately related to nature. Animals, plants, humans, and other components of the natural environment are the major subjects. This naturalistic art also has a religious significance, as nature and spirit are viewed as inseparable. Rock paintings with highly symbolic images of natural phenomena are found in most foraging societies. It is believed that this art is sacred and can be used to make contact with supernatural sources.

An example of Australian Aborigine rock painting illustrating mythical themes regarding how an individual was transformed into a turtle after violating the incest taboo.

Traditional Eskimo art products include many items made from ivory, one of the few rigid materials available in the Arctic. Human and animal figurines, which were worn as amulets to enhance supernatural powers and practices, dominate Eskimo artistic output. The Eskimo also carve masks in ivory (or sometimes wood) for use by their shamans.

The music of foraging societies is generally divided into recreational (folk or popular) and religious music. The Mbuti, for example, have no instrumental music, but they have many songs and dances. In their vocal music they have a precise sense of harmony, giving each singer one note to produce at a given moment. This leads to a harmonic pattern that is passed around a circle of people. This technique is often used in Mbuti recreational music.

The sacred music of the Mbuti is much more important than their recreational music, and much of it is linked to the *Elima* rites of passage discussed earlier. In the *Elima,* young girls and boys sing back and forth to one another in harmony. Other sacred songs are sung by males only. The intensity of the singing builds so as to reach the spirit of the rain forest. One of the hunters goes off into the forest to echo the song of his fellows so that the spirit may be sure to hear it. As in most societies, Mbuti ritual music usually has a standardized form, with little improvisation allowed. Ritual music helps sustain the cultural and spiritual traditions of the people. The lyrics of the music emphasize the sacred symbols that are maintained in Mbuti society. As the group chants the music together, a sense of sacredness is created in the community.

Music and religion are inextricably bound within the shamanistic rituals of the Eskimo. In the shamanistic performances, a drum is used to enhance the rhythmic songs. The shaman's songs are simple, chantlike recitations that have no actual words. Short phrases are repeated again and again. The drumming and song chants are used to establish contact with the spirits. Anthropologist Rodney Needham (1967) suggested that the use of instruments such as the drum in shamanistic rituals not only heightens the spiritual atmosphere of the ceremony but also affects psychological (and neurological) processes that produce altered states of consciousness in individuals.

SUMMARY

Unlike the hunter-gatherers, or foragers, of the Paleolithic period, modern foraging societies have adapted to marginal environments: deserts, tropical rain forests, and arctic regions. The subsistence patterns of band societies in these environments require a mobile, nomadic lifestyle. Foragers must move frequently to procure their basic food resources.

Population growth among foragers within specific territories is minimal. This slow growth rate is due to fissioning and other practices that minimize the number of individuals within a territory. Ethnologists have been studying foragers to determine whether low fertility rates are due to biological or cultural factors. The technology of foragers is refined to enable adjustments to the practical needs of their environmental conditions. They have developed economic patterns that depend on reciprocity and resource sharing to produce cooperative behavior. Generally, a foraging economy does not depend on private property but rather on kinship and family ownership.

The social organization of foraging societies is based on kinship, age, and gender. Kinship relations are maintained among different multifamily bands through marriage. Generally, people marry outside their own band. Gender relations are related to the division of labor: In most societies men hunt and women gather. To some extent, this division of labor determines the status of females. Age is also an important determinant of status in foraging societies. As individuals move through the life cycle they learn more about their society. As they reach old age, they are respected for their knowledge and teaching skills.

Political organization is limited in foraging societies. There is no formal, centralized political authority. Leadership is based on personal qualities and is not permanent. Although violence exists, usually among males, warfare is infrequent and restrained because of the limited political organization.

Religion in foraging societies is based on a unity between spiritual and material forces. Healers and shamans are the religious specialists who serve the people's spiritual needs. The art forms found among foragers reflect the spiritual aspects of their culture. The most common subjects are components of the natural environment, including plants, animals, and human beings.

STUDY QUESTIONS

1. What can we learn from studying hunter-gatherer societies that might help us understand and interpret life in industrial societies today?

2. How can the study of contemporary foragers provide us with an understanding of Paleolithic lifestyles?

3. What types of economic exchange would you expect to find in hunter-gatherer societies? Are the individuals in foraging societies more altruistic, magnanimous, and generous, or are they no more noble than other peoples?

4. Is private ownership of land a universal concept that applies to all societies? How much variation in "ownership" is found among forager groups?

5. Evaluate the hypothesis that in societies in which female contributions to the food supply are less critical or less valued than male contributions, female status is lower.

6. Would you rather be involved in warfare as a member of a forager society or as a member of an industrial nation? Why?

7. How are forager religions different from your own? Are there any similarities?

KEY TERMS

animism
balanced reciprocity
band
cross cousin
egalitarian
extended families

fissioning
foraging
generalized reciprocity
hunter-gatherer
infanticide
marginal environments

matrilocal residence
negative reciprocity
patriarchal
patrilocal residence
reciprocal economic system
reciprocity

INTERNET EXERCISES

1. Read over the introduction to the website **http:// www.mc.maricopa.edu/academic/cultsci/ anthro/exploratorium/diasporas/modern .html** and then click on the topic The Shortest People in the World. Why might the pygmies be short? How has the modern diet made industrialized people tall? What advantages accrue to the people of the forest for their limited height?

2. Look at the ecological model described by Flannery in **http://www.unl.edu/rhames/ courses/for97notes.htm.** What is meant by the phrase "ingenious team of lay botanists?" How does Flannery's view vary from that of Lubbock? Why do you think the differences between the two views are so great?

SUGGESTED READINGS

BICCHIERI, M. G., ed. 1972. *Hunters and Gatherers Today*. New York: Holt, Rinehart and Winston. A collection of eleven ethnographic portraits of foraging societies that exist in different parts of the world.

INGOLD, TIM, DAVID RICHES, AND JAMES WOODBURN, eds. 1991. *Hunters and Gatherers: History, Evolution and Social Change, Vol. 1*. New York: Berg. 1992. *Hunters and Gatherers: Property, Power and Ideology, Vol. 2*. New York: Berg. A two-volume collection of state-of-the-art essays on hunters and gatherers worldwide.

KATZ, RICHARD. 1982. *Boiling Energy: Community Healing among the Kalahari !Kung*. Cambridge, MA: Harvard University Press. An excellent descriptive account of the healers among the !Kung San and how they serve both spiritual and material needs.

SHOSTAK, MARJORIE. 1981. *Nisa: The Life and Words of a !Kung Woman*. New York: Vintage Books. An extensive biography of a San woman. It has become a modern classic of anthropology.

TURNBULL, COLIN. 1961. *The Forest People: A Study of the Pygmies of the Congo*. New York: Simon & Schuster. A wonderfully written book that evokes the personal lives of the Mbuti people of the Ituri Rain Forest.

9

Tribes

CHAPTER OUTLINE

**Environment and Subsistence
for Horticulturalists**
*Amazon Horticulturalists: The Yanomamö /
New Guinea Horticulturalists: The Tsembaga /
Horticulturalists in Woodland Forest Areas:
The Iroquois*

**Environment and Subsistence
for Pastoralists**
East African Cattle Complex

Demographics and Settlement

Technology
*Horticulturalist Technology / Pastoralist
Technology*

Economics
Money / Property Ownership

Social Organization
*Families / Descent Groups / Functions
of Descent Groups / Marriage / Gender / Age*

Political Organization
*Sodalities / How Leaders Are Chosen /
Pastoralist Tribal Politics / Explaining Tribal
Warfare / Law and Conflict Resolution*

Religion
*Animism and Shamanism in South America /
Witchcraft and Sorcery / Familistic Religion*

Art and Music
Musical Traditions

CHAPTER QUESTIONS

■ What problems do anthropologists encounter in trying to use the term tribe to classify various societies?

■ What are the basic environmental, demographic, technological, and economic features associated with tribal societies?

■ Compare the complexities of social organization in tribal societies with those in band societies.

■ What are the differences in gender relations in tribal societies compared to those in band societies?

■ What are the characteristics of tribal political relationships?

■ What are the unique expressions of religion, art, and music among tribal peoples?

IN CHAPTER 7 WE INTRODUCED THE TYPOLOGIES that anthropologists use to classify different forms of political systems. For example, hunter-gatherer societies are classified as band political systems. The term tribe is used loosely to characterize two different types of subsistence systems: horticulturalist and pastoralist. Unlike hunting-and-gathering societies, tribal societies are food-producing groups that depend on the limited domestication of plants and animals. Figure 9.1 shows the distribution of tribal societies around the world. Politically, tribes are noncentralized sociocultural systems in which authority is diffused among a number of kinship groups and associations. These characteristics are explored in this chapter.

Some anthropologists, most notably the late Morton Fried (1967, 1975), have objected to the use of the term tribe to characterize these societies. The word *tribe* is derived from the Latin term *tribus,* which was used by the Romans to refer to certain peoples who were not technologically advanced. Fried claimed that the term is often applied to a particular group by a more powerful group and usually has a pejorative connotation.

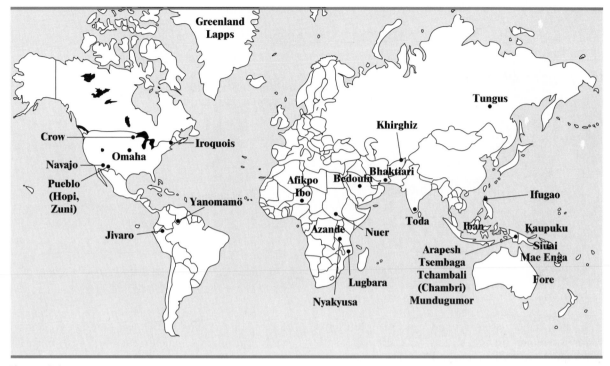

Figure 9.1 This map highlights many tribal societies, including those discussed in this chapter.

One aspect of Fried's criticism has created some theoretical controversy in anthropology. Fried argued that tribal organization is not an evolutionary stage emerging from the simpler stage represented by the foraging society, as most anthropologists had maintained. He suggested that, for the most part, tribes are usually "secondary" developments that evolve through contacts with other societies. This contact occurs when large, complex state societies, both agricultural and industrial, create tribal groups through the process of subjugation and domination. In many cases, these tribal groups become subjugated ethnic minorities in state societies. We examine these processes later in the text, especially in Chapter 13.

Fried's criticisms have sensitized most anthropologists to the vagueness of the term *tribe*. In the past and sometimes currently, the term has been used haphazardly to refer to an enormous range of societies that have almost nothing in common. Despite these reservations, the term is still used to categorize the many different types of horticulturalist and pastoralist societies and to denote a form of

political complexity and evolutionary development that bridges the gap between bands and centralized societies (Lewellen, 1983).

Environment and Subsistence for Horticulturalists

Horticulture is a form of agriculture in which people use a limited, nonmechanized technology to cultivate plants. One major type of horticulture is known as *slash-and-burn cultivation*. This system was once widespread but today is found primarily in tropical rain forests. Approximately 250 million people throughout the world currently engage in slash-and-burn cultivation (Moran, 1982).

Slash-and-burn cultivation involves the production of food without the intensive use of land, a large labor force, or complex technology. As generally practiced, it is a cyclical process that begins with clearing a tract of land by cutting down the trees and then setting fire to the brush. The burned

A tropical forest in the first stages of slash-and-burn horticulture.

vegetation and ashes remain, and the nutrients from them are unlocked and sink into the soil. After the land is cleared and burned, various crops are planted. In most cases women and children spend a great deal of time weeding and tending the gardens. Typically, after the crops are planted and harvested for several years, the garden plot is left fallow (unplanted) for three to fifteen years, and the cultivators must shift to a new location.

People who practice slash-and-burn cultivation must maintain a delicate balance with their environment. If the plot is not left fallow and is cultivated too often, grasses and weeds may colonize the area at the expense of forest regrowth. The land then becomes useless or overexploited. Some horticulturalists have recleared their land too often and brought devastation to some forest environments; others have been able to reside in one location for almost a century (Carneiro, 1961). In general, compared with foragers, slash-and-burn horticulturalists are less nomadic and more sedentary.

AMAZON HORTICULTURALISTS: THE YANOMAMÖ

One South American group introduced in Chapter 1, known as the Yanomamö, practices slash-and-burn cultivation. The Yanomamö have been studied by anthropologist Napoleon Chagnon for more than thirty years. Approximately 80 to 90 percent of their diet comes from their gardens (Chagnon, 1997). Yanomamö males clear the forest, burn the vegetation, and plant the crops; the females (and sometimes children) weed the garden and eventually harvest the crops. Generally, the Yanomamö do not work on subsistence activities for food production more than three to four hours per day. A Yanomamö garden lasts for about three years from the time of the initial planting; after this period, the garden is overrun with scrub vegetation, and the soil becomes depleted.

Early cultural ecologists assumed that slash-and-burn cultivators are forced to relocate because the soil becomes exhausted. Chagnon, however, has shown that Yanomamö decisions to move are not based simply on soil depletion. In fact, as the soil begins to lose its capacity to support crops, the Yanomamö make small adjustments such as extending a previous garden or clearing a new tract of land near the old one.

Chagnon discovered that major population movements of the Yanomamö are due instead to warfare and conflict with neighboring groups. Thus, a sedentary life in these Amazonian societies is not simply a product of ecological conditions; it also involves strategic alliances and political maneuvers designed to deal with human populations in nearby communities (Chagnon, 1997).

Although horticulture is the primary subsistence activity of many Amazonian tribes, hunting, fishing, and gathering typically supplement this activity. The Yanomamö gather wild foods, especially palm fruits and a variety of nuts, pods, tubers, mushrooms, and honey. They hunt game birds and a number of animals. In addition, they collect toads, frogs, and many varieties of insects.

NEW GUINEA HORTICULTURALISTS: THE TSEMBAGA

The Papua New Guinea highlands contain many horticulturalist populations, some of whom were not contacted by Western society until the 1950s and 1960s. Archaeologists have traced early horticultural developments in highland New Guinea to 7000 B.C. (White & O'Connell, 1982). One group, the Tsembaga Maring, has been studied thoroughly by anthropologist Roy Rappaport (1984).

The Tsembaga live in two river valley areas surrounded by mountains. They cultivate the mountain slopes with their subsistence gardens. Tsembaga males and females clear the undergrowth from the secondary forest, after which the men cut down the trees. When the cut vegetation dries out, it is stacked up and burned. The women then plant and harvest crops, especially sweet potatoes, taro, manioc, and yams; 99 percent of the Tsembaga diet by weight consists of vegetables, particularly these root crops. The Tsembaga also domesticate pigs, but these animals are usually consumed only during certain ritual occasions.

HORTICULTURALISTS IN WOODLAND FOREST AREAS: THE IROQUOIS

In the past, many Native American groups, such as the Iroquois, who resided in the eastern woodland region of North America, practiced horticulture. Rivers such as the St. Lawrence drain into the area, providing fertile ground for horticultural activities. These horticultural practices probably appeared between 2300 and 1000 B.C., although this time frame is not certain. The native peoples of this region began to raise maize and other crops along with local wild species. Most archaeologists have concluded that this horticultural pattern of maize, beans, and squash originated in Mesoamerica and then extended across the Gulf of Mexico and up the Mississippi River, spreading out to the Ohio River valley areas and eastward to Native American groups such as the Iroquois.

The Iroquois constructed their villages with longhouses in the center of the settlement. (Longhouses were large, multifamily housing built with upright posts that supported horizontal poles for rafters. Large slabs of bark, laced together with cords of plant fiber, covered the framework.)

Iroquois males cleared the primary forest around the village and burned the cut litter. In the spring the women planted fifteen varieties of maize, beans, squash, and other crops, which females later harvested and processed. The Iroquois left part of the primary forest standing so that deer, squirrels, fox, and bear were available for hunting. The forest also provided nuts, berries, and many species of wild plants.

After harvesting the crops in the fall, the men would concentrate their subsistence activities on game such as deer and bear. In the spring, while the women planted crops, the men fished in the many lakes and rivers and also captured birds. Like many other slash-and-burn cultivators, the Iroquois farmed their fields until the fields were no longer fertile, after which they cleared new fields while the old ones lay fallow. After a generation or so, depending on local conditions, the fertile fields were located far enough away from the village that the entire community moved so that it could be closer to the gardens.

Environment and Subsistence for Pastoralists

In central Asia, the Middle East, North and East Africa, and the subarctic regions, there were—and, in some cases, still are—**pastoralists,** groups whose subsistence activities are based on the care of domesticated animals. The use of herd animals differs from group to group. The Bedouins of Arabia, for example, use the camel mainly for transportation and other purposes and only sometimes consume the meat. Other pastoralist groups such as the Sami (Lapps) of Greenland have in the past completely depended on caribou, deriving most of their food and other vital resources from them. Although some pastoralists may have small gardens, most of them have only their herd animals for subsistence purposes.

The care of herd animals requires frequent moves from camp to camp and sometimes involves long

Bedouin pastoralist with camels in the Middle East.

migrations. Some groups such as the Tungus of Siberia, who are reindeer pastoralists, trek more than 1,000 miles annually. The Basseri of southern Iran, who keep goats, sheep, horses, and donkeys, migrate seasonally through mountainous regions in a strip of land 300 miles long, an area of about 2,000 square miles (Barth, 1961). These pastoralist migrations are not aimless; the groups know the layout of the land and move to territories that contain specific grazing pastures or water holes during different seasons.

EAST AFRICAN CATTLE COMPLEX

In an area stretching from southern Sudan through Kenya, Uganda, Rwanda, Burundi, Tanzania, Mozambique, and into parts of South Africa, various pastoralists herd cattle as their means of subsistence. Most of these groups do not depend entirely on their cattle for subsistence needs, but they plant gardens to supplement their food resources.

The Nuer Anthropologist E. E. Evans-Pritchard (1940, 1951, 1956) conducted a classic study of a pastoralist group called the Nuer. The Nuer reside along the upper Nile River and its tributaries in southern Sudan. Because of the flatness of this region, the annual flooding of the Nile during the rainy season, and the heavy clay soils, the Nuer spend the wet season on high, sandy ground, where they plant sorghum, a cereal grass used for grain. This horticulture is very limited, however, because strong rainfall, as well as elephants, birds, and insects, destroy the crops. Therefore, cattle are the most important subsistence resource for the Nuer.

The Nuer view cattle herding with a great deal of pride. In the dry season they move with their cattle into the grassland areas. The cattle transform the energy stored in the grasses, herbs, and shrubs into valuable subsistence products. Yet as is true of other herders in this area, the basis of the Nuer subsistence is not consumption of cattle. Rather, they depend heavily upon the blood and milk of their animals. Every few months during the dry season the cattle are bled by making small incisions that heal quickly. The Nuer boil the blood until it gets thick, then roast it and eat it. The cows are milked morning and night; some of the milk is used to make butter. The Nuer slaughter their old cattle, which then calls for elaborate ceremonies or sacrifices.

Demographics and Settlement

Generally, as humans developed the capacity to produce food through the domestication of animals and plants, the carrying capacity of particular territories increased to support a greater population density than had been possible for band societies. Whereas foraging populations had to live in small bands, tribal societies became much more densely populated. According to Murdock's (1967) cross-cultural tabulations, the median size of horticultur-alist societies ranges from 100 to more than 5,000 people in specific territories, and pastoralists have a median size of 2,000 people in particular niches. Some tribal populations have denser populations in large regions in which villages are connected through economic, social, and political relation-ships.

Compared with most foraging societies, tribal societies are relatively settled within fairly well-defined territories. As mentioned earlier, horticultural-ists are somewhat mobile, having to move to fertile lands every so often, but they generally settle in one locale for a number of years.

Of course, pastoralist societies are more no-madic, but their wanderings are limited to specific pastures and grasslands to care for their animals. Because pastoralists move seasonally from pasture to pasture, they place less intense population pressure on each area. Population densities for pastoralists range from 1 to 5 persons per square mile of land; however, in the richly endowed grassland environment of central Asia, the Kalmuk Mongols maintain an average density of about 18 people per square mile. In general, pastoralist populations are denser than are those of foragers, but both are spread thinly over the land (Sahlins, 1968b).

Like foraging societies, both horticulturalist and pastoralist societies experience only slow population growth because of limited resources. To regulate their populations, tribal societies have adopted the same strategies as bands, especially fissioning. Other cultural practices designed to control population growth include sexual abstinence, infanticide, abortion, and a prolonged period of nursing.

Technology

The whole range of tribal technologies is extremely broad and varies among differing populations depending on whether they are horticulturalists or pastoralists and to what types of environments they have had to adapt. Technological innovations found in tribal societies include wood-working, weaving, leather working, and the production of numerous copper ornaments, tools, and weapons.

HORTICULTURALIST TECHNOLOGY

Horticulturalist groups used sharpened digging sticks and sometimes wooden hoes to plant small gardens. Slash-and-burn horticulturalists such as the Yanomamö and the Iroquois used crude stone or wooden axes to fell the primary forest. It sometimes took weeks for a small group of males to cut down a wooded area for a garden.

Many horticultural societies also have developed technologies to aid in hunting and fishing to supplement their horticultural activities. For example, some Amazonian peoples such as the Jivaro of Ecuador and Peru often use blowguns, which propel poison darts up to 45 yards, to kill monkeys and birds deep in the forest (Harner, 1972). The Yanomamö use large, powerful bows, sometimes 5 to 6 feet long, and long arrow shafts with a splintered point, dipped in curare, a deadly poison (Chagnon, 1997). Amazonian horticulturalists also pour poisons into local waters, causing the fish to rise to the surface in a stupefied condition; they are then gathered for food (Harner, 1972; Chagnon, 1997).

The woodland Iroquois used both the blowgun and the bow (called the *self-bow*) and arrow to hunt game in surrounding forests. The Iroquois carefully selected light wooden branches for arrow shafts, dried them to season the wood, and then smoothed them with stone and bone tools. To make the arrow twist in flight they took feathers from eagles, turkeys, and hawks, which they then attached with a glue made from animal tissues, sinew, or horns. Arrowheads were made from wood, stone, horn, antler, shell, or raw copper (Garbarino, 1988).

Horticulturalists such as the Pacific Islanders, who were not slash-and-burn farmers and resided in more permanent locations, tended to have a more elaborate technology. In addition to the simple digging stick used to cultivate the irrigated gardens, they had many other sophisticated tools and utensils. Although the Pacific Islanders had no metals or clay for pottery, they had many specialized kinds of shell and woodworking tools for making jewelry, knives, rasps, and files.

PASTORALIST TECHNOLOGY

The mobility required by the pastoralist lifestyle prevented these groups from using an elaborate technology. Pastoralists such as the Mongols and the Bedouins carried all of their belongings with them in their yearly migrations. Their technologies aided them in these mass movements; for example, they had saddles for their horses and camels, weapons for hunting, equipment for taking care of their livestock and processing food, and tents that could be moved during migrations. Other pastoralists such as the Nuer of East Africa constructed huts of thatch in permanent locations that served as home bases where a certain number of people remained during the migration season.

Economics

As in hunting-and-gathering societies, reciprocity is the dominant form of exchange of economic resources in tribal economic systems. All three forms of reciprocity—generalized, balanced, and negative—are used by tribal societies. Generalized reciprocity tends to occur within close kinship groupings. Balanced and negative reciprocity occur among more distant kinship groupings. One example of balanced reciprocity occurs among the Yanomamö, who maintain a system of trade and feasting activities with other villages. One village will host a feast, inviting another village to attend. During the feast, the villagers exchange tools, pots, baskets, arrows, dogs, yarn, and hallucinogenic drugs. The feast activities sustain intervillage cooperation, marital exchanges, and political and military alliances (Chagnon, 1997). These transactions and exchanges are carefully calculated by the villagers to determine exact equivalencies. If an equal return is not given, then the original donor village will discontinue the exchange relationship. This may lead to hostilities and perhaps warfare between the villages.

MONEY

Unlike foragers, some tribal societies engage in monetary exchange, that is, transactions that involve money. **Money** is a medium of exchange based on a standard value. According to economists, money has four functions:

1. It enables people to pay for a good or service and then circulates to allow for subsequent purchases.
2. It serves as a uniform standard of value for goods and services within a society.
3. It has a store of value; that is, its standard of value does not fluctuate radically from one time to another.
4. It serves as a form of deferred payment; that is, it can express a promise to pay in the future with the same standard value. (Neale, 1976)

Economic anthropologists classify money into two types: *general-purpose money* (or multipurpose money) and *limited-purpose money* (or special-purpose money). General-purpose money serves all four of the above functions. It can be used as a medium of exchange for most of the goods and services in society. Limited-purpose money, in contrast, is restricted for the purchase of certain goods and services. The paper currencies used in the United States and other industrial societies are examples of general-purpose money. In contrast, most tribal societies that practice monetary exchange use limited-purpose money.

Peoples in some of the Pacific Islands and other coastal areas have used a variety of shells to conduct trade relations. In other tribal societies, livestock, cloth, salt, feathers, animal teeth, and, sometimes, women functioned as money. This type of money was used for specialized exchange circumstances. For example, the Siane of New Guinea exchanged food for other subsistence goods, and luxury items such as bird feathers were exchanged only for other luxury items. Another separate level of exchange took place with respect to prestige items such as certain forms of shell necklaces (Salisbury, 1962). These cases illustrate the use of limited-purpose money. One of the few tribal groups to use general-purpose money is the Kaupuku people of West Irian Jaya, an island in Indonesia; they developed a currency consisting of cowrie shells and necklaces (Pospisil, 1963).

PROPERTY OWNERSHIP

Ownership of property, especially land for horticulturalists and animals for pastoralists, takes on a significance in tribal societies that it does not have in band societies. The concept of property ownership becomes more clearly defined in tribal societies and is based on a web of social relations involving rights, privileges, and perhaps duties and obligations regarding the use of a particular piece of land, a herd of animals, or other objects.

In tribal societies, exclusive right to use property is rare; these rights are usually limited by others. Property rights in tribal societies are generally invested in family and wider kinship groupings. Tribal families have *use rights* to farmland, pastures, animals, and other items. The property of tribal societies is transferred to families through inheritance; individual access to property, however, is largely determined by status. In other words, in tribal societies, an individual gains certain rights, privileges, and obligations with respect to property through inheriting a particular status position. Status in tribal societies is usually determined by kinship, age, and gender, as we shall discuss later in the chapter.

Property rights in tribal societies are not completely static with respect to statuses. Rather, they may fluctuate according to the availability of basic resources. If land is plentiful in a specific tribe, for example, outsiders who need land may be granted rights to use the land. On the other hand, if there is a shortage of land, rights to that property may become more narrowly defined and may be defended if the land is intruded on. Grazing land for pastoralists or arable land for horticulturalists may become limited, and, if so, use rights may be defined more exclusively for particular family and kinship groupings. In contrast to foraging societies, in tribal societies warfare frequently results from encroachments on more narrowly defined property.

Tribal societies generally possess certain types of personal property. Horticulturalists typically have more personal property than do pastoralists, because they are more sedentary. Because of the demands of a nomadic life, pastoralist property tends to be more portable (saddles, tents, and similar objects), whereas much horticultural property tends to be immovable, like housing structures and land.

Because most tribal property is owned by families based in large kin groupings, individuals generally do not have the opportunity to amass concentrations of wealth. The limited technological capabilities and reciprocal economic system of tribal societies also restrict the capacity of individuals to accumulate stores of wealth. Consequently, tribal societies tend to be *egalitarian* with respect to the ownership of property.

Social Organization

Tribal societies differ from foraging societies in that tribal peoples produce most of their subsistence items through small-scale cultivation and the domestication of animals. The evolution of food-producing subsistence corresponds to the development of new forms of social organization. As is true among foragers, social organization among tribes is largely based on kinship. Rules concerning kinship, marriage, and other social systems, however, are much more elaborate in tribal societies, which have to resolve new types of problems including denser populations, control of land or livestock, and, sometimes, warfare.

New and diverse forms of social organization have enabled tribal societies to adjust to the new conditions of food production. Unlike foragers, who sometimes have to remain separate from one another in small, flexibly organized bands, food producers have had to develop social relationships that are more fixed and permanent. Tribal social organization is based on family, the descent group, gender, and age. The social organization of tribal societies is much more complex than that of band societies.

FAMILIES

The most common social grouping among tribal societies is the extended family. Most extended families consist of three generations—grandparents, parents, and children—although they can also contain married siblings with their spouses and children. Compared with the nuclear family, the extended family is a larger and more stable social unit that is more effective in organizing and carrying out domestic economic and subsistence activities (Pasternak, 1976). Even the extended family, however, cannot satisfy the complex needs of tribal societies for cooperation, labor, and reciprocity. To meet these needs, tribal groups have developed even more "extended" types of social organization, based on both kinship and nonkinship principles.

DESCENT GROUPS

One of the more extended social groupings that exist in tribal societies is the *descent group*. A **descent group** is a social group identified by a person to trace actual or supposed kinship relationships. Descent groups are the predominant social unit in tribal societies.

One major type of descent group is based on *lineage.* Anthropologists define **lineages** as descent groups composed of relatives, all of whom trace their relationship through consanguineal (blood) or affinal (marriage) relations to an actual, commonly known ancestor. Everyone in the lineage knows exactly how she or he is related to this ancestor.

Unilineal Descent Groups **Unilineal descent groups** are lineage groups that trace their descent through only one side of the lineage or through only one sex. The most common type of unilineal descent group is a **patrilineal descent group,** or *patrilineage,* composed of people who trace their

Figure 9.2 (top) A patrilineal descent system; (bottom) a matrilineal descent system.

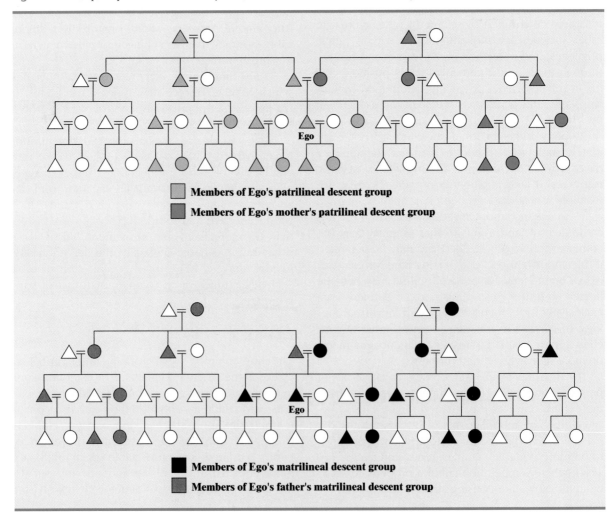

descent through males from a common, known male ancestor (see Figure 9.2a). Patrilineal descent groups are the predominant form of lineage in tribal societies (Pasternak, 1976).

Another form of unilineal descent group is the **matrilineal descent group,** or *matrilineage,* whose members calculate descent through the female line from a commonly known female ancestor (see Figure 9.2b). Matrilineal descent groups occur most frequently in horticultural societies, although they are not the most common organization. Matrilineal descent is found among a small number of North American tribal societies such as the Iroquois, Hopi, and Crow; among a number of tribes in southwestern Africa; and among a few peoples who live in the Pacific Islands.

One very rare type of unilineal grouping is based on *double descent,* a combination of patrilineal and matrilineal principles. In this type of social organization, an individual belongs to both his or her father's and mother's lineal descent groups. Several African tribal societies, such as the Afikpo Igbo in Nigeria, have a double-descent type of social organization (Ottenberg, 1965).

Ambilineal Descent Groups   One other form of descent group is known as *ambilineal descent.* An **ambilineal descent group** is formed by tracing relationships through either a male or a female line. The members of these groups are not all related to each other through a particular male or female. Therefore, technically, this form of descent group is not unilineal. Usually, once an individual chooses to affiliate with either the father's or mother's descent group, he or she remains with that descent group. Because each individual may choose his or her descent group, the ambilineal system offers more opportunity for economic and political strategizing. This choice frequently takes into account the relative economic resources or political power of the two family groups.

Bilateral Descent   A few tribal societies practice **bilateral descent,** in which relatives are traced through both maternal and paternal sides of the family simultaneously. This type of descent system does not result in any particular lineal descent grouping. For that reason, it is not common in tribal societies. In those cases in which bilateral descent is found among tribes, a loosely structured group known as a kindred is used to mobilize rela-

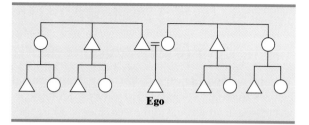

Figure 9.3   A kindred consists of relatives from both sides of a family that Ego recognizes as important kin relations.

tives for economic, social, or political purposes. **Kindreds** are overlapping relatives from both the mother's and father's side of a family that an individual recognizes as important kin relations (see Figure 9.3). In our own society, for example, when a person refers to all of his or her relatives, that person is designating a type of bilateral kindred.

Clans   A **clan** is a form of descent group whose members trace their descent to an unknown ancestor or, in some cases, to a sacred plant or animal. Members of clans usually share a common name but are not able to specify definitive links to an actual genealogical figure. Some clans are *patriclans,* a group distinguished by a male through whom descent is traced. Other clan groupings are *matriclans,* whose descent is traced through a female. Some tribal societies have both clans and lineages. In many cases, clans are made up of lineages that link their descent to an extremely vague person or sacred spirit. In such a system, clans are the larger groupings, consisting of several different lineages.

Phratries and Moieties   Other more loosely structured groups found in tribal societies include *phratries* and *moieties.* **Phratries** are social groupings that consist of two or more clans combined. Members of phratries usually believe they have some loose genealogical relationship to one another. **Moieties** (derived from the French word for "half") are composed of clans or phratries that divide the entire society into two equal divisions. In some cases, such as among the Hopi, the moiety divisions divide the village in half. People have to marry outside their own moiety. In addition, each moiety has specific functions related to economic and political organization and religious activities. Wherever phratries and moieties are found in tribal societies, they provide models for organizing social relationships.

FUNCTIONS OF DESCENT GROUPS

Descent groups provide distinctive organizational features for tribal societies. They may become corporate social units, meaning that they endure beyond any particular individual's lifetime. Thus, they can play a key role in regulating the production, exchange, and distribution of goods and services over a long period of time. Family rights to land, livestock, and other resources are usually defined in relation to these corporate descent groups.

Descent Groups and Economic Relationships

Descent groups enable tribal societies to manage their economic rights and obligations. Within the descent groups, individual nuclear families have rights to particular land and animals. For example, among patrilineal horticulturalist peoples, land is sometimes transmitted from generation to genera-

A depiction of a traditional Iroquois person.

tion through an eldest male, an inheritance pattern known as **primogeniture.** Another, less common, pattern is **ultimogeniture,** in which property and land are passed to the youngest son. In horticultural societies, separate families within patrilineages have joint rights to plots of land for gardening. For example, among the Yanomamö, villages are usually made up of two patrilineages; families within these lineages cultivate their own plots of land (Chagnon, 1997). In this sense, the Yanomamö patrilineage is an economic and territorial corporate group. The transmission of status, rights, and obligations through these patrilineages occurs without constant disputes and conflicts. In these tribal societies, land is usually not partitioned into individual plots and cannot be sold to or exchanged with other descent groups.

Iroquois tribal society was based on matrilineal corporate groupings. Matrilineages among the Iroquois resided together in longhouses and had collective rights over tools and garden plots. These matrilineages were also the basic units of production in the slash-and-burn cultivation for maize and other crops. Property was inherited through matrilineal lines from the eldest woman in the corporate group. She had the highest social status in the matrilineage and influenced decision making regarding the allocation of land and other economic rights and resources (Brown, 1970a).

Sometimes in societies with bilateral descent, kindreds are the basic labor-cooperative groups for production and exchange. People living in bilateral societies can turn to both the mother's and father's side of the family for economic assistance. The kindred is thus a much more loosely structured corporate group. The kindred is highly flexible and allows for better adaptation in certain environmental circumstances.

MARRIAGE

Corporate descent groups play a role in determining marital relations in tribal societies. Like foragers, most tribal peoples maintain exogamous rules of marriage with respect to different corporate groups. People generally marry *outside* their lineage, kindred, clan, moiety, or phratry. Marriages in tribal societies are guided by rules that

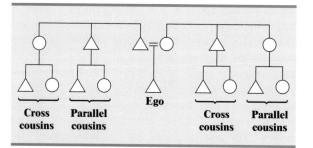

Figure 9.4   Different types of cousin marriage.

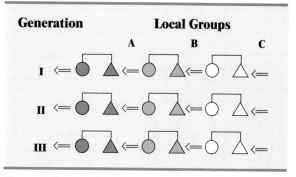

Figure 9.5   Matrilateral cross-cousin marriages among three lineages.

ensure the perpetuation of kinship ties and group alliances.

Some tribal societies practice different forms of cousin marriage, which are illustrated in Figure 9.4. For example, among the Yanomamö, cross-cousin marriage and patrilocal residence, in which a newly married couple resides with the husband's parents, are practiced among patrilineages in different villages. Males in one patrilineage, in effect, exchange sisters, whom they may not marry, with males of other patrilineages. When the sons of the next generation repeat this form of marriage, each is marrying a woman to whom he is already related by kinship. The woman whom the man marries is both his father's sister's daughter and his mother's brother's daughter. The woman is marrying a man who is both her mother's brother's son and her father's sister's son. This form of patrilineal exogamous marriage is common in many tribal societies. It is a type of restricted marriage exchange that helps provide for the formation of economic and political alliances among villages.

Some patrilineal tribal societies, including several in Southeast Asia, prefer a more specific rule of *matrilateral cross-cousin marriage*. In this system, males consistently marry their mother's brothers' daughters. This produces a marital system in which females move from one patrilineage to another. More than two lineages are involved in this system. The patrilineages become specialized as either wife givers or wife takers. In an example with three lineages—A, B, and C—anthropologists have noted cycles of marital exchange. Lineage B always gives women to lineage A but takes its wives from lineage C (see Figure 9.5). Claude Levi-Strauss (1969) refers to this type of marital system as *gen-*

eral exchange, in contrast to *restricted exchange,* which is practiced between two lineages.

Another form of cousin marriage found in some patrilineal societies is **parallel-cousin marriage,** in which a male marries his father's brother's daughter. Unlike the other forms of cousin marriage, parallel-cousin marriage results in endogamy—marriage within one's own descent group (see Figure 9.6). This form of marriage is found among the Bedouin and other tribes of the Middle East and North Africa.

Polygyny   Cross-cultural research has demonstrated that polygyny occurs most frequently in tribal societies. Anthropologists Kay Martin and Barbara Voorhies (1975) emphasized that polygyny is an ecologically and economically adaptive strategy for tribal populations. The more wives an individual male has, the more land or livestock he will control for allocation and exchange. This leads to an increase in both the labor supply and the overall productive value of the household. In addition, wealth in many of these tribal societies is measured in the number of offspring. Reproducing children for one's descent group is viewed as prestigious,

Figure 9.6   Patrilateral parallel-cousin marriage.

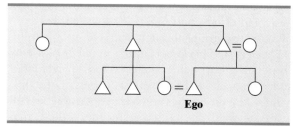

and the children also become productive members of the household.

Anthropologist Douglas White (1988) has done extensive cross-cultural research on polygyny. He described one widespread type of polygyny as a wealth-enhancing form of marriage in which elder males accumulate several wives for productive labor, which increases their wealth. Strongly correlated with this wealth-enhancing polygyny is the ability to acquire new land for expansion. As new land becomes available, the labor produced by co-wives is extremely valuable. According to White, this wealth-enhancing form of polygyny is also related to warfare and the capture of wives. In his cross-cultural research, White found that tribal warfare often involved the capture of women from other groups as a major means of recruiting new co-wives for elder males.

In addition to increasing wealth, polygyny enables certain individuals and lineages to have a large number of children. For example, roughly 25 percent of Yanomamö marriages are polygynous. One sample group of twenty Yanomamö political leaders had 71 wives and 172 children among them (Chagnon & Irons, 1979). One Yanomamö individual named Shinbone had 11 wives and 43 children (Chagnon, 1997).

Bridewealth Exchange   Among many tribal societies, marriages are accompanied by an exchange of wealth. The most common type of exchange, particularly among patrilineal societies, is called **bridewealth,** which involves the transfer of some form of wealth, sometimes limited-purpose money like shells or livestock, from the descent group of the groom to that of the bride. Bridewealth is not a commercial exchange that reduces a bride to a commodity; that is, the bride's family does not "sell" her to her husband's family. Nevertheless, in societies in which it occurs, females are usually low in status.

Bridewealth serves to symbolize and highlight the reciprocities and rights established between two descent groups through marriage. In a patrilineal society, the bride becomes a member of a new corporate group that acquires access to her labor and, eventually, to her offspring. In return, the husband's kin group has certain responsibilities toward the wife. The bridewealth reflects these mutual rights and obligations and compensates the bride's family for the loss of her labor. Thus, it helps to forge an alliance between the two kin groups. One recent cross-cultural study of marriage transactions suggests that bridewealth exchanges in tribal societies relate to the need to introduce new female labor into the household, the transmission of property, and the enhancement of status for males (Schlegel & Eloul, 1988). Failure to pay the bridewealth usually leads to family conflicts, including the possible dissolution of the marriage.

Polyandry   Not all tribal societies are polygynous: Some practice monogamy, and a few practice polyandry. Polyandrous marriage appears as a systematic pattern only in formerly tribal societies in the Himalayan regions of northern India and Tibet, and, until recently, among the Todas of southern India. The most common type of polyandry is *fraternal polyandry,* in which brothers share a wife.

The Toda were a buffalo-herding, pastoralist tribe of approximately 800 people. Traditionally, marriages were arranged by parents when the partners were young children. When a Toda girl married a specific individual, she automatically became a wife of his brothers, including those who were not yet born. Through patrilocal residence rules, the wife joined the household of the husband. There was little evidence of sexual jealousy among the co-husbands. If the wife became pregnant, the oldest male claimed paternity rights over the child. The other co-husbands were "fathers" in a sociological sense and had certain rights regarding the child, such as labor for their households. Biological paternity was not considered important. The most prevalent explanation for the development of polyandry among the Toda was that female infanticide was practiced, leading to a scarcity of females (Rivers, [1906] 1967; Oswalt, 1972; Walker, 1986).

The Levirate and Sororate   The corporateness of descent groups in some tribal societies is exemplified by two rules of marriage designed to preserve kin ties and fulfill obligations following the death of a spouse. These rules are known as the *levirate* and the *sororate.* The **levirate** is the rule that a widow is expected to marry one of her deceased husband's brothers. In some societies, such as the ancient Israelites of biblical times or the contemporary Nuer tribe, the levirate rule requires a man to cohabit with a dead brother's widow so that she can have children, who are then considered to be the deceased husband's. The essential feature of the levirate is that the corporate rights of the deceased husband and the lineage endure even after the husband's death. The **sororate** is a marriage rule that dictates that when a wife dies, her husband is expected to marry one of her sisters.

Both the levirate and sororate provide for the fulfillment of mutual obligations between consanguineal and affinal kin ties after death. Reciprocal exchanges between allied families must extend beyond the death of any individual. These marital practices emphasize the crucial ties among economic, kinship, and political factors in tribal societies.

Postmarital Residence Rules in Tribal Societies

Anthropologists find that the rules for residence after marriage in tribal societies are related to the forms of descent groups. For example, the vast majority of tribal societies have patrilineal descent groups and patrilocal rules of residence. Another, less frequent, pattern of postmarital residence is *matrilocal residence,* in which the newly wedded couple lives with or near the wife's parents. Yet another rule of residence found in matrilineal societies is known as *avunculocal,* in which a married couple resides with the husband's mother's brother.

Causes of Postmarital Residence Rules From studying the relationships between postmarital residence rules and forms of descent groups in tribal societies, anthropologists have found that residence rules often represent adaptions to the practical conditions a society faces. The most widely accepted hypothesis states that rules of postmarital residence usually develop before the form of descent groups in a society (Fox, 1967; Keesing, 1975; Martin & Voorhies, 1975). For example, limited land and resources, frequent warfare with neighboring groups, population pressure, and the need for cooperative work may have been important factors in developing patrilocal residence and patrilineal descent groups. The purpose of these male-centered rules of residence and descent may have been to keep fathers, sons, and brothers together to pursue common interests in land, animals, and people.

What, then, creates matrilocal rules and matrilineal descent? One explanation based on cross-cultural research by Melvin and Carol Ember (1971)

proposes that matrilocal rules developed in response to patterns of warfare. The Embers suggested that societies that engage in *internal warfare,* warfare with neighboring societies close to home, have patrilocal rules of residence. In contrast, societies involved in *external warfare,* warfare a long distance from home, develop matrilocal-residence rules. In societies in which external warfare takes males from the home territory for long periods of time, there is a strong need to keep the women of kin groups together. The classic example used by the Embers is the Iroquois, whose males traveled hundreds of miles away from home to engage in external wars, and this produced matrilocal residence and matrilineal descent.

Marvin Harris (1975, 1979) has extended the Embers' hypothesis to suggest that matrilocal rules and matrilineal descent emerge in societies in which males are absent for long periods, for whatever reason. For example, among the Navajo, females tended sheep near their own households, and males raised horses and participated in labor that took them away from their homes. The Navajo had matrilocal residence and matrilineal descent.

Generalizations on Marriage in Tribal Societies

It must be emphasized that descent, marriage, and residence rules are not static in tribal societies. Rather, they are flexible and change as ecological, demographic, economic, and political circumstances change. For example, tribal groups with rules of preference for marriage partners make exceptions to those rules when the situation calls for it. If a tribal society has norms that prescribe cross-cousin or parallel-cousin marriage and an individual does not have a cousin in the particular category, various options will be available for the individual.

There are usually many other candidates available for an arranged marriage. As anthropologist Ward Goodenough (1956) demonstrated, much strategizing goes on in tribal societies in determining marital choice, residence locales, and descent. Factors such as property and the availability of land, animals, or other resources often influence decisions about marital arrangements. Often, tribal elders will be involved in lengthy negotiations regarding marital choices for their offspring. These people, like others throughout the world, are not automatons responding automatically to cultural norms. Kinship and marital rules are ideal norms, and these norms are often violated.

Divorce   Among tribal peoples, especially those with patrilineal descent groups, divorce rates may be related to bridewealth exchanges. One traditional view suggested that in patrilineal-descent societies with a high bridewealth amount, marriages tend to be stable. In Evans-Pritchard's (1951) account of Nuer marriage, he noted that one of the major reasons for bridewealth is to ensure marital stability. In lineage societies, the man's family pays a bridewealth in exchange for the rights to a woman's economic output and fertility. The greater the bridewealth, the more complete is the transfer of rights over the woman from her own family to that of her husband. The dissolution of a marriage, which requires the return of bridewealth, is less likely to occur if the bridewealth is large and has been redistributed among many members of the wife's family (Gluckman, 1953; Leach, [1953]1954; Schneider, 1953). In contrast, when the bridewealth is low, marriages are unstable, and divorce is frequent.

As Roger Keesing (1981) has pointed out, however, this hypothesis raises a fundamental question: Is marriage stable *because* of high bridewealth costs, or can a society afford to have high bridewealth only if it has a stable form of marriage? Keesing's own theories concerning divorce focus on rules of descent. In general, societies with matrilineal descent rules have high divorce rates, whereas patrilineal societies have low rates. Among the matrilineal Hopi or Zuni, for example, a woman has only to put a man's belongings outside her house door to secure a divorce. The husband then returns to his mother's household, and the wife and children remain in the wife's household (Garbarino, 1988).

Marriages in matrilineal descent groups tend to be less enduring than those in patrilineal groups because of the clash of interests (or corporate rights) over children. When a woman's primary interests remain with her lineage at birth and the people of her descent group have control over her and her children, her bond to her husband and his lineage tends to be fragile and impermanent (Keesing, 1975). In contrast, in patrilineal societies, the wife has been fully incorporated into the husband's lineage. This tends to solidify patrilineal

rights over children, leading to more durable marital ties.

GENDER

Gender is an extremely important element of social structure in tribal societies. Cross-cultural ethnological research on tribal societies has contributed to a better understanding of male-female relations. Anthropologists are interested in the interrelationships among gender roles, subsistence practices, female status, patriarchy, and sexism in tribal societies.

Gender and Enculturation: Margaret Mead's Study   Although nineteenth-century anthropologists addressed the question of gender roles, their conclusions were largely speculative and were not based on firsthand research. In the twentieth century, anthropologists went into the field to collect information concerning the roles of males and females. The landmark ethnographic study of gender roles was carried out by Margaret Mead and involved three New Guinea societies: the Arapesh, the Mundugumor, and the Tchambuli. Mead's study was published in 1935 and was titled *Sex and Temperament in Three Primitive Societies.*

Mead described these three tribes as having totally different types of gender roles. Among the Arapesh, males and females had similar attitudes and behavior. Mead described both sexes as unaggressive, cooperative, passive, and sensitive to the needs of others. Based on U.S. standards of the time, Mead described the Arapesh as feminine. In contrast, Mead described Mundugumor males and females as aggressive, selfish, insensitive, and uncooperative, much like the U.S. stereotype of masculinity.

The Tchambuli, according to Mead, represented a complete reversal of U.S. conceptions of gender roles. Tchambuli females were dominant politically and economically, whereas males were submissive, emotionally dependent, and less responsible. Females were the breadwinners and the political leaders, and they engaged in warfare. Males stayed near the domestic camp and cared for children. One of their primary activities was artistic work such as dancing, painting, and jewelry making. Hence, by U.S. standards, Tchambuli women were masculine, and Tchambuli men were feminine.

Mead concluded that societies can both minimize and exaggerate social and cultural differences between males and females. She argued that gender differences are extremely variable from society to society.

Mead's study challenged the status quo in U.S. society regarding gender-role stereotypes. It also appealed strongly to the emerging feminist movement because it asserted that culture, rather than biology, determines (and limits) gender roles. Tchambuli women became an important symbol for the feminist movement in the United States during the 1960s.

Mead's Study Reappraised After restudying the Tchambuli (who actually call themselves the Chambri) during the 1970s, anthropologist Deborah Gewertz (1981) concluded that Mead's description of the reversal of gender roles was not accurate. She argued instead that the Chambri conform to traditional stereotypes of aggressive males and submissive females. Chambri males allocate and control the distribution of goods and valuables and hence are dominant politically and economically, despite the fact that females produce most of the goods.

Gewertz's reevaluation of Chambri gender-role patterns challenges the hypothesis presented by Mead regarding the tremendous flexibility of gender roles in human societies. Although Gewertz notes that cultural values do influence gender roles, a complete reversal of the male–female role was not evident in the Chambri case. According to Gewertz, Mead had viewed the Chambri at a time when they were going through a unique transition. For example, in the 1930s the Chambri had been driven from their islands by an enemy tribe. All of their physical structures and artwork had been burned. Consequently, the Chambri men were engaged near the domestic camps in full-time artwork and rebuilding at the time Mead conducted her study. Mead assumed that these were typical activities for males, when in fact they were atypical.

Patriarchy Despite Mead's conclusions concerning gender roles among the Tchambuli, most modern anthropologists agree that a pattern of *matriarchy,* in which females regularly dominate males economically and politically, is not part of the archaeological, historical, and ethnographic record (Bamberger, 1974; Friedl, 1975; Martin & Voorhies, 1975). Most tribal societies are patriarchal. Anthro-

pologists have offered many hypotheses to explain the prevalence of patriarchy.

Sociobiologists view patriarchy in tribal societies as a consequence of innate reproductive strategies, leading to enhanced reproductive fitness. In this view, males are unconsciously motivated to reproduce with as many females as possible to increase their chances of reproductive success. As we have seen, some tribal males have many more children than others. These reproductive strategies involve competition among males for females. According to this model, this male competition in turn leads to political conflict and increases in warfare. These factors produce the patterns of patrilocality, patrilineality, polygyny, and patriarchy in tribal societies (Van den Berghe & Barash, 1977; Chagnon, 1979).

Instead of referring to supposed innate biological drives, cultural materialists like William Divale and Marvin Harris (1976) maintain that patriarchy and gender hierarchy are caused by the scarcity of resources and recurring warfare in tribal societies. In general, when material resources are scarce, especially in horticultural societies, warfare between competitive tribes is prevalent. Because most warriors are male, both the status and the power of males in these societies become intensified. For example, warfare is an endemic feature of life for some tribes in the Amazon and in New Guinea. For these reasons, a male-supremacy complex develops.

Patriarchy and Sexism in Tribal Societies Other anthropologists emphasize that although biological or material considerations may contribute to male domination, the cultural values used to define "female" are extremely important in the maintenance of tribal patriarchies. Many tribal societies adhere to mythologies, beliefs, and ideologies that justify male domination and female subordination (Ortner, 1974). These mythologies, beliefs, and ideologies reinforce **sexism**—prejudice and discrimination against a person based on their sex.

Many patrilineal horticultural societies of New Guinea, for example, seclude females from males during menstruation because they believe that menstruating females are unclean and will harm the community (Lindenbaum, 1972). Another widely held belief in tribal societies is that the primary value of women is their ability to bear children, especially male children. Sherry Ortner

(1974) believed that women's reproductive value often causes them to be viewed as mere reproductive instruments.

These prejudices frequently lead to discriminatory practices against females. In many tribal societies, women are excluded from political and sacred ritual activities, as well as from military combat. This results in the cultural definition of males as the primary gender, who ensure the survival of society. Men are often admired by women and children for providing for the basic welfare of the tribal community.

Because of these views, women in some tribal societies are often subjected to social subordination, sexual segregation, excessive domination, and systematic physical abuse (Lindenbaum, 1972; Chagnon, 1997). At times, they are deprived of material resources during pregnancy, denied the same access to food as males, and physically mutilated. Sexist ideologies are often used to justify these practices.

Gender, Subsistence, and Female Status A number of anthropologists have proposed that, as in foraging societies, the status of women in tribal societies depends on their contributions to subsistence activities. As we have seen, both males and females are involved in horticultural production. Males usually clear the gardens, whereas women weed and harvest the crops. In a survey of more than five hundred horticultural societies, Martin and Voorhies (1975) found that women actually contribute more to cultivation activities in horticultural societies than do men. Nevertheless, patriarchy reigns in conjunction with a sexist ideology in most of these tribal groups. In some matrilineal horticultural societies, however, the status of females tends to be higher.

Female Status in Matrilineal Societies In matrilineally organized societies such as the Iroquois, Hopi, and Zuni of North America, and the Mundurucu of South America, women have considerable influence in economic and political decision making. Also, the mother and sisters of the wives in matrilineages can often offer support in domestic disputes with males. In addition, rights to property, including land, technology, and livestock, are embodied in the matrilineages. In general, however, males in matrilineal societies hold the influential positions of political power and maintain control over economic resources. In most matrilineal societies, the mother's brother has political authority and economic control within the family. Thus, matrilineality does not translate into matriarchy.

The Iroquois: Women in a Matrilineal Society The Iroquois offer a good example of the status of females in matrilineal societies. The Iroquois longhouses were occupied by families related through matrilineages. The elder matrons in these matrilineages had the power to appoint the sachem, a council leader of the Iroquois political system. Often they appointed their sons to this position. Women could also influence decisions about peace and warfare and determine whether prisoners of war should live or die (Brown, 1970a). As in most matrilineal societies, Iroquois women played an important role in organizing subsistence activities and allocating food.

Clearly, as the Iroquois case indicates, women influenced the political and economic dynamics in some matrilineal societies. In their cross-cultural survey, Martin and Voorhies (1975) found that the status of women is higher in horticultural societies that practice matrilineal descent. In many of these matrilineal societies, males developed political power only if they had strong support from the relatives of their wives. Nevertheless, these findings also indicate that in the matrilineal societies, males still exercise political authority and assume control over key economic resources. In these societies, women may be held in high regard, but they are still economically and politically subordinate to men.

AGE

As mentioned in Chapter 7, all societies have age grades, groupings of people of the same age. Within an age grade, people learn specific norms and acquire cultural knowledge. In some tribal societies, age grades have become specialized as groupings that have many functions.

Age Sets In certain tribal societies of East Africa, North America, Brazil, India, and New Guinea, specialized age groupings emerged as multifunctional institutions. In some tribal societies, age grades become much more formalized and institutionalized as age sets. **Age sets** are corporate groups of people of about the same age who share specific rights, obligations, duties, and privileges within their community. Typically, people enter an age set when they are young and then progress through various life stages with other members of the set. The transition from one age set to another is usually accompanied by a distinctive rite of passage. The corporate units provide for permanent mutual obligations that continue through time.

Age Sets among the Nyakyusa   The best-known age-set system is found among the Nyakyusa, an East African tribe that cultivates land and tends livestock. Nyakyusa men strive to accumulate many cattle and many wives. Cattle and wives are not only symbols of status; they are also instruments of power and security in old age. The Nyakyusa have age sets that influence their entire social organization. Young males reside in their father's home until the age of 10. From that time until they are 25, they reside with their own age-mates in separate villages, although they still visit and eat meals at their father's house. When they are about 25 they are allowed to marry.

After marriage, a Nyakyusa man is allowed to set up his household and accumulate land for horticultural production. Approximately ten years after marrying, these males undergo a series of elaborate rituals to enter a new age set that grants them senior status and political authority over the entire range of Nyakyusa affairs (Wilson, 1951). The age sets produce enduring social and political units that allow the Nyakyusa to manage, control, and organize their society without substantial conflict and disruption.

Age Grades among the Sebei Pastoralists   A number of tribal pastoralists of East Africa, such as the Karimojong, the Masai, the Nuer, the Pokot, the Samburu, and the Sebei, have specialized age-set and age-grade systems that structure social organization. The Sebei, for example, have eight age-set groups, each of which is divided into three subsets. The eight groups are given a formal name, and the subsets have informal nicknames. Sebei males join an age set through initiation, in which they are circumcised and exposed to tribal secret lore and indoctrination.

The Sebei initiations are held approximately every six years, and the initiation rituals extend over a period of six months. Those who are initiated together develop strong bonds. Newly initiated males enter the lowest level of this system, the

junior warriors. As they grow older, they graduate into the next level, the senior warriors, while younger males enter the junior levels. Groups of males then progress from one level to the next throughout the course of their lifetime (Goldschmidt, 1986).

The most important function of the Sebei age sets is military. The members of the age set are responsible for protecting livestock and for conducting raids against other camps. In addition, age sets are the primary basis of status in these societies. Among the most basic social rankings are junior and senior military men and junior and senior elders. All social interaction, political activities, and ceremonial events are influenced by the age-set system. In the absence of a centralized government, age sets play a vital role in maintaining social cohesion.

The Elderly   Among tribal pastoralists and horticulturalists, older people make use of ownership or control of property to reinforce their status. Societies in which the elderly control extensive resources appear to show higher levels of deference toward the aged (Silverman & Maxwell, 1983). The control of land, women, and livestock and their allocation among the younger generations are the primary means by which the older men (and sometimes older women, in matrilineal societies) exercise their power over the rest of society. In many cases, this dominance by the elderly leads to age stratification or inequalities. The system in which older people exercise exceptional power is called **gerontocracy**—rule by elders (usually male) who control the material and reproductive resources of the community.

In gerontocracies, elderly males tend to monopolize not only the property resources but also the young women in the tribe. Access to human beings is the greatest source of wealth and power in these tribal societies. Additionally, older males benefit from the accumulation of bridewealth. Through these processes, older men tend to have more secure statuses and economic prerogatives. They retire from subsistence and economic activities and often assume political leadership in tribal affairs. In this capacity they make important decisions regarding marriage ties, resource exchanges, and other issues.

Gerontocratic tribal societies have been prominent in the past as well as in the present. Among the ancient Israelites—once a pastoralist tribe—the elders controlled the disposition of property and marriages of their adult children, and the Bible mentions many examples of tribal patriarchs who were involved in polygynous marriages. In a modern pastoralist tribe—the Kirghiz of Afghanistan—the elderly enjoy extensive political power and status gained partially through the control of economic resources. In addition, the elders are thought to be wise, possessing extensive knowledge of history and local ecological conditions as well as medical and veterinary skills crucial to the group's survival (Shahrani, 1981). Thus, the possession of cultural knowledge may lead to the development of gerontocratic tendencies within tribal societies.

Political Organization

Like band societies, tribal societies have decentralized political systems in which authority is distributed among a number of individuals, groups, and associations. Political leadership is open to any male (especially older males) in the society and is usually based on personal abilities and qualities.

SODALITIES

Although anthropologists recognize that tribes are the most varied of all small-scale societies, Elman Service ([1962] 1971) attempted to distinguish the tribe from the band by referring to the existence of *sodalities* (associations). In tribal societies, two types of sodalities exist: *kinship sodalities,* including lineages and clans, and *nonkin sodalities,* voluntary and involuntary associations. Kinship sodalities are the primary basis for political organization in tribal societies. Nonkin sodalities, such as age sets, village councils of elders, male secret societies, and military societies, also have political functions and are mostly voluntary associations that cut across kinship ties by creating alliances outside the immediate kin groups.

In both horticulturalist and pastoralist societies, descent groups such as lineages and clans are the most common political sodalities. Intravillage and intervillage politics are based on these groups,

through which alliances are created that assist in maintaining peaceful and harmonious relationships within the tribe. As we have seen, these descent groups are instrumental in carrying out reciprocal exchanges involving bridewealth, women, and other goods, and they are often the only basis for maintaining order. Kinship is the primary basis for political activities and processes in tribal societies.

HOW LEADERS ARE CHOSEN

In horticulturalist and pastoralist societies, political leaders are recruited from within descent groups. As in band societies, however, these leaders do not have much coercive power and formal authority. Although many tribes engage in warfare, political leadership tends to be almost as weak and diffuse as it is in band societies. A number of anthropologists hypothesize that this decentralized and limited form of political leadership is due to the constant movement involved in slash-and-burn cultivation and to the nomadism associated with pastoralism (Vayda, 1961; Sahlins, 1968b). They suggest that permanent, long-term settlement in one locale is needed for the development of an effective, centralized form of political authority.

Village Headman   Some horticultural groups like the Yanomamö select a village headman. To become an effective leader, this individual must be "generous" and be able to motivate feasting and exchange activities among different lineages in the village. To become generous the individual must cultivate more land, which requires more productive labor. One way to be more productive is to have more wives. As we have seen, the Yanomamö leaders are polygynous. Thus, polygynous marital relations enable a Yanomamö headman to sustain his generosity and political status.

The Yanomamö headman has no recognized authority to enforce political decisions in the group; he has to lead more by example than by coercion (Chagnon, 1997). He must persuade people to obey the norms of the village, and he gives advice and suggestions on subsistence, economic, and ritual matters.

Big Man   Another style of political leadership and organization found among some horticultural groups, particularly in Melanesia, is the "big-man" system. One of the most detailed descriptions of this system was compiled by anthropologist Douglas Oliver (1955), who did fieldwork in the Solomon Islands among the Siuai tribe. According to Oliver, the aspiring Siuai big man has to collect as many wives as possible to form kinship alliances with other descent groups. In addition, he must accumulate a large number of pigs and grow the taro (an edible root crop) to feed them. Most of this productive labor is carried out by the man's wives. When a man has enough pigs, he has a pig feast in which he attracts followers while humiliating rival big men. If the leader is able to recruit a few hundred men through the "generosity" demonstrated by the feast, these followers may begin to build a "clubhouse" to demonstrate their political commitment to the big man.

The big-man political organization of the Siuai is both formidable and fragile. It is formidable in that the pig feasts can enable a man to attract more and more followers, and thus more power. This system provides the basis for political and war-making alliances. The big man is also able to command and sometimes coerce other people. At the same time, the political loyalties of the followers of the big man are not long lasting: The lineage of the big man does not assume any of his political power or authority. With the death of the big man the entire political organization collapses, and loyalties and allegiance shift to another or several other big men who compete through pig feasts for political supporters. Hence, the big man, like the hunter-gatherer leader, cannot pass on power or build permanent structures of authority.

PASTORALIST TRIBAL POLITICS

Pastoralist tribal groups tend to have similar political organizations, depending on the degree of their nomadic lifestyle. Some pastoralist societies depend on the agricultural societies within their region and are not completely self-sufficient. In these groups, leadership tends to become more permanent and centralized. The greater the degree of nomadic independence, isolation, and self-sufficiency within a group, however, the more diffuse and egalitarian is its political leadership (Lindholm, 1986).

Segmentary Lineage Systems   One traditional form of political organization found among such groups as the Nuer of East Africa and the Bedouins

is the *segmentary lineage system.* A **segmentary lineage system** is a type of political organization in which multiple descent groups (usually patrilineages) form at different levels and serve political functions. This system reflects a complex yet flexible arrangement of lineage groups. Among the Nuer, for example, the patrilineages are identified with particular territories in the tribal area. These patrilineages have both *maximal lineages,* which include descendants who trace their ancestors back through many generations, and *minimal lineages,* segments of the maximal lineage whose descendants trace their ancestry back only one or two generations. Minimal lineages are nested within the maximal lineage, and all members of the lineage can link themselves directly to the same maximal blood ancestor.

Complementary Opposition   The segmentary lineage system is composed of the various patrilineages, both maximal and minimal, that can be united for military or political purposes. The process by which alliances are formed and conflicts are resolved in this system is referred to as *complementary opposition.* **Complementary opposition** is the formation of groups that parallel one another as political antagonists. To understand this process, imagine a village with two different maximal lineages. We will call the maximal lineages A and B; the minimal lineages within A we will call A1 and A2; and the minimal lineages within B we will call B1 and B2 (see the diagram in Figure 9.7).

Figure 9.7   Model of segmentary lineage system.

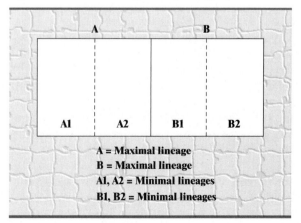

A = Maximal lineage
B = Maximal lineage
A1, A2 = Minimal lineages
B1, B2 = Minimal lineages

Now imagine that a member of B2 commits an offense against a member of B1. A feud may erupt, but it will usually be settled within the maximal lineage (B) to which both minimal lineages belong. However, should B2 commit an offense against A2, a different process unfolds. Both A2 and A1 will unite in opposition to B2, which in turn will join with B1. The result is a large-scale feud between maximal lineages A and B. This process can extend beyond the lineages to an entire population. For example, in the event of an outside attack, all of the maximal lineages will unite to defend the tribe.

Within the process of complementary opposition, then, kinspeople may be allies under one set of circumstances and enemies under another. Through this process, the segmentary lineage system can achieve political goals without any definitive type of centralized leadership, such as kings, chiefs, or headmen. The philosophy behind complementary opposition is summarized in an old Bedouin proverb:

> Me against my brother
> I and my brother against our cousins
> I and my brother and my cousins against non-
>   relatives
> I and my brother and my cousins and friends against
>   the enemies in our village
> All of these and the whole village against another
>   village. (Murphy & Kasdan, 1959)

Many other pastoralist societies have maintained segmentary lineage systems. For example, during their nomadic pastoralist existence prior to the establishment of the kingdom of Israel, the ancient Israelites appear to have been organized on the basis of segmentary lineages without any centralized political institutions. (In the Bible, patrilineal groups are referred to as *families*.)

Among segmentary lineage societies, feuds frequently erupt between lineages and result in retaliation or compensation without the imposition of force by a centralized authority. If a member of a particular lineage kills a member of another lineage, the victim's lineage may seek blood revenge. To prevent this, the Nuer attempt to reduce the tension between the victim's and the murderer's lineages. In Nuer society, an individual known as the *leopard skin chief* sometimes provides sanctuary for a murderer and attempts to negotiate compensation with the victim's lineage. In some in-

stances, compensation takes the form of cattle, a desired possession that can be used as bridewealth.

EXPLAINING TRIBAL WARFARE

Both internal and external warfare are far more common among tribes than among foragers. Several hypotheses have been developed to explain tribal warfare. Most anthropologists reject the notion that humans are by nature aggressive and warlike, possessing an instinct for violence. Instead, most theories focus on environmental, demographic, and other external political and cultural factors.

Among horticulturalist societies, members of one village frequently raid other villages for territory, women, or, occasionally, headhunting (removing the head of a slain enemy and preserving it as a trophy). In a detailed analysis of warfare among the Mae Enga of highland New Guinea, anthropologist Mervyn Meggitt (1977) noted that land shortages and ecological conditions are the most important causes of warfare. The Mae Enga, numbering more than thirty thousand, are organized into phratries, clans, and localized patrilineal groups. Meggitt distinguishes among different types of warfare involving phratries, clans, and patrilineages.

Phratry warfare involving the entire tribe is mostly ceremonial and serves to display status and prestige between big men and males. Phratry warfare is extremely limited. Interclan and interlineage internal warfare, however, is vicious and ongoing, with conquering kin groups seizing the land of the conquered patrilineages. Meggitt noted that 58 percent of cases of internal warfare were over land, and in 74 percent of the cases, the victors incorporated some or all of the land of the victims. The Mae Enga themselves interpret their internal warfare as a consequence of population growth in relation to the scarcity of land for cultivation.

The Yanomamö and Protein Shortages Cultural materialists Divale and Harris (1976) explain Yanomamö warfare in terms of ecological factors. They view the internal warfare of the Yanomamö as an indirect means of regulating population growth. Divale and Harris suggest that the Yanomamö institutions and values that relate to intervillage warfare emerge from the group's cultivation practices and nutritional deficiencies. They hypothesize that the Yanomamö expand their cultivation because they experience protein shortages. Thus, the intensification of warfare in which villages raid one another's game reserves is an adaptive Yanomamö response or mechanism that indirectly and unintentionally serves to inhibit population growth. The limited protein supplies are inadequate to support larger populations.

Other anthropologists have rejected the protein shortage explanation of Yanomamö warfare. Napoleon Chagnon and Raymond Hames (1979) measured the amount of protein consumed in different Yanomamö villages and encountered no clinical signs of shortages. Furthermore, they discovered that some villages that consumed high amounts of protein engaged in warfare as frequently as villages that consumed low amounts.

Sociobiological Hypotheses of Tribal Warfare

Anthropologist William Durham (1976) offered an evolutionary, sociobiological hypothesis of tribal warfare. An example of his model is his study of the Mundurucu of the Amazon, who had a reputation for continual warfare and headhunting against other tribes. Although Durham did not rule out competition for resources and land as explanations for warfare, he hypothesized that, ultimately, warfare is an adaptive reproductive strategy. In Durham's view, tribal warfare is a means of increasing inclusive fitness on a tribal level in competition with other tribal populations in the region. (Inclusive fitness was discussed in Chapter 6). If the population of a rival tribe is reduced, one's own tribe may increase its rate of survival and reproduction. Durham believed that increasing the number and survival of offspring (one's own genes) into the next generation is the underlying motivation for tribal warfare.

Multidimensional Explanations of Tribal Warfare
All of these hypotheses view warfare as having in some way an adaptive function for society. But many critics say that although population pressure, competition for land and livestock, and reproductive success may help explain tribal warfare, these variables need to be combined with cultural factors such as honor, prestige, and the enhancement of male status.

Anthropologist Walter Goldschmidt (1989) noted in an essay that males in tribal societies are in-

duced to go to war against other groups through institutionalized religious and cultural indoctrination. Although in some tribal societies warriors are given material rewards such as women or land, in most cases, nonmaterial rewards such as prestige, honor, and spiritual incentives are just as important. Most likely, this generalization applies to all societies that engage in warfare.

LAW AND CONFLICT RESOLUTION

Tribal societies that have no centralized political institutions for addressing internal conflicts must, for the most part, rely primarily on informal and formal sanctions to resolve conflicts. Because tribes have larger, more settled populations and more complex kinship networks than do bands, they cannot resolve disputes merely by having people

A Nuer leopard skin chief. These individuals are basically mediators who help resolve conflicts by building a consensus. They do not have the power to coerce other people.

CRITICAL PERSPECTIVES

Human Aggression: Biological or Cultural?

Throughout history, humans have been confronted with questions about violence and aggression. Indeed, it sometimes appears as if aggression is an inescapable aspect of life. In today's world of mass media, we are constantly confronted with accounts of violence and aggression, ranging from sports brawls to assaults and murders to revolutions and wars. The seeming universality of aggression has led some people to conclude that humans are "naturally" violent. What are the causes of human aggression? Is violence inbred, or is it learned?

Not surprisingly, anthropologists and other social scientists have examined these issues for decades, often arriving at conflicting conclusions. Disputes concerning the origins of violence reflect the biology-versus-culture debate. Some psychologists and ethologists attribute warfare and violence to humans' psychobiological-genetic heritage. For example,

ethologist Konrad Lorenz developed an elaborate biological hypothesis based on comparisons with animal behaviors. In his widely read book *On Aggression* (1966), Lorenz proposed that during humanity's long period of physical evolution certain genes were selected that provide humans with an aggressive instinct, which has survival value for the species. He argued that this instinct evolved through natural selection because of intergroup warfare and competition.

Lorenz noted that nonhuman animals usually do not kill within their species and that aggression among males within species is highly ritualized and rarely leads to death. Male deer, wolves, and other social animals fight each other, but this fighting establishes a hierarchy of dominant and submissive males and therefore helps to ensure order within the group. Thus, nonhuman animals have an instinct for inhibiting aggression

that is activated by the ritualized fighting behavior. Humans, in contrast, have evolved as physically weak creatures without sharp teeth, claws, beaks, or tremendous strength. Therefore, the instinct for inhibiting violence was not selected for the human species. According to Lorenz, this accounts for the prevalence of warfare in human societies and makes humans highly dangerous animals. Compounding this loss of instinctual inhibitions against violence is the human technological capacity to produce deadly weapons.

Many anthropologists challenged this concept of a universal instinct for aggression. Citing ethnographic evidence from sociocultural systems that experienced little violence, Ashley Montagu, Marshall Sahlins, and others proposed that cultural factors are more important than biological instincts in determining aggression (Montagu, 1968). They argued

move to another location. Thus, many tribal groups have developed more formalized legal techniques and methods of conflict resolution.

In general, tribal societies have no formal courts and no lawyers. However, ethnologists have found in such societies some individuals, usually older males, who are highly skilled in negotiation and conflict resolution. These individuals may become *mediators* who help resolve disputes among clans, lineages, and other descent groups. One example of a mediator is the Nuer leopard skin chief, who attempts to restore amicable relations between Nuer patrilineages after a homicide. It is important

to note that the chief has no authority to enforce legal decisions, a pattern typical of mediators in tribal societies. These mediators preside over the litigation procedures, but the final decision can be reached only when a consensus is achieved among the different descent groups.

Ordeals   Another, more formalized, legal mechanism found in some tribal societies is known as the *ordeal*. A classic case was described by anthropologist R. F. Barton (1919) for the Ifugao, a horticulturalist tribe of the Philippines. An Ifugao individual accused of a transgression and who wanted to claim that human behavior can be shaped and influenced in many ways. Humans can be extremely violent or extremely pacific, depending on the prevailing cultural values and norms.

During the 1980s, anthropologists such as Napoleon Chagnon hypothesized that aggression is related to strategies that have to do with reproduction and increasing one's ability to have more children. Although they denied the existence of an aggressive instinct, these anthropologists agreed with the biological school that humans possess an innate capacity or predisposition for violence. Violent behavior can be triggered by a number of factors that threaten humans' capacity to survive and reproduce, including scarcities of resources, excessive population densities, and significant ecological developments. They do, however, acknowledge that the norms and values of a particular sociocultural system can either inhibit or

enhance aggressive tendencies. Thus, the same pressure that would lead to warfare in one society might be resolved without violence in a society with a different set of values.

In our discussion of tribal societies in this chapter, we see that warfare is much more prevalent in these types of societies than those of the hunting-gathering bands of the last chapter. Tribal societies such as the horticulturalist Yanomamö or the pastoralist Nuer are frequently involved in violence and aggression. It appears that the cultivation of crops and the domestication of animals as food sources are related to the origins of warfare. Territories and land become more important within these tribal societies. Yanomamö lineages are important as social units that defend territories against raids and thefts of crops. Likewise, the Nuer lineages defend their cattle against theft or raids. Most of the tribal societies

are engaged in these defensive strategies involving warfare.

Anthropologists today generally concur that human aggression results from both biological and cultural factors, although they continue to disagree about the relative importance of each. Meanwhile, research into the origins of aggression has raised some basic questions concerning human behavior.

Points to Ponder

1. If cultural norms and values can promote violence, can they also eliminate or sharply reduce it?

2. Can you foresee a society (or a world) in which conflicts and problems are resolved peacefully? Or, will violence always be with us?

3. Given the complex relationships among various cultural and biological factors, what concrete steps can a society take to reduce the level of aggressive behavior?

innocence might submit to an ordeal. Barton described several types of ordeals found among the Ifugao. In one type, referred to as the hot-water ordeal, a person had to reach into a pot of boiling water to pull out a pebble and then replace it. In another, a red-hot knife was lowered onto a person's hand. If the party were guilty, his or her hand would be burned badly; if innocent, it would not be. If there were two disputants, they both had the hot knife lowered onto their hands. The one burned more severely was judged to be the guilty party. A third type of ordeal among the Ifugao involved duels or wrestling matches between the disputants.

All of these ordeals were supervised by a *monkalun,* or arbiter. The Ifugao assumed, however, that spiritual or supernatural intervention was the ultimate arbiter in these cases and that moral transgressions would be punished, not by the *monkalun,* but by cosmic religious forces and beings who oversee the social and moral order of Ifugaoan life. The *monkulan* interpreted the evidence and acted as an umpire in deciding the guilt or innocence of an individual.

Oaths and Oracles Some tribal societies use oaths and oracles to arrive at legal decisions. An

oath is an attempt to call on a supernatural source of power to sanction and bear witness to the truth or falseness of an individual's testimony. **Oracles,** individuals or sacred objects believed to have special prophetic abilities, are also used by some tribal groups to help resolve legal matters. Individuals who are believed to have oracular or prophetic powers are empowered to make legal decisions. One example is the Azande, a tribal group in East Africa described by Evans-Pritchard (1937). The Azande used oracles to help decide criminal cases.

In general, ordeals, oaths, and oracles are more common among tribal societies with weak authority structures, in which power is widely diffused throughout the society. Individuals in these societies lack the authority to enforce judicial rulings and therefore do not want to accept the full responsibility for making life-and-death decisions that would make them politically vulnerable (Roberts, 1967).

Religion

Given the immense diversity that exists from tribe to tribe, it is very difficult to generalize about tribal religions. Like hunter-gatherer religions, tribal religions tend to be cosmic religions. The concepts, beliefs, and rituals of these religions are integrated with the natural environment, seasonal cycles, and all living organisms. Animism and shamanism are common religious traditions.

ANIMISM AND SHAMANISM IN SOUTH AMERICA

The mingling of animism and shamanism is evident among some South American tribes. Some of these tribes use the extracts of certain plants for shamanistic practices. The Yanomamö, for example, use a hallucinogenic snuff called *ebene* to induce a supernatural state of ecstasy during which it is believed an individual will have direct contact with the spirit world. The *ebene* powder is blown through a bamboo tube into the nostrils to gain contact with the *hekura* spirits. These spirits, numbering in the thousands, are believed to reside in trees, rocks, and even within people's chests. Through the use of *ebene*, Yanomamö shamans fall into trances, en-

abling them to attract and control the *hekura* for various purposes.

The Jivaro of Ecuador use a tealike drink, *natema,* that enables almost anyone to achieve a trance state. *Natema* is concocted by boiling vines to produce a hallucinogenic drink containing alkaloids, which are somewhat similar to LSD and mescaline. Among the Jivaro, approximately one out of every four males is a shaman. Any adult, male or female, who desires to become such a practitioner simply gives a gift to an experienced shaman, who in turn gives the apprentices a drink of *natema,* as well as some of his own supernatural power in the form of spirit helpers. The spirit helpers, or "darts," are believed to be the major causes of illness and death. Some Jivaro shamans send these spirit helpers to infect enemies. Others gain the ability to cure illnesses through the use of their clairvoyant powers (Harner, 1972).

WITCHCRAFT AND SORCERY

Many tribal societies practice witchcraft and sorcery. Generally **witchcraft** refers to an innate, psychic ability of some people to harm others, whereas **sorcery** is a magical strategy in which practitioners manipulate objects to bring about either harmful or beneficial effects (Evans-Pritchard, 1937).

Anthropologists perceive witchcraft and sorcery as strategies for people to understand bad luck, illness, injustice, and other misfortunes that they cannot otherwise explain. Many tribal peoples perceive the cosmos as composed of various spirits that can affect human lives. Although these peoples accept cause-and-effect explanations for most occurrences, certain phenomena such as pain and suffering do not seem to have "natural" causes. These phenomena are therefore explained in terms of witchcraft and sorcery.

The Role of Witchcraft One classic example of witchcraft among tribal peoples was provided by Evans-Pritchard's study of the Azande. Among the Azande, witchcraft played a role in all aspects of life. Any misfortunes that could not be explained by known causes, such as the lack of game or fish, or crop failure, were attributed to witchcraft. The Azande believed that a person became a witch because of an inherited bodily organ or substance known as *mangu.* A male could inherit it only from another male, a female only from another female.

The Azande performed autopsies to determine whether witchcraft was carried in a family line.

Anthropologist Clyde Kluckhohn (1967) analyzed witchcraft beliefs among the Navajo Indians of the southwestern United States. Navajo witches were considered despicable monsters. The Navajo believed that the witches could transform themselves into animals. In these werewolflike transformations, they ate the meat of corpses and made poisons from dried and ground human flesh, especially that of children. These poisons were thrown into houses of enemies, buried in cornfields, or placed on victims. Fatal diseases were believed to result from the poisons. The Navajo had antidotes (the gall of an eagle, bear, mountain lion, or skunk) to forestall witchcraft activity, and they usually carried these antidotes with them into public situations.

Kluckhohn learned that the Navajo believed witchcraft was related to economic differences. The Navajo thought that those who had more wealth had gained it through witchcraft activities such as grave robbing and stealing jewelry from the dead. The only way a person could refute such an accusation was to share his or her wealth with friends and relatives. Thus, Kluckhohn hypothesized that the belief in witchcraft had the effect of equalizing the distribution of wealth and promoting harmony in the community.

The Role of Sorcery In tribal groups in Africa, New Guinea, and North America, sorcery is also used to influence social relationships. Among many tribes, one form of sorcery is used to promote fertility and good health and to avert evil spells. Another type is used to harm people whom the sorcerer hates and resents. In some cases, sorcery is used to reinforce informal sanctions.

One example of how societies use sorcery to explain misfortunes is provided by Shirley Lindenbaum's (1972) study of various New Guinea tribes. Among the Fore people, sorcery is often used to explain severe illnesses and death, whereas in other tribal groups, such as the Mae Enga, sorcery is not important. In particular, the Fore accuse sorcerers of trying to eliminate all women in their society, thereby threatening the group's survival. At the time of Lindenbaum's fieldwork, the Fore were faced with an epidemic disease that was devastating their population. Thus, according to Lindenbaum, sorcery aided in explaining fundamental survival questions.

FAMILISTIC RELIGION

In addition to animism, shamanism, witchcraft, and sorcery, tribal religions are intertwined with corporate descent groupings, particularly clans and lineages. Recall that clans are descent groups with fictive ancestors. Many of these clan ancestors are spiritual beings, symbolically personified by a deceased ancestor, animal, or plant found in specific environments. For example, among many Native American tribes, lineage groupings such as clans, moieties, and phratries divide the society into different groupings. Each group is symbolized by a particular animal, called a **totem,** that the group recognizes as its ancestor. Among the various totems are eagles, bears, ravens, coyotes, and snakes. There are as many tribal spirits or deities as there are constituent kin groupings. Although each grouping recognizes the existence of all the deities in the entire tribe, the religious activities of each group are devoted to that group's particular spirit.

Ghost Lineage Members among the Lugbara

The Lugbara of Uganda, in Africa, illustrate the familistic aspect of tribal religion (Middleton, 1960). The Lugbara believe that the dead remain as an integral part of the lineage structure of their society. Ancestors include all the dead and living forebears of a person's lineage. The spirits of the dead regularly commune with the elders of the lineages. Shrines are erected to the dead, and sacrifices are offered to ensure that the ancestors will not harm people. At the shrines it is believed that people have direct contact with their ancestors, especially during the sacrifices.

A Lugbara elder explained the relationship between the dead and the living:

A ghost watches a man giving food at sacrifice to him. A brother of that ghost begs food of him. The other will laugh and say "Have you no son?" Then he thinks, "Why does my child not give me food? If he does not give me food soon I shall send sickness to him." Then later that man is seized by sickness, or his wife and his children. The sickness is that of the ghosts, to grow thin and to ache throughout the body; these are the sicknesses of the dead. (Middleton, 1960: 46)

Art and Music

Art in tribal societies has both utilitarian and ceremonial functions. The expressive art of the tribes
of Papua New Guinea and of the U.S. Southwest is
used to decorate utensils such as baskets, bowls,
and other tools. It is also deeply connected with
religious and sacred phenomena. Various tribes in
the interior highlands of Papua New Guinea use
body decorations as their principal art form,
whereas the tribal peoples in the coastal regions
make large, impressive masks that symbolize male
power. These tribes also use various geometric designs to decorate their ceremonial war shields and
other paraphernalia.

The Pueblo Indians of the U.S. Southwest, such
as the Hopi and Zuni, use distinctive designs in
their artworks to represent a harmonious balance
among humans, nature, and the supernatural. The
groups create colorful sand paintings that are
erased after the ceremony is completed. In addition, they make masks and dolls to be used in the
katchina cult activities. *Katchinas* are spiritual figures that exercise control over the weather, especially rainfall, which is particularly important in this
arid region. *Katchina* art is used in various dance
ceremonies and is believed to help produce beneficial weather conditions. Because clay is abundant
in the Southwest, the Pueblo Indians developed
elaborate pottery with complex geometric motifs
and animal figures representing different tribal
groups in the area.

*A Katchina doll. The Katchina dolls represent some of the
forms of artistic production of the Pueblo Indians of the
Southwest.*

MUSICAL TRADITIONS

Music and musical instruments vary from one region to another. For example, various sub-Saharan
African tribes produce a vast range of musical instruments, including drums, bells, shells, rattles,
and hand pianos. The musical instruments are
heard solo and in ensembles. The hand piano, or
mbira, is a small wooden board onto which a
number of metal keys are attached. The keys are
arranged to produce staggered tones so that certain
melodic patterns can be improvised. Along with
the instrumentation, singing is used in many cases
to invoke specific moods: sadness, happiness, or a
sense of spirituality (Mensah, 1983).

Native American tribal musical traditions also
vary from region to region. The musical instruments consist primarily of percussive rattles and
drums. The drumming is done with a single
drumstick, although several other drum players
may accompany the drummer. The traditional tribal
music includes spiritual hymns, game songs, recreational dance music, war-dance music, and
shamanistic chanting. Most of the songs, even the
game and recreational songs, are inseparable from
sacred rituals related to crop fertility, healing, and
other life crises. Nearly all of the music is vocal,
sung by choruses. Many of the song texts contain
extensive use of syllables such as "yu-waw, yu-
waw, hi hi hi, yu-wah hi." These songs help to
create a hypnotic spiritual consciousness that
produces an appropriate sacred atmosphere (Mc-
Allester, 1983, 1984).

SUMMARY

Most anthropologists use the term tribe to refer to peoples who rely on horticulture, which is a limited form of agriculture, or pastoralism, which involves the maintenance of animals, for their basic subsistence. Most horticulturalists reside in tropical rain forests, whereas most pastoralists reside in eastern and northern Africa and the Middle East.

The population of tribal societies is larger than that of foragers because they have more abundant food supplies. The economic patterns of tribal societies are based on reciprocal exchanges, although some groups have developed special-purpose forms of monetary exchanges for certain goods. Property ownership is based on large kinship groups.

Social organization varies widely from region to region. Large extended families are the norm. Anthropologists generally find that tribal societies have extensive descent groups consisting of many extended families known as lineages (patrilineages and matrilineages), clans, phratries, and moieties that are multifunctional and corporate in nature.

Marriage in tribal societies tends to be polygynous and usually involves bridewealth exchanges. Marriage bonds are the basis of descent-group alliances among villages. Marital practices such as the levirate and sororate tend to cement social ties among descent groups in tribes.

Despite some early research that indicated women had a fairly high status in tribal societies, modern anthropologists find that patriarchy prevails in most tribes. At times, patriarchy is associated with sexism and the maltreatment of women. Anthropologists have been investigating the rela-

tionship among subsistence, warfare, and biology to explain the prevalence of patriarchy in tribal societies.

Age is another important feature of social organization in tribal society. In some tribes, age sets are the basis of economic, political, and religious organization. As people age in tribal societies, they often become more powerful, and in some cases gerontocratic societies arise.

Tribal political organization is usually decentralized and lacks permanent political offices. In horticulturalist tribes, village headmen and big men often organize and arrange intervillage political activities. In pastoralist tribes, the lack of centralized leadership often leads to segmentary lineage systems based on the consolidation of kinship principles to resolve feuds and disputes.

Warfare tends to be more prevalent among tribal societies than among foragers. Anthropologists have investigated the causes of tribal warfare by drawing on ecological, demographic, economic, and biological factors. Most anthropologists agree that no one of these factors explains tribal warfare and that they must use cultural variables such as honor, status, and glory to offer comprehensive explanations.

Religion in tribal society consists of animism, shamanism, witchcraft, and sorcery. These practices and beliefs help to explain illness, bad luck, and various crises. In addition, tribal religion is often familistic, with beliefs in ancestor worship and spirits that commune with the living members of descent groups.

STUDY QUESTIONS

1. What are some of the demographic differences one finds between foragers and food producers such as pastoralists and horticulturalists? Why do you think these differences exist?

2. Discuss the concept of property ownership in tribal societies. How does it differ from what generally occurs in band societies?

3. What is a descent group? What forms do descent groups take? What are some of their functions?

4. Discuss the functions of a descent group in managing the economic rights and obligations of a tribal society. Use specific examples to illustrate your points.

5. Why do you think a society would have marriage rules such as the levirate and sororate?

6. What are some of the explanations given for the fact that anthropologists have not found any truly matriarchal societies in the archaeological, historical, or ethnographic records?

7. What forms of political organization are found in tribal societies? What are some of the reasons that have been offered to explain these types of organization? How do these types of political organization differ from those found in forager groups?

8. How are descent groups associated with tribal religious practices?

◎ KEY TERMS

age sets	levirate	phratries
ambilineal descent group	lineages	primogeniture
bilateral descent	matrilineal descent group	segmentary lineage system
bridewealth	moieties	sexism
clan	money	sorcery
complementary opposition	oath	sororate
descent group	oracles	totem
gerontocracy	parallel-cousin marriage	ultimogeniture
horticulture	pastoralists	unilineal descent groups
kindreds	patrilineal descent group	witchcraft

◎ INTERNET EXERCISES

1. Visit the website **http://www.head-hunter.com/jivaro.html** and review the information on the Jivaro. What unique and unusual practice did they perform? Why would a horitcultural people be so fierce? Compare them to the Yanomamö also mentioned in this chapter.

2. When reading the website **http://www.fao.org/News/FOTOFILE/PH9819-e.htm,** determine the view of the United Nations Food and Agriculture Organization of pastoralism. How does this view compare to that of the chapter? How can camels help support desert-living people?

◎ SUGGESTED READINGS

BARTH, FREDRICK. 1961. *Nomads of South Persia.* New York: Humanities Press. An ethnography of the Basseri, a pastoralist group of southern Iran.

CHAGNON, NAPOLEON. 1997. *The Yanomamö,* 5th ed. New York: Holt, Rinehart & Winston. This frequently cited account of a tribal horticulturalist society has become a modern classic.

EVANS-PRITCHARD, E. E. 1940. *The Nuer.* Oxford: Clarendon Press. The classic ethnography of pastoralist life. It summarizes the ecological, economic, social, and political organization of this eastern African tribe.

FRIEDL, ERNESTINE. 1975. *Women and Men: An Anthropologist's View.* New York: Holt, Rinehart & Winston. A study of gender relations that focuses on tribal societies. Friedl examines how subsistence, economy, family, kinship, and politics influence gender relationships.

GLUCKMAN, MAX. 1965. *Politics, Law and Ritual in Tribal Society*. Chicago: Aldine. A comprehensive account of different political institutions and legal techniques developed in tribal societies. The focus of the text is on law.

HAAS, JONATHAN, ed. 1990. *The Anthropology of War*. Cambridge: Cambridge University Press. An excellent series of readings dealing with the various causes of warfare, with detailed cases of warfare among tribal peoples.

HARNER, MICHAEL, J. 1972. *The Jivaro: People of the Sacred Waterfall*. Garden City, NY: Natural History Press. A fascinating ethnography of horticultural Indians of Ecuador.

KEESING, ROGER M. 1971. *Kin Groups and Social Structure*. New York: Holt, Rinehart & Winston. A thorough summary of the different types of descent groupings and kinship relationships in tribal (and nontribal) societies.

KLUCKHOHN, CLYDE. 1967. *Navaho Witchcraft*. Boston: Beardon Press. An account of witchcraft among the Navajo emphasizing the positive benefits of witchcraft for the tribe.

SAHLINS, MARSHALL D. 1968. *Tribesmen*. Englewood Cliffs, NJ: Prentice Hall. An overall summary of the different forms of tribal groups and institutions found throughout the world. Although many of the author's generalizations have been criticized by modern theorists, this work remains valuable.

SOUTHALL, AIDAN. 1996. "Tribes," in Levinson, David and Ember, Melvin (eds.) *Encyclopedia of Cultural Anthropology*, Vol. 4. New York: Henry Holt. A recent critical and analytical essay on tribal societies. that surveys the concept within many different regions of the world.

Chiefdoms

CHAPTER OUTLINE

Environment, Subsistence, and Demography
Pacific Island Chiefdoms / African Chiefdoms / Native American Chiefdoms / Demography

Technology
Housing

Political Economy
Food Storage / Property Ownership / The Evolution of Chiefdoms / Economic Exchange

Social Organization
Rank and Sumptuary Rules / Marriage / General Social Principles / Gender / Age / Slavery

Law and Religion
Law / Religion / A Case Study: Law and Religion in Polynesia / Shamanism / Human Sacrifice

Art, Architecture, and Music
Music

CHAPTER QUESTIONS

- What are the characteristics of an environment that are conducive to the development of chiefdom societies?

- How is the political system of chiefdoms related to the economic system?

- How does the social structure of chiefdom societies compare to egalitarian societies?

- In what ways are the legal and religious traditions of chiefdoms different from those of tribal and band societies?

L IKE THE TERM TRIBE, THE TERM CHIEFDOM HAS caused a certain amount of confusion outside anthropology. A major reason for this is that chiefdoms have little to do with what people commonly refer to as "chiefs." For example, in Chapter 9 we discussed the Nuer leopard skin chief. The Nuer, however, are not classified as a chiefdom society. In addition, many Native American societies had leaders who were usually referred to as "chiefs," although these societies were usually tribes rather than chiefdoms. In the past, Western explorers, missionaries, and government officials used the label *chief* to describe any individual who held a leadership role in a non-Western, stateless society. But as we have learned in our previous discussions of band and tribal societies, political leadership was widely diffused in these groups, and many of these societies did not have permanent systems of leadership.

In contrast to this common usage, anthropologists use *chiefdom* to refer to a form of complex society that is intermediate between the band and tribal societies, discussed in Chapters 8 and 9, and the formally organized bureaucratic state societies, discussed in Chapters 11 and 12. A *chiefdom* is a political economy that organizes regional populations in the thousands or tens of thousands through a centralized hierarchy of leaders, or chiefs. **Chiefs** own, manage, and control the basic productive factors of the economy and have privileged access to strategic and luxury goods. These leaders are set off from the rest of society by various cultural practices and symbols, such as clothing, jewelry, specialized language, and social status. Thus, chiefdom societies are not egalitarian in the sense that band and tribal societies are.

Another reason that the term *chiefdom* is often unclear is that chiefdom societies vary greatly with respect to political, economic, and cultural forms. Hence, even anthropologists frequently disagree about which societies should be classified as chiefdoms. Some consider the chiefdom to be a subcategory of the tribe, whereas others view it as qualitatively different from tribes and bands (Service, [1962] 1971; Sahlins, 1968b). Although most anthropologists now recognize the limitations of the term *chiefdom* as it is applied to a vast range of societies in different circumstances, most also consider it a valuable category for cross-cultural and comparative research.

As with tribal and foraging societies, hundreds of chiefdoms existed during at least the past 12,000 years of human history. Chiefdoms were widespread throughout Polynesia, including the islands of Hawaii, Tahiti, and Tonga. They also flourished in parts of North, Central, and South America, sub-Saharan Africa, the Caribbean, Southeast Asia, and in Europe until the Roman Empire. Today, however, very few of these chiefdoms remain as an autonomous society. Therefore, the past tense is used to discuss these societies. Not surprisingly, a great deal of the research on chiefdoms is based on archaeological and historical documentation.

The transition to a chiefdom society from a prior form of society is not well documented in any part of the world. But through comparisons with tribal and foraging societies, anthropologists have developed various hypotheses to explain this transition. The central question is how one particular descent group (or several descent groups) managed to gain advantages or monopolies of resources over other descent groups. In other words, how did social stratification and economic inequality emerge from the egalitarian economic and political processes found in tribal or foraging societies? As we shall see in the descriptions of chiefdoms, ecological, demographic, economic, social, political, and religious factors all influenced the development of chiefdom societies. We begin with a description of the environments and subsistence activities of different chiefdoms.

Environment, Subsistence, and Demography

Most chiefdom societies have occupied ecological regions that contain abundant resources, usually more abundant than the resources in the areas inhabited by band and tribal societies.

PACIFIC ISLAND CHIEFDOMS

In the area known as Polynesia, which extends eastward from Hawaii to New Zealand and includes Samoa, Tahiti, and Tonga (see Figure 10.1), various chiefdoms existed. The arable land on

these Pacific islands is very fertile, and the soil is covered by a dense forest growth. Rainfall is plentiful, and the average temperature is 77°F year-round. Tahiti is a typical example of a Polynesian island on which most of the people resided on the coastal flatlands.

One important aspect of subsistence for the Tahitian people was the bountiful harvest from the sea. Fish and shellfish accounted for a substantial portion of their diet. The coconut palm, which grows abundantly even in poor soil, provided nourishment from its meat and milk, as well as oil for cooking. The breadfruit plant was another important foodstuff; if fermented, breadfruit can be stored in pits for long periods of time.

Like many other chiefdom societies, the Tahitians practiced **intensive horticulture,** in which one improves crop production by irrigating, fertilizing, hoeing, and terracing the land. Through intensive horticulture (and near-perfect weather conditions), the Tahitians were able to make efficient use of small parcels of arable land. Although this type of agriculture demanded labor, time, and energy, the agricultural yields it produced were much greater than those produced by tribal peoples who practiced slash-and-burn horticulture.

The Tahitians' most important crops were taro, yams, and sweet potatoes. Supplementing these crops were bananas, plantains, sugar cane, and gourds. Protein requirements were met by the consumption of seafood and such animals as domesticated pigs, chickens, and, on occasion, dogs. (The Polynesians did distinguish between dogs that were kept as pets and those that were used for food.) The native peoples of Hawaii, Samoa, Easter Island, and Cook Island had essentially the same ecological setting for the development of a highly productive subsistence strategy.

AFRICAN CHIEFDOMS

Anthropologist Jacques Maquet (1972) suggested that a very high proportion of precolonial African societies were chiefdoms. These savanna chiefdom societies included peoples such as the Kpelle of Liberia, the Bemba of Zambia, and the Luba and Songhe of central Africa. These chiefdoms developed in the dry forest, the woodland savanna, and the grassy savanna. In the savanna regions, the use of intensive horticulture, including the use of hoes,

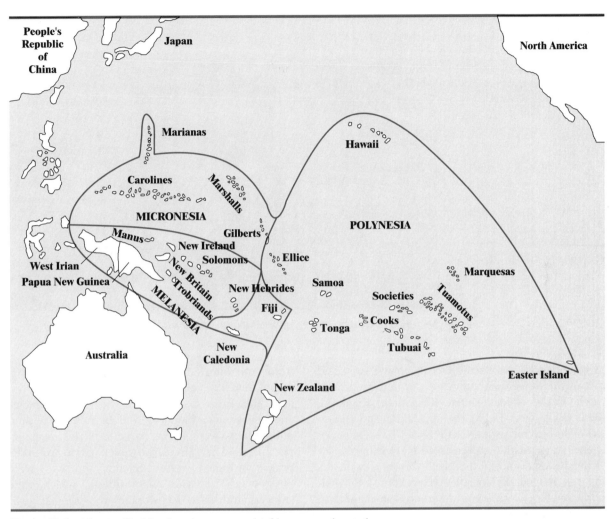

Figure 10.1 The Pacific Islands, where many chiefdoms were located.

produced a surplus of crops consisting of cereals such as sorghum, millet, cassava, and maize, and legumes such as peas and beans. Archaeologists have determined that sorghum, rice, and millet were cultivated as far back as 1000 B.C. (McIntosh & McIntosh, 1983).

NATIVE AMERICAN CHIEFDOMS

The Mississippi Region One prehistoric ecological region in North America where various chiefdom societies flourished was the region along the Mississippi River extending from Louisiana northward to Illinois. One of the primary cultural centers of the North American chiefdoms was the Ca-

hokian society, located near where the Mississippi and Missouri rivers come together. This area contained extremely fertile soil and abundant resources of fish, shellfish, and game animals. The Cahokian people also practiced intensive horticulture, using hoes and fertilizers to produce their crops. The Cahokian chiefdom society emerged around A.D. 950 and reached its peak by about 1100. At that point, it had evolved into an urban center with a population of about twenty thousand people.

The Northwest Coast Another region in North America that contains a vast wealth of natural resources is the area of the Northwest Coast. This area

An artist's re-creation of the Cahokia Mound around A.D. *1200.*

is bounded by the Pacific Ocean on the west and mountain ranges on the east. Numerous groups such as the Haida, Tlingit, Tsimshian, Kwakiutl, Bella Coola, Bella Bella, Nootka, Makah, and Tillamook lived in this region (see Figure 10.2). These societies are usually categorized as chiefdoms, although they do not fit the ideal pattern as neatly as do the Polynesian societies (Lewellen, 1983). Although there were some differences in respect to subsistence and adaptation for each group, the patterns were very similar for the entire region.

One of the major reasons the Northwest Coast groups do not fit as well into the chiefdom category is that they were essentially hunters and gatherers and did not practice any horticulture or agriculture. Because of their economic, social, and political features, however, they have been traditionally characterized as chiefdoms. The unique ecological conditions of the Northwest region enabled these societies to develop patterns not usually associated with the hunters and gatherers discussed in Chapter 8. Instead of residing in marginal environments as did many foragers, these peoples lived in environments rich with resources.

The ecological conditions on the Northwest Coast were as ideal as those of the Pacific Islands. The climate was marked by heavy rainfall, and the mountain barrier to the east sheltered the region

from cold winds from the continent. The region could therefore support rich forests of cedar, fir, and other trees. Game such as deer, bears, ducks, and geese were plentiful, and berries, roots, and other plants were easily harvested. The most important food resources, however, came from the coastal and inland waters. Streams and rivers were filled every fall with huge salmon, which were smoked and dried for storage, providing a year-round food source. The coastal waters supplied these groups with shellfish, fish, and sea mammals such as seals, sea otters, and porpoises.

The environments of the Pacific Islands, the Mississippi region, and the Northwest Coast of North America produced what is known as regional symbiosis. In **regional symbiosis,** a people resides in an ecological habitat divided into different resource areas; groups living in these different areas become interdependent. People in one region may subsist on fishing, in another region on hunting, and in a third region on cultivation. These groups exchange products, thus establishing mutual dependency.

DEMOGRAPHY

Anthropologists hypothesize that population growth is an important factor in the centralized administration and social complexity associated with chief-

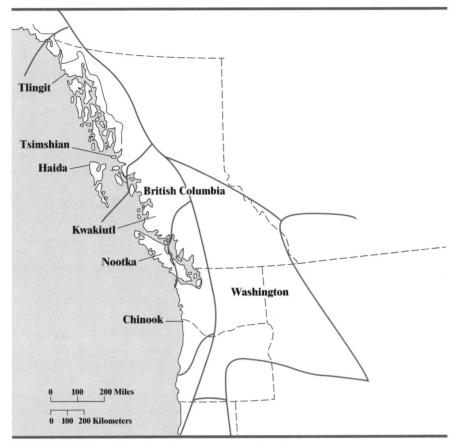

Figure 10.2   Map of the Northwest Coast showing where various chiefdoms were located.

doms (Carneiro, 1967; Dumond, 1972). Chiefdom populations, which range from 5,000 to 50,000 people, frequently exceed the carrying capacity of the region (Drennan, 1987; Johnson & Earle, 1987). Thus, population growth leads to an increased risk of shortages of food and other resources. To maintain adequate resources, these societies give certain individuals the power to organize systematically the production and accumulation of surplus resources (Johnson & Earle, 1987).

Technology

Chiefdom societies developed technologies that reflected their abundant and varied natural resources. Although the Polynesians relied primarily on digging sticks for intensive horticulture, they also had many specialized tools—including tools to cut shells and stones—for making jewelry, knives, fish-

hooks, harpoons, nets, and large canoes. Likewise, the Cahokian society had an elaborate technology consisting of fishhooks, grinding stones, mortars and pestles, hoes, and many other tools.

HOUSING

The dwellings used in chiefdom societies varied over regions, depending on materials available. The traditional Pacific Island housing of Tahiti and Hawaii was built with poles and thatched with coconut leaves and other vegetation. The island houses needed repair from time to time but generally were long-lasting dwellings. Similarly, the Cahokian people built firm housing by plastering clay over a wood framework. In the Northwest Coast villages, people lived in houses made of cedar planks, which were some of the most solid housing construction in all of America before European colonization. In all of these chiefdom societies, the housing structures of the chief's family were much more elaborate, spacious, and highly decorated than those of other people.

Political Economy

Because the economic and political aspects of chiefdom societies are so strongly interrelated, we discuss these variables together. As we shall see, as political centralization emerged in chiefdom societies, the economic system came under control of the chiefly elite.

FOOD STORAGE

One aspect of the economy that often played a key role in chiefdom societies was the storage of food. For chiefdoms to exist, resources had to be abundant, and people needed a technology for storing and preserving these resources. Food storage was a key variable in the ability of a society to become economically productive, creating the potential for economic and political stratification. Although there were occasional instances of food storage in some nomadic hunter-gatherer societies in marginal environments, food storage was not common among foragers or tribal societies (Testart, 1988).

The Northwest Coast Native Americans provide an example of food storage methods practiced by chiefdoms. These societies experienced two different seasonal cycles: In the summer, the groups engaged in fishing, hunting, and gathering; during the winter season, little subsistence activity occurred. During the winter these peoples lived on stored food, particularly smoked and preserved salmon. In these circumstances, certain descent groups and individuals accumulated surpluses, thereby acquiring a higher position in the society.

PROPERTY OWNERSHIP

Property ownership developed when a powerful individual, a chief, who was the head of a lineage, a village, or a group of interrelated villages, claimed exclusive ownership of the territory within the region. To use the land, other people had to observe certain restrictions on their production and turn over some of their resources to the chiefs.

In chiefdom societies, property ownership tended to become more closely identified with particular descent groups and individuals. For example, on the Northwest Coast, fishing sites with large and predictable runs of salmon tended to be owned and inherited by particular corporate kin groups. As another example, specific chiefs among the Trobriand Islands owned and maintained more or less exclusive rights to large canoes that were important in regional trade.

Political Aspects of Property Ownership   Anthropologists differ over how much exclusive ownership the chiefs had over their realm. As we will see later in the chapter, the political authority of a chief did have some limitations. Accordingly, the claim to exclusive rights over the territories may, in some cases, also have been restricted. For example, among the Kpelle of Liberia in West Africa, the land was said to be owned formally by the paramount chief (the highest-ranking chief), who divided it into portions for each village in the chiefdom. These portions were then distributed in parcels to families of various lineages. Once land was parceled out, it remained within the lineage until the lineage died out. In this sense, the paramount chief was only a steward holding land for the group he represented (Gibbs, 1965).

THE EVOLUTION OF CHIEFDOMS

A number of anthropologists, including Elman Service, hypothesize that in some cases chiefdom societies emerged because of regional symbiosis (Service, [1962] 1971). Because particular descent groups were strategically located among territories with different resources, these groups played a key role in the exchange and allocation of resources throughout the population. Eventually, some of the leaders of these descent groups became identified as the chiefs or centralized leaders. In other words, by regulating the exchange of resources, the chiefs held these formerly autonomous regions together under a centralized administration. In a detailed account of the evolution of chiefdoms, Service (1975) used cultural ideology as well as ecological variables to identify certain individuals and descent groups as chiefs. He argued that particular individuals and their descent group were recognized as having more prestige and status. A consensus thus emerged within the society regarding who became chiefs.

Based on his research of Polynesian chiefdoms, archaeologist Timothy Earle (1977, 1987) challenged the hypothesis that chiefdoms emerged through regional symbiosis. By analyzing the ecological conditions and reconstructing exchange networks in Hawaii and other Polynesian locations, Earle found that commodity exchanges were much more limited and did not involve large-scale exchanges among specialized ecological regions as described by Service and others. Exchanges were localized, and most households appear to have had access to all critical resources.

Earle (1987) suggested that the key factor in the evolution of chiefdoms was the degree of control over vital productive resources and labor. In the case of Hawaii, as population grew, land became a scarce commodity, and competition for the limited fertile land developed. Chiefs conquered certain agricultural lands, over which they claimed exclusive rights. Other people received use rights to small subsistence plots in return for their work on the chief's lands. This system permitted the chiefs to exercise much more extensive control over resources and labor. According to Earle, in contrast to the paramount chief as the steward of the land, these chiefs not only had "title" to the land but also effectively controlled the labor on the land.

ECONOMIC EXCHANGE

Chiefdom societies practiced a number of different types of economic exchange. Two basic types of exchange are reciprocal exchanges and redistributional exchanges.

Reciprocal Exchange Like all societies, chiefdoms engaged in reciprocal exchanges. One classic case of balanced reciprocal exchange occurred among the Trobriand Islanders, as described by Bronislaw Malinowski ([1922] 1961). The Trobrianders, intensive horticulturalists who raised yams and depended heavily on fishing, maintained elaborate trading arrangements with other island groups. They had large sea canoes, or outriggers, and traveled hundreds of miles on sometimes dangerous seas to conduct what was known as the *kula exchange.*

The Kula Exchange The *kula* was the ceremonial trade of valued objects that took place among a number of the Trobriand Islands. In his book *Argonauts of the Western Pacific* ([1922]

1961), Malinowski described how red-shell necklaces and white-shell armbands were ritually exchanged from island to island through networks of male traders. The necklaces traditionally traveled clockwise, and the armbands traveled counterclockwise. These necklaces and armbands were constantly circulating, and the size and value of these items had to be perfectly matched (hence, balanced reciprocity). People did not keep these items very long; in fact, they were seldom worn. There was no haggling or discussion of price by any of the traders.

Trobriand males were inducted into the trading network through elaborate training regarding the proper etiquette and magical practices of the *kula.* The young men learned these practices through their fathers or mothers' brothers and eventually established trading connections with partners on other islands.

A more utilitarian trade accompanied the ceremonial trade. Goods such as tobacco, pottery, coconuts, fish, baskets, and mats were exchanged through the Trobriand trading partners. In these exchanges the partners haggled and discussed price. Malinowski referred to this trade as *secondary trade,* or **barter,** the direct exchange of one commodity for another. He argued that the ceremonial *kula* trade created emotional ties among trading partners and that the utilitarian trade was secondary and incidental. Because of this argument, Malinowski is often referred to as one of the first substantivist economic anthropologists (see Chapter 7). He hypothesized that the economic production and exchange of the utilitarian goods were embedded in the social practices and cultural norms of the *kula* exchange, which was noneconomic.

Some formalist economic anthropologists, however, hypothesized that the ceremonial trade was only the ritual means for conducting the more utilitarian transactions for material goods. Annette Weiner (1987) reanalyzed the *kula* trade and in her interviews with older informants found that Malinowski had overlooked the fact that certain armbands or necklaces, known as *kitomu,* were owned by the chiefs. The *kitomu* could be used for bridewealth payments, funeral expenses, or to build a canoe. In other words, they were more like money. At times a chief would add some *kitomu* into the *kula* transactions to attract new partners and new wealth. These chiefs would take economic risks with these shells to accumulate valuable private profits. If a chief gained a new partner through these transactions he would be able to gain more wealth. If he was not able to gain new partners, however, he could lose some of his investments.

Thus, Weiner viewed the *kula* not as a system of balanced reciprocity but rather as a system of economic competition in which certain traders tried to maximize social and political status and to accumulate profits. Although the *kula* exchanges emphasized the notions of equality and reciprocity, this was in fact an illusion. In actuality, trading partners tried to achieve the opposite—to gain ever-larger profits and status.

Malinowski overlooked the fact that the trade items of the *kula* exchange, referred to as "wealth finances," were critically important in establishing a chief's social status and personal prestige. For example, only the chiefs were able to control the extensive labor needed to construct outrigger canoes, by means of which the trade was conducted. Thus, the chiefs benefited enormously from the *kula* exchange (Earle, 1987; Johnson & Earle, 1987).

Redistributional Exchange   The predominant form of economic exchange in chiefdom societies, and one that is not usually found in band and tribal societies, is **redistributional economic exchange,** which involves the exchange of goods and resources through a centralized organization. In the redistributional system, food and other staples, such as craft goods, are collected as a form of tax or rent. They are then redistributed by the chiefs (and sometimes subsidiary chiefs) back to the population at certain times of the year. This system thus assures the dispersal of food and resources throughout the community through a centralized agency.

Potlatch   A classic example of a chiefdom redistributional system was found among the Native Americans of the Northwest Coast. Known as the **potlatch,** it was described at length among the Kwakiutl by Franz Boas (1930) and was later interpreted by Ruth Benedict (1934).

The term *potlatch* is a Chinook word translated loosely as "giveaway." In a potlatch, local leaders gave away large quantities of goods and resources in what appeared to be a highly wasteful manner.

Potlatches were held when young people were introduced into society or during marriage or funeral ceremonies. Families would prepare for these festive occasions by collecting food and other valuables such as fish, berries, blankets, and animal skins, which were then given to local leaders in many different villages. In these potlatch feasts, the leaders of different villages competed in giving away or sometimes destroying more food than their competitors. In the view of the Northwest Coast Indians, the more gifts that were bestowed on the people or destroyed by a chief, the higher the status of that chief.

Benedict interpreted the potlatch feasts and rivalry among chiefs as the result of their megalomaniacal personalities. To substantiate this view, she presented this formal speech made by a Kwakiutl chief (1934: 191):

> I am the first of the tribes, I am the only one of the tribes. The chiefs of the tribes are only local chiefs. I am the only one among the tribes. I search among all the invited chiefs for greatness like mine. I cannot find one chief among the guests. They never return feasts. The orphans, poor people, chiefs of the tribes! They disgrace themselves. I am he who gives these sea otters to the chiefs, the guests, the chiefs of the tribes. I am he who gives canoes to the chiefs, the guests, the chiefs of the tribes.

Despite the apparent wastefulness, status rivalry, and megalomaniacal personalities suggested by Benedict, contemporary anthropologists view the potlatch feasts as having served a redistributional exchange process. For example, despite the abundance of resources in the Northwest Coast region, there were regional variations and periodic fluctuations in the supply of salmon and other products. In some areas people had more than they needed, whereas in other regions people suffered from frequent scarcities. Given these circumstances, the potlatch helped distribute surpluses and special local products to other villages in need (Piddocke, 1965).

Marvin Harris (1977) argued that the potlatch also functioned to ensure the production and distribution of goods in societies that lacked ruling classes. Through the elaborate redistributive feasts and conspicuous consumption, the chiefs presented themselves as the providers of food and security to the population. The competition among

Many of the Northwest Coast chiefdoms use the potlatch for redistributing goods and resources.

the chiefs meant that both the haves and the have-nots benefited from this system. According to Harris, this form of competitive feasting enabled growing chiefdom populations to survive and prosper by encouraging people to work harder and accumulate resources.

✔ **Redistribution in Polynesia** Another classic example of redistribution appears in the historical records of native Polynesian societies. In societies such as Tahiti and Hawaii, people who were able to redistribute goods and resources among various villages and islands emerged as leaders. After crops were harvested, a certain portion (the "first fruits of the harvest") was directed to local village leaders and then given to higher-level subsidiary chiefs who were more centrally located. These goods were eventually directed toward the paramount chiefs, who redistributed some of them back to the population during different periods of the year (Sahlins, 1958; Kirch, 1984). Along with coordinating exchanges, the chiefs could also decree which crops were to be planted and how they were to be used.

Redistributional exchange economies are similar to reciprocal economic systems in that they involve transfers of goods and other resources among related villagers. A major difference between the two systems is that the latter is predominant in societies that are highly egalitarian, whereas in the chiefdom societies that have redistributional economic systems, rank and status are unequal.

Within a redistributional system, local leaders and related individuals not only have a higher status and rank but are also able to siphon off some of the economic surplus for their own benefit. This inequality creates a **hierarchical society** in which some people have access to more wealth, rank, status, authority, and power than do other people. This redistributional exchange system among the Polynesian chiefdoms has been referred to as an early form of taxation (Johnson & Earle, 1987).

Political Authority among Chiefdoms Whereas the political structures of bands and tribes were impermanent and indefinite, chiefdom political structures were well defined, permanent, and corporate. The leadership functions were centralized in the institutionalized office of chief, with the personal qualities of the chief being unrelated to the responsibilities and prerogatives of the office. (An **office** refers to the position of authority assigned to a person.) The chief's office had clearly defined rules of succession. The office of the chief existed apart from the man who occupied it, and on his death the office had to be filled by a man from a similar chiefly family. This system differed markedly from the big-man system found in some tribes, in which leadership positions were attached to particular individuals based on personal characteristics. Tribal societies had no hereditary rules of succession; the big man's authority could not be passed on to his sons or to other kin.

In many of the Polynesian chiefdoms the rule of succession was based on primogeniture, in which the eldest son assumed the status (and realm) of the father. This form of political succession is prevalent in other chiefdom societies as well. The rule of primogeniture helped to avoid a power struggle when the chief died, and it provided for continuity for the overall political (and economic) system (Service, 1975).

As is evident from our previous discussions, the chiefs had a great deal of control over both surplus prestige goods and strategic resources, including food and water. This control enhanced chiefly status, rank, and authority, ensuring both loyalty and deference on the part of those from lower descent groups. In addition, it enabled the chiefs to exercise a certain amount of coercion. They could recruit armies, distribute land and water rights to families, and sentence someone to death for violating certain societal norms.

Limits on Chiefly Power Nevertheless, chiefs did not maintain absolute power over their subjects. They ruled with minimal coercion based on their control over economic production and redistribution rather than on fear or repression. This political legitimacy was buttressed by religious beliefs and rituals, which will be discussed later.

A Case Study: The Trobriand Islands The political systems of the Pacific Island societies had varying degrees of chiefly authority. Chiefly authority was more limited among the Trobrianders than among the Hawaiians and Tahitians. The Trobriand chief had to work to expand his arena of power and status and prevent other chiefs from destroying or diminishing his ancestral rights (Weiner, 1987). Much economic and political competition existed among the chiefs of matrilineal descent groups. A Trobriand chief gained rights, legitimacy, and authority through descent. That authority, however, also depended on what the chief accomplished in the way of redistribution and giving feasts to furnish food and other resources. Generosity was therefore one of the most important aspects of Trobriand chieftaincy. If generosity was not demonstrated, the chief's power, authority, and

legitimacy diminished. Chiefs were frequently replaced by other, more generous, people within the chiefly family.

A Case Study: Hawaii and Tahiti The aboriginal Hawaiian and Tahitian chiefdoms tended to be more fully developed than those of the Trobrianders. For example, Hawaiian society was divided into various social strata composed of descent groups. The highest-ranking noble strata, known as *ali'i,* were district chiefs and their families. Within the highest-ranking descent groups, the eldest son (or daughter) inherited the political and social status of the father. Above the *ali'i* were the paramount chiefs, or *ali'i nui,* who ruled over the islands.

The paramount chiefs and district chiefs were treated with reverence and extreme deference. They were carried around on litters, and the "commoners"—farmers, fishermen, craftsworkers, and "inferiors"—had to prostrate themselves before the nobles. Thus, political legitimacy and authority were much more encompassing than in the Trobriand case.

This does not mean, however, that the Hawaiian or Tahitian chiefs had absolute or despotic power. In fact, most of the evidence indicates that the political stability of Tahitian and Hawaiian chiefdoms was somewhat delicate. There were constant challenges to the paramount and district chiefs by rival leaders who made genealogical claims for rights to succession. These rivals used a variety of marital strategies, combined with the manipulation of genealogical status, to challenge a paramount chief's leadership.

In many cases, paramount chiefs had to demonstrate their authority and power not only through the redistribution of land, food, and prestige goods but also through warfare against rival claimants. If a paramount chief was unable to hold his territorial area, challengers could increase their political power, and the political legitimacy of the paramount chief might diminish substantially. Permanent conquest by rival chiefs over a paramount chief resulted in a new ranking system in which the lineage of the conquering group supplanted that of the paramount chief. When this occurred in Hawaii, the paramount chief's descent group became sacrificial victims to the new ruler's deities (Valeri, 1985). Thus, conquest did not result in the complete overthrow of the society's political structure. Rather, it consisted of revolts that minimally reordered the social and political ranking order. The basic fabric of the chiefdoms was not transformed; one noble lineage simply replaced another.

In some cases, the chiefs tried to institutionalize a more permanent basis of power and authority. For example, chiefs occasionally meted out a death sentence for those accused of treason or of plotting to overthrow a chief. Yet this use of force was rarely displayed. Despite the fact that authority was centralized, political legitimacy was based ultimately on consensus and goodwill from the populace rather than military coercion. Polynesian chiefs could normally expect to command a majority of the labor and military needed in their domains simply by occupying their political office. But if things were going badly, if the chief was not fair and generous in redistribution or settling disputes, armed revolts could begin, or political struggles would erupt—not to overthrow the political or social order but to substitute one chief for another.

Warfare   Warfare among chiefdom societies was more organized than among bands or tribes, pri-

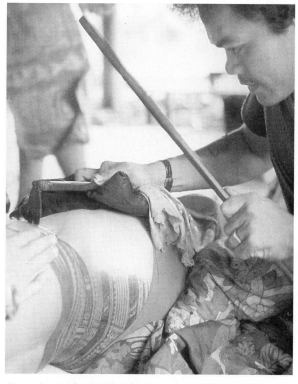

Tattooing in the Pacific islands was used frequently to symbolize status relationships.

marily because the political and economic mechanisms in chiefdoms were more centralized and formalized. In many cases, chiefs were able to recruit armies and conduct warfare in a systematic manner. Anthropologist Robert Carneiro (1970) views warfare as one of the decisive factors in the evolution of chiefdoms. The objective of many chiefs was to extend their chiefdom regionally so as to dominate the populations of surrounding communities and thereby control those communities' surplus production. As chiefdoms expanded through warfare and conquest, many of the people in the conquered territories were absorbed into the chiefdom. In certain cases, these chiefdoms succeeded because of their technological superiority. In many other cases, such as in Polynesia, they succeeded because the surrounding communities were circumscribed by oceans and had no choice but to become absorbed by the conquering chiefdom.

Social Organization

In Chapter 7, we discussed the concept of social stratification, the inequality among statuses within society. Chiefdom societies exhibit a great deal of stratification. They are divided into different **strata** (singular: *stratum*), a group of equivalent statuses based on ranked divisions in a society. Strata in chiefdom societies are not based solely on economic factors but rather cut across society based on prestige, power, and generalized religious conceptions.

RANK AND SUMPTUARY RULES

Chiefdom societies are hierarchically ranked societies. The various families and descent groups—households, lineages, and clans—have a specific ascribed rank in the society and are accorded certain rights, privileges, and obligations based on that rank. Social interaction between lower and higher strata is governed by sumptuary rules. **Sumptuary rules** are cultural norms and practices used to differentiate the higher-status groups from the rest of society. In general, the higher the status and rank, the more ornate the jewelry, costumes, and decorative symbols. Among the Natchez, Native Americans of the Mississippi region, the upper-ranking members were tattooed all over their bodies, whereas lower-ranking people were only partially tattooed.

Some of the Pacific chiefdoms had sumptuary rules requiring that a special orator chief instead of the paramount chief speak to the public. The highest paramount chiefs spoke a noble language with an archaic vocabulary containing words that commoners could not use with one another. Other sumptuary rules involved taboos against touching or eating with higher-ranking people. Sumptuary rules also set standards regarding dress, marriage, exchanges, and other cultural practices. In many of the chiefdoms, social inferiors had to prostrate themselves and demonstrate other signs of deference in the presence of their "social superiors." Symbols of inequality and hierarchy were thoroughly ingrained in most of these societies.

A Case Study: Polynesia and Stratified Descent Groups

The ethnohistoric data on the Polynesian Islands contain some of the most detailed descriptions of social stratification within chiefdom societies. The ideal basis of social organization was the *conical clan* (see Figure 10.3), an extensive de-

scent group having a common ancestor who was usually traced through a patrilineal line (Kirchoff, 1955; Sahlins, 1968b; Goldman, 1970). Rank and lineage were determined by a person's kinship distance to the founding ancestor, as illustrated in Figure 10.3. The closer a person was to the highest-ranking senior male in direct line of descent to the ancestor, the higher his or her rank and status. In fact, as Marshall Sahlins (1985) suggested, the Hawaiians did not trace descent but ascent toward a connection with an ancient ruling line.

Although Polynesian societies reflected a patrilineal bias, most had ambilineal descent groups (Goodenough, 1955; Firth, 1957). Local descent groups in the villages were headed by senior males. These local groups were ranked in relation to other larger, senior groups that were embedded in the conical clan. Because of ambilateral rules, people born into certain groups had the option of affiliating with either their paternal or maternal linkages in choosing their rank and status. In general, beyond this genealogical reckoning, these chiefdom societies offered little in the way of upward social mobility for achieved statuses.

Figure 10.3   Model of a conical clan.

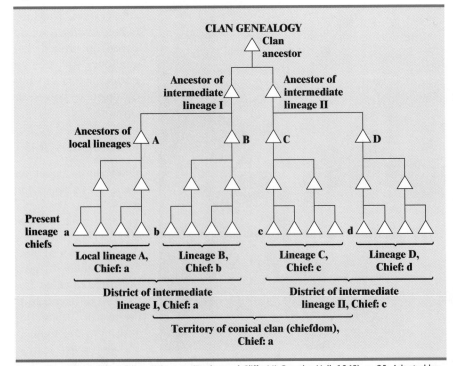

Source: From Marshall D. Sahlins. *Tribesmen* (Englewood Cliffs, NJ: Prentice Hall, 1968), p. 25. Adapted by permission of Prentice Hall.

MARRIAGE

As in tribal societies, most marriages in chiefdoms were carefully arranged affairs, sometimes involving cousin marriages from different descent groups. People who married outside of their descent group usually married within their social stratum. In some chiefdom societies, however, marriages were sometimes arranged between higher strata males and females of lower strata. Anthropologist Jane Collier (1988) noted that women in chiefdom societies that emphasized hereditary rank tended to avoid low-ranking males and tried to secure marriages with men who possessed more economic and political prerogatives.

One chiefdom in North America illustrates a situation in which marriage provided a systematic form of social mobility for the entire society. The Natchez Indians of the Mississippi region were a matrilineal society divided into four strata: The Great Sun chief (the eldest son of the top-ranking lineage) and his brothers; the *noble lineages;* the *honored lineages;* and the inferior "stinkards." All members of the three upper strata had to marry down to a stinkard. This resulted in a regular form of social mobility from generation to generation. The children of the upper three ranks took the status of their mother, unless she was a stinkard.

If a woman of the Great Sun married a stinkard, their children became members of the upper stratum. If a noble woman married a stinkard man, their children became nobles. However, if a noble man married a stinkard, their children would drop to the stratum of the honored status. Through marriage, all of the stinkard children moved up in the status hierarchy.

Although this system allowed for a degree of mobility, it required the perpetuation of the stinkard stratum so that members of the upper strata would have marriage partners. One way the stinkard stratum was maintained was through marriage between two stinkards; their children remained in the inferior stratum. In addition, the stinkard category was continually replenished with people captured in warfare.

Endogamy Marriages in chiefdom societies were both exogamous and endogamous. Although marriages might be exogamous among descent groupings, the spouses were usually from the same stra-

tum (endogamy). These endogamous marriages were carefully arranged so as to maintain genealogically appropriate kinship bonds and descent relations in the top-ranking descent group. This frequently involved cousin marriage between descent groups of the same stratum. Among Hawaiian chiefs, rules of endogamy actually resulted in sibling marriages, sometimes referred to as royal-incest marriage. One anthropologist categorized these sibling marriages as attempts to create alliances between chiefly households among the various Hawaiian Islands (Valeri, 1985).

Polygyny Many of the ruling families in chiefdom societies practiced polygyny. Among the Tsimshian of the Northwest Coast, chiefs could have as many as twenty wives, usually women from the high-ranking lineages of other groups. Lesser chiefs would marry several wives from lower-ranking lineages. In some cases, a Tsimshian woman from a lower-ranking lineage could marry up through the political strategies of her father. For example, a father might arrange a marriage with a high-ranking chief and his daughter. All of these polygynous marriages were accompanied by exchanges of goods that passed to the top of the chiefly hierarchy, resulting in accumulations of surplus resources and wives (Rosman & Rubel, 1986). Among the Trobriand Islanders, male chiefs traditionally had as many as sixty wives drawn from different lineages. High rates of polygyny in the high-ranking strata flourished in many chiefdom societies.

GENERAL SOCIAL PRINCIPLES

Among chiefdom societies, the typical family form was the extended family, with three generations living in a single household. In the Pacific region, for example, the basic domestic unit was usually made up of a household with three generations; in some cases, two or three brothers with their offspring were permanent residents of the household. The households in a specific area of a village were usually part of one lineage. The extended-family household was usually the basic economic unit for subsistence production and consumption in chiefdom societies.

Postmarital residence varied among chiefdoms. Patrilocal, matrilocal, and ambilocal types of residence rules were found in different areas. The ambilocal rule, found in many chiefdoms of the Pacific, enabled people to trace descent to ancestors (male or female) who had the highest rank in the society. This flexibility enabled some individuals to attain access to property, privileges, and authority in spite of the inherent restrictions on status mobility in chiefdom societies (Goodenough, 1956).

GENDER

Typically, gender relations were highly unequal in chiefdom societies, with males exercising economic and political dominance over females. Bridewealth payments, along with arranged marriages, enabled men to claim rights to the labor of children and women. This practice was particularly significant among the highest-status descent groups. A woman's chances of success depended entirely on the rank of her siblings and parents. Women with low-ranking brothers were frequently married by higher-ranking males who wanted to control and manage their marital relations, labor, and potential offspring.

If a woman was fortunate enough to be born or marry into a high-ranking descent group, her ascribed or achieved status was secured. Anthropologist Laura Klein described how some high-ranking women among the Tsimshian Indians were able to maintain considerably high status in their society (1980). According to Sahlins (1985), some wives of high-ranking chiefs married as many as forty males (a type of royal polyandry) to maintain their high status. Thus, the women of the ruling stratum had a higher status than men or women from other strata. Yet, generally, women in chiefdom societies were dominated economically and politically by males.

AGE

In many chiefdom societies, senior males had much more authority, rank, and prestige than other people. As in some tribal societies, this form of inequality produced gerontocratic systems. As people—especially in the higher-ranking descent groups—aged, they received more in the way of status, privileges, and deference from younger people. Because senior males controlled production, marriages, labor, and other economic activities, they became the dominant political authorities. Senior males also possessed special knowledge and controlled sacred rituals, reinforcing their authority. One

of their major responsibilities was to perpetuate the beliefs that rank depended on a person's descent group and that status was hereditary. As in some of the tribal societies, the combination of patriarchy and gerontocracy resulted in cultural hegemony, the imposition of norms, practices, beliefs, and values that reinforced the interests of the upper stratum. This cultural hegemony will become more apparent in the discussion of law and religion in chiefdom societies.

SLAVERY

Earlier in the chapter, we noted that chiefdoms frequently engaged in systematic, organized warfare. One consequence of this warfare was the taking of captives, who were designated as slaves. Slavery in chiefdoms generally did not have the same meaning or implications that it did in more complex state societies, and it usually did not involve the actual ownership of a human being as private property. In this sense, it was very different from the plantation slavery that developed later in the Americas. With some exceptions, most of the slaves in chiefdoms were absorbed into kin groups through marriage or adoption and performed essentially the same type of labor that most people did. Nevertheless, in contrast to the more egalitarian band and tribal societies, chiefdom societies did show the beginnings of a slave stratum.

We have already mentioned an example of a chiefdom slave system in our discussion of the Natchez. Recall, however, that upper-ranking members were obliged to marry members of the stinkard stratum; thus the Natchez did not have a hereditary slave population.

One exception to these generalizations involves some of the Northwest Coast Indians, who maintained a hereditary slave system. Because marrying a slave was considered debasing, slavery became an inherited status (Kehoe, 1992). The children of slaves automatically became slaves, producing a permanent slave stratum. These slaves—most of them war captives—were excluded from ceremonies and on some occasions were killed in human sacrifices. In addition, they were sometimes exchanged, resulting in a kind of commercial traffic of humans. Even in this system, however, slaves who had been captured in warfare could be ransomed by their kinfolk or could purchase their own freedom (Garbarino, 1988).

Law and Religion

Legal and religious institutions and concepts were inextricably connected in chiefdom societies. These institutions existed to sanction and legitimize the political economy and social structure of chiefdoms. They played a critical role in maintaining the cultural hegemony discussed earlier.

LAW

As with political economy, mechanisms of law and social control were more institutionalized and centralized in chiefdom societies. As we discussed earlier, in bands and tribes social norms were unwritten and social conflicts were resolved through kinship groups, often with the intervention of a leader who was respected but lacked political authority. In contrast, the authority structure in chiefdoms enabled political leaders to act as third-party judges above the interests of specific kin groupings and to make definitive decisions without fear of vengeance. Chiefs had the power to sanction certain behaviors by imposing economic fines or damages, by withholding goods and services, and by publicly reprimanding or ridiculing the offending parties. Chiefs could use their economic and political power to induce compliance. They were not just mediators; rather, they engaged in **adjudication,** the settling of legal disputes through centralized authority.

Within a chiefdom, a dispute between kin groups was handled in the same way it was handled in band and tribal societies—through mediation by the groups. Chiefdoms differed substantially from these other societies, however, in their treatment of crimes against authority. These crimes were of two general types: direct violations against a high-ranking chief and violations of traditional customs, norms, or beliefs, injuring the chief's authority (Service, 1975). Such crimes carried severe punishments, including death. The reason for such severe punishments is that these crimes were perceived as threatening the basis of authority in the chiefdom system.

RELIGION

Religious traditions in chiefdom societies were in some respects similar to the cosmic religions described for the band and tribal societies. That is, they reflected the belief that the spiritual and material aspects of nature could not be separated from one another. Religious worldviews were oriented to the cyclical pattern of the seasons and all other aspects of nature. The natural order was also the moral and spiritual order. The religious concepts in chiefdom societies were based on oral traditions perpetuated from generation to generation through elaborate cosmological myths. The most dramatic difference between chiefdom religions and band and tribal religions is the degree to which chiefdom religions legitimized the social, political, and moral status of the chiefs.

A CASE STUDY: LAW AND RELIGION IN POLYNESIA

Nowhere was the relationship between law and religion clearer than among the Polynesian Island chiefdoms. Hawaiian chiefs, for example, were believed to be either gods or sacred intermediaries between human societies and the divine world. Hawaiian chiefdoms have been referred to as **theocracies,** societies in which people rule not because of their worldly wealth and power but because of their place in the moral and sacred order. The political and legal authority of Hawaiian, Tonga, and Tahitian chiefs was reinforced by a religious and ideological system known as the *tabu* system, which was based on social inequalities. Social interaction in these societies was carefully regulated through a variety of tabus. Elaborate forms of deference and expressions of humility served to distinguish various strata, especially those of commoners and chiefs.

Religious beliefs buttressed the *tabu* system. The Polynesians believed that people are imbued with cosmic forces referred to as *mana*. These forces were powerful and sometimes dangerous. They were inherited and distributed according to a person's status and rank. Thus, paramount chiefs had a great deal of mana, subsidiary chiefs had less, and commoners had very little. Violations of certain *tabus*—for example, touching a member of a chiefly family—could bring the offender into contact with the chief's *mana,* which was believed to cause death.

These magical forces could also be gained and lost through a person's moral actions. Thus, the success or failure of a chief was attributed to the amount of *mana* he controlled. This was also reflected in the economic and political spheres, in that a chief who was a good redistributor and maintained order was believed to possess a great amount of mana. On the other hand, if things went badly, this reflected a loss of magical powers. When one chief replaced another, the deposed chief was believed to have lost his powers.

SHAMANISM

Shamanism was practiced in many chiefdoms, particularly among the Native American groups of the Northwest Coast. Like other social institutions, shamanism reflected the hierarchical structure of these societies. The shamans became the personal spiritual guides and doctors of the chiefs and used their knowledge to enhance the power and status of high-ranking chiefs. For example, it was believed that the shamans had the ability to send diseases into enemies and, conversely, to cure and give spiritual power to the chief's allies.

In addition, shamans danced and participated in the potlatch ceremonies on behalf of the chiefs (Garbarino, 1988). One widespread belief throughout the Northwest Coast was in a "man-eating spirit." These groups believed that a man could become possessed by an animal spirit, which transformed him into a cannibal. During the potlatch ceremonies, shamans would dance, chant, and sing, using masks to enact the transformation from human to animal form to ward off the power of the man-eating spirit. Through these kinds of practices, shamans could help sanction the power and authority of the high-ranking chiefs. The chiefs demonstrated their generosity through the potlatch, whereas the shamanistic ceremonies exhibited the supernatural powers that were under the control of the chiefs.

By associating closely with a chief, a shaman could elevate both his own status and that of the chief. The shaman collected fees from his chiefly clients, which enabled him to accumulate wealth. In some cases, low-ranking individuals became shamans by finding more potent spirits for a chief. No shaman, however, could accumulate enough wealth to rival a high-ranking chief (Garbarino, 1988).

HUMAN SACRIFICE

Another practice that reflected the relationships among religion, hierarchy, rank, and the legitimacy of chiefly rule was human sacrifice, which existed in some—but not all—chiefdoms. Among the Natchez Indians, for example, spectacular funerary rites were held when the Great Sun chief died. During these rites, the chief's wives, guards, and attendants were expected to sacrifice their lives, feeling privileged to follow the Great Sun into the afterworld. Parents also offered their children for sacrifice, which, they believed, would raise their own rank. The sacrificial victims were strangled, but they were first given a strong concoction of tobacco, which made them unconscious. They were then buried alongside the Great Sun chief in an elaborate burial mound.

Human sacrifice was also practiced in the Polynesian region. In Hawaii there were two major rituals: the *Mahahiki,* or so-called New Year's festival, and the annual rededication of the Luakini temple, at which human sacrifices were offered (Valeri, 1985). Some of the sacrificial victims had transgressed or violated the sacred *tabus.* These victims frequently were brothers or cousins of the chiefs who were their rivals. It was believed that these human sacrifices would help perpetuate the fertility of the land and the people. Human sacrifice was the prerogative of these chiefs and was a symbolic means of distinguishing these divine rulers from the rest of the human population. Such rituals effectively sanctioned the sacred authority of the chiefs.

Art, Architecture, and Music

Compared with band and tribal societies, chiefdom societies had more extensive artwork, which reflected two different tendencies in chiefdom societies: a high degree of labor organization and the status symbols associated with high-ranking chiefs. One of the most profound examples of the artwork of a chiefdom society is found on Easter Island.

Between 800 and 1,000 monumental stone figures known as *moai* have been discovered there. These figures vary in height from less than 2 meters to almost 10 meters (about 30 feet) and weigh up to 59 metric tons. After sculpting these figures in quarries, laborers dragged them over specially constructed transport roads and erected them on platforms. This project called for an extensive, regionwide labor organization. The symbolic design of the Easter Island statuaries evokes the power, status, and high rank of the chiefs of Easter Island (Kirch, 1984).

The large mounds associated with the Cahokian chiefdom complex also represented extensive labor projects and a hierarchical society. The city of Cahokia was surrounded by different types of earthen mounds. In the center of the city was a large, truncated, flat-top mound known as Monk's Mound. This mound is 100 feet high, covers 16 acres, and is built of earth, clay, silt, and sand. It took perhaps 200 years to construct. Monk's Mound is surrounded by hundreds of smaller mounds, some conical in shape, others flat-topped. Although the Cahokian society collapsed around A.D. 1450 (before European contact), archaeologists

A totem pole of the Kwakiutl, a Native American group of the Northwest Coast.

know from other remaining Mississippian chiefdom societies such as the Natchez Indians that the flat-topped mounds were used chiefly for residences and religious structures, whereas the conical mounds were used for burials.

Another example of the labor and status associated with chiefdom art forms comes from the Northwest Coast Native Americans. These groups produced totem poles, along with decorated house posts and wooden dance masks. The carved, wooden totem poles and house posts were the ultimate status and religious symbols, indicating the high social standing and linkages between the chiefs and the ancestral deities. Typically, a totem pole was erected on the beach in front of a new chief's house, which had decorated house posts. The symbolic messages transmitted through these poles expressed the status hierarchies in these societies.

MUSIC

We have already mentioned the important shamanic dance activities that accompanied the potlatch activities of the Northwest Coast chiefdoms. Most of the traditional music of chiefdom societies exemplified the interconnections among sociopolitical structure, religion, and art. The traditional music of Polynesia is a good example of these interconnections. Although work songs, recreational songs, and mourning songs were part of everyday life, formal music was usually used to honor the deities and chiefs (Kaeppler, 1980). In western Polynesia, on the islands of Tonga, Tikopia, and Samoa, much of the traditional music consisted of stylized poetry accompanied by bodily movements and percussion instruments such as drums.

In some ceremonies, formal poetic chants were sung in verses. In other contexts, people sang narrative songs, or *fakaniua,* describing famous places, past events, and legends, accompanied by hand clapping in a syncopated, complex rhythmic pattern.

The traditional formal musical style of eastern Polynesia, including the Hawaiian Islands, also consisted of complex, integrated systems of poetry, rhythm, melody, and movement that were multifunctional but were usually related to chiefly authority. The Hawaiians had a variety of musical instruments, including membranophones made of hollow wooden cylinders covered with sharkskin, mouth flutes, rhythm sticks, and bamboo tubes. In contrast to those of the other islands, traditional Hawaiian musical performers and dancers were highly organized and trained in specially built schools under the high priests. The major function of the Hawaiian performers was to pay homage to the chiefs and their ancestral deities through religious chants and narrative songs.

 # SUMMARY

Chiefdoms are intermediate forms of societies between tribal and large-scale state societies. They tend to consist of centralized economic and political sociocultural systems in contrast to those of foragers or tribes. In the past, they existed in many parts of the world, including the Pacific Islands, Africa, the Americas, and Europe.

Chiefdoms usually had greater populations and more extensive technologies than did tribes. The political economy of chiefdoms was based on redistributional economic exchanges, in which the upper stratum, the chiefly families, had greater access to wealth, power, and political authority than did other people. There were, however, many limitations on chiefly political authority and property ownership. Because many of these chiefdoms did not have regular police or a recruited military, the chiefs had to rule through popular acceptance rather than through coercion.

The social organization of chiefdom societies consisted of lineages, clans, and other descent groups. Yet unlike tribal societies, these descent groups were ranked in strata based on their relationship to a chiefly family. Marriages were frequently endogamous within a particular stratum. Many chiefdoms practiced polygyny, especially in the upper stratum. Gender relations in chiefdom societies tended to be patriarchal, although females in the chiefly stratum often had a high status. Senior males, especially in the upper stratum, often dominated chiefdom societies, resulting in a form of gerontocracy. Although slavery emerged in some chiefdom societies, it generally was not based on commercial exchanges of humans.

Law and religion were intertwined with the sociopolitical structure of chiefdom societies. Law was based on adjudication of disputes by chiefly authorities, especially in cases that threatened the chief's legitimacy. These laws were backed by supernatural sanctions such as the tabu system of Polynesia, which reaffirmed chiefly authority. The traditional art and music in chiefdom societies were also intended as a form of homage to the legitimacy of the chiefs and their ancestral deities.

STUDY QUESTIONS

1. How and why did chiefdoms come into existence? That is, how did economic inequality and social stratification arise from egalitarian foraging and tribal societies? What factors may have been involved in this change?

2. Aside from the prestige factors associated with the potlatch among the Northwest Coast Indians, what other functions did these ceremonies have, and what were the implications?

3. What role did kinship and descent play in the social structure of a chiefdom?

4. What was the role of trade and exchange in chiefdom societies? Give some specific examples of how goods were acquired and transferred from one individual to another.

5. How and why did the practices of reciprocity and redistribution in chiefdoms differ from the way they functioned in bands and tribes? What factors affected the way exchanges took place?

6. Describe the social structure of a chiefdom. What were the specific social rankings and how were these determined?

7. What was the role of supernatural forces in legitimizing the power of the chief? Illustrate your answer with specific concepts from ethnographic case studies.

KEY TERMS

adjudication

barter

chiefs

hierarchical society

intensive horticulture

kula

office

potlatch

redistributional economic
   exchange

regional symbiosis

strata

sumptuary rules

theocracies

INTERNET EXERCISES

1. Visit the website **http://www.siu.edu/~anthro/
muller/Salt/salt.html.** This is a summary report
by Jon Muller of the Great Salt Spring site. How
does the specialized economic behavior described
in this article relate to the concept of the chiefdom
as described in this chapter? What unusual environmental factors play into this discussion?

2. Explore the website **http://web.clas.ufl.edu/
users/abeltd/trobrial.htm.** What are the elements of the Throbriand Islands' simple chiefdom? How do these elements compare to the description of the chiefdom in this chapter? What
major differences do you see? Why do you think
these differences exist?

SUGGESTED READINGS

DRUCKER, PHILIP. 1965. *Cultures of the North Pacific.* San
Francisco: Chandler. One of the first attempts to clas-
sify and analyze the different types of chiefdoms of the
Northwest Coast of North America.

EARLE, TIMOTHY K. 1987. "Chiefdoms in Archaeological
and Ethnohistorical Perspective." *Annual Review of Anthropology* 16: 279–308. An excellent account of the
many variables that affected the development of chiefdoms. Earle is anthropology's foremost expert on chiefdoms.

HARDING, THOMAS G., AND BEN J. WALLACE, eds. 1970.
Cultures of the Pacific. Garden City, NY: Free Press. A
good collection of essays dealing with the multiplicity
of societies in the Pacific, including chiefdoms.

KIPP, RITA SMITH, AND EDWARD M. SCHORTMAN. 1989. "The
Political Impact of Trade in Chiefdoms." *American Anthropologist 91* (2): 370–385. A sophisticated and thorough discussion of the relationship between trade and

the development of the political economy in chiefdom
societies.

MALINOWSKI, BRONISLAW. 1922. *Argonauts of the Western
Pacific.* New York: Dutton. This classic ethnography
gives a full description of the kula exchange among the
Trobriand Islanders. It is the first substantivist (versus
formalist) treatment of economic behavior in anthropology.

————. *Crime and Custom in Savage Society.* [1926]
1959. Paterson, NJ: Littlefield, Adams. A classic treatment of law among the Trobriand Islanders, dealing
with a number of cases, such as suicide. Malinowski
treats law as an aspect of exchange and reciprocity between individuals in society.

SAHLINS, MARSHALL D. 1958. *Social Stratification in Polynesia.* Seattle: University of Washington Press. A classic
treatise comparing the different types of chiefdoms and
their institutions with other societies in Polynesia.

Agricultural States

CHAPTER OUTLINE

Demography

Technology
Agricultural Innovations / The Diffusion of Technology

Political Economy
The Division of Labor / Property Rights / The Command Economy versus the Entrepreneur / The Peasantry / Trade and Monetary Exchange

Social Organization
Kinship and Status / Marriage / Gender, Subsistence, and Status

Social Stratification
The Caste System / Racial and Ethnic Stratification

Law
Mediation and Self-Help

Warfare

Religion
Ecclesiastical Religions / Universalistic Religions / Divine Rulers, Priests, and Religious Texts

The Collapse of State Societies
Reasons for Collapse / Evaluating Theories

CHAPTER QUESTIONS

- How do the demographic characteristics of agricultural societies differ from those of small-scale societies?

- What are the features of the different forms of political economy that can be found in agricultural societies?

- What is the relationship among family, gender, and subsistence in agricultural societies?

- How does social stratification in agricultural societies differ from that in more egalitarian societies?

- What are the characteristics of law, warfare, and religion in state societies?

AS DISCUSSED IN EARLIER CHAPTERS, THROUGHOUT much of their history humans have relied on hunting wild animals and gathering wild plants. During the Neolithic period, however, a transition was made to a dependence on domesticated plants and animals. The Neolithic Period also saw increasing technological, political, and social complexity. As a result, many peoples developed **intensive agriculture,** the cultivation of crops by preparing permanent fields year after year, often using irrigation and fertilizers. In contrast to horticulture, intensive agriculture enables a population to produce enormous food surpluses to sustain dense populations in large, permanent settlements.

In some regions, beginning as much as 5,500 years ago, the intensification of agriculture was accompanied by the appearance of complex agricultural *states.* The term *state* is used by anthropologists to describe a wide range of societies that differ structurally from bands, tribes, and chiefdoms. The major difference between state and prestate societies is a bureaucratic organization (or government). The first states developed with the intensification of agriculture and are referred to as agricultural states. The other type of state society—industrial states—will be examined in Chapter 12.

Major agricultural states are sometimes referred to as *agricultural civilizations.* Although anthropologists disagree on the precise scientific meaning of *civilization,* the term usually implies a complex society with a number of characteristics, including dense populations located in urban centers; extensive food surpluses; a highly specialized division of labor with economic roles other than those pertaining to agricultural production; a bureaucratic organization or government; monumental works, including art and engineering projects that involve massive labor; and writing systems for record

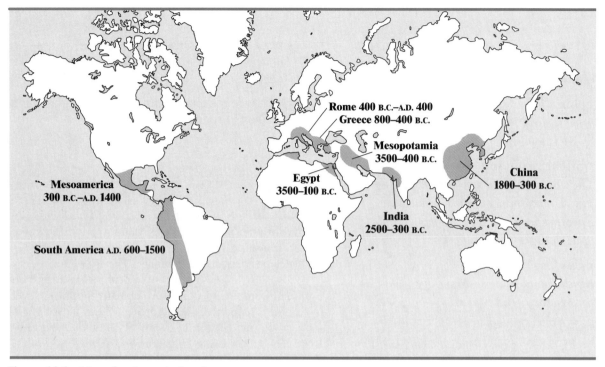

Figure 11.1 Map of major agricultural states.

keeping and religious texts. Figure 11.1 shows the location of some early agricultural states.

In this chapter, we examine some of the general characteristics associated with agricultural states. Developments in specific world areas are briefly explored in the regional chapters on Latin America, Africa, the Middle East, and Asia. As with bands, tribes, and chiefdoms, agricultural states no longer exist in the same form as in the past. The political economy, social organization, and religious traditions that emerged, however, have had consequences that persist up to the present.

Demography

After the transition to intensive agriculture, population began to increase dramatically along with increases in agricultural production, enabling people to settle in large urban areas. These population increases produced conditions that led to higher mortality rates. Poor sanitation coupled with the domestication of animals that were confined led to frequent epidemics that affected both animals and humans. The overwhelming evidence from fossil evidence and ethnographic evidence suggests that pre-Neolithic peoples had fewer health problems and less disease than the Paleolithic peoples. This debunks the notion that evolution always results in progress for humans, a nineteenth-century belief. Disease, warfare, and famines all contributed to higher mortality rates in agricultural societies than those found in bands, tribes, or chiefdoms. The majority of paleoanthropolgical and archaeological studies also suggest that life expectancy decreased with the development of intensive agriculture (Hassan, 1981; Harris & Ross, 1987; Cohen, 1994).

Despite increased mortality rates and decreased life expectancy, populations continued to grow at a significant rate because of increased fertility rates. Undoubtedly, higher birthrates reflected the socioeconomic benefits associated with increased family size in agricultural civilizations. Children provided additional labor for essential agricultural tasks such as planting, caring for animals, and harvesting, thereby freeing adults for other labor such as processing food and making clothing. The actual costs of rearing children were relatively low in agricultural states in which increased agricultural yields produced surplus foods to support large families. Clothing and shelter were manufactured domestically and were therefore inexpensive.

In addition, the mortality rates, particularly infant mortality rates, encouraged parents to have more children to ensure that some would survive into adulthood. Moreover, children were viewed as future assets who could take care of their parents in later life. In addition to the socioeconomic motives of parents, the political dynamics in agricultural civilizations encouraged high fertility rates. All of the agricultural states promoted the ideal of having large families (Harris & Ross, 1987). These societies depended on a large labor force to maintain their extensive agricultural production and military operations. Policies favoring high birthrates frequently were backed up by religious ideologies.

Technology

One major factor that contributed to the evolution of agricultural states was the development of a more sophisticated technology. To some extent, this represented modifications of existing technologies. For example, stone tools such as axes, hammers, knives, and scrapers were refined for more prolonged use. Increased knowledge of metallurgy enabled some agricultural peoples to create more durable tools. For example, copper, tin, and iron ores were smelted and cast into weapons, armor, ornaments, and other tools. Many technological innovations were dramatically expressed in a myriad of artwork and monumental construction, illustrated by such massive structures as the Pyramid of the Sun at Teotihuacan in Mexico, which rises more than 200 feet in the air and covers some 650 square feet.

AGRICULTURAL INNOVATIONS

Technological innovations were of key importance in increasing crop yields in agricultural states. Humans in various world areas developed specialized techniques to exploit local natural resources more efficiently. Initially, water had to be transported by hand, but later civilizations crafted devices such as the *shaduf,* a pole-and-lever device that is believed to have originated in southwest Asia more than 4,000 years ago. Many of the civilizations in southwest Asia, the Nile Valley, India, and the Americas created complicated irrigation systems that extended the amount of land that could be cultivated.

Old World agricultural civilizations reached a pivotal point with the advent of the plow, with which farmers could turn soil to a much greater depth than had previously been possible, radically transforming it by reaching deeper into the soil to replenish it with nutrients. The plow thus enabled

Large-scale monument building, like this Teotihuacan pyramid, required a ruling elite that organized peasants to provide labor to the state.

agricultural peoples to utilize fields on a more permanent basis and occupy the same land for many generations.

The first plows were modifications of the hoe and were probably pulled by the farmers themselves. Eventually, oxen were harnessed to the plows, and farmers gained the ability to cultivate large plots. Then, as people forged innovations in metallurgy, wooden-tipped plows were replaced by plows made first of bronze and then of iron. Oxen-drawn, iron-plowed agriculture spread widely, transforming civilizations throughout the Old World.

Early New World civilizations never used the plow. Instead, they devised a wide variety of other agricultural innovations in response to particular environmental settings. For example, in the Oaxacan Valley in Mexico the people practiced *pot irrigation,* in which farmers planted their crops near small, shallow wells and used pots to carry water to their fields (Flannery, 1968). More complicated irrigation techniques undergirded agriculture in other American agricultural states. In both the highland and lowland regions of Mesoamerica, the Mayan civilization (300 B.C.–A.D. 1500) created agricultural technology to support densely populated urban centers. Because no evidence of intensive agriculture had been discovered, archaeologists initially hypothesized that the Maya lived in widely dispersed villages with ritual centers consisting of

relatively few inhabitants. However, using more careful study techniques researchers have proved that the Maya devised sophisticated irrigation systems throughout lowland areas, which provided food for the large urban centers.

THE DIFFUSION OF TECHNOLOGY

In today's multicultural societies we take the diffusion, or exchange, of technological innovations for granted and, indeed, archaeologists have uncovered evidence that certain ideas—such as iron technology and plow agriculture—diffused over large areas during ancient times. However, the fact remains that before A.D. 1500, most regions of the world were comparatively isolated, and technological innovations were not spread as readily as today.

Certain areas experienced greater technological advances than did others. For example, the Near East, China, and parts of India had made remarkable technological and scientific achievements compared with those of Europe (Lenski & Lenski, 1982). Among the major innovations identified with China alone were papermaking, movable-type printing, paper money, guns and gunpowder, compasses, underwater mining, umbrellas, hot-air balloons, multistage rockets, and scientific ideas concerning the circulation of blood and the laws of motion (Frank, 1998). Little was known of these

Pot irrigation. These women are carrying pots of water for irrigation.

technological and scientific developments in Western societies until much later.

Political Economy

The scale of state organization varied in agricultural civilizations. In some areas there existed large-scale bureaucratic empires that organized and controlled wide-ranging territories. Examples are centralized governments in the Near Eastern empires such as Mesopotamia and Egypt; Rome, which controlled an empire that incorporated more than 70 million people throughout its long period of domination; China, in which a large centralized bureaucracy managed by government officials ruled over perhaps as many as 100 million people; and American empires such as those of the Mayas and Aztecs, which ruled over millions of people.

In contrast, state societies in Africa, India, and Southeast Asia were much less centralized and had less authority over adjacent regions. Anthropologist Aidan Southall (1956) applied the term *segmentary states* to African states in which the ruler was recognized as belonging to an appropriate royal segmentary lineage but had only symbolic and ritual authority over outlying regions. Centralized bureaucratic structures in such states did not effectively control peripheral areas.

Anthropologist Clifford Geertz (1980) used the term *theater state* to refer to the limited form of state society in Southeast Asia. The power of the theater state is mostly symbolic and theatrical, with many ceremonies to demonstrate the political legitimacy of the regime. The power and authority of the theater state have been compared with the light of a torch, radiating outward from the center and gradually fading into the distance, merging imperceptibly with the ascending power of a neighboring sovereign (Geertz, 1980).

Feudalism, a decentralized form of political economy based on landed estates, existed in agricultural civilizations during different historical periods. Usually, feudal regimes resulted from the breakdown of large-scale centralized states. Feudal political economies emerged at various times in western Europe and Japan. In these systems, lords were autonomous patrons who owned land and maintained control over their own military (knights and *samurai*) and demanded labor and tribute from their serfs. Political power varied from a decentralized form of authority (the nobles) to a more centralized form (a king or emperor). For example, during the Tokugawa period in Japan (1600–1868), the *daimyo* (lords) had to reside in the central capital, Edo (present-day Tokyo), for a year to demonstrate loyalty to the ruler, or *shogun*. This represented a more centralized form of feudalism.

THE DIVISION OF LABOR

The creation of substantial food surpluses, along with better food-storing technologies, led to new forms of economic relations in agricultural states. Many people could be freed from working in the fields to pursue other specialized functions. Hundreds of new occupations developed in the urban centers of agricultural states. Craftsworkers produced tools, clothing, jewelry, pottery, and other accessories. Other workers engaged in commerce, government, religion, education, the military, and other sectors of the economy.

This new division of labor influenced both rural and urban areas. Farm laborers were not only involved in essential food production, they also turned to craft production to supplement their income. Over time, some agricultural villages began to produce crafts and commodities not just for their own consumption but for trade with other villages and with the urban centers. Through these activities, rural villages became involved in widespread trading alliances and marketing activities.

PROPERTY RIGHTS

Despite the complex division of labor in agricultural states, the major source of wealth was arable land. In effect, the ownership of land became the primary basis for an individual's socioeconomic position. The governing elite in most of the agricultural states claimed ownership over large landholdings, which included both the land and the peasant or slave labor that went with it (Lenski & Lenski, 1982).

Two forms of property ownership predominated in agricultural states, depending on whether they were large-scale centralized states or decentralized feudal states. Eric Wolf (1966) identified one type of property ownership in which a powerful government claimed ownership of the land, appointed officials to supervise its cultivation, and collected the surplus agricultural production. In the other type of system, land was owned privately by a class of landlords who inherited it through family lines and who oversaw its cultivation. In certain cases, peasants could own land directly and produce surpluses for the elites.

Agricultural states thus developed major inequalities between those who owned land and those who did not. Bureaucratic and legal devices were developed by the elite to institute legal deeds and titles, and land became a resource that was bought, sold, and rented. A new form of economic system known as the *tributary* form became predominant. Tribute, in the form of taxes, rent, or labor services, replaced economic exchanges based on kinship reciprocity or chiefdom redistribution. Wolf (1982) has referred to this as a *tributary mode of production,* in contrast to the *kin-ordered mode of production* of nonstate societies. Under these conditions, a hierarchy emerged in which the elite who resided in the urban centers or on landed estates collected the tribute, and the peasants, who cultivated the land, paid tribute to this elite (Wolf, 1966, 1982).

THE COMMAND ECONOMY VERSUS THE ENTREPRENEUR

In the large-scale centralized states, a form of **command economy** emerged, wherein the political elite controlled production, prices, and trading. Some agricultural states became expansive world empires that extracted tribute and placed limits on people's economic activities. Although private trade and entrepreneurial activities did occur at times within these bureaucratic empires, most economic activity was controlled by state authorities (Adams, 1974). For example, China and Rome attempted to organize and control most aspects of their economy by monopolizing the production and sale of items like salt and iron.

At the same time, in the less centrally organized agricultural states, more independent economic activity was evident. For example, during the feudal periods in western Europe and Japan, the lack of a dominating elite that organized and managed the economic affairs of the society enabled more autonomous economic production and exchange to occur at the local level. Entrepreneurs had freedom to develop and innovate within the context of feudal political economies. This was a key factor in the later economic development of these regions.

THE PEASANTRY

Peasants are people who cultivate land in rural areas for their basic subsistence and pay tribute to elite groups. The socioeconomic status of the peasantry, however, varied in agricultural societies. As we have seen, rights to land differed between the bureaucratic empires and the less centralized societies. In most agricultural states, elites claimed rights to most of the land, and the peasantry in the rural areas paid tribute or taxes as a type of rent (Wolf, 1966). In other cases, the peasants owned the land they cultivated; nevertheless, they still paid tribute from their labor surplus or production. In the case of feudal Europe, the peasants, or serfs, were bound to the estates owned by lords, or nobles.

Whatever their status, all peasants had to produce a surplus that flowed into the urban centers. It is estimated that this surplus, including fines, tithes, and obligatory gifts, represented at least half of the peasants' total output (Lenski & Lenski, 1982). Also, in the bureaucratic civilizations such as Egypt and Teotihuacan, the peasantry provided much of the compulsory labor for large-scale government projects such as massive irrigation works and pyramids. Although research on peasants has demonstrated that they were often able to evade some of these obligations or contrived to hide some of their surpluses, most were subject to burdensome demands from the elites.

The Moral Economy   Despite the domination of the peasantry by the agricultural state or by landlords, the peasantry developed norms that emphasized community cooperation in production, distribution, consumption, and exchange in the village. These norms led to what some anthropologists have referred to as a *moral economy* for the peasantry. This moral economy involved sharing food resources and labor with one another in a reciprocal manner to provide a form of social and economic insurance so that individual families would not fall into destitution (Scott, 1976). Peasant families would exchange labor with each other to aid production of crops. In addition, rituals and festivals occurred at which peasants were encouraged to donate and exchange food and goods to be distributed throughout the community. Although the moral economy of the peasantry was not always successful, and individual families did become impoverished, in many cases it did help sustain the viability of the village community.

TRADE AND MONETARY EXCHANGE

As previously discussed, the production of agricultural surpluses and luxury items in agricultural states led to internal and external trade. This trade included raw materials for production, such as copper, iron ore, obsidian, and salt. Long-distance trade routes over both land and sea spanned immense geographical areas. Through constant policing, governing elites enforced political order and military security over these trade routes. In turn, this led to the security and maintenance of extensive road networks that aided commercial pursuits. For example, the Romans constructed roads and bridges that are still in use (Stavrianos, 1995).

Extensive caravan routes developed in areas such as the Near East and North Africa. The Bedouins, Arabic-speaking pastoralists, used camels to conduct long-distance trade, carrying goods from port cities in the Arabian peninsula across the desert to cities such as Damascus, Jerusalem, and Cairo. In Asia, other caravan routes crossed the

A woman selling food in a peripheral market area in Malaysia.

whole of China and central Asia, with connections to the Near East. In the Americas, long-distance trade developed between Teotihuacan and the Mayan regions.

In conjunction with long-distance trade, monetary exchange became more formalized. In the Near East (and probably elsewhere), foodstuffs such as grains originally could be used to pay taxes, wages, rents, and other obligations. Because grains are perishable and bulky, however, they were not ideal for carrying out exchanges. Thus, general-purpose money, based on metals, especially silver and copper, came into use. The sizes and weights of these metals became standardized and were circulated as stores of value. At first, bars of metal were used as money, but eventually smaller units of metal or coins were manufactured and regulated. After developing printing, the Chinese began to produce paper money as their medium of exchange.

The Rise of Merchants and Peripheral Markets

One result of the development of a formalized monetary system was the increased opportunity for merchants to purchase goods not for their own consumption but to be sold to people who had money. Merchants made up a new status category of those who, although below the elites, often prospered by creating demands for luxury goods and organizing the transportation of those goods across long distances. Much of the trade of the Near Eastern empires, followed by the Greek, Roman, Byzantine, and Islamic Mediterranean commercial operations, was stimulated by merchants who furnished imported luxury goods from foreign lands for consumption by internal elites (Wolf, 1982). Sometimes, as in the case of the Aztecs, the merchants of these empires also doubled as spies, providing information to governing authorities regarding peoples in outlying regions.

With increasing long-distance trade and other commercial developments, regional and local marketplaces as well as marketplaces in the urban areas began to emerge. Foodstuffs and other commodities produced by peasants, artisans, and craftsworkers were bought and sold in these marketplaces. In early cities such as Ur, Memphis, Teotihuacan, and Tikal, markets were centrally located, offering both imported and domestically manufactured items as well as food. In addition, marketplaces arose throughout the countryside. A steady flow of goods developed from villages to counties to regional and national capitals.

Although many goods were bought and sold in these regional markets, the vast majority of people—that is, the peasantry—did not receive their subsistence items from these markets. Nor were people engaged full time in producing or selling in these marketplaces (Bohannon & Dalton, 1962). The regional and local markets existed only as a convenient location for the distribution of goods. In many cases, the activity was periodic. For example, in medieval Europe, traveling fairs that went from city to city enabled merchants to bring their local and imported goods to be bought and sold.

Goods were bought and sold in markets through a system known as *haggling*. Haggling is a type of negotiation between buyer and seller that establishes the price of an item. The buyer asks a seller how much he or she wants for an item, the seller proposes a figure, and the buyer counters with a lower price until a price is finally agreed on.

Social Organization

Because agricultural states were more complex and highly organized than prestate societies, they could not rely solely on kinship for recruitment to different status positions. Land ownership and occupation became more important than kinship in organizing society. In the highly centralized agricultural societies, the state itself replaced kin groups as the major integrating principle in society.

KINSHIP AND STATUS

Nevertheless, family and kinship remained an important part of social organization. In elite and royal families, kinship was the basic determination of status. Royal incest in brother-sister marriages by both the Egyptian and Incan royalty shows the importance of kinship as a distinctive means of maintaining status in agricultural societies. The typical means of achieving the highest statuses was through family patrimony, or the inheritance of status. Access to the highest ranks was generally closed to those who did not have the proper genealogical relationships with the elite or the nobility.

The Extended Family   The extended family was the predominant family form in both urban and rural areas in most agricultural states. Family ties remained critical to most peasants; typically, the peasant extended family held land in common, and the members of the family cooperated in farm labor. To some extent, intensive agricultural production required the presence of a large extended family to provide the necessary labor to plant, cultivate, and harvest crops (Wolf, 1966). Large domestic groups had to pool their resources and labor to maintain economic production. To induce this cooperation, generalized reciprocal economic exchanges of foodstuffs, goods, and labor were maintained in these families.

Other Kinship Principles   In a cross-cultural survey of fifty-three agricultural civilizations, Kay Martin and Barbara Voorhies (1975) found that 45 percent had patrilineal kin groupings, another 45 percent had bilateral groupings, and 9 percent had matrilineal groupings. In some Southeast Asian societies such as Burma, Thailand, and Cambodia, bilateral descent existed along with kindred groupings. In some circumstances, these kindreds provided domestic labor in agricultural production through reciprocal labor exchanges. Families connected through kindreds would regularly exchange labor for the transplanting or harvesting of rice crops.

Family Structure among the Nayar   One matrilineal society, the Nayar of southern India, had unusual marriage practices that produced a remarkably different type of family structure. Prior to puberty, a Nayar female married a male as a rite of passage. This male, however, had no rights regarding the female, and the female had no obligations to the male. Later, the female could enter a number of marriages with males of her same caste and have children. The Nayar system was unusual because none of the husbands resided with the female. The matrilineal group assumed the rights over her and her children. Thus, the household family unit consisted of brothers and sisters, a woman's daughter and granddaughters, and their children.

From the Western viewpoint, the Nayar marital arrangement might not seem like a family because it does not tie two families together. This system, however, was a response to historical circumstances in southern India. Traditionally, most Nayar males joined the military. In addition, the land owned by the matrilineal group was worked by lower-caste, landless peasants. Therefore, young Nayar males had no responsibilities to the matrilineal group and were free to become full-time warriors (Mencher, 1965).

MARRIAGE

The significance of social ties in agricultural states is evident in the form of marriage practices found in these societies, all of which have economic and political implications. Because of these implications, the selection of marital partners was considered too important to be left to young people. Marriages were usually arranged by parents, sometimes with the aid of brokers, who assessed the alliances between the extended families with respect to landed wealth or political connections to the elite. In some cases (for example, China), arranged marriages were contracted when the children were young (see Chapter 4 on pages 77–78). As in chiefdom societies, elite marriages were frequently endogamous. Peasants, however, generally married outside their extended families and larger kin groups.

Dowry and Bridewealth Most agricultural states practiced some form of marital exchange involving land, commodities, or foodstuffs. In Asia and some parts of Europe, the most common type of exchange was the **dowry,** goods and wealth paid by the bride's family to the groom's family. In this sense, the dowry appears to be the reverse of *bridewealth,* in which the groom's family exchanges wealth for the bride. In actuality, the dowry represents an early inheritance for the woman, who is able to use it to arrange a marriage contract. Upon marriage the bride in an Indian or Chinese family was expected to bring material goods into her marriage.

In a cross-cultural comparison, Jack Goody (1976) found that bridewealth occurs more frequently in horticultural societies, whereas the dowry is found in complex, agricultural societies. In Europe and Asia, intensive agriculture was associated with the use of plows and draft animals, high population densities, and a scarcity of land. Goody hypothesized that one result of the dowry system was to consolidate property in the hands of

elite groups. As commercial and bureaucratic families expanded their wealth and increased their status, these groups began to move from bridewealth to dowry. As bridewealth was a means of circulating wealth among families through creating alliances between the groom's and bride's families, the dowry served to concentrate property and wealth in the already wealthy patrilineal families. Elites in India, China, and Greece relied on this form of marital exchange.

Although dowry exchanges were most significant in the upper socioeconomic groups in which wealth and status were of central significance, they were also supposed to be customary among the peasantry. However, bridewealth was not unknown in peasant society. In both northern and southern India, bridewealth became more common among the lower socioeconomic classes. In the poorest families, there was little to be inherited anyway, and the actual exchanges were mainly for the costs of the wedding feast and for simple household furnishings.

Polygyny In contrast to prestate societies, polygyny was rare in agricultural states, except among the elite. In some cases, the rulers of these societies would have large *harems,* in which many different women were attached to one ruler. The royal households of many agricultural states had hundreds of women at the disposal of the rulers. Individual males of the elite who were wealthy were sometimes able to keep mistresses or concubines in addition to their wives. For example, many Chinese males kept concubines or secondary wives, despite laws against this practice. Other agricultural states had similar polygynous practices for individuals in high-ranking socioeconomic positions.

For most of the populace, however, monogamy was the primary form of marriage. Economist Ester Boserup (1970) has argued that the general absence of polygyny in societies with plow agriculture is due to the lack of land that could be accumulated by adding wives to one's family. Similarly, Goody (1976) hypothesized that in agricultural societies where land is a scarce commodity, peasants cannot afford the luxury of polygyny. Obviously, wealth and status influenced the type of marriage patterns found in agricultural civilizations.

Divorce For the most part, divorce was rare in agricultural civilizations. The corporate nature of the extended family and the need for cooperative agricultural labor among family members usually led to normative constraints against divorce. In addition, marriage was the most important vehicle for the transfer of property and served as the basis for alliances between families and kin groups. Thus, families tended to stay together, and enormous moral, political, and social weight was attached to the marriage bond. In India, marriage was considered sacred, and therefore divorces were not legally permitted. Similar norms were evident in the feudal societies of Europe, where Christianity reinforced the sanctity of the family and the stability of marriage.

For women, however, marriage offered the only respectable career or means of subsistence. Most women faced destitution if a marriage were terminated. Thus, few women wanted to dissolve a marriage, regardless of the internal conflicts or problems. This pattern reflects the unequal status of males and females.

GENDER, SUBSISTENCE, AND STATUS

The transition to intensive agriculture affected the subsistence roles of both males and females. Martin and Voorhies (1975) noted that in agricultural systems the amount of labor that women contributed toward actual production of food declined. For example, the adoption of plow agriculture greatly diminished the need for weeding, a task that was primarily taken care of by women. They hypothesized that as women's role in agriculture decreased, their social status decreased accordingly. Thus, agricultural civilizations were even more patriarchal than were tribes or chiefdoms. Women were viewed as unable to contribute toward the household economy, and for the most part they were confined to cooking, child rearing, and caring for the domestic animals. They had little contact outside their immediate families.

Martin and Voorhies (1975) emphasized that a definite distinction arose in agricultural states between men's and women's roles. Women were restricted to inside (domestic) activities, whereas males were allowed to participate in outside (public) activities. In general, women were not allowed to own property, engage in politics, pursue educa-

tion, or participate in any activity that would take them outside the domestic sphere.

Female Seclusion This highly restricted female role was reflected in a number of cultural practices. For example, China adopted the tradition of foot binding, which involved binding a young female child's feet so the feet would not grow. Although this practice was supposed to produce beautiful feet (in the view of Chinese males), it had the effect of immobilizing women. Less of a handicap for upper-class females, who did not have to participate in the daily labor requirements of most women and were carried around by servants, foot binding was also practiced by the peasantry during various periods, which meant that peasant women had to work with considerable disabilities.

Similarly, many areas of the Near East, North Africa, and southern Asia practiced *purdah*, a system that restricted women to the household. *Purdah* is a Persian word translated as "curtain" or "barrier." In this system, women had to obtain permission from their husbands to leave the house to visit families and friends. In some of these regions, a woman had to cover her face with a veil when in public (Beck & Keddie, 1978; Fernea & Fernea, 1979).

Patriarchy and Sexism Sexist ideology developed in agricultural states as a means of reinforcing the seclusion of women. Females were viewed as inherently inferior and dependent on males. The so-called natural superiority of males was reinforced in most of the legal, moral, and religious traditions in agricultural states, including Confu-

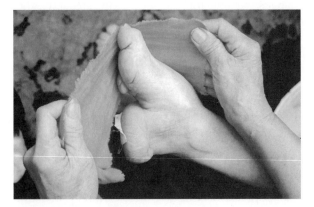

The binding of women's feet in traditional agricultural China led to results shown in this photo.

cianism, Islam, Hinduism, Judaism, and Christianity. Males were viewed as more intelligent, stronger, and more emotionally mature. In addition, many of these societies viewed women as sexually dangerous; women caught having premarital or extramarital sex were punished severely, in some cases by execution. In contrast, males were permitted to engage in extramarital affairs.

Variations in the Status of Women The role of women in agricultural civilizations varied by region. In some areas where soil conditions were poor, both male and female peasants had to work together in the fields to produce for the household, which tended to create more gender equality. In some mainland Southeast Asian countries such as Thailand and Cambodia, both males and females worked together in rice cultivation. In some cases, land was divided equally among all children regardless of gender, indicating that in these societies females had relative equality with males. However, even in these countries, women were confined to the domestic sphere and to household tasks (Keyes, 1977).

Ethnologists have discovered one exception regarding the role of peasant women in public in some agricultural civilizations. In China, Mesoamerica, and West Africa, many women participated as sellers in the marketplaces, taking some of the surplus produce or crafts made in the village to the marketplaces. This activity was generally restricted to older women whose children were grown, however, and the role of marketwoman did not lead to higher status. Moreover, these women had to perform their domestic chores as well as their marketplace activities.

Social Stratification

As previously mentioned, agricultural civilizations were highly stratified, and social mobility was generally restricted to people with elite-family or kinship backgrounds. Thus, anthropologists classify these societies as **closed societies,** in that social status was generally ascribed rather than achieved. For example, in traditional Chinese society, people born outside the emperor's family had two paths to upward mobility. One route was to be born into the *gentry,* the landowning class that made up

about 2 percent of Chinese families. The second route was to become a *mandarin*—a Chinese bureaucrat and scholar—by becoming a student and passing rigorous examinations based on classical Confucian texts. Although in theory this option existed for all males, in fact it was restricted to families or clans that could afford to spend resources for educating a son.

THE CASTE SYSTEM

India developed a much more restrictive form of social inequality known as the caste system. A **caste** is an endogamous social grouping into which a person is born and remains throughout his or her lifetime. Thus, an individual's status in a caste system is ascribed, and movement into a different caste is impossible. The Indian caste system evolved from four basic categories, or *varnas,* that were ranked in order from Brahmans (priests) to Ksaitryas (warriors) to Vaisyas (merchants) to Sudras (laborers). Hence, the caste into which a person was born determined that person's occupation. In addition, people were required to marry within their caste. Although contact among members of different castes was generally discouraged, the castes were interrelated through various mutual economic exchanges and obligations known as the *jajmani* system (discussed in Chapter 15).

Slavery Another form of social inequality and ascribed status was slavery. Slavery tends to increase as a society increases its productive technology, as trade expands, and as states become more centrally organized (Goody, 1980; Van den Berghe, 1981). For example, the Mediterranean empires of the Greeks, Romans, Arabs, and Turks used vast numbers of slaves in galleys, monument construction, irrigation works, plantation agriculture, and major public works projects.

Slave systems differed from one society to another. The Greeks and Romans reduced the status of the slave to a subhuman "thing" that was considered an instrument or tool, differing from inanimate tools only by the faculty of speech (Worsley, 1984). Indigenous African kingdoms practiced large-scale slavery in which nobles owned hundreds of slaves (Goody, 1980). Most of these slaves worked on plantations or in the household, although some became advisers and administrators for nobles. Although African slavery involved the capture and sale of human beings, eventually the slaves could be incorporated into the kinship groups.

In a comprehensive review of indigenous Asian and African slavery, anthropologist James Watson (1980) referred to open and closed forms of slavery. The indigenous African form of slavery was open in that slaves could be incorporated into domestic kinship groups and even become upwardly mobile. In contrast, the slave systems of China, India, Greece, and Rome were closed, with no opportunities for upward mobility or incorporation into kinship groups.

The two different types of slavery were correlated with specific demographic conditions and political economies. In societies such as Africa or Thailand, where land was relatively abundant and less populated, more open forms of slavery developed (Goody, 1971; Turton, 1980). In these societies, the key to power and authority was control over people rather than land. In political economies such as Greece, Rome, China, and India, where land was scarce and populations much more dense, closed forms of slavery emerged. The key to power and wealth in these societies was control over land and labor.

RACIAL AND ETHNIC STRATIFICATION

Related to slavery and a rigid social hierarchy was a pattern not found in nonstate societies: *racial and ethnic stratification*. Although "race" is not a scientifically useful concept (see Chapter 2 and 3), the term is often used to differentiate people according to skin color or other physical characteristics. In contrast, **ethnicity** refers to the cultural differences among populations, usually based on attributes such as language, religion, clothing, lifestyle, and ideas regarding common descent or specific territory.

As agricultural states expanded into surrounding environments, a variety of racially and ethnically different peoples were incorporated into the growing empires. Some of these groups were band, tribal, or chiefdom societies that spoke different languages and maintained different cultural or ethnic traditions. Once conquered or absorbed, they frequently found themselves under the rule of a particular dominant ethnic group. In many cases, the dominant group ascribed subordinate statuses

to them. Sometimes the conquered group became slaves. In other cases its members were viewed as racially or ethnically inferior and were given only limited opportunities for upward mobility. Thus, many ethnic and racial minorities were identified as subordinate classes and stigmatized as inherently inferior.

With the intensification of social stratification in agricultural states, social distance between the ruling elite and the rest of the population was accentuated not only by rights to land, wealth, and power but also by restrictive sumptuary laws. For example, among the Aztecs, patterns of deference and demeanor between the rulers and the ruled were highly formalized. The Aztec nobility were distinguished by clothing and jewelry, and they were believed to be vested with divine status (Berdan, 1982). Aztec commoners were required to prostrate themselves before the emperor and were not permitted to speak to him or look at him. Similar patterns of deference and social etiquette developed throughout the agricultural societies in the Old and New World.

Law

Agricultural states formalized legal decisions and punishments not only through laws but also through court systems, police, and sometimes legal specialists such as judges. In many of these societies, law became highly differentiated from customs, norms, tradition, and religious dogma (Vago, 1988). Writing systems enabled many of these societies to keep records of court proceedings.

The first recognized codified laws originated in the Near Eastern civilization of Babylon. The Babylonian code of law, known as the Laws of Hammurabi, was based on standardized procedures and precedents for dealing with civil and criminal offenses. Other agricultural states such as China, Rome, and India developed formalized legal systems, including court systems. Morton Fried (1978) used evidence from the Hammurabi codes to demonstrate that these laws reinforced a system of inequality by protecting the rights of the governing class while keeping the peasants in a subordinate status. In other words, the codes of Hammurabi were designed to allow those in authority to have access to scarce resources.

In contrast, anthropologists who adhere to the functionalist perspective emphasize the benefits of codified laws for the maintenance of society (Service, 1978b). They argue that the maintenance of social and political order was crucial for agricultural states. Serious disruptions would have led to the neglect of agricultural production, which would have had devastating consequences for all members of society. Thus, legal codes such as the Hammurabi codes, the Talmudic laws of the Israelites, the laws of Manu of India, the Confucianist codes of China, and the Roman imperial laws benefitted the peasants by maintaining social order, which made possible greater agricultural production.

Obviously, both of these perspectives provide useful insights into the role of law in agricultural states. Codified legal systems were developed by ruling elites, but they also functioned to control crime and institute political order.

MEDIATION AND SELF-HELP

Despite the emergence of codified systems, the practice of mediation and self-help in the redress of criminal offenses did not completely disappear. Rolando Tamayo demonstrated, for example, that these practices continued centuries after the development of the Greek state (Claessen et al., 1985). In addition, oaths, oracles, and ordeals remained as methods for determining legal decisions in many agricultural civilizations.

A Case Study: Law in China   The legal system of China evolved through various dynasties, culminating in the complex legal codes of the Han dynasty (206 B.C.–A.D. 220). Chinese criminal codes specified punishments for each offense, ranging from blows with a cane to execution by strangulation, decapitation, or even by slow slicing. Punishments also included hard labor and exile. Chinese civil law included rules on agricultural property, family, and inheritance.

Decisions involving civil law frequently were left to arbitration between the disputants in the local community. In this sense, many legal decisions depended on self-regulation of small groups. Use of written laws and the court system was generally restricted to cases that affected society as a whole. County magistrates familiar with the legal codes administered the law and recorded the decisions, which served as precedents for future cases.

A hierarchy of judicial bodies from the county magistrates to the imperial court served as courts of appeal for serious cases. Despite the existence of a highly formalized court system, however, most scholars concur that Chinese law was weak. Because local magistrates had hundreds of thousands of people under their jurisdiction and the police force was weak, law enforcement was ineffective at the local level. Basic law enforcement relied instead on informal processes and sanctions administered by community leaders (Clayre, 1985).

Warfare

Conflict theories view warfare as an integral aspect of agricultural state development. According to this view, the state emerged as a result of conflict and competition among groups that eventually led to the domination of a ruling group. Thus, warfare and conquest were instrumental in the rise of these state societies. Other theorists, who do not emphasize the role of warfare in their models of state development, agree that with the emergence of state societies warfare increased in scale and became much more organized. As governing elites accumulated more wealth and power, warfare became one of the major means of increasing their surpluses. Archaeologist Gordon Childe (1950), a conflict theorist, maintained that the ruling class in agricultural societies turned its energies from the conquest of nature to the conquest of people.

One cross-cultural study of external warfare found that the capacity for organized warfare is much greater in agricultural state societies than in band and tribal societies (Otterbein, 1970). State societies have a centralized political and military leadership as well as professional armies and military training. In addition, surpluses of foodstuffs and luxury items frequently attract outside invaders, particularly nomadic pastoralists. Keith Otterbein (1970) concluded that the primary motivation for warfare in state systems was to gain political control over other people. In the feudal societies of western Europe and Japan, professional classes of knights and samurai protected the interests and resources of nobles. In addition, these warrior classes were used to wage offensive warfare against neighboring estates to increase landholdings and the supply of manpower.

CRITICAL PERSPECTIVES

Aztec Warfare: A Puzzling Case

One case of offensive warfare that has generated controversy involves the Aztecs of Mesoamerica. Aztec warfare was directed toward controlling regions for economic tribute, but more important was capturing victims for human sacrifice. Scholars estimate that at the peak of the Aztec civilization (about A.D. 1490), the Aztecs were sacrificing thousands of people annually. Victims were led up the steps of a flat-topped pyramid, where four priests awaited them. The priests seized the victims, held them down, and cut open their chests with an obsidian knife. They then pulled out the victim's heart and hurled the body back down the steps (Harris, 1977; Berdan, 1982). Human sacrifices were daily events at small chapel centers in the Aztec region. To commemorate special events, thousands of people were sacrificed over several days in the large religious centers.

The traditional explanation for this practice involved the Aztec religious cosmology. The Aztecs believed that they were the "chosen people" who had to sacrifice individuals during certain dangerous times to keep the universe in equilibrium—more specifically, to keep the sun in the sky. However, some anthropologists, including Michael Harner (1977), have offered an alternative hypothesis based on ecological factors. These anthropologists question the religious motivation for such practices. Other state religions have driven societies to holy wars, but the Aztec warfare to gain sacrificial victims was unique. Although the pattern of human sacrifice has been associated with earlier Mesoamerican societies such as the Olmec, Maya, and Toltec, the Aztecs took this pattern to the extreme.

Harner suggested that because there were no major animal resources such as cattle, pigs, or sheep to supply meat, fats and proteins were scarce in Mesoamerica. The Mesoamericans ate maize, beans, and squash, which provided some of the essential amino acids, in combination with some dogs, turkeys, ducks, deer, rabbits, insects, and fish. But Harner noted that with a steadily growing population, approaching 25 million people, the Mexican Valley region experienced scarcities of fats and proteins. Harner hypothesized that some of the population consumed the bodies of their sacrificial victims to supplement their nutritional requirements.

In contrast, Francis Berdan (1982), a specialist on Aztec society, suggested that human sacrifice was essentially a terroristic device used to sanction and enforce the legitimacy of government power. Berdan emphasized that anyone could become a victim, and enemies were often invited to watch the sacrifices. This in itself helped extend Aztec political power and hegemony over various regions of Mesoamerica. On the other hand, Marvin Harris (1977), a proponent of the protein-shortage hypothesis, noted that although many other agricultural states had the same types of political problems, none of them resorted to widespread, formalized human sacrifice.

Many fundamental questions about Aztec sacrifices remain unanswered.

Points to Ponder

1. Which hypotheses do you find most convincing?

2. Is any one of them totally satisfactory?

3. What other types of evidence should anthropologists pursue to resolve these questions?

4. To what extent can we hope to understand behaviors that occurred in past societies with no written records and with norms that diverge from our own?

Religion

As state societies emerged, cultural elements such as political power, authority, and religion became much more closely intertwined. The religious traditions that developed in most of the agricultural states are referred to as **ecclesiastical religions,** in which there is no separation between state and religious authority. Generally, all people in the political jurisdiction are required to belong to the religion, and there is little toleration for other belief systems.

ECCLESIASTICAL RELIGIONS

Major ecclesiastical religious traditions emerged in agricultural civilizations around the world. Mesopotamia, Egypt, China, Greece, Rome, Mesoamerica, and South America developed some of the earliest ecclesiastical religions. These religious traditions were limited to the specific territory of these societies and were intimately tied to their particular state organization. For example, the Mesopotamian, Egyptian, Confucian (Chinese), Greek, Roman, Mayan, Aztec, and Incan religious traditions integrated both political and religious functions for their own people. State officials were often the priests who managed the rituals and maintained the textual traditions for these people.

UNIVERSALISTIC RELIGIONS

Other religious traditions that developed in early agricultural societies became **universalistic religions,** consisting of spiritual messages that apply to all of humanity rather than to just their own cultural heritage. There are two major branches of universalistic religions. One emerged in the Near East and led to the formation of the historically related religions of Judaism, Christianity, and Islam. The other developed in southern Asia and resulted in Hinduism and Buddhism.

These universalistic religious traditions are known as the great religious traditions. Although they began as universalistic traditions, in many cases they evolved into ecclesiastical religions identified with specific political regions. For example, many European nations established particular Christian denominations as state religions.

DIVINE RULERS, PRIESTS, AND RELIGIOUS TEXTS

Most of the early ecclesiastical religions taught that rulers have divine authority. For example, the rulers of Mesopotamia and the pharaohs of Egypt were believed to be divine rulers upholding the moral and spiritual universe. Various Greek and Roman rulers attempted to have themselves deified during different historical periods. In India and Southeast Asia, political rulers known as *rajahs* were thought to have a semidivine status that was an aspect of their religious traditions.

Ecclesiastical religious traditions are based on written texts interpreted by professionally trained, full-time priests, who became the official custodians of the religious cosmologies and had official roles in the political hierarchy. They presided over state-organized rituals called **rites of legitimation,** which reinforced the divine authority of the ruler. In these rituals, the priests led prayers, chants, and hymns addressed to the kings and the various deities (Parrinder, 1983). As in chiefdom societies, religion sanctified and legitimized the authority of political leaders.

One of the major functions of the priests was to standardize religious beliefs and practices for the society. Individualistic religious practices and beliefs were viewed as threatening to state authorities. For example, among the Maya, the shamanistic practice of taking hallucinogens to control spirits was perceived by state authorities as too individualistic. As the ecclesiastical religion developed, only the Mayan priests were allowed to take mind-altering drugs. Priests managed the use of these hallucinogens on behalf of state-organized ritual activities (Dobkin de Rios, 1984).

The Collapse of State Societies

Perhaps no aspect of agricultural states is more intriguing than the question of why they ceased to function. As discussed in the chapter opening, no agricultural states exist today: lost ruins, palaces hidden in tropical forests, and temples buried beneath shifting sand captivate the attention of archaeologists and the public alike. These images grip our attention all the more because of the lusterless prospect that the downfall of these ancient societies

CRITICAL PERSPECTIVES

The Downfall of the Moche

By 200 B.C. a number of small state-level societies had emerged in northwestern South America in what is today the coast and hinterland of Peru. The best-known of these is that of the Moche, which was centered in the Moche and nearby Chicama valleys. At its peak the state controlled satellite communities in a number of neighboring valleys, eventually extending its influence hundreds of miles to the north and south (Donnan & McClelland, 1979).

The archaeological record provides a rich testament to the wealth and power of the Moche. Ceremonial complexes, such as those near the modern city of Trujillo, include adobe brick temple platforms, pyramids, and associated room complexes that may have served as palaces. In 1987 the riches found in an undisturbed tomb of a Moche warrior-priest near the modern village of Sipán led some to dub the discovery "a

King Tut of the New World." Although the Moche possessed no writing system, the interpretation of the Sipán tomb and other Moche sites is aided by exquisite depictions of Moche life on pottery vessels.

The Moche kingdom flourished for almost 800 years. However, by 600 A.D. the classic Moche ceremonial centers were abandoned, and power shifted to other areas. Archaeological excavations and recent studies of photographs taken by the space shuttle Challenger have provided insights into what may have caused this collapse (Moseley & Richardson, 1992). Excavations during the 1970s provided part of the answer to the Moche mystery. Prior to that time, Moche ceremonial structures were known but no one had found any settlements, leading archaeologists to believe that the populations that had built the monumental structures had lived

elsewhere. Deep excavations at Moche sites during 1972, however, revealed residences, civic buildings, and high-status cemeteries buried under almost 30 feet of sand—evidence that the Moche centers had been destroyed at their peak of prosperity.

Interpretations of the archaeological findings have been aided by recent insights into the environmental conditions that may have ravaged the Moche sites and buried them with sand. Between A.D. 500 and 600 the Moche region experienced devastating rainfall and large-scale flooding characteristic of a climatic phenomenon today known as El Niño. During normal climatic conditions a cold stream of water known as the Humboldt or Peru current flows through the Pacific Ocean along the west coast of South America. This cold water limits rainfall along the coast, producing the New World's

offers insight into the limitations of our own civilization. As Joseph Tainter (1990: 2) notes: "Whether or not collapse was the most outstanding event of ancient history, few would care for it to become the most significant event of the present era."

In looking at their demise, it is important to note that many early agricultural states were exceedingly successful. They flourished in many different world areas for hundreds of years. The ancient Egyptian Old Kingdom, which spanned a period of almost 1,000 years, is particularly notable, but many lasted longer than the 200-odd years the United States has been in existence. The apparent success of these states makes the reasons for their

collapse all the more enigmatic: What accounts for the loss of centralized authority; the decline in stratification and social differentiation; the interruption of trade; and the fragmentation of large political units that seem to document the end of many different civilizations? These features extend beyond the end of specific governments or political systems; rather, they seem to reflect the breakdown of entire cultural systems.

REASONS FOR COLLAPSE

In examining the downfall of complex societies, writers have posited many different theories. Among driest desert in northern Chile and Peru. During an El Niño event, which may last 18 months, this pattern suddenly changes, with disastrous consequences. Warm water flows along the coast and the normally arid coastland is beset with torrential rains and flooding, while severe droughts plague the usually wetter highlands of Peru and Bolivia. Archaeological evidence indicates that flood waters possibly from one or more El Niño events destroyed Moche settlements and stripped as much as 15 feet from some sites. Although the Moche survived the flooding, by A.D. 600 sand dunes engulfed irrigation canals, fields, and architecture.

Recent studies of photographs taken by the space shuttle Challenger in 1983 and earlier satellite photos have helped explain the dune encroachment (Moseley & Richardson, 1992). The high-altitude photographs of the Peruvian coast link the formation of new beach ridges and dune systems to earthquakes and El Niño. The Challenger photographs indicate that a new beach ridge formed between 1970 and 1975. The ridge's appearance was linked to the Rio Santa earthquake of 1970, which caused massive landslides that dumped huge amounts of earth into the dry river valleys. The torrential rains of the El Niño event of 1972–1973 carried this debris into the ocean, where strong currents deposited it in a new beach ridge. The ridge, in turn, provided the sand for the dunes that swept inland.

The available evidence seems to support the theory that El Niño events, possibly exacerbated by earthquakes, may have contributed to the downfall of the Moche state. Additional evidence suggests that there may have been periods of extreme drought prior to A.D. 600. The combination of these environmental disasters beyond human control could have seriously undermined the state's ability to produce the agricultural surplus it needed to survive. In the absence of any means of overcoming these problems, the downfall of the Moche state may have been inevitable.

Points to Ponder

1. What other evidence could be used to evaluate this interpretation of the collapse of the Moche state?

2. Even if excellent evidence for environmental disasters is uncovered, can other reasons for the collapse of the Moche be ruled out?

3. Is it likely that it will be possible to create general models that will explain the collapse of societies in all cultural and environmental settings?

4. Do you think that study of ancient states offers any insights into problems facing modern societies?

---

the earliest were notions that collapse was somehow an innate, inevitable aspect of society, to be likened to the aging of a biological organism. Plato, for example, wrote that "since all created things must decay, even a social order . . . cannot last forever, but will decline" (quoted in Tainter, 1990: 74). Although romantically appealing, such interpretations lack explanatory value and cannot be evaluated by empirical observation.

More recent scholars have sought a more precise understanding of the factors that contributed to collapse. Many theories have focused on the depletion of key resources as a result of human mismanagement or climatic change. In an agricultural state,

conditions that interfered with or destroyed the society's ability to produce agriculture surplus would have had serious consequences. If the society was unable to overcome this depletion, collapse would result. Reasons such as this have been posited as contributing to the collapse of areas often included in discussions of the origins of complex societies, such as Mesopotamia (Adams, 1981), Egypt (Butzer, 1984), and Mesoamerica (Haas, 1982). The role of environmental degradation in the collapse of one society is examined in more detail in the box entitled "The Downfall of the Moche."

In some cases, researchers have suggested that resource depletion may be the result of sudden catastrophic events involving earthquakes, volcanic eruptions, or floods, which have an impact on agricultural lands as well as other resources. One of the most well-known theories of this kind links the destruction of Minoan civilization in the Mediterranean to the eruption of the Santorini volcano on the island of Thera (Marinatos, 1939).

Other theories have suggested that conditions within societies have led to collapse. Many of these stress the tension or conflict resulting from social stratification. For example, mismanagement, excessive taxes, demands for food and labor, or other forms of exploitation by a ruling class are seen as instigating revolts or uprisings by the disaffected peasant class. Without the support of the peasants the political system cannot function and the state collapses (Guha, 1981; Lowe, 1985; Yoffe, 1979).

Alternatively, some researchers have viewed collapse as the result of the societies' failure to respond to changing conditions. For example, Elman Service (1960: 97) argued: "The more specialized and adapted a form in a given evolutionary stage, the smaller its potential for passing to the next stage." Underlying this interpretation is the assumption that successful adaptation to a particular environmental or cultural setting renders a society inflexible and unable to adapt to changing conditions. In this setting less complex societies with greater flexibility overthrew older states.

EVALUATING THEORIES

Anthropologist Joseph Tainter notes in a survey that most of the models that have been presented focus on specific case studies, not on the understanding of collapse as a general phenomenon. He notes that most researchers assume that the decline in complexity associated with collapse is a catastrophe: "An end to the artistic and literary features of civilization, and the umbrella of service and protection that an administration provides, are seen as fearful events, truly paradise lost" (Tainter, 1990: 197). Tainter argues that in reality collapse instead represents a logical choice in the face of declining returns. When people's investment in complexity fails to produce benefits, they opt for disintegration.

Theories concerning the collapse of states can be evaluated in light of ethnographic, historical, and archaeological evidence. Upon surveying information from different states, it appears that reasons for collapse are exceedingly complex; the specific manifestation varies in individual settings—just as the specific features that define states differ. Adequate appraisal is dependent on the existence of a great deal of information about the society under study, including its technological capabilities, information on population, agricultural yields, and climatic conditions in the region. The difficulty involved in assessing competing models is perhaps best illustrated by the fact that very different theories have often been used to explain the decline of the same society.

 # SUMMARY

The transition from hunting and gathering to food production is known as the Neolithic. The Neolithic involved the domestication of plants and animals, which provided a more reliable food supply and thus allowed for population growth, the emergence of cities, the specialization of labor, technological complexity, and many other features that are characteristic of agricultural states.

States are societies that have bureaucratic organizations, or governments. State societies emerged with the development of intensive agriculture.

The demographic conditions of agricultural civilizations included a rise in mortality rates along with increases in fertility rates. Agricultural states often encouraged high fertility rates to raise population levels for political purposes. The technological developments associated with agricultural societies represented dramatic innovations in metallurgy, shipbuilding, papermaking, printing, and many scientific ideas.

The political economy of agricultural states varied from region to region. In some areas, large-scale, centralized empires emerged, such as in China and Egypt. In other areas, smaller-scale states developed that did not have complete political control over outlying regions. After the fall of some centralized states in Europe and Japan, a type of decentralized political economy known as feudalism developed.

Different forms of property relations developed, depending on whether an agricultural state was centralized or feudal. In the centralized states, property was owned and administered by the government, whereas in feudal regimes lords and nobles owned their estates. Long-distance trade and government-regulated monetary-exchange systems developed in agricultural societies. Within the context of long-distance trade and monetary exchange, merchants and markets emerged.

The social organization of agricultural states consisted of extended families and other descent groups, including lineages, clans, and kindreds. Marriages in agricultural societies were arranged by parents and based on political and economic considerations. In contrast to prestate societies, polygyny and bridewealth were not widespread among agricultural state societies. Instead, monogamy and dowry exchanges were the major patterns. Divorce was infrequent.

Gender relations became more patriarchal in agricultural societies, possibly reflecting the reduced participation of females in agricultural labor. Females were largely confined to the domestic sphere, and various patterns of female seclusion developed.

Social stratification in agricultural societies was based on class, caste, slavery, and racial and ethnic stratification. Some of these societies have been described as closed societies, with little opportunity for social mobility. Formalized legal systems developed, codifying laws administered by courts and government authorities. However, self-help and mediation were also used to resolve disputes.

Ecclesiastical religions developed in agricultural societies, with full-time priests, religious texts, and concepts of divine rulers associated with particular state societies. Some universalistic religious traditions developed in the Near East and Asia. The art and architecture of the agricultural societies included monuments such as pyramids.

One of the most intriguing questions concerning early agricultural states is the reason why they collapsed. Many of these complex societies functioned effectively for hundreds, even thousands, of years, yet all ended in fragmentation and declining complexity. Researchers have posited many different theories concerning the collapse of states, some more plausible than others. A survey of different models underscores the variation present in different societies and the difficulty in evaluating different theories of collapse.

STUDY QUESTIONS

1. How do agricultural states differ demographically from small-scale societies such as bands, tribes, and chiefdoms?

2. Discuss some of the technological innovations developed in agricultural states.

3. How do segmentary states and theater states differ from the Aztec, Roman, and Chinese empires?

4. How do property rights differ in agricultural states from those in forager and tribal societies?

5. What are some of the advantages of having an extended family organization in an agricultural state, as opposed to an autonomous nuclear family?

6. Are marriage patterns and social ties in agricultural states independent of economic and political considerations? If so, why? If not, what are some of the economic and political implications of marriage patterns and other social ties?

7. Discuss the relationships among gender, subsistence, and status in agricultural states. How does the picture that emerges differ from the one for any of the following groups: (1) foragers, (2) tribes, or (3) chiefdoms?

8. According to Morton Fried, codified laws reinforce a system of inequity by keeping peasants subordinate while allowing those in power to have access to scarce resources. Elman Service provides a different perspective. What is Service's perspective?

9. How does religion interact with state power and bureaucratic authority in agricultural civilizations? Give examples of the relationship between the state and religion in these agricultural societies.

10. What are some of the theories developed to explain the collapse of agricultural states? Are some more plausible than others? What type of evidence is needed to explain the collapse of a state society?

KEY TERMS

caste	ecclesiastical religions	peasants
closed societies	ethnicity	rites of legitimation
command economy	feudalism	universalistic religions
dowry	intensive agriculture	

INTERNET EXERCISES

1. While visiting the website **http://www.chass.utoronto.ca:8080/~reak/hist/earlyag.htm,** determine the meaning of the phrase "agricultural frontier." What is it? What is the basic industry of all modern countries? Why? What is the French "Physiocrats" view of all of this? Why did Thomas Jefferson equate farming with independence?

2. Look at the website **http://www.friesian.com/caste.htm.** While reviewing the introductory chart, examine the section on the "twice born." Who are the twice born? What is the meaning of the term *twice born?* How does skin color enter into Hindu caste structure? How does the caste system vary from open slavery?

SUGGESTED READINGS

ADAMS, ROBERT MCC. 1966. *The Evolution of Urban Society: Early Mesopotamia and Prehispanic Mexico.* Chicago: Aldine. A classic discussion by an archaeologist comparing Southwest Asian and American agricultural societies.

FAGAN, BRIAN. 1999. *Floods, Famines and Emperors: El Niño and the Fate of Civilizations.* New York: Basic Books. A new book by a well-known archaeologist who looks at the powerful effects of El Niño, a climatological pattern that had devastating effects on many of the ancient agricultural civilizations such as those in Egypt, India, and Peru.

GOODY, JACK. 1971. *Technology, Tradition and the State in Africa.* London: Oxford University Press. A cross-cultural comparison of agricultural states in Africa and other regions. This work contains many insightful, thought-provoking hypotheses regarding state development in different societies.

SERVICE, ELMAN. 1975. *Origins of the State and Civilization: The Process of Cultural Evolution.* New York: Norton. A good introduction to the various theories of state formation.

TAINTER, JOSEPH A. 1990. *The Collapse of Complex Societies.* New York: Cambridge University Press. A seminal attempt to provide a general model of collapse in complex societies. Although Tainter addressed mainly his own theoretical position, the volume provides an excellent survey and critique of previous work on the subject.

12

Industrial
States

The Commercial, Scientific, and Industrial Revolution
Modernization

Environment and Energy Use

Demographic Change
The Demographic Transition / Urbanization

Technology and Economic Change
Technology and Work / The Division of Labor / Economic Exchange / Perspectives on Market Economies / The Evolution of Economic Organizations

Social Structure
Kinship / Family / Marriage / Gender / Age

Social Stratification
The British Class System / Class in the United States / Class in Japan and the Former Soviet Union / Ethnic and Racial Stratification

Political Organization
Political Organization in Socialist States / Industrialism and State Bureaucracy

Law
Japanese Law

Warfare and Industrial Technology

Religion
Religion in Socialist States / Religion in Japan

CHAPTER QUESTIONS

- What were some of the historical changes that resulted in the industrial revolution?

- What are some of the energy use patterns and technological changes associated with industrial societies?

- What are the characteristics of the economy in industrial societies?

- How did the industrial revolution influence the status and role of family, gender, and age?

- Why are industrial societies considered to be more "open" in social stratification than preindustrial societies?

- What are the characteristics of politics, law, and warfare in industrial societies?

- What are the consequences of industrialization for religion in industrial societies?

T
HE INDUSTRIAL REVOLUTION IS THE TERM USED to describe the broad changes that occurred during the latter part of the eighteenth century in Europe. The roots of these dramatic changes in the structure and organization of society were there much earlier, however. This chapter considers the causes of the industrial revolution and its consequences for the states in which it occurred. This is an extremely important topic, because it emphasizes how anthropologists interpret and explain the development of the industrial revolution in Europe, rather than in other regions of the world. Traditionally, most ethnologists did research on preindustrial societies, which we covered in Chapters 8 through 11. However, many ethnologists have turned their attention to doing ethnography within the many industrial regions of the world including Europe, Russia, the United States, Canada, Australia, and Japan. These ethnologists have to be highly interdisciplinary drawing on the work of historians, economists, political scientists, and sociologists. The chapter uses much of the research of these other disciplines, as well as the studies of ethnologists.

An **industrial society** uses sophisticated technology based on machinery powered by advanced fuels to produce material goods. A primary feature of industrial societies in comparison with preindustrial societies is that most productive labor involves factory and office work rather than agricultural or foraging activities. This pattern has produced new forms of economic organization and social-class arrangements. In terms of political organization, industrial societies became the first well-developed

nation-states, political communities that have clearly defined territorial borders dividing them from one another. All modern industrial nation-states exercise extensive political authority over many aspects of the lives of their citizenry through the application of formalized laws and a centralized government.

The Commercial, Scientific, and Industrial Revolution

As seen in earlier chapters, especially Chapter 3, anthropologists reject the notion that there is a superior race of people such as the so-called Aryans, who were responsible for the development of civilizations. The so-called scientific racists that hold these views believe that Europeans are the descendants of this super race, that they are more intelligent, and, subsequently, that they were the ones who were responsible for the emergence of the industrial revolution in Europe. These racists believe that other races of people were incapable of developing the industrial revolution, and that is the reason that Europe was the center of the rise of industrial society. Again, anthropologists have refuted the basis of these racist arguments through systematic biological, archaeological, and cultural research throughout the world. However, historical research does indicate that Europe was the area that developed the industrial revolution. Anthropologists have attempted to address the question as to why Europe was the center of the industrial revolution by drawing on a wide range of historical sources from many regions of the world. A global perspective is the only way of trying to answer this question. Anthropologists such as Jack Goody (1996) and Eric Wolf (1997) have adopted this global perspective and have examined the interrelationships between the non-European world with Europe in order to help provide answers to this question.

A major factor leading to the emergence of industrial states in European society was the increased contact among different societies, primarily through trade. Although, as discussed in the last chapter, long-distance trade was present in agricultural states, the major regions of the world were relatively isolated from one another. Trade was conducted in Asia, the Near East, Europe, Africa, and internally within the Americas before A.D. 1500, but the difficulties of transportation and communication inhibited the spread of ideas, values, and technology among these regions. Although Europeans had contact with non-Europeans through religious wars such as the Crusades and the travels of adventurers such as Marco Polo, they did not engage in systematic relations with non-Europeans until after the year 1500.

The upper class and royalty of agricultural European society encouraged long-distance trade as a means of accumulating wealth. Their principal motivation was to build a self-sufficient economy as a basis for extending their centralized government. This type of economic system is often referred to as mercantilism. **Mercantilism** is a system in which the government regulates the economy of a state to ensure economic growth, a positive balance of trade, and the accumulation of gold and silver. One key mercantilist strategy was for the government to grant monopolies to trading companies so that these companies could accumulate wealth for the home country. The European upper classes were also attempting to compete with the Islamic and Asian trade that predominated in the East. These elites formed an alliance with merchants to support their endeavors (Wolf, 1997). Thus, for example, during the fifteenth and sixteenth centuries, the rulers of Spain and Portugal sponsored private traders who explored the world to search for wealth. These expeditions eventually established ports of trade in Africa, the Americas, and Asia.

Eventually European countries such as the Netherlands, Great Britain, France, and Russia became mercantile competitors with Spain and Portugal. They formed private trading companies, such as the British East India Company, that were subsidized by the government. These companies were given special rights to engage in trade in specific regions. In turn, they were expected to find both sources of wealth and luxury goods that could be consumed by the ruling classes.

One result of this mercantilist trade was the beginning of global unity (Chirot, 1986, Wolf, 1997). European explorers visited every part of the globe. An enormous diffusion of plants, animals, humans, technology, and ideas took place among Europe, America, and the rest of the world. Cultures from every region of the world began to confront each other. These encounters led to new patterns of trade, political developments, and the transmission of beliefs, ideas, and practices. European traders backed by military force began to compete with other traders from the Middle East and Asia. Soon, through the use of military force, European trade came to displace the Asian and Islamic trading empires. As economic wealth began to amass in Europe, through the accumulation of gold, silver, and other commodities from the Americas, Asia, Africa, and the Middle East, the political center of power also swung to Europe. These economic and political changes were accompanied by major transformations in non-Western societies. These changes in non-Western societies will be discussed in later chapters.

The global diffusion of philosophical and practical knowledge provided the basis for the scientific revolution in the West. Ideas and technology that were developed in the civilizations of China, India, the Middle East, Africa, and the Americas provided the stimulus for the emergence of the scientific enterprise in Europe. Eventually, scientific methods based on deductive and inductive logic (see Chapter 1) were allied with practical economic interests that help provide the basis for the industrial revolution in Europe. But, again, many of the ideas and technological developments that gave rise to the industrial revolution in Europe had emerged earlier in agricultural civilizations in other regions of the world. The scientific revolution would not have developed in Europe without the knowledge of scientific and mathematical concepts previously developed in India, the Middle East, and Asia. The notion that there was a unique European miracle that was associated with the so-called White Race is a fallacy. The idea that Europeans were superior geniuses that enabled them to develop the industrial civilization is also a fallacy. Without the diffusion of knowledge and technologies from other regions of the world, Europe would not have been able to develop the industrial revolution. Slowly and gradually, over a period of some 400 years or so, the combination of scientific and commercial alliances in Europe produced dramatic consequences that have transformed economic, social, and political structures through the process of **industrialization,** the adoption of a mechanized

means of production to transform raw materials into manufactured goods.

MODERNIZATION

The overall consequences of the industrial revolution are often referred to as **modernization,** the economic, social, political, and religious changes related to modern industrial and technological change. Modernization was not an overnight occurrence. It took more than 400 years, from 1600 on, to develop in the West, and it remains an ongoing process. It depended on the commercial transformations brought about through years of mercantilism that led to the accumulation of capital for investment and the gradual diffusion of practical knowledge and scientific methods that engendered technological innovations.

Environment and Energy Use

In earlier chapters, we saw how the availability of resources affects levels of political and economic development. States and chiefdoms emerged in areas with abundant resources, whereas other environments could support only bands and tribes. Environmental conditions also had an influence on the early phases of industrialization. Industrial societies still depended heavily on agricultural production to meet basic food requirements, but through industrialization, agricultural production itself was transformed. The major natural-resource requirements for industrial societies are based on harnessing new sources of energy, especially fossil-fuel energy.

In Chapter 6 we discussed Leslie White's attempt to explain sociocultural evolution in terms of energy use. He suggested that sociocultural evolution progressed in relationship to the harnessing of energy. Anthropologist John Bodley (1985) attempted to quantify White's ideas. He suggested that sociocultural systems can be divided into high-energy cultures and low-energy cultures, and that these categories have implications for the evolution of society. For example, before the industrial revolution, no states used more than 26,000 kilocalories per capita daily, and tribal hunters and farmers used between 4,000 and 12,000. These societies are classified as low-energy cultures. In contrast, early

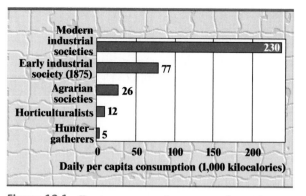

Figure 12.1   Energy consumption among the various types of societies. Note the dramatic increase in consumption in modern industrial societies.

Source: Adapted from Earl Cook, "The Flow of Energy in an Industrial Society," *Scientific American* 224(3) (1971): 136. By permission of the artist, Bunji Tagana.

industrial societies using fossil fuels almost tripled their consumption of energy to 70,000 kilocalories. Later phases of industrialization in high-energy cultures such as the United States experienced a quadrupling of energy consumption. Energy use and expenditure have risen dramatically in all industrial societies (see Figure 12.1).

In the low-energy, preindustrial societies, human and animal labor was the chief source of energy, supplemented by fire, wind, and sometimes waterpower. In contrast, in high-energy societies, fossil fuels such as coal, natural gas, and petroleum became the primary energy sources. During the early phases of the industrial revolution, societies in Europe and America relied on fossil fuels found in their own territories, but they eventually began to exploit resources from other regions. In later chapters we will examine the consequences of these patterns of high energy use on the different environments of the world.

Demographic Change

One major consequence of the early phases of the industrial revolution was a dramatic increase in population. The major reasons for this were technological developments in agriculture and transportation that enabled farmers to grow more food

and transport it to areas with food scarcities. In addition, scientific advances led to the control of some infectious diseases, such as the bubonic plague, diphtheria, typhus, and cholera, that had kept death rates high in preindustrial societies. As death rates declined, birthrates remained high. The combination of lower death rates with high birthrates produced major population increases of about 3 percent annually. Europe's population grew from about 140 million in 1750 to 463 million in 1914 (Stavrianos, 1995).

THE DEMOGRAPHIC TRANSITION

During later phases of industrialization (especially since the 1960s), population growth began to decline in societies like England, Western Europe, the United States, and Japan (Population Reference Bureau, 1986). Demographers refer to this change as the **demographic transition,** in which birthrates and death rates decline. In contrast to preindustrial societies, in which high birthrates were perceived as beneficial, many people in industrial societies no longer see large families as a benefit. One reason for this view is the higher costs of rearing children in industrial societies. In addition, social factors such as changing gender relations—more women in the work force and the reduction in family size—have contributed to lower fertility rates. (These social factors are discussed later in this chapter.) Increased knowledge of, and access to, contraceptives helped people to control family size.

URBANIZATION

Population increases, coupled with the movement of workers from farms to factories, resulted in the unprecedented growth of urban centers (see Table 12.1). During the nineteenth century, the populations of cities such as London, Paris, and Chicago soared into the millions. By 1930, one-fifth of all humanity, or approximately 415 million people, lived in urban areas (Mumford, 1961; Stavrianos, 1995). One of the major factors causing rapid urban growth was the increasing need for labor in the machine-based factory system. Factory towns like Manchester, England, grew into large industrial centers connected to financial and communications districts.

innovations ranging from automobiles to electronics to computers have continued to transform industrial societies. These technologies have not only made communication and transportation more efficient but have also contributed to a vast international global economic network in which all societies can interact.

TECHNOLOGY AND WORK

The technological revolution transformed basic work conditions. The factory system imposed a new work pace and led to a new form of discipline for laborers. Factory and mine workers were organized around the machine's schedule, and work became increasingly time-oriented. Most work in the early factories was highly routinized and repetitious.

Preindustrial workers had some control over the quantity and quality of their products and the pace of their labor, but early industrial workers had little control over these matters. Karl Marx, a major critic of industrial capitalism, saw that industrial workers were estranged and alienated from their work conditions and that they viewed their labor as meaningless and beyond their control.

THE DIVISION OF LABOR

The division of labor in industrial economies is much more complex than it is in preindustrial economies. Industrial economies have three identifiable sectors, which correspond to the division of labor. The **primary sector** represents the part of the industrial economy devoted to the extraction of raw materials and energy. This includes agriculture, lumber, fishing, and mining. The **secondary sector** includes the factories that take the raw materials and process them for consumption. The **tertiary sector,** sometimes referred to as the *service sector,* includes the financial and banking indus-

In industrial societies such as Japan, most couples prefer small families.

Technology and Economic Change

Industrialization was fueled by a series of technological innovations that occurred after the middle of the eighteenth century. The major change was a movement from human and animal labor to mechanical, or machine, labor. More recently, through science, engineering, and commerce, technological

Table 12.1	Population in Selected Industrial Cities	
City	1995 (thousands)	2015 (projected) density
Tokyo	26,959	28,887
New York	16,332	17,602
Los Angeles	12,410	14,217

Source: The World Almanac and Book of Facts. Mawah, NJ: World Almanac Books, 1999, p. 862.

tries and other industries such as automobile repair, communications, health care, computer services, government, and education.

In the first phases of industrialization, most of the labor force was engaged in the primary sector, extracting raw materials for industrial production. Further mechanization of industry led to an increase of the labor force in the secondary, or manufacturing, sector. These workers are the manual, or "blue-collar," workers. Finally, in the advanced phases of industrialization, an increasing percentage of the labor force has become located in the various service industries.

Currently, in the most advanced industrial societies such as the United States, the United Kingdom, Japan, Germany, Canada, and Australia the tertiary sector is the largest and most rapidly expanding component of the economy. Some sociologists refer to these societies as *postindustrial* societies, because more people are employed in service and technical occupations than in manufacturing. Information is the key component of a postindustrial economy, since people must acquire a great deal of technical knowledge to function effectively, and educational requirements for many jobs have increased substantially. To meet the demands of a postindustrial economy, an increasing percentage of the population attends college (and graduate and professional schools), and computer

skills have been integrated into the educational curriculum. With their capacity to process and manipulate vast amounts of data, computers have become essential in these societies.

ECONOMIC EXCHANGE

Like other types of societies, industrial states engage in reciprocal and redistributional economic exchanges. Reciprocal exchanges, such as Christmas gifts and gifts of funds for college tuition, frequently occur within the family. The graduated income tax in U.S. society represents one form of redistributional exchange—income is collected from some people and flows back to society. Taxes also represent a form of tributary economic exchange, which is characteristic of agricultural states.

Market Economies   In addition to these activities, industrial states developed a new pattern of exchange based on a *market economy*. A **market economy** is a pattern of economic exchange based on the value of goods and services determined by the supply and demand of these items. The evolution of the market economy, linked with industrial technological developments, radically changed the way goods and services were produced and exchanged in industrial societies. Goods and services are assigned monetary value and are bought and

The New York Stock Exchange represents the peak development of a market-driven economy.

sold with general-purpose money. The prices of these goods and services depend on the supply and demand of the goods and services on the world market.

Moreover, in the market economy the basic factors of production—land, labor, and capital—are assigned monetary prices and are bought and sold freely in the marketplace. Thus, rather than kinship or prominent leaders, market forces determine the general process of economic exchange.

In agricultural societies, goods and services were bought and sold in regional or local markets. These markets, however, were not based on market exchange; instead, buyers and sellers met and haggled over the price of goods. This is a type of nonmarket price determination. In contrast, in industrial societies, buyers and sellers do not have to meet face to face. Buyers can compare prices from different sellers, and the prices themselves are established according to supply and demand. Impersonality and lack of haggling between buyer and seller are the general patterns in market exchanges.

PERSPECTIVES ON MARKET ECONOMIES

Market forces based on the supply and demand of land, labor, and capital began to drive economic production, exchange, and consumption in industrial societies. The market process, which determined the prices of these factors of production, exerted tremendous influence over all aspects of these industrializing societies. The new economic forces and processes were described by the "father of modern economics," Adam Smith. In his book *The Wealth of Nations* (1776/1937), Smith argued that both buyers and sellers would reap rewards from market exchange and competition, because prices would be lower for consumers and profits higher for sellers. The result would be increased prosperity for all segments of society. Smith viewed the market economy as a mechanism for promoting progress.

In contrast, 100 years later, Marx offered a gloomier picture of industrial societies. Marx focused on how the market economy determined the price and organization of human labor, bringing about misery for millions of people. Marx believed that industrial-capitalist societies must be transformed to a new form of socialist society in which the factors of production would not be driven by

the market but would be controlled by the state to ensure an even division of profits among all classes.

Eventually, both capitalist and socialist forms of industrial societies developed in different regions of the world. To highlight some of the variations of industrial societies, we next examine the development of capitalism and socialism in some of these regions.

Capitalism   As is evident from the previous discussion, the industrial revolution was intricately connected with the emergence of capitalism in Western societies. **Capitalism** is an economic system in which natural resources as well as the means of producing and distributing goods and services are privately owned. Capitalist societies share three basic ideals. First, the factors of production are privately owned. An emphasis on private property has become the standard incorporated into all economic, legal, and political documents of capitalist societies. Second, companies are free to maximize profits and accumulate as much capital as they can. Finally, free competition and consumer sovereignty are basic to all economic activities. Ideally, people are free to buy and sell at whatever prices they can to satisfy their own interests. Also, government regulation of economic affairs is usually discouraged.

Capitalism in the United States   Capitalism spread into North America following the settling of colonies by British and other European peoples. The English had incorporated major portions of North America as a colony during the mercantile period. But eventually the English colonists began to control their own economic and political destinies, which led to the American Revolution of the late eighteenth century. Following independence, capitalist economic development and industrialization proceeded rapidly in the United States. Bountiful natural resources provided the raw materials for factory production, and millions of immigrants arrived from Europe, providing a source of cheap labor for factories. The U.S. economy grew quickly, and by 1894 the nation had the world's fastest-growing economy.

Despite the ideals of pure capitalism, which discouraged government regulation of the economy, the U.S. government actively encouraged industrial economic expansion through state subsidies, protective tariffs, and other policies. For example, the government promoted the development of a nationwide railroad system by providing large financial incentives, rights to land, and subsidies to individual capitalists. In addition, free land was given to people who wanted to settle frontier regions through the Homestead Act of 1862.

By the late nineteenth century, rapid economic expansion had produced a new monied class that held a great proportion of assets. A relatively small number of people controlled a large number of industries and other commercial enterprises of finance and capital. The wealthiest 1 percent of the population owned about one-third of all capital assets (wealth in land or other private property). Economic expansion also spurred the growth of a large middle class that exerted a powerful influence on both the economic and political structure of U.S. society.

Capitalism in Japan Japan was an agricultural feudal society from the period of the first shogunate in the twelfth century until about 1870, after which it rapidly industrialized. Following a period of historical isolation from the West during the Tokugawa period (1600–1870), Japan was forced to open its doors to outside powers such as the United States. The Japanese recognized the technological advancements of the Western world, and, to avoid being colonized like other Asian countries, they modified their society to accommodate industrial capitalism. But the socioeconomic and political conditions that made possible rapid capitalist development existed before Japan's intensive contact with the West.

During the Tokugawa period, internal trade and entrepreneurial developments flourished in highly developed urban centers such as Tokyo and Kyoto. Moreover, Japan had a highly educated class of samurai who were in a position to bring about innovations in society (Befu, 1971).

Following the opening of Japan to the West, the Japanese abandoned the feudal system and centralized their government under the Meiji emperor. With help from Western advisers (1868–1911), the Meiji government introduced a mandatory education system and modern military technology. The government also took concrete steps to help introduce capitalism (Geertz, 1963b). It taxed the peasants to raise money for industrialization and subsidized certain entrepreneurial families, the *zaibatsu*,

who gained control of the major industrial technologies. Families such as the Mitsubishi family were encouraged to invest in needed industries to compete with Western interests. Thus, the government developed key industries in Japan by cooperating with private interests and families.

Socialism A different type of economic system developed in some industrial societies as a historical response to capitalism. **Socialism** is an economic system in which the state, ideally as the representative of the people, owns the basic means of production. Although individuals may own some consumer goods such as housing and automobiles, they are not allowed to own stock in corporations or wealth-generating property related to the production of capital goods. Socialism evolved as a response to the considerable economic inequalities that existed in capitalist societies. To create more economic equality and less exploitation of working people, socialist philosophers promoted ideals that contrast with those of capitalism. Socialist ideals maintain that meeting the population's basic needs takes precedence over the enrichment of a small number of people.

Socialism in the Former Soviet Union In contrast to Marx's predictions that socialist revolutions would occur in industrial societies, socialism initially developed in Russia, which was primarily agricultural and feudal. From about A.D. 1000, the basic form of land tenure in Russia was based on

Soviet factory workers in the 1930s were mobilized by the state to develop heavy industry.

APPLYING ANTHROPOLOGY

Studying Industrial Corporations

The image of cultural anthropologists is changing. The typical image of an ethnologist is of a person dressed in a safari jacket copying detailed notes from an informant in a tropical region of the world. However, another role for cultural anthropologists has developed recently. In attempting to cut costs and improve productivity and competitiveness, many American and multinational corporations have begun to hire ethnologists to do studies of the "natives" in the factory, or in middle and upper management. In the past, corporations usually hired efficiency experts such as industrial engineers and industrial psychologists to help design their policies and work systems. But those programs usually involved little input and feedback from the employees themselves. In many cases, the implementation of the policies resulted in inefficient and unproductive practices (Garza, 1991).

Ethnologists study corporate life through participant observation and in-depth interviews with employees. These studies focus on gathering information about the corporate culture: the corporate norms, values, and practices that can be described only through

these anthropological techniques. John Seely Brown, former director of Xerox Corporation's Palo Alto Research Center, has admitted that the ethnologist of corporate life can deliver dramatic improvements in productivity. He goes on to say that "companies have to go beyond industrial psychology and reengineer the business process. They have to work from the bottom up. And anthropology is the field most attuned to that" (Garza, 1991).

In the mid 1980s, Xerox set out to devise more efficient and less costly methods to train its service technicians. Julian Orr, an anthropologist, was hired to determine whether Xerox could do its training more productively. Orr used participant research methods, taking the service training and going out on jobs himself to discover factors that affected the job. In the field, Orr found that the repair work was not the main job. Instead, he discovered that most of the service calls stemmed from customers who did not know how to run the machines rather than from technical breakdowns. Thus, the most important part of the job involved communication skills. Orr reasoned that service

technicians ought to be trained as teachers who can explain the technicalities of the new machines to customers who are using them. Through participant-observation research methods, ethnologists such as Orr can suggest remedies for improving relationships between companies and their clients.

Ethnologists are also being hired to bring their understanding of different cultures and their specialized research techniques to bear on the problems of multinational corporations. One study by anthropologist Margo L. Smith (1986) observed fifteen multinational corporations based in Chicago to determine what types of employees were selected for overseas assignments in foreign cultural environments and what types of cross-cultural skills these employees needed. She found that very few of the companies recognized the need for cross-cultural training for employees to be sent overseas on short-term assignments. Companies usually provided more culture and language training for upper-management personnel who were going to be assigned for more lengthy periods. Smith advised that the

---

the *mir,* or peasant commune, which was linked to feudal estates to which the serfs provided labor (Dunn & Dunn, 1988). During the nineteenth century, feudalism was abolished, and the serfs were freed from the estates. The Russian economy, however, remained largely dependent on wheat exports and Western capital (Chirot, 1986).

As in Japan, the Russian elites realized that they had to industrialize quickly if they were to survive. The central government subsidized industrialization by taxing the peasantry heavily and importing European industrial technology. As a result, Russia gradually began to industrialize. However, the new economic burdens on peasant society, a

companies underestimated the importance of language and culture skills, even for short-term assignments. Employees with short-term assignments represent the company's interests abroad as much as do those with longer-term assignments and may jeopardize the success of various projects by behaving improperly and saying something that could be interpreted as offensive to the local people.

General Motors hired anthropologists Elizabeth Briody and Marietta L. Baba to do research on overseas assignments. These anthropologists found that whereas upper management was promoting overseas assignments as a means of achieving improved business skills and managerial techniques, executives in the North American car and truck units discouraged the idea. The ethnologists discovered that GM's North American operation is run separately from the company's overseas subsidiaries and that within GM's corporate culture, employees perceived the North American operation as GM's elite. Therefore, a position overseas was perceived as a lower-status position. Many of the people who worked overseas were placed on slower career paths. In contrast, in

some component divisions of GM such as Delco, top executives were frequently assigned overseas and were viewed as valuable assets to the company.

Briody and Baba recommended that GM adopt a policy whereby managers assigned overseas would be given specific agendas that would lead to improvements in domestic car operations. For example, they could learn techniques from Europe on design, engineering, and manufacturing that could improve U.S. plants. They also suggested an exchange program to replace those sent overseas with a foreign counterpart. These exchanges would result in an improved understanding of global manufacturing, productivity, and competition.

A number of anthropologists are now directly employed in corporations or with marketing-research firms to find out about consumer preferences for different products. A company may want to know which type of advertising has successfully attracted consumers and which segment of a population represents the most promising market for future sales. Why do certain products appeal to some ethnic, age, or sex groups and not others? Why do some advertising campaigns result in

higher sales than others? Anthropologist Steve Barnett, who headed a cultural-analysis group at Planmetrics, a Chicago consulting firm (Lewin, 1986). Aside from directing research on management–union relations and other business-related topics for various corporations, he also does marketing research and gathers information on consumer preferences. He emphasizes participant observation in his research methods. For example, to report on consumer patterns of teenagers for fast-food chains, Barnett directs student researchers who participate in teen activities.

As corporations become more experienced with international business and strive to become more productive and competitive both domestically and internationally, anthropologists will increasingly be drawn into consulting and research roles. Anthropological research techniques and cultural knowledge have helped corporations throughout the world solve some of their practical problems. Perhaps future anthropologists may want to think about combining their coursework with some business and management courses to prepare for these new projects in anthropology.

military defeat by the Japanese in 1905, and the widespread suffering produced by World War I severely weakened the government of the emperor, or czar. The result was the Russian Revolution of 1917.

Under the leadership of Vladimir Lenin, the new Soviet state implemented a number of policies de-

signed to create a more egalitarian society that would meet the basic needs of all its people. All wealth-generating property (the means of production) was placed under government control. The government collectivized agriculture by taking land from landowners and distributing the peasant population on collective, state-controlled farms. Prices and wages were regulated systematically by state authorities. In addition, the government initiated a policy of rapid industrialization to try to catch up with the West.

Hybrid Economic Systems To some extent neither capitalism nor socialism exists in pure form according to the ideals espoused by their leading theorists. Government intervention in the economy exists in both types of economic systems. In some industrial societies such as Sweden and to a lesser extent in Western Europe and England, a hybrid form of economic system referred to as *democratic socialism* developed. In these societies, the key strategic industries that produce basic capital goods and services are government owned, as are certain heavy industries such as steel and coal, and utilities such as telephone companies. At the same time, much of the economy and technology is privately owned, and production takes place for private profit.

THE EVOLUTION OF ECONOMIC ORGANIZATIONS

As industrial economies developed in capitalist, socialist, and democratic-socialist societies, the major economic organizations increased in size and complexity. In capitalist societies, family businesses grew into corporations, which were established as legal entities to raise capital through the sale of stocks and bonds. Eventually these corporations increased their economic holdings and were able to concentrate their ownership of the society's major technology. Through expansion and mergers, they came to dominate economic production and exchange. The result was *oligopoly,* in which a few giant corporations control production in major industries. For example, in the United States in the early 1900s there were thirty-five domestic automobile companies, but in the 1980s only three remained.

This process of corporate expansion ushered in a phase of capitalism known as **monopoly capitalism,** a form of capitalism dominated by large corporations that can reduce free competition through the concentration of capital. This concentration of capital enables oligopolies to control prices and thereby dominate the markets.

In socialist societies such as the former Soviet Union, in which private ownership of technology was prohibited, the government controls and manages the major economic organizations. The equivalent of the large capitalist corporation is the state-owned enterprise that has some degree of financial autonomy, although production goals are established by government authorities. The majority of state enterprises were still small or medium in size, but the enterprises of the former Soviet state became more concentrated (Kerblay, 1983). These enterprises followed the production aims established by the various ministries, which were ultimately controlled by Communist party officials.

Multinational Corporations In the capitalist, socialist, and hybrid economic systems, corporations have increased in size to become large, multinational corporations with enormous assets. **Multinational corporations** are economic organizations that operate in many different regions of the world. Multinational corporations are based in their home countries but own subsidiaries in many other countries. For example, the American-based I.T.T., a multinational corporation with more than 400,000 employees, has offices in sixty-eight different countries. Although approximately 300 of the 500 largest multinational corporations are based in the United States, others, such as Unilever, Shell, and Mitsubishi, are based in England, Western Europe, and Japan, respectively. The socialist societies of the former Soviet Union and former Eastern European countries had large, state-owned multinational corporations that coordinated their activities through what was known as *Comecon* (a committee that coordinated multinational activities worldwide). The evolution of the multinational corporation has had tremendous consequences for the global economy. It is estimated that by the beginning of the 1990s, multinational corporations will control over 50 percent of the world's economic production.

Anthropologist Alvin Wolfe proposed that multinational corporations are beginning to evolve into supranational organizations that are stronger than the nation-state (1977, 1986). Reed Riner (1981) described how various multinational corporations are interconnected in the world global economy. The top CEOs in the various multinational corporations sit on one another's boards of directors. In addition, the multinational corporations are increasingly involved in joint ventures, consolidating their capital assets and technologies to produce goods and services throughout the world. We will consider the effects of these multinational corporations in different societies in later chapters.

Social Structure

The impact of industrialization on kinship, family, gender, aging, and social status has been just as dramatic as it has been on demography, technology, and economic conditions.

KINSHIP

Kinship is less important in industrialized states than in preindustrial societies. New structures and organizations perform many of the functions associated with kinship in preindustrial societies. For example, occupational and economic factors replace kinship as the primary basis of social status; a person no longer has to be part of an aristocratic or elite family to have access to wealth and political power.

As states industrialized, newly emerging middle-class families began to experience upward economic and social mobility, and economic performance, merit, and personal achievement rather than ascribed kinship relationships became the primary basis of social status. Of course, kinship and family background still have a definite influence on social mobility. Families with wealth, political power, and high social status can ensure that their children will have the best education. These families provide their offspring with professional role models and values that emphasize success. They also maintain economic and political connections that enhance their offspring's future opportunities. Hence, their children have a head start over children from lower socioeconomic categories. But kinship *alone* is not the fundamental determinant of social status and rank that it had been in most preindustrial societies.

FAMILY

In Chapter 7 we discussed the various functions of the family: socializing children, regulating sexual behavior, and providing emotional and economic

security. In industrial societies some of these functions have been transformed. The major transformation has been the diminishing importance of the extended family and the emergence of the smaller nuclear family. Some basic functions such as reproduction and the primary care and socialization of children are still performed in the nuclear family.

The family's economic role has changed dramatically. In industrial societies the family is no longer an economic unit linked to production. The prevalence of wage labor in industrial societies has been one of the principal factors leading to the breakdown of the extended family and the emergence of the nuclear family (Wolf, 1966). The extended family in peasant societies maintained cooperative economic production on the land. When employers began to hire individual workers for labor in mines, factories, and other industries, the extended family as a corporate unit no longer had any economically productive function.

During the early phases of industrialization, rural women, including these women who worked in the Lowell textile mill, often had to leave their rural extended families and, when married, formed nuclear families residing in urban areas.

Another factor leading to the diminishing importance of the extended family has been the high rate of geographical mobility induced by industrialization. Because much of the labor drawn into factories and mines initially came from rural areas, workers had to leave their families and establish their own nuclear families in the cities. Land tenure based on the extended family was no longer the driving force it had been in preindustrial societies. In addition, as manufacturing and service industries expanded, they frequently moved or opened new offices, requiring workers to relocate. Thus, the economic requirements of industrializing societies have had the effect of dissolving the extended family ties that had been so critical in preindustrial societies.

The disintegration of the extended family in industrial England, Europe, and North America has been studied by historians and sociologists for decades (e.g., Goode, 1963, 1982). A similar process occurred in Russia and Japan. In Russia, the nuclear family began to replace the extended family following the emancipation of the serfs (Kerblay, 1983). Yet, anthropologists have noted that the nuclear family is not the *ideal* norm in Russian society. Surveys indicate that the Russians do not consider it proper for older parents to live alone and that many consider the grandfather to be the head of the family. These ideal norms reflect the older traditions of the extended peasant family in Russia (Dunn & Dunn, 1988).

In Japanese society, the traditional family was based on the *ie,* (pronounced like the slang term "yeah" in American English). The *ie* is a patrilineal extended family that had kinship networks based on blood relations, marriage, and adoption (Befu, 1971; Shimizu, 1987). The *ie* managed its assets in land and property as a corporate group and was linked into a hierarchy of other branch *ie* families, forming a *dozoku*. The *dozoku* maintained functions similar to those of the peasant families of other agricultural societies. With industrialization, the rurally based *ie* and *dozoku* began to decline, and urban nuclear families called the *kazoku* began to develop (Befu, 1971, Kerbo and McKinstry, 1998). The shift from the *ie* and *dozuku* to the *kazoku* has been very sudden and recent. Many older people in Japan have not adjusted to this recent change.

Despite the general tendency toward the breakup of the extended family in industrialized societies, specific groups and regions in these societies may still retain extended family ties. For example, extended, peasant-type families exist in the rural regions, such as Uzbekistan, Azerbaijan, and Georgia, that were formerly part of the Soviet Union (Kerblay, 1983). Similar tendencies can be found in rural British, European, and Japanese societies. Even in the urban areas of nations such as the United States and Great Britain, some ethnic groups maintain extended family ties. In the United States, many African Americans and Latinos maintain extended family ties for economic and social purposes related to their relatively deprived status within the larger society (Stack, 1975; Macionis, 1999).

MARRIAGE

One of the major changes in marriage in industrialized societies is that it has become much more individualized; that is, the establishment of the union has come to involve personal considerations more than family arrangements. This individualistic form of marriage is usually based on *romantic love,* which entails a blend of emotional attachment with physical and sexual attraction. Naturally, romantic love existed in preindustrial societies (Fisher, 1992; Jankowiak and Fischer, 1992); there are many ethnographic descriptions of couples falling in love in both prestate and agricultural state societies. The classical literature of China, India, Greece, and Rome, as well as various religious texts such as the Bible, are filled with stories about romantic love. Shakespeare's play *Romeo and Juliet* underscores the conflict between romantic love and the familistic and practical considerations of marriage.

Before industrialization, however, most couples were married through the intervention of parents, who arranged their relationships. Romantic love may have existed in preindustrial societies (and in many cases it was the basis for extramarital relationships), but it did not become the primary basis of marriage until after the industrial revolution. This change first took place in England, the center of industrialized commercialization. As the extended family declined in significance, important decisions such as selection of a marriage partner increasingly were made by individuals rather than by families.

One exception needs to be noted with respect to the relationships among industrialization, commercialization, and the development of individualized decision making in the selection of marriage partners. In Japanese society, the traditional form of marriage was arranged through a go-between, a *nakoda,* who set up a meeting for a couple to get to know each other (Hendry, 1987). This pattern is known as the "samurai" form of marriage because it was practiced by these warrior-scholars during the Tokugawa period. The *nakoda* would establish an alliance between two extended households.

With industrialization in Japanese society, romantic love has had an effect on selection of marriage partners, and currently many Japanese individuals choose their own mates. But anthropologist Joy Hendry (1987) notes that "love marriages" are still held suspect and go up against the serious practical concerns of marital ties and the traditional obligations felt by people toward their parents. In many cases, *nakoda* are still used to arrange marriages in this highly modern society.

Approximately one third of the marriages in Japan are the result of arranged marriages. The couple is brought together in a formal meeting called an *omiai,* a formal meeting of a couple of marriageable age arranged by the *nakoda.* Love marriages based on romantic love, called *renai kekkon,* may result in marriage, but in most cases parents still have veto power over who their children marry (Kerbo and McKinstry, 1998). Marriage in Japan is still very much a family consideration, rather than just an individual's own choice or decision.

Divorce   All but a few industrialized societies have legalized divorce, and obtaining a divorce has become easier. In general, little social stigma is associated with divorce in industrialized societies (Quale, 1988). Divorce rates tend to be higher in industrial societies than in preindustrial societies.

Among the many factors that contribute to high divorce rates in industrialized societies is the dissatisfaction that some people experience in their marital relationships. People who contract a marital bond primarily on the ideals and expectations of romantic love may experience a conflict between those ideals and the actualities of marital life. In preindustrial societies, in which marriages were actually alliances between corporate kin groups, individuals typically did not have the freedom to dissolve the marital bond. As individualistic decision

making increased with the emergence of industrialization, however, partners in an unsatisfying relationship were more willing to consider divorce.

The divorce rates of most Western industrialized societies have ballooned during the last century. For example, the U.S. rate increased tenfold between 1890 and 1970 (Macionis, 1999). The same pattern is evident in Russia, where traditional taboos regarding divorce have been replaced by more tolerant attitudes (Kerblay, 1983).

In Japan, however, the divorce rate has *decreased* since industrialization (Befu, 1971). In contrast to most agricultural societies, prior to the Meiji period Japan had a fairly high divorce rate. This was not due to conflicts between husband and wife; instead, divorce resulted because elders in the husband's family rejected a young bride (because she did not conform easily enough to family norms, did not bring enough of a dowry, or other reasons). The traditional postmarital rule of residence was patrilocal, with the wife moving in with the husband's father's household (Goode, 1982). With industrialization and the breakdown of these traditional patterns, the divorce rate began to fall. More recently, however, the divorce rate has begun to increase in Japan, as industrialization creates the tensions experienced in all industrial societies. Yet, the divorce rate in Japan is still only one-fifth of that of the United States (Kerbo and McKinstry, 1998). To some extent, the traditional norms and expectations regarding the female gender role in Japanese society has undoubtedly had an influence on this lower divorce rate. Traditionally, Japanese women are not supposed to threaten the primacy of the husband's role as head of the family. The Japanese woman is supposed to dedicate herself to the husband and children. Work outside of the home should only be undertaken to boost family income when it is necessary, and upon having children, the Japanese woman is expected to be a full time homemaker (Kerbo and McKinstry, 1998).

GENDER

Industrialization has had a profound impact on gender relationships, particularly in England, Europe, and North America. The transition from an agricultural economy to an industrial-wage economy drew many women from the domestic realm into the workplace. Women thus have become more economically self-sufficient and less dependent on men for support.

Gender and the Division of Labor Although women in Western industrial societies have entered the work force in considerable numbers in the last several decades, most women work in a small range of occupations within the service economy, especially in underpaid clerical positions. In addition, women in industrial societies perform the majority of domestic tasks, such as household chores and child care, which are still considered by many the primary responsibility of women. Male occupations and the husband's income are usually considered the primary source of family income. Consequently, women in these societies have a dual burden of combining their domestic role with employment outside the home (Bernard, 1981).

Female Status in Industrial Societies To some degree industrialization undermined the traditional form of patriarchy. In most preindustrial societies, males held considerable authority and control over females. This authority diminished in industrial societies as women gained more independence and gender relations became more egalitarian. As we have seen, however, women are still restricted in the workplace and have a dual burden of combining outside work and domestic chores. This indicates that the cultural legacy of patriarchy still persists in most industrial societies.

As their economic role has changed, women have attempted to gain equal economic and political rights. The call for gender equality began with women from upper- and middle-class families. Unlike working-class women, these early women's rights advocates were financially secure and had much leisure time to devote to political activism. They eventually secured the right to vote in the United States and in other industrialized nations. In addition, with increasing educational levels and economic opportunities, more women entered the work force. For example, by the middle of the twentieth century, nearly 40 percent of all adult females in the United States were in the work force; by 1990 that number was almost 60 percent, as illustrated in Figure 12.2.

Feminism During the 1960s, a combination of economic and social forces fueled the feminist

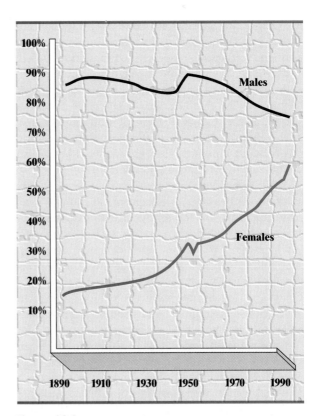

Figure 12.2 The labor force participation rates of women in the United States over the past century. What does this say about the effects of industrialization on traditional gender roles?

Source: Adapted from Francine D. Blau and Marianne A. Ferber, *The Economics of Women, Men, and Work* (Englewood Cliffs, NJ: Prentice Hall, 1986), p. 70 and *Statistical Abstracts of the United States* (Washington: USGPO, 1991), TABLE 635.

movement in many industrialized societies. **Feminism** is the belief that women are equal to men and should have equal rights and opportunities. The contemporary feminist movement has helped many women discover that they have been denied equal rights and dignity. This movement has a much broader base of support than the early women's rights movement. Among its supporters are career women, high school and college students, homemakers, senior citizens, and even many men.

Feminists have secured some concrete gains and helped change certain attitudes in the United States. For example, in a landmark legal decision in 1972, the American Telephone and Telegraph Company (AT&T), the world's largest employer of women, was forced to pay $23 million in immediate pay increases and $15 million in back pay to employees who had suffered sex discrimination. In addition, women have been admitted to many formerly all-male institutions such as the U.S. Military Academy at West Point.

Despite these gains, many female workers continue to be segregated into low-paying service occupations. To resolve this and other problems, the feminist movement supported the Equal Rights Amendment (ERA) to the U.S. Constitution to prohibit discrimination because of gender. Although the ERA was supported by almost three-fourths of American adults and passed by Congress in 1972, it failed to win ratification by the states in time. Apparently, the idea of full equality and equivalent pay for equivalent work has not received the full endorsement of U.S. society. Even in an advanced industrial society, the cultural legacy of patriarchy remains a persistent force.

In Japan the cultural legacy of patriarchy has retained its grip on the role of women. Even when women are in the work force in Japanese society, they tend to have a second-class status when compared to men. Many college educated women in offices are expected to wear uniforms, serve tea and coffee to the men, and are treated as if they are office servants (Hendry, 1987, Kerbo and McKinstry, 1998). They are expected to defer to men in the office and present themselves as infantile, which is interpreted as cute and polite. Most men in Japan perform almost no domestic chores, and are expected to be waited on by their wives. Despite this tradition of patriarchy in Japan, the Japanese woman has a powerful position within the domestic household. They manage the household budget, take charge of the children's education, and make long-term financial investments for the family. Thus, the outside-of-the-home, and the inside-of-the-home roles for women in Japan are still strongly influenced by patriarchal traditions. There are some women involved in a small-scale feminist movement in Japan that wants to transform gender roles, but traditional cultural expectations based on patriarchy are resistant to change.

AGE

Another social consequence of industrialization is the loss experienced by the elderly of traditional status and authority. This trend reflects the changes in the family structure and the nature of knowledge in industrial societies. As the nuclear family replaced the extended family, older people no longer lived with their adult children. Pension plans and government support programs such as Social Security replaced the family as the source of economic support for the elderly. At the same time, exchanges of resources between elders and offspring became less important in industrial societies (Halperin, 1987). Thus, elderly family members lost a major source of economic power.

The traditional role of the elderly in retaining and disseminating useful knowledge has also diminished. Sociologist Donald O. Cowgill (1986) hypothesizes that as the rate of technological change accelerates in industrial societies, knowledge quickly becomes obsolete, which has an effect on the status of elderly people. Industrialization promotes expanding profits, new products, and innovative

Although many elderly people have substantial economic resources, they no longer possess the political and social status they did in preindustrial societies.

services, all of which favor the young, who, through formal education and training, have greater access to technological knowledge. In addition, the amount of cultural and technical information has increased to the point where it can no longer be stored by the elderly. Instead, libraries, databases, and formalized educational institutions have become the storehouses of cultural knowledge.

The result of these changes, according to Cowgill, has been the rapid disengagement of the elderly from their roles in industrial societies. Although many elderly people remain active and productive, they no longer possess the economic, political, and social status they did in preindustrial societies. In some cases, the elderly are forced to retire from their jobs in industrial societies to make way for the younger generation. For example, in industrial Japan, the elderly are forced to retire at the age of 55 and often have difficulties adjusting to their senior years.

The status and roles of the elderly have changed much more dramatically in the West than in Japan and the former Soviet Union, where the elderly retain a great deal of authority and prestige in the family (Palmore, 1975; Kerblay, 1983). In Japanese society, the tradition of family obligations influenced by the Confucian values and ethos serves to foster the veneration of the elderly. In addition, about three-fourths of the elderly reside with their children, which encourages a greater sense of responsibility on the part of children toward their parents.

Theorists such as Cowgill suggest that because Japan and the former Soviet Union industrialized much later than Western societies, there has been less time to transform family structures and the status of the elderly. This view is supported by a comparison between the most modern industrialized urban sectors of these societies and the rural regions. For example, in the more rural regions in Russia and Japan, the extended family is still the norm, and the elderly remain influential and esteemed. Thus, the high status of the aged in Japan and Russia may represent delayed responses to industrialization (Cowgill, 1986).

Social Stratification

In earlier chapters we discussed the type of social stratification that existed in preindustrial societies. Bands and tribes were largely egalitarian, whereas chiefdoms and agricultural states had increased social inequality based on ascribed statuses. Chiefdoms and agricultural states are classified as *closed societies* because they offer little, if any, opportunity for social mobility. In contrast, industrial states are classified as **open societies** in which social status can be achieved through individual efforts. The achievement of social status is related to the complex division of labor, which is based on specialized occupational differences. Occupation becomes the most important determinant of status in industrial states. Societal rewards such as income, political power, and prestige all depend on a person's occupation.

This is not to say that industrial states are egalitarian. Rather, like some agricultural states, they have distinctive classes that consist of somewhat equivalent social statuses. The gaps among these classes in terms of wealth, power, and status are actually greater in industrial than in preindustrial societies. Thus, although people in industrial states have the opportunity to move into a different class from that into which they were born, the degree of stratification in these societies is much more extreme than it is in preindustrial societies. Let's examine the types of stratification systems found in some industrial states.

THE BRITISH CLASS SYSTEM

Some industrial states continue to reflect their agricultural past. Great Britain, for example, is made up of a class system that retains some of its estate-like social patterns. It has a symbolic monarchy and a nobility based on ascribed statuses passed down from generation to generation. The monarchy and nobility have titles such as "prince," "princess," "knight," "peer," and "earl." These individuals have to be addressed with the appropriate form: "sir," "lord," "lady." The British political system reflects its feudal past in the structure of the House of Lords, in which membership is inherited through family. This contrasts with the House of Commons, to which individuals are freely elected. Although the monarchy and the House of Lords have relatively little power today, they play an important symbolic role in British politics.

Class divisions in modern Britain are similar to those in many other European societies. They include a small upper class that maintains its position through inheritance laws and the education of children in elite private schools; a larger middle class that includes physicians, attorneys, business people, and other occupations in the service sector; and a large working class employed in the primary and secondary sectors of the economy. Yet social mobility in Great Britain is open, and people can move from one class to another.

The degree of social mobility in Great Britain, as well as in other industrial states, is to some extent a result of recent changes in the industrial economy. With advanced industrialization, an increasing percentage of jobs are found in the tertiary (service) sector, whereas the primary and secondary sectors have declined. Therefore, the number of white-collar workers has grown, and the number of blue-collar workers has decreased. Consequently, many of the sons and daughters of blue-collar workers have a higher social status than that of their parents. For example, in Great Britain approximately 40 percent of the sons of manual workers have moved into the middle class since the 1950s (Robertson, 1990). Sociologists refer to this as *structural mobility,* a type of social mobility resulting from the restructuring of the economy, producing new occupational opportunities. Technological innovations, economic booms or busts, wars, and other events can affect this mobility.

CLASS IN THE UNITED STATES

Most research demonstrates that the rate of social mobility in the United States is about the same as in other industrial states (Macionis, 1999). Although the United States differs from Great Britain in that it has never had an official class system with a titled aristocracy, it is not a classless society. The class structure of the United States consists of six basic categories based on equivalent social statuses, which are largely determined by occupation, income, and education (see Table 12.2).

One of the principal cultural ideals of the United States is that any person can move up the social ladder through effort and motivation. For this reason, Americans tend to believe that economic and social inequalities arise primarily from differences in individual abilities and work habits. They believe that equal opportunities are available to any individual. These cultural beliefs therefore help justify social inequity.

In fact, many factors besides individual efforts—such as family background and the state of the national (and world) economy—affect a person's location on the socioeconomic ladder. In addition, people's ethnic and racial backgrounds can inhibit or enhance their chances of social mobility. African Americans, Native Americans, and Latinos have lower rates of mobility than do Asian Americans and white, middle-class Americans.

CLASS IN JAPAN AND THE FORMER SOVIET UNION

Most research indicates that, despite the cultural emphasis on group harmony, class divisions and conflicts exist in Japan. Sociologist Rob Steven (1983) has identified five major classes in Japanese society: the bourgeoisie or capitalist class (the owners of the major industries), the petty bourgeoisie (small-business owners), the middle class (professional and other service workers), the peasantry (rural farmers), and the working class. The primary means of social mobility in Japanese society is the educational system, which is highly regimented and rigorous from the elementary years through high school. Higher education is limited to those students who excel on various achievement exams, a system that to some extent reflects class background. As in other industrial societies, middle- and upper-class students have better opportunities. The rate of social mobility in Japan is similar to that of other industrial states (Lipset & Bendix, 1967).

Ever since the Russian Revolution, the former Soviet Union claimed to be a classless society, because its system was not based on the private ownership of the means of production. In fact, however, it had a stratified class system based on occupation. Occupations were hierarchically ranked into four major status groups, based on income, power, and prestige. The highest-ranking statuses consisted of upper-level government officials, Politburo members who were recruited from the Communist party. The second tier consisted of those professional workers such as engineers, professors, physicians, and scientists, as well as lower-level government workers. The third tier was made up of the manual workers in the industrial economy, and the bottom rung was composed of the rural peasantry (Kerblay, 1983; Dunn & Dunn, 1988). Most sociologists agree

Table 12.2	The American Class System in the Twentieth Century: A Composite Estimate					
Class (and Percentage of Total Population)	Income	Property	Occupation	Education	Personal and Family Life	Education of Children
Upper class (1–3%)	Very high income, most of it from wealth	Great wealth, old wealth, control over investment	Managers, professionals, high civil	Liberal arts education at elite schools	Stable family life Autonomous personality	College education by right for both sexes
Upper middle class (10–15%)	High income	Accumulation of property through savings	and military officials Lowest unemployment	Graduate training	Better physical and mental health and health care	Educational system biased in their favor
Lower middle class (30–35%)	Modest income	Few assets Some savings	Small-business people and farmers, lower professionals, semiprofessionals, sales and clerical workers	Some college High school Some high school	Longer life expectancy Unstable family life	Greater chance of college than working-class children Educational system biased against them
Working class (40–45%)	Low income	Few to no assets No savings	Skilled labor Unskilled labor	Grade school	One-parent homes Conformist personality	Tendency toward vocational programs
Lower class (20–25%)	Poverty income (destitution)	No savings	Highest unemployment Surplus labor	Illiteracy, especially functional illiteracy	Poorer physical and mental health Lower life expectancy	Little interest in education, high dropout rates

Source: Daniel W. Rossides, *Social Stratification: The American Class System in Comparative Perspective,* 1990. Adapted by permission of Prentice-Hall, Inc., Upper Saddle River, NJ.

that this hierarchy of statuses reflects a class-based society.

ETHNIC AND RACIAL STRATIFICATION

In addition to social stratification based on occupation, many industrial states have a system of stratification based on ethnic or racial descent. For example, in the United States, various ethnic and racial groups such as African Americans, Native Americans, and Latinos have traditionally occupied a subordinate status and have experienced a more restricted type of social mobility. In contrast, most Western European countries traditionally have been culturally homogeneous, without many minority ethnic groups.

Recently, however, this situation has begun to change as many formerly colonized peoples, such as Indians, Pakistanis, and Africans, have moved to Great Britain, and other non-Western peoples have migrated to other European nations. This has led to patterns of ethnic and racial stratification and discrimination in these countries.

In the former Soviet Union, many ethnic minorities resided in regions such as Estonia, Lithuania, the Ukraine, and the Turko-Mongol areas such as Azerbaijan and Uzbekistan. These ethnic minorities lived outside the central Soviet territory, the heartland of the dominant Russian majority. Historically, the Soviet state had attempted to assimilate these national minorities by making the Russian language a compulsory subject in the educational system (Kerblay, 1983; Worsley, 1984). Although the Soviet state prided itself on its principles of equality and autonomy when applied to its national minorities, the outbreak of ethnic unrest and rebellion in these non-Russian territories in the mid 1990s demonstrated that these populations view themselves as victimized by the dominant ethnic Russian populace. Thus, ethnic stratification has been a component of industrial Soviet society.

Japan is one of the most homogeneous societies in the world; however, ethnologists have noted some patterns of ethnic stratification. For example, the small minority of Japanese of Korean ancestry have experienced widespread discrimination, even though they have adopted the Japanese language, norms, and values. In addition, a native-born Japanese population known as the *eta* or *burakumin,* consisting of about 2 million people, also occupies a lower status. Despite the fact that the *burakumin* are physically indistinguishable from most other Japanese, they reside in separated ghetto areas in Japan. They are descendants of peoples who worked in the leather-tanning industries, traditionally considered low-status professions. Most of the *burakumin* still work primarily in the shoe shops and other leather-related industries. Marriages between *burakumin* and other Japanese are still restricted, and other patterns of ethnic discrimination against this group continue (Befu, 1971; Hendry, 1987). This ethnic discrimination has resulted in poverty, lower education attainment, delinquency, and other social problems for the *burakumin,* just as it has for some ethnic minorities within the United States. As indicated in Chapter 3 in our discussion of I.Q. and race, the burakumin also score lower on I.Q. tests in Japan. As was emphasized in that discussion, since these people are not biologically or racially different from other Japanese people, this fact indicates that ethnic discrimination, poverty, and related environmental conditions are more responsible for differences in intelligence, than any purported biological differences.

Political Organization

As European and American societies began to industrialize, the nature of their political organization was transformed. Members of the middle class

grew economically powerful and were drawn to ideas of *popular sovereignty*—that is, that the people, rather than the rulers, were the ultimate source of political authority. In addition, because the middle classes (particularly the upper-middle class) were the primary beneficiaries of industrial capitalism, they favored a type of government that would allow them economic freedom to pursue profits without state interference. The feudal aristocratic patterns were thus eventually replaced with representative, constitutional governments. The overriding ideal in these democratic states is freedom or personal liberty, which includes freedom of expression, the right to vote, and the right to be represented in the government. Representation is based on the election of political leaders selected from various political parties that engage in competition for offices.

Though representative governments emerged in earlier centuries, their political ideals were not immediately realized. For example, in the United States, political rights, including the right to vote, were not extended to women and other minorities until the twentieth century.

Another aspect of political change was the growth of **nationalism,** a strong sense of loyalty to the nation-state based on shared language, values, and culture. Before the development of nationalism, the primary focus of loyalty was to the local community, religion, and the family (Anderson, 1983; Chirot, 1986; Stavrianos, 1995). For example, in agricultural states, peasants rarely identified with the interests of the ruling elites. In industrial states, however, with the increase in literacy and the development of a print technology, nationalism became a unifying force. Print technology was used to create what political scientist Benedict Anderson (1983) refers to as "imagined communities," an allegiance to a nation-state that is often far removed from everyday family or local concerns.

POLITICAL ORGANIZATION IN SOCIALIST STATES

The former Soviet Union was the first nation to declare that it had a socialist government that would be dominated by the working class—the proletariat—rather than the upper or middle classes. According to Marxist theory, this socialist government was to be only a transitional stage of state develop-

The Japanese Corporation: An Anthropological Contribution from Harumi Befu

During the past several decades, Japan has become one of the world's major economic powers. Many social scientists have investigated the organization and management techniques of Japanese corporations to determine how the Japanese economy has grown so rapidly.

One of the major conclusions of most of these studies is that Japanese corporations are run much differently from corporations in Western capitalist countries. According to these studies, Japanese corporations emphasize traditional values such as group harmony, or *wa,* and collective rather than individual performance (Ouichi, 1981; Lincoln and McBride, 1987). For example, rather than hiring managers based on their individual performance as indicated by grades in college, Japanese corporations recruit managers as groups from different universities. Japanese firms are more interested in how groups

and teams of managers will work together than they are in each person's individual effort or performance. Managers are hired, trained, and promoted as groups by the corporation, based on their ability to cooperate in teams. In contrast to Western countries, which emphasize individualism and independence, the Japanese stress mutual dependence and teamwork.

To ensure this collective performance, large Japanese corporations offer lifetime employment and a concern for their employees' general welfare. Employees are rarely fired or laid off. Corporations provide recreational facilities, parties, child care and other family-related services, and other benefits to enhance corporate loyalty. Corporate decision making is also based on collective principles. Typically, several younger managers are responsible for talking to sixty or seventy people who will be affected by a decision. Propos-

Harumi Befu.

als for a new plan or policy are discussed and then redrafted until a consensus is achieved. A decision requiring one or two phone calls to a division manager in a U.S. company may take two or three weeks in a Japanese corporation. Once a decision is reached, however, everyone involved becomes committed to the plan.

Japanese anthropologist Chia Nakane (1970) believed that this collective orientation results from the hierarchical nature of Japanese social organization. Nakane viewed Japanese society as consisting of hierarchically organized

---

ment, to be followed by a true form of communism in which the state would wither away. In Marx's view, in the communist stage there would be no need for the state, or government, because everyone's needs would be completely taken care of through people who would be free to produce and create for the community.

In the ensuing years, the ideals of the socialist state ruled by the proletariat and the movement toward an egalitarian communism were not realized in the Soviet Union. Instead, the Communist party

of the Soviet Union, with about 18 million members out of a total population of about 300 million, dominated the government, selecting the bureaucratic elite (the *apparatchiki*) of about 1 million to rule over the society. The former Soviet Union became a totalitarian state that controlled the economy, the political process, the media, the educational system, and other social institutions. During certain periods of extreme repression, such as under Joseph Stalin in the 1930s, millions of people were killed or exiled to forced labor camps.

groups with paternalistic leaders at the top who serve group needs. She believed that the psychological process supporting this group orientation is *amae,* an emotional dependence that develops between a child and his or her mother. Through enculturation, *amae* becomes the basis of a mutual dependence that develops between superiors and subordinates throughout society. This dependence is reinforced by provisions given by the superior to the subordinate and expectations of loyalty of the subordinate to the superior. In her classic study of Japan in the 1940s, Ruth Benedict (1946) explored similar themes.

Stanford anthropologist Harumi Befu (1980) has questioned this group model of Japanese society. Befu has a unique background and perspective from which to view this issue. He was born in the United States in 1930 but moved to Japan when he was 6 years old to receive his primary and secondary education. He returned to the United States in 1947 to carry out his undergraduate and graduate studies in an-

thropology. He subsequently remained in the United States and specialized in the ethnological study of Japanese society.

Befu criticized the group model of Japanese society for its tendency to overlook social conflict, individual competition, self-interest, and exploitation. Regarding the purported internal harmony of Japanese groups and society, Befu believed that many proponents of the group model have lost sight of many aspects of Japanese society. Befu believed that many of these theorists have failed to distinguish between the real and ideal norms of Japanese society. Although a president of a corporation may refer to his or her company as a harmonious, happy family at an induction ceremony for new recruits, he or she acts differently at a collective bargaining session in dealing with union demands.

Befu averred that not only Western scholars but the Japanese themselves have accepted this group-model concept as an integral aspect of their cultural identity. He argued that the group model is not really a social model

for Japanese society as much as a cultural model or belief system. He suggested that the group model as a social model is too simplistic to explain comprehensively a complex, postindustrial society such as Japan. Befu did not reject the group model entirely, however. Rather, he contended that the group model as well as a model based on individualism can be applied to both Japanese and Western institutions and bureaucracies. For example, at various times in both Japanese and Western corporations, individuals are in competition and conflict with one another over wealth, power, and status while simultaneously working on group projects that will benefit the corporation as a whole. Individual competition and conflict may take a different form in Japan than it does in Western countries; nevertheless, Befu emphasized that it does exist in both regions. To that extent, Befu suggested that Japanese corporations and social life may not be as unique as either the Japanese or Westerners think they are.

Citizens were prohibited from organizing politically, and official opposition to state policies was not tolerated. This form of totalitarian government also existed in the socialist countries of Eastern Europe that were dominated by the Soviet Union.

INDUSTRIALISM AND STATE BUREAUCRACY

One similarity among the governments of the West, Japan, and the Soviet Union is the degree to

which the state has become a highly developed bureaucracy. It appears that when an industrial economy becomes highly specialized and complex, a strong, centralized government develops to help coordinate and integrate the society's complicated political and economic affairs. Of course, as previously discussed, in the socialist societies such as the Soviet Union, this growth and centralization of the state is more extreme.

Law

Legal institutions are more formalized in industrial states. In general, the more complex the society, the more specialized the legal system (Schwartz & Miller, 1975). As discussed in Chapter 11, legal institutions became formalized in some of the intensive agricultural states with the emergence of codified written law, records of cases and precedents, courts and government officials such as judges, procedures for deciding cases, and a police force to enforce legal decisions. These innovations in legal systems have been expanded in modern industrial societies.

In industrial states, laws become more complex and bureaucratically formalized with the development of national and local statutes, private and public codes, the differentiation between criminal and civil laws, and more specialized law enforcement agencies. With the development of centralized national governments, a hierarchy of legal codes was formulated that ranged from national constitutions to regional and local codes. One of the most distinctive features of law in industrial societies is the proliferation of public and procedural law, referred to as *administrative law* (Vago, 1995). Administrative law reflects the emerging bureaucratic rules and technical requirements in the various legal institutions and agencies in industrial states. Courts in modern industrial states play an important role not only in adjudication but also in mediation and other methods of conflict resolution. In addition, the legal system is the most important means of inducing social change in complex industrial societies. For example, legislation was used to gain civil rights for ethnic minorities such as African Americans in the United States.

JAPANESE LAW

The unique configuration of Japanese values and norms, in comparison with Western or Soviet society, has produced a different form of legal system in Japan. The Confucian ethos and traditional Japanese norms emphasizing group harmony have deeply influenced legal processes and institutions. The Japanese generally adopt extrajudicial, informal means of resolving disputes and prefer legal compromises as opposed to assigning moral blame or deciding on the rightness or wrongness of an action. When a dispute arises a mediator is usually employed to bring about a reconciliation. The Japanese prefer the mediator to a lawyer, who is less likely to know the parties or to have a personal relationship with them. In this sense, the Japanese mediation system resembles those of small-scale tribal societies (Hendry, 1987).

In Japanese society, there tends to be no legal or societal pressure for absolute justice. The proper, moral action is to accept blame for a wrongdoing and resign oneself to the consequences. Conflict resolution outside the court system and codified law tends to be the rule with respect to civil law. Obviously, one of the differences between Japan and the United States is the overwhelming cultural homogeneity of Japan. In contrast, the United States is a highly heterogeneous society with many different ethnic groups and cultural backgrounds. The relative homogeneity of Japanese society facilitates resolving conflicts through informal means rather than through the legal system, as in the United States. However, a recent study indicates that Japan's rate of litigation is beginning to increase (Vago, 1988).

Warfare and Industrial Technology

We noted in Chapter 11 that warfare increased with the territorial expansion of the agricultural empires of China, Rome, and India. To some extent, this increase in warfare was linked to technological developments such as the invention of iron weapons. In addition, the nature of warfare began to change with the development of centralized state systems that competed with rival territories. These general tendencies were accelerated with the evolution of industrial states.

Industrial states began to develop military technologies that enabled them to carry on fierce nationalistic wars in distant regions. One of the prime motivations for these wars was to establish economic and political hegemony over foreign peoples. The industrial nation-states became much more involved in economic rivalry over profits, markets, and natural resources in other territories. Most historians conclude that these imperialist rivalries were the principal reasons for World War I.

Pablo Picasso, 'Guernica' 1937, Oil on Canvas. 11'5 1/2 x 25'5 3/4. Museo Nacional Centro de Arte Reina Sofia/©1998 Estate of Pablo Picasso/Artists Rights Society (ARS), New York.

World War I marked a watershed in the evolution of military warfare. It was a global war in which nation-states mobilized a high proportion of their male populations and reoriented their economic systems toward military production and support. The numbers of combatants and noncombatants killed far outnumbered those of any previous war in any type of society.

The combination of technological advances and centralized military organizations dramatically changed the nature of warfare. Tanks, airplanes, and other modern weapons enabled industrial states to wage tremendously destructive global warfare, as witnessed by World War II. This expanding military technology was inextricably linked to industrial technology. The rise of industries such as airlines, automobiles, petroleum and plastics, and electronics and computers were all related to the development of war technology. And, of course, the atomic era began in 1945 when the United States dropped atomic bombs on Hiroshima and Nagasaki.

Religion

Ever since the Enlightenment, Western industrial states have experienced extensive **secularization,** the decline in the influence of religion in society.

Scientists such as Galileo and Charles Darwin developed ideas that challenged theological doctrines. Secular philosophies increasingly proposed naturalistic (nonsupernatural), scientific explanations of both the natural and social worlds. Secularization has influenced all industrialized states. For example, most people in these societies do not perceive illness as the result of supernatural forces; rather, they rely on physicians trained in scientific medical practices to diagnose and cure diseases.

Despite the increase of secularization, however, religion has not disappeared from industrial states. For example, the United States has experienced a great deal of secularization, and yet it remains one of the most religious societies in the world. Polls indicate that almost 95 percent of all Americans profess a belief in some sort of divine power. Nearly two-thirds of Americans are affiliated with a religious organization, and about 90 percent identify with a particular religion (NORC, 1994). Most sociologists who have studied the question of how religious Americans are have concluded that this question is extremely complex because it relates to ethnic, political, and social-class issues. Many Americans claim religious affiliation in relationship to their communal or ethnic identity; others may belong to religious organizations to gain a sense of identity and belonging or as a source of social prestige. Whatever the reasons, secularization has

CRITICAL PERSPECTIVES

Graduation: A Rite of Passage in U.S. Society

As the United States continues to change from an industrial to a postindustrial society, more people are attending college to gain the skills and knowledge necessary to prepare them for careers. Consequently, one rite of passage that people increasingly look forward to is graduation from college. This rite of passage is similar to those in many other societies. Following an intensive four or five years of study, examinations, and research papers, students face the climactic rite of passage known as the commencement ceremony.

The commencement ceremony dates back to the twelfth century at the University of Bologna in what is now Italy. Shortly thereafter it spread to other European universities. The first U.S. graduates went through their commencement in 1642 at Harvard University. These first commencement ceremonies lasted several days and were accompanied by entertainment, wrestling matches, banquets, and dances.

The academic costumes worn by graduates come directly from the late Middle Ages and the Re-naissance. The black gowns and square caps, called mortarboards, were donned to celebrate the change in status. A precise ritual dictates that the tassel that hangs off the cap should be moved from the right side to the left side when the degree is conferred.

Like rituals of passage in other societies, graduation from college represents a transition in status. In Latin, *gradus* means a step, and *degradus* means a rung on a ladder. From the first we get the word graduation; from the second, degree. Both words are connected to a stage in life, the end of one period of life and the beginning of another. To graduate means to change by degrees.

Typically, the college graduate moves from the status of a receiver to that of a giver. Up to the point of graduation, many students are subsidized and nurtured by society and especially by parents. After graduation a person becomes a giver in all sorts of ways. A degree qualifies graduates to get jobs and to contribute to the workplace. In addition, degree holders will begin to subsidize others through taxes. Many will marry and accept such responsibilities as raising children and paying mortgages. This movement from receiver to giver represents a fundamental life-cycle transition for many U.S. students.

Points to Ponder

1. As you move toward your degree in college, do you believe that what you are learning has any relationship to what you will need after your change in status?

2. In what ways would you change the educational process so that it would help you to develop your potential?

3. Do you think the grading system used by most colleges and universities is a fair means of assessing your acquisition of knowledge and skills?

4. What would you suggest as a better means of evaluating students?

5. What kinds of expectations do you have about your change in status after you receive your degree?

---

not substantially eroded religious beliefs and institutions in the United States.

RELIGION IN SOCIALIST STATES

In the former Soviet Union, secularization had been an aspect of the ideological apparatus of the state. According to Marxist views, religion is a set of beliefs and institutions used by the upper classes to control and regulate the lower classes. The ultimate aim of socialist societies is to eradicate religion, thereby removing a major obstacle to equality. For this reason, the former Soviet Union and socialist Eastern European nations repressed religious organizations and officially endorsed atheism.

Despite these policies, however, in the former Soviet Union 15 percent of the urban population and 30 percent of the rural population practice religion. There are about 40 million Russian Orthodox

Catholics, 600,000 Protestants, and up to 45 million Muslims in a country that has proclaimed itself as atheistic for five decades (Kerblay, 1983). Thus, religious beliefs appear to have been a continuing source of inspiration and spiritual comfort for many citizens of the former Soviet state.

RELIGION IN JAPAN

Japan has also experienced a great deal of secularization as it has industrialized. Traditional Japanese religion was an amalgamation of beliefs based on an indigenous animistic form of worship referred to as Shintoism, combined with Confucianism, Taoism, and Buddhism, which spread from China. Most Japanese and Western observers agree that secularization has diminished the influence of these traditional faiths. Although the majority of Japanese still turn to Shinto shrines and Buddhist ceremonies for life-cycle rituals or personal crises, most modern Japanese confess that they are not deeply religious (Befu, 1971; Hendry, 1987).

Most anthropologists concur, however, that religious beliefs and practices are so thoroughly embedded in Japanese culture that religion cannot easily be separated from the national identity and way of life. For example, the Japanese refer to *nihondo* (the Japanese way) as the basis of their national, ethnic, and cultural identity. *Nihondo* refers to Japanese cultural beliefs and practices, including traditional religious concepts. Thus, it appears that religion is intimately bound with Japanese identity.

 # SUMMARY

The changes associated with the industrial revolution dramatically transformed the technologies, economies, social structures, political systems, and religions of various nations. The center of the first industrial revolution was in Europe. However, when taking a global perspective, anthropologists agree that this industrial revolution could not have occurred without the substantial influence of many other non-Western regions of the world. These changes brought about by the industrial revolution are referred to collectively as modernization. The use of industrial technology required increasing amounts of fossil fuels and other nonrenewable energy sources. In contrast to preindustrial societies, industrial societies are high-energy consumers. These societies also experienced decreasing fertility and mortality rates. This pattern is known as demographic transition. With the expansion of the factory system, people increasingly came to reside in dense urban areas.

The technological and economic changes of industrial societies led to a new, complex division of labor. Industrial economies consist of the primary, secondary, and tertiary sectors, with jobs increasingly located in the tertiary sector, consisting of white-collar, service industries. Industrialization also stimulated new exchange patterns, resulting in the development of the market economy. Both capitalist and socialist systems developed in industrial societies.

Industrial expansion transformed the social structure. Occupation replaced kinship as the most important determiner of status, and the nuclear family largely replaced the extended family. Marriage and divorce increasingly reflected personal choice rather than family arrangements. Gender relationships became more egalitarian, and a majority of women entered the work force. Still, the legacy of patriarchy and male domination continued to influence female status and the division of labor.

The status of the elderly declined in most industrial societies as a result of rapid technological change and new methods of acquiring and storing knowledge. Social stratification increased as class systems based on wealth and occupation emerged. Class systems developed in both capitalist and socialist societies. In addition, ethnicity and race influenced the patterns of stratification.

New forms of political systems, including democratic and totalitarian governments, took root in industrial societies. In both democratic-capitalist and totalitarian-socialist societies, state bureaucracies grew in size and complexity. New, complex forms of legal processes and court systems emerged.

Finally, scientific and educational developments influenced religious traditions in industrial states. Secularization has affected all of these societies, yet religion has not disappeared, and it remains an important component of all industrial societies.

STUDY QUESTIONS

1. Characterize the types of changes that led to the industrial revolution.
2. Compare high and low energy-using technologies.
3. What form does the division of labor take in industrial states? Where do you think the United States falls in this scheme?
4. Compare the principal tenets of capitalism and socialism. Would it be possible to create a functional economy that combined these two systems?
5. What is meant by the terms *market economy* and *capitalism*? What are the principal advantages and disadvantages of these systems for individual participants?
6. Using a specific example, describe what is meant by a multinational corporation. What are the processes by which this multinational corporation can affect the processes of both individual countries and the global economy?
7. How has industrialization affected the family, kinship, marriage, and divorce?
8. What is the difference between a closed society and an open society? Is the United States a closed or open society? What about Japan, the former Soviet Union, and Great Britain?
9. What are some of the characteristics of Japanese industrial corporations?
10. Define the term *feminism*. What are the goals of feminists in industrialized states? Do you agree with these goals? Why or why not?
11. What are the processes whereby industrialization affects the status of elderly individuals? How can we explain the higher status of the aged in societies like Japan and Russia?
12. How do political systems differ in industrial societies compared to preindustrial societies?
13. In your experience has secularization had an impact on your religious beliefs and practices?

 KEY TERMS

capitalism
demographic transition
feminism
industrialization
industrial society
market economy

mercantilism
modernization
monopoly capitalism
multinational corporation
nationalism
nation-states

open societies
primary sector
secondary sector
secularization
socialism
tertiary sector

INTERNET EXERCISES

1. When visiting **http://people.clemson.edu/ ~pammack/britir.htm,** note the changes to British economics and social life. List and describe several of each. What invention did James Watt improve and what did it do for British industrialism? Can one invention really make a difference to an economy? Explain your answer.
2. After reading the section of this chapter subtitled "Religion in Japan," go to the following website: **http://www.askasia.org/frclasrm/readings/ r000009.htm.** What is the Shinto religion? What is the Shinto worldview? How is the Shinto religion integrated with Buddhism? Are the Japanese really as secular as this subsection of the chapter implies? Why or why not?

SUGGESTED READINGS

BERNARD, JESSIE. 1981. *The Female World.* New York: Free Press. A comprehensive account of the changes in gender patterns and female status that have occurred in the industrial world.

CHIROT, DANIEL. 1986. *Social Change in the Modern Age.* San Diego, CA: Harcourt Brace Jovanovich. A global perspective on industrial change and its consequences for economic, social, and political development.

GOODE, WILLIAM J. 1982. *The Family.* 2d ed. Englewood Cliffs, NJ: Prentice Hall. A broad-based sociological analysis of the changes in family, marriage, and divorce that accompanied modernization.

GOODY, JACK. 1996. *The East in the West.* Cambridge: Cambridge University Press. A global analysis of how much influence non-Western societies especially China and the Islamic world had on the development of the industrial revolution in Europe. Goody critically examines the Eurocentric notions of how Europe was the first to develop science, industry, and other institutions that led to the industrial revolution.

HARRIS, MARVIN. 1987. *Why Nothing Works: The Anthropology of Daily Life.* New York: Simon & Schuster. A fascinating account by a prominent anthropologist of the transformations accompanying modern industrial change in contemporary U.S. society.

MUMFORD, LEWIS. 1961. *The City in History.* San Diego, CA: Harcourt Brace and World. A classic account of urbanization and its consequences for modern humans.

Globalization and Aboriginal Peoples

CHAPTER OUTLINE

Globalization: Theoretical Approaches
Modernization Theory / First, Second, and Third Worlds / Dependency Theory / World-Systems Theory / Anthropological Analysis and Globalization

Globalization and Prestate Societies

Vanishing Foragers
The Ju/'hoansi Foragers / The Dobe Ju/'hoansi / The Mbuti Pygmies / The Ik / The Siriono

Tribes in Transition
North American Horticulturalists / South American Horticulturalists / Pastoralist Tribes

Chiefdoms in Transition
The Hawaiian Islands

Forms of Resistance in Native Societies
Revitalization among Native Americans / New Guinea: The Cargo Cults

A Lost Opportunity?
A Case Study: Native American Knowledge / Preserving Indigenous Societies

CHAPTER QUESTIONS

- How are modernization and globalization interconnected?

- What are the differences between modernization and dependency theory?

- What are the advantages and disadvantages of using world-systems theory to understand globalization?

- How has globalization affected foragers, tribes, and chiefdom societies?

- In what ways have native societies tried to resist globalization?

- Why should we care about the plight of indigenous societies?

I N CHAPTER 12 WE DISCUSSED THE EMERGENCE OF industrial states. The rise of industrial states has led to what is referred to as **global industrialism,** or **globalization,** the impact of industrialization and its socioeconomic, political, and cultural consequences on the nonindustrialized societies of the world. Globalization has created substantial economic and political interconnections between the Western and non-Western worlds. The globalization process began with the expansion of Western industrial societies into the non-Western world through colonialism. Globalization continues to occur presently through the increasing spread of industrial technology, including electronic communications, television, the Internet, and the expansion of multinational corporations into the non-Western world. The next three chapters focus on these interconnections.

This chapter introduces some of the theoretical perspectives used to understand globalization. It also explores the influence of global-industrial expansion on small-scale aboriginal societies.

Globalization: Theoretical Approaches

Three major theoretical approaches have been used to examine globalization: modernization theory, dependency theory, and world-systems theory. Each provides a model for analyzing the impact of globalization on industrial and nonindustrial societies.

MODERNIZATION THEORY

Modernization theory, which was developed in the United States during the 1950s, is concerned with the process of economic, social, political, and religious change that accompanies industrial-technological change. Although modernization theory had its roots in Enlightenment ideas as espoused by anthropologists such as E. B. Tylor and later theorists such as Max Weber, it became the leading model of societal evolution in the 1950s in the context of the Cold War between the United States and the former Soviet Union. During that period, the two superpowers were competing for economic resources and the political allegiance of different nations. Modernization theory provided a model to explain how social and cultural change could take place in all societies through industrial capitalism.

One of the most influential proponents of modernization is the American economist W. W. Rostow. Rostow argued that although modernization occurred first in the West, it can occur in *all* societies, provided those societies meet certain preconditions. According to Rostow (1978), evolution from traditional preindustrial societies to modern industrial societies takes place through five general stages:

1. *Traditional stage.* Premodern societies are unlikely to become modernized because of *traditionalism*—persisting values and attitudes that represent obstacles to economic and political development. According to modernization theorists, traditionalism creates a form of "cultural inertia" that keeps premodern societies backward and underdeveloped. Traditionalism places great significance on maintaining family and community relationships, which inhibit individual freedom and initiative.

2. *Culture-change stage.* One of the preconditions for modernization involves cultural and value changes. People must accept the belief that progress is both necessary and beneficial to society and the individual. This belief in progress is linked to an emphasis on individual achievement, which leads to the emergence of individual entrepreneurs who will take the necessary risks for economic progress. Modernization theorists insist that these changes in values can be brought about through education and will result in the erosion of traditionalism.

3. *Takeoff stage.* As traditionalism begins to weaken, rates of investment and savings begin to rise. These economic changes provide the context for the development of industrial-capitalist society. England had reached this stage by about 1783, and the United States by about 1840. Modernization theorists believe that this stage can be reached only through foreign aid to support the diffusion of education and technology from industrial-capitalist societies into premodern societies. Many premodern societies have not yet achieved this stage of development.

4. *Self-sustained growth.* At this stage, the members of the society intensify economic progress through the implementation of industrial technology. This process involves a consistent reinvestment of savings and capital in modern technology. It also includes a commitment to mass education to promote advanced skills and modern attitudes. As the population becomes more educated, traditionalism will continue to erode.

5. *High economic growth.* This last stage involves the achievement of a high standard of living, characterized by mass production and consumption of material goods and services. Western Europe and the United States achieved this stage in the 1920s, and Japan reached it in the 1950s.

This model includes both economic and noneconomic factors such as cultural values as preconditions for modernization. In fact, as seen in Stage 2, the changes in attitudes and cultural values are the most important prerequisites for eliminating traditionalism and generating patterns of achievement. Thus, modernization theorists view cultural values and traditionalism as the primary reasons for the lack of economic development. The practical implication that derives from this model is that before a country should receive foreign aid, traditionalism and the values that support it must be transformed.

Like Rostow, theorist David McClelland (1973) maintained that a need for achievement represents the most important variable in producing the process of modernization. McClelland argued that this need for achievement is not just a desire for more material goods but rather an intrinsic need for satisfaction in achieving success. He believed that this desire for achievement leads to increased savings and accumulation of capital. McClelland claimed to have found evidence for this need in some non-Protestant countries such as Japan, Taiwan, and Korea, as well as in Western countries.

FIRST, SECOND, AND THIRD WORLDS

The modernization model led to the categorization of societies into three "worlds": the First, Second, and Third Worlds. According to the modernization theorists, the **First World** is composed of modern industrial states with predominantly capitalist or hybrid economic systems. Included in this group

Many people in underdeveloped countries such as Peru have the same need to achieve as other people in the West, but they lack basic economic opportunities.

are Great Britain, Western Europe, Japan, and the United States. The **Second World** consists of industrial states that have predominantly socialist economies. It includes the former Soviet Union and many of the former socialist countries of Eastern Europe—for example, Poland and Hungary. The **Third World** refers to premodern agricultural states that maintain traditionalism. The Third World encompasses the vast majority of the people in the world, including most of Latin America, Africa, the Middle East, and Asia.

Criticisms of Modernization Theory Modernization theory enabled anthropologists and other social scientists to identify various aspects of social and cultural change that accompany globalization. By the 1960s, however, modernization theory had come under attack by a number of critics. One of the major criticisms is that the applied model of modernization has failed to produce technological

and economic development in Third World countries. Despite massive injections of foreign aid and education projects sponsored by First World countries, most Third World countries remain underdeveloped. An **underdeveloped society** has a low gross national product (GNP), the total value of goods and services produced by a country.

Some critics view modernization theory as ethnocentric or "Westerncentric." They believe that this theory promotes Western industrial-capitalist society as an ideal that ought to be encouraged universally. These critics argue that Western capitalist societies have many problems, such as extreme economic inequality and the dislocation of community and family ties, and they question whether a Western model of modernization is suitable or beneficial for all societies. They do not agree that all societies must emulate the West to progress economically.

Modernization theorists have also been criticized for citing traditional values as obstacles to technological and economic development in the Third World. Critics consider this an example of blaming the victim. They charge that this argument oversimplifies both the conditions in Third World countries and the process of industrialization as it occurred in the West. For example, recall from Chapter 11 that individual entrepreneurs in the West and in Japan had a great deal of economic freedom, which encouraged independent initiative. Under feudalism, governments did not have systematic control over independent economic activities in local regions. Consequently, entrepreneurs had freedom to develop their technologies and trading opportunities. In contrast, many Third World people have a so-called need to achieve but lack the necessary economic and political institutions and opportunities for achievement.

Another criticism of modernization theory is that it neglects the factors of global economic and political power, conflict, and competition within and among societies. For example, the wealthier classes in Third World countries that have benefited from the new technology and other assets from the First World often exploit the labor of the lower classes. This conflict and division between classes may inhibit economic development. Modernization theorists also tend to view First, Second, and Third World countries as existing in isolation from one another.

One other major problem with the modernization theorists is that the terminology *First, Second, and Third World countries* is too simplistic today to account for the great diversity that anthropologists actually discover in these societies. Modernization theory was a product of Cold War politics, in which the capitalist West (the First World) was in global competition with the socialist East (the Second World), and the rest of the world (the Third World) was influenced by Cold War politics. However, as we shall see in Chapter 16, sweeping changes have been transforming the Eastern bloc countries, including those of the former Soviet Union, resulting in the dissipation of most of the Second World socialist societies. In addition, the term *Third World societies* tended to lump together many societies that were at different levels of socioeconomic development. For example, Saudi Arabia, rich in oil resources, cannot be compared with Bangladesh, which has very little natural resource wealth on which to draw. Some countries in the so-called Third World are much better off economically, with ten to twenty times the national wealth of other countries. Although the terms *First, Second,* and *Third Worlds* are still used in the media and elsewhere, we should be aware that this terminology is a legacy of the Cold War and is no longer relevant to an understanding of present-day societies.

DEPENDENCY THEORY

Criticism of modernization theory led to a new approach that emerged primarily from the underdeveloped world. Known as **dependency theory,** this approach is a model of socioeconomic development that explains global inequality as resulting from the historical exploitation of poor, underdeveloped societies by rich, developed societies. Dependency theory was influenced by Marxism and is associated with theorists such as Andre Gunder Frank, who denied that underdevelopment is the product of the persistence of traditionalism in preindustrial societies. These theorists instead contend that wealthy industrialized capitalist countries exploit underdeveloped precapitalist societies for the cheap labor and raw materials needed to maintain their own industrial technologies. Through this process, impoverished underdeveloped countries became economic and political *dependencies* of wealthy industrialized capitalist countries.

Dependency theorists suggest that mercantilism increased the prosperity and economic and political power of Western nations at the expense of poor nations. Especially after 1870, following the early phases of industrialism, a new type of relationship developed between industrialized and nonindustrialized societies. As manufacturing expanded, the industrial nations' needs for raw materials increased. Also, changing patterns of consumption created more demands for new foodstuffs and goods such as tea, coffee, sugar, and tobacco from nonindustrialized regions. The availability of cheap labor in underdeveloped countries contributed to increasing wealth and profits in industrial nations. Thus, according to dependency theorists, the wealth and prosperity of the industrial capitalist countries was due largely to the exploitation of the underdeveloped world.

The need for raw materials, consumer goods, cheap labor, and markets led to increasing **imperialism,** economic competition among industrial capitalist nations for control over nonindustrialized areas. Although imperialism had developed among preindustrial agricultural states, it did not involve the whole world. In contrast, industrial countries like Great Britain, the United States, France, Germany, the Netherlands, Belgium, Russia, and Japan divided the nonindustrialized areas into spheres of economic and political influence. Most of the nonindustrialized regions became **colonies** that exported raw materials and provided labor and other commodities for the industrialized nations.

Dependency theorists categorize the industrial capitalist countries as the *metropole* societies who maintain dependent *satellite* countries in the underdeveloped world. Through the organization of the world economy by the industrial capitalist societies, the surpluses of commodities produced by cheap labor flow from the satellites to the metropole. The satellites remain underdeveloped because of economic and political domination by the metropole. Despite the fact that many satellite countries have become politically independent from their former colonial rulers, the emergence of multinational corporations based in the industrialized capitalist societies has produced a new form of imperialism, *neoimperialism.* The industrial capitalist societies control foreign aid, international financial institutions such as the World Bank and the International Monetary Fund (IMF), and international political institutions such as the United Nations, all of which function to maintain their dominant position.

Criticisms of Dependency Theory Unlike modernization theory, the dependency approach demonstrates that no society evolves in isolation. By examining the political economy in industrial capitalist and precapitalist countries, theorists showed conclusively that some aspects of underdevelopment are related to the dynamics of power, conflict, class relations, and exploitation.

Critics, however, have noted a number of flaws in the dependency approach. Generally, dependency theory tends to be overly pessimistic. It suggests that dependency and impoverishment can be undone only by a radical restructuring of the world economy to reallocate wealth and resources from wealthy industrial capitalist countries to impoverished precapitalist countries. Economic development, however, has occurred in some countries that have had extensive contact with industrial capitalist societies. Notably, Japan moved from an underdeveloped society to a wealthy industrial capitalist position after the 1950s. Other countries such as Taiwan and South Korea have also developed. In contrast, some poor societies that have had less contact with the industrial capitalist societies remain highly undeveloped.

Critics also point out that dependency theorists neglect the internal conditions of underdeveloped countries that may inhibit economic development. Rapid population growth, famine and hunger, the excessive control of the economy by centralized governments, and, in some instances, traditional cultural values may inhibit economic development.

WORLD-SYSTEMS THEORY

The perspective known as **world-systems theory** maintains that the socioeconomic differences among various societies are a result of an interlocking global political economy. The world-systems model represents a response to both modernization and dependency theories. Sociologist Immanuel Wallerstein, who developed the world-systems approach, agrees with the dependency theorists that the industrial nations prosper through the economic domination and exploitation of nonindustrial peoples. His world-systems model (1974, 1979, 1980) places all countries in one of three general categories: core, peripheral, and semiperipheral. **Core societies** are the powerful industrial nations that exercise economic domination over other regions. Most nonindustrialized countries are classified as **peripheral societies,** which have very little control over their own economies and are dominated by the core societies. Wallerstein notes that between the core and peripheral countries are the **semiperipheral societies,** which are somewhat industrialized and have some economic autonomy but are not as advanced as the core societies (see Figure 13.1).

Unlike dependency theorists, Wallerstein believes that under specific historical circumstances a peripheral society can develop economically. For example, during the worldwide depression of the 1930s, some peripheral Latin American countries, such as Brazil and Mexico, advanced to a semiperipheral position. Wallerstein also explains the recent, rapid economic development of countries such as Taiwan and South Korea in terms of their favored status by core societies. Because the United States was in competition with the former Soviet Union and feared the emergence of communism in Asia, it invested huge amounts of money and capital in Taiwan and South Korea.

Criticisms of World-Systems Theory Although Wallerstein's world-systems theory has some advantages over modernization and dependency theories, critics note some weaknesses (Shannon, 1988). One criticism is that the theory focuses exclusively on economic factors at the expense of noneconomic factors such as politics and cultural traditions. In addition, it fails to address the question of why trade between industrial and nonindustrial nations must always be exploitative. Some theorists have noted that in certain cases peripheral societies benefit from the trade with core societies in that, for example, they may need Western technology to develop their economies (Chirot, 1986).

Although world-systems theory has been helpful in allowing for a more comprehensive and flexible view of global economic and political interconnections, it is not a perfected model. However, the terms used by Wallerstein, such as *core, semiperipheral,* and *peripheral,* have been adopted widely by the social sciences. These terms offer an

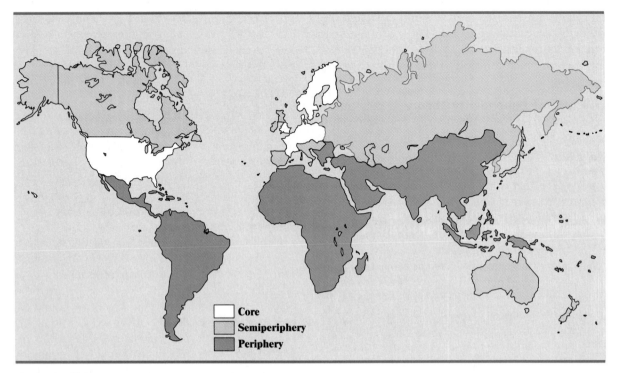

Figure 13.1(a)   The world system around 1900.

Source: From *Macrosociology: An Introduction to Human Societies* 3rd ed. by Stephen K. Sanderson. Copyright 1995 by HarperCollins College Publishers. Reprinted by permission of Addison-Wesley Educational Publishers Inc.

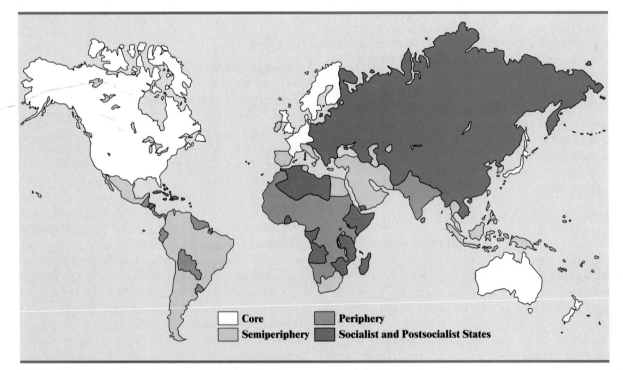

Figure 13.1(b)   The world system, 1990.

Source: From *Macrosociology: An Introduction to Human Societies* 3rd ed. by Stephen K. Sanderson. Copyright 1995 by HarperCollins College Publishers. Reprinted by permission of Addison-Wesley Educational Publishers Inc.

ANTHROPOLOGISTS AT WORK

Eric Wolf: A Global Anthropologist

Eric Wolf was born in Vienna, Austria, in 1923. After elementary school he went to gymnasium, a combined middle school and high school, in Czechoslovakia. At an early age, he was exposed to many diverse ethnic groups and nationalistic movements. His parents later sent him to England, where he first discovered the natural sciences. In 1940, he came to the United States to attend Queens College. He majored in a variety of subjects until he finally settled on anthropology. In 1943, he joined the U.S. Army and saw combat in Italy, returning with a Silver Star and a Purple Heart. After the war he completed his studies at Queens College and then went on to graduate from Columbia University, where he studied with Ruth Benedict and Julian Steward. He did ethnological fieldwork in Puerto Rico, Mexico, and the Italian Alps.

Having been exposed to peasant groups during his childhood in Europe, Wolf focused his studies on the peasantry in different parts of the world. Through his field-

work in areas such as Puerto Rico and Mexico, he became interested in how peasants adjust to global change. In a number of essays he refined the analytical approach to understanding the peasantry. His early books include *Sons of the Shaking Earth* (1959), an overview of the historical transformations in Mesoamerica caused by Spanish colonialism; *Peasants* (1966), an analytic treatment of peasants throughout the world; and *Peasant Wars of the Twentieth Century* (1969), an examination of peasant revolutions.

Because of the success of his early books and his global perspective in his comprehensive *Europe and the People without History* (1982), Wolf has exerted a tremendous influence on many anthropologists and other social scientists. *Europe and the People without History* won several awards. Wolf was awarded a grant from the MacArthur Foundation, frequently called the "genius" award. Candidates are recommended by 100 anonymous nominators, whose selections are re-

Eric Wolf.

viewed by panels of experts. Recipients can spend the grant money as they wish on their own research projects. Wolf wrote another influential text called *Envisioning Power* (1999) about ideology and its relationship to political economy, global developments, and culture.

Unfortunately Eric Wolf died in March 1999. His contributions to anthropological thought and his emphasis on the global perspective will endure forever within the profession.

---

improvement by helping to classify different types of global interrelationships and substitute for the older terminology of *First, Second,* and *Third Worlds.*

ANTHROPOLOGICAL ANALYSIS AND GLOBALIZATION

Ethnological research has uncovered limitations to all the approaches to globalization. Such labels as *traditional, modern, metropole-satellite,* and *peripheral* are too simplistic to classify realistically

the diverse economic and cultural traditions in the world. Anthropologists find that there are no predictable, unilineal, or unalterable patterns of societal evolution. They criticize the modernization, dependency, and world-systems theorists for neglecting the diverse precapitalist economic systems, specific histories, internal class relations, ethnic differences, political conditions, and dynamic cultural traditions.

Before the 1960s, many anthropologists were influenced by the modernization approach, which tended to view societies in isolation. Since the development of the dependency and world-systems perspectives, however, anthropologists have become more attuned to the global perspective. For example, a book by Eric Wolf, *Europe and the People without History* (1982), reflected these developments in anthropological thought. Wolf espoused a global perspective by drawing on modernization, dependency, and world-systems approaches while criticizing all of them for their weaknesses. Anthropologists today evaluate the claims of all three approaches by combining in-depth historical information with cultural data gathered through ethnological research. This strategy contributes to a more comprehensive understanding of the internal and external conditions that influence societal changes arising from globalization.

Globalization and Prestate Societies

In Chapters 8, 9, and 10 we discussed the major types of prestate societies studied by anthropologists: bands, tribes (horticultural and pastoral), and chiefdoms. Contrary to some popular stereotypes, these societies have never been entirely isolated, nor are they static. Since coming into contact with industrial societies, however, they have undergone dramatic transformations. These prestate societies are sometimes referred to as the *Fourth World,* as an additional classification to the First, Second, and Third World categories. Other terms for these societies include *native, indigenous, aboriginal,* or *first nation.* Extensive ethnological research has provided us with considerable documentation concerning the changes in these nonstate societies.

The expansion of globalization produced traumatic and violent changes in many prestate societies. These peoples were absorbed as subordinate ethnic groups in larger nation-states or in some cases have become extinct. When absorbed, they usually were forced to abandon their traditional language and culture, a process known as **ethnocide.** In other situations aboriginal peoples faced **genocide,** the physical extermination of a particular group or race of people. People such as the Tasmanians of Australia and some Native American groups were deliberately killed so that colonists could take their lands and resources. The following

sections focus on the impact of globalization on some first nation peoples.

Vanishing Foragers

As described in Chapter 8, contemporary bands, or foraging societies, have survived in marginal environments: deserts, tropical rain forests, and arctic regions. Because these lands are not suitable for agriculture, foragers lived in relative isolation from surrounding populations. Following the emergence of industrial states, however, these marginal areas became attractive as unsettled frontiers with low population densities and bountiful natural resources such as land, timber, energy resources, minerals and other valuable products. Industrial states have expanded into these regions in search of energy supplies and resources such as oil and minerals, in the deserts and arctic areas, and land and timber from the tropical rain forests. One result of this process has been increased contact between industrial and foraging societies, often with tragic results.

THE JU/'HOANSI FORAGERS

The bands of the African deserts and tropical rain forests have been devastated by confrontations with expanding industrial states. The Ju/'hoansi or San people of the Kalahari Desert, who, before the 1950s, had little contact with industrial nations, are now caught in the midst of forced change. Many of the Ju/'hoansi live in Namibia, which for many years was controlled by South Africa. Beginning in the 1960s, the South African government began to expand into the Kalahari Desert. In the process it restricted the Ju/'hoansi hunting territories and attempted to resettle them in a confined reservation. It further attempted to introduce the Ju/'hoansi to agriculture—the cultivation of maize, melons, sorghum, and tobacco—and cattle raising. Because of the unsuitability of the land and inadequate water supplies, however, these activities have not succeeded. Consequently, the Ju/'hoansi have become increasingly dependent on government rations of corn, salt, sugar, and tobacco.

In Namibia, the only economic opportunities for Ju/'hoansi males are menial chores, clearing fields, and building roads. The government initially paid

Ju/'hoansi laborers with mealie (ground corn), sugar, or tobacco, but eventually switched to money. The introduction of this cash economy transformed traditional relationships in Ju/'hoansi society. People who previously had embraced a reciprocal exchange system that enhanced their kinship and social ties now had to adjust to a system in which resources were managed for one's own family. Conflicts arose between those who wanted to share and others who were forced to become self-interested and hide resources even from their own kin.

In some of the areas where the Ju/'hoansi were settled, population began to increase. This is a typical consequence of a shift from a foraging to a settled life. With increased crowding came epidemics, particularly tuberculosis, that claimed many lives. Moreover, in response to the rapid transformation of their lifestyle, many Ju/'hoansi resorted to frequent drinking. Much of their newly acquired cash from employment went into alcohol consumption, and alcoholism became a problem for many.

Other Ju/'hoansi males were recruited by the South African military to engage in campaigns during the 1960s and 1970s against the South-West African People's Organization (SWAPO), guerrilla insurgents who opposed the South African regime. The Ju/'hoansi were valued as soldiers because they were good trackers and courageous fighters. Most of them, however, were unaware of the geopolitical strategies and racist policies of the South African government. They were simply attracted to military service by the promise of high wages.

Richard Lee believed that this involvement in the South African military has increased the amount of violence in Ju/'hoansi society. Lee documented only twenty-two cases of homicide among all the Ju/'hoansi between 1922 and 1955. In contrast, seven murders were recorded in a single village known as Chum!kwe during the brief period from 1978 to 1980, a major increase (Lee, 1984). According to Lee, the aggressive values and norms associated with militarism increased the tendency toward violence in Ju/'hoansi society.

Since Namibian independence in 1989–90, the situation of the Ju/'hoansi has improved. Under the new SWAPO (the South-West African People's Organization) government, their land is now protected by law, and they are working through a

grassroots development organization (the NYAE NYAE Farmers Cooperative) and outside agencies such as USAID, to provide schooling, health care and social services to the former foragers.

THE DOBE JU/'HOANSI

Lee (1993) has also studied the situation for the Ju/'hoansi of the Dobe area in the country of Botswana, who have not had to make the same types of adjustments as the Ju/'hoansi of Namibia. Generally, the nation of Botswana has not been subject to the same expansive South African policies as Namibia. Therefore, the Ju/'hoansi in Dobe have not been recruited into the South African army, nor has the government funded settlement reservations. However, Lee found that by the 1970s the Ju/'hoansi Dobe were beginning to adopt agriculture and herding. Although agriculture continues to be a very risky proposition in the desert area, herding and livestock production is beginning to become a viable source of income for the Dobe Ju/'hoansi.

Lee described how Ju/'hoansi Dobe males had also begun to migrate outside their own territories to work in South African mines for $18 to $25 a month. Upon returning home after months of working in the mines, they spent much of their cash wages on a home brew. This pattern of drinking increased the tendency toward alcoholism among some Ju/'hoansi Dobe.

The introduction of a cash economy disrupted traditional Ju/'hoansi Dobe patterns of egalitarianism and reciprocity. The availability of manufactured goods such as soap, foodstuffs, kerosene, and clothing led to the decline of indigenous technologies and crafts. Drinking, violence, and conflict increased. These problems heightened anxieties among the Ju/'hoansi Dobe, as they realized how dramatically their traditional lifestyle had changed. However, even in the late 1990s, much of the ethos of sharing and egalitarianism endures in spite of all the changes, giving some indications of the resilience of this way of life.

THE MBUTI PYGMIES

The late Colin Turnbull examined two cases of African foragers who have faced decimation through forced cultural change. Turnbull did the major ethnological study, discussed in Chapter 8,

The Mbuti pygmies have been traumatically influenced by globalization processes.

of the Mbuti Pygmies of the Ituri rain forest of Zaire. He noted (1963, 1983) that the Pygmies had been in contact with outsiders for centuries but had chosen to retain their traditional hunting-and-gathering way of life. During the colonial period in what was then the Belgian Congo, however, government officials tried to resettle the Mbuti on plantations outside the forest.

Following the colonial period, the newly independent government of Zaire continued the same policies of forced resettlement. In the government's view, this move would "emancipate" the Pygmies, enabling them to contribute to the economy and to participate in the national political process (Turnbull, 1983). The Pygmies would become national citizens and would also be subject to taxation. Model villages were built outside the forest with Mbuti labor. Convinced by government officials that they would benefit, many Mbuti at first supported these relocation projects.

The immediate results of this resettlement, however, were disastrous. Turnbull visited the model villages and found many of the Mbuti suffering from various diseases. Because the Mbuti were unaccustomed to living a sedentary life, they lacked knowledge of proper sanitation. Turnbull found that the Mbuti water had become contaminated and the change of diet from forest products to cultivated crops had created nutritional problems. Physiologically, the Mbuti could not adapt to living

and working outside the rain forest. Not having the rain forest to shield them from direct sunlight, they suffered from heat prostration. Additionally, working conditions in agricultural labor and construction presented new demands, and the Mbuti did not have the required musculature and physiology for this type of labor.

THE IK

In Uganda, Turnbull (1972) did ethnological research on another group of hunter–gatherers known as the Ik. Prior to World War II, the Ik were nomadic bands who moved throughout the countries of Kenya, Sudan, and Uganda. Their major hunting territory was the Kidepo Valley below Mount Morungole. After the war, Kidepo was turned into a national park, and the Ugandan government forced the Ik to move to the arid and barren mountains of northeastern Uganda. Although the Ik were resettled to become farmers, the mountain areas were unsuitable for agriculture, and famine was common.

Turnbull did his ethnological research on the Ik in their new surroundings in 1972. He was disturbed by the characteristics of Ik life that he observed. In contrast to the hospitality and reciprocity of hunting-and-gathering life that he observed among the Mbuti and that presumably had existed among the Ik before their resettlement, Turnbull found the Ik inhospitable, cruel, and insensitive. They had become self-interested to the point of not having any "social" life at all. Family and band unity had become completely fragmented, and individual survival had become their only governing principle.

The elderly were abandoned by the family; Turnbull described situations in which food was snatched out of the mouths of older people. Children were thrown out of their parents' homes when they reached the age of 3 and had to reside in age bands that foraged for themselves. Turnbull described the Ik's only shared value as *ngag,* or food. It was the only standard by which they evaluated right and wrong. Their word for "good" is *marang,* and it is defined with respect to food. Among the Ik a good person was a person with a full stomach.

THE SIRIONO

Many other hunter-gatherer societies are facing similar situations in their confrontation with industrializing societies and global processes. The Siriono foragers of eastern Bolivia were initially described by Allan Holmberg in an ethnography entitled *Nomads of the Long Bow* (1950). In contrast to the portrait of foragers elsewhere, Holmberg described the Siriono as living at the edge of starvation in conditions similar to those of the Ik. He presented the Siriono as so focused on food and hunger that they were largely ungenerous and did not have the same patterns of reciprocity practiced in other foraging societies. He further described them as having a rudimentary culture with little technology and no games, music, cosmology, myths, folktales, and ritual ceremonies. He hypothesized that the Siriono were so concerned with their immediate biological needs that they had no time for a reflective life.

Barry Isaac (1977) subsequently studied the historical conditions that affected the Siriono and challenged Holmberg's conclusions. As Isaac noted, although Holmberg understood that the Siriono were not an isolated society and had contact with Europeans and others, he underestimated the consequences of these contacts. The Spanish had been in the region for more than 400 years. Some of the Siriono observed by Holmberg were escapees from missions and plantations. In addition,

the Siriono population had been decimated by smallpox and influenza, as well as by raids by other Indian groups. The Siriono had become so dependent on European technology such as steel axes and knives that they had completely abandoned their traditional foraging activities for several generations.

In other words, the situation observed by Holmberg was that of a foraging society attempting to adapt to outside pressures while undergoing a traumatic transition. Instead of representing a rudimentary culture existing in the rain forest, the Siriono were adjusting to epidemics, exploitation, and warfare. The resulting depopulation accelerated the process of **deculturation,** the loss of traditional patterns of culture. In the case of the Siriono, the lost cultural elements included technology and subsistence practices as well as religious practices such as shamanism. Isaac maintained that the Siriono represented a fragile foraging society that, when confronted with external pressures, was easily tipped toward disintegration.

Tribes in Transition

Many horticulturalist and pastoralist tribes have also been adversely affected by the process of globalization. For example, many Native American societies suffered serious disruptions as a result of European colonization. The Spanish, French, Dutch, and British came to the Americas in search of precious metals, furs, and land for settlement. Each of these countries had different experiences with the indigenous peoples of North America. But wherever the Europeans settled, indigenous tribes were usually devastated through depopulation, deculturation, and, in many cases, physical extinction.

NORTH AMERICAN HORTICULTURALISTS

The collision of cultures and political economies between Native Americans and Europeans can be illustrated by the experiences of the Iroquois of New York State. The traditional horticulturalist system of the Iroquois has been described in Chapter 9. British and French settlers established a fur trade with the Iroquois and nearby peoples during the late 1600s. French traders offered weapons, glass beads, liquor, and ammunition to the Iroquois in exchange for beaver skins. Eventually the Iroquois abandoned their traditional economy of horticulture supplemented by limited hunting to supply the French with fur pelts. The French appointed various *capitans* among the Iroquois to manage the fur trade. This resulted in the decline of the tribe's traditional social and political order (Kehoe, 1995).

Meanwhile, the intensive hunting of beaver led to a scarcity of fur in the region, which occurred just as the Iroquois were becoming more dependent on European goods. The result was increased competition between European traders and various Native Americans who were linked to the fur trade. The Iroquois began to raid other tribal groups, such as the Algonquins, who traded with the British. Increasing numbers of Iroquois males were drawn into more extensive warfare (Blick, 1988). Many other Native American tribal peoples also became entangled in the economic, political, and military conflicts between the British and French over land and resources in North America.

The Relocation of Native Americans Beginning in the colonial period many Native American tribes were introduced to the European form of intensive agriculture, with plows, new types of grains, domesticated cattle and sheep, fences, and individual plots of land. The white settlers rationalized this process as a means of introducing Western civilization to indigenous peoples. However, whenever Native Americans became proficient in intensive agriculture, many white farmers viewed them as a threat. Eventually, following the American Revolution, the government initiated a policy of removing Indians from their lands to open the frontier for white settlers. A process developed in which Native Americans were drawn into debt for goods and then pressured to cede their lands as payment for these debts.

Ultimately, the U.S. government developed the system of reservations for resettling the Native American population. Under Andrew Jackson in the 1830s, many southeastern tribal groups were resettled into western regions such as Oklahoma. In many cases, Native Americans were forcibly removed from their land, actions that colonists justified as a way of bringing Western civilization and Christianity to these peoples. The removal policies

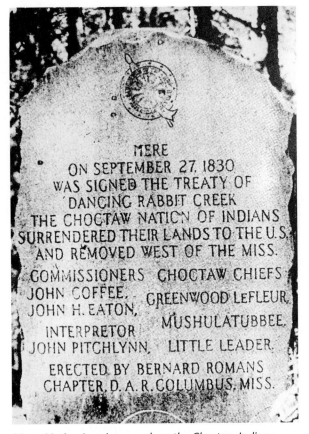

Many Native Americans such as the Choctaw Indians signed treaties with the U.S. government giving up their rights to land.

led to brutal circumstances such as the Trail of Tears, in which thousands of Shawnees and Cherokees living in Georgia and North Carolina were forced to travel hundreds of miles westward to be resettled. Many died of starvation and other physical deprivations on this forced march.

The patterns of land cession were repeated as white settlers moved westward. European Americans justified these behaviors through the concept of Manifest Destiny, the belief that they were responsible for extending the benefits of Western civilization throughout the continent. Military force frequently was used to overcome Indian resistance.

In 1890, Native Americans held title to 137 million acres of land. By 1934, these holdings had been reduced to 56 million acres. After suffering the dispossession of most of their lands, the majority of Native Americans were forced to live on reservations, most of which were unsuitable for agriculture. Lack of employment opportunities led to increased impoverishment for many of these people. Reservations were overseen by the Bureau of Indian Affairs (BIA). Before 1934, Native Americans were viewed as wards of the state, and the BIA established Indian schools to introduce "civilization" to Native American children. The BIA was empowered to decide whether Native Americans could sell or lease their land, send their children to boarding schools, or practice their traditional religion.

Native Americans in the Twentieth Century

Based on a survey of the Smithsonian's twenty-volume *Handbook of North American Indians,* Douglas Ubelaker (1988) estimated how dramatic the population decline precipitated by colonization and settlement was. The survey indicates that at the time of initial European contact, the Native American population ranged from 1.2 million to more than 2.6 million. This is an extremely conservative estimate. But, by 1890, when Native Americans made their last stand at Wounded Knee, South Dakota, their population had declined to about 250,000. This trend reflects the effects of warfare, forced marches, loss of traditional lands, and diseases such as smallpox, measles, influenza, and tuberculosis, to which Native Americans lacked immunity.

In the twentieth century, the Native American population has increased to about 2 million. Approximately two-thirds of this population live on reservations, and most of the remaining one-third live in major metropolitan areas. Native Americans are far below the average American in income and education.

Today, Native American reservation lands such as the Hopi and Navajo territories are sought by multinational corporations that want to develop reserves of coal, oil, natural gas, and uranium. Other companies have been making lucrative offers to lease Native American lands to be used as garbage landfills and toxic-waste dumps. These monetary offers have produced splits within Native American communities. Some favor the offers as a means of combating poverty whereas others condemn mining or any other commercial activity as a desecration of their sacred land. These issues present difficult decisions for Native American communities.

SOUTH AMERICAN HORTICULTURALISTS

In the Amazon rain forests of South America, tribal peoples such as the Yanomamö, the Jivaro, and the Mundurucu are facing dramatic changes resulting from globalization. Beginning in the 1950s, European and American missionaries representing different Christian denominations began to settle in the Amazon region and competed to "civilize" peoples such as the Yanomamö. In Venezuela the major missionary group are the Salesians, a Catholic mission. The missionaries attempted to persuade Yanomamö communities to reside in their mission stations. Those who did so became completely dependent on the missionaries, gradually abandoning their traditional means of subsistence and social life. The missionaries set up schools and teach the Yanomamö new methods of agriculture, and train them to spread these ideas among others. With the building of highways and increased settlement in the Amazon rain forest—developments sponsored by the Venezuelan and Brazilian governments—the Yanomamö became increasingly exposed to influenza, dysentery, measles, and colds. In some regions, almost 50 percent of the population have fallen victim to these diseases (Kellman, 1982).

One consequence of contact with the outside world was the Yanomamö's adoption of the shotgun for hunting in the forest. The Yanomamö originally obtained shotguns from the missionaries or other employees on the missions. Initially, Yanomamö hunters who knew the forest very well became proficient in obtaining more game. In time, however, the game in the rain forest grew more scarce. Consequently, the Yanomamö had to hunt deeper and deeper into the rain forest to maintain their diet. In addition, as indicated by ethnologist Raymond Hames (1979a), the Yanomamö had to expend much more labor in the cash economy to be able to purchase shotguns and shells to continue hunting. Additionally, some Yanomamö began to use the shotgun as a weapon in warfare and political intimidation and raiding with each other.

Recent Developments among the Yanomamö

The Amazon rain forest is experiencing new pressures. Prospectors, mining companies, energy companies, and government officials interested in industrial development are eager to obtain the gold, oil, tin, uranium, and other minerals in the 60,000 square miles of forest straddling the Brazilian and Venezuelan borders, where the Yanomamö live. A 1987 gold rush led to the settlement of at least 40,000 prospectors in Yanomamö territory. The prospectors hunt game in the forest, causing scarcities and increased malnutrition among the Yanomamö. Clashes between prospectors and the Yanomamö have led to many deaths. Most recently, in August 1993, gold miners massacred Yanomamö men, women, and children in Venezuela. After the attack, a Yanomamö leader described the massacre: "Many miners surrounded the lodge and started to kill Yanomamö. The women were cut in the belly, the breasts and the neck. I saw many bodies piled up" (Brooke, 1993, Chagnon, 1997).

Alarmed by these developments, concerned anthropologists, missionaries, and Brazilians have formed a committee to reserve an area for the Yanomamö to practice their traditional way of life. The Brazilian government and business leaders opposed this proposal, but eventually, the government alloted 8,000 square miles of land, which became known as Yanomamö Park. The land, however, was subdivided into small parcels that were impossible to defend against outsiders. In 1995 officials of the National Brazilian Indian Foundation (FUNAI) assured Napoleon Chagnon that there were no more than a few hundred illegal miners in the Yanomamö area and they were systematically trying to find and expel them (Chagnon, 1997). However, there are still news reports from Brazil indicating that more gold miners are infiltrating the area.

In Brazil, the drive toward economic development and industrialization has stimulated the rapid and tragic changes affecting the Yanomamö. The survival of the 9,000 Yanomamö in Brazil is in question. Their population has declined by one-sixth since the gold rush began in 1987. In contrast to Brazil, the Venezuelan government has been developing more humane and effective policies toward the Yanomamö natives. In 1991, then Venezuelan President Carlos Andres Perez took action to develop a reserve for the Yanomamö of some 32,000 square miles of rain forest as a "special biosphere" or national park that would be closed to mining and other development

(Chagnon, 1997). Then, in 1992, the Venezuelan government designated the Venezuelan Amazonas as a new state in its national political structure. State governments are being given more control over their own populations and resources. The resources of the new Amazonas state will probably include mineral wealth and tourism. Thus, the Yanomamö of Venezuela will become increasingly drawn into contact with outsiders. Whether this will mean more tragedy and epidemic diseases and economic problems for these natives is a question that can only be answered in the future. Anthropologists such as Napoleon Chagnon and Raymond Hames have been actively supporting the rights of the Yanomamö peoples as they themselves are becoming more aware of their future dilemma.

PASTORALIST TRIBES

Pastoralists have also been subjected to expanding industrial societies. The adaptive objectives of pastoralists tend to be at odds with the primary aims of state societies. Because of their nomadic way of life, pastoralists cannot be easily incorporated and controlled by state societies. They are not usually subject to the same processes of enculturation as settled peoples. They don't attend schools, and they may place their tribal loyalties above their loyalties to the state. Rapid change among pastoralist societies is evident in some Middle Eastern countries.

Middle Eastern Pastoralists: The Bedouins Anthropologist Donald Cole (1984) conducted research on the Bedouins of Saudi Arabia, groups of nomadic pastoralists. Cole focused on one particular group, the Al-Murrah, a tribe of 15,000 who live in the extreme desert conditions of Rub al-Khali. Traditionally, Al-Murrah subsistence was based on caravan trade, which depended on the care of camels and other animals. The Al-Murrah traded commodities with oasis centers for dates, rice, and bread. On average, they traveled about 1,200 miles annually during their migrations across the desert. They were also an autonomous military force, conducting raids and warfare.

The attempt to incorporate the Bedouin population into the Saudi state has been an ongoing process, going back to the early phases of state formation in the Arabian peninsula during the age of

Muhammad (A.D. 622–632). As Cole indicates, this process of settling and controlling the Bedouins accelerated following the emergence of the modern petroleum industry. To facilitate this process, the Saudi government drafted Al-Murrah males into their national guard.

The principal leader of the Al-Murrah, the emir, has been recognized by the Saudi government as the commander of this national guard unit. The government gives the emir a share of the national budget, and he distributes salaries to the tribespeople. Thus, the emir has become a dependent government official of the Saudi state.

The traditional subsistence economy based on nomadism and the care of herds of animals appears to be at an end. Camels are being replaced by pickup trucks. Bedouins are settling in cities and participating in the urban economy. All of the formerly self-sufficient Bedouin communities are being absorbed into nation-states throughout the Arabian peninsula.

The Qashqa'i   Ethnologist Lois Beck (1986) has written an in-depth study of the Qashqa'i pastoralist tribe of Iran. The Qashqa'i reside in the southern part of the Zagros Mountains. Beck emphasized that the Qashqa'i were to some degree a creation of state processes within Iran. In other words, the Qashqa'i tribe was not a self-contained entity but rather was formed through the long-term process of incorporating tribal leaders into the Iranian nation-state. During different historical periods, the state offered land and political protection to the Qashqa'i in exchange for taxes. Through that process the Qashqa'i leadership was able to maintain some autonomy. Eventually, the Qashqa'i political system became increasingly centralized around an economic and political elite. This is an example of how tribes may be formed as a result of an expansionist state political system.

As with other pastoralist societies, the Qashqa'i relationship with the central government in Iran was not always beneficial. During the 1960s, the Iranian government under Shah Pahlavi wanted to modernize and industrialize Iran rapidly with Western support (see Chapter 15). The government viewed the Qashqa'i as resisting modernization and used military force to incorporate them. This policy resulted in the establishment of strong ethnic boundaries between the Iranians and the Qashqa'i.

The Qashqa'i began to emphasize their own ethnic identity and to demand more autonomy.

In the initial stages of the Iranian Revolution led by Ayatollah Khomeini, the Qashqa'i joined demonstrations against the shah. Following the revolution, however, the Qashqa'i found themselves subject to patterns of discrimination and repression similar to those they had endured under the shah. Because they never accepted the revolutionary doctrines of the Khomeini regime, they were considered a threat to the ideals of the state. Consequently, they were harassed by Khomeini's Revolutionary Guards. Thus, Qashqa'i autonomy and local authority continued to erode under the pressures of the nation-state of Iran.

Chiefdoms in Transition

Some chiefdoms experienced a fate similar to that of many of the other nonstate societies we have just discussed. However, certain chiefdoms, most likely because they were more centrally organized, developed state organizations themselves following Western contact. The historical development of some Polynesian chiefdoms such as in Tahiti and Hawaii illustrates the evolution of state organization that occurred as a result of contact with the global economy.

Before contact with the West, Hawaii contained eight inhabited islands with a population of about 600,000. The Hawaiian chiefdom political structure was controlled by the paramount chiefs, who maintained a redistributional economic system and ruled through a belief in divine authority. The Hawaiian islands were contacted by the English expedition of Captain Cook in 1778, and the islands were eventually penetrated by traders, whalers, missionaries, and other outsiders. The impact of the Western encounter resulted in a unique religious "revolution" when compared with other aboriginal societies we have discussed in earlier sections.

Cook's expedition on the part of the British, which began in the 1760s, set the stage for the colonization of the Pacific. At the time of Captain Cook's discovery of Hawaii, the major paramount chief on the island of Hawaii was engaged in warfare with the chief of the island of Maui, who had already incorporated the islands of Oahu and Molokai under his chieftaincy. The reaction to

Cook's arrival during this period was shaped by the aboriginal religious culture. He appeared during the time of *Makahiki,* a time of religious-based human sacrifices (see chapter 10), and he was perceived as someone extremely powerful, perhaps as a god or at the least an important foreign chief. For a variety of different reasons, the Hawaiians ended up killing Captain Cook at this time (Sahlins, 1985, 1995, Obeyesekere, 1997).

Later, a man by the name of Kamehameha, who was a nephew of the Hawaiian chief, made a considerable reputation as a fearless warrior in the Maui campaign. When the chief of Hawaii died, Kamehameha became his successor. Because the island of Hawaii offered good anchorage and became a vital strategic point of contact with Europeans, Kamehameha had an advantage over any other rivals in trading with European ships. The Hawaiians began to trade their products such as sandalwood with Europeans, and in exchange Kamehameha received guns and light cannon. Eventually he was able to employ European help in conquering most of the other islands of Hawaii and transformed the Hawaiian chiefdoms into a unified, centralized military kingdom or state.

Kamehameha died in 1819 and was succeeded by his son Liholiho, later known as Kamehameha II. Since Western contact, Hawaii continued to be heavily influenced by Western culture. A number of traditional taboos of the Hawaiian culture were being violated on a regular basis. Some of the Hawaiian women were involved in sexual and romantic relationships with Westerners and openly ate with men, violating traditional taboos. Some of the commoner people began to trade openly with Europeans, which also violated traditional norms and taboos, causing tension between the rulers and commoners. Seeing practical advantages for trade with the Europeans and rule over their kingdom, in 1819, Liholiho, the new ruler, and other members of the royal family began to deliberately flout the most sacred traditional taboos of their ancient religion. The royal family began to systematically dismantle the aboriginal religious traditions and practices. This represented a revolutionary transformation in religious thought and culture for Hawaiian society. This transformation of religion was accomplished prior to the coming of Christian missionaries to Hawaii. This religious revolution was resisted by some of the more conservative peoples of Hawaii, and Liholiho had to arm his forces to defeat the more conservative faction within the kingdom. This Hawaiian revolution appeared to be an intentional strategy on the part of the ruling family to enhance their political control over the military kingdom.

The sandalwood trade declined in the 1830s and was transplanted by the whaling industry, which began to dominate commerce in Hawaii. Located within the vicinity of a major whaling area of the Pacific, New England whalers used Hawaii as a major base for provisioning and relaxation. However, during the 1830s, various companies began to develop sugar plantations in Hawaii, which eventually became more successful, resulting in the influx of more Europeans, including various Christian missionaries from the United States. Many of the missionaries were themselves sugar planters, or were connected with the sugar planters. Private property was introduced and land was commodified for sale. As the sugar plantations were developed, substantial native Hawaiian land was lost to the planters. Additionally, the native Hawaiians were subjected to devastating epidemics introduced by the Westerners. Whooping cough, measles, influenza, and other diseases led to rapid depopulation among the native peoples. As Hawaii became increasingly incorporated into the U.S. political economy during the nineteenth and twentieth centuries, the native population declined to a small minority of about forty thousand people. This depopulation resulted in a labor shortage for the sugar planters, who began to import labor from the Philippines, Japan, and China. In 1893, the United States, backed by American Marines, overthrew the Hawaiian monarchy, and five years later Hawaii was annexed as a colony. Following U.S. colonization, the Hawaiian islands were dominated by U.S. political and economic interests. Eventually, the native Hawaiian population became a marginal group in their own islands.

Eventually, through more contact with Western societies, the Pacific islands such as Hawaii and Tahiti experienced depopulation, deculturation, forced labor, and increased dependency on the global economy. Missionaries arrived along with whaling traders and the developers of sugar plantations. The American and European settlers imported labor from Asia, introduced the system of private property, abolished the traditional patterns of authority, and incorporated the islands into colonial empires. As these islands were integrated into colonial systems, the peoples were forced to adjust to the conditions of the global economy.

Through missionary schooling and activities the native Hawaiian people were forbidden to speak their native language or practice any of their traditional religious or cultural activities, which were deemed to be barbaric and uncivilized. These policies led to societal and cultural disintegration for the native population. Combined with the growing Asian population and new settlers from North America, who were rapidly developing the sugar economy, and the expansion of mass tourism to Hawaii from the mainland United States, the small modern Hawaiian population began to lose not only its native lands but also its cultural and ethnic identity (Friedman, 1992).

Forms of Resistance in Native Societies

As is evident from the preceding discussion, many nonstate societies resisted becoming incorporated into industrial states and colonial empires and have engaged in resistance movements, also known as *revitalization movements*. A **revitalization movement** is an attempt to reinstitute the traditional cultural values and beliefs of a group faced with dramatic changes. In some cases, revitalization movements take the form of violent military or political resistance. Generally, however, prestate peoples have lacked the technological capabilities to sustain armed resistance against more powerful societies. In most cases, therefore, these movements are nonviolent and have a strong religious element.

REVITALIZATION AMONG NATIVE AMERICANS

Native American societies developed a number of revitalization movements. One type of movement was associated with a particular prophet who was able to mobilize the population both politically and spiritually. In the Pueblo groups of the Southwest, a prophet leader known as Popé organized a rebellion against the Spanish rulers in 1680. The Pueblo tribes attacked the Spanish, killed the Catholic priests in the missions, and attempted to

reinstitute Pueblo traditions. Twenty years later, Spanish troops based in Mexico defeated this movement and reasserted their authority over the region.

Other Native American prophets such as Handsome Lake, Pontiac, Tecumseh, and Chief Joseph combined traditional religious values with military activities to resist European and American expansion into their territories. Eventually all of these leaders were defeated by the U.S. military.

The Ghost Dance   One of the best-known revitalization movements was the Ghost Dance movement of the late 1800s. The Ghost Dance spread through the region of Nevada and California, across the Rocky Mountains to Plains groups such as the Cheyenne, Arapaho, and Sioux. The movement became associated with the prophet Wovoka, a Paiute who was believed to have received spiritual visions of the future during an eclipse of the sun. Wovoka taught that if the Native American people did the Ghost Dance, a hypnotic dance with spiritual meanings, the whites would disappear and a train would come from the East with the ghosts of recently deceased Native Americans, signaling the restoration of Native American autonomy and traditions. Wovoka stressed nonviolent resistance and nonaccommodation to white domination (Kehoe, 1989).

Among the groups influenced by the Ghost Dance were the Lakota Sioux, who had been forced to reside on five reservations in South Dakota. In 1890, the Lakota Sioux leader, Kicking Bear, introduced a special shirt, called a "ghost shirt," that he claimed would protect the Sioux from the bullets of the white soldiers. The wearing of the ghost shirts precipitated conflicts between the U.S. military and the Sioux, culminating in a massacre of almost 200 Sioux at Wounded Knee, South Dakota, on December 29, 1890. Following that confrontation, Sioux leaders such as Kicking Bear surrendered themselves to the U.S. military.

Among the most common refrains of the Ghost Dance songs were

My children,/When at first I liked the whites,/I gave them fruits,/I gave them fruits. (Southern Arapaho)
The father will descend/The earth will tremble/ Everybody will arise,/Stretch out your hands. (Kiowa)
We shall live again./We shall live again. (Apache)
(Rothenberg, 1985:109–110)

Big Foot's frozen body after the Battle of Wounded Knee in 1890.

These Ghost Dance songs and dances are still heard among the Native Americans up to the present. For example, in February 1973, Wounded Knee once again became the site for a violent confrontation between the Plains Indians and the U.S. military forces. Led by leaders such as the Lakota Indians, Russel Means and spiritual leader Leonard Crow Dog, the Pine Ridge Indian reservation at Wounded Knee was taken over by the organization known as AIM, the American Indian Movement. AIM accused the tribal government leaders of political and economic corruption, and demanded justice and civil rights for all Native Americans. Leonard Crow Dog led a Ghost Dance ritual during the seventy-day occupation in order to create solidarity and spiritual renewal among the Sioux at Wounded Knee. (In addition, the Sun Dance ritual was also conducted at Pine Ridge in 1973). Fire fights between AIM and the FBI and U.S. forces were common throughout the longest siege in American history since the Civil War. The events of 1973 at Wounded Knee represented the frustration and resentment of many Native Americans regarding their conditions after a century of subordination by the U.S. government. The Ghost Dance led by Leonard Crow Dog symbolized the spiritual resurgence and religious renewal of contemporary Native Americans on the Plains.

The Peyote Cult Another form of revitalization movement developed among Native Americans on one Oklahoma reservation in the 1880s. It was also a nonviolent form of resistance, based on a combination of Christian and Native American religious beliefs. The movement is referred to as the *peyote cult*. *Peyote,* the scientific name of which is *Lophophora williamsii,* is a mild hallucinogenic drug contained in the bud of a cactus, which is either chewed or drunk as tea. It is a nonaddictive drug. Traditionally for thousands of years it has been used in some Native American rituals for inducing spiritual visions, especially in the southwest desert areas around the Rio Grande in both Mexico and North America. A number of Navaho Indians in the Southwest became involved in the ritual use of Peyote (Aberle, 1966). During their incarceration on the Oklahoma reservation, some of the Comanche, Kiowa, and other Plains Indians began to combine biblical teachings with the peyote ritual (Steinmetz, 1980). The ritual took place in a tepee, where the participants surrounded a fire and low altar and took peyote as a form of communal sacrament to partake of the "Holy Spirit." Eventually the peyote cult grew in membership and was legalized on the Oklahoma reservation as the Native American Church in 1914. It has spread throughout at least fifty other Native American tribes, and approximately 250,000 Indians are associated with the NAC.

MELANESIA AND NEW GUINEA: THE CARGO CULTS

As various Europeans colonized the islands of Melanesia the native peoples lives were forever transformed. The Dutch, French, British, and Germans claimed different areas as colonies. The Dutch from their colonial base in Indonesia took over the western half of New Guinea (now known as Irian Jaya, and a province of the country of Indonesia). In the 1880s, German settlers occupied the northeastern part of New Guinea. In the 1890s, gold was discovered in New Guinea, and many prospectors from Australia and other places began to explore the region. At the beginning of World War I in 1914, the Australians conquered the German areas. During World War II, the Japanese, Australians, and U.S. troops fought bitter battles in New Guinea. After the war, Australia resumed administrative control over the eastern half of the island until 1975, when Papua New Guinea was granted political independence. Today, the country of Papua New Guinea (PNG) occupies the eastern half of the island of New Guinea, and has about 4 million people.

The colonization of Melanesia and Papua New Guinea was both a dramatic and traumatic experience for native peoples as they faced new systems of economics with the introduction of cash wages, indentured labor, plantations, taxation, new forms of political control, and the unfathomable technologies and the apparently fabulous riches of the Europeans. Prospectors, traders, and soldiers during the World Wars created a highly unstable and unpredictable environment for Melanesian natives. One of the reactions to this rapid change that developed among the Melanesians took a religious and spiritual form. These Melanesian religious responses to Western impact were often loosely labeled as revitalization movements as so-called "cargo cults," a form of millenarian religious movement.

Beginning in the nineteenth century and continuing up to the present, these millenarian cult movements have spread throughout many areas of Melanesia. Generally, in New Guinea the coastal or seaboard peoples were contacted first by Europeans and by the end of the nineteenth century were subjected to intensive pressures from the outside world. The highland peoples were contacted much later and were not fully penetrated by the Europeans and Australians until after the 1930s. Many native peoples referred to the European or Australian goods that were loaded off ships or aircraft as *kago,* or as described by anthropologists as "cargo." The native peoples became aware of a dazzling array of goods such as steel axes, matches, medicines, soft drinks, umbrellas, and eventually jet planes and helicopters. Because these native peoples had no exposure to industrial production, they did not see how these Western goods were manufactured. Many, therefore, believed that these goods were generated through spiritual forces, which delivered "cargo" to humans through the spiritual means. Many of the tribal groups of this region attempted to discover the identity of the cargo spirits and the magical-ritual techniques used by Westerners to induce the spirits to deliver the particular commodities.

One New Guinean man who led a millenarian cult movement is known as Yali. Yali had lived in the coastal area of New Guinea, and in the 1950s was recognized as an important future leader of his people by the Australians. He had been a World

War II allied war hero fighting against the Japanese. The Australians took Yali to Australia to show him how the industrial goods were produced. Nevertheless, Yali maintained the belief that there must be a supernatural cause or divine intervention for the ability of Westerners to be able to produce cargo. He originated a millenarian cult movement known as *Wok bilong Yali* (Lawrence, 1964). Yali began to preach to hundreds of villages throughout New Guinea about how spiritual techniques needed to be developed to duplicate the white man's delivery of cargo. Over the years of this movement, Yali's teaching ranged from recommending close imitation of the Europeans to opposing white culture and returning to traditional rituals to help deliver the cargo. Although Yali openly rejected the millenarian cult movements beliefs in 1973, after his death many of his followers began to teach that Yali was a messiah equivalent to the white man's Jesus. In their religious literature they propagated these ideas of messiahship by using Yali's sayings to help develop a religious movement that was an alternative to Christianity.

However, some of the millenarian cult movements combined traditional rituals with Christian beliefs in the hope of receiving the material benefits they associated with the white settlers. One movement described by Paul Roscoe developed among the Yangoru Boiken of Papua New Guinea merged some of the millennial teachings of Canadian missionaries from the Switzerland-based New Apostolic Church (NAC) (1993). Roscoe describes how on Sunday, February 15, 1981, it was believed that Yaliwan, a leading spiritual and political leader was going to be crucified, ushering in the millennium. The villagers believed that the earth was going to rumble, hurricanes would arrive, and the mountains would flash with lightning and thunder, and a dense fog would cover the earth. Afterwards, Yaliwan would be resurrected as the native counterpart of Jesus, and the "two" Jesuses would judge the living and the dead. They believed that the whites and native members of the NAC would usher in a new "Kingdom of Rest," described as an earthly utopian paradise with an abundance of material goods and peaceful harmony between native peoples and whites. The millennial teachings of the NAC were interpreted and integrated with traditional Yangoru beliefs of spirits of the dead and other magical practices. Some of the traditional aboriginal beliefs had millenarian aspects promising the Yangoru economic prosperity and political autonomy. Therefore the NAC missionary teachings based on millenarian views were easily integrated with the traditional beliefs of the Yangoru. Though the crucifixion did not take place, various millenarian movements continue to have some influence on religious and political affairs in Papua New Guinea.

Various anthropologists have attempted to explain the development of the millenarian cult movements of Melanesia. One early explanation by anthropologist Peter Worsley views these millenarian cults as rational attempts at explaining unknown processes that appeared chaotic. The myths and religious beliefs of the cults also helped mobilize political resistance against colonialism. The cults provided an organizational basis for political action for the various Melanesia tribes. Groups who spoke different languages and maintained separate cultures joined the same religious cult. This enabled these people to form political organizations to challenge European and Australian colonial rule. Other explanations rely on more spiritually based phenomena emphasizing how the cargo cults represent the resurgence of aboriginal religious thought, which is more creative and authentic than that of the newer missionary religions that came to Melanesia. Yet, today, most anthropologists recognize that these millenarian cult phenomena are extremely varied.

As anthropologists learn more about these movements in different regions of Melanesia they discover that some have millenarian aspects, while others do not. Some of them integrate aboriginal beliefs and practices with the teachings of Christianity, a form of syncretism, while others feature a revival of the aboriginal elements and a rejection of the Christian teachings. A few of the movements have developed into vital political movements, and even violent rebellions, whereas others tend to have a purely spiritual influence. Anthropologists agree that the analysis of these cults is a fruitful area of investigation, and much more needs to be documented through interviews, historical examination and intensive ethnographic research.

A HAWAIIAN RELIGIOUS RENAISSANCE

As U.S. corporate capitalism and tourism became the dominant form of economy in Hawaii, every aspect of the traditional Hawaiian culture was affected. At present, the tourist industry generates close to 40 percent of Hawaii's income. Tourists crowd the hotels, restaurants, streets, highways, beaches, golf courses, and parks throughout Hawaii. The advertising industry attempts to promote the image of Hawaii as a romantic and exotic paradise setting where tourists can enjoy the traditional dancing, music, and culture of "primitive" peoples. Ads show skimpily clad women and men dancing before fires on near-deserted beaches. The tourist industry is involved in trying to preserve the traditional culture of Hawaii, because it is "good for business."

However, native Hawaiians have begun to resist the marketing of their culture. Beginning in the 1970s with a growing awareness of their marginal status in the U.S. political economy and more familiarity with the civil rights movement in the mainland U.S. led by various minorities, many Hawaiians have launched a movement known as the Hawaiian Renaissance. The Hawaiian Renaissance manifested itself as a resurgence of interest in aboriginal Hawaiian culture, including the traditional language and religious beliefs. The movement is fundamentally antitourist. Many contemporary native Hawaiians who are part of the new movement understand that their traditional culture has been mass-marketed and mass-consumed. They feel that their traditional culture has been overly commercialized, and they resent the tourist industry for selling the Hawaiian tradition.

Some of the spiritual elements of the native religious beliefs have been reintroduced and revitalized in the context of the Hawaiian Renaissance movement. For example, a number of native Hawaiians have become involved in environmental activism. In doing so, they draw on traditional religious beliefs. They are attempting to prohibit the destruction of the rain forests and other natural settings by developers. The native peoples emphasize a spiritual renewal and refer to traditional Hawaiian gods and goddesses that are associated with the natural areas in order to protect these areas from destructive tourist and commercial forces. In some areas, the native Hawaiians are restoring some of the ancient temples, or *heiaus*. Native Hawaiians can be seen making offerings to the god Pele at the rim of Halemaumau Crater in the Hawaii Volcanoes National Park. Some aboriginal young people complain about their parent's conversion to Christianity, and the negative views ex-

Many Native Hawaiians are beginning to emphasize their traditional ethnic heritage. In 1993 a march was held to commemorate the 100th anniversary of the Native Hawaiian monarchy.

pressed by Westerners about their traditional culture and religion. However, most importantly, the revitalization of their religious culture is part of an overall attempt to preserve their heritage and reclaim their cultural identity and selfhood. As these native peoples of Hawaii were subjected to overwhelming and traumatic cultural change, they found that they were marginalized in their own land. After losing their land, their autonomy, and their culture, these native Hawaiians have been involved in reconstructing and reinvigorating some of their aboriginal spiritual beliefs as a means of repossessing their cultural identity (Friedman, 1995).

A Lost Opportunity?

As Brian Fagan noted in his book *Clash of Cultures* (1984), which surveys the disappearance of many nonstate societies, the same confrontations between incompatible cultural systems were played out in many parts of the world during the late nineteenth century and continue to this day in the Amazon rain forests and other remote areas. Some government officials and businesspeople in industrial countries view the drastic modifications that took place and are taking place among prestate societies as necessary for the achievement of progress. This view is, of course, a continuation of the nineteenth-century unilineal view of cultural evolution, which overestimates the beneficial aspects of industrial societies. Depopulation, deculturation, fragmentation of the social community, increasingly destructive warfare, unemployment, and increases in crime, alcoholism, and degradation of the environment are only some of the consequences of this so-called progress. As Fagan (1984b:278) emphasized:

> *Progress has brought many things: penicillin, the tractor, the airplane, the refrigerator, radio, and television. It has also brought the gun, nuclear weapons, toxic chemicals, traffic deaths, and environmental pollution, to say nothing of powerful nationalisms and other political passions that pit human being against human being, society against society. Many of these innovations are even more destructive to non-Western societies than the land grabbing and forced conversion of a century and a half ago.*

As was discussed in previous chapters, prestate societies were not idyllic, moral communities in which people lived in perfect harmony with one another and their environment. Warfare, sexism, infanticide, slavery, stratification, and other harmful practices existed in many of these societies. Nonstate societies are not inherently good, and industrial societies are not inherently evil. Both types of societies have advantages and disadvantages, strengths and weaknesses. There are benefits associated with industrial societies, such as hospitals, better sanitation, and consumer goods that bring comfort and enjoyment, but nonstate societies also have benefits to offer to industrial societies.

Anthropological research has begun to alert the modern industrial world to the negative implications of the rapid disappearance of first nation peoples—specifically, the loss of extensive practical knowledge that exists in these populations. In the nineteenth-century view (and sometimes even in twentieth-century discourse), nonstate societies are described as backward, ignorant, and nonscientific. Ethnological research, however, demonstrates that these peoples have developed a collective wisdom that has contributed practical benefits for all of humankind.

A CASE STUDY:
NATIVE AMERICAN KNOWLEDGE

In a book titled *Indian Givers,* anthropologist Jack Weatherford (1988) summarized the basic knowledge, labor, and experience of Native American peoples that have contributed to humankind's collective wisdom. Native Americans introduced 300 food crops to the world, including potatoes and corn. Their experiments with horticultural diversity generated knowledge regarding the survival of crops in different types of environments. They recognized that planting a diversity of seeds would protect the seeds from pests and diseases. Only recently have farmers in the industrialized world begun to discover the ecological lessons developed by Native Americans.

The medical knowledge of Native Americans, which is based on experience with various plants and trees, has benefited people throughout the world. Weatherford uses the example of quinine, derived from the bark of the South American cinchona tree, which is used to treat malaria. Ipecac was made from the roots of an Amazonian tree as a cure for amoebic dysentery. Native Americans treated scurvy with massive doses of vitamin C, using a tonic made from the bark and needles of an evergreen tree. They also had developed treatments for goiter, intestinal worms, headaches (with a medication similar to aspirin), and skin problems. The lesson from Weatherford's book is that without the contributions of Native American soci-

eties, humankind may not have acquired this knowledge for years. As globalization brings about the disappearance of nonstate societies, humanity risks losing a great deal of knowledge. For example, as the Amazon rain forests are invaded and destroyed by governments and multinational interests, not only do we lose hundreds of species of plants and animals but we also lose the indigenous societies with their incalculable knowledge of those species. Thus, it is in humanity's best interests to abandon the view that deculturation, subjugation, and—sometimes—the extinction of nonstate societies represent a form of progress.

The most difficult issue that faces anthropologists, government officials, and aboriginal peoples is how best to fit traditional patterns in with the modern, industrial world. The fact that these nonstate societies were and are almost powerless to resist the pressures from global economic and political forces creates enormous problems. Multinational corporations, national governments, missionaries, prospectors, and other powerful groups and institutions place these indigenous societies in vulnerable circumstances. How will nonstate societies withstand these pressures and continue to contribute to humankind?

PRESERVING INDIGENOUS SOCIETIES

Most anthropologists argue that indigenous peoples should be able to make free and informed choices regarding their destiny, instead of being coerced into assimilating (Bodley, 1990, Hitchcock, 1988). As previously discussed, many nonstate societies have tried to resist domination by outside powers but generally lack the power to do so successfully. In some cases, anthropologists have assisted these peoples in their struggles. Anthropologists such as Napoleon Chagnon have set up foundations to collect money to aid indigenous peoples in their struggles against governments and economic interests who demand their territory. At Harvard University, anthropologists under the guidance of David Maybury-Lewis formed an organization known as Cultural Survival that seeks to aid nonstate societies in their confrontations with industrial and global pressures. Anthropologists such as Robert Hitchcock, a student of Richard Lee, has become an internationally known advocate of

APPLYING ANTHROPOLOGY

Marketing Products of the Rain Forest

Anthropologists are involved in using their cultural knowledge of different societies to solve some of the problems faced by indigenous peoples. One anthropologist actively engaged in trying to develop techniques to help native peoples cope with the new changes induced by globalization is Jason Clay. Clay is director of research at Cultural Survival, the major anthropological organization committed to aiding indigenous peoples in their adaptation to the processes of globalization.

Clay has recently developed a project to expand the market for products from tropical rain forests. Under his leadership, Cultural Survival has established a nonprofit trading company, Cultural Survival Imports. The major objective of this project is to use the world market to save the rain forest. (Destroying the forest leads to global problems such as the greenhouse effect and the disruption of indigenous societies.) Cultural Survival Imports has funded management projects for indigenous peoples who produce goods for the world market. These goods include nuts, roots, fruits, pigments, oils, and fragrances that can be regularly harvested without harming the rain forest. One

of the major clients of Cultural Survival Imports is Ben & Jerry's Homemade, an American ice cream company. In 1990, Ben & Jerry's ordered 200,000 pounds of Brazil nuts and 100,000 pounds of cashews. It set up a separate company, Community Products, to manufacture a nut brittle for Ben & Jerry's and other distributors to use in ice cream, cookies, and candy. The ice cream, called "Rainforest Crunch," is available in Ben & Jerry's stores. The company also markets rain forest sherbets and fruit ice creams, rotating flavors every four to six weeks to coincide with the seasons of the rain forest.

Another client of Cultural Survival Imports is the Body Shops, a cosmetic firm based in England. The company is interested in marketing oils, flours, nuts, fibers, fruits, and fragrances for developing organic cosmetic products. For example, in 1990, the company ordered 80 tons of copaiba oil, a product to be used for shampoos, face creams, lotions, soaps, and massage creams.

These orders for sustainable commodities have immediate benefits for the peoples of the rain forest. For example, in 1989, the nut collectors of Brazil received

only 3 to 4 cents per pound for nuts that sold for more than $1.50 a pound wholesale in New York City. Cultural Survival is using grants from international aid groups to help gatherers of forest products to form marketing and processing cooperatives. Through the strengthening of this marketing system, Cultural Survival can guarantee producers higher, more stable prices for these commodities.

Jason Clay has taken 350 product samples out of Brazil to exhibit to about forty companies in the United States and Europe. He predicts that American and European consumers will soon be using such products from the rain forest in sherbets, yogurts, oils, shampoos, and perfumes. In addition, Clay wants to expand the markets in the countries where these rain forests are located. Many people in cities such as São Paulo and Rio de Janeiro in Brazil have never eaten the most common fruits of the Amazon. Increased marketing in these nations will contribute to the preservation of the rain forests and also lead to improvements for the native populations of these areas, which will ultimately benefit all of humanity.

the rights of indigenous peoples such as the Ju/'ho-ansi.

Since the 1970s, many indigenous peoples themselves have become active in preserving their way of life. At a 1975 assembly on Nootka tribal lands on Vancouver Island, the World Council of Indigenous Peoples was founded. Fifty-two delegates representing indigenous peoples from nineteen countries established this council, which has become a nongovernmental organization of the

United Nations (Fagan, 1984b). The council endorsed the right of indigenous peoples to maintain their traditional economic and cultural structures. It emphasized that native populations have a special relationship to their languages and should not be forced to abandon them. It further stressed that land and natural resources should not be taken from native populations. Perhaps this new political awareness and activism will enable these inhabitants to exercise greater control over their future economic, political, and cultural adjustments in the modern world.

SUMMARY

Social scientists have developed three basic models for understanding the process of globalization. The first, known as modernization theory, maintains that traditionalism retards industrial expansion and social change in underdeveloped societies. Modernization theorists propose education and change in cultural values as prerequisites for economic and social development. Modernization theorists developed the terms First, Second, and Third Worlds.

The second perspective, dependency theory, developed as a critique of modernization. Dependency theorists view global change as the consequence of relationships between the industrial capitalist societies and underdeveloped precapitalist societies. They focus on the spread of the capitalist world economy and the political domination of the poor underdeveloped societies by wealthy nations.

The third approach is world-systems theory, which divides the world into core, peripheral, and semiperipheral nations, based on economic criteria. The world-systems approach has helped social scientists to understand worldwide changes based on the interconnections among different societies. Anthropologists evaluate these different models by collecting empirical data through ethnological studies.

Globalization has directly affected nonstate societies, or indigenous peoples. Ever since industrialist expansion began, foragers, tribes, and chiefdoms have undergone rapid changes. Among the negative consequences of globally induced change are depopulation, deculturation, the disintegration of social communities, and, in some cases, genocide.

Many nonstate peoples developed forms of resistance known as revitalization movements as they confronted the industrialized nations. Movements such as the Ghost Dance, the peyote cult, and the various cargo cults represented attempts at reinstituting traditional cultural patterns.

Anthropologists have warned that the disappearance of native societies leads to the loss of beneficial knowledge. Thus, it is in the interest of all of humanity to see that these populations do not become extinct. Recently, anthropologists have focused their activities on trying to give native peoples a choice in preserving their cultural heritage, land, and resources. Indigenous peoples are becoming politically aware and active in demanding their autonomy and human rights.

STUDY QUESTIONS

1. Describe the five stages by which a traditional society undergoes modernization to reach a level of high economic growth.

2. As the head of state of an underdeveloped nation, what are the public policies that you would implement if you wished to modernize your society?

3. Given a choice between modernization theory and dependency theory, which model do you prefer to explain the existence of vast inequities between industrialized capitalist societies and the precapitalist societies? What are the strengths of the model you prefer? What are its weaknesses?

4. What are the principal elements of Immanuel Wallerstein's world-systems theory? How has the theory been used in anthropology?

5. Describe some of the changes that have occurred in the Ju/'hoansi society as a result of global industrialization. What are some of the ways that the negative effects of industrialization can be reversed?

6. Discuss the principal factors that result in deculturation. What are some of the risks that deculturation poses for a traditional society?

7. What governmental policies contributed to the decline of Native American populations in the United States?

8. What do you think ought to be the policies of governments toward native peoples? Why?

KEY TERMS

colonies

core societies

deculturation

dependency theory

ethnocide

First World

genocide

global industrialism

imperialism

modernization theory

peripheral societies

revitalization movement

Second World

semiperipheral societies

Third World

underdeveloped society

world-systems theory

INTERNET EXERCISES

1. Review the Samuel's Memory at **http://pages.tca.net/martikw/samuel.html.** How does this story relate to the overall theme of the chapter? How does ethnocentrism allow for this behavior by the United States Army? What is the purpose of the Army? How does the Army function as a tool of the overall society?

2. Compare the author's view of globalization to that of the following website: **http://www.humanities.mcmaster.ca/~global/themeschool/globaliz.htm.** What are the similarities? What are the differences? How do modern corporations contribute to globalization?

SUGGESTED READINGS

BODLEY, JOHN H., ed. 1988. *Tribal Peoples and Development Issues: A Global Overview.* Mountain View, CA: Mayfield. A collection of essays dealing with human rights, development, health conditions, conservation, and policies affecting Fourth World peoples.

————. 1990. *Victims of Progress,* 3rd ed. Mountain View, CA: Mayfield. The most comprehensive treatment of the impact of globalization on Fourth World societies. Bodley details the plight of nonstate societies everywhere as they confront the industrialized world. He summarizes the different approaches taken by government officials and anthropologists in trying to aid indigenous peoples.

CHIROT, DANIEL. 1986. *Social Change in the Modern Era.* Orlando, FL: Harcourt Brace Jovanovich. A comprehensive account of the impact of the Western capitalist world economy; it draws on modernization, dependency, and world-systems approaches.

JOSEPHY, ALVIN M., Jr. 1976. *The Patriot Chiefs: A Chronicle of American Indian Resistance.* New York: Penguin Books. A good historical account of different Native American resistance leaders, including Handsome Lake, Pope, Pontiac, Tecumseh, Crazy Horse, and Chief Joseph.

WEYLER, REX. 1982. *Blood of the Land: The Government and Corporate War against the American Indian Movement.* New York: Vintage Books. A detailed account of how Native American peoples are deprived of their rights to land and resources by the U.S. government and multinational corporations.

The organization Cultural Survival Inc., located at 11 Divinity Avenue, Cambridge, MA 02138, publishes newsletters and studies on first nation peoples.

14

Globalization in Latin America, Africa, and the Caribbean

CHAPTER OUTLINE

Globalization and Colonialism
Latin America/ Africa / The Caribbean

Consequences of Globalization and Colonialism
Demographic Change / Economic Change / Religious Change

Political Changes: Independence and Nationalist Movements
Explaining Revolution

Uneven Development in Latin America, Africa, and the Caribbean
Peripheral Societies / Semiperipheral Societies

Ethnological Studies of the Peasantry in Latin America, Africa, and the Caribbean
African Peasants: A Unique Phenomenon?

Social Structure in Latin America, Africa, and the Caribbean
Latin American Social Relationships / African Social Relationships

Ethnicity in Latin America, Africa, and the Caribbean
Ethnicity in Latin America / Ethnicity in Africa / Ethnicity in the Caribbean

Patterns of Urban Anthropology

CHAPTER QUESTIONS

■ What were the early phases of Western colonialism like for Latin America, Africa, and the Caribbean?

■ What were the demographic, economic, political, and religious changes associated with globalization in Latin America, Africa, and the Caribbean?

■ Why did independence, nationalist, and revolutionary movements develop in Latin America, Africa, and the Caribbean?

■ How are the Latin American, African, and Caribbean countries situated in the global economy today?

■ What have anthropologists learned about the peasantry in in Latin America, Africa, and the Caribbean countries?

■ What are the characteristics of family and gender relationships in Latin America, Africa, and the Caribbean countries?

■ How has urbanization influenced Latin America, Africa, and the Caribbean countries?

Most anthropologists have focused on non-Western countries for their ethnological research. To understand how local conditions and cultures have been influenced by globalization processes, they have had to adopt a broad global perspective in their research. The non-Western countries of Latin America, the Caribbean, and Africa comprise a complex of diversified regions and cultures that cannot be characterized easily. The various countries in these regions are located in different types of environmental zones, ranging from highland mountain areas to lowland river valleys to small island regions to complex urban centers. Each country is made up of various ethnic groups in different proportions. As a result of globalization all of these countries are at different stages of political and economic development. In Chapter 13 we discussed various band, tribal, and chiefdom societies that exist in these different regions and how globalization has had an impact on their development. This chapter begins with an overview of the spread of globalization and colonialism in Latin America, Africa, and the Caribbean. We proceed with a discussion of some consequences of globalization processes on these regions. Finally, we discuss various ethnographic studies that have illuminated the effects of globalization on various institutions in these various countries.

Globalization and Colonialism in Latin America, Africa, and the Caribbean

LATIN AMERICA

Following Columbus's explorations in the 1400s, Spanish and Portuguese conquistadores led expeditions to the Americas. Recall that this was the period of mercantilism (see Chapter 13), when European states were competing to accumulate wealth to build their national treasuries. The Portuguese and Spanish were the first Europeans to engage in this mercantilist competition. Columbus believed that he had reached islands off Asia, and the Spanish and Portuguese were anxious to acquire access to this new trade route, in part to cut off the Muslim monopoly of trade in the Mediterranean and Asia. Thus, the primary objectives of the conquistadores were to find wealth and conquer the Americas.

The indigenous societies of Latin America consisted of three major types of sociocultural systems: some small-scale hunting-gathering bands; horticulturalist tribes, who lived in permanent or semipermanent villages and supplemented their diet by hunting, fishing, and gathering; and chiefdoms and agricultural empires, such as the Aztec and Inca, with great achievements in technology, architecture, economic organization, and statecraft.

In 1494, the Spanish and Portuguese governments agreed to the Treaty of Tordesillas, which divided the world into two major mercantilist spheres of influence. As a result, in the Americas the Portuguese took control of what is now Brazil, and the Spanish gained access to most of the remainder of Latin America.

Cortés and the Aztec Empire   The first major collision between the Spanish and the indigenous peoples occurred in 1519, when Hernando Cortés confronted the Aztec Empire in Mexico. After landing at Veracruz, Cortés encouraged many native groups who had been conquered and subjugated by the Aztecs to revolt against the Aztecs and their ruler, Montezuma. Besieged by these rebellious peoples and the superior weaponry of the Spaniards—especially guns and cannon—the Aztec state quickly crumbled. In 1521, Cortés and his Native American allies captured Tenochtitlan, establishing Spanish domination over the entire empire.

The Spanish then went on to conquer Mesoamerica, including Mexico, Honduras, and Guatemala, and areas in southeastern and southwestern North America. Similar conquests occurred in various regions of South America, such as Francisco Pizarro's conquest of the Incas. The Spanish ransacked these civilizations, taking the gold, silver, precious stones, and other valuables these people had accumulated. After this first phase of conquest and occupation, the Spanish began to exploit the sources of this wealth for the benefit of their home country. They developed systems of mining, commercial agriculture, livestock raising, and trading. These new forms of economic organization drastically transformed the sociocultural systems of the Americas.

The region of Brazil in South America contained no productive agricultural states such as those of the Aztecs or Incas, and the native population consisted of only about 1 million people. Therefore, instead of searching for wealth in gold, silver, and other precious goods, the Portuguese turned immediately to developing commercial agriculture and introduced sugar plantations. The plantation system initially relied on local labor, but because there were few natives in this area, the Portuguese also imported African slaves.

AFRICA

Mercantilist expansion into Africa began with the Portuguese, who came seeking gold; their explorers reached the West African coast in the second half of the fifteenth century. Although they did not find in Africa the vast amounts of gold that the Americas had yielded, they discovered another source of wealth: slaves.

Slave Trade   In earlier chapters, we noted that slavery was an accepted institution in some chiefdoms and agricultural states around the world. Slavery existed throughout much of the ancient agricultural world, including Egypt, Greece, Rome, the Middle East, and parts of Africa. Until the twentieth century, various Middle Eastern empires maintained an extensive slave trade based on African labor (Hourani, 1991). In Africa, agricultural states such as the Asante kingdom kept war captives and criminals as slaves. This slavery, however, was much different from that of later Western societies (Davidson, 1961; Goody, 1980). In Chapter 11 we discussed the

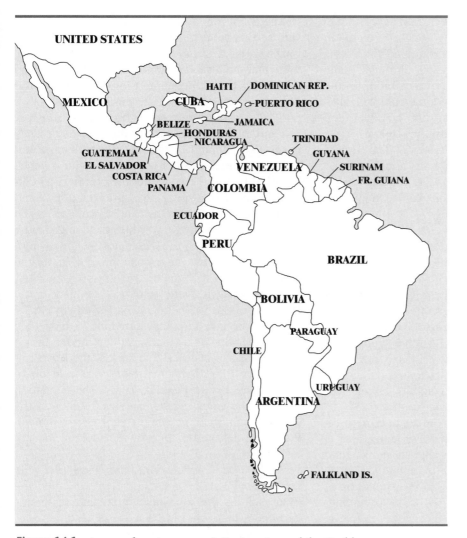

Figure 14.1   A map of contemporary Latin America and the Caribbean.

"open" forms of slavery associated with societies with abundant land and low populations. In Africa, this open system included slaves who were attached to extended families and became part of the domestic social unit. They could own property and marry, and they were protected from mutilation and murder by formalized norms or legal institutions.

The Portuguese initiated the European slave trade around 1440. They took slaves from coastal areas of West Africa to Portugal and to some islands in the Mediterranean. African slaves became the major source of labor for the expanding plantation systems in North and South America. Portugal, Holland, and—by the 1700s—England and France became the dominant slave-trading nations.

Unlike the "open" forms of slavery found in Africa, these Western countries classified slaves as property, with no personal rights, who could never be incorporated into the owner's domestic family or social system. These countries traded goods and weapons with certain African groups, who in turn supplied the Europeans with slaves. Sometimes African leaders simply relied on the local institutions of slavery to sell their own slaves to the Europeans. In many cases, however, coastal Africans raided inland villages for slaves. These practices had emerged in the earlier slave trade with the Islamic empires to the north.

Millions of slaves were taken from Africa and transported to the areas of Latin America and the Caribbean. The Atlantic slave trade declined in the early nineteenth century, when antislavery movements in Britain and France led to the prohibition of slave trading. British ships patrolled the coasts of Africa to capture slave traders, although many ships eluded this blockade. Slave trade to the United States ended in 1808, but the complete abolition of the slave trade was not possible until countries such as Brazil and the United States abandoned their plantation systems. The United States made slavery illegal in 1865, and Brazil did so in 1888 (Stavrianos, 1995). The devastating effects of the slave trade, however, continue to plague Africa up to the present.

Colonization   Europeans generally did not venture into the interior of Africa for colonization during the mercantilist phase. The threat of malaria and military resistance kept them in the coastal regions. During the late nineteenth century, however, European nations began to compete vigorously for African territories. To serve their needs for raw materials and overseas markets, the British, French, Dutch, Belgians, and Germans partitioned different areas of Africa into colonies, as reflected in the boundaries of present-day countries.

In West Africa, the difficult climate and the presence of diseases such as malaria discouraged large-scale European settlement. The British, French, and Germans, however, established commercial enterprises to control the production and exportation of products such as palm oil (used in soap making) and cocoa (Wolf, 1982).

In central Africa, King Leopold of Belgium incorporated the 900,000 acres of the Congo as a private preserve. He controlled the basic economic assets of the region through stock ownership in companies that were allowed to develop the rubber and ivory trade. In doing so, the king used brutal methods of forced labor that caused the population to decline by one-half (from 20 million to 10 million) during his reign, from 1885 to 1908 (Stavrianos, 1995).

In East Africa during the 1880s, the Germans and the British competed for various territories to develop plantations and other enterprises. This rivalry eventually resulted in treaties that gave the British the colony of Kenya and the Germans a large territory known as Tanganyika. British and German settlers flocked to these countries and took possession of lands from the native peoples.

The colonization of southern Africa began in the late seventeenth century, when Dutch explorers built a refueling station for their ships at Cape Town. From that site, Dutch settlers, called first "Boers" and later "Afrikaners," penetrated into the region. The Boers displaced, and often enslaved, the native peoples, including foragers such as the Ju/'hoansi or San and tribal peoples such as the Hottentots. They eventually adopted a racially based, hierarchical system in which the Boers held the highest ranks, followed by the coloreds (people of mixed parentage), the Bantu-speaking agriculturalists, and people like the Ju/'hoansi and Hottentots. Each group was segregated from the others and treated differently. Most of the Hottentots were eventually decimated by the Boers through genocidal policies.

As the Dutch were settling these lands, the British were also penetrating into southern Africa. They incorporated several kingdoms, which they transformed into native reservations under British control. Fearful of British expansion, the Boers migrated north into lands that had long been inhabited by the Bantu-speaking Zulus. This migration became known as the "Great Trek." Although the Zulus fought bitterly against this encroachment, they were defeated in 1838 by the superior military technology of the Boers.

As the Boers moved north, they established the republics of Natal, the Orange Free State, and the Transvaal. In the meantime, gold and diamonds had been discovered in these areas, leading to intense competition between the British and the Boers. In the Boer War of 1899–1902, the British defeated the Boers and annexed all of their republics. In 1910, the British established the Union of South Africa.

THE CARIBBEAN

The Caribbean islands consist of four distinct geographical regions. The first contains the Bahamas nearest to the coast of North America. The second group of islands are called the Greater Antilles consisting of Cuba, and Hispaniola (Haiti and the Dominican Republic), Jamaica, the Cayman islands, Puerto Rico, and the Virgin islands. The third region is referred to as the Lesser Antilles and includes Antigua, Barbuda, Dominica, St Lucia, St. Vincent, the Grenadines, Grenada, and St. Christopher-Nevis (St. Kitts). The fourth set of islands are off the coast of South America and includes Trinidad, Tobago, Barbados, Aruba, Cuacao, and Bonaire. Some of the islands such as Cuba, Haiti, and Puerto Rico came under Spanish rule by 1500. Others were divided up by other European powers such as the British, French, and Dutch. Unlike the mainland regions, these islands did not have large, complex agricultural states with accumulated treasures. Therefore, the colonial powers introduced commercialized agriculture usually in the form of sugar plantations, an agricultural system that had been developing in the Mediterranean region. As these sugar plantations were developed large numbers of African slaves were imported by the Europeans to labor on these plantations. When the African slave trade began to decline, the British replaced slave labor with East Indian workers on some of the islands. Thus, the islands of the Caribbean are an extremely culturally diverse region with Hispanic, French, Dutch, African, and East Indian influences.

An example of the strong traditional African influence is evident within Haiti, Jamaica, and other islands. For example, Carriacou, a small island located in the Eastern Caribbean between Grenada and St. Vincent, provides an example of the retention and reformulation of African beliefs and practices in the context of New World slavery. Most residents of Carriacou are descendants of African slaves brought to the island in the 17th and 18th centuries by first French, and later British, planters. After emancipation in the 1830s, most of the European planters left; the former slaves developed a relatively egalitarian society based on subsistence activities such as farming and fishing, supplemented by market activity and also by migration to places offering opportunities for wage labor.

This relative isolation allowed Carriacou people to maintain their connections to their African past in ways not available to former slaves in other places. For example, Carriacouans continue to trace their descent from particular African ethnic groups, some of which are Igbo, Yoruba, Mandingo, Congo, and Kromanti (Asante). Along with this knowledge, talented musicians keep alive the traditional drumming patterns associated with each group, and these have been combined over the years with new songs in Creole French and Creole English.

The songs and drumming patterns are the central feature of the ritual known as the Big Drum or Nation Dance, which is held to celebrate special occasions such as the launching of a boat, a marriage, the placing of a permanent tombstone, or a bountiful harvest. A Big Drum ceremony may also be held to honor a request for food from the ancestors; such requests come to the living through dreams, and are considered very important.

The Big Drum ceremony usually takes place at night in the yard of the ceremony's sponsor. An important feature of the ceremony, in addition to the drumming and singing, is food which is prepared in sufficient quantity to be shared with all who attend the ceremony. Some of the food is set aside for the ancestors; this food, called the *saraka* or "parents plate," is placed on a table inside the house and watched over by an elder woman called a *gangan*. This woman has "special sight" and can tell when the ancestors have come and eaten their fill; the *saraka* is then distributed among the children at the ceremony.

The ceremony, including the drumming and the sharing out of food, might be considered an example of egalitarian redistribution similar to that which takes place in some tribal societies, as it serves to reinforce the Carriacouan values of egalitarianism and sharing (Hill, 1977, McDaniel, 1998).

Consequences of Globalization and Colonialism

DEMOGRAPHIC CHANGE

The immediate impact of the West on Mesoamerica, South America, Africa, and the Caribbean was disastrous for local populations. In Mesoamerica, South America, and the Caribbean the native population began to decline drastically.

One of the major reasons for this decline was the introduction of diseases—smallpox, typhoid fever, measles, influenza, the mumps—to which the Indians had no resistance, because they had never been exposed to them before. In Brazil and the Caribbean, the importation of African slaves led to the introduction of diseases such as malaria and yellow fever. Although the numbers vary, archaeologists estimate that at least 25 million people lived in Mesoamerica alone when the Europeans arrived; by 1650, only 1.5 million remained (Wolf, 1982).

Rapid depopulation was also due to the stresses induced by the new forms of labor to which these peoples were subjected. Large-scale slave raiding decimated native populations. The rigorous forms of enforced labor—including slavery—in mining, plantations, and livestock raising created serious health problems and caused numerous deaths. In addition, the collapse of the indigenous patterns of intensive agriculture brought about famines and food shortages. All of these factors increased the social and biological stresses that aided the spread of disease in these populations (Wolf, 1982).

The demographic consequences of the slave trade in Africa were also immense. Historians estimate that as many as 40 million Africans were captured from the interior between 1440 and 1870 (Stavrianos, 1995). During this period, about 30 million Africans perished on their march from the inland regions or during the voyage to the New World. Approximately 12 million Africans were imported forcibly to the Americas (Lovejoy, 1989). Many of these were in their prime reproductive years, which, in conjunction with the wars between the coastal and interior regions, may account for the slow growth of Africa's population during this period (Wolf, 1982).

In the long run, however, Western expansion and colonialism in non-Western countries brought unprecedented demographic growth to the populations of these agricultural states. For example, the population of Mexico tripled in the nineteenth century from 2.5 million to 9 million, and Cuba's population increased from 550,000 to 5.8 million in 1953. Apparently, as Europeans began to remove the indigenous population from traditional subsistence peasant farming to the production of cash crops, fertility rates began to rise in the traditional villages. In the villages, there were labor shortages, and peasants responded by having larger extended families to try to maintain their subsistence peasant farming (Robbins, 1999). And, generally, fertility rates remain high in most of the countries of Latin America, Africa, and the Caribbean.

Eventually, new medical and sanitation practices introduced by modernization led to a tremendous reduction in death rates through the control of smallpox, plague, yellow fever, and malaria. Meanwhile, birthrates remained high. The combi-

nation of reduced death rates and high birthrates led to dramatic population increases. In Chapter 16 we will discuss some of the global effects of these population trends.

ECONOMIC CHANGE

The economic changes that occurred with globalization in Latin America, Africa, and the Caribbean countries wrought a dramatic transformation in these societies. In Latin America, the Spanish developed large-scale mining operations that used forced labor. In addition to gold, the Spanish discovered vast supplies of silver in Mexico and Bolivia. The American mines eventually became the major source of bullion accumulated by mercantile Spain. For example, of the 7 million pounds of silver extracted from these mines, 40 percent was collected by the Spanish Crown.

New patterns of economic organization in Latin America and the Caribbean were introduced after the Iberian (Portuguese and Spanish) conquest. In the Spanish areas, the Crown rewarded the conquistadores with the *encomienda,* or grant of Indian land, tribute, and labor, which, because it was based on forced labor, reduced the Indians to dependents.

Eventually, the *encomienda* system was superseded by the *hacienda* (in Brazil, *fazenda*), meaning large-scale farm. Established during the colonial period, *haciendas* and *fazendas* remained the major economic institutions in Latin America until the mid-twentieth century. The owners, called *hacendados* or *fazendieros,* acquired status, wealth, and power by owning the land and subjugating the tenants, or *peons,* who were tied to the *haciendas* through indebtedness and lived in shacks. In certain respects, the *haciendas* and *fazendas* were similar to the feudalistic manors of European societies described in Chapter 11.

Although the *haciendas* and *fazendas* were self-sufficient economic units providing the essential resources for the owners and tenants, they were not efficient (Wolf, 1969, 1982). The *hacendados,* preoccupied with their social prestige and comfortable lifestyle, did not attempt to produce cash crops for the world market or use their land productively. This pattern of inefficient, localized production and marketing of the *haciendas* is still visible in much of Latin America.

After three centuries of Iberian rule, much of Latin America consisted of these inefficient *haciendas,* economically deprived Indian communities with limited land, and a native population that was undernourished, maltreated, overworked, and reduced to bondage. An enormous social gap developed between the Indian peons and a class of individuals who identified with Iberian political and economic interests.

In Africa during the first phase of colonialism, the different European powers attempted to make their colonies economically self-sufficient. African labor was recruited for work on the commercialized plantations and in the gold and diamond mines. Native workers received substandard wages and were forced to pay head taxes to the colonial regimes. Head taxes were assessed for each individual and had to be paid in cash. By requiring cash payments, the colonial governments forced villagers to abandon subsistence agriculture and become wage laborers. In eastern and southern Africa, many choice agricultural lands were taken from the native peoples and given to British and Dutch settlers. As the demand for exports from Africa began to increase in the world-market system, the colonial powers began to develop transportation and communication systems linking coastal cities with inland regions. The purpose of these systems was to secure supplies of natural resources and human labor.

A major consequence of these colonial processes was the complete disruption of the indigenous production and exchange systems: Africans were drawn into the wage economy. Monetary systems based on European coinage were introduced, displacing former systems of exchange. The price of African labor and goods came to be determined by the world market. Global economic conditions began to shape the sociocultural systems and strategies of native peoples throughout Africa.

One major consequence of Western colonialism was the integration of many agricultural village communities into wider regional and global economic patterns. Although the precolonial traditional villages were probably never entirely self-sufficient and were tied to regional and national trading networks through Western colonialism, the village peasantry was no longer isolated from cities, and prices were determined by the global market for agricultural goods. The transformation of agricultural economies triggered dramatic changes in traditional peasant rural communities. Because few peasants had enough capital to own and manage land, much of the land fell into the hands of colonial settlers, large landowners, and moneylenders. In many cases, these changes encouraged absentee land-ownership and temporary tenancy. Long-term care of the land by the peasantry was sacrificed for immediate profits. Land, labor, and capital were thus disconnected from the village kinship structures of reciprocity and redistribution, or what has been referred to as the *moral economy* (see Chapter 11). Peasants were incorporated into the global capitalist cash economy.

RELIGIOUS CHANGE

Numerous religious changes occurred with globalization. The Catholic church played a major role in Latin American society during the colonial period.

A Yoruban man and family members.

Initially, the conquistadores were not sure whether the native peoples were fully human; that is, they were not certain that the natives had souls. After the Spanish authorities, backed by the pope, ruled that the Indians did indeed have souls and could be saved, various missionaries began to convert the Indians to Catholicism. The missionaries established the pueblos and villages where the Indians were relocated and attempted to protect the Indians from the major abuses of colonialism, but were too few and too spread out to do so.

In general, the Indians of Latin America readily accepted Catholicism. The indigenous religions of Mesoamerica, for example, were able to absorb foreign deities without giving up their own (Berdan, 1982). Many local religious conceptions were somewhat analogous to Catholic beliefs. A process of religious **syncretism** developed, in which indigenous beliefs and practices blend with those of Christianity. For example, the central theological tenet of Christianity, that Jesus sacrificed his life for the salvation of humanity, was acceptable to people whose religious traditions formerly included human sacrifices for the salvation of Mesoamerican peoples (see Chapter 11). The Indians were also attracted to the elaborate rituals and colorful practices associated with the Virgin Mary and the saints. Catholic beliefs and practices were assimilated into traditional indigenous cosmologies to become powerful symbolic images and rituals.

One well-known tradition that has endured in Mexico that represents a combination of pre-Hispanic and Spanish Catholic religious beliefs and practices is the *Dias de los Muertos* (the Day of the Dead). The Dias de los Muertos takes place on November 2, the day after All Saints' Day (*Todos Santos*). This is the time when the souls of the dead return to earth to visit their living relatives. Dias de los Muertos is a time when families get together for feasting. They contruct altars to the dead and offer food and drink and prayers to the souls of their dead relatives. The altars usually have a photo of the dead person, along with an image of Jesus or the Virgin Mary. For those who died as children, there may be toys or sugar treats made in the shape of animals on the altar. Mexicans prepare for this day many months ahead of time. They prepare candy skulls, *calaveras,* which are given out to everyone in the family and friends. A substantial expense goes into preparing the foods, chocolate sauces (*mole*), and drinks, along with flowers, candles, and incense for the festivities. Food, drinks, and gifts of the *calaveras* are exchanged to symbolize strong linkages among family members both living and dead. It is the most important ritual in Mexico exemplifying the crucial links between the past pre-Hispanic symbolic culture and the present. The Dia de los Muertos represents the persistence of cultural traditions despite the globalizing processes induced by colonialism (Norget, 1996, Garciagodoy, 1998).

An Indian peasant woman in Peru.

Candy skulls, called **calaveras**, are given to family and friends to celebrate the Day of the Dead in Mexico.

Despite the official position of the Catholic church in Latin America and the Caribbean, indigenous religious traditions have survived for centuries, partly because Catholicism had evolved over a long period in Europe, during which it absorbed a number of indigenous pagan traditions. Thus, Catholicism was predisposed to accommodate pagan traditions in the Americas (Ingham, 1986).

In addition, the slaves that were imported from Africa to Latin America and the Caribbean brought traditional religious ideas and practices that were also absorbed in Catholicism. In Brazil these religious traditions are referred to as *Umbanda* and *Macumba*. In Northeast Brazil these traditions are known as *Candomble*. Catholic traditions are mixed with African beliefs and practices. In Cuba these syncretic traditions are called *Santeria*. On the island of Haiti the vast majority of the people believe in the tradition known as *Vodoun*. *Vodoun* is a similar combination of African and a blend of other traditions. Vodounists believe that they communicate directly with spirits. Vodoun traditions have evolved into a code of ethics, education, and a system of politics that are evident throughout Haitian society. Secret vodoun societies control everyday life in Haiti. These secret vodoun societies trace their origins to escaped slaves that organized revolts against the French colonizers. They meet at night and use traditional African drumming

A Voodoo altar and celebration in Haiti.

ANTHROPOLOGISTS AT WORK

Kristin Norget: Research in Mexico

Kristin Norget's involvement with anthropology was never a single, conscious choice but rather a result of a series of decisions concerning how she preferred to live her life and what was meaningful to her. When she was a child growing up in the prairie city of Winnipeg, in central Canada, the subject of *anthropology* was embodied by the big, thick book that sat on the living room table, filled with photos of apes and archaeologists unearthing treasures from ruins in far-off places. It was not something to which she could relate readily. However, she always had the urge to travel, to see the possibility for ways of viewing and being in the world that were different from her immediate world of experience. Her first "fieldwork" was during her last year of high school when she spent two weeks in Jamaica doing research on Rastafarianism for a paper in a course on comparative politics. This experience, though brief, left a strong impact, and inspired her to seek ways to find the same kind of connection with and understanding about people and culture

not accessible through books and formal education alone.

Norget's first direct contact with anthropology as a more encompassing body of ideas about humanity and culture came in her first year at the University of Victoria when anthropology was just one of several courses that she took as part of a general arts program that included languages, art history, philosophy and English literature. In a course on cultural anthropology, she was intrigued by what anthropology offered for an immersion in themes which had always captivated her interests: art, symbolism, religion, and other creative domains of culture; people's ways of making sense of their worlds; and their innovation and richness of spirit in situations of material impoverishment. After completing her undergraduate degree in anthropology, she moved to England to begin her graduate studies at Cambridge University. There she was exposed to the classical works of British social anthropology and experienced the culture shock that came from living within a particularly

Kristin Norget.

privileged and rare slice of English society. Although her time in Cambridge was overwhelming in some respects, it was also highly stimulating and enriching.

Norget chose as the focus of her master's research the Mexican festival of the Day of the Dead, a topic which she saw could encompass her real interests in anthropology related to religion, ritual, art, and the expressive realms of culture. She had already visited Mexico as a tourist and had been fascinated by its history, art, and literature, and had been moved by the warmth and generosity of the Mexicans she had met. Her master's dissertation was the first stage

and celebrations. The vodounists have a complex belief system that involves practices of priest or priestesses that can do harm to people. One practice is known as *zombification*. Using the poison of a puffer fish, they can cause an individual to die, and then recover several days later. The victims of the poisoning remain conscious, but are not able to speak or move. Zombification and the threat of zombification was used by the secret societies to

police the Haitian rural communities and maintain order (Davis, 1997, Metraux, 1989) All of these syncretic traditions combining traditional African religions and Catholicism are sometimes called *spiritism* and are evident in many parts of Latin America and the Caribbean.

With European colonization in Africa came missionaries who established schools to spread Christianity. As in Latin America, many of the misof her exploration of the Day of the Dead (the Mexican commemoration of the Catholic festival and All Souls' and All Saints' Days), which later evolved into a doctoral research project. She was already familiar with the Day of the Dead from museums exhibitions she had attended in England and Mexico and from the colorful popular art and iconography inspired by the festival which she had come across during her travels. Much of what she had previously seen and read about the Day of the Dead struck her as offering a rather one-dimensional, romanticized portrayal of the festival as simply a folkloric tradition with strong roots in pre-Hispanic religiosity and in a supposed quintessentially "Mexican" obsession with death. She wanted to explore the significance of the festival in a more contemporary framework, as well as to learn more about the ritualization of death in Mexico. She chose as her fieldsite the southern Mexican city of Oaxaca, located in one of the poorest and most indigenous regions of the country. The urban milieu of Oaxaca enabled her to examine the Day of the Dead in a dynamic setting in which traditional lifeways came into direct interaction with tourism, commercialization, and other influences.

Norget situated her investigation of the Day of the Dead in the context of Oaxacan urban popular culture, popular Catholicism, and other rituals concerned with death. During her fieldwork, she immersed herself in the local community of the neighborhood in which she lived, especially in the religious dimension of people's everyday lives, taking part in Bible discussion groups, masses, and other church activities, but especially in funerals and other death-related rituals. She discovered that death in Oaxaca was the inspiration for an elaborate series of ritual events and cultural discourses concerned with the reinvigoration of traditional ideas of collectivism and community in a rapidly changing and unstable social context in which such norms and values are being severely eroded. Her research deepened her fascination with the very practical way in which people use ritual as an arena for the imaginative and creative reconstruction of their social world.

Since completing her doctorate in 1993, Norget has been teaching anthropology at McGill University in Montreal. While she finds teaching very rewarding, she is most content when she is in Mexico immersed in research, writing, and spending time with the wide community of friends she has amassed there over the past ten years. In 1995, she was able to extend her interests in popular religiosity and Catholicism into a new research project investigating the relation between liberation theology and indigenous movements in southern Mexico. Through her work on this project, she finds an avenue for her continuing fascination with the ways that people use religion as a powerful means for articulating and actualizing their desires for a transformation of their social environment. It has also brought her into a practical involvement with the human rights struggle in Mexico as well as in Montreal, where she is an active member of various local Mexican human rights and refugee rights organizations. Norget has published articles based on her research in various international journals and is currently in the final stages of writing a book on death and its ritualization in Oaxacan popular culture.

sionaries in Africa were paternalistic toward the native peoples and tried to protect them from the worst abuses of colonialism. Mission schools served as both hospitals and education centers. Many people sent their children to the Christian schools because this education offered opportunities for better jobs and higher social status. Many people educated in the mission schools became part of the elite.

At the same time, however, the missionaries attempted to repress traditional religious beliefs and practices. The missionaries believed that to be "saved," the Africans had to abandon their customary practices and embrace the Christian faith. To some extent, the ethnocentrism of the missionaries in Africa had tragic consequences for many native peoples. Through the educational system, Africans were taught that their traditional culture was shameful, something to be despised. In many cases this led to a loss of ethnic and cultural identity and sometimes induced feelings of self-hatred.

As various Christian denominations missionized throughout Africa, and number of syncretistic movements began to emerge among the indigenous peoples. They became known as Independent African Church denominations referred to as "Zionist," "Spiritual," or "Prophet." The leaders of these churches are often called Prophets, and are known for their charismatic powers of healing. Facing the crisis created by colonialism, and the loss of their traditional culture, many indigenous Africans turned to these traditions for relief. In some cases, these syncretic traditions combining traditional spiritual beliefs and Christianity have played a pivotal role in political movements throughout Africa (Comaroff, 1985).

Political Changes: Independence and Nationalist Movements

One important consequence of globalization and colonialism in various Latin America, Africa, and the Caribbean areas was the development of political movements that emphasized independence and nationalistic ideas. Some of the indigenous peoples became educated under the colonial regime and began to assert their independence. After approximately 300 years of European domination, the various regions of Latin America and the Caribbean began to demand their political autonomy from the colonial regimes. An educated descendant of the ancient Incans, Tupac Amaru, led a rebellion in Peru against the Spanish rulers. Simon Bolivar (1783–1830), a national hero among both Venezuelans and Colombians, led a broad-based independence/nationalist movement. In the French colony of Saint Domingue (modern-day Haiti), a slave uprising became a warning for all the various colonial regimes in the region.

During the decades following World War II, European colonial rule ended in Africa; by the 1970s, no fewer than thirty-one former colonies had won their independence. The first country to do so, the West African nation of Ghana, became independent of Britain in 1957. The Ghanian independence

movement was led by Kwame Nkrumah, a charismatic leader who mobilized workers, youths, professionals, and farmers to speed up the pace of decolonization. Ghana's success intensified independence movements elsewhere. By the early 1960s, all of the West African countries, including the French colonies of Niger, Mali, Senegal, and Dahomey, had gained their independence, making a fairly smooth transition to independent political control.

In the Congo region, however, because of the Belgians' rigid exploitative political and economic policies, the independence movement was much more difficult. Belgian colonial policies had brutalized the native population, and the inadequate educational system had failed to produce an elite, affording Africans in the Belgian colonies little opportunity to gain political training for self-rule or nation building. When Belgium finally granted independence to the Congo in 1960, it was due more to international pressure than to nationalist movements. In 1971, the Congo changed its name to Zaire.

In East Africa, the large numbers of white settlers vigorously resisted nationalist movements. In Kenya, for example, hostility between the majority Kikuyu tribe and white settlers who had appropriated much of the best farmland contributed to the Mau Mau uprisings, which resulted in thousands of deaths and the imprisonment of thousands of Kikuyu in detention camps. Jomo Kenyatta, a British-educated leader who had completed an anthropological study of the Kikuyu, led Kenya to independence in 1963 with his call for *uruhu* ("freedom" in Swahili). In the colony of Tanganyika, nationalist leader Julius Nyerere organized a mass political party insisting on self-rule. Tanganyika achieved independence in 1961 and in 1964 merged with Zanzibar to form the nation of Tanzania.

In South Africa, colonization and independence eventually produced a system of racial stratification known as **apartheid,** in which different populations are assigned different statuses with varying social and political rights, based on racial criteria. Dutch settlers, or Afrikaners, inaugurated the apartheid system when they came to power after World War II, and apartheid was the official policy of South Africa until recently.

Apartheid was based on white supremacy and assumed that the culture and values of nonwhite Africans rendered them incapable of social, politi-

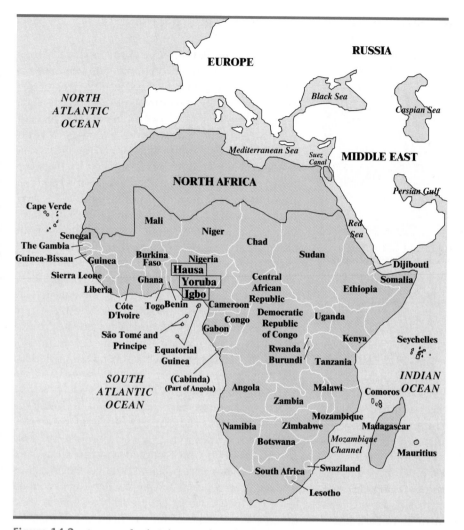

NORTH
ATLANTIC
OCEAN

EUROPE

RUSSIA

Black Sea

Caspian Sea

Mediterranean Sea *Suez Canal* **MIDDLE EAST**

NORTH AFRICA

Persian Gulf

Cape Verde

Mali

Niger

Chad

Red Sea

Senegal
The Gambia
Guinea-Bissau   Guinea

Burkina
Faso

Nigeria

Sudan

Djibouti

Sierra Leone   Ghana

Hausa
Yoruba
Igbo

Central
African
Republic

Somalia

Ethiopia

Liberia

Côte
D'Ivoire Togo Benin Cameroon

Congo

Democratic
Republic
of Congo

Uganda

São Tomé and
Principe   Equatorial
Guinea

Gabon

Kenya

Seychelles

SOUTH
ATLANTIC
OCEAN

(Cabinda)
(Part of Angola)

Rwanda
Burundi

Tanzania

INDIAN
OCEAN

Angola

Malawi

Comoros

Zambia

Namibia

Zimbabwe

Mozambique

Madagascar

Botswana

*Mozambique
Channel*

Mauritius

South Africa Swaziland

Lesotho

Figure 14.2   A map of sub-Saharan Africa, highlighting some of the peoples discussed in the chapter.

cal, and economic equality with whites. The government enforced this system through legal policies designed to bring about strict segregation among the different "races." The population was stratified into a hierarchy with whites, who number about 4.5 million, at the top. Approximately 60 percent of the whites are Afrikaners, and the rest are English-speaking. An intermediate category consists of "coloreds"—the 2.6 million people of mixed European and African ancestry—and Asians, primarily immigrants from India and Malaysia, who number about 800,000.

At the bottom of the hierarchy are the approximately 21 million black South Africans, who are divided into four major ethnic groupings: the Nguni,

which includes the Xhosa, the Zulu, the Swazi, and the Ndebele; the Sotho; the Venda; and the Tsonga (Crapanzano, 1986). Important cultural and linguistic differences exist among these groups.

The policies of apartheid have affected every aspect of life in South Africa. Blacks have been segregated socially and forced into lower-paying—and frequently hazardous—occupations. They could not vote or take part in strikes, and until recently they had to carry passes and observe curfews. In 1963, the South African government created a series of black states called Bantustan homelands, to which millions of black South Africans were forcibly removed.

Opposition to apartheid led to the emergence of various resistance and liberation movements, in-

Nelson Mandela, the first black elected president of South Africa.

cluding the major resistance group, the African National Congress (ANC), formed in 1912. Although the ANC began as a moderate political organization calling for a unified South Africa representing all races in the government, it turned to armed struggle in response to ruthless suppression by the government. Many people were killed, and resistance leaders such as Nelson Mandela were imprisoned.

In the 1980s and early 1990s, forced by international pressures, the government implemented some reforms, abolishing laws that had once confined blacks to the rural homelands, forbade them to join legal trade unions, reserved skilled jobs for whites, and prohibited interracial marriages. Black nationalist groups and the clergy, led by Archbishop Desmond Tutu, negotiated with the government for other political reforms.

In April 1994, all South Africans participated in a national election for the first time, electing Nelson Mandela's African National Congress (ANC) with a solid majority. Mandela, who became president, agreed to share power with whites during a five-year transitional period and tried to implement an economic blueprint for South Africa that included providing new homes, electrification projects, free and mandatory education, and millions of new jobs. In June of 1999, South Africa's parliament chose Thabo Mbeki as the nation's second freely elected president. Mbeki, also a member of the ANC, is striving to carry out Nelson Mandela's programs.

EXPLAINING REVOLUTION

In some of the countries of Latin America, Africa, and the Caribbean, revolutionary movements developed as a response to the consequences of globalization and colonialism. Anthropologists have been examining the causes of revolution in Latin America and other non-Western countries. A **revolution** is a dramatic, fundamental change in a society's political economy brought about by the overthrow of the government and the restructuring of the economy. The classical understanding of revolution is derived from the writings of Karl Marx, who explained revolutions as the product of the struggle between the propertied and nonpropertied classes. For example, Marx predicted that the discontented proletariat would rise up against their bourgeois masters and overthrow capitalism (see Chapter 6). The revolutions in most non-Western countries, however, have not followed the Marxist model. Most countries in Latin America, Africa, or the Caribbean did not have a substantial proletariat and bourgeoisie. Rather, revolutions were identified with the peasants.

Social scientists have found, however, that the poorest peasants did not organize and participate in peasant revolutions. People living in extreme poverty were too preoccupied with everyday subsistence to become politically active. Severe poverty tends to generate feelings of fatalism and political apathy. Consequently, anthropologists and other social scientists turned from the traditional Marxist model to find alternative models to explain revolutions. These models involve the concepts of *rising expectations* and *relative deprivation*.

Rising expectations refers to how a particular group experiences improvements in economic and political conditions. Often these improvements stimulate the desire for even more improvements. For example, revolutions sometimes occur in the midst of political and economic reform. Groups that experience improvements brought about by their governments may become politically active and protest for even broader changes. **Relative deprivation** refers to a group's awareness that it lacks economic opportunities and political rights in comparison with other groups in a society. Even though a particular group may have experienced improved economic and political conditions, it still perceives it is suffering from injustice and inequality compared with other groups. The combination of rising expectations and relative deprivation helps explain revolutionary movements in areas such as Latin America, Africa, and the Caribbean.

Although the first independence movements in Latin America brought about certain reforms, some groups were affected by rising expectations and relative deprivation. The emerging middle class, which consisted of intellectuals and business-people, as well as some peasants who were benefiting from the introduction of the global economy, began to organize against the *hacendados* and the governing elite. For example, the Indians and peasants played a vital role in the Mexican Revolution of 1910–1920. At that time, 1 percent of the Mexican population owned 85 percent of the land, whereas 95 percent owned no land at all (Wolf, 1969; Chirot, 1986). Peasant leaders such as Emiliano Zapata, who called for the redistribution of land, carried out guerrilla campaigns against the *hacendados*. Although the revolution did not establish an egalitarian state, it did bring about the redistribution of land to many of the Indian communities.

In Latin American and Caribbean countries where power remained in the hands of the elites, revolutionary movements continued to develop throughout the twentieth century. From the Cuban Revolution of the 1950s through the Nicaraguan Revolution of the 1980s, peasants joined with other dissatisfied elements in overthrowing elite families. Countries such as El Salvador continue to experience peasant revolutions. The *hacienda* system produced tenant farmers, sharecroppers, and day laborers on large estates, a situation that will inevitably make peasant guerrillas a continuing presence in some Latin American nations.

Uneven Development in Latin America, Africa, and the Caribbean

Throughout the twentieth century, the countries of Latin America, Africa, and the Caribbean have increasingly been incorporated into the global economy. These countries, however, differ in degree of integration into this global economy. Some nations are peripheral agricultural states that produce a few cash crops for the international market. Others, such as Mexico, Venezuela, Brazil, and Nigeria, have a significant industrial sector and are clearly semiperipheral. In some regions, small-scale industrialists produce manufactured goods alongside the crops and cattle of the plantations. In many cases, however, these industrialists have to depend on Europe and North America for their machinery. They also discover that the internal market for their products is extremely limited because their own societies lacked a consuming middle class.

PERIPHERAL SOCIETIES

Anthropologists find that many countries in Latin America, Africa, and the Caribbean remain peripheral societies. The core societies developed these countries as export platforms, that is, nations whose economies concentrate almost exclusively on the export of raw materials and agricultural goods to the core nations. Through economic aid and military assistance, core countries such as the United States supported elite families and local capitalists in these peripheral countries. The elites minimized restrictions on foreign investments and encouraged the production of cash crops for the export economy. The entire economy in these peripheral societies was reorganized to produce profits and commodities for the core societies.

A Case Study: The United Fruit Company An example of the development of a peripheral country by a multinational corporation involves the U.S.–based United Fruit Company in Central America. United Fruit obtained rights to thousands of acres of empty tropical lowlands in Central America for banana plantations. It enlisted local Indians, *mestizos,* and blacks from the Caribbean islands to work the plantations. Anthropologist Phillipe Bourgois (1989a) studied one of the plantations operated by United Fruit, which expanded in 1987 to become the multinational Chiquita Brands. He investigated the archival records of United Fruit to determine how the North Americans managed the plantations.

Focusing on the Bocas Del Toro plantation, Bourgois observed the interactions among the various ethnic groups on the plantation. He discovered that the North Americans used race and ethnicity as a form of manipulation. He described the relationship between management and labor as based on a hierarchy in which each of the four ethnic groups—blacks, *mestizos,* Indians, and white North Americans—worked at different tasks. Indian workers were used to spread corrosive fertilizers and dangerous pesticides. The management rationale for this practice was that "the Indian skin is thicker, and they don't get sick." Indians were not paid a full wage because, according to superiors, "the Indian has low physiological needs. . . . The Indian only thinks of food; he has no other aspirations. He works to eat" (1989a: x).

Blacks worked in the maintenance department's repair shops and electrical division because, Bourgois was told, they are "crafty and don't like to sweat." The *mestizo* immigrants from Nicaragua were worked as hard as the Indians because they "are tough, have leathery skin [*cueron*], and aren't afraid of sweating under the hot sun" (1989a: xi). The white North Americans were the top management because "they are the smartest race on earth." Management used these stereotypes to classify the workers, thereby segregating each ethnic group in a separate occupation and preventing the workers from uniting to organize labor unions. Bourgois found that racism, ethnicity, inequality, exploitation, and class conflict were all interrelated in a continuing process in the day-to-day realities of a banana-plantation economy.

SEMIPERIPHERAL SOCIETIES

A number of countries in Latin America and Africa, because of their valuable strategic resources, have emerged as semiperipheral societies. Two examples of peripheral societies that have become semiperipheral are Mexico and Nigeria.

Mexico Following political revolution, Mexico gradually achieved stability under the control of a single political party, the Party of the Institutionalized Revolution (PRI). One-party rule, however, fostered corruption and inefficiency, resulting in personal enrichment for political officials. The government nationalized the key industries, including the important oil industry, which had been developed by foreign multinational corporations. Despite political authoritarianism and corruption, the Mexican economy continued to grow with gradual industrialization.

During the 1970s, as the industrial world experienced major oil shortages, the Mexican government implemented a policy of economic growth through expanded oil exports. International lending agencies and financial institutions in the core countries offered low-interest loans to stimulate industrial investment in Mexico. As a result of these policies, Mexico initially experienced an impressive growth rate of 8 percent annually and moved from a peripheral to a semiperipheral nation.

This progress was short-lived, however. Surpluses on the petroleum market in the early 1980s led to falling prices for Mexican oil. Suddenly Mexico faced difficulties in paying the interest on the loans that came due. The government had to borrow more money, at higher interest rates, to cover its international debt, which exceeded $100 billion. This excessive debt began to undermine government-sponsored development projects. Foreign banks and lending organizations such as the International Monetary Fund (IMF) demanded that the government limit its subsidies for social services, food, gasoline, and electricity. These new policies led to inflation and a new austerity that has adversely affected the standard of living of the poor and the middle classes of Mexico.

Another development influencing Mexico's economic status is the expansion of U.S. multinational corporations into Mexico. Since the 1980s, thousands of U.S. companies have established plants inside Mexico to take advantage of the low wage rates, lax environmental standards, and favorable tax rates there. These plants, known as *maquiladoras,* have drawn hundreds of thousands of peasants and workers from rural communities to expanding cities such as Juarez, a border city (Shirk & Mitchell, 1989). Among the companies that have established plants in Mexico are Fisher-Price, Ford, Emerson Electric, Zenith, Sara Lee, and General Electric.

Faced with mounting debts and unemployment, the Mexican government did everything possible to attract multinational corporations. This was also seen as a solution to the problem of the migration of Mexican workers to the United States as illegal aliens. The *maquiladoras* employ approximately 500,000 people and account for 17 percent of the Mexican economy. Although many *maquiladora* workers appear satisfied with their jobs, the

A maquiladora factory on the Mexican-U.S. border.

maquiladoras have created a number of problems for Mexico. Because they pay such low wages, they have not yet transformed workers into consumers, which has restricted economic expansion. Other problems include occupational health hazards, the taxing of sewer systems and water supplies, and high turnover rates among workers.

Nigeria   Under British rule, Nigeria developed an export economy centered on palm oil and peanut oil, lumber, cocoa, and metal ores. Like Mexico, after independence, a new commodity was discovered that had major consequences for Nigerian society—oil. The discovery of oil appeared to be an economic windfall for Nigeria, and the government saw it as the foundation for rapid economic growth. Many Africans from other nations immigrated to Nigeria in search of opportunity.

By the 1980s, over 90 percent of Nigeria's revenues came from the sale of petroleum. These monies were used to fuel ambitious economic development schemes. Unfortunately, the Nigerian economy fell into disarray when oil prices dropped during the first half of the 1980s. In spite of

tremendous economic expansion during the 1970s, unemployment rose, and the Nigerian government expelled virtually all non-Nigerian workers and their families, forcing millions of Africans to return to their former homelands, where the local economies could not absorb them.

By the late 1980s, cocoa was the only important Nigerian agricultural export. Oil production and the vast wealth that it represented for Nigeria had actually contributed to the decline of agriculture because the government invested heavily in the petroleum industry, neglecting the agricultural sector (Rossides, 1990). Consequently, Nigeria now depends on core countries for imported foods. In addition, much of its oil wealth was spent on imported goods such as automobiles, motorcycles, and televisions, which fueled inflation and did not benefit an underdeveloped industrial sector. Today, the industrial sector accounts for only 10 percent of Nigeria's economic production. In 1995, Nigeria's annual per capita income was $600, one of the highest figures of any African country but far below that of many other semiperipheral societies (Ramsay, 1995).

Ethnological Studies of the Peasantry in Latin America, Africa, and the Caribbean

As Latin American, African, and Caribbean countries were drawn increasingly into the global economy, the status and lifestyles of the peasantry were transformed. Anthropologists have been studying this transformation of the peasantry for many decades. For example, ethnologists such as Redfield (1930), Villa Rojas (Redfield & Villa Rojas, 1934), Lewis (1951), and Goldkind (1965) have been studying peasant communities in Latin America and the Caribbean since the 1920s.

A problem in generalizing about behavior in rural communities of non-Western countries is the tremendous variation from one community to another. As these countries became integrated into the global economy, the peasantry became more heterogeneous. This variation is due to the different historical processes that have influenced these communities. For example, research by Eric Wolf (1955, 1957) led to some important insights regarding the different types of peasant communities in some regions of Latin America and Asia. Wolf distinguished between closed peasant communities and open peasant communities. The **closed peasant community** is made up of peasants who lived in the highland regions of Mexico and Guatemala or in isolated areas of Indonesia. In these communities, a person had ascribed economic and social status, and there was a great deal of internal solidarity and homogeneity. The peasants produced primarily for subsistence rather than for the world market. Many closed peasant communities in Central America, such as Chan Kom, consisted of Indian refugees who attempted to isolate themselves from the disruptive effects of Spanish colonial policies. They held their land in common, but much of this land was marginal. In Indonesia these closed peasant communities were isolated from the Dutch colonial authorities.

An **open peasant community** consisted primarily of peasants who were directly drawn into the world market. These communities were located in the lowland areas of Latin America and Indonesia. Land was owned individually rather than held in common. The open peasant community evolved in response to the intrusion of colonialism, which engendered the development of plantations and the production of commodities for the core societies.

In open communities some peasants sold as much as 90 to 100 percent of their produce to outside markets, which enabled some individuals to achieve access to sources of wealth, power, and prestige in the wider society. Wolf (1955) suggested that the market and the developing global economy were the integrating factors influencing local, regional, national, and international levels.

AFRICAN PEASANTS: A UNIQUE PHENOMENON?

Anthropologists David Brokensha and Charles Erasmus (1969) maintained that Africans were not typical peasants because of the distinctive nature of precolonial African states. They suggested that most of the precolonial states had very limited control over their populations and that Africans were able to retain control over their land and their economic production. Other anthropologists suggested that sub-Saharan Africans could not be characterized as peasants because in many cases they were still horticulturalists (Goldschmidt & Kunkel, 1971).

Anthropologists Godfrey Wilson and Max Gluckman of the Rhodes-Livingstone Institute in southern Africa have engaged in detailed studies of African society. They distinguished six types of regions based on an array of factors such as degree of urbanization and industrialization, relative importance of subsistence and cash cropping, and nature of the work force. They also examined such related phenomena as rural-to-urban migration, depopulation, unionization, and prevailing political issues. These and other studies helped produce an improved understanding of how the global economy directly affected the African people (Vincent, 1990).

Most anthropologists now agree that the general term *peasants* does not apply to the diverse conditions found in the African agricultural states. In some regions there were rural peoples who could be designated "peasants," whereas in other regions the term was not applicable. The historical experience of Africa was much different from that of medieval Europe, Latin America, or Asia. Environmental, economic, and political circumstances varied from region to region, involving different types of societal adaptations. In addition, the presence of so many colonial powers in Africa created greater diversity than was the case in Latin America, which was colonized almost exclusively by the Spanish and Portuguese. Thus, the current political economy of Africa is more heterogenous than that of many other regions.

Social Structure in Latin America, Africa, and the Caribbean

Ethnological studies have illuminated aspects of the social structure, including family and gender relations, of various countries of Latin America, Africa, and the Caribbean. As in most rural agricultural societies, the traditional family unit was an extended family that provided aid for people living in marginal subsistence conditions. But with the growth of industry and wage labor and the redistribution of land from communities to individuals, many large, extended families were forced to break up. Thus, the typical family in many urban areas today is the nuclear family. Ethnographers, however, have found some unique features of kinship and social structure in these countries.

LATIN AMERICAN SOCIAL RELATIONSHIPS

Many peasant communities maintain **fictive kinship ties**—that is, extrafamilial social ties that provide mutual-aid work groups for the planting and harvesting of crops and for other economic and political activities. George Foster described one type of fictive kinship tie in Mexican peasant communities that is known as the **dyadic contract,** a reciprocal exchange arrangement between two individuals (a *dyad*). According to Foster (1967), to compensate for the lack of voluntary organizations or corporate groups beyond the nuclear family in these communities, males and females established dyadic contracts to exchange labor, goods, and other needed services. Dyadic contracts can be established with people of equal or superior status or with supernatural beings such as Jesus, the Virgin Mary, and the saints. People develop dyadic contracts with these supernatural sources in hopes of inducing specific spiritual and material benefits. They care for the shrines of Jesus, the Virgin Mary,

and the saints to demonstrate their loyalty and obedience.

Dyadic contracts between individuals of equal status are based on generalized reciprocal exchanges: continuing exchanges that are not short term but rather bind two people in cooperative relationships for many years.

The dyadic contracts between people of unequal status, known as **patron-client ties,** are informal contracts between peasant villagers and nonvillagers (including supernatural beings). The patron is an individual who combines status, power, influence, and authority over the client. Patrons include politicians, government employees, town or city friends, and local priests.

One type of dyadic contract found in Latin America is known as the *compadrazgo*. Ethnologists have investigated *compadrazgo* relationships extensively (Redfield, 1930; Wolf & Mintz, 1950; Foster, 1967). This institution, brought to the Americas with Catholicism, has become an integral aspect of Latin American social relationships. During the colonial period, the *hacendado* often served as godparent to the children of *peons*. The result was a network of patron-client ties involving mutual obligations and responsibilities. The godparent had to furnish aid in times of distress such as illness or famine. In return, the *peon* had to be absolutely loyal and obedient to the hacendado.

The *compadrazgo* system eventually spread throughout peasant and urban areas. Every individual has a *padrino* (godfather) and *madrina* (godmother) who are sponsors at baptismal rituals. The sponsors become the coparents (*compadres, comadres*) of the child (Davila, 1971; Romanucci-Ross, 1973). The most important social relationship is the one between the *compadres* and the parents, who ideally will assist one another in any way possible. The *compadrazgo* is a remarkably flexible extra-kin relationship that sometimes reaches across class lines to help peasants cope with the tensions and anxieties of modern life in Latin America.

Machismo   Gender relationships in Latin America have been strongly influenced by the Spanish and Portuguese colonial experience. The basic traditional values affecting gender relations are known as *machismo*, the explicit code for the behavior of Latin American males. As a part of this code, the "true man" (*macho*) is supposed to be courageous, sexually viral and aggressive, and superior to women. A woman, in contrast, is supposed to be passive, sexually conservative and faithful, obedient, and completely devoted to her mate. These ideals and values have affected gender relations throughout Latin America.

Yet many ethnologists who have done research in Latin American peasant communities have observed that the actual behaviors of males and females do not conform completely to the ideals of *machismo*. Lewis (1951) observed that in Tepotzlan, males were not the dominant authoritarian figures in the family that they wanted to be, and wives were not completely submissive. Instead, in many families he found conflict between the spouses over authority. Most families tended to follow a middle course: The wife did little to challenge the authority of her husband, and the husband was not too overbearing toward his wife. May Diaz (1966) also showed that the ideals of *machismo* conflict with the actual behavioral realities of gender relations in Mexico. She observed in her study of Tonala, a small town near Guadalajara, that females often effectively opposed male domination within their family and their community.

AFRICAN SOCIAL RELATIONSHIPS

Because many African societies are composed of horticulturalist or pastoralist peoples in transition to different forms of peasantry, their social organization largely centers on lineages and extended families. But as in other regions of the world, as industrialization and the commercialization of agriculture proceed, social organization inevitably changes.

Some ethnologists have challenged basic concepts regarding the African family. For example, Niara Sudarkasa (1989), an anthropologist who did ethnological research on the Yoruba and other West African groups, has challenged anthropologists such as George Murdock, who believe that all families worldwide can be reduced to the nuclear family (see Chapter 7). Murdock (1949) argued that the extended family, or polygamous African family, really consists of multiple nuclear families with a common husband and father.

Sudarkasa saw this hypothesis as a distortion of the basic elements of the African family. She argued that the male-female dyad and offspring do not perform the basic functions of the family in African society. That is, the nuclear family is not the unit of economic production or consumption, not the unit of socialization, and not the unit providing emotional support. A typical African family such as that of the Yoruba consists of a group of brothers, their wives, their adult sons and grandsons and their wives, and any unmarried children. Marriages usually are polygynous, and the husband has a room separate from his wives. Every wife has a separate domain with her own cooking utensils and other furnishings. Co-wives depend on the senior wife to be a companion and confidante. Sudarkasa concluded that the nuclear family is not the basic "building block" for the African family. She further maintained that Western ethnologists misunderstand and distort the practice of polygyny in African society. She noted that most of the anthropological literature emphasizes the negative characteristics of polygyny, such as rivalry and discord among co-wives. Her research demonstrated that co-wives develop important emotional and social bonds with one another that create a nurturing environment for both co-wives and children.

Although not all anthropologists have accepted Sudarkasa's views, most concur that there are many variations of the African family, depending on sociocultural conditions. In the urban areas of Africa, the extended family and polygyny are declining in influence. Several factors are responsible for these changes. As employment opportunities develop outside agriculture, prompting migration from rural to urban areas, extended family ties break down. Wage employment in mines and industrial firms tends to disrupt extended families that are tied to agricultural land. In addition, African governments often promote "modern" family and marriage practices to alter traditional ways of behavior, which they perceive as impeding economic development. To some extent, the elites of these societies accept Western conceptions of the family, romantic love, and monogamy.

Gender in Africa   Most African societies tend to be patriarchal, placing women in a subordinate status. In 1988, for example, women provided approximately 60 to 80 percent of the household food needs in many parts of Africa (Smith-Ivan, 1988). They often worked ten to twelve hours a day, and in many instances their workload increased after colonization and independence. As colonial regimes forced males to migrate to mines for employment, women were forced to assume the major subsistence roles for the family. Because their husbands' wages were meager, women had to grow and collect food for their families. In most cases the lack of formal education prohibited females from entering the wage-labor economy, so that they were unable to buy property and send their children to school.

Despite providing much of the agricultural labor and household food needs, women in rural Africa tend to be the poorest people on the world's poorest continent. The European colonial powers often allocated land to males, but African women were given rights to the land only through their relationship to males (Henn, 1984; Tandon, 1988). This tended to decrease the status of females in African society. Males were considered the head of the household and earned income, whereas females were viewed as the providers of the family's social needs (such as child care) and the producers of the future labor force. Following independence, males were given access to credit, training, and new skills to improve agricultural production. Because females did not have collateral through land ownership, they were denied the credit and training needed for commercialized agriculture.

Urban Women   African women in the urban regions often receive a formal education and tend to have more independence than do rural women. In West Africa, where females have traditionally been employed in urban markets, some educated women have become prominent self-employed entrepreneurs. In general, however, even highly educated women are confined to the service sector of the urban economy, working in clerical or secretarial occupations (Robertson, 1984; Smith-Ivan, 1988). Urban women without formal education who lack the support of extended families and village communities are especially vulnerable to exploitation and alienation. Without extended family ties to assist in child care, women often are restricted to unskilled, low-wage occupations, such as making clothing, that require them to remain at home.

Because South Africa was largely a settler colony and possesses a strong economy, the role of women there is somewhat different from that in other parts of Africa. Some African women are employed as domestics in white homes or as clerical and textile workers in the industrial sector. Despite their valuable contribution to these sectors of the economy, however, they earn 20 percent less than the minimum wage (Smith-Ivan, 1988).

Patterns of Ethnicity in Latin America, Africa, and the Caribbean

As a result of European conquest and colonization, the ethnicity of Latin America, Africa, and the Caribbean became increasingly diverse and heterogeneous.

ETHNICITY IN LATIN AMERICA

In Latin America, a small minority of Spanish and Portuguese rulers, never exceeding more than 5 percent of the total population, dominated the native population. Following the conquest, people born in Spain and Portugal went to Latin America to improve their social status. The Europeans eventually intermarried with native Indian women. The offspring of these marriages were called *mestizos,* a new social class in Latin America. After three centuries, the mestizo population grew to become the majority in Latin America, representing approximately 60 percent of the population. In addition, in Brazil and the Caribbean, the intermarriages of Africans and Europeans produced a group known as *mulattos.*

Gradually, in certain regions of Latin America and the Caribbean, the new populations of mestizos and mulattos began to outnumber the indigenous peoples. The relative populations of these different groups vary from region to region. For example, only about 10 percent of the Mexican population speaks an Indian language, as opposed to about 50 percent in Guatemala, which is more geographically isolated. Brazil's population is about 11 percent black and 33 percent mulatto. Other areas in Bolivia, Peru, and Ecuador that are farther from the commercial coastal regions are primarily mestizo and Indian; only 10 percent of their populations are European or white. In contrast, in the coastal areas of Argentina and Uruguay, the

European component of the population is more prominent.

In countries such as Mexico and Guatemala the Indian population as a minority has faced obstacles in attaining economic and political opportunities. Ethnographers have found that one of the only routes to upward social and economic mobility for the Indian population was *assimilation,* the adoption of the culture and language of the dominant group in society (Nash, 1989). Some Indians did assimilate by adopting the Spanish language, clothing, and culture of the dominant majority, and thereby becoming *ladino.* The ethnic distinction between a ladino and Indian was based on a cultural boundary. However, many Indians have tried to maintain their ethnic distinctiveness and have recently been involved in asserting their Indian ethnic identity in an attempt to attain economic and political rights.

For example, in southern Mexico, especially in the province of Chiapas, the Mayan Indians have been mobilized politically into what is referred to as the Zapatista movement. The Zapatista movement is named after Emiliano Zapata and has been using armed guerilla warfare tactics against Mexican government forces in order to attain political and economic rights from the state. In this area, the Maya Indian population is dominated economically and politically by a wealthy group of landowners and ranchers. Traditionally, the Maya Indians had a certain amount of communal land or *ejidos* that they could share. In the 1980s, in order to encourage private enterprise and capitalism in agriculture, the Mexican government declared that *ejido* land could be sold. The Maya lost their communal land, which they had been using for their basic subsistence. For these reasons, the Zapatistas led by a mysterious charismatic leader known as Sub-Comandante Marcos declared war on the Mexican government. This movement has drawn on their traditional ethnic roots as a means of mobilizing a political struggle against a dominant majority in the midst of globalization (Nash, 1997).

ETHNICITY IN AFRICA

In Africa, as another example, the term *tribe* has negative connotations and is seldom used. Consequently, peoples of different language groupings and culture refer to themselves as ethnic groups.

Anthropologist Herbert Lewis (1992) has estimated that there are no fewer than 1,000 distinct ethnic groups among the more than fifty countries in Africa. As independence movements spread, many people hoped that the new African nations would develop as plural societies in which diverse ethnic groups would share power and tolerate cultural differences. These plural societies, however, generally have not developed. Anthropologists find that political parties are linked with specific ethnic groups. As one ethnic group assumes power, it usually forms a one-party state and establishes a military government that dominates other groups. This has become one of the major problems in African society. One country that has been the subject of much ethnological research on ethnic relationships is Nigeria. The resolution of ethnic problems in Nigeria may provide a model for other African countries.

Nigeria is the most populous nation of Africa, with about 98 million people, consisting of many different ethnic groups. Approximately 300 different languages are recognized by the Nigerian government. The three major ethnic divisions, which make up two-thirds of the Nigerian population, are the Yoruba, the Hausa, and the Igbo (Ibo).

More than 12 million Yoruba live in the southwest region of Nigeria and across its borders in neighboring Benin. The Yoruba were the most highly organized precolonial urban people in West Africa. The majority of the Yoruba were subsistence peasant farmers. The men traditionally supplemented their diet through hunting and fishing.

British colonialism changed the political economy of Nigeria. Aside from commercialized agriculture emphasizing cocoa production, railways, automobiles, new manufactured goods, Christian churches and schools, and industry entered Yoruban society. One-fifth of the people live in the urban areas of Nigeria such as Lagos and Ibadan. Wage employment and industrialization are rapidly transforming the society of the Yoruba, creating new class structures and integrating the traditional kingdom into the Nigerian nation and the global economy.

To the north of the Yoruba live the Hausa, who number about 20 million. Like the Yoruba, the Hausa had developed large, urban areas with extensive trade routes. Hausa cities had elaborate markets that offered different types of foodstuffs and crafts produced by peasants and craftspeople. British anthropologist M. G. Smith (1965) conducted extensive ethnological and historical research on Hausa society.

The Hausa made their home in a savanna where the peasants cultivated various crops and maintained cattle for trade and consumption. Hausa craftsmen smelted iron and crafted iron tools for farming, sewing, leather work, and hunting. As with the Yoruba, most Hausa peasants were engaged in subsistence agriculture, but cash crops such as cotton and peanuts were introduced by the British and changed the nature of economic production and consumption.

The third major ethnic group in Nigeria is the Igbo people of the southeastern region. Igbo anthropologist Victor Uchendu (1965) completed a major ethnological study of the Igbo. His descriptions of Igbo society are extremely insightful because he blends an anthropological focus with an insider's perspective.

Most of the Igbo were primarily root-crop, subsistence farmers who grew yams, cassava, and taro. Unlike some of the other West African peoples in the area, both Igbo males and females were engaged in agricultural production. Like most other traditional West African societies, the Igbo used some of their agricultural production for exchanges within the villages and trade outside the region. Women dominated trade in the rural village markets, whereas men dominated trade with other regions.

Uchendu described the traditional political system of the Igbo as unique. Igbo villages were essentially autonomous. At the village level, a form of direct democracy operated in which all adult males participated in decision making. Leadership was exercised by male and female officeholders who had developed power and influence gradually. Executive, legislative, and judicial functions were divided among leaders, lineages, and age-grade associations.

After Nigeria became independent in 1960, it was confronted with the types of ethnic problems that beset many other African nations. The British had drawn political boundaries without any respect to the traditional territorial areas of indigenous kingdoms or ethnic groups. For example, the Yoruba live in both Benin and Nigeria, and the Hausa reside in both Niger and Nigeria. Consequently, when Nigeria achieved independence, the

presence of various ethnic groups inhibited the political unification of the new nation. Most of the Hausa, Igbo, and Yoruban peoples identified with their own ethnic group and territories.

Ethnologist Abner Cohen, who examined the role of ethnicity and political conflict in Nigeria, focused on Hausa traders in the Yoruban city of Ibadan. Cohen (1969, 1974) described how ethnic distinctions between the Hausa and Yoruba became the basis of political and economic competition. Cohen used the term *retribalization* to refer to the Hausa strategy of using ethnic affiliations as an informal network for economic and political purposes. These networks were in turn used to extend and coordinate Hausa cattle-trading activities in Ibadan. Cohen's ethnographic research in Ibadan has become a model for analyzing ethnic trends in urban areas throughout the world. Cohen demonstrated how ethnic processes and the meaningful cultural symbols used by ethnic groups can mobilize political and economic behavior. These cultural symbols aided ethnic groups in Nigeria in their struggle to attain a decent livelihood and political power in the urban communities. This process, however, generated tensions among the various ethnic groups.

Nigeria's multicultural society was racked by interethnic, religious, and political competition and conflict. In the mid 1960s, these conflicts erupted into civil war. Because the Igbo people had had no historical experience with a centralized state, they resented the imposition of political authority over them. This led to conflict among the Igbo, the Yoruba, and the Hausa. Following the collapse of a civilian government in the 1960s, the Igbo were attacked and massacred in northern Nigeria. The Igbo fled as refugees from the north and called for secession from Nigeria. In 1967, under Igbo leadership, eastern Nigeria seceded and proclaimed itself the independent Republic of Biafra. The result was a civil war in which non-African powers assisted both sides. After three years of bitter fighting and a loss of about 2 million people, Biafra was defeated, and the Igbo were reincorporated into Nigeria.

Under a series of military-dominated regimes, Nigeria has succeeded in healing the worst wounds of its civil war. One strategy was to incorporate all ethnic and religious groups into the military leadership. In addition, the country was carved into nineteen states, the boundaries cutting through the

APPLYING ANTHROPOLOGY

Famines and Food Problems in Africa

Although Africa has the land and resources to produce more food than its current population requires, many African countries face famine conditions. A *famine* is starvation that is epidemic in scale and causes death from starvation-related diseases. Agencies of the United Nations estimate that more than 14 million people continually face starvation in Africa. In the 1980s, widespread famine occurred in twenty-two African nations. Ethiopia confronted famines in 1984 and 1989. In 1992, six countries were suffering from severe famine, including Somalia and the Sudan. Despite international relief and tens of millions of dollars of food aid, African agricultural production has been stifled.

A number of anthropologists have been researching famines to provide a knowledge base for countries that face these conditions. One area that has been investigated concerns the causes of famine conditions (Shipton, 1990). Researchers have found that many factors are responsible for the widespread famines in Africa. Climatic conditions, particularly droughts, decimate crops and diminish the fertility of the land. In some cases, political instability and civil war prevent food from reaching hungry people. For example, the Sudan has been destabilized by a civil war between the Muslim north and the Christian south. Both sides use food as a weapon, withholding needed grains to weaken the opposition. Similar conditions exist in Somalia, where rival tribes compete for political power by using food. In addition, in impoverished regions such as the Sudan, Somalia, and Ethiopia, poor transportation and communication facilities inhibit the shipment and distribution of food. Despite the work of international relief agencies, food frequently does not reach the famine-stricken population.

In addition, the colonial heritage of these nations contributes to the abysmal state of agricultural production. In substituting export crops for subsistence agriculture, the colonial powers promoted the growing of a single crop. This practice resulted in the loss of cultivable land, which, combined with population growth, led to problems in food production. In addition, the decrease in the availability of land resulted in fewer economic opportunities in rural

Harvesting sugarcane.

territories of the Yoruba, Hausa, and Igbo. This encouraged the development of multiethnic coalitions and a federalist political system (Ramsay, 1995). Nigerians hope that when ethnic and religious factions develop new social ties based on education, class backgrounds, and new forms of nationalism, older forms of association will weaken. Presently, however, ethnic loyalties and identities appear to be very powerful bases for social and political life in Africa. This has produced the potential for political disintegration in many African states (Lewis, 1992).

Nation-building projects that unify different ethnic groups remain the most formidable challenge facing Nigeria and other African countries.

ETHNICITY IN THE CARIBBEAN

Ethnicity in the Caribbean is a complex, diverse mixture of imported African slaves, East Indian laborers, and various Europeans. One conventional ethnic classification is based on skin color, especially the distinction between *black* and *brown*. Beginning regions and increased migration to overcrowded cities.

The growth of a single crop has also led to widespread environmental deterioration, including soil erosion, desertification, and deforestation. This agricultural pattern depletes the soil, turning grazing land into desert. Since the late 1970s, the Sahara Desert has been expanding southward at a rate of about 12 miles per year. The country of Ethiopia loses about a billion tons of topsoil annually as a result of intensive cultivation for cash crops. The use of firewood for fuel in Africa has resulted in severe deforestation. All of these developments have impeded food production.

As African countries became integrated into the world economy, food problems were intensified by declining commodity prices. Western industrial nations with large-scale mechanized agriculture have produced huge surpluses of wheat, corn, rice, and soybeans. Large multinational companies based in Minneapolis and Chicago have been able to dominate the world grain trade. These compa-

nies are able to lower the prices of these grains, which has driven thousands of African farmers out of business. In many cases, government officials living in African cities support low prices for food to gain political loyalty from urban residents. Yet falling prices lower the export earnings of African states, which were already confronted with rising interest rates and debts to core nations. These developments negated government plans to increase food production. As a result, food imports have increased throughout Africa. For example, wheat imports rose by 250 percent from 1969 to 1982, just before the widespread Ethiopian famine (Connell, 1987).

To resolve this food crisis, some Africans have called for increased regional trade within Africa and less reliance on the world market and global economy (Okigbo, 1988). Both anthropological researchers and Africans have also called for production of underutilized African food plants that would broaden their food base. They suggest growing a variety of different plant species to improve

the productive capacity of the land. In addition, anthropologists suggest restoring some traditional, small-scale subsistence production to provide a more balanced system of agriculture. This would involve providing credit and education to peasant farmers. Moreover, African governments must devote greater resources to research on land use and technology.

Western and African anthropologists, in cooperation with other specialists, have been working to resolve these problems. For example, in 1984, the American Anthropological Association set up a Task Force on African Famine, which included anthropologists with fieldwork experience in Africa, specialists in food security, and members of private voluntary organizations such as Oxfam, which deal with famine.

Anthropologists have a great deal of knowledge that is needed by agencies dealing with famine and food supply. The ethnographic data on local conditions in different communities are extremely valuable in famine relief and development planning to prevent future famines in Africa.

with the illicit offspring of European whites and slave women, a category of mulattoes began to gain certain advantages. At present, *brown* in many Caribbean islands such as Jamaica is synonymous with middle class, and these people are associated with the professional occupations (Eriksen, 1993). After the arrival of *East Indians* into the Caribbean, new ethnic relations began to develop. In contrast to the *blacks,* these East Indians were free to develop their own ethnic communities. Thus, in the Caribbean, the East Indian descendants are divided

among different linguistic and cultural groups. There are Hindu and Muslim ethnic communities, as well as Tamil and other language communities. Many of the Indians have used these ethnic ties to form effective career networks to enhance their professional careers. In response to the large Indian communities in islands such as Trinidad, the black community began to strengthen its own ethnic identity. The blacks began to develop stereotypes, such as the "backwardness" of the Indian communities and the "progressive" Europeanized black

A squatter settlement in Santo Domingo, the Dominican Republic. Wealth and poverty coexist throughout the Caribbean.

communities. Many of the black, brown, and Indian communities have been revitalizing their own ethnic identity in the context of globalization within the Caribbean region.

Urban Anthropology

Urban anthropologists who have done research in Latin America, Africa, and the Caribbean have helped improve our understanding of issues such as poverty and rural-to-urban migration. These topics are of vital interest to government officials and urban planners, economists and development technicians, and other international agencies. Population growth and urbanization in non-Western underdeveloped nations have posed global problems that urgently need to be resolved. Urban anthropologists working in these regions are providing data that can be used to help resolve these global problems.

The mass movement of people from rural areas to the cities is a major trend in these regions. Between 1950 and 1980, the proportion of the population living in urban areas increased from 41 to 65 percent (De Blij & Muller, 1985). Cities such as Mexico City, Rio de Janeiro (Brazil), Buenos Aires (Argentina), San Juan (Puerto Rico), and Lagos (Nigeria) are among the largest metropolitan areas in the world. For example, in 1990, the population of Mexico City exceeded 20 million (World Almanac, 1991). It is projected that in the first years of the new century, if growth rates remain the same, Mexico City will be the world's largest city, with more than 28 million inhabitants.

Much of this urban growth is due to internal migration. Migrants are pushed away from the countryside by poverty, lack of opportunity, and the absence of land reform. They are pulled to the city by the prospects of regular employment, education and medical care for their children, and the excitement of urban life. Rapid urbanization has led to the development of illegal squatter settlements, or high-density shantytowns, in and outside urban areas. Shantytowns provide homes for the impoverished and unskilled migrants. Anthropologists have found that in some of these settlements, some people are optimistic about finding work and improving their living conditions. In the shantytowns, the new migrants take advantage of city services such as running water, transportation, and electricity. However, in the worst slums in non-Western cities, many of these new migrants are so poor that they are forced to live in the streets.

Some anthropologists have focused their research on the poverty conditions of many of the non-Western urban centers. One well-known pioneer is Oscar Lewis, who studied families of slum dwellers in Mexico City (1961) and San Juan (and New York) (1966). From these studies, and from other evidence collected by urban anthropologists, Lewis concluded that the cultural values of the slum dwellers inhibited them from pursuing economic opportunities. He referred to these values as the **culture of poverty.**

Lewis described the people who maintain this culture of poverty as having a sense of fatalism, apathy, and hopelessness with respect to aspirations for economic or social mobility. They tended to be suspicious and fearful, disdained authority, and did not plan for the future. Alcoholism, violence, and unstable marriages were common. According to Lewis, these values were passed on to children through the enculturation process. Thus, poverty and hopelessness were perpetuated from generation to generation.

To be fair, Lewis stressed that the culture of poverty was a result of the lack of economic opportunities in the slum neighborhoods. Moreover, he carefully noted that these attitudes affected only about 20 percent of the people living in these areas. Nevertheless, many critics have charged that Lewis's hypothesis is an example of blaming the victim; that is, it attributes poverty to the negative attitudes of poor people themselves rather than to the economic and social stratification of their society. Some anthropologists have challenged the assertion that these attitudes are widespread among slum residents. For example, Helen Safa (1974) conducted research on a shantytown in San Juan and did not find the hopelessness and apathy that were portrayed in Lewis's studies. Safa found that the poor in the shantytowns have values emphasizing hard work, thrift, and determination. Her data contained little to confirm Lewis's characterization of the poor as having a pathological culture.

Safa and other anthropologists emphasize that these culture-of-poverty values are not perpetuated from generation to generation as Lewis suggested. Rather, each individual develops attitudes and strategies toward achievement depending on the availability of real economic opportunities. According to Safa, a sense of achievement based on individual initiative had relatively little effect on real economic and social mobility. She observed that, because of rapid economic growth in Puerto Rico, a few privileged people were able to attain upward mobility. This limited mobility led poor people to believe that economic and social advancement is due to individual and personal initiative rather than socioeconomic factors. In fact, Safa contends, socioeconomic conditions in Puerto Rico are to a great extent a consequence of global economic processes beyond the control of individuals in the shantytowns.

Other anthropologists are investigating the patterns of rural to urban migrations in non-Western countries. For example, during the 1970s, a comprehensive study of highland Guatemalan Mayan Indians of San Pedro La Laguna by anthropologists William Demarest and Benjamin Paul (1981) found a significant pattern of rural-to-urban mobility among Indian males. Although the Indians were extremely resourceful in gaining employment in urban areas such as Guatemala City, the low wages did not allow them to support families. Consequently, many of them resettled in San Pedro, where they looked for wives.

SUMMARY

Globalization has had a major effect on the countries of Latin America and the Caribbean, Africa, the Middle East, and Asia. These countries were either directly or indirectly affected by Western colonialism. Demographically, the countries of Latin America, the Caribbean, and Africa were devastated by diseases or slavery. In the long run, all of these countries were affected by declining death rates brought about by Western colonialism, but populations began to increase rapidly because of high birthrates.

Economically, these societies were drawn into the global economy and were transformed by producing commodities that were demanded by the wealthier core societies. Patterns of land ownership were reordered, and many peasants were producing for economic elites. Religious changes occurred in all of these countries because of Western expansion and missionary influence.

Western colonialism eventually gave way to political movements based on nationalist, independence, and sometimes revolutionary tendencies.

These movements represented anticolonial sentiments and resulted in many new countries around the world.

These countries were absorbed into the global economy at different levels depending on the resources that were available in their regions. Some countries remain poor and underdeveloped because their economies are heavily dependent on the wealthy core countries. Other countries, including Mexico and Nigeria, had oil resources that could be used to help develop their economies. Despite oil resources, these non-Western countries still find themselves with various obstacles to developing their economies.

Ethnographers have conducted research on the peasantry, social structures, family life, and gender in these countries. Each region has unique structures based on its cultural beliefs and practices. The peasantry differs in various countries based on the people's traditional relations and new global relationships to the world market. Family structures and gender relations are illuminated by ethnographers as they study patterns that develop in relationship to the emergence of new urban areas and the changing rural areas.

Ethnologists are also studying the overall patterns and consequences of urbanization in these societies, including the issues of poverty and rural-to-urban migration. They find that peoples throughout these countries, despite their hardships, continue to adapt their traditional social and cultural mechanisms to help them adjust to the effects of globalization.

STUDY QUESTIONS

1. Compare and contrast the effects of colonialism on Latin America, Africa, and the Caribbean.

2. How did globalization impinge on the traditional economies of Latin America, Africa, and Caribbean countries?

3. What were some of the religious changes that came with Western expansion into Latin America, Africa, and the Caribbean?

4. Compare the independence movements in Latin America and Africa.

5. What are some of the differences between the peripheral and semiperipheral countries in Latin America, Africa, and the Caribbean?

6. What do you think will enable the peripheral and semiperipheral countries in Latin America, Africa, and the Caribbean to sustain their economies in the future?

7. How is the peasantry different in various Latin America, Africa, and Caribbean countries?

8. Compare and contrast the social structure of Latin America with that of Africa.

9. How have family and gender patterns in Latin America, Africa, and the Caribbean been influenced by globalization?

10. Discuss some of the patterns of ethnicity in Latin America, Africa, and the Caribbean.

11. What are the effects of urbanization in Latin America, Africa, and the Caribbean?

KEY TERMS

apartheid

closed peasant community

culture of poverty

dyadic contract

fictive kinship ties

open peasant community

patron-client ties

relative deprivation

revolution

rising expectations

syncretism

◎ INTERNET EXERCISES

1. Look at the following website: **http://www. english.upenn.edu/~afilreis/50s/zinn-chap 16.html#guatemala.** What was the purpose of the overthrow of the President of Guatemala, Jacobo Arbenz? Why was the United States involved? How does this type of action by the United States subvert the needs of the people of the region? Why are human rights not more important to the United States government in this situation?

2. Review the website titled CIA involved in Guatemala coup, 1954: **http://www.english. upenn.edu/~afilreis/50s/guatemala.html.** Why was simple land reform such a threat to the United States? How does the United Fruit Company play into this? How is Guatemala a peripheral nation, as are many other countries in Central America?

◎ SUGGESTED READINGS

COMAROFF, JEAN. 1985. *Body of Power, Spirit of Resistance.* Chicago: University of Chicago Press. An incisive and moving anthropological analysis of a religious-based resistance movement among the Tshidi of South Africa.

CRAPANZANO, VINCENT. 1986. *Waiting: The Whites of South Africa.* New York: Random House. A fascinating ethnological study that examines the deep convictions, fears, and religious fervor mixed with racism of white South Africans as they assess their dilemma.

GIBBS, JAMES L., JR., ed. 1965. *Peoples of Africa.* New York: Holt, Rinehart and Winston. An anthology containing some classic descriptions of African societies including the Igbo, the Swazi, and the Yoruba.

KOTTAK, CONRAD. 1983. *Assault on Paradise: Social Change in a Brazilian Village.* New York: Random House. This is a detailed description of a Brazilian community responding to the changes brought about by the modern global economy.

KUPER, LEO, and M. G. SMITH, eds. 1971. *Pluralism in Africa.* Berkeley: University of California Press. A theoretical attempt at understanding ethnicity, colonialism, and social change in various African societies.

LEWIS, OSCAR. 1959. *Five Families: Mexican Case Studies in the Culture of Poverty.* New York: Wiley.

————. 1961. *The Children of Sanchez.* New York: Random House. These two books by Oscar Lewis are based on in-depth interviews with rural migrants who face problems in urban Mexico. They remain worthwhile descriptions of people coping with poverty, although the culture-of-poverty thesis has been challenged by many anthropologists.

OLMOS, MARGARITE FERNANDEZ, ed. 1997. *Sacred Possessions: Vodou, Santeria, Obeah, and the Caribbean.* New Brunswick, NJ: Rutgers University Press. A broad overview of the various syncretic religious movements such as Vodoun and Santeria that have influenced the people of the Caribbean islands.

RICH, EVELYN JONES, and IMMANUEL WALLERSTEIN. 1972. *Africa: Tradition and Change.* New York: Random House. A dated but useful introduction to the peoples of Africa. It includes many Africans speaking for themselves about their condition.

SMITH, CAROL, ed. 1990. *Guatemalan Indians and the State: 1540–1988.* Austin: University of Texas Press. An anthology of readings on the relationship between the Indian communities and economic and political developments in Guatemala.

15

Globalization in the Middle East and Asia

CHAPTER OUTLINE

**Colonialism and Globalization
in the Middle East and Asia**
Middle East / Asia

**Consequences of Colonialism
for the Middle East and Asia**
*Demographic Change / Economic Changes /
Religious Change / Political Change:
Independence and Nationalism /
Revolutionary Movements in Asia*

**Uneven Development in the Middle East
and Asia**
*Oil and the Middle East / Withdrawal
from the Global Economy*

**Ethnographic Studies of the Societies
in the Middle East and Asia**
*A Middle Eastern Village in Transition /
Middle Eastern Family, Marriage, and
Gender / Social Structure, Family, and
Gender in India and South Asia / Family
and Gender in China*

**Ethnic Tensions in the Middle East
and Asia**

Islamic Revitalization
*A Case Study: The Islamic Revolution
in Iran / The Islamic Revolution / Islamic
Revitalization in Afghanistan*

CHAPTER QUESTIONS

■ What were the most important consequences of colonialism in the Middle East and Asia?

■ What creates uneven development in the Middle East and Asia?

■ What are the basic features of the family and gender relations in the Middle East and Asia?

■ How does globalization result in ethnic tensions in the Middle East and Asia?

■ What is the link between globalization and Islamic movements?

AS IN LATIN AMERICA, AFRICA, AND THE CARIBBEAN, the process of globalization has been going on in the Middle East and Asia since the exploration of these regions by Europeans. The Middle East and Asia are vast heterogeneous regions with different ethnic groups and cultures that have had contact with each other through trade and exploration since the first millennium. For the purposes of this chapter, the Middle East includes the area of North Africa and Southwest Asia (Figure 15.1). Most of these regions were influenced by the development of Islamic culture and the Arabic language. Traditionally, this area was referred to as the "Near East" to distinguish it from the "Far East." At other times, it is mistakenly labeled the the "Arab world." The term *Arab* refers to people who speak the Arabic language. Included within this category of Arabic-speaking regions are the countries of Jordan, Syria, Iraq, Saudi Arabia, Yemen, Oman, and the Persian Gulf states such as Kuwait and the United Arab Emirates. However, the Middle Eastern region also contains non-Arabic-speaking countries such as Israel, Turkey, and Iran. Thus, the Middle East as described in this chapter is comprised of peoples with different histories, languages, ethnicities, and religions.

Asia is also a culturally diverse continent with a wide variety of sociocultural systems. This chapter focuses on three regions: South Asia, East Asia, and Southeast Asia (Figure 15.2). These regions contain most of the world's population, over 3 billion people. Different forms of societies have developed in these regions, ranging from hunter-gatherer and horticultural societies of the tropical rainforests, to the pastoral nomads of northern China, to the advanced industrial society of Japan. This chapter focuses primarily on the agricultural societies in Asia that have been transformed by globalization processes.

This chapter discusses the findings of anthropologists who use a global perspective that reflect the ongoing changes and transitions in the societies of the Middle East and Asia.

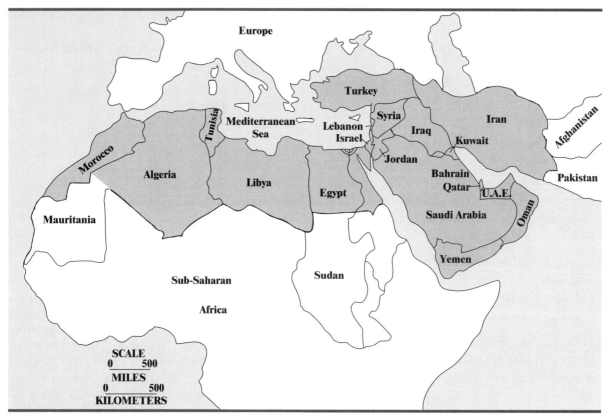

Figure 15.1   The Middle East.

Source: Adapted from Dale Eickelman, *The Middle East and Central Asia: An Anthropological Approach,* 4th ed. (Upper Saddle River, NJ: Prentice Hall). © 1998, p. 3. Reproduced with permission.

Colonialism and Globalization in the Middle East and Asia

THE MIDDLE EAST

Aside from the Portuguese, most Europeans did not have much direct contact with the Middle East until the 1800s. As European countries industrialized, however, they came to view the Middle East as an area ripe for imperial control. In the European view, the Middle East could supply raw materials and serve as markets for manufactured goods. Napoleon Bonaparte led an expedition to Egypt in 1798, bringing it under French rule for a brief period. He planned to incorporate Egypt as a colony that would complement French economic interests. Because of British rivalry following the Napoleonic Wars, the French had to evacuate Egypt; nevertheless, Europeans gradually attained more influence in the region.

Although Egypt was not colonized directly until 1882 by the British, various European advisers in-fluenced Egyptian rulers to develop specific products for the world market. Egyptian rulers and the upper classes cooperated with Western interests in these activities to induce economic growth. Factories were built for processing sugar, and cotton became the most important agricultural commodity in the country. The most important development project that affected ties between the Middle East and the West was the Suez Canal, which connects the Mediterranean Sea with the Gulf of Suez. Completed in 1869, the Suez Canal was financed through capital supplied by French and British interests. The canal shortened the distance between East and West, thereby drawing the Middle East into the orbit of the core nations.

To offset British expansion in the Middle East, the French began to build a North African empire, taking control of Algeria, Tunisia, and Morocco. Morocco was considered the most "perfect" French colony, in which, through indirect rule, the French devised a "scientific colony" that required only a small number

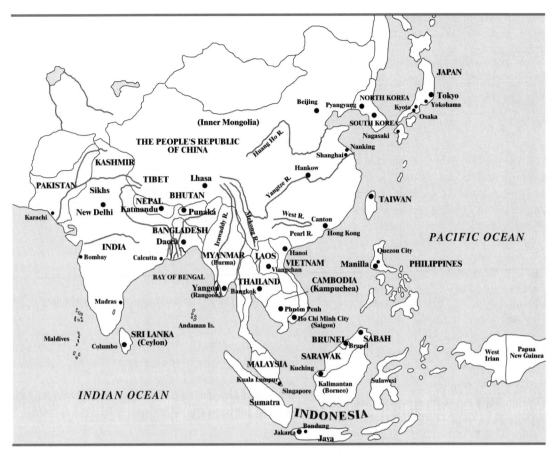

Figure 15.2 A map of contemporary Asia.

of French officials to supervise a vast territory. Thus, the French ruled through urban elites, rural leaders, and Moroccan religious officials. They developed large commercial enterprises such as railroads and mining as well as various agricultural operations. These commercial enterprises enabled the colony to pay for itself, a definite asset for the French.

European expansion in the Middle East continued throughout the nineteenth and early twentieth centuries. Although not directly colonized, Turkey, which was then part of the Ottoman Empire, came under the economic control of Western interests. To reduce the disparity in economic development between their country and Europe, Turkish rulers gave concessions to French and British interests to develop industries and services in Turkey. These enterprises produced cheap goods that undermined native Turkish businesses. By the end of the nineteenth century, Turkey had become a peripheral society exporting raw materials, providing cheap labor, and depending on core societies for

manufactured goods. This led to the end of the Ottoman Empire.

Although not as industrialized as many other European countries, Russia began to expand toward the Middle East during the mid 1800s and eventually assumed control over various regions of central Asia, absorbing the Muslim populations of Samarkand, Tashkent, and Turkestan. To secure access to the warm waters of the Persian Gulf, Russia also moved into Iran (formerly Persia), taking control of the northern half of the country. The British, who through their naval fleet maintained control of commerce in the Persian Gulf, were thus threatened by this Russian expansion. As a countermeasure, they moved into southern Iran and funneled capital into the region by developing a tobacco monopoly and financing other economic projects. Eventually, in 1907, the British and Russians agreed to divide Iran into three spheres, with northern and central Iran, including Tehran, in the Russian sphere; southeastern Iran in the British sphere; and an area between in the neutral zone. The Iranians were neither consulted nor informed about the terms of this agreement (Keddie, 1981).

Another area that was contested between the Russians and the British is the country of Afghanistan. Geographically, Afghanistan is situated between the Middle East and South Asia. It is a country made up of various ethnic groups who were Muslims that were involved in agricultural practices, and also nomadic pastoralism among the various rugged mountains and deep valleys, deserts, and arid plateaus. Afghanistan is a remnant of one of the major Muslim empires founded in the seventeenth century. In the nineteenth century, the Russians tried to colonize Afghanistan by completing a railway to the Afghan border, and the British countered by building a railway from their colonized portion of South Asia northward. This "Great Game" played out between the British and Russians left Afghanistan as a buffer state between these colonial powers. Various Afghan leaders had to negotiate between these powers and give concessions to these powers to maintain their independence.

Following World War I, the European powers divided the Middle East into different spheres of influence. In addition to their North African empire, the French gained the countries of Lebanon and Syria as direct colonies. Other areas such as Turkey and the Arabian peninsula remained politically independent but became peripheral states.

The British took Egypt, Iraq, and Palestine as direct colonies. The British also allowed European Jews to immigrate to Palestine. Because Jewish communities had faced discrimination and persecution for centuries in European society, Jewish leaders in Europe called for the resettlement of Jews in their original homeland in Palestine. This movement, known as Zionism, influenced British policy, which led to the immigration of thousands of Jews to Palestine, with dramatic consequences for the Middle East.

Asia

Intensive economic and political contact between Asia and the West began during the period of European mercantilism. The first phase of Western expansion into Asia began with the Portuguese trade in India, China, and Southeast Asia. The next phase involved the Dutch, French, and British, who established private trading companies in Asia to secure access to exportable goods.

India, Burma, and Malaysia   Western nations resorted to direct colonization in Asia following the industrial revolution. For example, Britain colonized India, gaining control over the production of export cash crops such as jute, oil seeds, cotton, and wheat. Because India did not have a strong centralized state, it could not resist British colonization. The opening of the Suez Canal facilitated Britain's management of its Asian colonies, and, by 1900, the British had established direct economic and political control over 300 million South Asians (Warshaw, 1989b).

From their base in India, the British initiated a series of wars to incorporate Burma as a direct colony. Eventually, the British expanded their colonial domination southward to the region of Malaysia. To satisfy industrial societies' increasing demand for commodities such as tin (for the canning industry) and rubber, the British developed mining and plantations in both Burma and Malaysia. In addition, as the demand for rice grew in the world market, the British commercialized rice production for export.

China   The industrial nations also attempted to carve out colonies in China. Although the country had been open to European trade ever since the Portuguese established ports in Macao in the sixteenth century, China successfully resisted direct colonization by the West, for several reasons. First, it was farther from the West than were other Asian countries. Second, China had a highly centralized state empire in which mandarin officials controlled local regions and thus was a more formidable empire than were other Asian countries. Third, the Chinese government was not impressed with Western goods and technology. Officials had been familiar with Western products from the time of Marco Polo in the fifteenth century and forbade the importation of Western commodities.

Despite this resistance, the British eventually gained access to China through the introduction of opium. Attempts by the Chinese government to prohibit the illegal smuggling of this drug into the country led to the Opium Wars of 1839–1842 between Great Britain and China. Britain defeated China, subsequently acquiring Hong Kong as a colony and securing other business concessions.

Eventually, international settlements were established in cities such as Shanghai, which became sovereign city-states outside the Chinese government's control (Tweddell & Kimball, 1985).

The Dutch Empire The Dutch expanded into the East Indies, eventually incorporating the region—now known as Indonesia—into their colonial empire. By the nineteenth century, the Dutch had developed what they referred to as the Kultur-System, which lasted until 1917. Through this system, Indonesian peasants were allowed to grow only certain cash crops, such as sugar, coffee, tobacco, and indigo, for the world market. These crops were developed at the expense of subsistence crops such as rice. The policy of coerced labor and exploitation of the peasantry held back the economic development of the Indonesian islands (Geertz, 1963a).

French Indo-China French imperial rivalry with Britain had direct consequences for Southeast Asia. By 1893, the French had conquered and established direct colonial rule over Cambodia, Vietnam, and Laos, a region that became known as Indo-China. In northern Vietnam, French settlers directed the production of coal, zinc, and tin; in the southern areas near the Mekong River, they developed the land to produce rubber and rice exports.

Thailand: An Independent Country One country in Southeast Asia that did not become directly colonized was Thailand. The Thai monarchy, which had some experience with Western interests, developed economic and political strategies to play European rivals against one another while adopting Western innovations. European business interests were allowed to aid in the development of some goods, but not to exercise direct political control. To some extent, this suited the geopolitical strategies of both the British and the French, who preferred Thailand as a buffer state between their colonial domains.

The Philippines The Philippines were directly colonized first by Spain, then by the United States. Spain took control of most of the Philippine Islands during the sixteenth century. As in Latin America, the Spanish established *pueblos* (towns) in which colonial officials directed Filipino peasant labor and collected tribute. Eventually, *encomiendas*—land grants to Spanish settlers—developed into *hacien-das*, on which tobacco, sugar, and indigo were planted for export to the world market. Aside from these agricultural enterprises, the Spanish encouraged few commercial developments. During the Spanish-American War of 1898, the United States defeated Spanish forces in both the Philippines and the Caribbean. Many Filipinos sided with the United States in the hopes of achieving independence from Spain. When the United States refused to recognize Philippine independence, numerous Filipinos redirected their resistance efforts against the United States. After a protracted war in which 600,000 Filipinos lost their lives and many more were placed in concentration camps, the Philippines were directly colonized by the United States. The United States continued to organize native Filipino labor to produce cash crops such as tobacco, sugar, and indigo as export commodities for the world market (Warshaw, 1988).

Consequences of Colonialism for the Middle East and Asia

DEMOGRAPHIC CHANGE

Western expansion and colonialism in non-Western countries brought unprecedented demographic growth to the populations of these agricultural states. Just as we saw in the areas of Latin America, Africa, and the Caribbean, the development of intensive cash-crop cultivation often resulted in rapid population growth. As labor shortages developed in subsistence agriculture as a result of moving labor into cash-cropping agriculture for the European market, peasant farmers began to increase their family size (Robbins, 1999). This increase in fertility led to rapid population growth in many of the Middle East and Asian societies. Eventually, Europeans introduced new medical and sanitation practices that led to a tremendous reduction in death rates through the control of smallpox, plague, yellow fever, and malaria. Meanwhile, birthrates remained high. The combination of reduced death rates and high birthrates led to dramatic population increases. For example, the population of India increased by one-third between 1881 and 1931 and then doubled between 1931 and 1971. In Chapter 16 we will discuss some of the global effects of these population trends.

Unlike in the West, population growth in non-Western countries was not coupled with rapid industrialization. The expanding Middle Eastern and Asian populations therefore had to be absorbed by the intensification of agricultural production. For example, population growth in Indonesia under the Dutch led to what Clifford Geertz has referred to as agricultural involution (1963a). The commercialization of agriculture and the use of coerced labor increased production somewhat, but the rates of increase could not keep pace with population growth. Agricultural yields per day of labor actually decreased. In addition, as the population grew, land became more scarce. Thus, the system of intensified agriculture was increasingly unable to feed the growing population.

As a result of colonialism, major urban centers grew quickly in the Middle East and Asia. For example, the cities of Cairo in Egypt and Tehran in Iran began to grow at tremendous rates. In India, the British created port cities such as Calcutta, Bombay, and Madras that became international trading and financial centers. In China, Shanghai and Nanking developed into major urban centers as a result of the expansion of Western businesses. Southeast Asian cities such as Rangoon, Bangkok, Saigon, Jakarta, Kuala Lumpur, Singapore, and Manila expanded rapidly. These cities attracted rural migrants who crowded into squatter settlements and slums.

ECONOMIC CHANGES

The economies of the countries of the Middle East and Asia during the nineteenth century were directed toward the production of agricultural goods such as tea, sugar, tobacco, cotton, rice, tin, and rubber for export. Prices of these goods were subject to fluctuations in the world market. Land that had been converted to growing these export crops could no longer support peasant villages. Native handicrafts declined dramatically in importance in comparison with export-oriented commodity production. In addition, as in other colonized areas of the world, imported Western manufactured goods flowed into Middle Eastern and Asian nations. Thus, these societies became more dependent on the core industrial societies.

As in Latin America, Africa, and the Caribbean, one major consequence of Western colonialism was the integration of many agricultural village communities into wider regional and global economic patterns. Although the precolonial traditional villages were probably never entirely self-sufficient and were tied to regional and national trading networks. Under Western colonialism, the village peasantry in the Middle East and Asia was no longer isolated from cities, and prices were determined by the global market for agricultural goods. The transformation of agricultural economies triggered dramatic changes in non-Western rural communities. Because few peasants had enough capital to own and manage land, much of the land fell into the hands of colonial settlers, large landowners, and moneylenders. In many cases, these changes encouraged absentee landownership and temporary tenancy. Long-term care of the land by the peasantry was sacrificed for immediate profits. Just as we saw with the peasants of Latin America, Africa, and the Caribbean, land, labor, and capital were thus disconnected from the village kinship structures of reciprocity and redistribution, or what has been referred to as the moral economy (see Chapter 11). As globalization occurred these peasants were incorporated into the capitalist cash economy.

RELIGIOUS CHANGE

The major religious traditions of most of the societies in the Middle East and Asia were Islam, Hinduism, and Buddhism. The Islamic tradition dates to the life of Muhammad, who was born in A.D. 570 in the city of Mecca, which is now in Saudi Arabia. Muslims believe that Muhammad is the final prophet in the long line of prophets referred to in the Bible. They share with Christians and Jews the faith that Abraham was the founder and first prophet of their tradition. Unlike Christians and Jews, however, they believe that Muhammad began receiving revelations from God that culminated in the major religious text known as the Qur'an (Koran). The traditions of Islam spread widely throughout areas of the Middle East and various areas of Asia.

Two other southern Asian religions that have influenced civilizations throughout the region are Hinduism and Buddhism. Both developed in India and are associated with three major doctrines. The first doctrine is known as *samsara,* or *reincarna-*

tion, which refers to how an individual's soul trans-migrates and is reborn in a new organism in a new cycle of existence. The second doctrine is *karma,* the belief that an individual's destiny is affected by his or her behaviors in previous lives. Hinduism emphasizes that an individual must live a dutiful and ethical life to produce good karma for future existences. The third doctrine is *moksha,* or *nirvana*—spiritual enlightenment—the ultimate aim and spiritual goal for all Hindus and Buddhists. Enlightenment represents the final escape from the cycle of life, death, rebirth, and suffering into an ultimate spiritual state of existence.

The Middle East and Asia already had the major highly literate religious traditions of Islam, Hinduism, and Buddhism, which meant that Western missionaries had a much more difficult time trying to convert native populations in these regions. However, in many cases, the Western missionaries in these Middle Eastern and Asian countries were instrumental in teaching some of the basic cultural values of the Western world, including political ideas regarding democratic institutions, civil liberties, and individual freedom.

POLITICAL CHANGE: INDEPENDENCE AND NATIONALISM

During the nineteenth and twentieth centuries, the extension of Western power into the Middle East and Asia elicited responses ranging from native reformist activities to nationalist independence movements. Because most people in these regions were Muslims, Hindus, or Buddhists, many of the anticolonial responses reflected a religious orientation. In response to Western colonialism, Muslim, Hindu, and Buddhist leaders called for a rethinking of their religious traditions to accommodate pressures from the West. Reformers such as Muhammad Abduh in Egypt and Tagore in India argued that the sources of Western strength evolved in part from early Eastern contributions to science, medicine, and scholarship. Thus, the reformists exhorted believers to look to their own religious traditions as a source of inspiration to overcome Western domination. Reformist movements spread throughout the Muslim world, especially among the urban, educated classes, paving the way for later nationalist and independence movements throughout the region.

Similarly, most of the anticolonial, nationalist, and independence movements that emerged in Asia were linked to local religious or political developments. They also were associated with the rise of Western-educated groups that articulated nationalist demands.

A Case Study of a Nationalist and Independence Movement: India   As in other colonies, the British desired an educated class of Indians to serve as government clerks and cultural intermediaries between the British and the colonized people. The British sponsored a national educational system that included universities and training colleges, which educated thousands of Indians. These educated people became part of a literate middle class, familiar with Western liberal thought regarding human rights and self-determination. A small, powerful merchant class that benefited from British economic policies also emerged.

Whereas India formerly had been fragmented into separate language groups, the colonial educational system provided the educated middle classes with a common language—English. Improved communication and transportation media such as railroads, print technology, and the telegraph accelerated the movement for national unity. In addition, the educated classes became increasingly aware of the hypocrisy of British values such as equality and democracy, being exposed to racism and discrimination in the form of exclusion from British private hotels, clubs, and parks, for example.

The majority of the Indian population, however, was not middle class but was made up of peasants who lived in rural village communities and did not speak English. Thus, the middle-class nationalist movement did not directly appeal to them. This gulf between the middle classes and the peasants was bridged by a remarkable individual, Mohandas Gandhi, later called the Mahatma, or "great soul." Although from the middle class, Gandhi fused Hindu religious sentiments with Western political thought to mobilize the peasantry against British domination (Fox, 1989).

Hindu traditions provided the model for Gandhi's strategies of nonviolent resistance. He called for the peaceful boycott of British-produced goods, telling the villagers to maintain their traditional weaving industries to spin their own cloth.

Through his protests and boycotts he rallied millions of Indians in a mass movement that eventually could not be resisted. In 1947, two years after the end of World War II, the British were forced to relinquish their empire in South Asia (Warshaw, 1989b).

REVOLUTIONARY MOVEMENTS IN ASIA

As in Latin America, Africa, and the Caribbean, a number of revolutionary movements developed in the Middle East and Asia as a result of globalization and contact with Western colonialism and power. The revolutions that developed in Asia had worldwide repercussions. In China a grassroots revolutionary movement developed out of anti-Western, nationalistic movements. In the early twentieth century Sun Yat-sen, a doctor educated in Hawaii and Hong Kong, championed the formation of a democratic republic in China, gaining support among the peasants by calling for the redistribution of land. The movement toward democracy failed, however. Instead, the military under Chiang Kai-shek, who did not sympathize with peasant resistance movements or democratic reforms, assumed control of China. These developments encouraged the growth of the Chinese Communist party under Mao Zedong. Mao's guerrillas engaged in a protracted struggle against Chiang Kai-shek's forces in the 1940s.

Mao Zedong was familiar with the writings of Karl Marx and Marx's prediction that the revolutions toward socialism and communism would be directed by the urban proletariat. Mao, in contrast, believed that the peasantry could become the backbone of a communist revolution (Wolf, 1969). Through the Chinese Communist party, Mao began to mobilize the peasantry. Calling for the overthrow of the landlords and Western forms of capitalism that he blamed for social and economic inequality, Mao made Marxism comprehensible to Chinese peasants. By 1949, after two decades of struggle, Mao and his peasant-based armies gained control of the country, renaming it the People's Republic of China (Welty, 1984).

Vietnam experienced the most dramatic nationalist and revolutionary movement of any of the French colonies of Southeast Asia. After World War II, the French attempted to reestablish their colonial regime in IndoChina. Leading the opposition was Ho Chi Minh, who like many other Vietnamese, was frustrated by French colonialism and its negative impact on his society. Ho believed in the communist ideal but, like Mao Zedong, adapted Marxist ideology to the particular concerns of his nationalist struggle (Wolf, 1969). His well-organized peasant army, the Vietminh, defeated the French forces at Dien Bien Phu in 1954. This defeat led to the withdrawal of the French from Vietnam.

Following Dien Bien Phu, the French and the Vietminh agreed to a temporary division of the country into North Vietnam under Ho Chi Minh

Mao Zedong.

Ho Chi Minh.

and South Vietnam under Ngo Dinh Diem. The nation was to be unified through elections in 1956, but the elections were never held. As a Cold War strategy the United States, meanwhile, committed itself to the survival of an independent, noncommunist South Vietnam, supplying Diem with massive economic, political, and military support. Diem lacked widespread support among the South Vietnamese population, however, and he brutally repressed dissent against his regime. He was overthrown in a military coup in 1963.

As communist opposition, supported by North Vietnam, escalated in the South, the United States dramatically increased its level of military involvement. By 1967, more than 500,000 U.S. troops were stationed in Vietnam. Unable to defeat the Vietnamese guerrillas, the United States entered into a long period of negotiation with the Vietnamese communists, finally signing a peace treaty in January 1973. Two years later, North Vietnam overran the South, thereby unifying the nation.

Uneven Development in the Middle East and Asia

By redirecting economic development toward an export-oriented global economy, Western colonialism and globalization transformed most of the formerly agricultural countries into peripheral, dependent economies. The core, wealthy industrial societies of the West provided economic and political support to those elites who instituted policies to promote economic growth. Many of these elites in the Middle East and Asia minimized restrictions on foreign investment and opened their borders to multinational corporations. In addition, some of these societies had vital resources that enabled them to develop a special type of relationship with the wealthy industrialized core societies. However, a number of these societies especially in Asia, began to attempt to withdraw from globalization and capitalism and develop self-sufficient economies.

OIL AND THE MIDDLE EAST

The discovery of vast sources of oil—60 percent of the world's known reserves—in the Middle East has revolutionized trade and politics and has

brought tremendous social change to the region. Oil became the major energy source for the industrial world. Multinational corporations based in the core societies developed these resources, controlling both oil production and prices, to maintain economic growth in their home countries. As nationalist independence movements spread, however, many countries demanded control over their oil. Nations such as Libya, Iran, Saudi Arabia, Iraq, and Kuwait began to nationalize their oil industries, and the multinational corporations eventually lost their controlling interests in the region.

The rapid increase in the price of oil since the 1970s has enabled the oil-producing countries of the region to accumulate vast wealth and has fueled worldwide inflation that raised the costs of all goods and raw materials. The per capita incomes of some Middle Eastern countries eventually surpassed those of many core countries. Realizing that

Oil production in countries such as Saudi Arabia has had global consequences.

they were dependent on a single export commodity, however, Middle Eastern countries took certain steps to diversify their economies. Smaller countries, such as Saudi Arabia, with a population of 8 million people, and Kuwait, with only 1 million, both ruled by royal families, financed some capital-intensive industries such as cement and detergent manufacturing and food processing. In doing so, these small Arab countries ensured high incomes for most of their population, which enhanced their political legitimacy and stability.

Larger oil-rich countries such as Iran and Iraq pursued rapid economic development to increase national wealth and legitimize their political regimes. Shah Muhammad Reza Pahlavi of Iran and Saddam Hussein of Iraq invited multinational corporations and consultants from core countries to help diversify their industries and develop their military forces. In contrast to the smaller countries, however, Iraq and Iran, with their larger populations (18 million and 42 million, respectively), had more difficulty raising economic standards for everyone immediately.

The vast majority of the people of the Middle East, however, do not live in oil-rich countries: These nations include Egyptian, Syria, Jordan, Lebanon, and Morocco. Although all of these countries have developed some industries to diversify their economies, they remain peripheral societies dependent on the wealthier industrial core societies.

WITHDRAWAL FROM THE GLOBAL ECONOMY

Some countries, by adopting a socialist form of economic system, tried to develop economically outside of the capitalist global economy. In China following his victory in 1949, Mao Zedong implemented an economic development plan modeled on that of the former Soviet Union. He collectivized agriculture by appropriating the land owned by the elite and giving it to the peasants. Mao established cooperatives in which a number of villages owned agricultural land in common, and he also sponsored the development of heavy industries to stimulate economic growth. Communist party officials, known as cadres, managed both the agricultural cooperatives and industrial firms.

When these policies failed to generate economic growth, Mao launched a radically different effort in 1958 favoring a decentralized economy. This plan, known as the Great Leap Forward, established locally based rural and urban communes that organized the production and distribution of goods and services. Each commune, consisting of 12,000 to 60,000 people, was subdivided into brigades of 100 to 700 households, production teams of about thirty-five households, and work teams of eight to ten households. Each commune was supposed to be self-sufficient, containing its own banking system, police force, schools, day-care centers, mess halls, hospitals, and old-age centers. The communes established their own production goals and reinvested their profits in the commune.

Although some aspects of the Great Leap Forward were successful, especially those involving health care and literacy, the program failed to promote agricultural and industrial development. In fact, it was marked by famine, political corruption, and economic retardation.

Mao then initiated an ideological campaign to eliminate corruption and political "deviance" while restoring revolutionary consciousness. This campaign, known as the Cultural Revolution, lasted from 1966 to 1976. Mao organized young people into groups called the Red Guards to purify China of any capitalist, traditional Confucianist, or Western tendencies. Millions of people, primarily the educated classes, were arrested and forced to work on rural communes as punishment for their deviance from the communist path. By 1976, at the time of Mao's death, the Cultural Revolution had paralyzed economic development by eliminating the most skilled and educated classes, those who could have contributed to the nation's growth (Welty, 1984).

Vietnam also tried to withdraw from the world capitalist system, implementing a socialist government based on Marxist–Leninist principles. After the end of the Vietnam War, the government instituted a five-year plan that collectivized agriculture and relocated people from urban to rural communities. By 1978, 137 collective farms had been established; 4 million people, including half the population of Ho Chi Minh City (formerly Saigon), were resettled in what were called new economic zones. These zones were organized to produce crops and light industry as a means of encouraging economic self-sufficiency. They were managed by Communist party officials, many of whom had no direct experience in agriculture or industry.

By 1981, Vietnam had become one of the poorest peripheral nations in the world. While food production and labor productivity decreased, inflation and unemployment rose. Military expenditures drained the economy of needed funds for capital development. Part of the reason that Vietnam is underdeveloped was the war itself. For example, the defoliation of forests as a result of U.S. bombing and the use of Agent Orange impeded the growth of timber. At the same time, however, many of the problems were a direct result of inflexible ideological commitments and lack of expertise on the part of Communist party bureaucrats (Pike, 1990).

Ethnological Studies of the Societies in the Middle East and Asia

A MIDDLE EASTERN VILLAGE IN TRANSITION

Studies of peasant villages in the Middle East have contributed to a more comprehensive understanding of the interconnections between peripheral and core nations. Ethnologist Hani Fakhouri (1972) studied the Egyptian village of Kafr El-Elow, which at the time of Fakhouri's study (1966–1968) was undergoing substantial changes. About 80 percent of the Egyptian population lived in about 4,000 rural villages, many of which were being drawn into the global economy through rapid industrialization and the commercialization of agriculture.

Kafr El-Elow is located 18 miles south of Cairo. Before the 1920s, it was a relatively small farming community in which the *fellaheen* (peasants) practiced small-scale subsistence agriculture. After British colonization in the nineteenth century, the *fellaheen* began to grow cotton as an export commodity. By the 1920s, water pumps had been introduced into the village, and several industries had begun to develop. Roads were constructed, linking Kafr El-Elow with nearby industrializing communities.

After the 1950s, industrialization accelerated, and subsistence farming was no longer the primary aspect of the Kafr El-Elow economy. Instead, many nearby industries related to steel, natural gas, cement, textiles, railways, aircraft, and other products drew increasing numbers of fellaheen into the industrial work force. Many villagers continued cultivating their crops after factory hours and on weekends to supplement their incomes, however.

By the 1960s, only about 10 percent of the community was made up of peasants. Although the remaining Fellaheen continued to plow their fields with draft animals, they also used some modern machinery such as crop sprayers and irrigation pumps. At the time of Fakhouri's study, agricultural productivity was very high, and the *fellaheen* were able to harvest three or four crops a year. Wheat

Traditional Egyptian peasants.

and corn were cultivated for domestic consumption, primarily for making bread, and vegetables were grown for cash crops and home consumption. Cash crops became important enough that the Egyptian government built refrigerated bins to store the farmers' seeds and cuttings for replanting.

Industrialization brought to Kafr El-Elow new patterns of social mobility, an influx of migrants for urban labor, and rising incomes, which created new socioeconomic classes. These new classes demanded a variety of consumer goods and services not familiar to the traditional population. Bicycles, wristwatches, radios, and electricity for households became increasingly common. Preferences for Western clothing, housing, entertainment, and other commodities contributed to the decline of traditional handicraft industries and the rise of new businesses. Six businesses existed in 1930; in 1966, Fakhouri counted seventy-eight.

MIDDLE EASTERN FAMILY, MARRIAGE, AND GENDER

An enormous amount of ethnological research is available on family, marriage, and gender in Arab, Turkish, and Iranian societies. In all of these societies, the ideal form of the family has been patrilineal, endogamous, polygynous, and patriarchal. The main sources for the ideals of the Muslim family are Islamic religious texts, principally the Qur'an and the Sharia. Ethnologists have discovered, however, that the ideals of the Muslim family do not always coincide with the realities of social life in the Middle East and North Africa.

In much of the Arab world, the term *hamula* is used to refer to an idealized descent group (a patrilineage or patriclan) that members view as a kinship group. The hamula is associated with a patronym, the name of a particular male who is thought to be a paternal ancestor. In rural areas, the typical hamula is a clan that embraces various patrilineages. The head of the clan is referred to as a *sheik,* a hereditary position. He resolves disputes and encourages cooperation among members of the clan. The hamula has always been a source of pride and loyalty in rural Arab communities.

Despite the descriptions of the hamula as a patrilineal descent grouping and its association with a particular patronym, enthnologists find that it is frequently a loosely structured group combining patrilineal, affinal, matrilineal, and neighborhood relations (Eickelman, 1998). Nevertheless, it serves to coordinate economic, political, and ceremonial affairs. Research on urban and rural communities in Lebanon, Kuwait, and other Arab countries suggests that loyalty to the hamula remains a basic aspect of social organization throughout the Muslim world (Al-Thakeb, 1985).

The Family   As in most other agricultural states, the extended family is the ideal in the Middle East. The traditional household espoused by Arabs, Turks, and Iranians is made up of the patriarch, his wife, one or more married sons and their families, and unmarried daughters and sons. Yet, as in the case of the hamula, these ideals are often not realized (Bates & Rassam, 1983). Economic and demographic conditions such as landlessness, poverty, and geographical mobility frequently influence the size and dimension of the Muslim family.

As industrialization and consequent urbanization influence the Middle East, the nuclear family is becoming the normative pattern. Survey research on the Muslim family from Egypt, Syria, Libya, Jordan, Lebanon, Iraq, Bahrain, and Kuwait suggests that the nuclear family has become the predominant form in both rural and urban areas (Al-Thakeb, 1981, 1985). Variability in family type is often related to socioeconomic status. The ideal of the nuclear family appears to be most prevalent among the middle and upper classes, which are most influenced by globalization. Among the lower socioeconomic classes, especially families involved in agriculture, the extended family retains its importance. Yet even when the nuclear family predominates, wider kinship relations, including the hamula, remain important (Al-Thakeb, 1985; Eickelman, 1998).

Marriage   Marriage is a fundamental obligation in the Islamic tradition. Unless financially or physically unable, every Muslim male and female is required to be married. Marriage is regarded as a sacred contract between two families that legalizes intercourse and the procreation of children. In the Islamic tradition, there are no cultural beliefs or practices such as monasticism that sanction any form of life outside of marriage.

Islamic societies are known for practicing polygyny. Polygyny is mentioned once in the Qur'an (iv:3):

Marry of the women, who seem good to you, two, three, or four, and if ye fear that ye cannot do justice [to so many] the one [only].

Although polygynous marriage is permitted and to some extent represents the ideal norm in Muslim societies, ethnologists find that most marriages are monogamous. For example, less than 10 percent of married Kuwaiti males and about 1 percent of married Egyptian males are involved in polygynous marriages (Al-Thakeb, 1985; Eickelman, 1998). In Kafr El-Elow, Fakhouri (1972) found that only a few males had multiple wives. In questioning males involved in polygynous marriages, Fakhouri noted that the major rationales for taking a second wife were either the first wife's infertility or poor health or the desire of wealthy males to demonstrate their high status.

Wealthy males in both urban and rural areas contract polygynous marriages. In the traditional pattern found in rural communities, a wealthy male from the landed elite contracts a parallel-cousin marriage and then takes a wife from another family (Bates & Rassam, 1983). Polygyny is also found among the new elite in some of the wealthy oil-producing countries. However, economic limitations and the fact that the Islamic tradition prescribes equal justice for all wives encourage monogamous marriages among the majority of Muslims. Arranged marriage based on parental decision making still predominates in Islamic societies. Until recently, for example, Saudi Arabian males did not even view their wives until their wedding day. Some indicators suggest, however, that a degree of individual choice in marriage may become more prevalent. Anthropological research from Kuwait in the mid-1980s indicates that an individual's freedom to select a spouse varies according to education, socioeconomic status, age, and sex (Al-Thakeb, 1985). As males become more educated and achieve greater economic independence from their parents, they enjoy greater freedom in mate selection. Females generally have much less choice.

Divorce Like polygyny, divorce in traditional Islamic societies was a male prerogative. To obtain a divorce a male does not need much justification; Islamic law specifies several means whereby a male can easily repudiate his wife. It also empowers a husband to reclaim his wife without her consent within a four-month period after the divorce. Traditionally, a Muslim wife did not have the same rights to obtain a divorce. A woman could, however, divorce her husband for reasons such as impotence, insanity, and lack of economic support; but to prove these accusations, she would need a very sympathetic judge (Esposito, 1991).

Ethnologists find it difficult to generalize about divorce and marriage in the Muslim world. In countries such as Egypt, Turkey, and Morocco, which have greater exposure to outside influences, divorce laws for women have become liberalized. These countries have educated middle classes that support reform. In conjunction with these reform movements, along with the modification of divorce laws, some Muslim feminists have called for the abolition of polygyny. Certain countries—for example, Tunisia and Turkey—have prohibited this practice, and others have restricted it (Eickelman, 1998).

Gender The Western image of the Arab or Muslim woman is frequently that of a female hidden behind a veil and completely dominated by the demands of a patriarchal society. Early Western scholars painted a grim and unwholesome portrait of the female in the Muslim household. Ethnologists find that this image obscures the complexity of gender relations in the Middle East.

The patriarchal ideal and the status of the female in the Muslim world cannot be understood without reference to two views in the Islamic doctrine. First, according to the Islamic tradition, before the origins of Islam, females were treated negatively. For example, in the pre-Islamic period, the Bedouins regularly practiced female infanticide by burying the unwanted child in sand. The Qur'an explicitly forbids this practice. Thus, Islam was viewed as having had a progressive influence on the role of women. Second, Islam condemns all sexual immorality, prescribing severe penalties for adultery. The Qur'an enjoins both males and females to be chaste and modest.

Islamic religious texts prescribe a specific set of statuses and corresponding roles for females to play in the Muslim family as daughter, sister, wife, and mother. Each of these statuses carries certain obligations, rights, privileges, and duties. These statuses are influenced by the patriarchal ideals of the Islamic texts. One passage of the Qur'an (iv:34) is often cited when referring to the role of women:

Men are in charge of women, because god hath made the one of them to excel the other, and because they spend of their property (for the support of women). So good women are the obedient.

This passage provides the context for the development of various laws that have influenced the status of Muslim women. For example, traditionally a woman could inherit only a one-half share of her parents' estate, whereas her brothers inherited full shares. This law assumed that a woman is fully cared for by her family and, when she marries, her husband's family will provide for her material needs. Thus, a Muslim woman does not need the full share of inheritance.

Another traditional code in the Islamic law illustrates the patriarchal attitudes toward women in respect to political and legal issues. In legal cases a woman is granted half the legal status of a man. For example, if a crime is committed, two women as opposed to one man are needed as legal witnesses for testimony. This legal equation of "two females equals one male" reflects the traditional Islamic image of women as less experienced and less capable than men in political and legal affairs.

Ethnological research since the 1970s has demonstrated that male–female relations in these societies are far more complex than the religious texts might imply. By focusing exclusively on Islamic texts and laws, early researchers distorted and misunderstood actual practices and relations between males and females. In addition, before the 1970s, much of the ethnological research in Muslim societies was done by males, resulting in a skewed understanding of the position of women, because male ethnologists did not have the same access to female informants as did female ethnologists. Eventually, female ethnologists such as Nikki Keddie, Lois Beck, and Elizabeth Fernea began to study the Muslim female world.

Female ethnologists discovered that the position of Muslim women cannot be categorized uniformly. One major reason for variation is the extent to which Islamic countries have been exposed to the West. Some, like Tunisia, Egypt, and Turkey, have adopted legal reforms that have improved the status of women. For example, Egyptian women

have had access to secondary education since the early 1900s and have had career opportunities in medicine, law, engineering, management, and government. The Egyptian constitution accords women full equality with men, and—ideally—prohibits sexual discrimination in career opportunities. Muslim feminist movements dedicated to improving the status of women have emerged in those countries most affected by the West.

In contrast to Egypt, religiously conservative Saudi Arabia has highly restrictive cultural norms regarding women. Saudi Arabia was not colonized and thus was more isolated from Western values. The Saudi Arabian government has interpreted the Islamic law to declare that any mingling of the sexes is morally wrong. Saudi women are segregated from men; they attend separate schools and upon finishing their education can seek employment only in exclusively female institutions such as women's hospitals, schools, and banks. Saudi women are forbidden by law to drive cars, and when riding on public buses they have to sit in special closed sections. All Saudi public buildings must have separate entrances and elevators for men and women (May, 1980).

Despite legal reforms and access to education in some Muslim societies, the notion that women are subordinate to men remains firmly entrenched. For example, in Egypt a woman trained in law cannot become a judge or hold any position with legislative authority. Also, in Egypt polygyny remains legal, and men can obtain divorces with minimal justification (May, 1980). In many respects, the patriarchal family remains the center of Islamic social organization. Hence, in some cases attempts to reform women's status have been perceived as heretical assaults on the Islamic family and morality. Some of the recent Islamic revival movements have reactivated conservative, patriarchal cultural norms.

The Veil and Seclusion   To many Westerners, the patriarchal order of the Islamic societies is most conspicuously symbolized by the veil and the other shapeless garments worn by Muslim women. As a female approaches puberty, she is supposed to be restricted and kept from contact with males. The veil is an outward manifestation of a deep cultural pattern (Beck & Keddie, 1978; Fernea & Fernea, 1979). The wearing of the veil and the enforced seclusion of the Muslim woman are known as *purdah*. These practices reinforce a separation

An Afghan woman with child.

In addition, in countries such as Egypt, Turkey, and Iran that had formerly abandoned traditional dress codes, many educated, middle-class women have opted to wear the veil and the all-enveloping garments. To some extent, this return to traditional dress reflects the revival movements now occurring throughout the Islamic world. For many Muslim women, returning to the veil is one way in which they can affirm their Islamic religious and cultural identity and make a political statement of resistance to Western power and influence.

SOCIAL STRUCTURE, FAMILY, AND GENDER IN INDIA AND SOUTHERN ASIA

In the aftermath of independence and the retreat of western colonial authority in South Asia, ethnologists began to explore the various societies of the region. Much ethnological research centered on rural communities of India, with ethnologists such as McKim Marriott, Oscar Lewis, Milton Singer, and Alan Beals investigating the Indian peasantry.

Origins of the Caste System The caste system of India was briefly introduced in Chapter 11. Most scholars associate the origins of the caste system with the Aryan peoples who settled in northern India after 1500 B.C. Various social divisions in Aryan society developed into broad ideological categories known as varnas. At the top were the *brahmans* (priests), followed by the *kshatriyas* (warriors), the *vaisyas* (merchants), and the *sudras* (commoners). This fourfold scheme provided the ideological framework for organizing thousands of diverse groups.

The functional groupings in the varna categories are the subcastes, or, more precisely, what Indians refer to as *jatis,* of which there are several thousand, hierarchically ranked. Jatis are based on marital, economic, and ritual relations. Marriages are endogamous with respect to jati; jatis are thus ranked endogamous descent groups. In addition, each jati is a specific hereditary occupational group. A person's jati places him or her within a rigid form of social stratification.

Ethnologists have found that jati relationships are intimately linked with what is known as the *jajmani* economy of rural Indian villages. The typical Indian village consists of many different castes, with one caste dominating the village both eco-

between the domestic private sphere of women and the male-dominated public sphere.

Veiling and purdah tend to be associated with urban Muslim women. Most scholars believe that the tradition of veiling originated in urban areas among upper-class women (Beck & Keddie, 1978). Many peasant and Bedouin women in the Middle East and North Africa do not wear the veil and generally have more freedom to associate with men than do Muslim women who live in towns and cities. Many urban Muslim women report that the veil and accompanying garments offer practical protection from strangers and that when in public they would feel naked and self-conscious without these garments (Fernea & Fernea, 1979).

CRITICAL PERSPECTIVES

The Sacred Cow

From the Western perspective, the Hindu conception of the cow as a sacred animal seems irrational. Because India has severe economic problems including malnutrition and underdeveloped agricultural production, Westerners are usually critical of Hindu norms prohibiting the consumption of cattle. Cattle wander the streets unharmed, and elderly cows sometimes are kept in government-sponsored "old-age homes." Western peoples often consider these practices to be the primary source of poverty in India.

Anthropologists, however, have studied these practices in terms of the needs of the Indian population. Marvin Harris (1985), for example, has used a cultural-ecology approach in analyzing Hindu norms concerning cattle. He hypothesized that there are highly practical reasons for these norms. First, cows generally don't consume the same kinds of foods as humans and therefore don't compete with humans for scarce resources. More important, cows produce oxen (neutered offspring of cows), which are used for plowing fields. Peasant farmers who sold or killed their cows for food would be destroying the "factories for producing their natural "tractors." in many cases, farmers would have to abandon their farms or increased production. Thus, the short-term benefits of consuming the cow would be more than offset by the long-term consequences of increased land-lessness and starvation. In addition, cows produce manure, which is used for both fertilizer and cooking fuel.

Thus, in Harris's analysis, living cows are sound, long-term investments. In the context of the traditional, labor intensive agricultural system of India, Hindu attitudes toward cows make good practical sense.

Harris went on to explain that while the development of an Indian beef industry would strain the ecological relationships in the country, in the United States, for example, over three-quarters of all crop lands are used to feed cattle. To produce these cattle, the U.S. farmer depends on very expensive, energy-consuming , machinery, fertilizers, and pesticides. If this highly inefficient, capital-intensive form of agriculture were introduced into India, the economy would be severely shaken. India would have to depend on high-cost petrochemicals and other expensive capital technology. Developing a beef industry in India would be a highly irrational decision.

Do you find Harris's arguments convincing? When examined in anthropological terms, do Hindu attitudes toward cattle seem more rational? Why, in your opinion, do Westerners perceive these attitudes as irrational? Is the maintenance of a large-scale cattle industry in the United States a rational response to U.S. needs and resource availability? What can you conclude about cross-cultural analysis from this study of the sacred cow?

nomically and politically. Traditionally, all of these castes were interconnected through economic exchanges within the jajmani economy. The dominant caste controlled the land and exchanged land-use rights for other goods and services. For example, members of the dominant caste would have their hair cut and fingernails trimmed by a barber. Then, at harvest time, the barber would get a stipulated amount of grain from his client. In addition, the barber, carpenter, potter, and water carrier would exchange their goods and services with one another in a type of barter system. Every caste, even the lowest-ranking, had access to housing, furniture, food, credit, and other goods and services through these exchanges.

More recent ethnological studies have concluded that the jajmani system is collapsing because of the introduction of new goods and technology into Indian villages. When people can use safety razors to shave, buy imported dishware and glasses, and use electric pumps to obtain water, many of the old occupations become superfluous. Consequently, many artisans and service workers leave their villages to market their skills elsewhere or, in many cases, to join the increasing number of unskilled migrants flooding the cities.

Although the jajmani system is disappearing, ethnologists find that the caste system persists. Contemporary India has caste hotels, banks, hospitals, and co-ops. Caste organization continues to delineate political factions in India. Most elections are decided by caste voting blocs, and politicians must therefore appeal to caste allegiances for support. Thus, caste remains one of the most divisive factors facing the democratic process in India.

Ethnologists find that the caste system is reinforced by the worldview of Hinduism. The doctrines of karma and reincarnation reinforce concepts of purity and pollution that correlate with caste hierarchy. An individual's karma determines his or her status and ritual state. It is believed that individuals born into low castes are inherently polluted, whereas higher-caste individuals such as brahmans are ritually pure. This state of purity or pollution is permanent.

The late French anthropologist Louis Dumont (1970) argued that from the Hindu viewpoint humans have to be ranked in a hierarchy; egalitarian relationships are inconceivable. Dumont asserted that in this worldview, caste relations produce interdependency and reciprocity through exchanges and ritual relationships. He concluded that the cultural understandings of caste rules and ritual purity and pollution have created a system of stratification based on widespread consensus.

In contrast, cultural materialists ground caste relationships in prevailing economic and political conditions, maintaining that Hindu beliefs about caste were primarily ideological justifications for a system that emerged from longstanding inequalities in which a dominant group accumulated most of the land and other resources. They deny that a consensus exists concerning the appropriateness of caste relationships, citing as evidence the situation of the *harijans,* or untouchables, at the bottom of the caste hierarchy, who daily face discrimination and exploitation. Based on her research in southern India, anthropologist Joan Mencher (1974) reported that the *harijans* resent, rather than accept, this treatment.

Other anthropologists have refined their analyses of caste relations by combining both material and cultural variables. For example, ethnologists such as Jonathan Parry and Gloria Raheja have described the complex interplay of material interests and cultural meanings of exchanges among castes in the jajmani system. They note how upper-caste brahmans accept gifts and other material items from lower-caste members but in this exchange they ritually absorb the sins of the donors (Parry, 1980; Raheja, 1988). Raheja (1988) emphasizes that in these jajmani exchanges, the lower- and upper-caste groups become equal, and strict hierarchy is undermined. Thus, the exchanges are based on material factors and on the symbolic conceptions of Hinduism.

Family and Marriage in South Asia   The most typical form of family in South Asia is the extended family, which consists of three generations: grandparents, parents, and children. It may also include brothers and their wives and children within the same household. The extended family is the ideal norm for South Asian villages because it provides a corporate structure for landowning, labor, and other functions. Ethnologists find, however, that families actually go through development cycles—an extended family at one point, a large extended family at another time, and a nuclear family at still other times. But despite modernizing influences, the cultural ideal of the joint family persists, even in most urban areas (Maloney, 1974; Tyler, 1986).

Marriages in South Asia are arranged by parents. As noted, in northern India people marry outside their patrilineage and village but inside their caste grouping. A married woman must switch allegiance from her father's descent group to that of her husband. After marriage, a woman moves into her husband's joint family household and must adjust to the demands of her mother-in-law. In Pakistan and Bangladesh, parallel-cousin marriage is often preferred, and polygynous marriages, in accordance with Muslim practices, are sometimes found.

The Dowry   Another marital practice, found especially in northern India, is the dowry. The Indian bride brings to the marriage an amount of wealth that to some extent represents her share of the household inheritance. Typically, the dowry includes clothing and jewelry that the bride retains for her personal property, household furnishings, and prestige goods (Tambiah, 1989). Upper-caste families try to raise a large dowry payment as a sign of their elevated status. In these cases, the dowry creates alliances between elite families.

Gender and Status in South Asia   The status of women in South Asia varies from one cultural area to another. In Pakistan and Bangladesh, which are influenced by the Islamic tradition, women are secluded according to the prescriptions of purdah. Until recently, Hindu women of northern India were subject to similar norms. Today, however, many do not wear the veil and accompanying clothing, thereby distinguishing themselves from Muslims. Traditionally, in both Islamic and Hindu regions, a woman was expected to obey her father, her husband, and, eventually, her sons. Women ate after the men were finished and walked several paces behind them.

Older women, particularly mothers-in-law, gained more respect and status in the family. In certain cases, older women became dominant figures in the extended family, controlling the household budget.

As some urban South Asian women have become educated, they have begun to resist the patriarchal tendencies of their societies. Some have even participated in emerging feminist political activities. As industrialization and urbanization continue, an increase in feminist activity would be expected. However, because about 80 percent of the population still resides in rural communities, patriarchal tendencies remain pervasive.

FAMILY AND GENDER IN CHINA

Ethnological research in China was severely restricted by the Chinese communist government. During the 1970s the United States and China developed a more formal cooperative relationship, and China began to allow some ethnologists to conduct research within its borders. In the 1970s, Norman Chance became the first american ethnologist allowed to conduct fieldwork in both rural and urban communes. His detailed ethnography of Half Moon Village in Red Flag Commune, near Beijing, offers important insights into the economic, social, political, and cultural developments of that period. Half Moon Village was one sector of the Red Flag Commune, which was one of the largest communes in China when it was formed in 1958. Red Flag occupied 62 square miles and contained 85,000 inhabitants in 17,000 households, organized into production brigades and work teams. The state owned the land and the sideline industries associated with the commune. The commune work force consisted of more than 40,000 people, most of whom did agricultural work. Many of the commune's crops were sent to Beijing markets, providing a steady income for the villagers. Approximately 15 percent of the labor force worked in the commune's industrial sector.

The Family, Marriage, and Kinship in Red Flag Commune   Following the Chinese revolution, the government initiated a campaign to eradicate the patriarchal nature of the Chinese family and clan. The communist leadership viewed the traditional family, clan, and male dominance as remnants of precommunist "feudal" China, as well as major sources of inequality. The Chinese communist party passed legislation such as the marriage laws of 1950 to destroy the traditional clan and extended-family ties and create more equal relationships between males and females. The marriage laws required free choice in marriage by both partners, guaranteed monogamy, and established a woman's right to work and obtain a divorce without losing her children.

Norman Chance's (1984) research indicated, however, that despite government attempts to alter family and kinship relations, Half Moon Village residents sought to maintain strong kinship ties for economic security. Chance discovered that many decisions concerning access to various jobs in the commune were based on kinship relationships. To ensure kinship ties, families maneuvered around government officials and decisions. In addition, younger family members looked to their elders for knowledge and advice. Chance found that within the family, harmonious relationships were emphasized according to the centuries-old Confucianist traditions.

The role and the status of women have been strongly influenced by the ideals of the Chinese communist party leadership. Based on his study of Half Moon Village, Chance (1984) concluded that the status of women had improved under the communist regime and that in general the new marriage laws had disrupted the confucian pattern of rigid patriarchy. Young girls were no longer married off or sold. Women were no longer confined to the home; rather, they were encouraged to work along with the men in agriculture and industry.

Chance noted some other changes in the status of women. He regularly observed young men taking care of their children and doing tasks such as cooking, chores that were previously performed only by women. In addition, women had assumed decision-making roles in certain areas, especially in respect to family planning—a high priority for the Chinese government after 1976. After China adopted the well-known one-child policy, the

A sign advertising the importance of the one-child policy and family planning in the People's Republic of China.

communist party paid bonuses to families that had only one child. Families had to return the bonus to the government if they had a second child. Women were responsible for administering and monitoring this policy.

Despite these changes, however, Chance found that some remnants of the older patriarchal norms were still evident. For example, peasant women engaged in agricultural labor were unable to develop skills that would lead to better job opportunities in the factories and other sideline occupations of the commune. In contrast to men, women were restricted to unskilled jobs. In addition, women did not hold administrative positions on commune committees.

Chance also found that women's role in the family did not change dramatically. Typically, patrilocal residence rules prevailed at Half Moon Village. Chance noted that this often led to conflicts between the mother-in-law and daughter-in-law in the modern Chinese family, just as it had for centuries in the traditional Chinese family. In addition, despite the passage of the marriage laws, matchmaking and arranged marriages remained the norm, and villagers strongly disapproved of divorce. Couples still preferred male over female children to perpetuate family interests. Party officials frequently postponed efforts to alter these patriarchal patterns because such changes might cause stress and conflicts in the family unit.

Ethnic Tensions in the Middle East and Asia

Ethnic tensions divide some Middle Eastern countries. Anthropologist Dale Eickelman notes how difficult it is to maintain a rigid primordialist perspec-

Many Sikhs in India would like to have their own country.

ANTHROPOLOGISTS AT WORK

Susan Brownell: Ethnography in China

Susan Brownell traces her interest in China back to the stories told by her grandmother. Her grandmother's father, Earl Leroy Brewer, was governor of Mississippi, a civil rights proponent, and lawyer for the Mississippi Chinese Association in the 1910s and 1920s. Brownell's love of anthropology began as an undergraduate at the University of Virginia, where she took Victor Turner's famous seminar, in which the participants reenacted different rituals from around the world. She wrote her first paper on sports for Turner's seminar in 1981, and his ideas continued to inspire her over the years. She was also a nationally ranked track and field athlete (in the pentathlon and heptathlon) from 1978 to 1990. She was a six-time collegiate All-American while

at Virginia, and competed in the 1980 and 1984 U.S. Olympic Trials. In 1980 she also worked for six weeks as a stunt double for the feature film *Personal Best*, which depicted four years in the life of a young pentathlete played by Mariel Hemingway. After starting the Ph.D. program at the University of California, Santa Barbara, she decided to try to combine her various interests in a dissertation on Chinese sports. While at Beijing University in 1985–86 for a year of Chinese language studies, she joined the track team. She was chosen to represent Beijing in the 1986 Chinese National College Games, where she won a gold medal and set a national record in the heptathlon, earning fame throughout China as the American girl who won glory for Beijing

Susan Brownell.

University. She returned to China to study sport theory at the Beijing University of Physical Education (1987-88). She was awarded her Ph.D. in 1990. After teaching at Middlebury College, the University of Washington, and Yale University, she joined the Department of Anthropology at the University of Missouri, St. Louis, in

tive on ethnicity when viewing the population known as the Kurds (1995). Kurdish ethnic identity is constructed and shifted to adjust to many different circumstances and conditions. The Kurdish minority crosses several international borders. About 20 percent live in Turkey (about 10 million), several million live in Iran and Iraq, and others live in Syria. Their Kurdish identity is constructed and treated differently within these various countries of the Middle East. In general, the Kurds view themselves as an oppressed ethnic minority in all of the countries in which they live and have faced considerable persecution and discrimination by all of these countries. They have struggled within all of these different countries to form an autonomous country called Kurdistan, but thus far they have not succeeded.

Ethnologists have studied the ethnic problems that confront some Asians. One such problem in-

volves the Sikhs, a population of about 18 million who live in the Punjab region bordering India and Pakistan. The Sikh religion developed in the fifteenth century as a syncretic blend of Hindu and Islamic beliefs. Sikhism is a mystical religious tradition centered on venerated leaders who founded a military fraternity that offered protection from both Muslims and Hindus. The Sikhs pride themselves on their warrior spirit. Every male carries the name Singh, which translates as "lion." the Sikhs have built a major house of worship—the golden Temple of Amritsar in the Punjab.

Anthropologist Richard Fox (1985) conducted ethnological research among the Sikhs in 1980–81. Using historical material and ethnographic data, he focused on the development of Sikh ethnic and religious identity as a response to external pressures. The Sikhs, who had freed themselves from Muslim and Hindu the fall of 1994 and was promoted to associate professor in 1998.

Brownell drew on her direct experience of Chinese athletics in *Training the Body for China: Sports in the Moral Order of the People's Republic* (University of Chicago Press, 1995), an insightful look at the culture of sports and the body in China. This was the first book on Chinese sports based on fieldwork in China by a Westerner. She is an internationally recognized expert on Chinese sports and has acted as a consultant and expert on the topic for different media, including *Sports Illustrated, The Los Angeles Times, The Atlanta Journal and Constitution, The Asian Wall Street Journal, The Sports Factor* on Australian Broadcasting Corp. Radio, *The Ultimate Athlete* on The Discovery Channel, the NBC Sports Olympic Unit, China

Central Television, and many others. She has participated in national and international conferences bringing together officials of the International Olympic Committee, the International Olympic Academy, the U.S. Olympic Committee, the Atlanta Committee for the Olympic Games, the Amateur Athletic Foundation, sports journalists, sports scholars, and others. On these occasions, she has spoken on topics such as women in Chinese sports, doping in Chinese sports, sports television broadcasting in China, and Western misconceptions of the world record-setting female long-distance runners. In all of these settings, her goal has been to promote a deeper understanding of Chinese sports that moves beyond the stereotype of the "Big Red Machine" with a centralized doping system. She has attempted

to nudge members of the Olympic Movement and the press toward comprehending that Chinese sports people are "like us" in the problems they face due to sexism, commercialization, the complexities of international telecasting, and drug use; but that they are "unlike us" in the cultural background they bring to sports, which includes different sentiments about gender, nationalism, "fair play," and—more generally—the meaning of sports.

In 1995–96, Brownell also began a new project on "The Body in Consumer Culture in Beijing." She did fieldwork on cosmetic surgery, fashion models, and upscale fitness clubs as a way of gauging how concepts of beauty, health, and fitness are changing under the growth of consumerism.

domination, were confronted with colonialism and the capitalist world system that penetrated the Punjab. The British viewed the Sikhs as an important military shield that could be used for extending their control over India. They therefore treated the Sikhs as a separate race, which reinforced Sikh separateness from Muslims, Hindus, and other groups.

Eventually the Sikhs recognized that the incorporation of their territory into the British empire would reduce their political and economic autonomy. They therefore initiated reform movements that sought to unify urban workers and rural peasants. These movements led to violent resistance against the British and, following national independence in 1947, to secessionist movements against the Indian government.

In 1984, a group of militant armed Sikhs occupied the golden Temple of Amritsar, demanding

political autonomy from India. The government responded by sending military troops into the Punjab, some of whom entered the temple. This violation of their sacred temple outraged many Sikhs. Later in 1984, as resistance to Hindu domination grew, a Sikh militant assassinated Prime Minister Indira Gandhi. Conflict between Sikhs and Hindus will probably remain a problem into the twenty-first century.

Another South Asian country facing severe ethnic problems is Sri Lanka. Prior to independence from the British in 1948, this island country was called Ceylon. Under colonialism, Tamil-speaking Hindus were imported from southern India to work on rubber plantations. (Although Tamil-speaking Hindus were already in residence in Sri Lanka, British policies increased their population.) The indigenous population of Sri Lanka are Sinhalese-speaking Buddhists. By 1980, the Tamil Hindus made up 18 percent of the population and constituted a majority in northern Sri Lanka. They considered themselves victims of discrimination by the Sinhalese.

Tamil militants formed an organized paramilitary group, the Tamil tigers, who called for the liberation of northern Sri Lanka as an independent Tamil state. Violence broke out between Tamils and Sinhalese in the north. The Sinhalese army responded with an invasion and indiscriminate killings in the Tamil communities. The Tamils responded in kind. In 1987, India sent soldiers to quell the violence. Pressured by the Sri Lankan government, India withdrew in 1989. Meanwhile, the violence continues. As anthropologist Stanley Tambiah notes, the ethnic fratricide that is ongoing in Sri Lanka is exacerbated by the continuing delivery of strategic arms from the industrialized world into the hands of these various ethnic groups (1991).

As is obvious, in the Middle East and Asia many different ethnic and cultural traditions are rapidly colliding with the process of globalization. The process of globalization is disrupting the traditional values and practices within the region. In some cases, the overall reaction to this rapid process of change is to revert back to a nostalgic past in which the traditional rural communities maintain the moral economy, the extended family, and other communal practices. This reaction to the process of rapid globalizing forces has at times led to tensions among political, religious, and ethnic groups throughout these regions. Continuing ethnological research is needed within these regions to help people understand each other's traditions as one major step in helping to reduce these tensions.

Islamic Revitalization

One pervasive trend throughout the Muslim world since the 1970s is Islamic fundamentalism. Contemporary fundamentalist movements have their roots in earlier reformist movements that sought to combine Islam with Western values as a means of coping with colonialism and industrialism. In countries such as Egypt, however, fundamentalist groups such as the Muslim brotherhood rejected reform in favor of the total elimination of secular, Western influences. These movements encouraged the reestablishment of an Islamic society based on the

Qur'an and Sharia. Some groups sought to bring about these changes peacefully, whereas others believed that an Islamic state could be established only through violent revolution.

Ethnological studies have contributed to a better understanding of the sources of Islamic revival movements. One critical factor was the 1967 Arab–Israeli War, which resulted in the crushing defeat of the Arab states and the loss of Arab territories to Israel. This event symbolized to many the economic and political weakness of the Islamic nations and inspired many Muslims to turn to their faith as a source of communal bonds and political strength. Another significant factor was the oil boom. Many fundamentalists believed that by bestowing these societies with rich oil reserves, Allah was shifting power from the materialist and secular civilizations of the west to the Islamic world (Esposito, 1998). The oil revenues of countries such as Libya, Iran, Saudi Arabia, and Kuwait have been used to support fundamentalist movements throughout the Muslim world.

A CASE STUDY: THE ISLAMIC REVOLUTION IN IRAN

Many Western social scientists were surprised by the Islamic revivalistic movements in the Middle East. They assumed that with modernization and globalization these societies would become increasingly secularized and that the role of religion in economic, social, and political affairs would be reduced. Instead, most Muslim countries experienced Islamic movements that were linked to national, political and economic issues.

One of the regions of the Middle East most affected by Islamic fundamentalist tendencies is Iran. Through their ethnological, historical, and comparative research, anthropologists Mary Hegland, Michael Fischer, William Beeman, Henry Munson, and others have contributed to an understanding of the Islamic revival in Iran. They cite a number of factors that converged to produce this revival.

Iran is predominantly a Shi'a Islamic society. After the death of the prophet Muhammad, the Islamic community was divided into the Sunni versus the Shi'a sect. In the sixteenth century, Shah Ismail of the Safavid dynasty proclaimed Shi'ism as the official religion of Iran. From that time, many Shi'a migrated to Iran for protection from the dominant Sunni rulers elsewhere. Traditional Shi'a theology does not distinguish between religion and politics; instead, based on the doctrine of the imamate, the Shi'a maintain that their religious leaders have both theological and political authority. Consequently, Shi'a religious leaders constantly emphasize that Islamic beliefs and doctrine show no separation between religion and politics.

During the nineteenth century, the Iranian rulers, or shahs, offered a large number of concessions to British and Russian bankers and private companies and also attempted to modernize Iran's military and educational system along Western lines. These policies generated internal opposition. The newly educated classes, who had acquired Western ideals of democracy and representative government, opposed the Shahs' absolute power. The clergy opposed secularization and Western education, which interfered with traditional education, which they controlled.

In 1925, the Pahlavi dynasty came to power in Iran. Reza Shah Pahlavi viewed the Shi'a religious leaders as obstacles to his plans for rapid modernization. He attempted to reduce their power by appropriating their lands, thus depriving them of income. Reza Shah decreed that secular laws would replace the Sharia and that women would no longer have to wear the veil.

During World War II, Muhammad Reza Pahlavi, supported by Russian and Western interests, replaced his father as ruler. The new Shah continued the modernization and secularization policies of his father. By the 1960s, he had centralized all political authority in his hands. Many Western multinational corporations were attracted to Iran because of its vast oil reserves and growing gross national product. By the 1970s, about forty-three thousand Americans were living in Iran. The Iranian economy became increasingly dependent on Western imported goods, while internally, aside from oil production, few native industries were developed.

In 1963, the Shah announced the White Revolution which included the commercialization of agriculture through land reforms and the expansion of capitalism. It also included public ownership of companies and voting rights for women. The land reforms disrupted the traditional peasant economy, creating a class of landless peasants. These peasants flocked to Iranian cities in search of scarce opportunities. The White Revolution further mobi-

lized the opposition of the religious clergy, who saw the plight of the peasants. The Shah was perceived as a puppet of the United States (the Great Satan) and Western imperialism. One of the major critics was the Ayatollah Khomeini, who was arrested and exiled in 1963.

In addition to religious clerics, the Shah's policies alienated many other sectors of Iranian society. To buttress his power, the Shah, along with his secret police, the savak, brutally crushed any opposition to his regime. The Westernized middle classes, the university students, the merchants in the bazaars, and the urban poor began to sympathize with any opposition to the Shah's regime. These groups began to ally themselves with the Muslim clergy and the clergy's call for an Islamic revolution. For fifteen years, Khomeini continued to attack the Shah in pamphlets and taped sermons smuggled into Iran.

THE ISLAMIC REVOLUTION

Although united in their opposition to the Shah, various segments of Iranian society viewed the Islamic revolution in different terms. The rural migrants who flooded into the Iranian cities steadfastly supported the Islamic clergy. The Western-

Ayatollah Khomeini.

ized middle class viewed the Islamic revolution in terms of its own democratic aspirations, believing that the religious leaders would play a secondary role in the actual administration of the Iranian state. Many university students had been influenced by the writings of Ali Shariati, who interpreted Shi'a Islam as a form of liberation theology that would free their society from foreign domination. These elements in Iranian society formed a coalition that encouraged the social and political revolution led by Khomeini and the religious clerics. A cycle of demonstrations, violent protests, and religious fervor led to the downfall of the Shah, and, in 1979, Khomeini returned to Iran to lead the revolution.

Ever since the overthrow of the Shah, the religious clerics have assumed nearly all of the important political positions. Khomeini announced the establishment of the Islamic republic of Iran, a theocratic state ruled by the Shi'a clergy, who used the mosques as the basic building blocks of political power. All Iranians were forced to register at a mosque, which functioned as an amalgam of government office, place of worship, and local police force. A systematic campaign was waged to purge Iranian society of its Western influences. Alcohol, gambling, prostitution, and pornography were strictly forbidden; women were required to wear head scarves, and those who refused were sent to "reeducation centers." the Shi'a regime believed it had a religious duty to export its revolution to other areas of the Islamic world.

Since the Islamic revolution, most ethnological research has been forbidden in Iran, so collecting data on recent trends has been difficult. From press reports it is clear that the revolution has radically changed the nature of Iranian society. The revolution was not only political but also a total social and cultural transformation. Iran is, however, racked with internal conflicts among different classes, religious factions, and political groups. Economic problems exacerbated by the reduction in oil prices and a ten-year war against Iraq have led to infighting among radical militants, conservative fundamentalists, and moderates.

In May 1997, Mohammad Khatami, a moderate Muslim cleric, won Iran's presidential election in a landslide victory over more conservative candidates. Khatami attracted a broad coalition of centrists, women, youth of both genders, and middle-class intellectuals to his cause. He is believed to be a direct descendant of the Prophet Muhammad, which helped him consolidate support. While Katami's victory is unlikely to result in immediate changes in the country's Islamic fundamentalist path, his election will most likely restrain the more conservative factions of the clergy that has ruled the country since 1979. One leading Ayatollah, Hussein Ali Montazeri has been questioning openly the legitimacy of Iran's clerical rule. Only time will tell whether Iran will be able to overcome factionalism and resolve its political and economic problems.

ISLAMIC REVITALIZATION IN AFGHANISTAN

Another region in which Islamic revitalization is playing a profound role is in the country of Afghanistan. Afghanistan has a troubled history. As we saw above, the British and Russians tried to colonize the area during the nineteenth century in the so-called "Great Game" between these powers. During the nineteenth century, with British support, Afghan leaders such as Abdul Rahman attempted to modernize and unify its many ethnic groups by building roads and pacifying fractious tribes throughout the country. During the 1920s and 1930s with increased education, many Afghan intellectuals were exposed to ideas based on constitutional democracy and nationalism. Some of these leaders tried to institute democratic processes, however, economic development programs were failing. Consequently, class-based Marxist movements began to emerge in Afghanistan, with the support of the Soviet Union. In 1973, a pro-Soviet Marxist leader staged a military coup and proclaimed himself as President of the Republic of Afghanistan. Five years later, another military coup installed a communist government with the patronage of the Soviet Union.

The communist leadership and the Soviet Union underestimated the strength of the Islamic and multiethnic assertiveness within the country of Afghanistan. The ethnic groups of Afghanistan include the Pashtuns (the largest group comprised of about 47 percent of the population), Tajiks, Uzbeks, Turkmen, Kirghiz, Hazara, Baluchis, and others. The Sunni Muslim constitute about 88 percent of the population, and the Shi'a comprise about 12 percent (Dupree, 1980, Shahrani & Canfield, 1984). These ethnic and religious coalitions

ANTHROPOLOGISTS AT WORK

David Edwards: Ethnography in Afghanistan

David Edwards became interested in Afghanistan before he ever thought about anthropology. As a child growing up in the Midwest, he was captivated by stories of travel, especially those his grandmother would tell him. Edwards's grandmother was widowed at a relatively young age and thereafter set off to see as much of the world as she could, often aboard inexpensive freighters that took on a half-dozen or so paying passengers. One of the stories she told her grandson was about watching camel caravans unloading their wares in the central bazaar in Kabul, Afghanistan. The story caught in his imagination and he was determined to make his way to Central Asia, which he managed to do right after graduating from Princeton University in 1975.

After spending two years teaching English in Afghanistan, Edwards went back to the United States with the idea of going to graduate school in a field that would allow him to delve more fully into Afghan culture. Never having taken an anthropology course as an undergraduate, he stumbled on this field as the right one for his interests when he read a book by Clifford Geertz. The book's blend of elegant writing and insightful cultural analysis

captured for him a sense of what he hoped to accomplish in his own research and writing, and he began graduate school in that discipline in the fall of 1977.

While he initially hoped and expected to return to Afghanistan to conduct fieldwork in a small mountain village, Edwards had to change course after the Marxist revolution, which happened towards the end of his first year of graduate school. Thereafter, Edwards redirected his research primarily towards studies of refugees and guerrilla movements, which became the focus of his own fieldwork, the first stint of which took place in and around Peshawar, Pakistan, between 1982 and 1984. Peshawar is right across the border from Afghanistan and was the headquarters for most of the Islamic political parties that worked to dislodge the Marxist regime in Afghanistan from power. Edwards's research dealt mostly with the internal dynamics of these parties and their conduct of the war inside Afghanistan, but also included an extended study of a camp of some 30,000 Afghan refugees located on the outskirts of Peshawar. Subsequent fieldtrips in 1986 and 1995 have taken him back to Pakistan and Afghanistan and have allowed him to follow Afghan political developments, in-

David Edwards.

cluding the recent takeover of the Taliban militia.

The publications that have resulted from this field research have mostly focused on the evolution of Islamic political authority in Afghanistan and the social transformations brought about by the Islamic political parties in their quest for power. These publications include a book published by the University of California Press, titled *Heroes of the Age: Moral Fault Lines on the Afghan Frontier*, and a second book, *Children of History: Genealogies of the Afghan Jihad*, which he is completing for publication while enjoying a year's sabbatical at the School of American Research in Santa Fe, New Mexico. In between sabbatical leaves and research trips to Pakistan and Afghanistan, Edwards lives in Williamstown, Massachusetts, with his wife and two children and teaches anthropology at Williams College.

began to resist the Soviet Union and the Marxist communist government. A nation-wide Islamic struggle was launched, referred to as a *jihad*, or "holy war" by a group of "holy warriors" called the *Mujahidin*. The former USSR invaded Afghanistan in 1979 to repress this Islamic resistance led by the Muhajidin. Cold War politics began to influence this struggle against the USSR, with many Western governments offering financial and military assistance to the Muhajidin. Many Afghans were driven out of their country into neighboring Pakistan. However, with increasing internal weaknesses within the USSR, and the fierce resistance of the Muhajidin, the Soviets withdrew from Afghanistan in 1989.

Following the withdrawal of the Soviet Union ethnic differences and varying Islamic traditions and movements presented obstacles in the unification of the Afghans. Various Islamic and ethnic factions that had developed during the Soviet occupation began to fight for power, resulting in years of warfare in Afghanistan during the 1980s and 1990s. The Western governments that patronized the Muhajidin during the Cold War withdrew support, fearing an Islamic revolution similar to the Iranian one. Consequently, the factional fighting among ethnic and religious groups resulted in political disorder and chaos in Afghanistan.

One Islamic faction that emerged in Afghanistan in 1994 is known as the Taliban. Anthropologist David Edwards has described the social and religious background of the Taliban (1998). The majority of the Taliban are Afghan religious students recruited from Islamic religious schools. The term *taliban* refers to religious student. The Taliban served as a militia that scored a series of victories against other ethnic and religious factions throughout Afghanistan. They have consolidated control over most of the regions in Afghanistan. The Taliban have received a lot of international attention because of their stringent Islamic guidelines and norms. Men are forbidden to trim their beards. Afghan women are strictly secluded from any contact with men, are not allowed to work outside of the home, and have to wear the traditional Islamic full veil and covering known as the *burqa*. Edwards emphasizes that many of the Taliban were socialized and trained in Pakistan, outside the confines of traditional ethnic and tribal affinities within Afghanistan. Therefore, young men from different backgrounds were able to unify an Islamic revitalization movement based on a sense of frustration over twenty years of conflict, factionalism, and political disorder. The Taliban have managed to provide order and stability throughout Afghanistan, and many Afghans support them despite their attempt to impose a purified Islamic culture on the country. One unusual aspect of the Taliban movement is the lack of a charismatic leader such as a Khomeini. At this time in Afghan history, the Taliban movement appears as a movement that is opposed to any form of personal leadership, and has emerged as a religious movement based on exhaustion and frustration with a very troubled political history.

One conclusion resulting from the many ethnological studies of Islam in the Middle East and Asia is that this religious tradition, like all religious traditions, can have different interpretations depending on the context. The Islamic religion can be combined with diverse types of political activity. It can provide ideological support for revolutionary change, as the case of Iran suggests, or it can help sustain a specific socioeconomic and political order, as in contemporary Saudi Arabia, where some two thousand princes control the entire political economy. Thus, Islam can be used by political and religious leaders to advance social justice, justify political oppression, or further the goals of one particular political group.

SUMMARY

As in Latin America, Africa, and the Caribbean, globalization has had dramatic consquences on the countries in the Middle East and Asia. These countries were either directly or indirectly affected by Western colonialism. Demographically, in the long run, all of these countries were affected by declining death rates brought about by Western colonialism, and populations began to increase rapidly because of economic circumstances and the maintenance of high birthrates.

Economically, these societies were drawn into the global economy and were transformed by producing commodities that were demanded by the wealthier core societies. Patterns of landownership were reordered, and many peasants were producing for economic elites. Religious changes occurred, however, since most of the population in the Middle East and Asia were committed to the traditions of Islam, Hinduism, or Buddhism, Christianity did not make significant inroads into these colonized areas.

Western colonialism eventually gave way to political movements based on nationalist, independence, and sometimes revolutionary tendencies. These movements represented anticolonial sentiments and resulted in many new countries in the Middle East and Asia. Some leaders in the Middle East such as Gamal Nasser in Egypt tried to develop a Pan-Arabic movement directed against Western colonialism. Countries such as India were led by charismatic leaders such as Mahatma Gandhi, who mobilized millions of people to develop a national identity and notions of self-determination. In China and Vietnam revolutionary leaders such as Mao Zedong and Ho Chi Minh organized millions of peasants to bring about new social and political orders based on Marxist ideals mixed with indigenous cultural ideals.

These countries were absorbed into the global economy at different levels depending on the resources that were available in their regions. Some countries remain poor and underdeveloped because their economies are heavily dependent on the wealthy core countries. In the Middle East, some countries had tremendous oil resources that were to be used to help develop their economies. Despite oil resources, these Middle Eastern countries still find themselves dependent on the wealthy core industrialized nations. Many of the countries in both the Middle East and Asia face internal population problems and underdeveloped economic systems that tend to make them marginal to the global economy. Some countries such as China, Burma, and Vietnam tried to withdraw from the global economy through a commitment to a socialist program.

Ethnographers have conducted research on the peasantry, social structures, family life, and gender in these countries. The peasantry is rapidly changing in the Middle East and Asia, as globalization introduces the cash economy, new consumer goods, and other changes. The peasantry differs in various countries based on the people's traditional relations and new global relationships to the world market. Family structures and gender relations are illuminated by ethnographers as they study patterns that develop in relationship to the emergence of new urban areas and the changing rural areas. Each region has unique structures based on its cultural beliefs and practices. In the Middle East, the Islamic tradition and Arab cultural practices influences the patterns of family life and gender. However, ethnographers find a great deal of variation within these Islamic societies based on the contact these societies have had with Western countries. In addition, there are some basic misconceptions and stereotypes of the Islamic family, marriage, and gender practices that have been debunked through systematic ethnographic research.

Ethnographers in Asia have focused on some of the traditional practices regarding family and gender that have remained despite globalization and revolutionary movements in countries such as China. However, globalization is having a transformative effect on all of these institutions throughout Asia.

One of the consequences of globalization is the resurgence of Islamic movements in countries such as Iran and Afghanistan. Ethnographers have brought their analytical skills to try to comprehend and explain these Islamic revitalization movements in these countries of the Middle East and Asia.

 STUDY QUESTIONS

1. Compare and contrast the Western impact on India and on China.

2. How did demographic change occur as a result of globalization in the Middle East and Asia?

3. How did globalization impinge on the traditional economies of the Middle East and Asia?

4. How did religion change as a result of colonialism and Western influence in the Middle East and Asia?

5. Compare the independence movements in India with the revolutionary movement in China.

6. What are some of the differences between the oil-producing countries of the Middle East and non-oil producers?

7. How has the peasantry changed as a result of globalization in the Middle East and Asian countries?

8. What are some of the stereotypes of family, marriage, and gender patterns in the Middle Eastern Islamic countries?

10. Discuss some of the problems of ethnicity in the Middle East and Asia that have been influenced by globalization?

11. What are some of the factors discovered by ethnographers that have influenced the Islamic revitalization movement in the Middle East?

KEY TERMS

hamula

jajmani

jati

purdah

INTERNET EXERCISES

1. Read the article by W. Judd Peak on U.S. strategic interests in the Middle East on the following website: **http://www.is.rhodes.edu/Modus_ Vivendi/Peak.html.** How are United States interests in the Middle East different from the earlier imperial goals of Britain and France? How have our strategic interests changed since the fall of the Soviet Union? How do these concepts relate to the current chapter?

2. Read the Amnesty International report on Algeria on the following website: **http://www.** **amnesty.org/ailib/aipub/1999/MDE/528002 99.htm.** Why would a country that had escaped colonial rule (France in 1962) use techniques of terror on its citizenry? Look at the section on the Algerian economy in the CIA Fact Book page (**http://www.odci.gov/cia/publications/fact- book/ag.html**) and see if you can identify any reasons for this behavior? Describe your opinion using examples from this chapter and the Fact Book to support it.

SUGGESTED READINGS

BECK, LOIS, and NIKKI KEDDIE, eds. 1978. *Women in the Muslim world.* Cambridge, MA: Harvard University Press. A fine collection of essays dealing with the role of women in Middle Eastern societies.

EICKELMAN, DALE F. 1989. *The Middle East: An Anthropological Approach,* 2d ed. Englewood Cliffs, NJ: Prentice Hall. An excellent summary of the ethnological and historical research on the Middle East.

FERNEA, ELIZABETH WARNOCK. 1965. *Guests of the Sheik.* Garden City, NY: Doubleday Anchor. A classic ethnography of an Iraqi village. It is one of the first accounts by a female ethnologist of the role of women in an Islamic society.

SPENCER, WILLIAM. 1990. *The Middle East,* 3d ed. Guilford, CT: Dushkin Publishing Group. A country-by-country survey of the Middle East, containing recent general data on the political economies of the region. It also includes articles from the world press on various topical issues.

TAMBIAH, S. J. 1976. *World Conqueror and World Renouncer: A Study of Buddhism and Polity in Thailand against a Historical Background.* Cambridge: Cambridge University Press. An investigation of how religion interconnects with politics in the development of Thailand as a modern nation.

16

Contemporary Global Trends

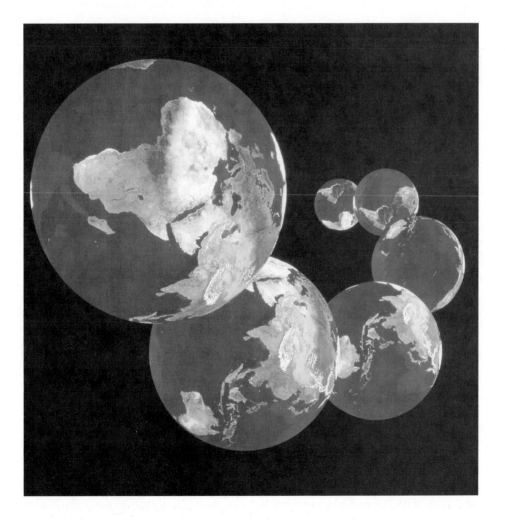

CHAPTER OUTLINE

Environmental Trends
*Mechanized Agriculture and Pollution /
Air Pollution*

Population Trends
The Demographic-Transition Model Applied

Technological Change
*Energy Consumption Patterns / Loss
of Biodiversity*

**Pessimists versus Optimists on Global
Issues**
*The Doomsday Model / The Optimists:
The Logic-of-Growth Model / The
Pessimists and the Optimists: An
Assessment / The Sustainability Model*

Economic Trends
*Multinational Corporations / Case Study:
The Potlatch Corporation / Emerging
Economic Trends*

Political Trends

Ethnic Trends

Religion and Secularization

The Role of Anthropology

CHAPTER QUESTIONS

- What are some of the environmental trends that are a consequence of globalization?

- How do demograpic trends differ in various societies?

- What are the results of globalization on technology and energy use?

- How does the logic-of-growth model compare with the sustainability model?

- What are some of the economic consequences of globalization?

- What are some of the political, ethnic, and religious tendencies resulting from globalization?

A S WE HAVE SEEN THROUGHOUT THIS TEXT, GLOBAL interdependence or what we have called 'globalization' has become an undeniable fact in the contemporary world. This process began after the Neolithic revolution, when small-scale societies were either absorbed into larger states or became dependent on those states. Ever since the Industrial Revolution, the trend toward interdependence has escalated, especially through the process of colonialism. As the world shrinks and industrial societies continue to expand, interconnections are developing among different societies, creating a global village. The global village has been described as a world in which all regions are in contact with one another through the mass media, instantaneous communication, and highly integrated economic and political networks. This chapter reviews some of the recent trends associated with the development of this global village.

Environmental Trends

Hunting-gathering, horticulturalist, pastoralist, and intensive agriculture societies survived by extracting natural resources from a particular biome. In these societies, people were directly linked with nature and the environment, and they lived in relative harmony with the natural environment. This is not to suggest that humans in preindustrial societies did not harm their environments in any manner—slash-and-burn horticulture, intensive agriculture, pastoralism, and sometimes even foraging caused some environmental damage. Overgrazing, soil erosion, and the depletion of certain species have always been part of humankind's evolution.

With the development of globalization, however, the negative consequences for the environment have multiplied rapidly. Ironically, many people in industrial societies came to believe that they had gained mastery over the natural environment and were therefore free from its constraints. But in recent decades, people have become more aware that they are as dependent on the natural environment as were preindustrial peoples. It has become evident that the pollution created by global industrialization is threatening the ecological balance of the planet and the health of plant and animal species, including the human species. One major source of pollution is commercialized, mechanized agriculture, known as **agribusiness.**

MECHANIZED AGRICULTURE AND POLLUTION

Mechanized agriculture or agribusiness depends on the use of fossil fuels, chemical fertilizers, large tracts of land, and toxic poisons such as herbicides and pesticides to increase agricultural yields. This form of agriculture is prevalent not only in the industrialized world; it is also becoming common in developing countries. For example, some farmers in societies such as Mexico, India, and Indonesia have adopted mechanized agriculture. The spread of mechanized agriculture has been labeled the Green Revolution (Schusky, 1990). Through *biotechnology research,* sometimes known as genetic engineering, and other methods, scientists have produced hybrid species of wheat and rice seeds that generate higher agricultural yields. To take advantage of these yields, however, farmers must use expensive, capital-intensive technology for irrigation and cultivation; nonrenewable fossil fuels such as gasoline and oil; synthetic chemical fertilizers; and toxic weed killers or herbicides, and pesticides.

The use of capital intensive agricultural, however, can have negative consequences for the global environment. One of the most tragic cases resulting from the Green Revolution occurred in 1984 in Bhopal, India, where toxic fumes leaking from a chemical-fertilizer plant killed and injured thousands of people. Many of the consequences of mechanized agriculture, however, are much less dramatic (and therefore less publicized), although perhaps just as dangerous. For example, research has shown that much of the food produced in both industrialized and developing countries contains traces of pesticides and other poisons. Even when governments ban the use of chemicals, the residues may remain in the food chain for many years. Because many new synthetic chemicals

are being produced for agribusiness every year, the danger to the environment continues to increase.

AIR POLLUTION

Air pollution, especially from the emissions of motor vehicles, power generators, and waste incinerators, continues to be a major problem for industrializing societies. As less developed countries industrialize, the degree of global air pollution steadily multiplies. It appears that atmospheric pollution is depleting the earth's ozone layer, which absorbs 99 percent of the ultraviolet radiation from the sun. These pollutants could irreversibly alter the earth's ability to support life. Satellite data show that during the period from 1978 to 1984, the ozone layer eroded at an average annual rate of 0.5 percent. In addition, acid rain produced by the burning of fossil fuels such as coal and gasoline has become a global problem, spreading across national boundaries and wreaking havoc on forests, lakes, and various species of aquatic life.

Some scientists hypothesize that the increased levels of carbon dioxide produced by the burning of fossil fuels and tropical rainforests will create a **greenhouse effect.** According to this hypothesis, after solar rays reach the earth's surface, the carbon dioxide in the atmosphere traps the heat and prevents it from radiating back into space. This process could eventually melt the polar ice caps, raise sea levels, flood major coastal cities, create violent weather patterns, and turn tropics into deserts.

Population Trends

As discussed in Chapter 12, with industrialization, new demographic trends have arisen. A recent model used to measure population trends is based on the **demographic-transition theory,** which assumes a close connection between fertility and mortality rates and socioeconomic development (Figure 16.1). According to the demographic-transition model, societies pass through three major phases of population change. During Phase 1, a high fertility rate is counterbalanced by a high mortality rate, resulting in minimal population growth. Phase 1 describes preindustrial societies. At first, societies used various methods of population regulation such as self-induced abortions, or infanticide, or migration to limit population growth. As

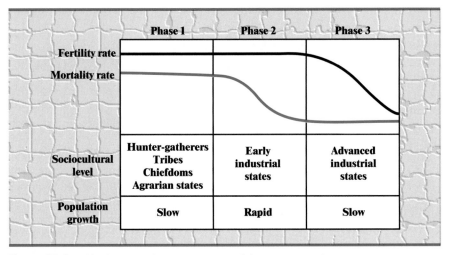

Figure 16.1 The demographic-transition model.

they developed intensive agriculture, population began to increase, but disease, famine, and natural disasters kept mortality rates fairly high, thus limiting growth.

In Phase 2, population tends to increase rapidly because of continued high fertility rates coupled with lower mortality rates. Mortality rates decline because of increases in the food supply, the development of scientifically based medical practices, and improved public sanitation and health care. Improvements in nutrition and health care enable people to control certain diseases, thus diminishing infant mortality rates and increasing life expectancy. Consequently, during Phase 2, population growth is dramatic. Growth of this magnitude was associated with the early phases of industrialization in Western Europe and North America, but it is also visible in many Third World societies that are now in the early stages of industrialization.

Phase 3 of the demographic-transition model represents the stage when fertility rates begin to fall along with mortality rates. According to the model, as industrialization proceeds, family planning is introduced, and traditional institutions and religious beliefs supporting high birthrates are undermined. Values stressing individualism and upward mobility lead couples to reduce the size of their families. Phase 3 describes the stage of advanced industrial societies such as Western Europe, the United States, and Japan. Other trends, such as geographic mobility and the increased expense of rearing children, also affect reproductive decisions in industrial societies. Hence, in advanced industrial societies, as the birthrate or fertility rate falls, population growth begins to decline.

THE DEMOGRAPHIC-TRANSITION MODEL APPLIED

The demographic-transition model seems to have some validity when applied to global population trends. The world population during the Paleolithic period (Phase 1) is estimated to have been about 10 million (Hassan, 1981). Following the agricultural revolution, around the year A.D. 1, the global population was approximately 300 million. But after the early stages of industrialization (Phase 2), from 1650 to 1900, world population had tripled from 510 million to 1.6 billion. By 1950, the global population had risen to 2.5 billion, and, by 1970, another billion people had been added. By 1990, the world population was approximately 5.4 billion, with 150 babies being born every minute (Figure 16.2). At this rate, in the year 2000, the world population exceeded 6 billion, and by 2050, the global population will reach 10.2 billion.

Thomas Robert Malthus (1766–1834), a British clergyman and economist, is known as the father of demography. Malthus predicted that human populations would increase at a rapid, or exponential, rate. In contrast, the production of food and other vital resources would increase at a lower rate. Thus, populations would always grow more quickly than the food supply to support them. As a result, human societies would constantly experience hunger, increases in warfare, resource scarcities, and poverty.

To measure the exponential growth rate, demographers use the concept of **doubling time,** the period it takes for a population to double. For example, a population growing at 1 percent will double in 70 years, one growing at 2 percent will take 35 years to double, and one growing at 3 percent will double in 23 years.

The industrial nations of Western Europe, the United States, and Japan have reached Phase 3 of the demographic-transition model. The U.S. population is growing at only 0.7 percent. Countries such as Germany, Hungary, and Japan actually have negative growth rates, which means that they are not replacing the number of people dying with new births. For a society to maintain a given level of population, each woman must give birth to an average of 2.1 children. At this point, the society has achieved *zero population growth* (ZPG), meaning that the population is simply replacing itself. When the average number of births falls below 2.1, a society experiences negative growth. Thus, Japan, with an average of 1.8 births, is actually experiencing a population decline (Martin, 1989). De-

Globalization creates dense traffic problems in major cities such as Bangkok.

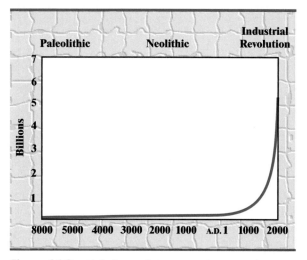

Figure 16.2 Global population growth. From about ten million people in the Paleolithic period, the world population reached one billion by 1850. Following the Industrial Revolution and decreases in mortality rates, the world population has increased to over five billion people.

creased growth rates in industrialized nations have helped lower the global growth rate from 2 to 1.7 percent.

The demographic-transition model provides a conceptual scheme for evaluating global population trends, especially for the core industrial societies, yet it must be used carefully, as a hypothesis. Although the industrial societies of North America, Western Europe, and Japan have reached Phase 3, the vast majority of the world's people reside in societies that are in Phase 2, with exponential growth rates. Population growth in African countries such as Kenya is almost 4 percent (doubling every 15 years), and Mexico's growth rate is 2.6 percent (doubling every 27 years).

Thus, the demographic-transition hypothesis explains population trends in industrial societies, but it may not accurately predict population growth elsewhere for Phase 3. Suggesting that all societies will follow the path of development of the advanced industrial societies is somewhat naive. As we have seen from our discussion of industrial societies in Chapter 12, it took at least 500 years of historical experience for these countries to become fully industrialized societies and reach Phase 3 of the demographic model.

Most peripheral societies maintain high birthrates related to their agricultural lifestyles. As these societies become industrialized, however, death rates fall, leading to dramatic population increases. These societies have not had an extended time period to adjust to the demographic trends related to industrialization. Consequently, predicting a movement to Phase 3 is problematic. Most underdeveloped countries can attain population decline only through changes in technology, political economy, and social and cultural practices. One developing country that has taken steps to drastically reduce their population growth is China.

The One-Child Policy in China   In the 1950s Mao Zedong perceived China's revolution as being based on peasant production and small-scale, labor-intensive technology. For this reason, he encouraged population growth among the peasantry. After Mao's death, however, a new leadership group emerged that reversed his policies regarding population growth.

In 1979, a demographic study was presented at the Second Session of the Fifth National People's Congress. This study indicated that if the existing average of three children per couple were maintained, China's population would reach 1.4 billion by the year 2000 and 4.3 billion by the year 2080. Alarmed by the implications of these statistics, the government introduced a one-child policy designed to achieve zero population growth (ZPG) by the year 2000. Families that restricted their family size to one child were given free health care and free plots of land. In addition, their children would receive free education and preferential employment treatment. Families that had more than one child would be penalized through higher taxes and nonpreferential treatment. The one-child policy continues to be enforced through neighborhood committees at the local level, and contraceptives, sterilization, and abortion services are provided free of charge. Neighborhood committees

monitor every woman's reproductive cycle to determine when she is eligible to have her one child.

With some exceptions, the one-child policy has been remarkably effective. Between 1980 and 1990, the birthrate in China was reduced, and the annual growth rate fell from 2.0 percent to 1.4 percent, a record unmatched by any developing nation. This rate is similar to those of the most advanced industrial societies (*World Population Data Sheet,* 1991). For example, the United States has a growth rate of 0.7 percent. Incentives, propaganda campaigns, and government enforcement combined to produce a new image of the Chinese family, one that had only a single child. Billboards and TV ads throughout China showed radiant mothers nurturing their one child.

Because the one-child policy is an attempt to reverse family patterns that have existed for thousands of years, it has created controversies and problems. In the agricultural areas, it has generated a great deal of resentment. In addition, many Chinese prefer sons to daughters, a long-established Confucian tradition. In some cases, couples that have a daughter may practice female infanticide so that they may have a son to assume family responsibilities. Although infanticide is a criminal offense in China, it appears to be increasing in rural areas. Moreover, anthropologist Steven Mosher (1983) has reported that government officials sometimes forced women to undergo abortions to maintain the one-child policy.

In response to some of these conflicts, the Chinese government relaxed the one-child policy in 1989. Rural families can now have two children, whereas urban families are restricted to one. Additionally, the various minority groups have no restrictions on the number of children they can have. The minorities argue that through the one-child policy, their groups would be quickly dominated by the majority population in China. They view the policy as an attempt to reduce their population and have pressured the government to relax restrictions on their population growth. The Chinese government believes that the key to the success of its population-control efforts is the system of rewards offered to compliant families. Whether the people are willing to transform their fundamental cultural traditions to conform to government regulations is a question to be answered in the future.

Technological Change

Ever since the Industrial Revolution, the scale of technological change has become global rather than local. Industrial technology, including computers, electronics, and advances in global communications, has spread from the core nations to the developing countries. For example, as previously discussed, the Green Revolution has altered the nature of food production. Technical information on agricultural production is spread through television and satellites to villages in countries such as India and Pakistan.

ENERGY-CONSUMPTION PATTERNS

High energy consumption is not only creating environmental hazards; it has also led to increased depletion of resources. High-energy, industrialized societies such as the United States consume a major portion of the world's nonrenewable energy and resources. For example, in 1987, the United States used over 2 billion tons of energy (the equivalent of coal), and the former Soviet Union used 1.8 billion. In contrast, Mexico used 140 million; Egypt, 33 million; Bangladesh, 6.8 million; and the Sudan, 1.5 million tons (*Information Please Almanac,* 1991). The 23 percent of the world's population residing in industrialized countries is consuming 80 to 90 percent of the energy reserves that the planet is capable of producing.

Were semiperipheral and peripheral countries, with 77 percent of the world's population, to adopt the same consumption patterns as the core nations, nonrenewable energy supplies and resources might not be sufficient to support global economic development (Schusky, 1989). For example, as peripheral countries adopted mechanized farming, they increased their consumption of fossil fuels, leading to a worldwide jump in energy use. Between 1950 and 1985, the energy used to produce a ton of grain increased from 0.44 barrels of oil per ton to 1.14 barrels. By 1985, fossil-fuel energy used in farming totaled 1.7 billion barrels, about one-twelfth of the world oil output of 21 billion barrels per year (Brown, 1988).

LOSS OF BIODIVERSITY

One of the major concerns regarding the consequences of globalization on the planet is the loss of biodiversity. **Biodiversity** is the genetic and biological variation within and among different species of plants and animals. Biologists are not exactly certain of how many species of plants and animals exist; new species are discovered every day. Some biologists think that there may be as many as 30 to 100 million species, or even more. Approximately 250,000 flowering plant species, 800,000 lower-plant species, and 1.5 million animal species have been identified (Raven, Berg, & Johnson, 1993). About 50 percent of these species live in tropical rainforests. As humans, we are dependent on these living organisms for survival; in both preindustrial and industrial societies people rely on plants and animal species for basic foodstuffs and medicinal applications.

Many plant and animal species are threatened with extinction, causing a loss of biodiversity. Biologists estimate that at least one species becomes extinct each day. And as globalization continues, it is estimated that perhaps as many as a dozen species will be lost per day. Biologist E. O. Wilson writes in his book *In Search of Nature* (1996) that each year an area of rain forest half the size of Florida is cut down. If that continues, by 2020, the world will have lost forever 20 percent of its existing plant species. That is a loss of 30,000 species per year, 74 per day, 3 per hour. He goes on to say that we know almost nothing about the majority of plants and animals that comprise the rain forest. We haven't even named 90 percent of them, much less studied their properties or tapped their potential value. Wilson suggests that it is likely that a substantial portion of the planet's biodiversity will be eliminated within the next few decades. With the increase of industrialism, mechanized agriculture, and deforestation, as many as one-fourth of the world's higher-plant families may become extinct by the end of the next century. Wilson believed that we are entering the greatest period of mass extinction in the planet's history.

We have very limited knowledge of the world's plant and animal species. For example, there are approximately 250,000 different flowering plant species, but 225,000 of them have never been evaluated with respect to their agricultural, medicinal, or industrial potential (Raven, Berg, & Johnson, 1993). One out of every four prescription drugs come from flowering plants. Yet less than 1 percent have been studied for pharmacological potential. Many of these plants could be exploited as new food crops, pharmaceuticals, fibers, or petroleum substitutes. As long as biodiversity can be preserved, it represents a wealth of information and potential resources that can be extremely beneficial for humanity. In addition, with the new developments in genetic engineering, which depends on biodiversity (genetic variation), humanity may be able to find new resources that provide solutions for food and health problems.

Pessimists versus Optimists on Global Issues

Two basic perspectives—one negative, one positive—have influenced the analyses of global trends affecting the environment, population, and technology.

THE DOOMSDAY MODEL

The negative perspective is sometimes referred to as the Doomsday Model, or the neo-Malthusian approach. This model predicts that if current population, environmental, and technological trends continue, they will produce a series of ecological disasters that will threaten human existence. In the 1970s, a group of scientists and academics known as the Club of Rome assessed these global trends and predicted worldwide scarcities and a global economic collapse. Using elaborate computer models developed at the Massachusetts Institute of Technology, these scientists concluded that current global trends in population growth, energy-consumption patterns, and environmental pollution will exhaust the world's natural resources within the next 100 years.

THE OPTIMISTS: THE LOGIC-OF-GROWTH MODEL

The Doomsday Model has been challenged by optimists such as Julian Simon (1981), who foresee a more promising future for humankind. Simon

noted that health improvements, including a decrease in infant mortality and an increase in life expectancy, are a global trend. Simon also argued that pollution has abated in most societies that have experienced economic growth. Simon believed that as development and economic improvements continue in different societies, people will spend money to solve pollution problems.

Sometimes this perspective is referred to as the *logic-of-growth model*. This **logic-of-growth model** assumes that natural resources are infinite and that economic growth can continue indefinitely without long-term harm to the environment. For example, this model notes that Malthus had not foreseen the biotechnological revolution in agriculture that made land much more productive than was true in eighteenth-century England. Economists such as Simon believed that food-production problems in regions such as Africa can be attributed to farm collectivization, government attempts to control the prices of agricultural commodities, and other institutional problems. Simon cites statistics indicating that on a worldwide level, food prices per person are decreasing and food production per person is increasing.

The logic-of-growth theorists cite evidence showing that the costs of energy and other natural resources have actually fallen over time because humans have found creative technological solutions for producing and extracting these resources. For example, Simon argues that the increase in the price of oil in the 1970s was purely political. The cost of producing a barrel of oil is still about 15 to 25 cents. He noted how people in the past responded to shortages in firewood used for heating by turning to coal, and to coal shortages by using oil. Simon believed that this ongoing process of creative innovation will continue.

Simon and other logic-of-growth theorists further suggest that population growth is a stimulus for, rather than a deterrent to, economic progress. The title of Simon's major book is *The Ultimate Resource* (1981), which he considers to be the human mind. Productivity and solutions for economic and environmental problems come directly from the human mind. In the long run, therefore, population growth helps to raise the standard of living in society by providing more creative ideas and technologies from which to extract solutions. Although Simon and other logic-of-growth theorists admit that, in the short term, population growth may inhibit economic development, he concluded that countries ought not to restrict population growth forcibly and that eventually technological innovations and human creativity will solve our problems, just as they have in the past.

THE PESSIMISTS AND THE OPTIMISTS: AN ASSESSMENT

Most likely, both the pessimistic and the optimistic predictions regarding global problems are exaggerated. Predicting the future is risky for any social scientist, and to project complex global trends regarding population growth, environmental destruction, and technological change over many decades is highly problematic. The optimists believe that, ever since the beginnings of civilization, humanity has benefited from technological progress. A comprehensive view of the past, however, challenges this assumption. For example, we saw in Chapter 11 that the emergence of intensive agriculture—one of the major developments in human history—produced benefits for small segments of the population but adversely affected the majority of people by contributing to higher disease rates, increased inequality, and other problems. Conversely, the pessimists tend to underestimate the human capacity to devise technological solutions to global problems.

Anthropological research may help assess these global issues in a more cautious and analytic manner. With its holistic approach, anthropology has always been concerned with precisely those aspects of human interaction with the environment that are now being recognized widely by scientists studying global environmental change. The U.S. Committee on Global Change (1988) has called for the development of an interdisciplinary science for understanding global change. The discipline of anthropology represents a prototype or model for the interdisciplinary science that would be needed to understand these changes (Rayner, 1989). Anthropological data can help assess the causes of such phenomena as the greenhouse effect by examining land-use choices and the impacts of economic activities. Anthropology may assist in the development of policies on matters such as agriculture, biotechnology, pollution, and population growth by providing information on the links between local practices and global processes.

Ethnological Research on the Green Revolution

An example of how ethnological research can illuminate global problems involves studies of the Green Revolution in underdeveloped countries. Optimists such as Simon cite the Green Revolution as one of the advancements made through technology and human creativity. In their view, the Green Revolution contradicts the basic assumptions made by the neo-Malthusians that population will outgrow the finite resources (food) of a particular area of land. Using hybrid species of high-yield wheat and rice and highly mechanized agricultural techniques has increased food production to a degree that could not have been anticipated by Malthusians of past ages.

However, many ethnologists who have studied the adoption of mechanized agriculture in developing countries have found that these innovations have created unintended economic and social

Vaccinating cattle before they are shipped to a feedlot. Industrial societies have changed the nature of agricultural production. Large corporate farming that depends on expensive energy and heavy capital investment has resulted in the decline of family farming.

problems. In most cases, only wealthy farmers have the capital to invest in irrigation equipment, chemical fertilizers, and large tracts of land. To extend their landholdings, wealthy farmers buy out smaller farmers, creating a new class of landless peasants and a small group of wealthy farmers, which intensifies patterns of inequality and related economic and social problems (Schusky, 1989).

In addition, ethnologists find that in areas such as Mexico, where the Green Revolution was adopted enthusiastically, the increased agricultural yields in grains are often used to feed animals raised for human consumption. Anthropologist Billie DeWalt (1984) discovered that more than 50 percent of the annual grain production in Mexico was used to feed animals such as pigs, chickens, and cattle. His research indicates that people who can afford meat have benefited from the Green Revolution. By increasing inequalities, however, the Green Revolution has reduced the percentage of the population that can afford meat. DeWalt concluded that the commercialization and industrialization of agriculture has not only widened the gap between rich and poor in Mexico, it has led to the underutilization of food energy and labor, thus hindering rather than promoting agricultural development.

Case Study: The Green Revolution In Shahidpur   One ethnological study has shown that when the Green Revolution is carried out under the right conditions it can be successful. Ethnologist Murray Leaf (1984) studied the effects of the Green Revolution in the Punjab region of northern India. Leaf conducted research in a Sikh village called Shahidpur from 1964 to 1966 and then returned in 1978. The years 1965 and 1978 mark the onset and complete adoption, respectively, of the Green Revolution in Shahidpur. Thus, Leaf was able to view the beginning and end of the process. During this period, the village switched from subsistence to mechanized agriculture.

The villagers adopted new strains of wheat, tractors, insecticides, and an irrigation technology on an experimental basis to determine whether this would increase their yields. Wealthy farmers adopted the technology readily, investing their capital in equipment and land. Poor peasants, however, also took the needed capital investment risks (with the support of government develop-

ment agencies), and the risks paid off. Leaf's research demonstrates that, in contrast to modernization theory, poor peasants are not constrained by traditional cultural patterns that might inhibit rational strategies of investment and savings. When these peasants saw they would directly benefit from these investments, they were willing to accept the economic risks.

More important, the villagers were willing to acquire the knowledge and technical skills needed to manage and ensure the continuity of their agricultural production. Through a university extension center, new plant varieties and technologies were adopted on an experimental basis. The people could directly see the results of their agricultural experiments and respond appropriately to various conditions. The education was a low-cost investment with government-subsidized tuition even for the poorest families. Furthermore, the university center provided training in the maintenance and repair of farm equipment and in other nonagricultural employment fields.

Leaf suggested that a key to the success of the Green Revolution in this region (in contrast to many other rural areas) is that government officials were more interested in development than in control. Government advice was always linked to the actual reactions among the villagers. Channels of communication were always open between local and regional levels. Leaf's valuable ethnological study has some suggestive insights for those interested in furthering the Green Revolution in the Third World. Much more ethnological research needs to be done, however, to evaluate the successes and problems in implementing the Green Revolution.

Case Study: The Conservation of Wood in Haiti   Another area in which ethnological research has increased our understanding of a global problem is the growing shortage of wood for fuel and construction in developing societies. This problem is most acute in regions where growing populations practice intensive agriculture. Peasant farmers spend several hours each day searching for firewood, the principal cooking fuel in poor households. This practice results in the cutting of forests, which take a long time to grow back. Deforestation has become a worldwide ecological challenge.

Anthropologist Gerald Murray (1989), who conducted research among the rural peasants in Haiti, helped design a plan to solve the problem. European powers such as the French had developed Haiti as a sugar-exporting colony. They found it profitable to cut forests to clear land for sugarcane, coffee, and indigo for European consumers. After Haiti became independent in the nineteenth century, foreign lumber companies continued to cut and export most of the nation's hardwoods. These activities, combined with population growth that created land scarcities, greatly reduced the amount of forest area. The Haitian government tried to develop a reforestation project but failed to secure the cooperation of most of the peasants. The government blamed traditional peasant attitudes and patterns of land use for the project's failure.

In contrast, Murray argued that neither traditional land-use patterns nor peasant attitudes were responsible for the failure of reforestation. He discovered that the peasants did not cooperate with the project because they did not see any immediate benefits. Most of the trees with which the peasants were familiar took many years to grow. Moreover, the peasants believed that planting trees on their small tracts of land would interfere with crop cultivation. They also feared that even if they reforested the land, the government would assume ownership of the trees and thereby deprive them of the use of the land.

Because of his study, Murray was invited to help design a reforestation plan. With assistance from other anthropologists and development specialists, he designed a program that introduced fast-growing hardwood trees as an additional cash crop for peasant farmers. The increasing demand for this type of wood for charcoal and construction made it an ideal commodity. Thousands of trees were planted all across Haiti. In addition, the plan called for the trees to be completely owned and managed by the peasantry rather than by the government. The peasants could harvest the trees whenever needed, and they knew that they would receive the direct benefits from the project. After several years, the peasants constructed their houses and sold charcoal from the new woods. Murray views this type of peasant-managed, cash-crop production as a feasible option for many Third World peasant communities.

A Global Solution for Global Problems In June 1992 in Rio de Janiero, Brazil, representatives of 178 nations gathered at what was known as the Earth Summit. These representatives tried to set the stage for managing the planet Earth through global cooperation. The issues were the environment, climate change induced by the greenhouse effect and global warming, population growth, deforestation, the loss of biodiversity, air and water pollution, and the threats of globalization throughout the world. Although the Earth Summit was successful because it received so much international attention and created worldwide awareness of global issues, the specifics of how soon problems were going to be solved, how much it would cost, and who was going to pay became extremely complicated.

Not surprisingly, many of the leaders of developing countries blamed the industrialized countries for many of their problems. Many leaders in developing countries view themselves as victims of industrialized countries. For example, the Rio Declaration was going to contain a statement of principles on deforestation that would legally bind developing countries from burning their tropical rainforests. The developing countries objected to this statement because it was unfairly focused on the tropical forests and included nothing regarding the deforestation of the old-growth forests in the United States, Canada, and Europe. When a compromise could not be reached, the legally binding statement was scrapped for a weaker statement with no legal implications. In addition, the industrialized countries, including the United States, were very reluctant to participate in some issues. For example, with respect to global warming, Japan and the European community have established limits on carbon dioxide emissions. Germany intends to reduce its carbon dioxide emissions by 25 percent by 2005. So far, the United States has resisted adopting specific carbon dioxide limits.

Many of the developing countries at Rio feel that their number-one priority is economic survival rather than saving the environment. Many of the leaders in these developing countries want to adopt industrialization as rapidly as possible to induce economic development. Although they agreed to some of the environmental mandates of industrialized countries, they did so only by requiring the industrialized countries to contribute large sums of money toward those efforts. This resulted in various conflicts between the have and have-not countries.

THE SUSTAINABILITY MODEL

Obviously, the problems resulting from globalization are extremely complex and are not going to be solved without some sort of global unity. Anthropological research in countries throughout the world has resulted in a perspective sometimes known as the *sustainability model*. The **sustainability model** suggests that societies throughout the world need environments and technologies that provide sustenance, not only for the present generation, but also for *future* generations. This model encourages the use of resource management that does not degrade the environment for future generations. The sustainability model is opposed to the logic of growth model, which assumes that economic and technological growth will inevitably bring progress. The sustainability model is more realistic in assessing environmental and technological change, and recommends policy changes to inhibit problems that are induced by globalization. Some countries are beginning to adopt this sustainability model of development by limiting their emissions, curbing population growth, and cleaning up pollution. However, these global problems cannot be solved by country-by-country solutions. The challenge for this generation is to provide a global, internationally based organizational context for the resolution of these problems. Neglecting these global problems is bound to result in massive difficulties for the future of humanity. Anthropological research can help in assessing these global problems and thereby promote the model of sustainability.

Economic Trends

As indicated in earlier chapters the contemporary global economy began with European expansion in the mercantilist and colonialist periods. Ever since World War II, this world economic system has been divided into core, semiperipheral, and peripheral countries, with the United States the leading core country. Multinational corporations and international organizations such as the World Bank and the International Monetary Fund were controlled by the trading and financial institutions in the capitalist world. The industrial-socialist countries of Eastern Europe and the former Soviet Union tried not to participate directly in the capitalist world economic system and also tried to create their own client states in areas such as Cuba, Angola, and Afghanistan. By the 1980s, however, new developments in the world economy were producing a radical restructuring of the world economic system.

MULTINATIONAL CORPORATIONS

One of the major factors behind the emergence of the global economic network is the multinational corporation. In Chapter 12, we discussed multinational corporations as they have evolved in both the capitalist and socialist world. In many ways, multinational corporations have opened the door for globalization by promoting the spread of technical and cultural knowledge to non-Western societies.

In the modern era, the multinational corporations have expanded to the point that some anthropologists consider them a new societal institution beyond the state. For example, anthropologist Alvin Wolfe (1977, 1986) discussed how multinational corporations have integrated the manufacturing processes at a supranational level. Multinational corporations have reorganized the electronics industry, garment manufacturing, and the automobile industry. Today, products might be manufactured in several different countries, and the financing and organization of labor carried out by the multinational corporation. Wolfe suggested that this process will continue: the multinational corporations will eventually assume the management of global affairs, and the nation-state will disappear.

Jobs and Growth: A Positive Assessment
Given their power and influence, multinational corporations have become highly controversial. With their tremendous capital assets, they can radically alter a society. Some theorists believe that multinational corporations can enhance global economic development, thereby reducing poverty and hunger. As these corporations expand into Latin America, Africa, the Middle East, and Asia, they bring capital and technology and provide employ-

ment. From this vantage point, they create jobs and spur both short- and long-term economic growth.

Neocolonialism: A Negative Assessment Dependency theorists, however, suggest that multinational corporations have actually intensified the problems of developing countries. They contend that these corporations create benefits for a wealthy elite and a small, upwardly mobile middle class, while the vast majority of the population remains in desperate poverty. Because the multinational corporations tend to invest in capital-intensive commodities, the majority of the population does not participate in the modernization of the economy. Furthermore, the entire society becomes dependent on corporations that are based outside the region, which inhibits self-sufficiency and the development of a more diversified economy.

According to this view, multinational corporations are simply the forerunners of a new form of neocolonialism, aimed at supplying the industrial world with natural resources and cheap labor. Multinational corporations based in core societies encourage peripheral societies to incur loans to produce a limited number of export-oriented commodities, a process that creates a cycle of economic indebtedness and increased dependency. In contrast to the older forms of colonialism, the core countries do not incur the expenses of maintaining direct political control over these societies; rather, they keep the peripheral nations in a state of dependency and maintain indirect political control by making contributions and paying bribes to politicians. In certain cases, however, when core countries feel threatened by political developments in peripheral nations, they resort to direct military intervention.

CASE STUDY: THE POTLATCH CORPORATION

As with other global developments, these issues can benefit from ethnological research. In one example, anthropologist Paul Shankman (1975, 1978) researched the changes generated by a multinational corporation on the island of Western Samoa. The corporation studied by Shankman was a large wood-product firm called the Potlatch Corporation (named after the famed redistributional exchanges of Native Americans in that region; see Chapter 10), based in the Northwest coast region of the United States. The Potlatch Corporation surveyed the tropical hardwood trees in a portion of Western Samoa and found a dozen species that could be used for furniture and veneers. To facilitate the leasing of large amounts of land in Western Samoa (bypassing traditional landholding arrangements), the Potlatch Corporation requested that the Samoan government set up an agency to act as a broker on behalf of the corporation. Potlatch eventually won a number of concessions from the Samoan Parliament.

Although Potlatch claimed to be committed to the economic development of Western Samoa, Shankman found that the monetary rewards from leasing the land did not prove as great as the people had expected. For example, Potlatch leased 28,000 acres of land for $1.40 an acre. In one project in which it leased land from a group of seven villages, the average yearly income from leasing amounted to less than $11 per person. Royalties paid on cut timber were also low, amounting to 4 cents per cubic foot, part of which was to go back to the government for reforestation.

The Potlatch Corporation did provide jobs for three hundred people in Western Samoa, making it one of the island's largest employers. Shankman discovered, however, that most of these people were formerly employed in agriculture, civil service, and light industry. Through the Potlatch projects, labor was simply shifted from other sectors of the economy to forestry. Thus, Potlatch did not really create jobs; rather, it simply shifted them to new sectors. Shankman believed that Potlatch's leasing policies will ultimately create a scarcity of land, and more peasants will be forced to produce on marginal land. Moreover, Shankman suggested that the inflated cost of living generated by the company, through higher wage notes in addition to the negative consequences such as erosion of the rainforest caused by rapid lumbering, may result in long-term negative costs to the people of Samoa.

Shankman noted that the risks assumed by the people of Western Samoa were much greater than those of the multinational corporation. If Potlatch were successful, it could recoup its initial investments very quickly. Were it to lose revenue, it could simply leave the area. In contrast, the peasants did not have any capital to fall back on were they to lose their land. Moreover, they had to live permanently with the economic, social, and ecological changes brought about by Potlatch's policies. Eventually, the Potlatch Corporation pulled out of the region. As Shankman (1990, 1999) concluded: "So much for the commitment to economic development of Western Samoa."

Other anthropologists are conducting research similar to Shankman's. The consensus at this point appears to confirm his charges that the expansion of multinational corporations has created new forms of economic dependency and neocolonialism. Thus, in the short run, the global changes wrought by multinational corporations appear to have had negative consequences for developing societies. Whether this will be true over the long run remains to be seen.

EMERGING ECONOMIC TRENDS

Driven by new technological and scientific developments in areas such as biotechnology, telecommunications, microprocessor information systems, and other high-tech industrialization, the world economy continues to undergo rapid changes. The globalization of the world economy has produced a vast array of products and services in interlocking markets. World trade has accelerated over the last few decades, stimulating greater economic interdependency. These increasing trends have resulted in a restructuring of the world economic system.

Changes in Socialist Countries   The globalization of the economy has had traumatic consequences for the industrial, socialist-based economies of the former Soviet Union and Eastern Europe and other peripheral socialist economies such as China and Vietnam. These state-administered economies did not produce the extensive economic development that they had promised. Government officials in these countries promoted five-year plans for economic development, but these plans did not lead to the production of prized consumer goods or a higher standard of living.

Anthropologist Marvin Harris (1992) advocates a cultural-materialist approach in explaining the downfall of the former Soviet Union and Eastern European communism. Harris suggested that the infrastructure, which encompasses the technological, economic, demographic, and environmental activities directed at sustaining health and well-being, has a primary, determinant role in the functioning of a sociocultural system. The serious deficiencies and weaknesses in the infrastructure of the former Soviet Union and Eastern Europe undermined the entire fabric of society. For example, the basic energy supply based on coal and oil production became stagnant, and the generating plants for electricity were antiquated, leading to periodic blackouts and frequent breakdowns.

Harris described how the agricultural and marketing system for the production and distribution of food resulted in severe shortages, delays in delivery, hoarding, and rationing. In addition, increasing problems with and costs incurred by industrial pollution led to the deterioration of the socialist economies. According to Harris, the infrastructural deficiencies of these socialist systems had fundamental consequences for the basic health, safety, and ultimate survival of the people in these societies. These deficiencies eventually led to the systemic breakdown of these societies.

The industrial-socialist societies faced major economic crises. Repeated failures in agricultural and industry led to frustration and unrest among the populace. Global communications with other societies, particularly those with much greater access to consumer goods, caused many people in socialist states to become frustrated with the inadequacy of their systems. These people began to question the aims and policies of their leaders.

The Soviet Union: *Perestroika* and *Glasnost*   In the former Soviet Union, Communist party leader Mikhail Gorbachev responded to the people's criticisms and the economic crisis facing the country by instituting a series of reforms and economic restructuring known as *perestroika*. In effect, this policy involved the reintegration of the former Soviet Union into the world-capitalist system. New joint ventures with capitalist firms were undertaken; McDonald's and other multinational corporations from the West and Japan were invited to participate in the Soviet economy. Soviet industrial corporations were reorganized to emphasize competition and the maximization of private profits for individual firms. Wages and salaries in Soviet industries were no longer to be controlled by the government; rather, they would reflect market conditions and individual productivity.

McDonald's restaurants are one sign of globalization in non-Western countries.

To carry out *perestroika,* Gorbachev had to confront the bureaucratic elite that dominated the Soviet political economy (see Chapter 12). Because these reforms directly threatened the bureaucratic control of the political economy, he faced much resistance by government officials. Some of these bureaucrats were ideologically committed to the Marxist–Leninist model of communism and did not want the Soviet Union integrated into the world-capitalist economy. Others believed that tinkering with the economy with these reforms would induce more hardship for the Soviet people. For example, since the introduction of *perestroika* and the removal of government-controlled price restraints, the costs of food and other basic commodities have skyrocketed.

As a means of implementing his economic reforms, Gorbachev also called for *glasnost,* usually translated as "openness," which involved the freedom to criticize government policies and officials. Newspapers and other media were allowed to express views that were in opposition to Communist party dictates. *Glasnost* also permitted greater political freedom of expression as well as democratic elections and a multiparty political system. The policy of *glasnost* led to mass demonstrations against the former Soviet government and eventually to criticism and the downfall of Gorbachev himself.

As a result of the severe economic difficulties and subsequent political crises in the Soviet Union, many of the non-Russian republics began to declare sovereignty and independence. Regions such as Estonia, Lithuania, the Ukraine, Kazakhstan, Uzbekistan, Turkmenistan, and Azerbaijan cut their political ties with the Soviet Union. Although Gorbachev attempted to frustrate these developments, sometimes with a show of military force, the Soviet empire began to collapse. Eventually, all of the non-Russian regions formed their own independent republics. The independent republics not only cut political ties, leaving the Russian republic by itself, they also began to restrict the export of their domestic commodities into Russia. This exacerbated the difficult economic conditions within the Russian state itself.

The successor to Mikhail Gorbachev, Boris Yeltsin, has attempted to further the *perestroika* and *glasnost* policies of his predecessor. Yeltsin's primary goal is to transform the remains of the state-managed centralized economy of Russia into an economy in which managerial and consumer decisions are based on market forces and the economy is in private hands. The Yeltsin government has tried to radically restructure the political economy by ending price and wage controls, reducing or eliminating subsidies to factories and farms, slashing military expenditures, introducing new taxes, and balancing the national budget. This economic shock therapy has had some positive consequences, but most economists agree that the peculiarities of the Soviet system are bound to prolong the process of economic reform. In the meantime, many Russians who were accustomed to subsidies and government benefits have had to endure substantial hardships. The question for future developments in Russia is whether the people can be patient enough to endure these economic difficulties (Goldman, 1996).

Eastern Europe Stimulated by the policies of *perestroika* and *glasnost*, the Eastern European nations of East Germany, Poland, Czechoslovakia, Hungary, Romania, Bulgaria, and Yugoslavia began reforms of their socialist political economies. These countries had been restricted to trading primarily with the Soviet Union and among themselves. In the German Democratic Republic (East Germany), mass demonstrations and migrations of people to West Germany led to the fall of the Communist government and the destruction of the Berlin Wall. The government of Poland was toppled by a popular movement directed by Solidarity, an outlawed labor union led by Lech Walesa. Polish workers demanded economic reforms and a better standard of living than that offered by the socialist model. Democratic elections led to Walesa's becoming prime minister. Walesa subsequently visited the United States and other Western countries in search of foreign investment. Many of the Eastern European socialist-bloc societies actively sought reintegration into the world-capitalist economy as a means of stimulating both economic growth and democratic freedom.

In a book entitled *What Was Socialism and What Comes Next* (1996) anthropologist Katherine Verdery, who did most of her ethnographic work in the East European country of Romania, summarizes some of the problems and dilemmas facing this region. She writes about how a different sense of time prevailed during the socialist period in Eastern Europe, and the new forms of capitalism and its industrial work rhythms based on progress and linear models are disrupting these societies. Verdery notes that new resurgent patterns of gender inequality based on older patriarchal forms are re-emerging in these postsocialist Eastern European countries. During the socialist period, gender relations were supposed to have been equalized. However, Verdery describes how the socialist governments in Romania reconfigured gender roles,

making women dependent on a patrilineal-paternalistic state. After the downfall of socialism, Romania, as well as Poland, Hungary, and other postsocialist countries have been emphasizing a return to "traditional values" regarding gender, which positions the woman once again in the home and household chores. To some extent this gender organization of postsocialist society defines housework as "nonwork." As these Eastern European economies become more capitalistic, women will probably be drawn into the work force, but in the meantime these women are returning to the older patriarchal forms of family life.

In the final chapter of her book, Verdery comments on how the transformation of Eastern Europe and Russian societies may take a much different path towards capitalism than the Western European or U.S. societies have taken. The privatization of property is likely to involve much different processes than in Western societies. Former socialist leaders will undoubtedly use the legal and political process to develop economic opportunities for themselves, as they transfer the state enterprises into private hands. Verdery suggests that black markets, organized crime, and the manipulation of the legal and state apparatus by former socialist bureaucrats will all have consequences for these postsocialist societies. The future of these postsocialist societies cannot be predicted based on models of how Western capitalist states developed.

China Since Mao Zedong's death, China, under leaders such as Deng Xiaoping, introduced many tenets of capitalism. Instead of relying on Communist party cadre who wanted to instill egalitarian ideals, the new leadership sought to develop leaders with technical, agricultural, and scientific expertise. They encouraged students to obtain education in the United States and other Western nations. They abolished the commune system and reorganized agricultural and industrial production based on individual profits and wages for farmers and workers. The Chinese government has called for modernization in agriculture, industry, science, and defense.

Although promoting economic change, the Chinese government has not endorsed political reform. Party bureaucrats remain entrenched in power and resist all pressure to relinquish their authority. The absence of political freedom resulted in mass demonstrations by students and others in

Tiananmen Square in Beijing in 1989. The Chinese government crushed this freedom movement with military force and has continued to repress any form of political dissent that threatens its authority. Whether economic development and reintegration into the world economic system can work in China without corresponding political freedom is a question that remains to be answered.

Vietnam   Confronted with being one of the poorest countries in the world, the Vietnamese government in 1981 introduced a series of economic reforms called *doi moi* (Pike, 1990). Some of the younger politicians in Vietnam are calling for greater participation in the world economic system, the introduction of private enterprise, and individual material benefits in the form of wages and salaries. The Vietnamese reformers face the same problem as those in China and the Soviet Union. With their memories of their colonial experience and wars against the capitalist nations, conservative bureaucrats who are committed to Marxist–Leninist ideology oppose reintegration into the world economic system. Reformers, in contrast, actively seek support from capitalist countries and the international community to pursue their economic-liberalization policies and democratization. Recently, it appears that reformers are having the stronger influence regarding state policies. For example, they were instrumental in the negotiations that resulted in the United States lifting its trade embargo against Vietnam in January 1994. This shift in U.S. policy will undoubtedly lead to increasing trade and capitalist economic activity in Vietnam.

Changes in the Core Societies: The United States and Japan   The globalization of the world economy has also had dramatic effects on the core industrial societies such as the United States and Japan. The United States currently exports about one-fifth of its industrial production. This is double what it was exporting in the 1950s, and that proportion is rapidly increasing. About 70 percent of those exported goods compete directly with goods produced by other nations. Some U.S. states depend heavily on the international economy. For example, approximately one-half of the workers in Ohio work directly on exports such as tires and automobiles. Most American corporations now conduct business on a global level. Although the United States remains the world's largest economy, with a gross national product twice the size of that of its nearest competitor, it no longer dominates as it did in the past. In fact, at the end of the 1990s, the United States had one of the largest trade deficits and largest foreign debt of any nation.

In contrast, Japan has maintained a trade surplus. During the past several decades, the United States and Japan have engaged in global economic

Japanese factories are moving to new areas of the world such as Indonesia.

competition. This competition needs to be considered in the context of the world economic system.

In the 1920s, in the early phases of Japanese industrialization, Japan's population began to expand. Lacking adequate natural resources such as fertile land, raw materials, and energy supplies, Japan became increasingly dependent on imported food and other raw materials. To secure a food supply to support its growing population, the Japanese began to act as an imperial power in Asia, colonizing Korea and Taiwan and expanding into China. Japanese imperialism in Asia was one of the direct causes of World War II.

During its occupation of Japan following World War II, the United States encouraged the development of corporate capitalism. The U.S. government viewed Japan as a capitalist center that could be used to forestall the spread of communism in Asia. Some of Japan's *zaibatsu*, wealthy family conglomerates, were broken up into smaller concerns. Others, such as the Mitsui and Mitsubishi families, were encouraged to invest in new equipment and technologies to induce rapid capitalist growth. Large sums of U.S. capital were funneled into corporations such as Sony to stimulate corporate capitalism. These policies led to the "economic miracle" in Japan that occurred in the 1960s. By the end of that decade, Japan had become one of the world's leading exporters.

The Japanese government, however, realized that it was still dependent on energy and food from other regions of the world. The government constantly reminded its population that Japan must "develop exports or die." The government organized the Ministry of International Trade and Industry (M.I.T.I.) to mobilize industrial firms to export products such as automobiles and electronics to ensure a balance of funds to pay for its heavy imports of food and energy. The M.I.T.I. helps finance Japan's huge exporting corporations so that it can maintain a favorable balance of trade. By the late 1980s, Japan had a large trade surplus. However, it imported approximately 8 tons of fuel, food, wood, and other raw materials for every ton of goods it exported.

Both Japan and the United States, as well as other core capitalist countries, have become postindustrial societies, with a large component of their economy devoted to the service sector (see Chapter 12). At the same time, many of the basic manufacturing plants of these industrial economies are relocating into developing countries to exploit the cheaper labor supply. Japanese multinational corporations have relocated auto factories and other industries to developing Asian countries such as Indonesia and Thailand. Ford Motor Company has relocated an engine manufacturing plant in Mexico. As the core countries become increasingly internationalized, economic interdependency accelerates. Some theorists believe that this interdependency may become a key component in resolving conflict among nations in the global village.

The Semiperipheral NICs   Another result of the globalization of the economy is the rise of the newly industrializing economies (NICs) from a peripheral to a semiperipheral status in the world economic system. Included here are the nations of South Korea, Hong Kong, Singapore, and Taiwan. Popularly known as the Little Dragons of Asia, they compete with the economic might of Japan. Both Taiwan and Korea were colonies of Japan, whereas Hong Kong and Singapore were colonies of Great Britain. As with other colonized nations, they became peripheral dependencies. These countries, however, are rapidly industrializing and have broken their bonds of dependency. In some industries, such as electronics, these nations have marketed products that compete with core countries like Japan.

The success of the NICs reflects the changing division of labor in the world economic system. As the multinationals relocated some of their labor-intensive industries to low-wage regions, the NICs were able to absorb some of these jobs. Like Japan, their success is partially due to U.S. economic support. In particular, during the 1950s and 1960s, the United States viewed South Korea and Taiwan as part of the capitalist bloc in Asia. The United States invested large sums of capital and foreign aid into these countries, thereby enabling them to develop as capitalist centers. In addition, as in Japan, the governments in these countries directed the modernization of the economy through massive investment into export industries.

The NICs have changed the context of the world economy through low-cost production methods and aggressive marketing. They have created a unique niche in the world economic system by exporting products that compete directly with those produced by the core countries. In many cases, they have expanded their overseas markets through joint ventures with multinational firms based in core countries. In other cases, they have produced their own multinational corporations. For example, NIC multinational corporations have become global competitors as producers of semiconductors for electronic and computer equipment. The world's largest plastic firm is Formosa Plastics, based in Taiwan. The best-selling imported car in Canada is the Pony, made by Hyundai in South Korea.

Political Trends

As the world economy becomes more integrated, major political changes are taking place in the global network. During the 1950s, some modernization theorists (Chapter 13) predicted that the various nations would become very similar as they were brought closer together in the global economy. People everywhere would share the same goods and services and eventually the same cultural values. This similarity would set the stage for a unified world government. Certain current trends indicate that such a movement may be taking place; for example, in 1999, twelve European countries agreed to accept the "Euro" as the form of currency exchange in order to facilitate trade and to help develop a unified European economy.

In addition, a unified European parliament has been established and Europeans no longer need passports to visit among the twelve different countries. At the same time, however, other political tendencies seem to indicate movement in the opposite direction, in many areas the nation-state appears to be fragmenting along linguistic, ethnic, and religious lines.

In considering these global political trends, many anthropologists suggest that the nation-state is too small for the immense problems in the world political economy: capital flows, economic development, management of technology, environmental and demographic trends, production of commodities, and labor problems. Organizations such as the United Nations, International Monetary Fund, World Bank, General Agreement on Tariffs and Trade (GATT), and the multinational corporations appear to be in the process of displacing the nation-state in the management of the global econ-

omy. Although the United Nations has not been effective in producing an international consensus on global problems, it may become more important in the future. At the same time, the nation-state may be too large to care for the different needs of people at the local level. Government officials representing the nation-state may not have enough contact with the populace in local areas to respond to their needs, which can range from housing and food to the opportunity to express their cultural values. One sign of the fragmentation of the nation-state into smaller components is the increasing ethnic and religious tensions at the local level.

Ethnic Trends

Ethnic unrest and tension are prevalent in today's world. Newspapers and television news are rife with stories about ethnic violence among the peoples of the former Soviet Union and Eastern Europe, Africa, Sri Lanka, India, Ireland, the Middle East, and the United States.

Anthropologists have been systematically examining ethnicity since the 1960s. As we saw in Chapter 3, an *ethnic group* is a collectivity of people who believe they share a common history and origins. Members of ethnic groups often share cultural traits such as language, religion, dress, and food. Today, as we saw in Chapters 14 and 15, the countries of Latin America, Africa, the Caribbean, the Middle East, and Asia are plural societies that contain many ethnic groups.

As globalization occurs with the rapid integration of nation-states, markets, and information technology, and the management of economic and political development goes to the World Bank, the IMF, and the U.N., many peoples at the local level feel threatened by these global processes. Citizens of various countries lose faith in their governments to represent their interests in these pluralistic societies. These globalization processes often exacerbate ethnic tensions and conflicts. In previous chapters, we have looked at ethnic tensions and conflicts in Latin America, the Caribbean, Africa, the Middle East, and Asia. Undoubtedly, these ethnic conflicts are to some extent a result of earlier colonial policies, and new post-Cold War trends in globalization. Many ethnic groups have expressed a desire to return to a more

APPLYING ANTHROPOLOGY

World Migration and Refugees

It has been estimated that some 100 million people are migrating from their homelands to other countries. Of this number, about 17 million are refugees and another 20 million have fled violence, drought, and environmental destruction (Popline, 1993). The vast majority of the migration and refugee problems involve Africa, Latin America, the Middle East, and Asia. However, during the 1990s thousands of refugees in Europe, primarily from Bosnia and Kosovo began a forced migration out of their homelands. Although some of the migrants and refugees come to wealthier countries in North America or Europe, the majority are marking time or trying to carve out a new existence in underdeveloped regions. Approximately 87 percent of the 17 million refugees are residing in underdeveloped countries, countries that have rapidly growing populations and severe economic and environmental problems.

A number of anthropologists are actively engaged in research projects and planning activities directed at resolving some of the basic problems that confront refugee populations. An organization known as the Committee on Refugee Issues (CORI) has developed as a division of the American Anthropological Association to sponsor and encourage research and problem-solving projects among refugee populations. A variety of anthropologists are doing research on the Southeast Asian

migrants who came to the United States following the aftermath of the Vietnam War. Refugees from Vietnam, Laos, and Kampuchea (Cambodia) are being studied by anthropologists, most of whom are actively involved in attempting to help these refugees adapt to conditions in the United States.

Anthropologist Pamela DeVoe (1992) has been doing research among Southeast Asian refugees in the St. Louis area. DeVoe has found that Southeast Asian refugees enter the work force at the unskilled and semiskilled level within the first six months of their arrival in the United States. She found that the key problem for these refugees is the lack of adequate health benefits to cover their families. DeVoe found that there is a lack of federal planning for a comprehensive refugee health program and an inadequate, uncoordinated state network of health services for them. Consequently, these refugees, who have to cope with traumatic experiences as a result of the stresses of migration and relocation, have few opportunities for adequate health care.

After interviewing the employers of the refugees, DeVoe discovered that many of the Southeast Asian refugee workers quit their jobs suddenly, for no apparent reason. She found that job absenteeism and abrupt quitting occurred frequently, indicating that these refugees were having difficulties adjusting to U.S. society.

DeVoe found that in some cases the refugees do not understand the system of health care and the benefits available to them. Hospitals will treat illnesses and bill patients over time using a sliding scale to determine how much a person has to pay for a service. Because of the lack of language skills, however, these refugees did not understand what the health-care system could do for them or what it would cost. This causes delays in health-care treatment. Generally, when these delays develop, the refugees buy over-the-counter medications or use folk remedies to treat themselves. In some cases this results in more severe illnesses or dangerous treatments.

DeVoe found that about 40 percent of the refugees employed in metropolitan St. Louis have work-related health-insurance benefits. Generally, as for other Americans, the expense of buying private health insurance is too costly for most refugees. Thus, health insurance is the critical problem for many of the Southeast Asian refugees in the work force in the St. Louis area. DeVoe suggested that a national comprehensive health-care system would eliminate many of the problems for these refugees and help them become more self-sufficient, productive members of American society.

Other anthropologists have been using their research skills and problem-solving techniques to assist migrants who have been detained in refugee camps in different parts of the world. Anthropologist Nancy Donnelly (1991) has been studying the Vietnamese refugees that have been confined in detention centers in Hong Kong. Vietnamese refugees have been coming to Hong Kong as asylum seekers since the end of the Vietnam War. Since 1979, about 180,000 men, women, and children have arrived in Hong Kong in boats. Approximately 64,000 remain in refugee detention camps awaiting acceptance to other countries. In 1989, Hong Kong attempted to force some of the refugees to return to Vietnam, but international pressure forced Hong Kong to reverse its policy, and it has focused instead on assisting refugees to return voluntarily, if they wish to do so.

Donnelly conducted her research in 1991, visiting thirteen detention camps and agency offices that manage the camps in Hong Kong. She found that most of the camps are much like prisons that are strictly controlled by the Correctional Services Department in Hong Kong. As many as three hundred people live together in Quonset huts that are surrounded by double chain-link fences topped by barbed wire. These camps contain Vietnamese who are waiting for screening to determine their eligibility for resettlement. They have little to do most of the time. Camp life is described as rule-bound and boring, punctuated by occasional violent episodes. In general, Donnelly found that these refugees are treated as criminals. On the other

hand, Donnelly found that most of the refugees found their status in the camps preferable to their lives in Vietnam. Everyone expressed hopes regarding freedom and a better life.

Drawing on anthropological research, Holly Ann Williams (1990) has attempted to highlight general trends for family situations for people detained in refugee camps. In the initial decision-making stages of choosing to flee one's country, refugee families often face upheaval, disruption, disorientation, and possible death for friends and family members. The breakdown of customary family roles and the new, unfamiliar patterns of social organization often result in multiple stresses. In some cases, extended family units fragment into smaller nuclear units to safeguard resources and food. In other cases, when families are fleeing war conditions, males stay behind as resistance fighters. This leads to the development of many female-headed households in the refugee camps. The vast majority of the refugees in camps in Third World societies are women and children.

Once situated in the camps, scarce resources, limited food, communicable diseases, minimal health care, and overcrowding place more stress on the families. Families are crowded into living quarters with little privacy, often leading to increased marital and family conflicts, including more cases of wife and child abuse. Within the camps, refugee families experience a loss of control over

their destiny; they describe camp life as a waste of time, meaningless, and pacifying.

Despite this loss of autonomy and self-determination and the consequent disintegration of the family unit, Williams reported that in many cases the individuals often try to re-create the family structure as a basis of social support. Women begin to develop new leadership roles, economic responsibilities, and coping skills required for family maintenance in the camps. Although women experience more hardship than men in refugee camps, often being subjected to personal violence, rape, and abduction, they are sometimes able to assume leadership roles and create social support for family members. Williams, who completed her specific research on Cambodian refugees, called on anthropologists to do more research on family dynamics in refugee camps, to better understand these coping mechanisms.

The United Nations High Commissioner for Refugees (UNHCR) is the organization responsible for ensuring that refugee camps maintain minimum standards of health and safety conditions. Anthropologists are engaged in studies that provide information and problem-solving strategies that can be used by various voluntary agencies and UN officials to help improve the lives of refugees confined to these camps. This has become an increasingly important project for anthropologists who can use their knowledge and research techniques in solving various global problems.

Vietnamese boat people.

simple way of life and traditional culture and behavior. They distrust the new global managers in attending to their needs. New resurgent forms of ethnicity as described in earlier chapters are reactions to these globalization tendencies. Restoring ethnic autonomy is sometimes seen as a strategy to rectify the globalization process. The revival of local ethnic tendencies and identities is developing in non-Western countries as well as the West. Anthropologists are studying the ethnic resurgence of the Scots and why they want more independence in the U.K., and why Quebec wants to separate from the rest of Canada (Cohen, 1996; Handler, 1988). These local ethnic movements for autonomy and separatism are a response to the weakening of older nation-state processes, induced by globalization. As globalization is fraught with anxieties and produces uncertainties in structures and institutions as it develops in anarchic, haphazard fashions carried along by economic, technological, and cultural imperatives, the ethnic group becomes the refuge for people who feel as if they have no control over these new forces.

Religion and Secularization

Just as ethnic trends have created contradictory political trends, there are ongoing, contradictory religious trends in the context of globalization. In Chapter 12 in the discussion of industrial societies, we discussed the process of secularization. Generally, traditional religious beliefs and rituals become separated from economic, social, and political institutions in industrial societies. Religion becomes a private affair for most people.

After the Enlightenment, social thinkers such as Auguste Comte and Karl Marx, as well as early anthropologists, predicted that as societies became increasingly industrialized and modernized, secularization would eradicate religious institutions and beliefs. Though secularization has occurred, however, religion has not disappeared in these societies. Even in places such as the former Soviet Union and Poland, where religious beliefs and institutions were prohibited by government authorities, religion has remained a vital force.

To some extent, religious institutions have survived in industrial societies because religious leaders have emphasized many of the cultural values—for example, nationalism—espoused by other institutions. In addition, the persistence of religion may also be a product of the secularization process itself. Many recent religious revivals have occurred in those societies that have been most affected by modernization. We saw this in the case of the Iranian Islamic revolution in Chapter 15. As globalization introduces sweeping political, social, and ideological changes, many traditional beliefs and values are challenged. To cope with these destabilizing transformations, many people are reemphasizing traditional cultural values, including religion. For example, the fundamentalist movements in North America, whether Catholic, Jewish, or Protestant, can be partially understood as a reaction against secularization and modernization. The same can be said of Buddhist, Hindu, and Islamic fundamentalism in other parts of the world. As more people recognize that globalization is not incidental to their lives, but rather a recog-nizable transformation in their everyday circumstances, they draw on religious substance as a means of restoring power over their lives. The reconstruction and reinvigoration of their religious identity gives some people a sense of greater control in what appears to be a runaway world. Fundamentalist movements articulate the uncertainties and distress brought about by expanding globalization. These religious movements advocate alternative ways of organizing life on a more localized level.

The Role of Anthropology

Although the political, ethnic, and religious trends discussed in this chapter are essentially global, they also obviously affect people on the local level. Not surprisingly, therefore, ethnologists are actively documenting the local responses to global political and religious trends of people in the agricultural regions of Latin America, Africa, the Middle East, Asia, and nonstate societies, as well as in industrialized societies. Ethnologists have recorded the various dislocations of global political and religious processes in these societies and the ways in which people have attempted to cope with these global changes. The continuing agony of separatist, ethnic, and religious conflicts in Bosnia, Kosovo, Sri Lanka, and elsewhere threatens people throughout the world. Existing institutions such as the nation-state have not been able to manage this local conflict. Perhaps by understanding the specific aspirations of these different peoples, national governments and the international community will be more responsive to their diverse needs and interests. As anthropologists identify the cultural variations that can block international coordination, they may help to contribute to the reduction of ethnic and religious tensions worldwide. Anthropologist John Bennett (1987) recommended that anthropologists synthesize their local studies (the micro level) with studies of global conditions (the macro level) to identify trends that militate against international cooperation. Anthropologists should make a concerted effort to understand the underlying historical and cultural motivations that contribute to ethnic and religious conflicts. In doing so, they may aid in humankind's understanding of its existence and the need for cooperation in the global village.

Jerry Falwell, a Christian fundamentalist.

SUMMARY

Numerous global trends are altering the way of life in all societies. Environmental changes induced by globalization are creating new problems that may threaten the existence of our planet, including the greenhouse effect, the depletion of the ozone layer, and atmospheric pollution. Population growth has declined in the core countries but has risen in many Third World societies because of a combination of reduced mortality rates and continued high birthrates. Technological changes resulting from industrialism have increased the consumption of energy and other raw materials.

Global environmental, demographic, and technological changes have led to two different perspectives: one pessimistic, and the other optimistic. Pessimists predict that population growth and expanded industrialism will result in global economic collapse. Optimists tend to see human creativity and technological solutions as the salvation for humanity. Both the pessimistic and optimistic views are probably exaggerated. Anthropologists have examined specific cases regarding the adoption of mechanized agriculture and reforestation projects to understand better these worldwide problems.

Various global economic trends have developed in recent decades. Multinational corporations are creating more economic interdependency among nations. Ethnological research, however, indicates that the changes introduced by multinational corporations may not always generate economic development in Third World societies. Other global economic trends include the reintegration of socialist societies into the world-capitalist system. Russia, Eastern Europe, China, and Vietnam are abandoning orthodox forms of socialism to join the world-market system.

The core countries such as the United States and Japan compete with one another in the global economy. This competition has resulted in the expansion of multinational corporations into various areas, leading to a new global division of labor. Countries such as South Korea and Taiwan have been moving from peripheral to semiperipheral status in the world-market system.

In contrast to global economic interdependency and modernization, political, ethnic, and religious trends often move in the opposite direction. Ethnic separatist movements often divide people, making the promotion of national goals difficult. Religious fundamentalist movements often result from the rapid modernization processes that erode traditional cultural beliefs. Anthropological studies of these trends improve our understanding of both local aspirations and global processes.

STUDY QUESTIONS

1. In your view what are the positive and negative consequences of globalization?
2. What is the demographic transition theory? Do you think that this model applies to all cultures in the world?
3. Why is there concern over the loss of biodiversity?
4. What is the Doomsday Model (neo-Malthusian approach)? How does it differ from the logic-of-growth model?
5. How can an anthropologist make a difference in the changing world of today? Or, is the world in need of engineers and technicians who can invent new ways of solving problems? That is, how can the anthropological perspective be used to examine global issues such as overpopulation, deforestation, global warming, and the loss of biodiversity?
6. What types of unanticipated problems has the implementation of the Green Revolution caused in areas where it was introduced? Are there any success stories, or is the verdict all negative?
7. What is the global economy? What types of changes have occurred in the world recently that are related to the globalization of the world economy?
8. What types of contributions can anthropologists make by studying ethnic conflict and religious movements?

KEY TERMS

agribusiness
assimilation
biodiversity

demographic-transition theory
doubling time
greenhouse effect

logic-of-growth model
sustainability model

 ## INTERNET EXERCISES

1. While reading the website **http://www.con-verge.org.nz/pirm/dtoxgrev.htm,** please note that alternative forms of agriculture are now being developed for hybrid crops that require a large amount of pesticides and fertilizers. What makes these newer organic approaches better? Can it be that the world will be able to feed itself with organic methods?

2. Look at the following website on Hungary: **http://www.interlog.com/~photodsk/mag-yar/negbirth.html.** What is the concern here? How does it compare to the birthrate in Japan as described in the book? Are these serious concerns, or are they just driven by group pride?

 ## SUGGESTED READINGS

BERNARD, H. R., and P. J. PELTO, eds. 1987. *Technology and Social Change,* 2d ed. Prospect Heights, IL: Waveland Press. A fine series of essays by anthropologists examining the consequences of technological change in different societies.

BODLEY, JOHN H. 1985. *Anthropology and Contemporary Human Problelms,* 2d ed. Palo Alto, CA: Mayfield. A broad overview of how an anthropological perspective can be brought to bear on problems such as environmental pollution, population growth, energy consumption, and political problems.

HUTCHINSON, JOHN and SMITH, ANTHONY (eds.) 1996. *Ethnicity.* Oxford: Oxford University Press. A comprehensive collection of essays, both classic and contemporary on the topic of ethnicity. Many of the essays are by anthropologists.

VAN DEN BERGHE, PIERRE. 1981. *The Ethnic Phenomenon.* New York: Elsevier Science. A sociobiological view of ethnicity that examines ethnic interaction around the world. Although the sociobiological hypothesis is questionable, the empirical data on ethnic relations are superb.

WILSON, E. O., ed. 1989. *Biodiversity.* Washington, DC: National Academy Press. A comprehensive series of essays by distinguished scientists on the topic of biodiversity and threats to it.

Applied
Anthropology

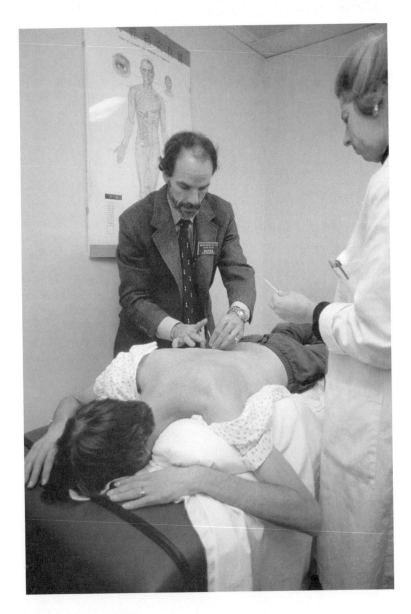

CHAPTER OUTLINE

The Roles of Applied Anthropologists in Planned Change
The Informant Role / The Facilitator Role / The Analyst Role / The Representative Role / The Future of Applied Anthropology

Medical Anthropology
Applied Anthroplogy and Substance Abuse

Applied Archaeology: Cultural Resource Management
Preserving the Past

Cultural Relativism and Human Rights
Relativism Reconsidered / A Possible Resolution to the Problem of Relativism / The Problem of Intervention / Universal Human Rights / The Role of Applied Anthropology

CHAPTER QUESTIONS

- What types of projects are conducted by applied anthropologists?

- What are the different roles of applied anthropologists in various projects?

- What type of research is identified with medical anthropology?

- How are archaeologists involved in applied anthropology?

- How have applied anthropologists become involved in human rights research?

A S THE PRECEDING CHAPTERS ILLUSTRATED, AN-thropologists are engaged in extensive research in the four basic subfields of the discipline: physical anthropology, archaeology, linguistics, and ethnology. Within these fields, different specializations have emerged that allow for the in-depth gathering of data and the testing and evaluation of specific hypotheses regarding human societies and behavior. As mentioned in Chapter 1, however, one of the most important developments in the field of anthropology is **applied anthropology,** the use of data from the research in anthropology to offer practical solutions to problems faced by a society.

The preceding chapter focused on the various global trends and problems that face humankind. This chapter introduces some of the research and problem-solving techniques in the area of applied anthropology that may help solve some of these problems.

Applied anthropologists research environmental, demographic, technological, economic, social, and health-care problems for the purpose of devising solutions. They rely on basic ethnological methods, especially participant observation and in-depth interviewing techniques, to investigate variables that may impede or foster the resolution of these problems. They frequently work as consultants to various government and private agencies. Applied anthropologists are often referred to as *practicing anthropologists* and are involved at some level in the planning process for implemental change to resolve various societal problems.

The Roles of Applied Anthropologists in Planned Change

In a broad overview of applied anthropology, Erve Chambers (1985) classified the different roles of applied anthropologists. One role is the *representative role,* in which the anthropologist becomes the spokesperson for the particular group being studied when policies are being developed for them. For example, in the 1940s and 1950s, applied anthropologists often represented Native

American communities in negotiations with state and federal authorities.

The second role discussed by Chambers is the *facilitator role.* In the facilitator role, applied anthropologists actively help bring about change in the community being researched. For example, they may take a proactive, participative role in bringing about economic or social change to improve conditions for the community. The third role is the *informant role,* in which the applied anthropologist transfers cultural knowledge obtained from ethnological studies to the government or other agency that wants to promote change in a particular direction. Chambers discussed how the U.S. government has recently employed applied anthropologists as on-site researchers to provide data on how local-level service clients and delivery agencies respond to government policy.

The fourth role of applied anthropologists is the *analyst role.* Rather than being just a provider of data, the applied anthropologist sometimes becomes engaged in the actual development of policy. More opportunities are developing in this area, as applied anthropologists become more skilled in technical and administrative issues regarding development. Another role specified by Chambers in his overview is the *mediator role.* The mediator role involves the applied anthropologist as an intermediary among different interest groups who are participating in a development project. This may include private developers, government officials, and the people who will be affected by the project. The anthropologist as mediator must try to reconcile differences among these groups, facilitating compromises that ideally will benefit all parties involved in the project.

THE INFORMANT ROLE

Over the years, most applied anthropologists have worked in the informant role. To assist governments, private developers, or other agencies, applied anthropologists are hired because of their ethnological studies of particular societies. Government and private agencies often employ applied anthropologists to prepare **social-impact studies,** research on the possible consequences that change will have on a community. Social-impact studies involve in-depth interviews and ethnological studies in local communities to determine how various

policies and developments will affect social life in those communities.

One well-known social-impact study was carried out by Thayer Scudder and Elizabeth Colson (1979) in the African country of Zambia. Scudder and Colson had conducted long-term ethnological research for about thirty years in the Gwembe Valley in Zambia. In the mid-1950s, the Zambian government subsidized the development of a large-scale dam, which would provide for more efficient agricultural activities and electrification. Because of the location of the dam, however, the people in the Gwembe Valley would be forced to relocate. Scudder and Colson used their knowledge from their long-term research and subsequent interviews to study the potential impact of this project on the community.

From their social-impact study, Scudder and Colson concluded that the forced relocation of this rural community would create extreme stresses that would result in people clinging to familiar traditions and institutions during the period of relocation. Scudder did social-impact studies of other societies in Africa experiencing forced relocation from dams, highways, and other developments. These studies enabled Scudder and Colson to offer advice to the various African government officials, who could then assess the costs and benefits of resettling these populations and could plan their development projects taking into consideration the impact on the people involved.

THE FACILITATOR ROLE

Applied anthropologists often serve as consultants to government organizations, such as the Agency for International Development (AID), that formulate policies involving foreign aid. For example, anthropologist Patrick Fleuret (1988), a full-time employee of AID, studied the problems of farmers in Uganda after the downfall of Idi Amin in 1979. Fleuret and other AID anthropologists discovered that, on the heels of the political turmoil in Uganda, many of the peasants had retreated into subsistence production rather than participate in the market economy. They also found that subsistence production was affected by a technological problem—a scarcity of hoes for preparing the land for cultivation. In response, AID anthropologists helped design and implement a system to distribute hoes through local cooperative organizations.

Applied anthropologists often act as consultants for farmers in underdeveloped areas such as rural India.

This plan for the distribution of hoes reflects the development of new strategies on the part of AID and the facilitator role for applied anthropology. Most of the development work sponsored by AID and applied anthropology in the 1950s and 1960s was aimed at large-scale development projects such as hydroelectric dams and other forms of mechanized agriculture and industrialism. Many of these large-scale projects, however, have resulted in unintended negative consequences. In the preceding chapter, we saw how the Green Revolution frequently led to increasing inequality and a mechanized agriculture system that was expensive, inefficient, and inappropriate. Often these large-scale projects were devised in terms of the modernization views proposed by economists such as Walt Rostow (see Chapter 13) and were designed to shift an underdeveloped country to industrialism very rapidly.

Most recently, AID and applied anthropologists have modified their policies on development projects in many less developed countries. They now focus on projects that involve small-scale economic change with an emphasis on the development of appropriate technologies. Rather than relying on large-scale projects to have "trickle-down" influences on local populations, applied anthropologists have begun to focus more realistically on determining where basic needs must be fulfilled. After assessing the needs of the local population, the applied anthropologist can help facilitate change by helping people learn new skills.

THE ANALYST ROLE

One project that placed applied anthropologists in decision-making and analytical roles was run by Allan Holmberg of Cornell University. In the 1950s and 1960s, Holmberg and Mario Vasquez, a Peruvian anthropologist, developed what is known as the Vicos Project in the Andean highlands. Vicos is the name of a *hacienda* that was leased by Cornell in 1952 as part of a program to increase education and literacy, improve sanitation and health care, and teach new agricultural methods to the Andean Indians. Prior to the Vicos Project, these Indians were peasant farmers who were not able to feed themselves. Their land on the *hacienda* was broken into small plots that were insufficient to raise potato crops. The Indians were indebted to the *hacendado* and were required to work on the hacendado's fields without pay to service their debts.

Although the applied anthropologists took on the role of a new patron to the Indians, the overall aim was to dissolve historic patterns of exploitation and to guide the Indians toward self-sufficiency (Holmberg, 1962; Chambers, 1985). The Indians were paid for their labor and were also introduced to new varieties of potatoes, fertilizers, and pesticides. New crops such as leafy vegetables and foods such as eggs and fruit were introduced into their diet.

Through an educational program, the Indians became acquainted with forms of representative democratic organization. Developing more independence, they eventually overturned the traditional authority structure of the *hacienda*. In 1962, the Indians purchased the land of the *hacienda* from its former owners, which gave the Indians a measure of self-sufficiency. Overall, the Vicos Project led to basic improvements in housing, nutrition, clothing, and health conditions for the Indians. It also served as a model for similar projects in other parts of the world.

THE REPRESENTATIVE ROLE

Problems sometimes arise between applied anthropologists and private developers or government officials. Many developers and governments want to induce modernization and social change as rapidly as possible with capital-intensive projects, hydroelectric dams, and manufacturing facilities. In many cases, anthropologists have recommended against these innovations because of their expense and inefficient use of labor resources and the heavy cost to communities. (For example, as discussed in Chapter 16, anthropologist Billie DeWalt argued that the majority of Mexicans were not receiving benefits from the adoption of mechanized agriculture, which was being encouraged by the government.) Political officials, however, often ignore these recommendations because they are committed to programs that serve their political and personal interests. In these circumstances, applied anthropologists are often forced to take an advocacy approach, or the representative role, which means supporting the interests of the people who will be directly affected by policies and projects.

In Chapter 13, we discussed the activities of advocacy organizations such as Cultural Survival, founded by David Maybury-Lewis in 1972, which is actively engaged in trying to reduce the costs imposed by globalization on small-scale societies. Driven by trade deficits and gigantic foreign debts, many governments in developing countries want to extract as much wealth as possible from their national territories. Highway expansion, mining operations, giant hydroelectric projects, lumbering, mechanized agriculture, and other industrial developments all intrude on the traditional lifestyle and territory of small-scale societies. Applied anthropologists connected with groups such as Cultural Survival try to obtain input from the people themselves and help them represent their interests to the government or private developers.

Maybury-Lewis (1985) admits that the advocacy role in anthropology is extremely difficult, requiring great sensitivity and complex moral and political judgments. Most recently, as discussed in Chapter 13, many small-scale societies and minority groups in developing countries are organizing themselves to represent their own interests. This has resulted in the diminished role of the applied anthropologist as advocate or representative. Generally, anthropologists are pleased when their role as advocates or representative is diminished because these roles are called for only when native people are dominated by forces from globalization that are beyond their control.

THE FUTURE OF APPLIED ANTHROPOLOGY

An increasing number of anthropologists have become practitioners of applied anthropology rather than pursuing careers in basic research or academia. The National Association of Applied Anthropologists (NAPA) numbers about five hundred members, approximately 10 percent of the profession. The Society for Applied Anthropology is a well-established group publishing a respected scholarly journal titled *Human Organization* as well as the bulletin *Practicing Anthropology*. According to a 1990 survey, 50 percent of those with doctorates in anthropology develop careers outside the academic arena (Givens & Fillmore, 1990). Many of these graduates are employed in public agencies such as AID and the National Institutes of Health (NIH), but some also work for private firms.

Medical Anthropology

Another branch of applied anthropology is known as **medical anthropology,** the study of disease, health-care systems, and theories of disease and curing. Medical anthropologists study **epidemiology,** which examines disease patterns in different societies. For example, these anthropologists provide nutritional data to help determine whether coronary (heart) disease or cancer is related to particular dietary habits, such as the consumption of foods high in sodium or saturated fats. They also study various methods of treating illnesses—for example, shamanism. These studies can often help health providers to design more effective means for delivering health care.

An illustration of medical anthropology is the work of Louis Golomb (1985), who conducted ethnological research on the curing practices among different ethnic and religious communities in Thailand. Golomb did research on Buddhist and Muslim medical practitioners who rely on native spiritualistic beliefs to diagnose and cure diseases. These practices are based on earlier Hindu, magical, and animistic beliefs that had been syncretized with Buddhist and Muslim traditions. Many of these medical practitioners are themselves Buddhist monks or Muslim religious teachers.

ANTHROPOLOGISTS AT WORK

John McCreery: Applying Anthropology in Japan

This chapter has some examples of anthropologists who work outside the academic setting. John McCreery is an anthropologist who has lived in Japan since 1980 and has developed a productive and fruitful career in the area of advertising. For a number of years, he worked as a copywriter and creative director for Hakuhodo Incorporated, Japan's second largest advertising agency. In 1984, he and his wife and business partner Ruth McCreery founded The Word Works, a supplier of translation, copywriting, and presentation support services to Japanese and other clients with operations in Japan. While earning his living as Vice President and Managing Director of The Word Works, he is also a lecturer in the Graduate Program in Comparative Culture at Sophia University in Tokyo. There he teaches seminars on "The Making and Meaning of Advertising" and "Marketing in Japan." When asked, "How did an anthropologist get into advertising?" he replies, "In Taiwan I studied magicians. In Japan I joined the guild."

As an undergraduate in the Honors College at Michigan State University, McCreery had studied Philosophy and Medieval History. In the summer after his junior

year, a friend recommended that he take a course in East African Ethnography taught by anthropologist Marc Swartz. The course and the thought of doing research that involved travel to exotic places were fascinating. Another friend was studying Chinese, and noting that an anthropologist should have some experience with a non-Indo-European language, McCreery decided to study Chinese as well. One thing led to another, and he wound up in graduate school at Cornell University, doing a Ph.D. in anthropology and preparing to do research in Chinese anthropology. McCreery's first field research was in Puli, a market town in central Taiwan, where he and Ruth McCreery lived and worked from September 1969 to August 1971. He returned to Taiwan in 1976–77, the summer of 1978, and again in 1983.

At Cornell University McCreery studied with Victor Turner. In Taiwan, McCreery focused his ethnographic study on religious traditions and worked with a Taoist master Tio Se-lian. Both Victor Turner and Tio Se-lian were teachers with a willingness to listen, a flair for the dramatic, a passion for detail, and a breadth of humanity that moved all those with whom they came in contact. They, and

John McCreery.

senior creative director Kimoto Kazuhiko, who shared these earlier mentors' traits and gave McCreery his job at Hakuhodo, are the models he tries to emulate in his work.

McCreery's essays on Chinese religion and ritual have appeared in *The Journal of Chinese Religions* and *American Ethnologist.* He is also the author of a forthcoming book on Japanese consumer behavior, *Japanese Consumer Behavior: From Worker Bees to Wary Shoppers.* McCreery maintains his contact with other anthropologists through an internet listserve, Anthro-list, which provides lively discussions on ethnographic and theoretical issues in the field. Anthropologists from many backgrounds participate on this listserve. As a student you may want to become involved in lurking or participating on this listserve yourself.

These practitioners acquire and use a wide variety of knowledge involving astrology, faith healing, massage, folk psychotherapy, exorcism, herbs, and charms and amulets to treat patients. Although most of these practitioners acquire their initial training in rural areas, many move to urban regions such as Bangkok to treat patients. Two major types of practitioners exist in Thailand. The most traditional practitioners are curer-magicians or shamans, who diagnose and treat every illness as an instance of spirit possession or spirit attack. Other practitioners are more skeptical of supernatural causation of illness and diagnose health problems in reference to natural or organic causes. They frequently use herbal medicines to treat illnesses.

Golomb discovered that even when Western-based scientific forms of medicine are available, many Thais still rely on traditional practitioners. He found that even the urban-educated elite, including those who had studied in the United States and other Western countries, adhered to both supernatural and scientific cosmological views. Golomb referred to this as *therapeutic pluralism*. Patients in Thailand do not rely on any single therapeutic approach; they use a combination of therapies combining elements of ritual, magic, and modern scientific medications. Parasites or germs are rarely accepted as the only explanations of disease; a sick person may go to a clinic to receive medication to relieve symptoms but may then seek out a traditional curer for a more complete treatment. Golomb emphasized that the multiplicity of alternative therapies encourages people to play an active role in preserving their health.

In Thailand, as in many other countries undergoing modernization, modern medical facilities have been established based on the scientific treatment of disease. Golomb studied the impact of the introduction of modern health care on the traditional systems of medicine. He found that personnel in these facilities are critical of traditional medical practices and that many traditional healers have incorporated modern medicines such as antibiotics into their therapies. Other modern medicines to treat colds, headaches, and diarrhea are available in the village shops.

Golomb discovered that although the people in the villages often respect the modern doctor's ability to diagnose diseases and prescribe medications to relieve symptoms, in most cases they don't accept the scientific explanation of the disease. In addition, villagers feel that modern medical methods are brusque and impersonal, because doctors do not offer any psychological or spiritual consolation. Doctors do not make house calls and rarely spend much time with patients. The impersonality of the doctor-patient relationship is also due to social-status differences based on wealth, education, and

Medical anthropologists do studies to help improve basic health care delivery in countries around the world.

power. Golomb found that many public-health personnel expected deference from their rural clientele. For these reasons, many people preferred to rely on traditional curers.

Through his study of traditional medical techniques and beliefs, Golomb isolated some of the strengths and weaknesses of the introduction of modern medicine to Thailand. His work contributed to a better understanding of how to deliver health-care services to rural and urban Thais. For example, the Thai Ministry of Public Health began to experiment with ways of coordinating the efforts of modern and traditional medical practitioners. Village midwives and traditional herbalists were called on to dispense modern medications and pass out information about nutrition and hygiene. Some Thai hospitals have established training sessions for traditional practitioners to learn modern medical techniques. Golomb's studies in medical anthropology offer a model for practical applications in the health field for other developing societies.

APPLIED ANTHROPOLOGY AND SUBSTANCE ABUSE

Another area of research and policy formulation for applied medical anthropologists is substance abuse. For example, Michael Agar (1973, 1974) did an in-depth study of heroin addicts based on a description of U.S. society, and its therapeutic agencies in particular, from the addict's point of view. His research involved taking on the role of a patient himself so that he could participate in some of the problems that exist between patients and staff. From that perspective he was better able to understand the "junkie" worldview.

Through his research, Agar was able to isolate problems in the treatment of heroin addiction. For example, he found that when the drug methadone was administered by public-health officials as a substitute for heroin, many heroin addicts not in treatment became addicted to methadone, which was sold on the streets by patients. This street methadone would often be combined with wine and pills to gain a "high." In some cases, street methadone began to rival heroin as the preferred drug, being less expensive than heroin, widely available, and in a form that could be taken orally rather than injected. By providing this information, Agar helped health officials monitor their programs more effectively.

In a more recent study, Philippe Bourgois spent three and a half years investigating the use of crack cocaine in Spanish Harlem in New York City. In his award-winning ethnography *In Search of Respect: Selling Crack in El Barrio* (1996), Bourgois noted that policymakers and drug-enforcement officials minimize the influences of poverty and low status in dealing with crack addiction. Through his investigation of cultural norms and socioeconomic conditions in Spanish Harlem, Bourgois demonstrated

Some applied anthropologists have been doing studies of drug addiction to assist agencies in the prevention of drug use.

402 CHAPTER 17 Applied Anthropology

that crack dealers are struggling to earn money and status in the pursuit of the American Dream. Despite the fact that many of crack dealers have extensive experience with the jobs, they find that most of the jobs, such as in construction and factory work, are reserved for non-Hispanics. Other unpleasant experiences in the job world lead many to perceive crack dealing as the most realistic route toward upward mobility. Most of the inner-city youths who deal crack are high school dropouts who do not regard entry-level, minimum-wage jobs as steps to better opportunities. In addition, they perceive the underground economy as an alternative to becoming subservient to the larger society. Crack dealing offers a sense of autonomy, position, and rapid, short-term mobility. Bourgois compared the use of crack to the millenarian movements such as the Ghost Dance of Native Americans or the cargo cults of Melanesia. As he observed:

Substance abuse in general, and crack in particular, offer the equivalent of a millenarian metamorphosis. Instantaneously, users are transformed from being unemployed, depressed high school dropouts, despised by the world—and secretly convinced that their failure is due to their own inherent stupidity, "racial laziness," and disorganization—into being a mass of heart-palpitating pleasure, followed only minutes later by a jaw-gnashing crash and wideawake alertness that provides their life with concrete purpose: get more crack—fast! (1989b: 11)

Bourgois's depictions of the culture and economy of crack dealers and users provided policy suggestions. He concluded that most accounts of crack addiction deflect attention away from the economic and social conditions of the inner city and that by focusing on the increases of violence and terror associated with crack, U.S. society is absolved from responsibility for inner-city problems. He suggested that rather than use this "blame-the-victim" approach, officials and policymakers need to revise their attitudes and help develop programs that resolve the conditions that encourage crack use.

Applied Archeology: Cultural Resource Management

One subfield of applied anthropology is applied archaeology. One of the problems that faces humanity is how to preserve the cultural heritage of peoples from the past. Preservation of the past is a key concern to archaeologists, as archaeological sites are being destroyed at an alarming rate. This destruction is the result of a number of factors. One is the natural environment: erosion and the decomposition of organic material contribute to the disappearance of archaeological sites. By far the greatest threat to the archaeological record, however, is human activity—collectors prize treasures from the past such as arrowheads and pottery. To fulfill the demands of the antiquities market, archaeological sites in many world areas are looted by *pot hunters* who dig into sites to retrieve artifacts for collectors, ignoring the traces of ancient housing, burials, and cooking hearths. Removed from their context with no record of where they came from, such artifacts are of limited value to archaeologists.

The destruction of archaeological sites also results from the conflict of the present with the past. Construction projects such as dams, roads, buildings, and pipelines all disturb the ground and can destroy archaeological sites in the process. In many instances, archaeologists work only a few feet ahead of construction equipment, trying to salvage any information they can before a site disappears forever. One of the most spectacular examples of salvage archaeology arose as a result of the construction of a dam across the Nile River at Aswan, Egypt, in the 1960s. The project offered many benefits, including water for irrigation and the generation of electricity. However, the rising water behind the dam threatened hundreds of archaeological sites that had lain undisturbed and safely buried by desert sand for thousands of years. Among the threatened sites was the temple of Pharaoh Rameses II at Abu Simbel, a huge monument consisting of four colossal figures carved from a cliff face on the banks of the Nile. With help from the United Nations Educational, Scientific, and Cultural Organization (UNESCO), the Egyptian government was able to cut the monument into over a thousand pieces, some weighing as much as 33 tons, and reassemble them above the floodwaters. Today the temple of Rameses can be seen completely restored only a few hundred feet from its original location. Numerous other archaeological sites threatened by the flooding of the Nile were partly salvaged or recorded. Unfortunately, countless other sites throughout the world have not been so lucky.

The rate at which archaeological sites are being destroyed is particularly distressing because the archaeological record is a *nonrenewable resource;* that is, after the sites are destroyed, no others will be created to replace them. In many parts of the world, recognition of this fact has led to legislation aimed at protecting archaeological sites.

PRESERVING THE PAST

The first legislation in the United States designed to protect historic sites was the Antiquities Act of 1906, which safeguards archaeological sites on federal lands (see Table 17.1). Other, more recent legislation has extended protection to sites threatened by projects that are funded or regulated by the government. This legislation has had a dramatic impact on the number of archaeologists in the United States and has created a new area of specialization generally referred to as **cultural resource management (CRM).** Whereas most archaeologists had traditionally found employment teaching or working in museums, many are now working as applied archaeologists, evaluating, salvaging, and protecting archaeological resources that are threatened with destruction. Applied archaeologists conduct surveys before construction begins to determine if any sites will be affected. Government agencies such as the Forest Service have developed comprehensive programs to discover, record, protect, and interpret archaeological resources on their lands (Johnson & Schene, 1987).

The restoration of Abu Simbel in Egypt. Preserving artifacts from past civilizations will present a major challenge for anthropologists in the coming decades.

Unfortunately, current legislation in the United States leaves many archaeological resources unprotected. In many countries, excavated artifacts, even those located on privately owned land, become the property of the government. This is not the case in the United States. One example of the limitations of the existing legislation is provided by the case of Slack Farm, located near Uniontown, Kentucky (Fagan, 1995). Archaeologists had long known that an undisturbed Native American site of the Late Mississippian period was located on the property. Dating roughly to between 1450 and 1650, the site

Table 17.1   Major Federal Legislation for the Protection of Archaeological Resources in the United States

Antiquities Act of 1906	Protects sites on federal lands
Historic Sites Act of 1935	Provides authority for designating National Historic Landmarks and for archaeological survey before destruction by development programs
National Historic Preservation Act of 1966 (amended 1976 and 1980)	Strengthens protection of sites via National Register and integrates state and local agencies into national program for site preservation
National Environmental Policy Act of 1969	Requires all federal agencies to specify impact of development programs on cultural resources
Archaeological Resources Protection Act of 1979	Provides criminal and civil penalties for looting or damaging sites on public and Native American lands
Convention on Cultural Property of 1982	Authorizes U.S. participation in 1970 UNESCO convention to prevent illegal international trade in cultural property
Cultural Property Act of 1983	Provides sanctions against U.S. import or export of illicit antiquities

Source: From Wendy Ashmore and Robert J. Sharer, *Discovering Our Past: A Brief Introduction to Archaeology* (Mountain View, CA: Mayfield, 1988), p. 203.

was particularly important because it was the only surviving Mississippian site from the period of first contact with Europeans. The Slack family, who had owned the land for many years, protected the site and prevented people from digging. When the property was sold in 1988, however, conditions changed. Anthropologist Brian Fagan (1995: 18) described the results:

> Ten pot hunters from Kentucky, Indiana, and Illinois paid the new owner of the land $10,000 for the right to "excavate" the site. They rented a tractor and began bulldozing their way through the village midden to reach graves. They pushed heaps of bones aside and dug through dwellings and potsherds, hearths, and stone tools associated with them. Along the way, they left detritus of their own—empty pop-top beer and soda cans—scattered on the ground alongside Late Mississippian pottery fragments. Today Slack Farm looks like a battlefield—a morass of crude shovel holes and gaping trenches. Broken human bones litter the ground, and fractured artifacts crunch underfoot.

The looting at the site was eventually stopped by the Kentucky State Police, using a state law that prohibits the desecration of human graves. Archaeologists went to the site attempting to salvage what information was left, but there is no way of knowing how many artifacts were removed. The record of the prehistoric past of America was irrevocably damaged.

Regrettably, the events at Slack Farm are not unique. Many states lack adequate legislation protecting archaeological sites on private land. For example, Arkansas had no laws protecting unmarked burial sites until 1991. As a result, Native American burial grounds were systematically mined for artifacts. In fact, a recent article was titled "The Looting of Arkansas" (Harrington, 1991). Although Arkansas now has legislation prohibiting the unauthorized excavation of burial grounds, the professional archaeologists of the Arkansas Archaeological Survey face the impossible job of trying to locate and monitor all of the state's archaeological sites. As in other states, much of their success is largely due to the active involvement of amateur archaeologists and concerned citizens who bring archaeological remains to their attention. The preservation of the past needs to be everyone's concern.

Cultural Relativism and Human Rights

A recent development that has had wide-ranging consequences for applied anthropology and ethnological research involves the ways in which anthropologists assess and respond to the values and norms of other societies. Recall our discussion of *cultural relativism,* the principle that other societies must be understood through their own cultural values, beliefs, norms, and behaviors. Some critics have charged that anthropologists (and other people) who adopt this position cannot (or will not) make value judgments concerning values, norms, and practices of any society. If this is the case, then how can anthropologists encourage any conception of human rights that would be valid for all of humanity? Must anthropologists accept such practices as infanticide, caste and class inequalities, and female subordination out of fear of forcing their own values on other people?

RELATIVISM RECONSIDERED

These criticisms have led some anthropologists to reevaluate the basic assumptions regarding cultural relativism. In his 1983 book *Culture and Morality: The Relativity of Values in Anthropology,* Elvin Hatch recounted the historical acceptance of the cultural-relativist view. As we saw in Chapter 6, this was the approach of Franz Boas, who challenged the unilineal-evolutionary models of nineteenth-century anthropologists like E. B. Tylor, with their underlying assumptions of Western cultural superiority. Boas's approach, with its emphasis on tolerance and equality, appealed to many liberal-minded Western scholars.

However, belief in cultural relativism led to the acceptance by some anthropologists of the early twentieth century to **ethical relativism,** the notion that we cannot impose the values of one society on other societies. Ethical relativists argued that because anthropologists had not discovered any universal moral values, each society's values were valid with respect to that society's circumstances and conditions. No society could claim any superior position over another regarding ethics and morality.

As many philosophers and anthropologists have noted, the argument of ethical relativism is a circular one that itself assumes a particular moral position. It is in fact a moral theory that encourages people to be tolerant toward all cultural values, norms, and practices. Hatch notes that in the history of anthropology many who accepted the premises of ethical relativism could not maintain these assumptions in light of their data. Ethical relativists would have to tolerate practices such as homicide, child abuse, human sacrifice, torture, warfare, racial discrimination, and even genocide. In fact, even anthropologists who held the ethical-relativist position in the early period of the twentieth century condemned many cultural practices. For example, Ruth Benedict condemned the practice of the Plains Indians who cut off the nose of an adulterous wife. Boas himself condemned racism, anti-Semitism, and other forms of bigotry. Thus, these anthropologists did not consistently adhere to the ethical-relativist paradigm.

The horrors associated with World War II eventually led most scholars to reject ethical relativism. The argument that Nazi Germany could not be condemned because of its unique moral and ethical standards appeared ludicrous to most people. In the 1950s, some anthropologists such as Robert Redfield suggested that general standards of judgment could be applied to most societies. However, these anthropologists were reluctant to impose Western standards on prestate societies. In essence, they suggested a double standard in which they could criticize large-scale, industrial state societies but not prestate societies.

However, this double standard of morality poses problems. Can anthropologists make value judgments about homicide, child abuse, warfare, torture, rape, and other acts of violence in a small-scale society? Why should they adopt different standards in evaluating such behaviors in prestate societies as compared with industrial societies? In both types of societies, human beings are harmed. Don't humans in all societies have equal value?

A POSSIBLE RESOLUTION TO THE PROBLEM OF RELATIVISM

There may be a possible resolution to these philosophical and moral dilemmas. First, he emphasized that we need to distinguish between cultural relativism and ethical relativism. In other words, to understand the values and worldviews of another

people does not mean to accept all of their practices and standards. Second, we need to realize that the culture of a society is not completely homogeneous or unified. In Chapter 3, we noted how culture was distributed differentially within any society. For example, the same "culture" is not shared by men and women in any society. Ethnographic experience tells anthropologists that there are always people who may not agree with the content of the moral and ethical values of a society. Treating cultures as 'uniform united wholes' is a conceptual mistake. For one thing it ignores the power relationships within a society. Those who impose harmful practices upon others may be the beneficiaries of those practices.

To get beyond the problem of ethical relativism, we ought to adopt a humanitarian standard that would be recognized by all people throughout the world. This standard would not be derived from any particular cultural values—such as the U.S. Declaration of Independence—but rather would involve the basic principle that every individual is entitled to a certain standard of "well-being." For example, no individual ought to be subjected to bodily harm through violence or starvation.

Of course, we recognize certain problems with this solution. Perhaps the key problem is that people in many societies accept—or at least appear to accept—behaviors that we would condemn as inhumane. For example, what about the Aztec practice of human sacrifice? The Aztecs firmly believed that they would be destroyed if they did not sacrifice victims to the sun deity. Would an outside group have been justified in condemning and abolishing this practice? A more recent case involves the West Irian tribe known as the Dani, who engaged in constant warfare with neighboring tribes. They believed that through revenge they had to placate the ghosts of their deceased kin killed in warfare, because unavenged ghosts bring sickness and disaster to the tribe. Another way of placating the ghosts was to bring two or three young girls related to the deceased victim to the funeral site and chop two fingers off their hands. Until recently, all Dani women lost from two to six fingers in this way (Heider, 1979; Bagish, 1981). Apparently these practices were accepted by Dani males and females.

Other examples of these types of practices, such as headhunting, slavery, female subordination, torture, and unnecessarily dangerous child labor, also fall into this category. According to a universal humanitarian standard suggested here, all of these practices could be condemned as harmful behaviors.

THE PROBLEM OF INTERVENTION

The condemnation of harmful cultural practices with reference to a universal standard is fairly easy. The abolition of such practices, however, is not. Anthropologists recommend that one should take a pragmatic approach in reducing these practices. Sometimes intervention into the cultures in which practices such as genocide is occurring would be a moral imperative. This intervention would not proceed from the standpoint of specific Western values but from the commonly recognized universal standards of humanitarianism.

Such intervention, however, must proceed cautiously and be based on a thorough knowledge of the society. In addition, the cultural practice must be shown to clearly create pain and suffering for people. When these elements are present, intervention should take place in the form of a dialogue.

As is obvious, these suggestions are based on the highly idealistic standards of a universal humanitarianism. In many cases, intervention may not be possible, and in some cases, intervention to stamp out a particular cultural practice may cause even greater problems. In Chapter 13, we saw how outside intervention adversely affected such peoples as the Ju/'hoansi, the Mbuti, and the Yanomamö. Communal riots or group violence may result from the dislocation of certain cultural practices. Thus caution, understanding, and dialogue are critical to successful intervention.

UNIVERSAL HUMAN RIGHTS

Nevertheless, the espousal of universally recognized standards to eradicate harmful practices is a worthwhile, albeit idealistic, goal. Since the time of the Enlightenment, Western societies have prided themselves on extending human rights. Many Western theorists emphasize that human rights have spread to other parts of the world through globalization, thus providing the catalyst for social change, reform, and political liberation. At the same time, as people from other non-Western societies can testify, the West has also promoted intolerance, racism, and genocide. Western society has not always lived up to the ideals of its own tradition.

THE ROLE OF APPLIED ANTHROPOLOGY

Ethnologists and applied anthropologists have a role in helping to define the universal standards for human rights in all societies. By systematically studying community standards, applied anthropologists can determine whether practices are harmful and then help provide solutions for reducing these harmful practices. This may involve consultation with local government officials and dialogue with members of the community to resolve the complex issues regarding the identified harmful practices.

An illustration of this type of research and effort by applied anthropologists is the work of John Van Willigen and V. C. Channa (1991), who have done research on the harmful consequences of the dowry in India. As discussed in Chapter 15, India, like some other primarily agricultural societies, has the cultural institution known as the *dowry,* in which the bride's family gives a certain amount of cash or other goods to the groom's family upon marriage. Recently, the traditions of the dowry have led to increasing cases of what has been referred to as "dowry death" or "bride burning." Some husbands or their families have been dissatisfied with the amount of the dowry that the new wife brings into the family. Following marriage, the family of the groom begins to make additional demands for more money and goods from the wife's family. These demands result in harassment and abuse of the wife, culminating in murder. The woman is typically burned to death after being doused with kerosene, hence the use of the term bride burning.

Dowry deaths have increased in recent years. In 1986, 1,319 cases were reported nationally in India. There are many other cases in which the evidence is more ambiguous, however, and the deaths of these women might be reported as kitchen accidents or suicides (Van Willigen & Channa, 1991). In addition, another negative result of the burdens imposed by the dowry tradition has led many pregnant women to pay for *amniocentesis* (a medical procedure to determine the health status of the fetus) as a means to determine the sex of the fetus.

If the fetus is female, in many cases Indians have an abortion partly because of the increasing burden and expense of raising a daughter and developing a substantial dowry for marriage of the daughter. Thus, male children are preferred and female fetuses are selectively aborted.

Van Willigen, an American anthropologist, and Channa, an Indian anthropologist, studied the dowry problem together. They found that the national laws established against the institution of the dowry (the Dowry Prohibition Act of 1961, amended in 1984 and 1986) are very tough. The law makes it illegal to give or take a dowry, but the laws are ineffective in restraining the practice. In addition, a number of public-education groups have been organized in India. Using slogans such as Say No to Dowry, they have been advertising and campaigning against the dowry practices. Yet, the problem continues to plague India.

After carefully studying the dowry practices of different regions and local areas of India, Van Willigen and Channa concluded that the increase in dowry deaths was partially the result of the rapid inflationary pressures of the Indian economy as well as the demands of a consumer-oriented economy. Consumer price increases have resulted in the increasing demands for more dowry money to buy consumer goods. It has become increasingly difficult to save resources for a substantial dowry for a daughter or sister that is satisfactory to the groom's family. Van Willigen and Channa found that aside from wealth, family "prestige" that comes with wealth expenditures is sought by the groom's family.

From the perspective of the bride's family, dowry payments provide for present consumption and future earning power for their daughter through acquiring a husband with better connections and future earning potential. In a less developed society such as India, with extremely high unemployment and rapid inflation, the importance of investing in a husband with high future earning potential is emphasized. When asked why they give a dowry when their daughters are being married, people respond, "because we love them." The decision by the groom's family to forgo the dowry would also be very difficult.

There appears to be a very positive commitment to the institution of the dowry in India. Most people have given and received a dowry. Thus, declaring dowry a crime technically makes many people criminals. Van Willigen and Channa recommended that to be effective, the antidowry practices must be displaced by other, less problematic practices, and that the apparent causes of the practice be attacked. Women's property rights must be examined so as to increase their economic access. Traditional Hindu cultural norms regarding inheritance, which give sons the right from birth to claim the so-called ancestral properties, must be reformed. At present, male descendants inherit property, but females must pay for marriage expenses and dowry gifts. Van Willigen and Channa asserted that a gender-neutral inheritance law in which women and men receive equal shares ought to be established to help reduce the discrepancy between males and females in India.

In addition, Van Willigen and Channa recommended the establishment of universal marriage registration and licenses throughout India. This may enable the government to monitor dowry abuses so that antidowry legislation could be more effective. These anthropologists concluded that a broad program to increase the social and economic status of women, along with more rigorous control of marriage registration and licensing, will be more effective in solving the dowry death problem in Indian society.

Applied anthropologists utilize their research to help develop human rights for women in India and in other areas of the world.

This example of applied anthropology, based on the collaboration between Western and non-Western anthropologists to solve a fundamental human rights issue represents a commendable strategy for applied anthropologists in the future. It is hoped that through better cross-cultural understanding aided by ethnological research, and through applied anthropology, universally recognized and humanitarian standards will become widely adopted throughout the world. Many anthropologists are promoting *advocacy anthropology,* the use of anthropological knowledge to further human rights. Universal human rights would include the right to life and freedom from physical and psychological abuse, including torture; freedom from arbitrary arrest and imprisonment, freedom from slavery and genocide, the right to nationality, freedom of movement and departure from one's country, the right to seek asylum in other countries because of persecution in one's own country, rights to privacy, ownership of property, freedom of speech, religion, and assembly, the rights of self-determination, and the right to adequate food, shelter, health care, and education (Sponsel, 1996). Obviously, not all of these rights exist in any society at present. However, most people will probably agree that these rights ought to be part of any society's obligations to its people.

As people everywhere are brought closer together with the expansion of the global village, different societies will experience greater pressures to treat one another in sensitive and humane ways. We live in a world in which our destinies are tied to one another more closely than they have ever been. Yet it is a world containing many different societies with varied norms and practices. Sometimes this leads to mutual distrust and dangerous confrontations.

Anthropologists may be able to play a role in helping to bring about mutual understanding, to help to understand one another's right to existence. Perhaps through this understanding we may be able to develop a worldwide, pluralistic *metaculture,* a global system emphasizing fundamental human rights, with a sense of political and global responsibility. This cross-cultural understanding and mutual respect for human rights may be the most important aspect of anthropological research today.

SUMMARY

Applied anthropology is one of the specializations that has offered new opportunities for anthropologists to serve as consultants to public and private agencies to help solve local and global human problems. Applied anthropologists cooperate with government officials and others in establishing economic development projects, health-care systems, and substance-abuse programs. They serve in a variety of roles to help bring about solutions to human problems.

Recent development within the field of archaeology is cultural resource management, or applied archaeology. Legislation passed by state and federal authorities in the United States requires the preservation of both prehistoric and historic materials. Applied archaeologists are involved in identifying important sites that may be endangered by development. They con-

duct surveys and excavations to preserve data that are important to understanding the cultural heritage of the United States. Cultural resource management offers new career opportunities for archaeologists in government agencies, universities, and consulting firms.

Early ethnologists who accepted the tenets of cultural relativism sometimes also embraced ethical relativism, the idea that a person could not make value judgments about other societies. Although most anthropologists reject ethical relativism, the issue of universal standards to evaluate values and harmful cultural practices is still problematic. Proposing universal standards to make value judgments and help reduce harmful cultural practices remains one of the most important tasks for applied anthropology and future ethnological research.

STUDY QUESTIONS

1. What is applied anthropology? Erve Chambers suggests that there are five roles that applied anthropologists play. Discuss each of these roles as they apply to present-day applied anthropological studies.

2. Why do you think the advocacy role in anthropology is so difficult, requiring great sensitivity and complex moral and political judgment? Can you give an example of this type of applied anthropology?

3. What is medical anthropology? What are some of the types of things that medical anthropologists do?

4. What is cultural resource management?

5. Examine the concepts of cultural relativism and ethical relativism. Can an anthropologist be involved in applied anthropology and adhere to either of these principles or views? Are there any problems associated with an ethical relativist perspective?

6. Is it possible to understand the values and worldview of another culture and not accept all of their practices and standards? In other words, can one be a cultural relativist and not an ethical relativist at the same time?

7. Do you think it is possible to adopt a humanitarian standard that would be accepted by everyone in the world? What might this view entail?

8. Is there such a thing as universal human rights?

KEY TERMS

applied anthropology
cultural resource management

epidemiology
ethical relativism

medical anthropology
social-impact studies

INTERNET EXERCISES

1. Please visit the website **http://www.falcon-one.com/arch.html** and read about the cultural landscape of the Hudson River. How have historical archaeologists "discovered" that a landscape is an artifact? What is the purpose of this type of study? Why is historical archaeology necessary, as history records events during periods covered by these studies? How does the particular study in this website relate to cultural resource management?

2. Review the World Health Organization press release at **http://www.who.org/whr/1999/en/** **pressrelease.htm.** Look at the table on life expectancies. How can the field of applied anthropology help in understanding the differences in life expectancies between countries? When looking at the table on malaria mortality rates, notice that worldwide rates have dropped dramatically, whereas sub-Saharan Africa rates have not dropped much. What can applied anthropologists do to help reduce these rates?

SUGGESTED READINGS

CHAMBERS, ERVE. 1985. *Applied Anthropology: A Practical Guide*. Englewood Cliffs, NJ: Prentice Hall. A thorough introduction to the field of applied anthropology, with many examples of how anthropologists resolve social problems.

JOHNSON, RONALD W., and MICHAEL G. SCHENE. 1987. *Cultural Resources Management*. Malabar, FL: Robert E. Krieger. A compilation of essays focusing on the management of archaeological resources and the preservation of standing historic monuments. The work serves as a useful introduction to cultural resource management and the diverse problems confronting archaeologists in their efforts to preserve the past.

PARTRIDGE, WILLIAM, ed. 1984. *Training Manual in Development Anthropology*. Special publication of the American Anthropological Association and the Society for Applied Anthropology, no. 17. A series of essays by applied anthropologists who served as consultants for development projects. These essays identify the potential conflicts that arise in planning and consulting on such projects and provide illustrations of how the conflicts were resolved.

PODOLEFSKY, AARON, and PETER J. BROWN, eds. 1997. *Applying Cultural Anthropology: An Introductory Reader,* 3rd ed. Mountain View, CA: Mayfield. A reader containing state-of- the-art essays on how cultural anthropologists apply their research skills and knowledge to solve problems in health care, economic development, business, agricultural development, and law.

Glossary

Acheulian   The technology associated with *Homo erectus*.

achieved status   A status that results at least in part from a person's specific actions.

adaptation   The process in which an organism makes a successful adjustment to a specific environment.

adjudication   The settling of legal disputes through a formal, centralized authority.

age grades   Statuses defined by age, through which a person moves in the course of his or her lifetime.

age sets   Corporate groups of people who are about the same age and share specific rights, obligations, duties, and privileges in their community.

age stratification   The unequal allocation of wealth, power, and prestige among people of different ages.

agribusiness   Commercialized, mechanized agriculture.

ambilineal descent group   A corporate kinship group formed by choosing to trace relationships through either a male or a female line.

anatomically modern *Homo sapiens*   The most recent form of human, distinguished by a unique anatomy that differs from that of earlier, archaic *Homo sapiens*.

animism   The belief that the world is populated by spiritual beings such as ghosts, souls, and demons.

anthropology   The systematic study of humankind.

apartheid   A political, legal, and social system developed in South Africa in which the rights of different population groups were based on racial criteria.

applied anthropology   The use of data gathered from the other subfields of anthropology to find practical solutions to problems in a society.

archaeology   The discipline that focuses on the study of the artifacts from past societies to determine the lifestyles, history, and evolution of those societies.

archaic *Homo sapiens*   The earliest form of *Homo sapiens,* dating back more than 200,000 years.

artifacts   The material products of past societies.

artificial selection   The process in which people select certain plants and animals for breeding.

ascribed status   A status that is attached to a person from birth, for example, sex, caste, and race.

assimilation   The adoption of the language, culture, and ethnic identity of the dominant group in a society by other groups.

authority   Power generally perceived by members of society as legitimate rather than coercive.

balanced reciprocity   A direct type of reciprocal exchange with an explicit expectation of immediate return.

band   The least complex and, most likely, the oldest form of a political system.

barter   The direct exchange of one commodity for another; it does not involve the use of money.

beliefs   Specific cultural conventions concerning true or false assumptions shared by a particular group.

bilateral descent   A descent system that traces relatives through both maternal and paternal sides of the family simultaneously.

biodiversity   The genetic and biological variation within and among different species of plants and animals.

biome   An area dominated by a particular climate and distinguished by the prevalence of certain types of plants and animals.

bipedalism   The ability to walk erect on two hind legs.

bridewealth   Transfer of some form of wealth from the descent group of the groom to that of the bride.

capitalism   An economic system in which natural resources as well as the means of producing and distributing goods and services are privately owned.

cargo cult   Revitalization movements in Papua New Guinea that involve beliefs that Western goods are produced by supernatural forces.

carrying capacity   The upper limit of the size of a population that a specific environment can support.

caste   A social grouping into which a person is born and remains throughout his or her lifetime.

chief   A person who owns, manages, and controls the basic productive factors of the economy and has privileged access to strategic and luxury goods.

411

chiefdom A political system with a formalized and centralized leadership, headed by a chief.

circumstantial model A model of ethnicity that focuses on the situations and circumstances that influence ethnic interaction.

clan A form of descent group in some societies whose members trace their descent to an unknown ancestor or, in some cases, to a sacred plant or animal.

closed peasant communities Indian communities in highland areas of Latin America that were isolated from colonialism and the market economy.

closed society A society in which social status is generally ascribed rather than achieved.

Clovis hypothesis The hypothesis that the first humans entered the Americas about 13,500 B.C.

colonies Societies that are controlled politically and economically by a dominant society.

command economy An economic system in which a political elite makes the decisions concerning production, prices, and trade.

communication The act of transferring information.

complementary opposition A system in which kinship groups within a segmentary lineage organization can be allies or antagonists.

composite tool Tools made from several components, such as harpoons or spears.

conflict approach A major anthropological perspective; it argues that benefits accrue only to the dominant groups and that state organization is very costly to the subordinate groups such as the peasantry.

core societies Powerful industrial nations that have exercised economic hegemony over other regions.

correlation The simultaneous occurrence of two variables.

cosmologies Ideas that present the universe as an orderly system, including answers to basic questions about the place of humankind.

cross-cousin marriage A system in which a person marries the offspring of parental siblings of the opposite sex; for example, a male marries his mother's brother's daughter.

crude birthrate The number of live births in a given year for every thousand people in a population.

crude death rate The number of deaths in a given year for every thousand people.

cultural anthropology The subfield of anthropology that focuses on the study of contemporary societies.

cultural ecology The systematic study of the relationships between the environment and society.

cultural hegemony The control over values and norms exercised by the dominant group in a society.

cultural materialism A research strategy that focuses on technoenvironmental and economic factors as key determinants in sociocultural evolution.

cultural relativism The view that cultural traditions must be understood within the context of a particular society's responses to problems and opportunities.

cultural resource management The attempt to protect and conserve artifacts and archaeological resources for the future.

cultural universals Essential behavioral characteristics of humans found in all societies.

culture A shared way of life that includes material products, values, beliefs, and norms that are transmitted within a particular society from generation to generation.

culture of poverty The hypothesis that sets of values sustaining poverty are perpetuated generation after generation within a community.

culture shock A severe psychological reaction that results from adjusting to the realities of a society radically different from one's own.

deculturation The loss of traditional patterns of culture.

deductive method A scientific research method that begins with a general theory, develops a specific hypothesis, and tests it.

demographic transition theory A model used to understand population changes within a society through different stages, concluding in the decline of fertility and mortality rates in advanced industrial societies.

demography The study of population and its relationship to society.

dependency theory The theory that underdevelopment in Third World societies is the result of domination by capitalist, industrial societies.

dependent variable A variable whose value changes in response to changes in the independent variable.

descent group A corporate group identified by a person that traces his or her real or fictive kinship relationships.

dialect Linguistic patterns involving differences in pronunciation, vocabulary, or syntax that occur within a common language family.

dialectical materialism A view of sociocultural evolution that focuses on the continuous interactions among the infrastructure, structure, and superstructure.

diffusionism The spread of cultural traits from one society to another.

division of labor The specialization of economic roles and activities within a society.

dominance hierarchy The relative social status or ranking order found in some primate social groups.

doubling time The period of time required for a population to double.

dowry Goods and wealth paid by the bride's family to the groom's family.

drives Basic, inborn, biological urges that motivate human behavior.

dyadic contract A reciprocal exchange arrangement between two individuals.

ecclesiastical religions Religious traditions that develop in state societies and combine governmental and religious authority.

ecology The study of living organisms in relationship to their environment.

economy The social relationships that organize the production, distribution, and exchange of goods and services.

egalitarian A type of social structure that emphasizes equality among different statuses.

enculturation The process of social interaction through which people learn their culture.

endogamy Marriage between two people of the same social group or category.

environmental determinism A theory based on the assumption that the physical environment directly causes human action and thought.

environmental niche A locale that contains various plants, animals, and other ecological conditions to which a species must adjust.

environmental possibilism The theory that the physical environment limits or selects certain possibilities for sociocultural development.

epidemiology The study of disease patterns in a society.

ethical relativism The belief that the values of one society should never be imposed on another society.

ethnic group A group that shares a culture.

ethnicity Cultural differences among populations usually based on attributes such as language, religion, lifestyle, and cultural ideas about common descent or specific territory.

ethnocentrism The practice of judging another society by the values and standards of one's own.

ethnocide A process in which a dominant group or society forces other groups to abandon their traditional language and culture.

ethnogenesis The emergence of a new ethnic group.

ethnography A description of a society written by an anthropologist who conducted field research in that society.

ethnology The subfield of anthropology that focuses on the study of different contemporary cultures throughout the world.

ethologist A scientist who studies the behaviors of animals in their natural setting.

ethos Socially acceptable norms in a society.

evolution Process of change within a species over time.

evolutionary psychology The study of the mind using evolutionary findings.

exogamy Marriage between people of different social groups and categories.

extended family A type of family made up of parents, children, and other kin relations residing together as a social unit.

false consciousness The inability of groups in a society to discern their own interests.

family A social group of two or more people related by blood, marriage, or adoption who reside together for an extended period, sharing economic resources and caring for their young.

family of orientation The family into which people are born and receive basic enculturation.

family of procreation The family within which people have or adopt children of their own.

famine Epidemic starvation and widespread death from starvation-related diseases.

fecundity The potential number of children women are capable of bearing.

feminism The belief that women are equal to men and should have equal rights and opportunities.

fertility The number of births in a society.

feud A type of armed combat between groups in a community.

feudalism A decentralized form of political economy based on landed estates, which existed during different historical periods in agrarian societies.

fictive kinship ties   Extrafamilial social ties that provide mutual-aid work groups.

First World   The sector of the global economy that is composed of modern industrialized capitalist societies.

fissioning   The movement of people from one group to another area when their population begins to increase and food or other resources become scarce.

folkways   Norms guiding ordinary usages and conventions of everyday life.

foraging society   Another classification used for a hunting-and-gathering society.

forensic anthropology   The identification of human skeletal remains for legal purposes.

fossil   The preserved remains of bones and living materials from earlier periods.

functionalism   An anthropological perspective based on the assumption that society consists of institutions that serve vital purposes for people.

gender   Specific behavioral traits attached to each sex by a society and defined by culture.

generalized reciprocity   A type of reciprocal exchange based on the assumption that an immediate return is not expected and that the value of the exchange will balance out in the long run.

genes   Discrete units of hereditary information that determine specific physical characteristics of organisms.

genetics   The study of genes, the units of heredity.

genocide   The physical extermination of a particular ethnic group in a society.

genotype   The specific genetic constitution of an organism.

gerontocracy   Rule by elders (usually males) who control the material and reproductive resources within the community.

globalization   The worldwide impact of industrialization and its socioeconomic, political, and cultural consequences on the world.

goods   Elements of material culture produced from raw materials in the natural environment, ranging from the basic commodities for survival to luxury items.

grammar   A finite set of rules that determines how sentences are constructed to produce meaningful statements.

greenhouse effect   Global warming caused by the trapping of heat from solar rays by carbon dioxide, preventing it from radiating back into space.

hamula   Arabic term for clan-like organization.

heredity   The origin of variations within populations of plants and animals associated with the passing on of traits from one generation to another.

hierarchical society   A society in which some people have greater access than others to wealth, rank, status, authority, and power.

historical linguistics   The comparison and classification of different languages to explore the historical links among them.

historical particularism   An approach to studying human societies in which each society has to be understood as a unique product of its own history.

holistic   A broad comprehensive approach to the study of humankind drawing on the four fields of anthropology, integrating both biological and cultural phenomena.

hominid   The family of primates that includes modern humans and their direct ancestors who share distinctive types of teeth, jaws, and bipedalism.

horticulture   A form of agriculture in which a limited, nonmechanized technology is utilized to cultivate plants.

hunter-gatherer   A society that depends on hunting animals and gathering vegetation for subsistence.

hypodescent concept   A system in which children of mixed parentage acquire the social and racial status of the parent whose social and racial status is lower.

hypothesis   A testable proposition concerning the relationship among different variables within the collected data.

ideal culture   What people say they do or should do.

ideology   Cultural symbols and beliefs that reflect and support the interests of specific groups in a society.

imperialism   Economic and political domination and control over other societies.

incest   Sexual relations or marriage between certain relatives.

incest avoidance   Avoidance of sexual relations and marriage with members of one's own family.

incest taboo   Strong cultural norms that prohibit sexual relations or marriage with members of one's own family.

independent variable   Causal variable that produces an effect on another variable, the dependent variable.

inductive method   A method of investigation in which a scientist first makes observations and collects data and then formulates a hypothesis.

industrial society   A society that uses sophisticated technology based on machinery powered by advanced fuels to produce material goods.

industrialization   The use of machines and other sophisticated technology to satisfy the needs of society.

infanticide Deliberate abandonment or killing of infants 1 year of age or younger.

infant mortality rate The number of babies per thousand births in any year who die before reaching the age of 1.

instincts Fixed, complex, genetically based, unlearned behaviors that promote the survival of a species.

integrationist perspective A school of thought within political anthropology that assumes that society as a whole benefits from the organization of the political state.

intensive agriculture The cultivation of crops by preparing permanent fields year after year, often including the use of irrigation and fertilizers.

intensive horticulture A method of crop production by irrigating, fertilizing, hoeing, and terracing hillsides.

jati Hindi term for caste.

jajmani Hindi term for traditional caste-based economy in India.

kindred Overlapping relatives from both sides of a family whom an individual recognizes as being part of his or her descent group.

kinesics The study of body motion and gestures used in nonverbal communication.

knowledge The storage and recall of learned information.

kula A form of reciprocal exchange involving ceremonial items in the Trobriand islands.

language A system of symbols with standard meanings through which members of a society communicate with one another.

laws Norms defined by political authorities as principles that members of a society must follow.

levirate The rule that a widow is expected to marry one of her deceased husband's brothers.

lexicon The basic vocabulary needed to cope in a particular environment.

life expectancy The average number of years a person can expect to live.

lineages Descent groups comprised of relatives, all of whom trace their relationship through consanguineal or affinal relations to an actual, commonly known ancestor.

linguistic relativism The theory that language molds habits of both cognition and perception.

linguistics The study of language.

logic-of-growth model The model and set of values that suggest that economic growth and technological developments will always represent progress for society.

marginal environment An environment that is not suitable for intensive agriculture.

market economy A pattern of economic exchange based on the value of goods and services as determined by the worldwide supply and demand of these items.

marriage A social bond between two or more people sanctioned by society that involves economic cooperation and culturally approved sexual activity.

material culture Tangible products of human society.

matrilineal descent group A corporate descent group within which members calculate descent through the female line from a commonly known female ancestor.

matrilocal residence A rule of postmarital residence in which a man resides with his wife's parents.

medical anthropology The study of disease, health care systems, and theories of disease and curing in different societies.

mercantilism A system in which the government regulates the economy of a state to ensure economic growth, a positive balance of trade, and the accumulation of wealth, usually gold and silver.

middens Artifacts often found in sites of ancient dumps or trash heaps.

migration rate The rate at which people move into and out of a specific territory.

modernization Economic, social, political, and religious change that is interrelated with modern industrial and technological developments.

modernization theory A theory that the forces associated with industrialization will eventually transform all societies into modern, industrial states.

moieties Descent groups made up of clans or phratries that form two groups, dividing the entire society into equal divisions.

molecular dating A system for dating the divergence among different species by comparing amino acid sequences or DNA material.

money A durable medium of exchange, based on a standard value, that is used to purchase goods and services.

monocropping An agricultural system in which land is utilized exclusively to produce one crop.

monogamy A form of marriage that involves one spouse of each sex.

monopoly capitalism A form of capitalism dominated by oligopolies that can reduce free competition through the concentration of capital.

mores Stronger norms than folkways; violators are usually punished severely.

morphemes The smallest units of a language that convey meaning.

morphology The study of morphemes.

mortality The incidence of death in a society's population.

Mousterian technology The technology associated with Neanderthal in Europe.

multinational corporation A transnational economic organization that operates in many different regions and is not necessarily associated with any one country.

multiregional evolutionary hypothesis The view that *Homo sapiens* evolved from *Homo erectus* concurrently in different regions of the world.

myth Assumed knowledge about the universe, the natural and supernatural worlds, and humanity's place therein.

nationalism Strong sense of loyalty to the nation-state based on shared language, values, and culture.

nation-states Political communities that have clearly defined territorial borders with centralized authority.

natural selection A theory presented by Darwin and Wallace that nature or environmental circumstances determine which characteristics are essential for survival. Individuals with these characteristics survive and pass them on to their offspring.

negative reciprocity The opposite of reciprocity involving getting something for nothing.

neocolonialism The argument that multinational corporations exploit the nonindustrialized world to supply the industrialized world with natural resources and cheap labor.

Neolithic The New Stone Age, representing the shift from food gathering to food production.

net migration The total movement of a population into and out of a territory.

niche A locale that contains various plants, animals, and other ecological phenomena to which a species must adjust.

nonmaterial culture Intangible products of human society, including values, beliefs, and knowledge.

norms Shared rules that define how people are supposed to behave under certain circumstances.

nuclear family A family that is composed of two parents and their immediate biological offspring or adopted children.

oath The attempt to call on a supernatural source of power to sanction and bear witness to the truth or falseness of an individual's testimony.

office A formal, corporate position of authority in a group or society.

Oldowan The earliest types of tools found in the Olduvai Gorge in East Africa.

one-drop rule American social and legal custom of classifying anyone with one black ancestor, regardless of how far back, as black.

open peasant communities Communities in which peasants are involved in producing some of their crops for the world market.

open society A society in which social status can be achieved through individual efforts.

oracle A person, sacred object, or shrine believed to have special or supernatural abilities.

paleoanthropology The study of human evolution through the analysis of fossil remains.

paradigm A set of beliefs, assumptions, techniques, ideals, and research strategies that influence observations and conclusions.

parallel-cousin marriage A system in which a person marries the offspring of parental siblings of the same sex; for example, a male marries his father's brother's daughter.

participant observation The method by which the ethnologist learns the culture of the group being studied by participating in the group's daily activities.

pastoralists Groups whose subsistence activities center on the care of domesticated animals.

patriarchal Male-dominated societies.

patrilineal descent group A corporate group made up of people who trace their descent through males from a common, known male ancestor.

patrilocal residence A postmarital residence rule in which a newly married couple must reside with the husband's father.

patron-client ties Informal contracts between people of unequal status.

peasants People who cultivate land in the rural areas for their basic subsistence and pay tribute to elite groups.

peripheral societies Societies that exercise little control over their own economies and are dominated by the core industrial societies.

personality Stable patterns of thought, feeling, and action associated with a specific person.

phenotype The characteristics of an organism that are shaped in part by the genotype and the organism's unique life history in a particular environment.

phoneme A basic unit of sound that distinguishes meaning in a language.

phones Units of sound in a language.

phonology The study of the sounds made in speech.

phratries Umbrella-like social groupings that consist of two or more clans.

plural society A society made up of different ethnic groups.

political power The ability to achieve personal ends in spite of opposition.

polyandry Marriage between a female and more than one male.

polygamy Marriage involving a spouse of one sex and two or more spouses of the opposite sex.

polygyny Marriage between one male and two or more females.

population A group of organisms that interbreeds and occupies a given territory at the same time.

postindustrial society A society in which the tertiary or service sector of the economy predominates.

potlatch A form of redistributional exchange found among many Northwest Native American groups.

pre-Clovis hypothesis The hypothesis that humans entered the Americas about 30,000 years ago, a much earlier date than that proposed by the Clovis hypothesis.

priest A full-time, formally trained, male religious specialist.

priestess A full-time, formally trained, female religious specialist.

primary sector The sector of an industrial economy that is devoted to the extraction of natural resources.

primates A diverse order of mammals, including humans, monkeys, and apes, that share similar characteristics.

primatology The study of primates.

primogeniture An inheritance pattern in which land or other wealth is transmitted from generation to generation through the eldest male.

primordial model A model of ethnicity emphasizing the fundamental determinants of language, descent, locale, or religion.

protolanguage The parent language for many ancient and modern languages.

proxemics The study of how people in different societies perceive and use space.

psychological anthropologist An anthropologist who studies the interrelationship between the individual and culture, or enculturation.

purdah Arabic term for seclusion of women from men in public.

qualitative data Nonstatistical information that tends to be the most important aspect of ethnological research.

quantitative data Data that can be expressed as numbers, including census materials, dietary information, and income and household-composition data.

racism Beliefs and practices that advocate the superiority of certain races and the inferiority of others.

random sample A representative sample of people of various ages or statuses in a society.

real culture People's actual behaviors, as opposed to ideal culture.

reciprocal economic system An exchange system based on transactional exchanges among family groups that allocate goods and services throughout the community.

reciprocity The exchange of goods and services among people.

redistributional economic exchange A system that involves the exchange of goods and services through a centralized organization.

regional symbiosis The pattern in which a particular society resides in an ecological habitat divided into different resource areas that become interdependent.

relative deprivation A group's awareness of the absence of economic opportunities and political rights for its members in contrast to those for other groups.

replacement model A paleoanthropological hypothesis that *Homo sapiens* evolved in one area of the world and replaced earlier hominid populations.

revitalization movement A social movement by people faced with dramatic changes that is designed to reinstitute traditional cultural values and beliefs.

revolution Sudden, dramatic, sweeping change that usually involves the overthrow of a government.

rising expectations The process in which a particular group begins to experience improvements in living conditions, stimulating the desire for further improvements.

rites of legitimation Rituals that reinforce the authority of a ruler.

rites of passage   Rituals associated with the life cycle and the movement of people between different age-status levels.

rituals   Repetitive behaviors that communicate sacred symbols to members of society.

role   A set of expected behavior patterns, obligations, and norms attached to a particular status.

Sapir–Whorf hypothesis   A hypothesis that assumes a close relationship between language and culture; it claims that language defines people's experiences.

scientific method   A method used to investigate the natural and social world; it involves critical thinking, logical reasoning, and skeptical thought.

secondary sector   The sector of an industrial economy that is devoted to processing raw materials into manufactured goods.

Second World   In the terminology of the Cold War, the industrial socialist societies in the global economy.

secularization   The decline in the influence of religion in a society.

segmentary lineage system   A type of political organization in which multiple descent groups form at different levels and serve political functions.

semantics   The meaning of words, phrases, and sentences.

semiperipheral societies   Societies that have some degree of industrialization and some economic autonomy in the world economy but are not as advanced as core societies.

services   Elements of nonmaterial culture derived from cultural knowledge in the form of specialized skills that benefit others, such as giving spiritual comfort or medical care.

sex   Biological and anatomical differences between males and females.

sexism   Prejudice and discrimination against people based on their sex.

shamans   Part-time religious specialists who are believed to be linked with supernatural beings and powers.

signs   Meanings that are directly associated with concrete physical phenomena.

situational learning   A type of learning in which organisms adjust their behavior in response to direct experience.

social-impact studies   Research on the possible consequences of change in a society.

socialism   An economic system in which the state owns the basic means of production.

social learning   A type of learning in which an organism observes another organism's response to a stimulus and then adds that response to its own collection of behaviors.

social stratification   Inequality of statuses in a society.

social structure   The sum of the patterns of relationships in a society.

society   A group of people who reside within a specific territory and share a common culture.

sociobiology   The systematic study of the biological basis of social behavior, including the development of culture.

sociolinguistics   The systematic study of language use in various social settings to explore the links between language and social behavior.

sodalities   Groups based on kinship, age, gender, or other principles that provide for political organization.

sorcery   A conscious magical strategy, often using different objects, that is believed to bring about either harmful or beneficial results.

sororate   The marriage rule requiring a widower to marry one of his deceased wife's sisters.

species   Groups of organisms with similar physical characteristics that can potentially interbreed successfully.

state   A form of political system with centralized bureaucratic institutions to establish power and authority over large populations in clearly defined territories.

status   A recognized position that a person occupies in a society.

strata   A group of equivalent statuses based on ranked divisions within a society.

structural linguistics   An area of research that investigates the structure of language patterns as they presently exist.

subsistence patterns   The means by which people obtain their food supply.

sumptuary rules   Cultural norms and practices that are used to differentiate higher-status groups from lower-status groups.

sustainability model   A model that emphasizes the conservation and preservation of environmental resources for future generations.

symbolic anthropology   The study of culture through the interpretation of a society's symbols, values, beliefs, and ethos.

symbolic learning   The ability to use and understand symbols.

symbols Arbitrary units of meaning that can stand for different concrete or abstract phenomena.

syncretism The blending of indigenous religious beliefs and practices with those introduced by outside groups.

syntax Rules for phrase and sentence construction in a language.

technology All the human techniques and methods of reaching a specific goal in subsistence or in modifying or controlling the natural environment.

tertiary sector The sector of an industrial economy devoted to services.

theocracy A society in which people are believed to rule not because of their worldly wealth and power but because of their place in the moral and sacred order.

theodicy Religious-based, meaningful explanations for unknown phenomena.

theories Interconnected hypotheses that offer general explanations of natural or social phenomena.

Third World In the terminology of the Cold War, premodern, nonindustrialized societies in the global economy.

totem A mythical ancestor, usually a plant or animal, that symbolizes a particular group.

trial-and-error learning Another phrase used for situational learning, in which organisms adjust their behavior in response to direct experience.

tribe Complex societies having political institutions that unite horticulturalist or pastoralist groups into a political system.

ultimogeniture An inheritance system in which property and land are passed to the youngest son.

underdeveloped society A country with a low gross national product.

unilineal descent group A lineage group that traces its descent through only one side of the lineage or through only one sex.

unilineal evolution The belief, widespread during the nineteenth century, that societies were evolving in a single direction toward complexity and industrial progress.

universalistic religions Religions whose spiritual messages apply to all of humanity.

Upper Paleolithic The late Stone Age, dating back to about 40,000 years ago.

values Standards by which a society defines what is desirable and undesirable.

variable A datum that varies from case to case.

voluntary association A political, religious, recreational, or occupational group that people can join freely.

warfare Armed combat among territorial or political communities.

witchcraft The innate, unconscious psychic ability of some people, which is believed to bring about harmful effects.

world-systems theory The view that core societies dominate peripheral and semiperipheral societies to create a global economic system.

worldview An integrated system of beliefs and cosmologies about natural and supernatural realities.

References

ABERLE, DAVID F. 1961. "'Arctic Hysteria' and Latah in Mongolia." In Yehudi Cohen, ed., *Social Structure and Personality. A Casebook*. New York: Holt, Rinehart and Winston.

———. 1966. *The Peyote Religion Among the Navajo*. New York: Wenner-Gren Foundation for Anthropological Research, Inc.

ABU-LUGHOD, JANET. 1961. "Migrant Adjustment to City Life: The Egyptian Case." *The American Journal of Sociology* 62:22–32.

ABU-LUGHOD, LILA. 1987. *Veiled Sentiments: Honor and Poetry in a Bedouin Society*. Berkeley: University of California Press.

ADAMS, ROBERT MCC. 1966. *The Evolution of Urban Society*. Chicago: Aldine.

———. 1974. "Anthropological Perspectives on Ancient Trade." *Current Anthropology* 15(3):239–258.

———. 1981. *Heartland of Cities*. Chicago: Aldine.

AGAR, MICHAEL. 1973. *Ripping and Running*. New York: Academic Press.

———. 1974. *Cognition and Ethnography*. Minneapolis: Burgess.

———. 1980. *The Professional Stranger: An Informal Introduction to Ethnography*. New York: Academic Press.

AL-THAKEB, FAHAD. 1981, July–December. "Size and Composition of the Arab Family: Census and Survey Data." *International Journal of Sociology of the Family* 2:171–178.

———. 1985. "The Arab Family and Modernity: Evidence from Kuwait." *Current Anthropologist* 25(5):575–580.

ALVERSON, HOYT. 1994. *Semantics and Experience: Universal Metaphors of Time in English, Mandarin, Hindi, and Sesotho*. Baltimore, MD: Johns Hopkins University Press.

AMERICAN ANTHROPOLOGICAL ASSOCIATION. 1976. Rev. ed. 1983. *Professional Ethics: Statements and Procedures of the American Anthropological Association*. Washington, DC: American Anthropological Association.

ANDERSON, BENEDICT. 1983. *Imagined Communities: Reflections on the Origin and Spread of Nationalism*. London: Verso.

ANDERSON, RICHARD L. 1989. *Art in Small-Scale Societies*. Englewood Cliffs, NJ: Prentice Hall.

ANUMAN-RAJADHON, PHYA. 1961. "Thai Traditional Salutation." *Journal of the Siam Society* 49(2):161–171.

BAGISH, HENRY H. 1981. *Confessions of a Former Cultural Relativist*. Santa Barbara, CA: Santa Barbara City College Publications.

BAKER, LESLIE. 1989. "Cultural Survival Imports: Marketing the Rain Forest." *Cultural Survival Quarterly* 13(3):64–67.

BALIKCI, ASEN. 1970. *The Netsilik Eskimo*. Garden City, NY: Natural History Press.

BAMBERGER, JOAN. 1974. "The Myth of Matriarchy: Why Men Rule in Primitive Society." In Michelle Zimbalist Rosaldo and Louise Lamphere, eds., *Women, Culture, and Society*. Stanford, CA: Stanford University Press.

BANTON, MICHAEL. 1998. *Racial Theories*. Cambridge: Cambridge University Press.

BARASH, DAVID P. 1987. *The Hare and the Tortoise: Culture, Biology, and Human Nature*. New York: Penguin.

BARKOW, J. H., L. COSMIDES, AND J. TOOBY, eds. 1992. *The Adapted Mind: Evolutionary Psychology and the Generation of Culture*. New York: Oxford University Press.

BARNOUW, VICTOR. 1985. *Culture and Personality*, 4th ed. Homewood, IL: Dorsey Press.

BARRETT, LEONARD E. 1977. *Rastafarians: Sounds of Cultural Dissonance*. Boston: Beacon Press.

BARRETT, RICHARD A. 1984. *Culture and Conduct: An Excursion in Anthropology*. Belmont, CA: Wadsworth.

BARRET, RICHARD E. AND LI, FANG. 1999. *Modern China*. New York: McGraw-Hill.

BARTH, FREDERICK. 1961. *Nomads of South Persia: The Basseri Tribe of the Khamseh Confederacy*. Boston: Little, Brown.

———. 1969. *Ethnic Groups and Boundaries*. Boston: Little, Brown.

———. 1975. *Ritual and Knowledge Among the Baktaman of New Guinea*. Oslo: Universitets Forlaget; New Haven, CT: Yale University Press.

BARTON, R. F. 1919. "Ifugao Law." *Publications in American Archeology and Ethnology*, Vol. 15, No. 1, pp. 92–109. Berkeley: University of California Press.

BASCOM, WILLIAM. 1969. *The Yoruba of Southwestern Nigeria*. New York: Holt, Rinehart and Winston.

BASSIS, MICHAEL S., RICHARD J. GELLES, AND ANN LEVINE. 1991. *Sociology: An Introduction*, 4th ed. New York: McGraw-Hill.

BATES, DANIEL G., AND AMAL RASSAM. 1983. *Peoples and Cultures of the Middle East*. Englewood Cliffs, NJ: Prentice Hall.

BECK, LOIS. 1986. *The Qashqa'i of Iran*. New Haven, CT: Yale University Press.

BECK, LOIS, AND NIKKI KEDDIE, eds. 1978. *Women in the Muslim World*. Cambridge, MA: Harvard University Press.

BEEMAN, WILLIAM O. 1986. *Language, Status, and Power in Iran*. Bloomington: Indiana University Press.

BEFU, HARUMI. 1971. *Japan: An Anthropological Introduction*. San Francisco: Chandler.

———. 1980. "A Critique of the Group Model of Japanese Society." *Social Analysis* 5(6):205–225.

BELL, DANIEL. 1973. *The Coming of the Post-Industrial Society: A Venture into Social Forecasting*. New York: Basic Books.

BELLAH, R., R. MADSEN, W. SULLIVAN, A. SWIDLER, AND S. M. TIP-
TON. 1985. *Habits of the Heart: Individualism and Commitment in American Life.* New York: Harper & Row.

BENEDICT, RUTH. 1928. "Psychological Types in the Cultures of the
Southwest." Reprinted in Margaret Mead, ed., *An Anthropologist
at Work: Writings of Ruth Benedict.* Boston: Houghton Mifflin.

———. 1934. *Patterns of Culture.* Boston: Houghton Mifflin.

———. 1946. *The Chrysanthemum and the Sword.* Boston:
Houghton Mifflin.

BENNETT, JOHN W. 1987. "Anthropology and the Emerging
World Order: The Paradigm of Culture in an Age of Interde-
pendence." In Kenneth Moore, ed., *Waymarks: The Notre
Dame Inaugural Lectures in Anthropology.* Notre Dame, IN:
University of Notre Dame Press.

BERDAN, FRANCES F. 1982. *The Aztecs of Central Mexico: An Imperial Society.* New York: Holt, Rinehart and Winston.

BERLIN, BRENT, AND PAUL KAY. 1969. *Basic Color Terms: Their
Universality and Evolution.* Berkeley: University of California
Press.

BERNARD, JESSIE. 1981. *The Female World.* New York: Free Press.

BERNARD, RUSSELL H. 1992. "Preserving Language Diversity."
Human Organization 51(1):82–89.

BERNARD, R. H., PERTTI PELTO, O. WERNER, J. BOSTER, K. A. ROM-
NEY, A. JOHNSON, C. EMER, AND A. KASAKOTT. 1986. "The Con-
struction of Primary Data in Cultural Anthropology." *Current
Anthropology* 27(4):382–396.

BERNARD, RUSSELL H., AND JESÚS SALINAS PEDRAZA. 1989. *Native
Ethnography: A Mexican Indian Describes His Culture.* New-
bury Park, CA: Sage.

BICKERTON, DEREK. 1985. *Roots of Language.* Ann Arbor, MI:
Karoma Publishing.

BINFORD, LEWIS. 1968. "Post-Pleistocene Adaptations." In Lewis
R. Binford and Sally Binford, eds., *New Perspectives in Archaeology,* pp. 313–341. New York: Academic Press.

BINFORD, LEWIS R., AND SALLY BINFORD. 1966. "A Preliminary
Analysis of Functional Variability in the Mousterian of Leval-
lois Facies." *American Anthropologist* 68(2):238–295.

BIRDSELL, JOSEPH B. 1968. "Some Predictions for the Pleisto-
cene Based on Equilibrium Systems Among Recent Hunter-
Gatherers." In Richard B. Lee and Irven Devore, eds., *Man the
Hunter.* Chicago: Aldine.

BIRDWHISTLE, RAY. 1970. *Kinesics and Context.* Philadelphia:
University of Pennsylvania Press.

BISHOP, J. A., L. M. COOK, AND J. MUGGLETON. 1978. "The Response of Two Species of Moths to Industrialization in Northwest England: II. Relative Fitness of Moths and Population
Size." In *Philosophical Transactions Royal Society of London*
B281:517–542.

BLICK, JEFFREY P. 1988. "Genocidal Warfare in Tribal Societies as
a Result of European-Induced Culture Conflict." *Man* 23:
654–670.

BLOCH, MAURICE. 1977. "The Past and the Present." *Man*
12:278–292.

———. 1983. *Marxism and Anthropology.* Oxford: Oxford University Press.

———. 1985. "From Cognition to Ideology." In R. Fardon, ed.,

*Power and Knowledge: Anthropological and Sociological Ap-
proaches.* Edinburgh: Scottish Academic Press.

BLURTON JONES, NICHOLAS. 1986. "Bushman Birth Spacing: A Test
for Optimal Intervals." *Ethology and Sociobiology* 7(2):91–106.

———. 1987. "Bushman Birth Spacing: Direct Tests of Some
Simple Predictions." *Ethology and Sociobiology* 8(3):183–204.

BOAS, FRANZ. 1930. *The Religion of the Kwakiutl,* Vol. 10, Part II.
New York: Columbia University Contributions to Anthropology.

———. [1940] 1966. *Race, Language, and Culture.* New York:
Free Press.

BODLEY, JOHN H. 1985. *Anthropology and Contemporary
Human Problems,* 2d ed. Mountain View, CA: Mayfield.

———. 1990. *Victims of Progress,* 3d ed. Mountain View, CA:
Mayfield.

BOEHM, CHRISTOPHER. 1993. "Egalitarian Behavior and Reverse
Dominance Hierarchy." *Current Anthropology* 34(3):227–254.

BOHANNON, PAUL, AND GEORGE DALTON. 1962. *Markets in Africa.*
Evanston, IL: Northwestern University Press.

BOOTH, WILLIAM. 1989. "Warfare Over Yanomamo Indians." *Science* 243:1138–1140.

BORDES, FRANÇOIS. 1968. *The Old Stone Age.* New York: Mc-
Graw-Hill.

BOSERUP, ESTER. 1965. *The Conditions of Agricultural Growth:
The Economics of Agrarian Change Under Population Pressure.* Chicago: Aldine.

———. 1970. *Women's Role in Economic Development.* London:
Allen & Unwin.

BOSTER, JAMES. 1987. "Agreement Between Biological Classification Systems Is Not Dependent on Cultural Transmission."
American Anthropologist 89(4):914–919.

BOURGOIS, PHILIPPE. 1989a. "Crack in Spanish Harlem: Culture
and Economy in the Inner City." *Anthropology Today* 5(4):
6–11.

———. 1989b. *Ethnicity at Work: Divided Labor on a Central
American Banana Plantation.* Baltimore: Johns Hopkins University Press.

———. 1996. *In Search of Respect: Selling Crack in El Barrio.*
Cambridge, England: Cambridge University Press.

BOURGUIGNON, ERIKA. 1979. *Psychological Anthropology: An Introduction to Human Nature and Cultural Differences.* New
York: Holt, Rinehart and Winston.

BRAIDWOOD, ROBERT J. 1960. "The Agricultural Revolution." *Scientific American* 203:130–141.

BROKENSHA, DAVID, AND CHARLES ERASMUS. 1969. "African 'Peasants' and Community Development." In David Brokensha and
Marion Pearsall, eds., *The Anthropology of Development in
Sub-Saharan Africa.* Society for Applied Anthropology Monograph No. 10, pp. 85–100.

BROOKE, JAMES. 1993, August 23. "Brazil's Outrage Intensifies as
Toll in Massacre Hits 73." *The New York Times,* p. A6.

BROWN, CECIL H. 1984. *Language and Living Things: Uniformities in Classification and Naming.* New Brunswick, NJ: Rutgers University Press.

BROWN, DONALD E. 1976. *Principles of Social Structure: Southeast Asia.* London: Duckworth Press.

———. 1991. *Human Universals*. New York: McGraw-Hill.

BROWN, JUDITH K. 1970a. "Economic Organization and the Position of Women Among the Iroquois." *Ethnohistory* 17: 151–167.

———. 1970b. "A Note on the Division of Labor by Sex." *American Anthropologist* 72:1073–1078.

BROWN, KAREN MCCARTHY. 1992. *Mama Lola: A Voodoo Priestess in Brooklyn* (Comparative Studies in Religion and Society, No. 4). Berkeley: University of California Press.

BROWN, LESTER R. 1988, March/April. "The Vulnerability of Oil-Based Farming." World Watch. Reprinted in Robert Jackson, ed., *Global Issues 90/91*. Sluice Dock, Guilford, CT: Dushkin Publishing Group, 1990.

BROWN, MICHAEL H. 1990. *The Search for Eve*. New York: HarperCollins.

BRUMFIEL, ELIZABETH. 1983. "Aztec State Making: Ecology, Structure, and the Origin of the State." *American Anthropologist* 85(2):261–284.

BURCH, ERNEST J., JR. 1970. "Marriage and Divorce Among the North Alaskan Eskimos." In Paul Bohannon, ed., *Divorce and After,* pp. 152–181. Garden City, NY: Doubleday.

BUTZER, KARL W. 1984. "Long-Term Nile Flood Variation and Political Discontinuities in Pharonic Egypt." In J. Desmond Clark and Steven A. Brandt, eds., *From Hunters to Farmers: The Causes and Consequences of Food Production in Egypt,* pp. 102–112. Berkeley: University of California Press.

CALLENDER, CHARLES, AND L. KOCHEMS. 1983. "The North-American Berdache." *Current Anthropology* 24:443–470.

CAMPBELL, BERNARD G. 1983. *Human Ecology: The Story of Our Place in Nature from Prehistory to the Present*. Chicago: Aldine.

———. 1987. *Humankind Emerging,* 5th ed. Glenview, IL: Scott, Foresman.

CANN, R. L., W. M. BROWN, AND A. C. WILSON. 1987. "Mitochondrial DNA and Human Evolution." *Nature* 325:31–36.

CARLISLE, R., ed. 1988. *Americans Before Columbus: Perspectives on the Archaeology of the First Americans*. Pittsburgh: University of Pittsburgh Press.

CARLISLE, R. C., AND J. M. ADAVASIO. 1982. *Collected Papers on the Archaeology of Meadowcroft Rockshelter and the Cross Creek Drainage*. Pittsburgh: Department of Anthropology, University of Pittsburgh.

CARNEIRO, ROBERT. 1961. "Slash and Burn Cultivation Among the Kuikura and Its Implications for Cultural Development in the Amazon Basin." In Johannes Wilbert, ed., *The Evolution of Horticultural Systems in Native South America, Causes and Consequences: A Symposium, Anthropologica*. Supplement Publication No. 2, pp. 47–67.

———. 1967. "On the Relationship Between Size of Population and Complexity of Social Organization." *Southwestern Journal of Anthropology* 23:234–243.

———. 1970, August 21. "A Theory of the Origin of the 'State.'" *Science,* pp. 733–738.

———. 1988. "Indians of the Amazonian Forest." In Julie Sloan Denslow and Christine Padoch, eds., *People of the Tropical Rain Forests*. Berkeley: University of California Press.

CARTER, GEORGE F. 1988. "Cultural Historical Diffusion." In Peter J. Hugill and Bruce D. Dickson, eds., *The Transfer and Transformation of Ideas and Material Culture*. College Station: Texas A & M University Press.

CATON, STEVEN C. 1986. "Salam Tahiyah: Greetings from the Highlands of Yemen." *American Ethnologist* 13(2):290–308.

CHAGNON, NAPOLEON A. 1974. *Studying the Yanomamö*. New York: Holt, Rinehart and Winston.

———. 1997. *Yanomamö,* 5th ed. Fort Worth, TX: Harcourt Brace College Publishers..

CHAGNON, NAPOLEON, AND RAYMOND HAMES. 1979. "Protein Deficiency and Tribal Warfare in Amazonia: New Data." *Science* 20(3):910–913.

CHAGNON, NAPOLEON, AND WILLIAM IRONS. 1979. *Evolutionary Biology and Human Social Behavior*. North Scituate, MA: Duxbury Press.

CHAMBERS, ERVE. 1985. *Applied Anthropology: A Practical Guide*. Englewood Cliffs, NJ: Prentice Hall.

CHANCE, NORMAN. 1984. *China's Urban Villagers: Life in a Beijing Commune*. New York: Holt, Rinehart and Winston.

CHANG, KWANG-CHIH. 1975. "From Archaeology to History: The Neolithic Foundations of Chinese Civilization." In Chang Chun-shu, ed., *The Making of China: Main Themes in Premodern Chinese History,* pp. 38–45. Englewood Cliffs, NJ: Prentice Hall.

———. 1976. *Early Chinese Civilization: Anthropological Perspectives*. Cambridge, MA: Harvard University Press.

———. 1986. *The Archaeology of Ancient China,* 4th ed. New Haven, CT: Yale University Press.

CHASE, P. G., AND H. L. DIBBLE. 1987. "Middle Paleolithic Symbolism: A Review of Current Evidence and Interpretations." *Journal of Anthropological Archaeology* 6:263–293.

CHILDE, V. GORDON. 1936. *Man Makes Himself*. London: Watts.

———. 1950. "The Urban Revolution." *Town Planning Review,* 21, 3–17.

———. 1952. *New Light on the Most Ancient East*. London: Routledge & Kegan Paul.

CHIROT, DANIEL. 1986. *Social Change in the Modern Era*. San Diego, CA: Harcourt Brace Jovanovich.

CHOMSKY, NOAM. 1980. *Rules and Representation*. New York: Columbia University Press.

CLAESSON, H. J. M., P. VAN DE VELDE, AND E. M. SMITH. 1985. *Development and Decline: The Evolution of Sociopolitical Organization*. South Hadley, MA: Bergin & Garvey.

CLAYRE, ALASDAIR. 1985. *The Heart of the Dragon*. Boston: Houghton Mifflin.

CLIFFORD, JAMES. 1983. "On Ethnographic Authority." *Representations* 1:118–146.

COE, MICHAEL. 1977. *Mexico,* 2d ed. New York: Praeger.

COE, MICHAEL, DEAN SNOW, AND ELIZABETH BENSON. 1986. *Atlas of Ancient America*. New York: Facts on File.

COHEN, ABNER. 1969. *Custom and Politics in Urban Africa*. Berkeley: University of California Press.

———. 1974. *Urban Ethnicity*. London: Tavistock.

COHEN, ANTHONY. 1996. "Personal nationalism: A Scottish View of some rites, rights, and wrongs." *American Ethnologist*, 23 (4),802-815.

COHEN, MARK NATHAN. 1977. *The Food Crisis in Prehistory*. New Haven, CT: Yale University Press.

———. 1994. Demographic Expansion: Causes and Consequences. In Ingold, Tim (ed.) *Companion Encyclopedia of Anthropology*. New York: Routledge.

COHEN, RONALD. 1978. "Introduction." In R. Cohen and E. Service, eds., *Origins of the State: The Anthropology of Political Evolution*. Philadelphia: ISHI.

COLE, DONALD POWELL. 1984. *Nomads of the Nomads: The Al-Murrah Bedouin of the Empty Quarter*. Prospect Heights, IL: Waveland Press.

COLE, MICHAEL, AND SYLVIA SCRIBNER. 1974. *Culture and Thought: A Psychological Introduction*. New York: Wiley.

COLLIER, JANE FISHBURNE. 1988. *Marriage and Inequality in Classless Societies*. Stanford, CA: Stanford University Press.

COMAROFF, JEAN. 1985. *Body of Power, Spirit of Resistance*. Chicago: University of Chicago Press.

CONNAH, GRAHAM. 1990. *African Civilizations: Precolonial Cities and States in Tropical Africa: An Archaeological Perspective*. Cambridge: Cambridge University Press.

CONNELL, DAN. 1987. "The Next African Famine." In *Dollars and Sense*. Reprinted in Robert Jackson, *Global Issues 90/91*, 6th ed. Sluice Dock, Guilford, CT: Dushkin Publishing Group, 1990.

COWGILL, DONALD O. 1986. *Aging Around the World*. Belmont, CA: Wadsworth.

CRAPANZANO, VINCENT. 1986. *Waiting: The Whites of South Africa*. New York: Random House.

CUSACK, JOHN T. 1986. "The International Narcotics Control System: Coca and Cocaine." In Deborah Pacini and Christine Franquenmont, eds., *Coca and Cocaine: Effects on People and Policy in Latin America*. Cultural Survival Report 23. Cambridge, MA: Cultural Survival, Inc.; Latin American Studies Program, Cornell University.

DAHLBERG, FRANCES, ed. 1981. *Woman the Gatherer*. New Haven, CT: Yale University Press.

D'ANDRADE, ROY G. 1989. "Cultural Cognition." In M. Posner, *Foundations of Cognitive Science*. Cambridge, MA: MIT Press.

DARWIN, CHARLES, AND E. MAYR. [1859] 1966. *The Origin of Species*. Facsimile of the 1st ed. Cambridge, MA: Harvard University Press.

DASEN, PIERRE, ed. 1977. *Piagetian Psychology: Cross-Cultural Contributions*. New York: Gardner Press.

DAVIDSON, BASIL. 1961. *The African Slave Trade*. Boston: Atlantic; Little, Brown.

DAVILA, MARIO. 1971. "Compadrazgo: Fictive Kinship in Latin America." In Nelson Graburn, ed., *Readings in Kinship and Social Structure*. New York: Harper & Row.

DAVIS, WADE. 1997. *The Serpent and the Rainbow*. New York: Touchstone Books.

DEBLIJ, HARM J., AND PETER O. MULLER. 1985. *Geography: Regions and Concepts,* 4th ed. New York: John Wiley.

DEGLER, CARL N. 1991. *In Search of Human Nature: The Decline and Revival of Darwinism in American Social Thought*. New York: Oxford University Press.

DEMAREST, WILLIAM J., AND BENJAMIN D. PAUL. 1981. "Mayan Migrants in Guatemala City." *Anthropology, UCLA* 11(12):43–73.

D'EMILIO, JOHN. 1988. *Intimate Matters: A History of Sexuality in America*. New York: Harper & Row.

DEVOE, PAMELA. 1992. "Refugee Work and Health in Mid-America." In Devoe, Pamela (ed.) *Selected Papers on Refugee Issues*. Arlington, VA: American Anthropological Association.

DEWALT, BILLIE. 1984. "Mexico's Second Green Revolution: Food for Feed." *Mexican Studies/Estudios Mexicanos* 1:29–60.

DIAMOND, JARED. 1993, February. "Speaking with a Single Tongue." *Discover*, pp. 78–85.

———. 1997. *Guns, Germs, and Steel: The Fates of Human Societies*. New York: W. W. Norton & Co.

DIAZ, MAY N. 1966. *Tonala: Conservatism, Responsibility and Authority in a Mexican Town*. Berkeley: University of California Press.

DICKEMANN, MILDRED. 1979. "Female Infanticide, Reproductive Strategies, and Social Stratification." In N. Chagnon and W. Irons, eds., *Evolutionary Biology and Human Social Behavior: An Anthropological Perspective*, pp. 321–367. North Scituate, MA: Duxbury Press.

DILLEHAY, THOMAS D. 1989. *Monte Verde: A Late Pleistocene Settlement in Chile,* Vol. 1. Washington, DC: Smithsonian Institution Press.

DILLEHAY, THOMAS D., AND DAVID J. MELTZER. 1991. *The First Americans: Search and Research*. Boca Raton, FL: CRC Press.

DIVALE, WILLIAM, AND MARVIN HARRIS. 1976. "Population, Warfare, and the Male Supremacist Complex." *American Anthropologist* 78:521–538.

DOBKIN DE RIOS, MARLENE. 1984. *Hallucinogens: Cross-Cultural Perspectives*. Albuquerque: University of New Mexico Press.

DONNAN, CHRISTOPHER B., AND McCLELLAND, DONNA. 1979. *The Burial Theme in Moche Iconography*. Washington, DC: Dunbarton Oaks.

DONNELLY, NANCY D. 1992. "The Impossible Situation of Vietnamese in Hong Kong's Detention Centers" in Devoe, Pamela (ed.) *Selected Papers on Refugee Issues*. Arlington, VA: American Anthropological Association.

DRENNAN, ROBERT D. 1987. "Regional Demography in Chiefdoms." In Robert D. Drennan and Carlos A. Uribe, eds., *Chiefdoms in the Americas*. New York: University Press of America.

DUMOND, DON E. 1972. "Population Growth and Political Centralization." In Brian Spooner, ed., *Population Growth: Anthropological Implications*. Cambridge, MA: MIT Press.

DUMONT, LOUIS. 1970. *Homo Hierarchicus: An Essay on the Caste System*. Trans. Mark Sainsburg. Chicago: University of Chicago Press.

DUNN, STEPHEN P., AND ETHEL DUNN. 1988. *The Peasants of Central Russia*. Prospect Heights, IL: Waveland Press.

DUPREE, LOUIS. 1980. *Afghanistan*. Princeton: Princeton University Press.

DURHAM, WILLIAM H. 1976. "Resource Competition and Human Aggression. Part I: A Review of Primitive War." *Quarterly Review of Biology* 51:385–415.

424   References

DURKHEIM, ÉMILE. 1915. *The Elementary Forms of Religious Life.* Trans. Joseph Ward Swain. London: Allen & Unwin.

DYSON-HUDSON, RADA, AND ERIC ALDEN SMITH. 1978. "Human Territoriality: An Ecological Reassessment." *American Anthropologist* 80(1):21–41.

EARLE, TIMOTHY. 1977. "A Reappraisal of Redistribution: Complex Hawaiian Chiefdoms." In T. Earle and J. Ericson, eds., *Exchange Systems in Prehistory.* New York: Academic Press.

———. 1987. "Chiefdoms in Archaeological and Ethnohistorical Perspective." *Annual Review of Anthropology* 16:299–308.

EATON, BOYD S., MARJORIE SHOSTAK, AND MELVIN KONNER. 1988. *The Paleolithic Prescription: A Program of Diet and Exercise and a Design for Living.* New York: Harper & Row.

EBERHARD, WOLFRAM. 1977. *A History of China,* 4th ed. Berkeley: University of California Press.

EDWARDS, DAVID. 1998. "Learning from the Swat Pathans: Political Leadership in Afghanistan, 1978–97." *American Ethnologist,* 25(4), 712–728.

EHRET, CHRISTOPHER, AND MERRICK POSNANSKY. 1982. *The Archaeological and Linguistic Reconstruction of African History.* Berkeley: University of California Press.

EICKELMAN, DALE F. 1976. *Moroccan Islam: Tradition and Society in a Pilgrimage Center.* Modern Middle East Series, Vol. 1. Austin and London: University of Texas Press.

———. 1982. "The Study of Islam in Local Contexts." *Contributions to Asian Studies* 17:1–16.

———. 1998. *The Middle East and Central Asia: An Anthropological Approach.* Upper Saddle River, NJ: Prentice Hall.

———. 1995. "Ethnicity." In John L. Esposito, ed., *The Oxford Encyclopedia of the Modern Islamic World,* Vol. I. New York: Oxford University Press.

EKMAN, PAUL. 1973. "Cross-Cultural Studies of Facial Expressions." In P. Ekman, ed., *Darwin and Facial Expression: A Century of Research in Review.* New York: Academic Press.

EKMAN, PAUL, WALLACE V. FRIESEN, AND JOHN BEAR. 1984. "The International Language of Gestures." *Psychology Today,* pp. 64–69.

ELIADE, MIRCEA. 1959. *The Sacred and the Profane: The Nature of Religion.* New York: Harper & Row.

EMBER, CAROL. 1978. "Myths About Hunter-Gatherers." *Ethnology* 17:439–448.

EMBER, MELVIN. 1975. "On the Origin and Extension of the Incest Taboo." *Behavior Science Research* 10:249–281.

EMBER, MELVIN, AND CAROL EMBER. 1971. "The Conditions Favoring Matrilocal Versus Patrilocal Residence." *American Anthropologist* 73:371–574.

———. 1979. "Male-Female Bonding: A Cross-Species Study of Mammals and Birds." *Behavior Science Research* 14:37–56.

ENDICOTT, KIRK. 1988. "The Basis of Egalitarian Social Relations Among the Batak Foragers of Malaysia." Paper read at the Eighty-Seventh Annual Meeting of the American Anthropological Association, Phoenix, AZ.

"Energy, Petroleum, and Coal, by Country." 1991. *Information Please Almanac,* 44th ed., pp. 146–147. Boston: Houghton Mifflin.

ERIKSEN, THOMAS HYLLAND. 1993. *Ethnicity and Nationalism: Anthropological Perspectives.* London: Pluto Press.

ERRINGTON, FREDERICK, AND DEBORAH GEWERTZ. 1987. "Of Unfinished Dialogues and Paper Pigs." *American Ethnologist* 14(2):367–376.

ESPOSITO, JOHN. 1998. *Islam: The Straight Path,* 3rd ed. London: Oxford University Press.

ESTIOKO-GRIFFIN, AGNES, AND BION P. GRIFFIN. 1978. "Woman the Hunter: The Agta." In Frances Dahlberg, ed., *Woman the Gatherer,* pp. 121–152. New Haven, CT: Yale University Press.

EVANS-PRITCHARD, E. E. 1937. *Witchcraft, Oracles and Magic Among the Azande.* Oxford: Clarendon Press.

———. 1940. *The Nuer.* Oxford: Clarendon Press.

———. 1951. *Kinship and Marriage Among the Nuer.* Oxford: Clarendon Press.

———. 1956. *Nuer Religion.* New York: Oxford University Press.

FAGAN, BRIAN. 1984a. *The Aztecs.* New York: W. H. Freeman.

———. 1984b. *Clash of Cultures.* New York: W. H. Freeman.

———. 1995. *People of the Earth: An Introduction to World Prehistory,* 8th ed. Glenview, IL: Scott, Foresman.

FAKHOURI, HANI. 1972. *Kafr El-Elow: An Egyptian Village in Transition.* New York: Holt, Rinehart and Winston.

FARB, PETER. 1974. *Word Play: What Happens When People Talk.* New York: Knopf/Bantam.

FARLEY, JOHN E. 1990. *Sociology.* Englewood Cliffs, NJ: Prentice Hall.

FARR, GRANT M. 1999. *Modern Iran.* McGraw-Hill.

FEDER, KENNETH L. 1990. *Frauds, Myths, and Mysteries: Science and Pseudoscience in Archaeology.* Mountain View, CA: Mayfield.

FEDIGAN, LINDA M. 1986. "The changing role of women in models of human evolution." *Annual Review of Anthropology,* 15, 25-66.

FELL, BARRY. 1980. *Saga America.* New York: Times Mirror.

FERDON, EDWIN N. 1981. *Early Tahiti as the Explorers Saw It.* Tucson: University of Arizona Press.

FERNEA, ELIZABETH W., AND ROBERT A. FERNEA. 1979. "A Look Behind the Veil." In *Human Nature.* Reprinted in *Anthropology 1989/90.* 1989. Sluice Dock, Guilford, CT: The Dushkin Publishing Group.

FIRTH, RAYMOND. 1957. "A Note on Descent Groups in Polynesia." *Man* 57:4–8.

FISHER, HELEN E. 1992. *Anatomy of Love: The Natural History of Monogamy, Adultery, and Divorce.* New York: W. W. Norton.

FLANNERY, KENT. 1968. "Archaeological systems theory and early Mesoamerica." In Betty Meggars (Ed.), *Anthropological Archaeology in the Americas* (pp. 67–87). Washington, DC: Anthropological Society of Washington.

FLEURET, PATRICK. 1988. "Farmers, Cooperatives, and Development Assistance in Uganda: An Anthropological Perspective." In David Brokensha and Peter D. Little, eds., *Anthropology of Development and Change in East Africa.* Boulder, CO: Westview Press.

FOSSEY, DIAN. 1983. *Gorillas in the Mist*. Boston: Houghton Mifflin.

FOSTER, GEORGE M. 1967. *Tzintzuntzan: Mexican Peasants in a Changing World*. Boston: Little, Brown.

FOUTS, R. S., AND R. L. BUDD. 1979. "Artificial and Human Language Acquisition in the Chimpanzee." In D. A. Hamburg and E. R. McCown, eds., *The Great Apes*, pp. 374–392. Menlo Park, CA: Benjamin/Cummings.

FOX, RICHARD G. 1985. *Lions of the Punjab: Culture in the Making*. Berkeley: University of California Press.

————. 1989. *Gandhian Utopia: Experiments With Culture*. Boston: Beacon Press.

FOX, ROBIN. 1967. *Kinship and Marriage: An Anthropological Perspective*. Baltimore: Penguin.

FRANK, ANDRE GUNNER. 1993. "Bronze Age World System Cycles." *Current Anthropology* 34(4):383–429.

————. 1998. *Reorient: Global Economy in the Asian Age*. Berkeley: University of California Press.

FRANKE, RICHARD W. 1974. "Miracle Seeds and Shattered Dreams." *Natural History* 83(1):10.

FRAZER, SIR JAMES. [1890] 1911. *The Golden Bough: A Study in Magic and Religion*, 12 vols., 3d rev. ed. London: Macmillan.

FREEMAN, DEREK. 1983. *Margaret Mead and Samoa: The Making and Unmaking of an Anthropological Myth*. Cambridge, MA: Harvard University Press.

FREUCHEN, PETER. 1961. *Book of the Eskimos*. Cleveland: World Publishing Co.

FREUD, SIGMUND. 1913. *Totem and Taboo: Some Points of Agreement Between the Mental Lives of Savages and Neurotics*. Trans. James Strachey. New York: W. W. Norton.

FRIED, MORTON. 1953. *Fabric of Chinese Society: A Study of the Social Life of a Chinese County Seat*. New York: Praeger.

————. 1967. *The Evolution of Political Society: An Essay in Political Anthropology*. New York: Random House.

————. 1975. *The Notion of Tribe*. Menlo Park, CA: Cummings.

————. 1977. "First Contact and Political Theory." In Ronald K. Wetherington, ed., *Colloquia in Anthropology*, Vol. 1. Taos, NM: Fort Burgwin Research Center, Southern Methodist University.

————. 1978. "The State, the Chicken and the Egg: Or What Came First?" In R. Cohen and E. R. Service, eds., *Origins of the State: The Anthropology of Political Evolution*, pp. 35–48. Philadelphia: ISHI.

FRIEDL, ERNESTINE. 1975. *Women and Men: An Anthropologist's View*. New York: Holt, Rinehart and Winston.

FRIEDMAN, JONATHAN. 1974. "Marxism, Structuralism, and Vulgar Materialism." *Man* 9:444–469.

————. 1992. "Narcissism, Roots, and Postmodernity: The Constitution of Selfhood in the Global Crisis." In Scott Lash and Jonathan Freidman, eds., *Modernity and Identity*. Oxford: Basil Blackwell.

————. 1995. *Culture Identity and Global Process*. London: Sage Publications.

GARBARINO, MERWYN. 1988. *Native American Heritage*, 2d ed. Prospect Heights, IL: Waveland Press.

GARCIAGODOY, JUANITA. 1998. *Digging the Days of the Dead: A Reading of Mexico's Dias De Muertos*. Niwot, CO: University Press of Colorado.

GARDNER, HOWARD. 1983. *Frames of Mind: The Theory of Multiple Intelligences*. New York: Basic Books.

GARDNER, PETER. 1991. "Foragers Pursuit of Individual Autonomy." *Current Anthropology* 32:543–558.

GARDNER, R. A., AND B. T. GARDNER. 1969. "Teaching Sign Language to a Chimpanzee." *Science* 16:664–672.

GARN, STANLEY. 1971. *Human Races*, 3d ed. Springfield, IL: Chas. C Thomas.

GARZA, CHRISTINA ELNORA. 1991, September 30. "Studying the Natives on the Shop Floor." *Business Week*, pp. 74–78.

GEERTZ, CLIFFORD. 1960. *The Religion of Java*. Glencoe, IL: Free Press.

————. 1963a. *Agricultural Involution: The Processes of Ecological Change in Indonesia*. Berkeley and Los Angeles: University of California Press.

————. 1963b. *Peddlars and Princes: Social Change and Modernization in Two Indonesian Towns*. Chicago: University of Chicago Press.

————. 1966. "Religion as a Cultural System." In Michael Banton, ed., *Anthropological Approaches to the Study of Religion*. Association of Social Anthropologists Monographs, No. 3.

————. 1973. *The Interpretation of Cultures: Selected Essays by Clifford Geertz*. New York: Basic Books.

————. 1980. *Negara: The Theatre State in Nineteenth Century Bali*. Princeton, NJ: Princeton University Press.

————. 1983. "Common Sense as a Cultural System." In Clifford Geertz, ed., *Local Knowledge: Further Essays in Interpretive Anthropology*. New York: Basic Books.

GEWERTZ, DEBORAH. 1981. "A Historical Reconsideration of Female Dominance Among the Chambri of Papua New Guinea." *American Ethnologist* 8(1):94–106.

GIBBS, JAMES L. 1965. "The Kpelle of Liberia." In James L. Gibbs, ed., *Peoples of Africa*. New York: Holt, Rinehart and Winston.

GILKEY, LANGDON. 1986. "The Creationism Issue: A Theologian's View." In Robert W. Hanson, ed., *Science and Creation: Geological, Theological, and Educational Perspectives*. New York: Macmillan.

GILSENAN, MICHAEL. 1973. *Saint and Sufi in Modern Egypt*. Oxford: Oxford University Press.

GIVENS, DAVID, AND RANDOLPH FILLMORE. 1990, May. "AAA Pilot Survey of Nonacademic Departments: Where the MAs Are." *Anthropology Newsletter* 31(5).

GLADKIH, M. I., N. KORNEITZ, AND O. SEFFER. 1984. "Mammoth-Bone Dwelling on the Russian Plain." *Scientific American* 251(5):164–175.

GLASCOCK, ANTHONY P. 1981. "Social Assets or Social Burden: Treatment of the Aged in Nonindustrial Societies." In C. L. Fry, ed., *Dimensions: Aging, Culture and Health*. New York: Praeger.

GLUCKMAN, MAX. 1953. "Bridewealth and the Stability of Marriage." *Man* 53:141–142.

GOLDKIND, VICTOR. 1965. "Social Stratification in a Peasant Community: Redfield's Chan Kom Reinterpreted." *American Anthropology* 67:863–884.

GOLDMAN, IRVING. 1970. *Ancient Polynesian Society*. Chicago: University of Chicago Press.

GOLDMAN, MARSHALL. 1992, October. "Needed: A Russian Economic Revolution." *Current History*, pp. 314–320.

GOLDMAN, MINTON, ed. 1996. *Russia: The Eurasian Republics, and Central/Eastern Europe*, 6th ed. Sluice Dock, Guilford, CT: Dushkin Publishing Group/Brown & Benchmark Publishers.

GOLDSCHMIDT, WALTER. 1986. *The Sebei: A Study in Adaptation*. New York: Holt, Rinehart and Winston.

———. 1989. "Inducement to Military Participation in Tribal Societies." In Paul R. Turner, David Pitt et al., eds., *The Anthropology of War and Peace: Perspectives on the Nuclear Age*, pp. 15–29. Granby, MA: Bergin & Garvey.

GOLDSCHMIDT, WALTER, AND EVELYN J. KUNKEL. 1971. "The Structure of the Peasant Family." *American Anthropologist* 73:1058–1076.

GOLDSTEIN, MELVYN. 1987. "When Brothers Share a Wife." *Natural History* 96(3):39–48.

GOLOMB, LOUIS. 1985. *An Anthropology of Curing in Multiethnic Thailand*. Urbana: University of Illinois Press.

GOODALE, JANE. 1971. *Tiwi Wives: A Study of the Women of Melville Island, North Australia*. Seattle: University of Washington Press.

GOODALL, JANE VAN LAWICK. 1971. *In the Shadow of Man*. New York: Dell.

———. 1986. *The Chimpanzees of Gombe*. Cambridge, MA: Harvard University Press.

GOODE, WILLIAM J. 1963. *World Revolution and Family Patterns*. New York: Free Press.

———. 1982. *The Family*, 2d ed. Englewood Cliffs, NJ: Prentice Hall.

GOODENOUGH, WARD H. 1955. "A Problem in Malayo-Polynesian Social Organization." *American Anthropologist* 57:71–83.

———. 1956. "Residence Rules." *Southwestern Journal of Anthropology* 12:22–37.

GOODMAN, JEFFREY. 1981. *American Genesis*. New York: Berkley.

GOODY, JACK. 1971. *Technology, Tradition, and the State in Africa*. London: Oxford University Press.

———. 1976. *Production and Reproduction: A Comparative Study of the Domestic Domain*. Cambridge: Cambridge University Press.

———. 1977. *The Domestication of the Savage Mind*. Cambridge: Cambridge University Press.

———. 1980. "Slavery in Time and Space." In James L. Watson, ed., *Asian and African Systems of Slavery*, pp. 17–42. Berkeley and Los Angeles: University of California Press.

———. 1987. *The Interface Between the Written and the Oral*. Cambridge: Cambridge University Press.

———. 1996. *The East in the West*. Cambridge: Cambridge University Press.

GOODY, JACK, AND STANLEY J. TAMBIAH. 1973. *Bridewealth and Dowry*. Cambridge: Cambridge University Press.

GOUCHER, CANDICE L. 1981. "Iron Is Iron 'til It Is Rust!: Trade and Ecology in the Decline of West African Iron Smelting." *Journal of African History* 22(1):179–184.

GOULD, JAMES L. 1986. "The Locale Map of Honey Bees: Do Insects Have Cognitive Maps?" *Science* 232:861–863.

GOULD, JAMES L., AND PETER MARLER. 1987. "Learning by Instinct." *Scientific American* 256:74–85.

GOULD, S. J. 1977. *Ever Since Darwin*. New York: W. W. Norton.

———. 1987. "Bushes All the Way Down." *Natural History* 87(6):12–19.

GRABER, ROBERT B., AND PAUL B. ROSCOE. 1988. "Introduction: Circumscription and the Evolution of Society." *American Behavioral Scientist* 31:405–415.

GREEN, ERNESTINE, ed. 1984. *Ethics and Values in Archaeology*. New York: Free Press.

GREENBERG, JOSEPH H. 1986. "The Settlement of the Americas." *Current Anthropology* 27:477–497.

GREENBERG, JOSEPH H, DENNING, KEITH, KEMMER, SUZANNE (eds.) 1990. *On Language: Selected Writings of Joseph H. Greenberg*. Palo Alto, Stanford University Press.

GRIFFIN, DONALD. 1985. *Animal Thinking*. Cambridge, MA: Harvard University Press.

GUHA, ASHOK S. 1981. *An Evolutionary View of Economic Growth*. Oxford: Clarendon Press.

HAAS, JONATHAN. 1982. *The Evolution of the Prehistoric State*. New York: Columbia University Press.

HALL, EDWARD T. 1969. *The Hidden Dimension*. New York: Anchor Press.

———. 1981. *The Silent Language*. New York: Anchor Press.

HALPERIN, RHODA. 1987. "Age in Cross-Cultural Perspective: An Evolutionary Approach." In Philip Silverman, ed., *The Elderly as Modern Pioneers*. Bloomington: Indiana University Press.

HALVERSON, JOHN. 1987. "Art for Art's Sake in the Paleolithic." *Current Anthropology* 28:63–89.

HAMES, RAYMOND B. 1979a. "A Comparison of the Efficiencies of the Shotgun and the Bow in Neotropical Forest Hunting." *Human Ecology* 7(3):219–252.

———. 1979b. "Relatedness and Interaction Among the Ye'Kwana: A Preliminary Analysis." In N. Chagnon and W. Irons, eds., *Evolutionary Biology and Human Social Behavior: An Anthropological Perspective*, pp. 238–251. North Scituate, MA: Duxbury Press.

HAMMEL, E. A., AND NANCY HOWELL. 1987. "Research in Population and Culture: An Evolutionary Framework." *Current Anthropology* 28(2):141–160.

HANDLER, RICHARD. 1988. *Nationalism and the Politics of Culture in Quebec*. Madison, Wisc: Wisconsin University Press.

HARDMAN-DE-BAUTISTA, M. 1978. Linguistic Postulates and Applied Anthropological Linguistics. In Honsa, V and Hardman-de-Bautista, M. (eds.) *Papers on Linguistics and Child Language*. The Hague: Mouton Publishers.

HARNER, MICHAEL J. 1972. *The Jivaro: People of the Sacred Waterfalls*. Garden City, NY: Natural History Press.

———. 1977. "The Ecological Basis for Aztec Sacrifice." *American Ethnologist* 4:117–135.

HARRINGTON, SPENCER P. M. 1991. "The Looting of Arkansas." *Archaeology* 44(3):22–30.

HARRIS, MARVIN. 1964. *Patterns of Race in the Americas.* New York: Norton Press.

———. 1977. *Cannibals and Kings: The Origins of Cultures.* New York: Random House.

———. 1979. *Cultural Materialism: The Struggle for a Science of Culture.* New York: Random House.

———. 1985. *The Sacred Cow and the Abominable Pig: Riddles of Food and Culture.* New York: Simon & Schuster.

———. 1988. *Culture, People, Nature: An Introduction to General Anthropology,* 5th ed. New York: Harper & Row.

———. 1992. "Distinguished Lecture: Anthropology and the Theoretical and Paradigmatic Significance of the Collapse of Society and East European Communism." *American Anthropology* 94(2):295–305.

HARRIS, MARVIN, AND ERIC ROSS. 1987. *Death, Sex, and Fertility: Population Regulation in Preindustrial and Developing Societies.* New York: Columbia University Press.

HART, C. W. M., ARNOLD PILLING, AND JANE GOODALE. 1988. *The Tiwi of North Australia,* 3d ed. New York: Holt, Rinehart and Winston.

HASSAN, FEKRI A. 1981. *Demographic Archaeology.* New York: Academic Press.

HATCH, ELVIN. 1973. *Theories of Man and Culture.* New York: Columbia University Press.

———. 1983. *Culture and Morality: The Relativity of Values in Anthropology.* New York: Columbia University Press.

HAWKES, K., HILL, K. AND O'CONNELL, J. F. 1982. "Why hunters gather: optimal foraging and the Ache of eastern Paraguay," *American Ethnologist,* 9:379-98.

HEFNER, ROBERT W. 1983. "The Culture Problem in Human Ecology: A Review Article." *Comparative Studies in Society and History* 25(3):547–556.

———. 1987. "Islamizing Java? Religion and Politics in Rural East Java." *The Journal of Asian Studies* 46(3):533–554.

HEIDER, KARL. 1979. *Grand Valley Dani: Peaceful Warriors.* New York: Holt, Rinehart and Winston.

———. 1991. *Landscapes of Emotion: Mapping Three Cultures of Emotion in Indonesia.* Cambridge: Cambridge University Press.

HENDRY, JOY. 1987. *Understanding Japanese Society.* London: Croom Helm.

———. 1992. "Introduction and Individuality: Entry into a Social World." In Roger Goodman and Kirsten Refsing, eds., *Ideology and Practice in Modern Japan.* London: Routledge Press.

HENN, JEANNE K. 1984. "Women in the Rural Economy: Past, Present, and Future." In Margaret Jean Hay and Sharon Stichter, eds., *African Women South of the Sahara,* pp. 1–19. London: Longman.

HERDT, GILBERT. 1987. *The Sambia: Ritual and Custom in New Guinea.* New York: Holt, Rinehart and Winston.

HERDT, GILBERT, AND ROBERT J. STOLLER. 1990. *Intimate Communications: Erotica and the Study of Culture.* New York: Columbia University Press.

HERRING, GEORGE C. 1979. *America's Longest War: The United States and Vietnam.* New York: John Wiley.

HERRNSTEIN, RICHARD J. AND MURRAY, CHARLES. 1994. *The Bell Curve: Intelligence and Class Structure in American Life.* New York: Free Press.

HICKERSON, NANCY PARROTT. 1980. *Linguistic Anthropology.* New York: Harper & Row.

HILL, D. 1977. *The Impact of Migration on the Metropolitan and Folk Society of Carriacou, Grenada.* New York: American Museum of Natural History.

HILL, K., H. KAPLAN, K. HAWKES, AND A. M. HURTADO. 1985. "Men's Time Allocation to Subsistence Work Among the Ache of Eastern Paraguay." *Human Ecology* 13:29–47.

HILL-BURNETT, JAQUETTA. 1978. "Developing Anthropological Knowledge Through Application." In E. Eddy and W. Partridge, eds., *Applied Anthropology in America.* New York: Columbia University Press.

HINDE, ROBERT A., AND JOAN STEVENSON-HINDE. 1987. *Instinct and Intelligence,* 3d ed. Burlington, NC: Scientific Publications Department, Carolina Biological Supply Company.

HITCHCOCK, ROBERT. 1988. *Monitoring Research and Development in the Remote Areas of Botswana.* Gaborone: Government Printer.

HOBBES, THOMAS. [1651] 1958. *Leviathan.* New York: Liberal Arts Press.

HOCKETT, CHARLES F., AND R. ASCHER. 1964. "The Human Revolution." *Current Anthropology* 5:135–168.

HOEBEL, E. ADAMSON. [1954] 1968. *The Law of Primitive Man.* New York: Atheneum.

HOLMBERG, ALLAN R. [1950] 1969. *Nomads of the Long Bow: Siriono of Eastern Bolivia.* Garden City, NY: Natural History Press.

———. 1962. "Community and Regional Development: The Joint Cornell-Peru Experiment." *Human Organization* 17:12–16.

HOLMES, LOWELL D. 1987. *Quest for the Real Samoa: The Mead/Freeman Controversy and Beyond.* South Hadley, MA: Bergin & Garvey.

HOPKINS, KEITH. 1982. "Aspects of the Paleogeography of Beringia During the Late Pleistocene." In D. Hopkins, J. Matthews, C. Schweger, and S. Young, eds., *The Paleoecology of Beringia,* pp. 3–28. New York: Academic Press.

HOURANI, ALBERT. 1991. *A History of the Arab Peoples.* Cambridge: Cambridge University Press.

HOWELL, NANCY. 1976. "The Population of the Dobe Area !Kung." In Richard B. Lee and Irven DeVore, eds., *Kalahari Hunter-Gatherers.* Cambridge, MA: Harvard University Press.

———. 1979. *Demography of the Dobe !Kung.* New York: Academic Press.

HOWELLS, W. W. 1976. "Explaining Modern Man: Evolutionists versus Migrationists." *Journal of Human Evolution* 5:477–496.

HSU, FRANCIS. 1948. *Under the Ancestor's Shadow: Chinese Culture and Personality.* New York: Columbia University Press.

———. 1981. *Americans and Chinese: Passage to Differences,* 3d ed. Honolulu: University of Hawaii Press.

HUMBOLDT, W. VON. [1836] 1972. *Linguistic Variability and Intellectual Development.* Trans. C. G. Buck and F. Raven. Philadelphia: University of Pennsylvania Press.

HUNTINGTON, ELSWORTH. 1924. *Civilization and Climate.* New Haven, CT: Yale University Press.

INFORMATION PLEASE ALMANAC. 1991 New York: Houghton and Mifflin Co.

INGHAM, JOHN M. 1986. *Mary, Michael, and Lucifer: Folk Catholicism in Central Mexico.* Austin: University of Texas Press.

ISAAC, BARRY L. 1977. "The Siriono of Eastern Bolivia: A Reexamination." *Human Ecology* 5:137–154.

JANKOWIAK, WILLIAM R., AND EDWARD F. FISCHER. 1992. "A Cross-Cultural Perspective on Romantic Love." *Ethnology* 3(2):149–155.

JENSEN, ARTHUR. 1980. *Bias in Mental Testing.* New York: Free Press.

JETT, STEPHEN C. 1978. "Precolumbian Transoceanic Contacts." In Jesse D. Jennings, ed., *Ancient North Americans.* San Francisco: W. H. Freeman.

JOHANSON, DONALD, AND MAITLAND EDEY. 1981. *Lucy: The Beginnings of Humankind.* New York: Simon & Schuster.

JOHNSON, ALLEN W. 1975. "Time Allocation in a Machiguenga Community." *Ethnology* 14:301–310.

JOHNSON, ALLEN, AND TIMOTHY EARLE. 1987. *The Evolution of Human Societies: From Foraging Group to Agrarian State.* Stanford, CA: Stanford University Press.

JOHNSON, RONALD W., AND MICHAEL G. SCHENE. 1987. *Cultural Resources Management.* Malabar, FL: Robert E. Krieger.

JOLLY, ALISON. 1985. *The Evolution of Primate Behavior,* 2d ed. New York: Macmillan.

JURMAIN, ROBERT, HARRY NELSON, AND WILLIAM A. TURNBAUGH. 1990. *Understanding Physical Anthropology and Archaeology,* 4th ed. St. Paul, MN: West.

KAEPPLER, ADRIENNE L. 1980. "Polynesian Music and Dance." In Elizabeth May, ed., *Musics of Many Cultures.* Berkeley: University of California Press.

KARNOW, STANLEY. 1984. *Vietnam: A History.* New York: Penguin.

KEDDIE, NIKKI R. 1981. *Roots of Revolution: An Interpretive History of Modern Iran.* New Haven, CT: Yale University Press.

KEESING, ROGER M. 1975. *Kin Groups and Social Structure.* New York: Holt, Rinehart and Winston.

———. 1981. *Cultural Anthropology: A Contemporary Perspective.* New York: Holt, Rinehart and Winston.

KEHOE, ALICE BECK. 1989. *The Ghost Dance: Ethnohistory and Revitalization.* New York: Holt, Rinehart and Winston.

———. 1995. *North American Indians: A Comprehensive Account,* 2d ed. Englewood Cliffs, NJ: Prentice Hall.

KELLMAN, SHELLY. 1982, May. "The Yanomamös: Portrait of a People in Crisis." *New Age Journal.* Reprinted in *Anthropology 88/89.* 1988. Sluice Dock, Guilford, CT: Dushkin Publishing Group.

KERBLAY, BASILE. 1983. *Modern Soviet Society.* New York: Pantheon.

KERBO, HAROLD R. AND MCKINSTRY, JOHN A. 1998. *Modern Japan.* McGraw-Hill.

KEYES, CHARLES F. 1977. *The Golden Peninsula: Culture and Adaptation in Mainland Southeast Asia.* New York: Macmillan.

KIRCH, PATRICK V. 1984. *The Evolution of the Polynesian Chiefdoms.* Cambridge: Cambridge University Press.

KIRCHOFF, PAUL. 1955. "The Principles of Clanship in Human Society." *Davidson Anthropological Journal* 1:1. Reprinted in Morton H. Fried, ed., *Readings in Anthropology,* 2 vols. New York: Thomas Y. Crowell, 1958.

KITCHER, PHILLIP. 1982. *Abusing Science: The Case Against Creationism.* Cambridge, MA: MIT Press.

KLEIN, LAURA. 1980. "Contending with Colonization: Tlingit Men and Women in Charge." In Mona Etienne and Eleanor Leacock, eds., *Women and Colonization.* New York: Praeger.

KLEINFELD, JUDITH. 1975. "Positive Stereotyping: The Cultural Relativism in the Classroom." *Human Organization* 34(3):269–274.

KLUCKHOHN, CLYDE. 1944. "Navajo Witchcraft," XII. *Papers of the Peabody Museum of American Archaeology and Ethnology.*

———. 1967. *Navajo Witchcraft.* Boston: Beacon Press.

KNAUFT, BRUCE. 1988. "Reply to Betzig, Laura. On Reconsidering Violence in Simple Human Societies." *Current Anthropology* 29(4):629–633.

KONNER, MELVIN. 1982. *The Tangled Wing: Biological Constraints on the Human Spirit.* New York: Holt, Rinehart and Winston.

KRAYBILL, DONALD B. AND OLSHAN, MARC A. (eds.) 1994. *The Amish Struggle with Modernity.* Hanover, N.H.: University Press of New England.

KROEBER, ALBERT. 1939. *Cultural and Natural Areas of Native North America.* Berkeley: University of California Press.

KROPP, DAKUBU M. E., ed. 1988. *The Languages of Ghana.* London: Kegan Paul International.

KUHN, THOMAS. 1970. *The Structure of Scientific Revolutions,* 2d ed. Chicago: University of Chicago Press.

KUPER, ADAM. 1988. *The Invention of Primitive Society.* London: Routledge Press.

KURIN, RICHARD. 1980. "Doctor, Lawyer, Indian Chief." *Natural History* 89(11):6–24.

KURTZ, DONALD V. 1982. "The Virgin of Guadalupe and the Politics of Becoming Human." *Journal of Anthropological Research* 38:194–210.

LAITMAN, JEFFREY T. 1984. "The Anatomy of Human Speech." *Natural History* 93(8):20–27.

LAKOFF, GEORGE. 1987. *Women, Fire, and Dangerous Things.* Chicago: University of Chicago Press.

LANE, H. 1979. *The Wild Boy of Aveyron.* London: Paladin.

LAWRENCE, PETER. 1964. *Road Belong Cargo: A Study of the Cargo Movement in the Southern Madang District, New Guinea.* Manchester: Manchester University Press.

LEACH, EDMUND. [1953] 1954. "Bridewealth and the Stability of Marriage." *Man* 53:179–180; *Man* 54:173.

———. 1966. "Ritualization in Man in Relation to Conceptual and Social Development." *Philosophical Transactions of the Royal Society of London, Series B* 251:(772):403–408.

———. 1988. "Noah's Second Son." *Anthropology Today* 4(4):2–5.

LEAF, MURRAY J. 1984. *Song of Hope: The Green Revolution in a Punjab Village.* New Brunswick, NJ: Rutgers University Press.

LEAP, WILLIAM. 1988. "Indian Language Renewal." *Human Organization* 47(4):283–291.

LEE, RICHARD B. 1968. "What Do Hunters Do for a Living, Or How to Make Out on Scarce Resources." In R. B. Lee and Irven DeVore, eds., *Man the Hunter,* pp. 30–43. Chicago: Aldine.

———. 1969. "Kung Bushman Subsistence: An Input-Output Analysis." In A. P. Vayda, ed., *Environment and Cultural Behavior: Ecological Studies in Cultural Anthropology.* Garden City, NY: Natural History Press.

———. 1972a. "The Intensification of Social Life Among the !Kung Bushmen." In Brian Spooner, ed., *Population Growth: Anthropological Implications,* pp. 343–350. Cambridge, MA: MIT Press.

———. 1972b. "Population Growth and the Beginning of Sedentary Life Among the !Kung Bushmen." In Brian Spooner, ed., *Population Growth: Anthropological Implications,* pp. 330–342. Cambridge, MA: MIT Press.

———. 1979. *The !Kung San: Men, Women, and Work in a Foraging Society.* Cambridge: Cambridge University Press.

———. 1981. "Politics, Sexual and Nonsexual in an Egalitarian Society: The !Kung San." In Gerald Berreman, ed., *Social Inequality: Comparative and Developmental Approaches,* pp. 83–101. New York: Academic Press.

———. 1993. *The Dobe Ju/'hoansi.* Fort Worth, TX: Harcourt Brace College Publishers.

LEE, RICHARD B., AND IRVEN DEVORE, eds. 1968. *Man the Hunter.* Chicago: Aldine.

LENSKI, GERHARD, AND JEAN LENSKI. 1982. *Human Societies: An Introduction to Macrosociology.* New York: McGraw-Hill.

LETT, JAMES. 1987. *The Human Enterprise: A Critical Introduction to Anthropological Theory.* Boulder, CO: Westview Press.

LEVI-STRAUSS, CLAUDE. 1944. "The Social and Psychological Aspects of Chieftainship in a Primitive Tribe: The Nambikuara of Northwestern Matto Grosso." *Transactions of the New York Academy of Sciences* 7:16–32.

———. 1966. *The Savage Mind.* Trans. George Weidenfeld and Nicholson, Ltd. Chicago: University of Chicago Press.

———. 1969. *The Elementary Structures of Kinship,* rev. ed. Trans. J. H. Bell. Boston: Beacon Press.

LEWELLEN, TED C. 1983. *Political Anthropology: An Introduction.* South Hadley, MA: Bergin & Garvey.

LEWIN, TAMAR. 1986, May 11. "Profile of an Anthropologist Casting an Anthropological Eye on American Consumers." *New York Times.*

LEWIS, HERBERT. 1992, December 28. "Ethnic Loyalties Are on the Rise Globally." *Christian Science Monitor.* Reprinted in Jeffress Ramsay, ed., *Africa,* 5th ed. Guilford, CT.: Dushkin Publishing Group, 1993.

LEWIS, OSCAR. 1951. *Life in a Mexican Village: Tepotzlan Restudied.* Urbana: University of Illinois Press.

———. 1955. "Peasant Culture in India and Mexico: A Comparative Analysis." In McKim Mariott, ed., *Village India: Studies in the Little Community.* Chicago: University of Chicago Press.

———. 1961. *The Children of Sanchez: Autobiography of a Mexican Family.* New York: Random House.

———. 1966. *La Vida: A Puerto Rican Family in the Culture of Poverty—San Juan and New York.* New York: Random House.

LIEBERMAN, PHILIP. 1984. *The Biology and Evolution of Language.* Cambridge, MA: Harvard University Press.

LINCOLN, JAMES R. AND MCBRIDE, KERRY. 1987. "Japanese Industrial Organization in Comparative Perspective." *Annual Review of Sociology* 13:289–312.

LINDENBAUM, SHIRLEY. 1972. "Sorcerers, Ghosts, and Polluting Women: An Analysis of Religious Belief and Population Control." *Ethnology* 2(3):241–253.

LINDHOLM, CHARLES. 1986. "Kinship Structure and Political Authority: The Middle East and Central Asia." *Comparative Study of Society and History* 28(2):334–355.

LINDHOLM, CHARLES, AND CHERRY LINDHOLM. 1980, November-December. "What Price Freedom?" *Science Digest,* pp. 50–55.

LINTON, RALPH. 1936. *The Study of Man.* New York: Appleton-Century-Crofts.

———. 1942. "Age and Sex Categories." *American Sociological Review* 7:589–603.

LIPSET, SEYMOUR MARTIN, AND REINHARD BENDIX. 1967. *Social Mobility in Industrial Society.* Berkeley: University of California Press.

LITTLE, KENNETH L. 1957. "The Role of Voluntary Associations in West African Urbanization." *American Anthropologist* 59:579–596.

———. 1970. *West African Urbanization: A Study of Voluntary Associations in Social Change.* Cambridge: Cambridge University Press.

LIZOT, JACQUES. 1976. *The Yanomamo in the Face of Ethnocide.* Copenhagen: IWGIA Documents.

———. 1977. "Population, Resources, and Warfare Among the Yanomamo." *Man* 12:497–517.

LLOYD, PETER C. 1965. "The Yoruba of Nigeria." In James L. Gibbs, ed., *Peoples of Africa.* New York: Holt, Rinehart and Winston.

LOEHLIN, J. C., LINDZEY, G., and SPUHLER, J. N. 1975. *Race Differences and Intelligence.* San Francisco: W. H. Freeman.

LORENZ, KONRAD. 1966. *On Aggression.* New York: Harcourt, Brace & World.

LOWE, JOHN W. G. 1985. *The Dynamics of Apocalypse: Systems Simulation of the Classic Maya Collapse.* Albuquerque: University of New Mexico Press.

LUCY, JOHN. 1992. *Grammatical Categories and Cognition: A Case Study of the Linguistic Relativity Hypothesis.* Cambridge: Cambridge University Press.

MACIONIS, JOHN. 1999. *Sociology,* 7th ed. Upper Saddle River, NJ: Prentice Hall.

MAINE, HENRY. [1861] 1931. *Ancient Law.* London: Oxford University Press.

MALINOWSKI, BRONISLAW. 1922/1961. *Argonauts of the Western Pacific*. New York: Dutton.

———. 1927. *Sex and Repression in Savage Society*. New York: Meridian Books.

MALONEY, CLARENCE. 1974. *Peoples of South Asia*. New York: Holt, Rinehart and Winston.

MALOTKI, EKKEHART. 1983. *Hopi Time: A Linguistic Analysis of the Temporal Concepts in the Hopi Language*. Berlin: Mouton.

MAQUET, JACQUES. 1972. *Civilizations of Black Africa*. London: Oxford University Press.

MARANO, LOU. 1982. "Windigo Psychosis: The Anatomy of an Emic-Etic Confusion." *Current Anthropology* 23:385–412.

MARINATOS, SPIRIDON. 1939. "The Volcanic Destruction of Minoan Crete." *Antiquity* 13:425–439.

MARSELLA, ANTHONY J. 1979. "Cross-Cultural Studies of Mental Disorders." In Anthony J. Marsella, Ronald G. Tharp, and Thomas J. Cibrowski, eds., *Perspectives on Cross-Cultural Psychology*. New York: Academic Press.

MARSHALL, LORNA. 1976. *The !Kung of Nyae Nyae*. Cambridge, MA: Harvard University Press.

MARTIN, KAY, AND BARBARA VOORHIES. 1975. *Female of the Species*. New York: Columbia University Press.

MARTIN, LINDA G. 1989, July. "The Graying of Japan." *Population Bulletin* 44(2):1–43. Population Reference Bureau, Washington, DC: U.S. Government Printing Office.

MARTIN, SAMUEL. 1964. "Speech Levels in Japan and Korea." In Dell Hymes, ed., *Language in Culture and Society: A Reader in Linguistics and Anthropology*. New York: Harper & Row.

MARX, KARL. [1859] 1959. *A Contribution of the Critique of Political Economy*. New York: International Publishers.

MAUSS, MARCEL. 1985. "A Category of the Human Mind: The Notion of Person; the Notion of Self." Trans. W. D. Halls. In Michael Carrithers, Steven Collins, and Steven Lukes, eds., *The Category of the Person: Anthropology, Philosophy, History*. Cambridge: Cambridge University Press.

MAY, DARLENE. 1980. "Women in Islam: Yesterday and Today." In Cyriac Pullapilly, ed., *Islam in the Contemporary World*. Notre Dame, IN: Cross Roads Books.

MAYBURY-LEWIS, DAVID. 1985. "A Special Sort of Pleading: Anthropology at the Service of Ethnic Groups." In R. Paine, ed., *Advocacy and Anthropology*. St. John's Newfoundland: Institute of Social and Economic Research, Memorial University of Newfoundland.

McALLESTER, DAVID P. 1983. "North American Native Music." In Elizabeth May, ed., *Music of Many Cultures: An Introduction*. Berkeley: University of California Press.

———. 1984. "North America/Native America." In Jeff Todd Titon, ed., *Worlds of Music: An Introduction to the Music of the World's Peoples*. New York: Schirmer Books.

McCLELLAND, DAVID. 1973. "Business Drive and National Achievement." In A. Etzioni and E. Etzioni-Halevy, eds., *Social Change*. New York: Basic Books.

McDANIEL, L. 1998. *The Big Drum Ritual of Carriacou: Praise Songs in Memory of Flight*. Gainesville: University Press of Florida.

McINTOSH, S. K., AND McINTOSH, R. J. "Current directions in West African Prehistory." *Annual Review of Anthropology*, 12, 215-258.

McMAHON, FRANK, AND JUDITH H. McMAHON. 1983. *Abnormal Behavior: Psychology's View*. Homewood, IL: Dorsey Press.

MEAD, MARGARET. 1928. *Coming of Age in Samoa*. New York: Morrow.

———. 1935. *Sex and Temperament in Three Primitive Societies*. New York: Mentor.

MEGGITT, MERVYN. 1977. *Blood Is Their Argument: Warfare Among the Mae Enga Tribesmen of the New Guinea Highlands*. Palo Alto, CA: Mayfield.

MELLARS, P. A. 1989. "Major Issues in the Emergence of Modern Humans." *Current Anthropology* 30(3):349–385.

MENCHER, JOAN P. 1965. "The Nayars of South Malabar." In M. F. Nimkorr, ed., *Comparative Family Systems*, pp. 162–191. Boston: Houghton Mifflin.

———. 1974. "The Caste System Upside Down: Or the Not-So-Mysterious East." *Current Anthropology* 15:469–494.

MENSAH, ATTA ANNAM. 1983. "Music South of the Sahara." In Elizabeth May, ed., *Music of Many Cultures: An Introduction*. Berkeley: University of California Press.

MERNISSI, FATIMA. 1975. *Beyond the Veil: Male-Female Dynamics in a Modern Muslim Society*. Cambridge, MA: Schenkman.

MESSENGER, JOHN. 1971. "Sex and Repression in an Irish Folk Community." In Donald S. Marshall and Robert C. Suggs, eds., *Human Sexual Behavior: Variations in the Ethnographic Spectrum*. New York: Basic Books.

METRAUX, AFRED, CHARTERIS, HUGO, AND MINTZ, SIDNEY 1989. *Voodoo in Haiti*. New York: Schocken Books.

MIDDLETON, JOHN. 1960. *Lugbara Religion*. London: Oxford University Press.

———. 1978. *Peoples of Africa*. New York: Arco.

MOERMAN, MICHAEL. 1966. "Kinship and Commerce in a Thai-Lue Village." *Ethnology* 5:360–364.

MOLNAR, STEPHEN. 1997. *Human Variation: Races, Types, and Ethnic Groups*. 4th edition. Upper Saddle River, NJ: Prentice Hall Press.

MONAGHAN, L, HINTON, L., & KEPHART, R. 1997. "Can't teach a dog to be a cat?: a dialogue on Ebonics." *Anthropology Newsletter*, 38 (3),1,8,9.

MONTAGU, ASHLEY, ed. 1968. *Man and Aggression*. London: Oxford University Press.

———. 1997. *Man's Most Dangerous Myth: The Fallacy of Race*. 6th edition. Walnut Creek, CA: Altamira Press.

MORAN, EMILIO F. 1982. *Human Adaptability: An Introduction to Ecological Anthropology*. Boulder, CO: Westview Press.

MORGAN, LEWIS HENRY. [1877] 1964. *Ancient Society*. Cambridge, MA: Harvard University Press.

MOSELEY, MICHAEL E., AND JAMES B. RICHARDSON. 1992. "Doomed by Natural Disaster." *Archaeology* 45(6):44–45.

MOSHER, STEVEN W. 1983. *The Broken Earth: The Rural Chinese*. Glencoe, IL: Free Press.

MUMFORD, LEWIS. 1961. *The City in History: Its Origins, Its Transformations, and Its Prospects*. New York: Harcourt, Brace & World.

MURDOCK, GEORGE. 1945. "The Common Denominator of Cultures." In Ralph Linton, ed., *The Science of Man in the World Crisis,* pp. 123–142. New York: Columbia University Press.

———. 1949. *Social Structure.* New York: Macmillan.

———. 1967. "Ethnographic Atlas: A Summary." *Ethnology* 6:109–236.

———. 1968. "The Current Status of the World's Hunting and Gathering Peoples." In Richard Lee and Irven DeVore, eds., *Man the Hunter,* pp. 13–20. Chicago: Aldine.

———. 1981a. *Atlas of World Cultures.* Pittsburgh: University of Pittsburgh Press.

———. 1981b. *Ethnographic Atlas.* Pittsburgh: University of Pittsburgh Press.

MURPHY, R. F., AND L. KASDAN. 1959. "The Structure of Parallel Cousin Marriage." *American Anthropologist* 61:17–29.

MURRAY, GERALD F. 1989. "The Domestication of Wood in Haiti: A Case Study in Applied Evolution." *Anthropological Praxis.* Reprinted in Aaron Podelfsky and Peter J. Brown, eds., *Applying Anthropology: An Introductory Reader.* Mountain View, CA: Mayfield, 1994.

MYERS, DAVID G. 1998. *Psychology,* 5th ed. New York: Worth Publishers.

NAKANE, CHIA. 1970. *Japanese Society.* Rutland, VT: Charles Tuttle.

NANDA, SERENA. 1990. *Neither Man nor Woman: The Hijras of India.* Belmont, CA: Wadsworth.

NASH, JUNE. 1997. "The Fiesta of the Word: The Zapatista Uprising and Radical Democracy in Mexico." *American Anthropologist* 99(2):261–274.

NASH, MANNING. 1989. *The Cauldron of Ethnicity in the Modern World.* Chicago: University of Chicago Press.

NATIONAL OPINION RESEARCH CENTER. 1994. *General Social Surveys. 1972–1994: Cumulative Codebook.* Chicago: University of Chicago.

NEALE, WALTER. 1976. *Monies in Societies.* San Francisco: Chandler.

NEEDHAM, RODNEY. 1967. "Percussion and Transition." *Man* 2:606–614.

NELSON, HARRY, AND ROBERT JURMAIN. 1988. *Introduction to Physical Anthropology,* 4th ed. St. Paul, MN: West.

NORGET, KRISTIN. 1996. "Beauty and the Feast: Aesthetics and the Performance of Meaning in the Day of the Dead, Oaxaca, Mexico." *Journal of Latin American Lore* 19, 53–64.

OBEYESEKERE, GANANATH. 1992. *Apotheosis of Captain Cook: European Mythmaking in the Pacific.* Princeton: Princeton University Press.

O'CONNOR, MARY I. 1989. *Descendants of Totoliguoqui: Ethnicity and Economics in the Mayo Valley.* University of California Publications in Anthropology, Vol. 19. Berkeley: University of California Press.

OKIGBO, BEDE N. 1988, September-October. "Food: Finding Solutions to the Crisis." *Africa Report.*

OLIVER, DOUGLAS. 1955. *A Solomon Island Society: Kinship and Leadership Among the Siuai of Bougainville.* Cambridge, MA: Harvard University Press.

———. 1974. *Ancient Tahitian Society,* 3 vols. Honolulu: University of Hawaii Press.

OLMOS, M. F. 1997. *Sacred Possessions: Vodou, Santeria, Obeah, and the Caribbean.* New Brunswick, NJ: Rutgers University Press.

O'MEARA, TIM J. 1990. *Samoan Planters: Tradition and Economic Development in Polynesia.* New York: Holt, Rinehart and Winston.

ORTNER, SHERRY. 1974. "Is Female to Male as Nature Is to Culture?" In Michelle Zimbalist Rosaldo and Louise Lamphere, eds., *Woman, Culture, and Society,* pp. 67–87. Stanford, CA: Stanford University Press.

OSWALT, WENDELL H. 1972. *Other Peoples, Other Customs: World Ethnography and Its History.* New York: Holt, Rinehart and Winston.

———. 1976. *An Anthropological Analysis of Food-Getting Technology.* New York: John Wiley.

OTTENBERG, PHOEBE. 1965. "The Afikpo Ibo of Eastern Nigeria." In James L. Gibbs, ed., *Peoples of Africa.* New York: Holt, Rinehart and Winston.

OTTERBEIN, KEITH. 1970. *The Evolution of War.* New Haven, CT: HRAF Press.

———. 1974. "The Anthropology of War." In John Honigmann, ed., *Handbook of Social and Cultural Anthropology.* Chicago: Rand McNally.

OUICHI, WILLIAM G. 1981. *Theory Z: How American Business Can Meet the Japanese Challenge.* New York: Avon Books.

PALAKORNKUL, ANGKAB. 1972. *A Sociolinguistic Study of Pronominial Strategy in Spoken Bangkok Thai.* Doctoral Dissertation, University of Texas, Austin.

PALMORE, ERDMAN BALLAGH. 1975. *The Honorable Elders: A Cross-Cultural Analysis of Aging in Japan.* Durham, NC: Duke University Press.

PARRINDER, GEOFFREY. 1983. *World Religions: From Ancient History to the Present.* New York: Hamlyn Publishing Group.

PARRY, JONATHAN. 1980. "Ghosts, Greed and Sin: The Occupational Identity of the Benares Funeral Priests." *Man* 21:453–473.

PASTERNAK, BURTON. 1976. *Introduction to Kinship and Social Organization.* Englewood Cliffs, NJ: Prentice Hall.

PATTERSON, FRANCINE, AND DONALD COHN. 1978. "Conversations with a Gorilla." *National Geographic* 154:454–462.

PATTERSON, FRANCINE, AND EUGENE LINDEN. 1981. *The Education of Koko.* New York: Holt, Rinehart and Winston.

PAUL, ROBERT A. 1989. "Psychoanalytic Anthropology." *Annual Review of Anthropology* 18:177–202.

———. 1996. *Moses and Civilization: The Meaning Behind Freud's Myth.* New Haven: Yale University Press.

PFEIFFER, JOHN. 1985. *The Emergence of Man,* 4th ed. New York: Harper & Row.

PHILLIPS, HERBERT P. 1965. *Thai Peasant Personality.* Berkeley: University of California Press.

PHILLIPSON, DAVID W. 1985. *African Archaeology.* New York: Cambridge University Press.

PIDDOCKE, STUART. 1965. "The Potlatch System of the Southern Kwakiutl: A New Perspective." *Southwestern Journal of Anthropology* 21:244–264.

PIKE, DOUGLAS. 1990. "Change and Continuity in Vietnam." *Current History* 89(545):117–134.

PINKER, STEVEN. 1994. *The Language Instinct: How the Mind Creates Language.* New York: HarperCollins.

POLYANI, KARL. 1944. *The Great Transformation.* New York: Rinehart.

POPLINE: WORLD POPULATION NEWS SERVICE. 1993, July-August. "1993 State of World Population Edition," Vol. 15.

POPULATION REFERENCE BUREAU. 1986. *Population Data Sheet.* Washington, DC: Population Reference Bureau.

———. 1991. *World Population Data Sheet.* Washington, DC: Population Reference Bureau.

POSPISIL, LEONARD. 1963. *The Kapauku Papuans of West New Guinea.* New York: Holt, Rinehart and Winston.

———. 1967. "The Attributes of Law." In Paul Bohannon, ed., *Law and Warfare: Studies in the Anthropology of Conflict.* Garden City, NY: Natural History Press.

POTTER, JACK M. 1976. *Thai Peasant Social Structure.* Chicago: University of Chicago Press.

POWDERMAKER, HORTENSE. 1966. *Stranger and Friend: The Way of an Anthropologist.* New York: W. W. Norton.

PRICE, DOUGLAS T. AND BROWN, JAMES A. 1985. *Prehistoric Hunter-Gatherers: The Emergence of Cultural Complexity.* New York: Academic Press.

QUALE, ROBIN G. 1988. *A History of Marriage Systems.* New York: Greenwood Press.

QUINN, NAOMI, AND DOROTHY HOLLAND. 1987. "Culture and Cognition." In D. Holland and N. Quinn, eds., *Cultural Models in Language and Thought.* Cambridge: Cambridge University Press.

RADCLIFFE-BROWN, A. R. 1922/1964. *The Andaman Islanders.* New York: Free Press.

RAHEJA, GLORIA. 1988. *The Poison in the Gift: Ritual, Prestation, and the Dominant Caste in a North Indian Village.* Chicago: University of Chicago Press.

RAMSAY, JEFFRESS F., ed. 1995. *Africa,* 6th ed. Guilford, CT: Dushkin Publishing Group.

RAPPAPORT, ROY. 1979. *Ecology, Meaning, and Religion.* Richmond, VA: North Atlantic Books.

———. 1984. *Pigs for the Ancestors: Ritual in the Ecology of a New Guinea People.* New Haven, CT: Yale University Press.

RATHJE, WILLIAM L., AND CHERYL K. RITENBAUGH. 1984. "Household Refuse Analysis: Theory, Method, and Applications in Social Science." *American Behavioral Scientist* 28(1):5–153.

RAVEN, PETER H., LINDA R. BERG, AND GEORGE B. JOHNSON. 1993. *Environment.* Fort Worth, TX : Saunders College Publishing.

RAYNER, STEVE. 1989. "Fiddling While the Globe Warms." *Anthropology Today* 5(6):1–2.

REDFIELD, ROBERT. 1930. *Tepotzlan: A Mexican Village: A Study of Folk Life.* Chicago: University of Chicago Press.

REDFIELD, ROBERT, AND ALFONSO VILLA ROJAS. 1934. *Chan Kom, A Maya Village.* Washington, DC: Carnegie Institute.

REISS, SPENCER. 1990, December 3. "The Last Days of Eden." *Newsweek,* pp. 48–50.

RELETHFORD, JOHN H. 1997. *The Human Species: An Introduction to Biological Anthropology,* 3d ed. Mountain View, CA: Mayfield.

RENFREW, COLIN. 1989. *Archaeology and Language: The Puzzle of Indo-European Origins.* Cambridge: Cambridge University Press.

RICKFORD, JOHN R. 1997. "Suite for Ebony and Phonics." *Discovery* 18(2):82-87.

RIGHTMIRE, G. P. 1981. "Patterns in the Evolution of Homo erectus." *Paleobiology* 7:241–246.

RINDOS, DAVID. 1984. *The Origins of Agriculture: An Evolutionary Perspective.* New York: Academic Press.

RINER, REED. 1981. "The Supranational Network of Boards of Directors." *Current Anthropology* 22(2):167–172.

RIVERS, W. H. O. [1906] 1967. *Todas.* London: Macmillan.

ROBBINS, RICHARD H. 1999. *Global Problems and the Culture of Capitalism.* Boston: Allyn and Bacon.

ROBERTS, JOHN M. 1967. "Oaths, Autonomic Ordeals, and Power." In Clellan S. Ford, ed., *Cross-Cultural Approaches: Readings in Comparative Research.* New Haven, CT: HRAF Press.

ROBERTSON, CLAIRE C. 1984. "Women in the Urban Economy." In Margaret Jean Hay and Sharon Stichter, eds., *African Women South of the Sahara.* London: Longman.

ROBERTSON, IAN. 1990. *Sociology,* 4th ed. New York: Worth Publishers.

ROMANUCCI-ROSS, LOLA. 1973. *Conflict, Violence and Morality in a Mexican Village.* Palo Alto, CA: National Press Books.

ROSCOE, PAUL B. 1994. "Amity and Aggression: A Symbolic Theory of Incest." *Man* 28:1–28.

——— 1993. "The Brokers of the Lord: The ministrations of a Christian Faith in the Sepik Basin of Papua New Guinea." In Lockwood, V., Harding, T., and Wallace, B. (eds.) *Contemporary Pacific Societies: Studies in Development and Change.* Upper Saddle River, NJ: Prentice Hall Press.

ROSEBERRY, WILLIAM. 1982. "Balinese Cockfights and the Seduction of Anthropology." *Social Research* 49:1013–1038.

ROSENBERG, MICHAEL. 1990. "The Mother of Invention: Evolutionary Theory, Territoriality, and the Origins of Agriculture." *American Anthropologist* 92(2):399–415.

ROSMAN, ABRAHAM, AND PAULA G. RUBEL. 1986. *Feasting with Mine Enemy: Rank and Exchange Among Northwest Coast Societies.* Prospect Heights, IL: Waveland Press.

ROSSIDES, DANIEL W. 1990a. *Comparative Societies: Social Types and Their Interrelations.* Englewood Cliffs, NJ: Prentice Hall.

———. 1990b. *Social Stratification: The American Class System in Comparative Perspective.* Englewood Cliffs, NJ: Prentice Hall.

ROSTOW, WALTER W. 1978. *The World Economy: History and Prospect.* Austin: University of Texas Press.

ROTHENBERG, JEROME. 1985. *Technicians of the Sacred: A Range of Poetries from Africa, Asia, Europe, and Oceania.* Berkeley: University of California Press.

RUMBAUGH, DUANE M., ed. 1977. *Language Learning by a Chimpanzee.* New York: Academic Press.

SACKETT, JAMES R. 1982. "Approaches to Style in Lithic Archaeology." *Journal of Anthropological Archaeology* 1:59–112.

SAFA, HELEN I. 1974. *The Urban Poor of Puerto Rico: A Study in Development and Inequality*. New York: Holt, Rinehart and Winston.

SAHLINS, MARSHALL. 1958. *Social Stratification in Polynesia*. Monograph of the American Ethnological Society. Seattle: University of Washington Press.

———. 1961. "The Segmentary Lineage: An Organization of Predatory Expansion." *American Anthropologist* 63:322–343.

———. 1965. "On the Sociology of Primitive Exchange." In M. Banton, ed., *The Relevance of Models for Social Anthropology*, pp. 139–227. London: Tavistock.

———. 1968a. "African Nemesis: An Off Broadway Review." In Ashley M. F. Montagu, ed., *Man and Aggression*. New York: Oxford University Press.

———. 1968b. *Tribesmen*. Englewood Cliffs, NJ: Prentice Hall.

———. 1972. *Stone Age Economics*. Chicago: Aldine.

———. 1976. *The Use and Abuse of Biology: An Anthropological Critique of Sociobiology*. Ann Arbor: University of Michigan Press.

———. 1981. *Historical Metaphors and Mythical Realities: Structure in the Early History of the Sandwich Islands*. Ann Arbor: University of Michigan Press.

———. 1985. *Islands of History*. Chicago: University of Chicago Press.

———. 1995 *How 'Natives' Think, About Captain Cook, For Example*. Chicago: University of Chicago Press.

SALISBURY, R. F. 1962. *From Stone to Steel: Economic Consequences of a Technological Change in New Guinea*. Cambridge: Cambridge University Press.

SALZMAN, PHILIP. 1989. "The Lone Stranger and the Solitary Quest." *Anthropology Newsletter* 30(5):16, 44.

SANDERS, WILLIAM T., AND BARBARA J. PRICE. 1968. *Mesoamerica: The Evolution of a Civilization*. New York: Random House.

SAPIR, EDWARD. 1921. *Language*. New York: Harcourt Brace Jovanovich.

SARDESAI, D. R. 1989. *Southeast Asia: Past and Present*. Boulder, CO: Westview Press.

SAUER, CARL O. 1952. *Agricultural Origins and Dispersals*. New York: American Geographical Society.

SAVAGE-RUMBAUGH, SUE E. 1986. *Ape Language from Conditioned Response to Symbol*. New York: Columbia University Press.

SCARR, S. AND WEINBERG R. A. 1978. "Attitudes, Interests, and IQ." *Human Nature* 1(4):29–36.

SCHAFFT, GRETCHEN. 1999. "Professional Denial" *Anthropology Newsletter*. 40(1):56–54 (January).

SCHALLER, GEORGE. 1976. *The Mountain Gorilla—Ecology and Behavior*. Chicago: University of Chicago Press.

SCHIEFFELIN, BAMBI B. 1990. *The Give and Take of Everyday Life: Language Socialization of Kaluli Children*. New York: Cambridge University Press.

SCHIEFFELIN, BAMBI AND OCHS, ELINOR (Eds.) *Language Socialization Across Cultures (Studies in the Social and Cultural Foundations of Languages, No 3)*. Cambridge: Cambridge University Press.

SCHLEGEL, ALICE, AND ROHN ELOUL. 1988. "Marriage Transactions: Labor, Property, and Status." *American Anthropologist* 90(2):291–309.

SCHNEIDER, DAVID. 1953. "A Note on Bridewealth and the Stability of Marriage." *Man* 53:55–57.

SCHUSKY, ERNEST L. 1990. *Culture and Agriculture*. New York: Bergin and Garvey.

SCHWARTZ, RICHARD, AND JAMES C. MILLER. 1975. "Legal Evolution and Societal Complexity." In Ronald L. Akers and James C. Miller, eds., *Law and Control in Society*. Englewood Cliffs, NJ: Prentice Hall.

SCOTT, JAMES. 1976. *The Moral Economy of the Peasant: Rebellion and Subsistence in Southeast Asia*. New Haven: Yale University Press.

SCUDDER, THAYER, AND ELIZABETH COLSON. 1979. "Long Term Research in Gwembe Valley, Zambia." In G. Foster, ed., *Long Term Field Research in Social Anthropology*. New York: Academic Press.

SCUPIN, RAYMOND. 1988. "Language, Hierarchy and Hegemony: Thai Muslim Discourse Strategies." *Language Sciences* 10(2):331–351.

SEBEOK, THOMAS A., AND JEAN UMIKER-SEBEOK, eds. 1980. *Speaking of Apes: A Critical Anthology of Two Way Communication with Man*. New York: Plenum Press.

SERVICE, ELMAN. 1960. "The Law of Evolutionary Potential." In Marshall D. Sahlins and Elman R. Service, eds., *Evolution and Culture*, pp. 93–122. Ann Arbor: University of Michigan Press.

———. [1962] 1971. *Primitive Social Organization: An Evolutionary Perspective*. New York: Random House.

———. 1975. *Origins of the State and Civilization: The Process of Cultural Evolution*. New York: W. W. Norton.

———. 1978a. "Classical and Modern Theories of the Origin of Government." In Ronald Cohen and E. R. Service, eds., *Origins of the State: The Anthropology of Political Evolution*. Philadelphia: ISHI.

———. 1978b. *Profiles in Ethnology*. New York: Harper & Row.

———. 1979. *The Hunters*, 2d ed. Englewood Cliffs, NJ: Prentice Hall.

SERVICE, ELMAN, AND MARSHALL SAHLINS. 1960. *Evolution and Culture*. Ann Arbor: University of Michigan Press.

SEXTON, JAMES D., ed. 1981. *Son of Tecun Uman: A Maya Indian Tells His Life Story*. Tucson: University of Arizona Press.

SHAHRANI, M. NAZIF. 1981. "Growing in Respect: Aging Among the Kirghiz of Afghanistan." In P. Amoss and S. Harrell, eds., *Other Ways of Growing Old: Anthropologist Perspectives*. Stanford, CA: Stanford University Press.

SHAHRANI, M. NAZIF AND CANFIELD, ROBERT (eds.) 1984. *Revolutions and Rebellions in Afghanistan: Anthropological Perspectives*. Berkeley: University of California Press.

SHANKMAN, PAUL. 1975. "A Forestry Scheme in Samoa." *Natural History* 84(8):60–69.

———. 1978. "Notes on a Corporate 'Potlatch': The Lumber Industry in Samoa." In A. Idris-Soven, E. Idris-Soven, and M. K. Vaugh, eds., *The World as a Company Town: Multinational*

Corporations and Social Change. The Hague: Mouton World Anthropology Series.

———. 1990. Personal correspondence.

———. 1998. "Margaret Mead, Derek Freeman, and the Issue of Evolution" *Skeptical Inquirer* 22(6):35–39.

———. 1999. "Development, Sustainability, and the Deforestation of Samoa. *Pacific Studies,* (forthcoming).

SHANNON, THOMAS RICHARD. 1988. *An Introduction to the World-System Perspective.* Boulder, CO: Westview Press.

SHARP, LAURISTON, HAZEL M. HAUCK, AND R. B. TEXTOR. 1953. *Siamese Rice Village: A Preliminary Study of Bang Chan,* Bangkok: Cornell Research Center.

SHATTUCK, R. 1980. *The Forbidden Experiment.* New York: Farrar, Straus & Giroux.

SHEEHAN, TOM. 1976. "Senior Esteem as a Factor in Socioeconomic Complexity." *The Gerontologist* 16(5):433–440.

SHEPHER, JOSEPH. 1983. *Incest: A Biosocial View.* New York: Academic Press.

SHIMIZU, AKITOSHI. 1987. "Ie and Dozuku: Family and Descent in Japan." *Current Anthropology* 28(4):S85–S90.

SHIPMAN, PAT. 1984. "Scavenger Hunt." *Natural History* 4(84):20–27.

———. 1986a. "Baffling Limb on the Family Tree." *Discover* 7(9):86–93.

———. 1986b. "Scavenging or Hunting in Early Hominids: Theoretical Frameworks and Tests." *American Anthropologist* 88:27–43.

SHIPTON, PARKER. 1990. "African Famines and Food Security: Anthropological Perspectives." *Annual Review of Anthropology* 19:353–394.

SHIRK, MARTHA, AND O'DELL MITCHELL JR. 1989, June 25. "One Company Evolving in Two Lands." *St. Louis Post-Dispatch.*

SHORE, BRADD. 1982. *Sala'ilua. A Samoan Mystery.* New York: Columbia University Press.

SHOSTAK, MARJORIE. 1981. *Nisa: The Life and Words of a !Kung Woman.* New York: Vintage Books, Random House.

SHREEVE, JAMES. 1992, September. "The Dating Game." *Discover,* pp. 76–83.

SHWEDER, RICHARD. 1991. *Thinking Through Cultures: Expeditions in Cultural Psychology.* Cambridge, MA: Harvard University Press.

SILVERMAN, PHILIP, AND ROBERT J. MAXWELL. 1983. "The Role and Treatment of the Elderly in 95 Societies." In Jay Sokolovsky, ed., *Growing Old in Different Cultures,* pp. 43–55. Belmont, CA: Wadsworth.

SIMMONS, LEO. 1945. *The Role of the Aged in Primitive Society.* London: Oxford University Press.

SIMON, JULIAN L. 1981. *The Ultimate Resource.* Princeton, NJ: Princeton University Press.

SMITH, ADAM. [1776] 1937. *An Inquiry into the Nature and Causes of the Wealth of Nations.* New York: The Modern Library.

SMITH, BRUCE D. 1989. "Origins of Agriculture in Eastern North America." *Science* 246:1566–1571.

SMITH, HUSTON. 1986. *The Religions of Man.* New York: Harper & Row.

SMITH, MARGO L. 1986. "Culture in International Business: Selecting Employees for Expatriate Assignments." In Hendrick Serrie, ed., *Anthropology and International Business.* Williamsburg, VA: Department of Anthropology, William and Mary.

SMITH, M. G. 1965. "The Hausa of Northern Nigeria" in Gibbs, James L. Jr. (ed.) *Peoples of Africa.* New York: Holt, Rinehart, and Winston.

SMITH-IVAN, EDDA. 1988. "Introduction." In Edda Smith-Ivan, Nidhi Tandon, and Jane Connors, eds., *Women in Sub-Saharan Africa, Report No. 77.* London: Minority Rights Group.

SOLWAY, JACQUELINE S., AND RICHARD B. LEE. 1990. "Foragers, Genuine or Spurious?" *Current Anthropology* 31(2):109–146.

SOUTHALL, AIDAN. 1956. *Alur Society: A Study in Processes and Types of Domination.* Cambridge: Heffer.

SOWELL, THOMAS. 1994. *Race and Culture.* New York: Basic Books.

———. 1995. "Ethnicity and IQ." In Fraser, Steven (ed.) *The Bell Curve Wars: Race, Intelligence and the Future of America.* New York: Basic Books.

SPIRO, MELFORD. 1952. "Ghosts, Ifaluk, and Teleological Functionalism." *American Anthropologist* 54:497–503.

———. 1971. *Buddhism and Society: A Great Tradition and Its Burmese Vicissitudes.* Berkeley: University of California Press.

———. 1982. *Oedipus in the Trobriands.* Chicago: University of Chicago Press.

SPONSEL, LESLIE. 1996. "Human Rights and Advocacy Anthropology." In M. Ember and D. Levinson, eds., *Encyclopedia of Cultural Anthropology,* Vol. 2. New York: Henry Holt and Company.

STACK, CAROL B. 1975. *All Our Kin: Strategies for Survival in a Black Community.* New York: Harper & Row.

STANNER, W. E. H. 1979. "The Dreaming." In W. A. Lessa and E. Z. Vogt, eds., *Reader in Comparative Religion,* 4th edition. pp. 513–523. New York: Harper & Row.

STAVENHAGEN, RODOLFO. 1975. *Social Classes in Agrarian Societies.* Garden City, NY: Anchor Press.

STAVRIANOS, L. S. 1995. *A Global History: From Prehistory to the Present,* 6th ed. Englewood Cliffs, NJ: Prentice Hall.

STEINBERG, DAVID J., ed. 1985. *In Search of Southeast Asia: A Modern History.* Honolulu: University of Hawaii Press.

STEINMETZ, PAUL. 1980. *Pipe, Bible and Peyote among the Oglala Lakota.* Stockholm: Almquist and Wiksell International.

STEVEN, ROB. 1983. *Classes in Contemporary Japan.* Cambridge: Cambridge University Press.

STEWARD, JULIAN H. 1938. "Basin-Plateau Aboriginal Sociopolitical Groups." *Bureau of American Ethnology,* Bulletin 120.

———. 1955. *Theory of Culture Change: The Methodology of Multilinear Evolution.* Urbana: University of Illinois Press.

STIEBING, WILLIAM H., JR. 1984. *Ancient Astronauts: Cosmic Allusions and Popular Theories About Man's Past.* Buffalo, NY: Prometheus Books.

STINI, WILLIAM A. 1975. *Ecology and Human Adaptation.* Dubuque, IA: William C. Brown.

STRINGER, C. B. 1985. "Middle Pleistocene Hominid Variability and the Origin of Late Pleistocene Humans." In E. Delson, ed., *Ancestors: The Hard Evidence,* pp. 289–295. New York: Alan R. Liss.

STRINGER, C. B., AND P. ANDREWS. 1988. "Genetic and Fossil Evidence for the Origin of Modern Humans." *Science* 239:1263–1268.

STRUG, DAVID L. 1986. "The Foreign Politics of Cocaine: Comments on a Plan to Eradicate the Coca Leaf in Peru." In Deborah Pacini and Christine Franquemont, eds., *Coca and Cocaine: Effects on People and Policy in Latin America. Cultural Survival Report 23.* Cambridge, MA: Cultural Survival, Inc.; Latin American Studies Program, Cornell University.

SUDARKASA, NIARA. 1989. "African and Afro-American Family Structure." In Johnetta Cole, ed., *Anthropology for the Nineties: Introductory Readings,* pp. 132–160. New York: Free Press.

SULLIVAN, JO. 1989. *Africa,* 3d ed. Sluice Dock, Guilford, CT: Dushkin Publishing Group.

SWADESH, MORRIS. 1964. "Linguistics as an Instrument of Prehistory." In Dell H. Hymes, ed., *Language and Society.* New York: Harper & Row.

SWARTZ, MARC, VICTOR TURNER, AND ARTHUR TUDEN, eds. 1966. *Political Anthropology.* Chicago: Aldine.

SWEET, LOUISE. 1965. "Camel Raiding of North Arabian Bedouin: A Mechanism of Ecological Adaptation." *American Anthropologist* 67:1132–1150.

SYMONS, DONALD. 1979. *The Evolution of Human Sexuality.* Oxford: Oxford University Press.

TAINTER, JOSEPH A. 1990. *The Collapse of Complex Societies.* Cambridge: Cambridge University Press.

TALMON, YONINA. 1964. "Mate Selection in Collective Settlements." *American Sociological Review* 29:491–508.

———. 1989. "Bridewealth and Dowry Revisited: The Position of Women in Sub-Saharan Africa and North India." *Current Anthropology* 30(4):413–435.

TAMBIAH, STANLEY J. 1989. "Bridewealth and Dowry Revisited: The Position of Women in Sub-Saharan Africa and North India." *Current Anthropology* 30(4):413–435.

———. 1991. *Sri Lanka: Ethnic Fratricide and the Dismantling of Democracy.* Chicago: University of Chicago Press.

TANDON, NIDHI. 1988. "Women in Rural Areas." In Edda Smith-Ivan, Nidhi Tandon, and Jane Connors, eds., *Women in Sub-Saharan Africa. Report No. 77.* London: Minority Rights Group.

TANNER, NANCY M. 1981. *On Becoming Human.* London: Cambridge University Press.

———. 1987. "Gathering by Females: The Chimpanzee Model Revisited and the Gathering Hypothesis." In Warren G. Kinsey, ed., *The Evolution of Human Behavior,* pp. 3–27. Albany: State University of New York Press.

TARLING, D. H. 1985. *Continental Drift and Biological Evolution.* Burlington, NC: Carolina Biological Supply Co.

TAX, SOL. 1953. *Penny Capitalism: A Guatemalan Indian Economy.* Smithsonian Institution, Institute of Social Anthropology. Publication No. 16. Washington, DC: U.S. Government Printing Office.

TEMPLE, ROBERT. 1989. *The Genius of China: 3000 Years of Science, Discovery and Invention.* New York: Simon & Schuster.

TEMPLETON, ALAN R. 1993. "The 'Eve' Hypothesis: A Genetic Critique and Reanalysis." *American Anthropologist* 95(1):51–72.

———. 1998. "Human Races: A Genetic and Evolutionary Perspective." *American Anthropologist* 100(3):632-650.

TERRACE, HERBERT S. 1986. *Nim: A Chimpanzee Who Learned Sign Language.* New York: Columbia University Press.

TESTART, ALAIN. 1988. "Some Major Problems in the Social Anthropology of Hunter-Gatherers." Trans. Roy Willis. *Current Anthropology,* 29(1):1–31.

THOMAS, E. M. 1958. *The Harmless People.* New York: Random House.

THOMASON, SARAH G., AND TERRENCE KAUFMAN. 1988. *Language Contact, Creolization, and Genetic Linguistics.* Berkeley: University of California Press.

TURNBULL, COLIN. 1963. *The Forest People: A Study of the Pygmies of the Congo.* New York: Simon & Schuster.

———. 1972. *The Mountain People.* New York: Simon & Schuster.

———. 1983. *The Mbuti Pygmies: Change and Adaptation.* New York: Holt, Rinehart and Winston.

TURNER, VICTOR. 1967. *The Forest of Symbols: Aspects of Ndembu Ritual.* Ithaca: Cornell University Press.

———. 1974. *Dramas, Fields, and Metaphors: Symbolic Action in Human Society.* Ithaca, NY: Cornell University Press.

TURTON, ANDREW. 1980. "Thai Institutions of Slavery." In James L. Watson, ed., *Asian and African Systems of Slavery,* pp. 251–292. Berkeley: University of California Press.

TWEDDELL, COLIN E., AND LINDA AMY KIMBALL. 1985. *Introduction to the Peoples and Cultures of Asia.* Englewood Cliffs, NJ: Prentice Hall.

TYLER, STEPHEN A. 1986. *India: An Anthropological Perspective.* Prospect Heights, IL: Waveland Press.

TYLOR, EDWARD B. 1871. *Primitive Culture.* London: J. Murray.

———. 1889. "On a Method of Investigating the Development of Institutions, Applied to Laws of Marriage and Descent." *Journal Royal Anthropological Institute* 18:245–272.

UBELAKER, DOUGLAS H. 1988. "North American Indian Population Size, A.D. 1500 to 1985." *American Journal of Physical Anthropology* 77:289–294.

UCHENDU, VICTOR C. 1965. *The Igbo of Southeast Nigeria.* New York: Holt, Rinehart and Winston.

US. CENSUS BUREAU. 1998. *Statistical Abstracts of the United States: 1998.*

U.S. COMMITTEE ON GLOBAL CHANGE. 1988. *Toward an Understanding of Global Change.* Washington, DC: National Academy Press.

VAGO, STEVEN. 1995. *Law and Society.* 2nd Edition. Upper Saddle River, NJ: Prentice Hall.

VALERI, VALERIO. 1985. *Kingship and Sacrifice: Ritual and Society in Ancient Hawaii.* Trans. Paula Wissing. Chicago: University of Chicago Press.

VAN DEN BERGHE, PIERRE. 1979. *Human Family Systems: An Evolutionary View.* New York: Elsevier Science Publishing Co.

———. 1980. "Incest and Exogamy: A Sociobiological Reconsideration." *Ethology and Sociobiology* 1:151–162.

———. 1981. *The Ethnic Phenomenon.* New York: Elsevier Science Publishing Co.

VAN DEN BERGHE, PIERRE, AND DAVID BARASH. 1977. "Inclusive Fitness Theory and the Human Family." *American Anthropologist* 79:809–823.

VAN GENNEP, ARNOLD. 1960. *The Rites of Passage*. Chicago: University of Chicago Press.

VAN WILLIGEN, JOHN, AND V. C. CHANNA. 1991. "Law, Custom, and Crimes Against Women: The Problem of Dowry Death in India." *Human Organization* 50(4):369–377.

VAYDA, ANDREW, ed. 1969. *Environment and Cultural Behavior*. Garden City, NY: Natural History Press.

VAYDA, ANDREW P. 1961. "Expansion and Warfare Among Swidden Agriculturalists." *American Anthropologist* 63:346–358.

VERDERY, KATHERINE. 1996. *What Was Socialism, and What Comes Next*. Princeton: Princeton University Press.

VINCENT, JOAN. 1990. *Anthropology and Politics: Visions, Traditions, and Trends*. Tucson: University of Arizona Press.

VOGT, EVON Z. 1969. *Zinacantan: A Maya Community in the Highlands of Chiapas*. Cambridge, MA: Harvard University Press.

VOLKMAN, TOBY ALICE. 1982. *The San in Transition. Vol. 1: A Guide to N!ai, The Story of A !Kung Woman*. Cambridge, MA: Cultural Survival.

VON DANIKEN, ERICH. 1970. *Chariots of the Gods*. New York: Bantam.

VON DER MEHDEN, FRED R. 1974. *Southeast Asia, 1930–1970: The Legacy of Colonialism and Nationalism*. New York: W. W. Norton.

VON FRISCH, KARL. 1967. *The Dance Language and Orientation of Bees*. Trans. L. E. Chadwick. Cambridge, MA: Harvard University Press.

WAFER, JIM 1991. *The Taste of Blood: Spirit Possession in Brazilian Candomble* (Contemporary Ethnography Series). Philadelphia: University of Pennsylvania Press.

WALKER, ANTHONY. 1986. *The Toda of South India: A New Look*. Delhi: Hindustan Publishing Company.

WALLACE, ANTHONY K. C. 1972. "Mental Illness, Biology, and Culture." In Francis Hsu, ed., *Psychological Anthropology*. Cambridge, MA: Schenkman.

WALLERSTEIN, IMMANUEL. 1974. *The Modern World-System: Capitalist Agriculture and the Origins of the European World-Economy in the Sixteenth Century*. New York: Academic Press.

———. 1979. *The Capitalist World-Economy*. New York: Cambridge University Press.

———. 1980. *The Modern World-System: II. Mercantilism and the Consolidation of the European World-Economy, 1600–1750*. New York: Academic Press.

———. 1986. *Africa and the Modern World*. Trenton, NJ: Africa World Press.

WANG, YU-CH'UAN. 1975. "The Central Government of the Former Han Dynasty." In Chun-shu Chang, ed., *The Making of China: Main Themes in Premodern Chinese History*. Englewood Cliffs, NJ: Prentice Hall.

WARSHAW, STEVEN. 1988. *Southeast Asia Emerges*. Berkeley, CA: Diablo Press.

———. 1989a. *China Emerges*. Berkeley, CA: Diablo Press.

———. 1989b. *India Emerges*. Berkeley, CA: Diablo Press.

WATSON, JAMES L. 1980. "Slavery as an Institution, Open and Closed Systems." In James L. Watson, ed., *Asian and African Systems of Slavery*. Berkeley: University of California Press.

WATSON, PATTY JO. 1971. *Explanation in Archaeology: An Explicitly Scientific Approach*. New York: Columbia University Press.

———. 1984. *Archaeological Explanation: The Scientific Method in Archaeology*. New York: Columbia University Press.

WATSON, WILLIAM. 1961. *China Before the Han Dynasty*. New York: Praeger.

WAX, ROSALIE. 1971. *Doing Fieldwork: Warnings and Advice*. Chicago: University of Chicago Press.

WEATHERFORD, JACK. 1988. *Indian Givers: How the Indians of the Americas Transformed the World*. New York: Crown.

WEBER, MAX. [1904] 1958. *The Protestant Ethic and the Spirit of Capitalism*. New York: Scribner.

———. 1927. *General Economic History*. New Brunswick, NJ: Transaction Books.

WEEKS, JOHN R. 1988. "The Demography of Islamic Nations." *Population Bulletin, Vol. 43, No. 4*. Washington, DC: Population Reference Bureau.

WEINER, ANNETTE B. 1987. *The Trobrianders of Papua New Guinea*. New York: Holt, Rinehart and Winston.

WELTY, PAUL THOMAS. 1984. *The Asians: Their Evolving Heritage*, 6th ed. New York: Harper & Row.

WEST, FRED. 1975. *The Way of Language: An Introduction*. New York: Harcourt Brace Jovanovich.

WHITE, DOUGLAS. 1988. "Rethinking Polygyny: Co-Wives, Codes, and Cultural Systems." *Current Anthropology* 29(4):529–553.

WHITE, JOHN PETER, AND JAMES F. O'CONNELL. 1982. *A Prehistory of Australia, New Guinea and Sahul*. New York: Academic Press.

WHITE, LESLIE. [1949] 1971. "The Symbol: The Origin and Basis of Human Behavior." In Leslie White, ed., *The Science of Culture: A Study of Man and Civilization*. New York: Farrar, Straus & Giroux.

———. 1959. *The Evolution of Culture*. New York: McGraw-Hill.

WHITE, RANDALL. 1982. "Rethinking the Middle/Upper Paleolithic Transition." *Current Anthropology* 23:169–192.

WHITING, BEATRICE B. AND WHITING, JOHN W. M. 1975. *Children of Six Cultures*. Cambridge, MA: Harvard University Press.

WHORF, BENJAMIN. 1956. *Language, Thought, and Reality: The Selected Writings of Benjamin Lee Whorf*. Cambridge, MA: MIT Press.

WIKAN, UNNI. 1991. *Behind the Veil in Arabia: Women in Oman*. Chicago: University of Chicago Press.

WILK, RICHARD R. 1996. *Economies and Cultures: Foundations of Economic Anthropology*. Boulder, CO: Westview Press.

WILLIAMS, HOLLY ANN. 1990. "Families in Refugee Camps." *Human Organization* 49(2):100–109.

WILLIAMS, ROBIN M., JR. 1970. *American Society: A Sociological Interpretation*, 3d ed. New York: Knopf.

WILSON, E. O. 1975. *Sociobiology: The New Synthesis*. Cambridge, MA: Harvard University Press.

———. 1978. *On Human Nature*. Cambridge, MA: Harvard University Press.

———. ed. 1988. *Biodiversity*. Washington, DC: Smithsonian Institution, National Academy of Sciences.

———. ed. 1989. *Biodiversity*. Washington, DC: National Academy Press.

———. 1992. *The Diversity of Life*. Cambridge, MA: Harvard University Press.

WILSON, E.O. AND SOUTHWORTH, LAURA SIMONDS. 1996. *In Search of Nature*. New York: Island Press.

WILSON, MONICA. 1951. *Good Company: A Study of Nyakyusa Age-Villages*. Boston: Beacon Press.

WITTFOGEL, KARL W. 1957. *Oriental Despotism: A Comparative Study of Total Power*. New Haven, CT: Yale University Press.

WOLF, ARTHUR. 1970. "Childhood Association and Sexual Attraction: A Further Test of the Westermarck Hypothesis." *American Anthropologist* 72:503–515.

WOLF, ERIC R. 1955a. "Closed Corporate Communities in Mesoamerica and Java." *Southwestern Journal of Anthropology* 13(1):1–18.

———. 1955b. "Types of Latin American Peasantry: A Preliminary Discussion." *American Anthropologist* 57(3), Part 1:452–471.

———. 1958. "The Virgin of Guadalupe: A Mexican National Symbol." *Journal of American Folklore* 71:34–39.

———. 1959. *Sons of the Shaking Earth*. Chicago: University of Chicago Press.

———. 1966. *Peasants*. Englewood Cliffs, NJ: Prentice Hall.

———. 1969. *Peasant Wars of the Twentieth Century*. New York: Harper & Row.

———. 1997 [1982]. *Europe and the People Without History*. Berkeley: University of California Press.

———. 1987. "Cycles of Violence. The Anthropology of War and Peace." In Kenneth Moore, ed., *Waymarks: The Notre Dame Inaugural Lectures in Anthropology,* pp. 127–151. Notre Dame, IN: University of Notre Dame Press.

———. 1999. *Envisioning Power: Ideologies of Domination and Crisis*. Berkeley: University of California Press.

WOLF, E. R., AND S. MINTZ. 1950. "An Analysis of Ritual Coparenthood (Compadrazgo)." *Southwestern Journal of Anthropology 6*. Reprinted in Jack A. Potter, May Diaz, and George Foster, eds., *Peasant Society: A Reader,* pp. 174–199. Boston: Little, Brown, 1967.

WOLFE, ALVIN. 1977. "The Supranational Organization of Production: An Evolutionary Perspective." *Current Anthropology* 18:615–635.

———. 1986. "The Multinational Corporation as a Form of Sociocultural Integration Above the Level of the State." In Hendrick Serrie, ed., *Anthropology and International Business*. Publication No. 28. Williamsburg, VA: Studies in Third World Societies.

WOLPOFF, MILFORD H. 1980. *Paleoanthropology*. New York: Knopf.

WOODBURN, JAMES. 1982. "Egalitarian Societies." *Man* 17:431–451.

WORLD ALMANAC AND BOOK OF FACTS. 1991. New York: Scripps Howard Company.

WORSLEY, PETER. 1957. *The Trumpet Shall Sound*. New York: Schocken.

———. 1984. *The Three Worlds: Culture and World Development*. Chicago: University of Chicago Press.

WRIGHT, HENRY T. 1977. "Recent Researches of the Origin of the State." *Annual Review of Anthropology* 6:355–370.

YELLEN, JOHN. 1985. "Bushmen." *Science* 85:40–48.

YOFFEE, NORMAN. 1979. "The decline and rise of Mesopotamian Civilizaton." *American Antiquity*. 44, 5–35.

YENGOYAN, ARAM A. 1986. "Theory in Anthropology: On the Demise of the Concept of Culture." *Comparative Studies in Society and History* 28(2):357–374.

Photo Credits

CHAPTER 1   Raymond B. Hames, 1; The Granger Collection, 3; Y. Nagata/United Nations, 5; C. Loring Brace, 6; David H. Kilper/Washington University, 8; Bambi B. Schieffelin, 9; Napoleon A. Chagnon, Anthro-Photo, 11; Japan National Tourist Organization, 16.

CHAPTER 2   Paul A. Souders/Corbis, 20; David L. Brill/David L. Brill Photography, Brill Atlanta, 25; Hank Morgan/Hank Morgan Photography, 29; Archiv fur Kunst und Geschichte, Berlin, 31; J.P. Brain/Peabody Museum/Anthro-Photo, 32; Susan Meiselas/Magnum Photos, Inc., 33; Bill Losh/FPG International LLC, 34.

CHAPTER 3   Alain Evrard/Liaison Agency, Inc., 37; Susan Hogue/Anthro-Photo, 40 (top, left); Tom McHugh/Photo Researchers, Inc., 40 (bottom, left); Paul Conklin/Monkmeyer Press, 40 (top, right); Art Resource, N.Y., 42; Rapho/Photo Researchers, Inc., 45; Daniel Laine/Corbis, 51; Sylvain Grandadam/Tony Stone Images, 57.

CHAPTER 4   David Hiser/Tony Stone Images, 62; Jen and Des Bartlett/Photo Researchers, Inc., 65; Corbis, 68; The Institute for Intercultural Studies, Inc., 68; Mark Wexler/Woodfin Camp & Associates, 71; ASAP/Sarit Uzieli/Photo Researchers, Inc., 77; Michael Busselle/Tony Stone Images, 81.

CHAPTER 5   James Stanfieldngs/National Geographic Society, James Stanfieldngs/NGS Image Collection, 90; Susan Kuklin/Science Inc. Source/Photo Researchers, 92; ChromoSohm/Sohm/The Stock Market, 98; AP/Wide World Photos, 101; Dilip Mehta/CONT/Woodfin Camp & Associates, 103; Vivienne della Grotta/Photo Researchers, Inc., 107; Nancy Durrell McKenna/Photo Researchers, Inc., 112; Paul Conklin/Monkmeyer Press, 114 (top, left); Suzanne Szasz/Photo Researchers, Inc., 114 (top, right); UPI/Corbis, 114 (bottom, left); Teri Stratford/Pearson Education/PH College, 114 (bottom, right); Noboru Komine/Photo Researchers, Inc., 115.

CHAPTER 6   Paul Chesley/Tony Stone Images, 118; Corbis, 122; Corbis, 124; Bernard Pierre Wolff/Photo Researchers, Inc., 127; Tony Howarth/Daily Telegraph/Woodfin Camp & Associates, 128.

CHAPTER 7   Katrina Thomas/Photo Researchers, Inc., 133; Anthro-Photo, 136; SuperStock, Inc., 144; Kaluzny/Thatcher/Tony Stone Images, 149; R. Ian Lloyd/The Stock Market, 151; Fred Lombardi/Photo Researchers, Inc., 153; Steven Weinberg/Tony Stone Images, 155.

CHAPTER 8   John Eastcott/Yva Momatiuk/Woodfin Camp & Associates, 160; Irven DeVore/Anthro-Photo, 163; American Museum of Natural History, Neg. no. 2a3766. Courtesy Dept. of Library Services, American Museum of Natural History. 164; Marjorie Shostak/Anthro-Photo, 173; Jim Steinberg/Photo Researchers, Inc., 180.

CHAPTER 9   Christopher Arnesen/Tony Stone Images, 183; Karl Weidmann/Photo Researchers, Inc., 186; Lorne Resnick/Tony Stone Images, 188; Corbis, 194; J.F.E. Bloss/Anthro-Photo, 205; Mimi Forsyth/Monkmeyer Press, 210.

CHAPTER 10   George Holton/Photo Researchers, Inc., 214; Cahokia Mounds State Historic Site, William R. Iseminger/Cahokia Mounds State Historic Site, 218; Corbis, 223; Tim O'Meara, 225; SEF/Art Resource, N.Y., 231.

CHAPTER 11   Yann Layma/Tony Stone Images, 234; Jim Fox/Photo Researchers, Inc., 237; SuperStock, Inc., 238; Malaysia Tourism Promotion Board, 241; Explorer/Y. Layma/Photo Researchers, Inc., 244.

CHAPTER 12   George Haling/Photo Reseachers, Inc., 255; Joan Lebold Cohen/Photo Researchers, Inc., 260; Eugene Gordon/Pearson Education/PH College, 261; UPI/Corbis, 263; American Textile History Museum, Lowell, Mass., E042-276-089, 267; Jim Whitmer/Stock Boston, 271; Harumi Befu, 276; Artists Rights Society Society, Museo Nacional Centro de Arte Reina Sofia, 279.

CHAPTER 13   Michael K. Nichols/National Geographic Society, Michael Nichols/NGS Image Collection, 284; Sean Sprague/Stock Boston, 287; Eric Wolf, 291; Wendy Stone/Liaison Agency, Inc., 294; Library of Congress, 296; The Granger Collection, 302; Bruce Asato/The Honolulu Advertiser, 305.

CHAPTER 14   SuperStock, Inc., 310; Owen Franken/Stock Boston, 317; Arvind Garg/Photo Researchers, Inc., 318; Peter Menzel/Stock Boston, 319 (top); Marc Bernheim/Woodfin Camp & Associates, 319 (bottom); Kirstin Norget, 320; Doug Mills/AP/Wide World Photos, 324; B. Daemmrich/The Image Works, 327; Jack Fields/Corbis, 334; Hubertus Kanus/Photo Researchers, Inc., 336.

CHAPTER 15   Paul Harris/Tony Stone Images, 340; Hulton-Deutsch Collection/Corbis, 348 (left); Hulton Getty/Liaison Agency, Inc., 348 (right); L. Van Der Stockt/Liaison Agency, Inc., 349; R.T. Nowitz/Photo Researchers, Inc., 351; Rick Smolan/Stock Boston, 355; Alon Reininger/Woodfin Camp & Associates, 359 (top); Arvind Garg/Liaison Agency, Inc., 359 (bottom); Prof. Susan Brownell, 360; Hulton Getty/Liaison Agency, Inc., 363; David Edwards, 365.

CHAPTER 16   Tom Van Sant/Geosphere Project, Santa Monica/Science Photo Library/Photo Researchers, Inc., 369; Lindsay Hebberd/Woodfin Camp & Associates, 373; Photo Researchers, Inc., 377; Mark Richards/PhotoEdit, 383; Pagnotta/REA/SABA Press Photos, Inc., 385; AP/Wide World Photos, 390; Ron Edmonds/AP/Wide World Photos, 391.

CHAPTER 17   Tim Crosby/Liaison Agency, Inc, 394; M & E Bernheim/Woodfin Camp & Associates, 397; John L. McCreery, 399; Steven Rubin/The Image Works, 400; Grant LeDuc/Monkmeyer Press, 401; Hamilton Wright/Photo Researchers, Inc., 403; Paul W. Liebhardt, 407.

Index

A

Abduh, Muhammad, 347
Aberle, David, 85
Abnormality, concept of, 84–85
Aborigines, Australian
  religious beliefs of, 178–79
  rock paintings of, 180
  subsistence pattern of, 163
  technology of, 167
Abuse, 175, 200
Abu Simbel, 402, 403
Ache foragers, 165, 170
Acheulian technology, 26
Achievement, need for, 286, 287
Acid rain, 371
Adaptation
  extreme form of, 126
  failures in, 252
  food and, 49–50
  human success in, 141
  predisposition for, 82, 83
Adapted Mind, The (Tuoby, Cosmides), 82, 83
Ade behavior, 72–73
Adjudication, 229
Adolescence, 68–69, 70, 151
Advocacy anthropology, 408
Affluence, 169–70
Afghanistan, 344, 364–66
Africa
  chiefdoms in, 216–17
  colonialism in, 312–14
  demographic change in, 315–16, 373
  early humans in, 24–26, 30
  economic development in, 317, 325, 327
  ethnic diversity in, 46, 332–34
  migration in, 336–37, 396
  peasantry in, 328–29
  political movements in, 322–25
  religious change in, 320–22
  slave trade in, 245–46, 312–14
  social relationships in, 330–31
African Americans
  demographic changes among, 46, 47
  family ties of, 268
  IQ scores of, 53–54
  language of, 105
  one-drop rule for, 55

African Famine Task Force, 335
African National Congress (ANC), 324
Afrikaners, 314, 322–24
Afterlife, 27
Agar, Michael, 401
Age grades, 151, 200, 201
Agency for International Development (AID), 397
Age roles
  among foragers, 174–76, 178
  in chiefdoms, 228
  in industrial societies, 271–72
  tribal, 200–202, 211
Age sets, 200–201
Age stratification, 150–51
Aggression, origins of, 206–7
Agribusiness, 142, 371
Agricultural revolution, 125, 372, 373
Agricultural states
  collapse of, 249–52
  demography of, 236–37
  emergence of, 125, 235
  law in, 246–47
  norms of, 45
  political economy of, 239–42
  religion in, 249
  social organization in, 242–46
  technology of, 237–39
  warfare in, 247–48
Agriculture. *See also* food production; horticulture; intensive agriculture; subsistence patterns
  African, 334–35
  collectivized, 265, 350
  global trends in, 258–59, 376
  innovations in, 237–38
  in marginal environments, 292, 293
  Native American, 8
  women's role in, 244
Agta foragers, 174
Air pollution, 371
Alaska, 102
Alcoholism, 293
Alternative therapies, 398, 400–401
Altruism, 168–69
Alverson, Hoyt, 107
Amaru, Tupac, 322
Amazonas, Venezuelan, 298
Amazon rain forest, 186–87, 297–98, 306, 307

Ambilateral descent, 226
Ambilineal descent, 193
Ambilocal residence, 227–28
American Anthropological Association, 335, 388
American Indian Movement (AIM), 302
American Revolution, 262
American Sign Language (ASL), 92
American Standard English, 105–6, 110, 111
American Telephone and Telegraph (AT&T), 270
Amin, Idi, 397
Amish society, 57–58
Amok disorder, 85
Analyst role, 396, 397
Ancient Society (Morgan), 120, 169
Andean Indians, 397
Anderson, Benedict, 275
Animals
  aggression among, 206
  bioprograms of, 65, 66, 87
  communication of, 92–95
  extinction of, 375
  humans as, 64–65
Animism, 178, 208, 281, 398
Anthro-list, 399
Anthropoids, 24
Anthropology. *See also specific subfields*
  "armchair," 122, 124
  British, 123–124
  goals of, 3, 119
  holistic approach to, 10–12, 134, 140, 377
  humanities and, 15–16
  interdisciplinary, 10–12, 377
  Marxist, 127–28
  modern economic, 146–47
  postmodern, 138–39
  research ethics in, 140
  role of, 391
  science of, 12–15
  significance of, 16–17
  subfields of, 3–10, 13, 17
Anticolonial movements, 347–48
Antiquities Act (1906), 403
Antislavery movements, 314
Apartheid, 322–24
Ape Language From Conditioned Response to Symbol (Terrace), 93

439

Apes, communicating with, 92–94
Apollonian culture, 67
Apparatchiki (bureaucratic elite), 276
Applied anthropology
 defined, 12, 395
 future of, 398
 intercultural workshops in, 47
 research focus of, 13
 resource management in, 402–4
 roles in, 395–98, 406–8
Applied archaeology, 402
Applied research, 13
Arabic language, 341
Arab-Israeli War (1967), 362
Arapesh tribe, 198
Arbitrariness, linguistic, 94–95
Arbitration, 207, 247
Archaeological Explanation (Watson
  et al.), 8
Archaeological research, 7–8, 44
Archaeological Resources Protection Act
  (1979), 403
Archaeological sites, 27, 29, 30, 402–4
Archaeology, 3, 6–8
 basic research in, 13
 humanistic issues in, 15
 subfields of, 5
Architecture, 230–31
Arctic tundra, 143, 164–65
Ardipithecus ramidus, 24
Arena, political, 152
Argentina, 33
Argonauts of the Western Pacific
  (Malinowski), 221
Aristotle, 22
Arkansas Archaeological Survey, 404
Armstrong, Neil, 2, 3
Art
 abstract, 279
 of agricultural states, 237, 238
 of chiefdoms, 230–31
 Cro-Magnon, 31
 naturalistic, 179–80
 study of, 15–16
 tribal, 210
 Upper Paleolithic, 35
Artifacts, 6, 7, 28, 29, 402–4
Arunta foragers, 163
"Aryan race," 52–53, 257, 258
Aryan society, 355
Asch, Timothy, 11
Ascribed status, 147
Asia
 colonialism in, 344–45
 demographic change in, 345–46
 economic development in, 346, 349,
  350–51
 ethnic diversity in, 46, 360–62
 languages in, 97, 102
 religion in, 346–47

revolutionary movements in, 348–49
 socialism in, 350–51
 social structure in, 355–59
Asian Americans, 47
Assimilation, 56, 57, 332
Aswan Dam, 402
Atheism, 280
Atlas of World Cultures (Murdock), 156
Atomic era, 279
Australopithecines, 24–25, 96, 97
Authority
 age-related, 228, 271–72
 agricultural state, 239
 among foragers, 176
 chiefly, 220, 224–25
 divine, 229–30, 249
 justification of, 44
 legal, 154
 in matrilineal societies, 200
 political, 151–52
 tribal, 202
Autonomy, 176, 390
Avunculocal residence, 197
Aymara language, 108
Azande tribe, 44, 208–09
Aztec Indians
 conquest of, 312
 religious practices of, 42, 43, 405
 social organization among, 246
 warfare by, 248

B

Baba, Marietta L., 265
Babylonian code of law, 246, 247
Baktaman people, 136
Balanced reciprocity, 168, 190
Balikci, Ansen, 164, 173
Balinese society, 138
Bands, 152, 161, 171. *See also* foraging
  societies
Barkow, Jerome, 83
Barnett, Steve, 265
Barrett, Richard, 130
Barter system, 222
Barth, Frederick, 56, 136
Barton, R. F., 206–07
Basseri tribe, 188
Batak foragers, 174
Beals, Alan, 355
Beck, Lois, 299, 354
Bedouins of Arabia
 culture of, 298–99
 infanticide among, 353
 proverb of, 204
 subsistence patterns of, 187, 188
 technology of, 190
Beeman, William, 362

Befu, Harumi, 276–77
Behavior. *See also* instincts
 abnormal, 84–85
 animal, 65–66, 87
 biological vs. cultural, 49
 conditioning of, 39
 double standard for, 404–6
 Freud's theory of, 73–74
 individual patterns of, 86
 innate, 66, 67, 128, 129
 learned, 65–66
 measuring, 15
 predicting, 119
 stereotyped, 51–52
 universal patterns of, 58, 64
Behaviorist model, 100, 115
Belgium, 322
Beliefs, 38
 double standard for, 404–6
 interpreting, 129
 Neanderthal, 27
 types of, 44–45
Bell Curve, The (Herrnstein, Murray),
  53–54
Benedict, Ruth, 67–68, 69, 70, 83, 84, 87,
  123, 222–23, 277, 405
Ben & Jerry's Homemade, 307
Bennett, John, 391
Berdaches (homosexuals), 79
Berdan, Francis, 248
Beringia, 32
Bering Strait, 32
Berlin, Brent, 99–100
Berlin Wall, 384
Bernard, Russell, 103
Bhopal, India, 371
Bible, 22, 202
Bickerton, Derek, 104–5
Big Drum ceremony, 315
"Big man" system, 202–3
Bilateral descent, 193, 194, 242
Bilingual Education Act, U. S., 103
Bilingualism, 103
Binet, Alfred, 53
Biodiversity, 28, 375–76
Biology, 64, 87
Biomes, 142, 143, 157. *See also* environ-
  ment
Bioprograms, 66
Biotechnology research, 371
Bipedalism, 24
Birdsell, Joseph, 166
Birth control, 259, 374. *See also* popula-
  tion control
Birth rates
 in agricultural states, 236–37
 in colonized societies, 316
 crude, 142, 144
 cultural influences on, 145
 ethnic minority, 46

in industrial states, 259
in non-Western societies, 345
trends in, 372, 374
Black English (BE), 105–6
Black Madonna of Czestochowa, 43
Blades, 28
Blended families, 173
Bloch, Maurice, 81
Blood quanta rules, 55
Boas, Franz, 53, 55, 68, 74, 122–23, 131, 222, 404–5
Boat people, Vietnamese, 389
Bocas Del Toro plantation, 325–26
Bodley, John, 258
Body language, 113–14, 116
Body Shops, 307
Boehm, Christopher, 176
Boer War (1899–1902), 314
Bolivar, Simon, 322
Bonaparte, Napoleon, 342
Borers, 28
Boserup, Ester, 243
Boster, James, 100
Bourgeoisie, 273, 324
Bourgois, Philippe, 325–26, 401–2
"Bowwow" theory, 95
Brace, C. Loring, 6
Braidwood, Robert, 8
Brain, human
evolution of, 24, 25–26, 27, 82–83
intelligence and, 53, 123
speech centers in, 95–96
Brazil, 55, 298, 314
breast-feeding, 166
Brewer, Earl Leroy, 360
Bride burning, 406–7
Brideservice, 172
Bridewealth, 196, 198, 228, 243
Briody, Elizabeth, 265
Britain. See Great Britain
British East India Co., 257
British English, 111
Broca's area, 96
Brokensha, David, 328
Brown, Donald E., 58, 83
Brown, John Seely, 264
Brownell, Susan, 360–61
Buddhism
doctrines of, 346–47
greetings in, 113
medical practices of, 398, 400–401
rituals in, 137
Budding hypothesis, 26
Burakumin people, 54, 275
Bureaucracy, 152, 277
Bureau of Indian Affairs (BIA), 297
Burial sites, 27, 403–4
Burins, 28
Burma, 344
Butler, Joyce, 92

C

Cahokian society, 217–19, 231
Cajuns, 144
Call systems, 93
Cambodian refugees, 390
Capitalism, 44
Asian withdrawal from, 350–51
Chinese, 384
corporate, 266, 386
dependency on, 288
development of, 127
individualism and, 74, 75
in industrial states, 262–63
Capitalist class, 127, 273
Caravan trade, 241, 298–99
Carbon dioxide emissions, 371, 379
Cargo cults, 302–4
Caribbean, 313
colonialism in, 314–15
Creoles of, 105
cultural diversity in, 311
demographic change in, 315–16
economic development in, 325
ethnicity in, 334–36
peasantry in, 328
political movements in, 322, 324–25
religious practices in, 319–20
urban migration in, 336–37
Carneiro, Robert, 225
Carriacou society, 315
Carrying capacity, 144–45
Cash economy, 293, 297, 346
Caste system, 245, 355–57
Catholicism, 42–43, 151, 317–18, 319. *See also* Christianity
Cattle, 188, 356
Cause-and-effect relationships, 140–41
Cave bear cult, 27
Caves, 8, 30, 31
Ceremonial complexes, Moche, 250
Chagnon, Napoleon, 11, 186, 205, 207, 298, 306
Chamberlain, Houston Stewart, 53
Chambers, Erve, 395–96
Chance, Norman, 358
Channa, V. C., 406, 407
Chiang Kai-shek, 348
Chiefdoms
art and music of, 230–32
cultural change in, 299–301
demography of, 218–19
Latin American, 312
law and religion in, 229–30
political system of, 152, 220–25
social organization in, 225–29
subsistence in, 215–18
technology of, 219–20
Childbirth, 166, 199–200

Childe, Gordon, 247
Childhood familiarity hypothesis, 77–78
Children
in agricultural states, 236–37
cognitive development in, 80–82
emotional development in, 84
enculturation of, 68–69, 70–73
of foragers, 174–75, 176, 178
language acquisition in, 101
multicultural education for, 47
Children of History (Edwards), 365
Children of Six Cultures, 71
Chimpanzees, communicating with, 92–94, 95, 96
Chimpsky, Nim (chimpanzee), 92
China
colonialism in, 344–45
early humans in, 25
economic reform in, 384–85
foot binding in, 244
individualism in, 75
legal system of, 247
origin myth in, 22
revolutionary movements in, 348
socialism in, 350
social structure in, 99, 245, 358–59
sports in, 360–61
technology of, 238–39
Chippewa tribe, 85
Choctaw tribe, 296
Chomsky, Noam, 100–101, 104, 105, 115
Chopper tools, 25
Christianity. *See also* Catholicism
African, 320–22
in feudal societies, 244
medieval, 74–75
origin myth in, 22
sexism in, 245
Circumstantialist model, 56–57
Civilization, 130, 235–36
savagery vs., 120, 121
Clans, 193, 226
Clash of Cultures (Fagan), 305
Classical archaeologists, 5, 6
Classification systems, 82
Class struggle, 127
Class systems, 272–274. *See also* caste system; social stratification
Clay, Jason, 307
Clifford, James, 138, 139
Climate
adaptation to, 49, 50
famine due to, 334
of Pleistocene, 26, 31–32
Closed peasant community, 328
Clothing, 27, 50, 167
Clovis spear points, 32
Club of Rome, 376
Cognitive anthropology, 99
Cognitive development, 80–82, 87

Cohen, Abner, 333
Cold War, 285–86, 288, 366
Cole, Donald, 298–99
Cole, Michael, 82
Collective ownership, 169
Collier, Jane, 227
Colonialism
    in Africa, 312–14
    in Asia, 344–45
    in Caribbean, 314–15
    consequences of, 315–22, 345–49
    famine due to, 334
    industrialization and, 285
    in Latin America, 312
    in Middle East, 342–44
    political change due to, 322–25
    racist promotion of, 5
    resistance to, 304
Colonies, exploitation of, 288
Color classification, 99–100
Colson, Elizabeth, 396
Columbus, Christopher, 312
Comecon, 266
Coming of Age in Samoa (Mead), 69
Command economy, 240
Commencement ceremonies, 280
Commercial revolution, 256–58
Committee on Global Change, U. S., 377
Committee on Refugee Issues (CORI), 388
Commodities, 145, 220–21, 307
Commonsense knowledge, 12–13, 44
Communes, Chinese, 350, 358–59
Communication. *See also* language
    animal, 92–95
    defined, 91
    evolution of, 26
    interethnic, 58
    nonverbal, 113–14, 116
    symbolic, 39–40, 50–51
Communism, 127, 382–85
Communist party
    Asian, 350, 351
    Chinese, 348, 358
    economic control by, 266
    Polish, 43
    repression by, 276–77
Compadrazgo relationships, 329
Competition, global, 385–86, 392
Complementary opposition, 203–4
Composite tools, 28–29
Computers, 103, 137
Comte, Auguste, 390
Concrete-operational stage, 81
Conditioning, behavioral, 39, 40, 100
Confidentiality, 140
Conflict resolution, 178, 205–8, 278
Conflict theory, 247
Confucian ethos, 244–45, 272, 278, 358
Congo (Zaire), 294, 314, 322
Conquistadores, 312, 316

Consumerism, 75, 265
Continental shelves, 32
Convention on Cultural Property (1982), 403
Cook, Captain, 299–300
Cooperatives, agricultural, 350
Copernicus, 22
Core societies
    control by, 381
    defined, 289
    economic changes in, 385–86
    location of, 290
Corporate culture, 264, 276–77
Corporate descent, 194, 209
Corporations, 264–65, 266, 276–77. *See also* multinational corporations
Correlation, statistical, 140
Cortés, Hernando, 312
Cosmic religions, 178–79
Cosmides, B., 82
Cosmides, Leda, 82
Cosmologies, 21, 42, 248. *See also* myths
Court system, 247, 248, 278
Cousin marriage, 171, 172, 195, 227
Cowgill, Donald O., 271–72
Crack cocaine, 401–402
Crafts, 239
Cranial capacity, 24–25, 27, 123
Cree Indians, 85
Creole languages, 104–106
Crime, in chiefdoms, 229
Critical thinking, 16–17
Cro-Magnon, 30–31
Cross-cousin marriage, 171, 172, 195
Cross-cultural analysis, 17, 58
Crow Dog, Leonard, 302
Crow Indians, 103
Cuba, 316, 325
Cultural anthropology. *See* ethnology
Cultural ecology, 125, 126, 141–42
Culturalism, 130
Cultural materialism, 126–27, 382
Cultural Property Act (1983), 403
Cultural relativism, 49, 122, 404–6
Cultural resource management (CRM), 402–404
Cultural Revolution, Chinese, 350
Cultural Survival, 307, 398
Culture. *See also* enculturation
    archaeological, 29
    breakdown of, 250–252
    characteristics of, 38–39
    components of, 41, 44–45, 47, 59
    diffusion of, 121–22
    diversity of, 17, 48–51, 83–84
    high- vs. low-energy, 258–59
    ideal, 48
    IQ scores and, 53–55
    language in, 106–108
    learning, 39–41

mass-marketing of, 304
mental illness and, 84–86
personality and, 67–73
phenomena in, 15
population growth and, 145
of poverty, 336–37
prehistoric, 28–32
race and racism in, 51–55
universals in, 58–59, 81–82
vs. biology, 64, 66–67
Culture and Morality (Hatch), 404
Culture-and-personality theory, 67–69, 87, 123
Culture core, 125
Culture shock, 11, 137, 140
Czestochowa shrine, 43

D

D'Andrade, Roy, 41
Dani tribe, 405
Darwin, Charles, 6, 22–23, 34, 52, 119–20, 141, 279
Data, ethnological, 135–37
    analysis of, 140–41
Database, ethnographic, 137, 156, 157
Day of the Dead, 318, 320–21
Death, dowry, 406–7
Deculturation, 295, 300–301
Deductive method, 14
Deforestation, 335, 375, 378–79, 379
Demarest, William, 337
Democratic socialism, 266
Democratic states, 275
Demographic anthropology, 142
Demographics
    in agricultural states, 236–37, 252
    assessment models for, 376–80
    in chiefdoms, 218–19
    colonialism and, 315–16
    elements of, 142, 144–45
    in foraging societies, 165–67
    global trends in, 371–75, 392
    in industrial states, 259, 260
    in non-Western societies, 345–46
    tribal, 188–89
    U. S. trends in, 46–47
Demographic transition theory, 371–74
Deng Xiaoping, 384–85
Dependency theory, 288–89, 381
Dependent variables, 140–41
Depopulation, 295, 297, 298, 300, 316–17
Depression, mental, 86
Deprivation, relative, 324–25
Descartes, René, 100
Descent groups, 192–94, 226
Desertification, 335
Desert subsistence, 162–63

Detention camps, 388–89
Determinism, 70, 146
DeVoe, Pamela, 388
DeWalt, Billie, 378, 398
Dialects, 110–11
Diaz, May, 330
Diego, Juan, 42–43
Dien Bien Phu, 348
Diet
  among foragers, 162–65,
    169–70
  in chiefdoms, 216–18
  cultural diversity in, 49–50
  horticulturalist, 186–87
  Mesoamerican, 248
  Upper Paleolithic, 30
Diffusionism, 121–22, 130
"Ding-dong" theory, 95
Dionysian culture, 68
Disease
  in aboriginal societies, 294, 297
  anthropological studies of, 398
  in colonized societies, 315–16
  control of, 259
  rise in, 236
Displacement, linguistic, 94
Distribution, defined, 146
Divale, William, 199, 204
Divine rulers, 229–30, 249
Divorce, 173, 198, 244, 269, 353
Dobuan people, 68
Doctor-patient relationship, 400–401
Doi moi reforms, 385
Donnelly, Nancy, 389
Doomsday Model, 376
Dordogne site, 30
Double descent, 193
Dowries, 243, 357, 406–407
Dreadlock hairstyle, 50–51
Dreamtime, the, 178–79
Dress codes
  Amish, 57–58
  Islamic, 45, 48, 79, 354–55
  symbolism of, 50–51
Drives, biological, 66, 78
Drug addiction, 401–2
Duality of patterning, 95
Dumont, Louis, 75, 357
Durham, William, 205
Dutch Empire, 345
Dyadic contract, 329
Dyson-Hudson, Rada, 169

E

Earle, Timothy, 221
Earth Summit (1992), 379
Easter Island, 230–31

Eastern Europe, 384
Ebene powder, 208
Ebonics (Black English), 105–6
Ecclesiastical religions, 249, 253
Ecological anthropology, 125
Ecology, 141
Economic anthropology, 222
Economic exchange. See also mercantil-
    ism; reciprocal exchange; trade
  among foragers, 168–69
  in chiefdoms, 221–24
  of commodities, 220–21
  defined, 146
  in industrial states, 261–62
Economics, 12, 194, 380–87
Economic systems, 240, 266–67
Economies. See also global economy
  anthropological approaches to, 146–47
  Chinese, 384–85
  of core societies, 385–86
  Eastern European, 384
  foraging, 167–70
  industrial, 260–67
  jajmani, 355–57
  moral, 240–41
  non-Western, 316–17, 346
  semiperipheral, 386–87
  Soviet, 382–84
  tribal, 190–91, 211
  underground, 402
  Vietnamese, 385
Education
  assimilation policies in, 56
  goal of, 17
  IQ scores and, 54
  Japanese, 273
  liberal arts, 16
  multicultural, 47, 264–65
Edwards, David, 365, 366
Egalitarian societies, 168, 293
Ego, 73
Egypt
  colonialism in, 342
  cultural diffusion in, 121
  female status in, 354
  industrialization of, 351–52
  Old Kingdom of, 250
Eickelman, Dale, 359
Ekman, Paul, 113
Elderly
  in foraging societies, 175, 178
  in industrial societies, 271–72
  roles for, 150–51
  tribal, 201–2
Eliade, Mircea, 178
Elima (puberty ritual), 175, 180
Elite, bureaucratic, 276
Elite class, 239–40, 242, 243
Ember, Carol, 177, 197
Ember, Melvin, 78, 197

Emirs, Saudi Arabian, 299
Emotions, 83–84, 113–14
Encomiendas (land grants), 316, 345
Enculturation. See also culture; socializa-
    tion
  age and, 150
  during childhood, 70–72
  cognition and, 80–82
  defined, 39, 63
  early studies of, 67–70
  emotions and, 83–84
  ethnic, 56
  of gender, 149, 198–99
  language and, 110
  limits of, 86
  primordialist view of, 57
  psychoanalytic approaches to, 73–76
  religious, 154
  sex drive and, 78–80
  two-way, 72–73
Endogamy, 148
  in agricultural states, 243
  in chiefdoms, 227
  Middle Eastern, 352
  tribal, 195
Energy
  consumption of, 258–59, 375, 376
  resources for, 144–45
  in sociocultural development, 124–25,
    126–27
Enga, Mae, 204
English language
  dialects of, 105–6, 111
  gender bias in, 108
  greetings in, 111–12
  kinship terms in, 99
  Native American adoption of, 102, 103
  nonhuman understanding of, 93
  structure of, 98, 101
Enlightenment, the, 119
Enterprise, state-owned, 266
Entrepreneurs, 240, 263
Environment. See also biomes
  African, 335
  assessment models for, 376–80
  energy resources in, 258–59
  of foragers, 162–65
  global trends in, 370–71, 392
  instinctive behavior and, 65
  IQ scores and, 53–55
  mental illness and, 85
  natural selection and, 23, 35
  of Pleistocene, 26, 31–32
  population size and, 144–45
  in sociocultural development, 125,
    126–27
  subsistence in, 141–42, 157
  of tribal societies, 185–88
Environmental disasters, 250–52
Envisioning Power (Wolf), 291

Epidemics, 236, 293, 300
Epidemiology, 398
Equality, gender, 270–71
Equal opportunity, 273
Equal Rights Amendment (ERA), 271
Erasmus, Charles, 328
Eskimo society
    economy of, 168, 169
    language of, 107–108
    mental illness in, 85
    religious beliefs in, 179
    social organization in, 172–73, 174, 175
    song duel of, 178
    subsistence patterns of, 164–65
    technology of, 167
Essai sur l'inegalité des races humaines
        (Gobineau), 52–53
Essences (humors), 51–52, 55
Ethical relativism, 404–6
Ethics, in research, 140
Ethiopia, 334–35
Ethnic groups, 56, 387
    African, 332
    in agricultural states, 246
    Asian, 360–62
    circumstantialist view of, 56–57
    demographic changes in, 46–47
    dominant, 45
    family ties in, 268
    IQ studies of, 54
    Middle Eastern, 359–60
    primordialist view of, 57–58
Ethnicity, 55–56
    anthropological models for, 56–58
    diversity in, 46–47
    exploitation based on, 326–27
    global trends in, 387, 390, 392
    Latin American, 331–32
    vs. race, 246
Ethnic stratification, 246, 274–75
Ethnocentrism
    among missionaries, 321
    defined, 48
    in diffusionistic theory, 121
    in modernization theory, 287
    in social evolution, 120
    vs. cultural relativism, 49
Ethnocide, 292
Ethnogenesis, 57
Ethnographic Atlas (Murdock), 156, 173
Ethnographies, 10, 17
    data analysis for, 140
    databases for, 156, 157
    postmodernist, 139
Ethnological research
    basic, 13
    conceptual framework for, 39
    examples of, 9, 11
    future of, 138–39
    interdisciplinary focus of, 256

methodology in, 49
objectives of, 44, 156–57
roles in, 10, 264
strategies for, 135–37
variables in, 140
Ethnology, 10
    fieldwork in, 122, 134–41
    humanistic issues in, 15
    social sciences and, 11–12
    specializations in, 3, 5
    value judgments in, 49
Ethnomusicology, 15, 16
Ethnopoetics, 15
Ethnosemantics, 99
Ethological research, 93–94
Ethos, 45, 153
Etiquette, standards of, 45, 48
Europe
    colonialist expansion by, 342–45
    dietary practices in, 49
    early humans in, 25, 30–31
    Industrial Revolution in, 256,
        257–58
    political organization in, 275
    population growth in, 259
    racism in, 52–53
    slave trading by, 313
European Americans, 53–54
Europe and the People without History
        (Wolf), 291, 292
Evans-Pritchard, E. E., 188, 198, 208
"Eve hypothesis," 28
Evolution
    cultural, 305
    cultural-physical, 6–7
    defined, 22
    early human, 24–28, 82–83
    research in, 4
    social, 52
    theories of, 21–24
    types of, 125
Evolutionary psychology, 66, 82–83
Evolutionism, 119–21, 124–26
Exogamy, 148, 227
Expectations, rising, 324
Explanation in Archaeology (Watson et
        al.), 8
Exploration, world, 257
Exports, 385, 386–87
Extended families
    African, 330, 331
    in agricultural states, 242–43
    among foragers, 171
    in chiefdoms, 227
    defined, 148
    in industrialized states, 267–68, 272
    Middle Eastern, 362
    South Asian, 357
    tribal, 191–192
Extinction, of species, 375

F

Facial expressions, 113–14
Facilitator role, 396, 397
Factory system, 259, 260
Fagan, Brian, 305, 404
Faith, 13
Fakhouri, Hani, 351
Falk, Dean D., 7
Families
    African, 330
    in agricultural states, 236–37, 242–43
    Chinese, 358–59
    evolution of, 120
    incest taboo in, 77–78
    in industrial states, 259, 267–68
    Middle Eastern, 352
    refugee, 389–90
    South Asian, 357
    tribal, 191–92
    types and functions of, 148
Family planning, 358–59, 372
Famine, 294–95, 316, 334–35
Fazendas (farms), 316–17
Fecundity, 144
Federal Bureau of Investigations (FBI), 302
Fedigan, Linda Marie, 174
Fellaheen (peasants), 351–52
Feminist movement, 199, 270–71
Fernea, Elizabeth, 354
Fertility rates
    in agricultural states, 236–37
    among foragers, 166–67
    cultural influences on, 145
    in industrial states, 259
    measuring, 142, 144
    in non-Western societies, 316, 345
    trends in, 371–72
Fertilizers, chemical, 371
Feudalism
    entrepreneurship in, 240
    Japanese, 263, 287
    political economy of, 239
    Russian, 263–64
    warfare and, 247
Feuds, 152
Fictive kinship ties, 329
Field notes, 137
Fieldwork, ethnological, 122, 134–41. *See
        also* ethnological research
Fire, early use of, 26, 27, 30
First contact, 2
First World, 286–87, 288
Fischer, Michael, 138, 362
Fissioning, 166, 189
Flags, national, 40–41, 42
Fleuret, Patrick, 397
Flinn, Mark, 82
Folkways, 45, 48, 55. *See also* norms; values

Food. *See also* diet
shortages of, 316, 334–35
storage of, 170, 220, 239
Food production. *See also* agriculture; subsistence patterns
development of, 161
environmental capacity for, 144–45
global trends in, 376, 378
surplus, 239, 240
Upper Paleolithic, 30
Foot binding, 244
Foraging, 142
Foraging societies. *See also* bands
characteristics of, 125
cultural change among, 292–95
defined, 161
demographics of, 165–67
economic systems of, 167–70
Latin American, 312
mores of, 48
political organization of, 176–78
religion of, 178–80
social organization of, 170–76
subsistence patterns of, 162–65
technology of, 167
Upper Paleolithic, 30
Ford Motor Co., 386
Forensic anthropology, 33
Forests, 143, 187. *See also* rain forests, tropical
Fore tribe, 114, 209
Formalist approach, 146
Formal-operational stage, 81
Fossil fuels, 258–59, 371, 375
Fossils, 4, 24–27
Foster, George, 329
Fourth World, 292
Fouts, Roger, 92
Fox, Richard, 360
France
archaeological sites in, 30, 31
colonialist expansion by, 342–43, 345, 348–49
fur trade of, 295–96
slave trade of, 313
Frank, Andre Gunder, 288
Freedom movement, Chinese, 384–85
Freeman, Derek, 69–70
Freud, Sigmund, 73–74, 76, 87
Fried, Morton, 2, 177, 184–85, 246
Functionalism, 123–24, 127
Fundamentalist movements, 156, 362–66, 391
Fur trade, 295–96

G

Gacy, John Wayne, 33
Galileo, 22, 279
Galton, Francis, 52
Gandhi, Indira, 361
Gandhi, Mohandas, 347–48, 367
Garbage studies, 6, 7
Gardner, Allen, 92
Gardner, Beatrice, 92
Gardner, Howard, 54
Gardner, Peter, 176
Geertz, Clifford, 12, 138, 154, 239, 346, 365
Gender, views on, 12–13
Gender bias, 108
Gender relations. *See also* women, status of
in agricultural states, 244–45, 253, 281
among foragers, 173–76, 181
in chiefdoms, 228, 232
Chinese, 358–59
Indian, 406–7
in industrial states, 269–71
issues concerning, 148–50
Latin American, 329–30
Middle Eastern, 353–55
Romanian, 384
South Asian, 357–58
tribal, 198–200
General exchange, 195
Generalized reciprocity, 168, 190
General Motors, 265
Generative grammar model, 101
Genes. *See also* Heredity
defined, 23
inbreeding and, 76–77, 78
perpetuation of, 128–29
skin-color, 34
violence-promoting, 206
Genetic engineering, 371
Genetics, 23, 35, 66, 67. *See also* biodiversity; heredity
Genocide, 292
Gentry class, 245
Geological sciences, 22
German Democratic Republic, 384
Gerontocracy, 201–2, 228
Gestures, 113
Gewertz, Deborah, 199
Ghana, 322
Ghost Dance, 301–2
Ghost lineage, 209
Give and Take of Everyday Life, The (Schieffelin), 9
Glaciers, 26, 31–32
Glasnost, 382–84
Global economy, 266, 350–51, 380–87. *See also* economies
Globalization. *See also* industrialization
Africa and, 312–14
Asia and, 344–45
Caribbean and, 314–15
cultural change through, 257–58, 315–22
environmental impact of, 370–71
foragers and, 292–95
Latin America and, 312
Middle East and, 342–44
political consequences of, 322–25
resistance to, 301–5
theories of, 285–92, 308
tribal societies and, 295–99
Global perspective, 12, 16–17, 257
Glottochronology, 110
Gluckman, Max, 328
Gobineau, Joseph Arthur de, 52–53
Goldschmidt, Walter, 205
Golomb, Louis, 398, 400–401
Gombe Game Reserve, Africa, 93
Goodall, Jane, 93–94
Goodenough, Ward, 197
Goods, 145, 146, 261–62
Goody, Jack, 243, 257
Gorbachev, Mikhail, 382, 383
Gorillas, communicating with, 92, 93
Government. *See also* political organization
of agricultural states, 239
centralized, 277
economic intervention by, 266
ideological basis for, 44
representative, 275
Government, U.S.
archaeological legislation by, 403
assimilation policies of, 56
blood quanta rules of, 55
industrialization efforts of, 262–63
multicultural programs of, 47
Native American relations with, 296, 302
Grammar, 100–101, 106, 110
Grasslands, temperate, 143
Great Britain
class system in, 273–74
colonialist expansion by, 342–45, 346, 364
fur trade of, 295–96
India and, 347–48
slave trading by, 313
Great Leap Forward, 350
"Great Trek," 314
Greece, ancient, 22, 51–52, 245
Greenberg, Joseph, 98
Greenhouse effect, 371
Green Revolution, 371, 377–79, 397
Greetings, 111–13
Gross national product (GNP), 287, 385
Group model, 276–77
Guatemalan Indians, 146
Guernica (Picasso), 279
Gullah language, 105
Gusii people, 71

H

Haciendas (plantations), 316–17, 325, 345, 397

Hadza society, 174
Haggling system, 242, 262
Haimes, Raymond, 205
Hairstyles, symbolism of, 50
Haiti, 319–20, 378–79
Hall, Edward T., 114
Hallucinogens, 208, 249, 302
Hames, Raymond, 297, 298
Hammer stones, 25
Hammurabi codes, 246, 247
Hamula (kinship group), 352
Handbook of North American Indians
    (Ubelaker), 297
Hardman-de-Bautista, M. J., 108
Harems, 243
Harner, Michael, 248
Harris, Marvin, 49–50, 126, 131, 197, 199,
    204–205, 223, 248, 356, 382
Hatch, Elvin, 404
Hausa people, 332–34
Hawaii
    colonialism in, 299–300
    commodity exchange in, 221
    language of, 99
    music of, 231–32
    political system in, 224–25
    religion in, 229–30, 304–5
    social structure in, 226, 227
Hawaiian Renaissance, 304–5
Hawkes, Kristin, 165
Headhunting, 204
Headman, village, 202
Healers
    African, 322
    among foragers, 179, 181
    native, 156
    Thai, 398, 400–401
Health care systems, 388, 398, 400–401
Hegemony, cultural
    in chiefdoms, 228, 229
    defined, 44–45
    examples of, 56, 57
    source of, 130
Hegland, Mary, 362
Heider, Karl, 83–84
Hendry, Joy, 71–72, 269
Herbicides, 371
Herd animals, 187–88
Herdt, Gilbert, 79
Heredity, 23, 53, 64. *See also* genetics
Hermaphrodites, 12
Herodotus, 48
Heroes of the Age (Edwards), 365
Heroin addiction, 401–2
Herrnstein, Richard, 53–54
Heterogeneity, cultural, 278
Hijras (eunuchs), 79
Hill, Kimberly, 165
Hill-Burnett, Jacquetta, 47
Hindu culture, 75, 79, 81, 107

Hinduism, 245, 346–47, 356, 357,
    398
Hinton, Robert, 7
Hippocrates, 51–52
Hiroshima, 279
Hispanic Americans, 46–47, 268
Historical archaeologists, 5, 6
Historical linguistics, 10, 108–10, 116
Historical particularism, 122–23, 131
Historic Sites Act (1935), 403
History, field of, 12
Hitchcock, Robert, 306–7
Hitler, Adolf, 53
Ho Chi Minh, 348, 367
Holmberg, Allan, 295, 397
Holocaust, the, 53
Homestead Act (1862), 263
Homicide, 177, 293
Hominids, 24–28, 96–97
Homo erectus, 24, 25–26, 28, 97
Homogeneity, 102, 278
Homo habilis, 24, 34, 44, 97
Homo Hierarchicus (Dumont), 75
Homo sapiens
    archaic, 26–27, 96, 97
    evolution of, 24
    modern, 27–32, 96
    neanderthalensis, 6
Homosexual behavior, 79–80
Hong Kong, 386, 389
Honorifics, 111
Hopi (playground), 174–75
Hopi society, 106–7, 193, 198
Horticulturalist societies
    cultural change in, 295–98
    female status in, 200
    Latin American, 312
    political organization in, 202–3
    population densities of, 189
    subsistence patterns in, 185–87
    warfare in, 204
Horticulture, 142, 185, 216, 306. *See also*
    agriculture
Hottentots, 314
Housing, of chiefdoms, 219–20
Howell, Nancy, 166
Hsu, Francis, 75
Humanitarianism, 405, 406, 408
Humanities, 15–16
Human nature, 63, 64–67
Human Relations Area Files (HRAF),
    156–57
Human rights, 33, 406–8
Humans, 64–65, 66, 87
Human sacrifice, 228, 230, 248, 300
Human Universals (Brown), 58
Humboldt, William von, 94
"Humoral-environmental" essentialist the-
    ory, 51–52
Hunter-gatherers. *See* Foraging societies

Hussein, Saddam, 350
Hxaro system, 168
Hypodescent concept, 55
Hypotheses, 14, 15, 140

I

Iberian conquest, 312, 316
Ice Age. *See* Pleistocene period
Id, 73, 74
Ideal culture, 48
Identity
    cultural, 304–5
    ethnic, 29, 57–58, 332
Ideology, defined, 44–45
Ifaluk people, 74
Ifugao society, 206–7
Igbo (Ibo) people, 332–34
Ik society, 294–95
Immigration, 46, 54
Imperialism, 52, 278–79, 288, 386
Incest, 76–78, 180
    royal, 76, 227, 242
Inclusive fitness, 128–29, 205
Independence movements, 322–25,
    347–48
Independent African Church, 322
Independent variables, 140–41
India
    colonialism in, 344
    dowry deaths in, 406–7
    Green Revolution in, 378
    languages in, 102
    nationalist movement in, 347–48
    origin myth in, 22
    population growth in, 345
    social structure in, 355–57
Indian Givers (Weatherford), 306
Indigenous societies, 306–8
Individualism
    American value of, 45
    enculturation and, 86
    in Japanese society, 71, 72, 277
    multicultural view of, 74–75
Indochina, 345, 348
Indo-European languages, 108–10
Indonesia (East Indies), 345
Inductive method, 14
Industrialism, global, 285. *See also*
    globalization
Industrialization, 258. *See also*
    globalization
    in Amazon rain forest, 298
    bureaucratic growth during, 277
    demographic change due to,
    371–74
    extinction due to, 375
Industrial melanism, 23

Industrial Revolution, 125, 256–58, 262, 281
Industrial states
  demographic change in, 259, 373–74
  emergence of, 256–58
  energy use by, 258–59, 375
  law in, 278
  Marxist view of, 127
  political organization in, 275–78
  religion in, 279–81
  social structure in, 150–51, 267–72, 272–75
  strengths and weaknesses of, 305–6
  technology of, 260–61, 278–79
  warfare in, 278–79
Inequality, status-based, 147
Infanticide, 166, 189, 196, 353, 374
Infant mortality rates, 144, 237, 372, 376. *See also* mortality rates
Infants, language acquisition in, 100
Informant role, 396
Infrastructure, of sociocultural systems, 126, 382
Inheritance patterns, 194. *See also* heredity
Inis Beag Islanders, 79
In Search of Nature (Wilson), 375
In Search of Respect: Selling Crack in El Barrio (Bourgois), 401
Instincts, 65–67
  aggressive, 206, 207
  emotions as, 83
  human nature and, 64
Intelligence, 53–55, 121, 123
  testing, 53–55, 92
Intensive agriculture, 142, 235. *See also* agribusiness; agriculture; food production
  environmental consequences of, 371, 375, 377
  Native American, 296
  population growth due to, 345–46
  productivity of, 376, 378
Interactionist perspective, 64, 78, 83–84, 100
Intercultural workshops, 47
Interdependence, 370, 386
International Monetary Fund (IMF), 289, 326, 380
International Phonetic Alphabet (IPA), 97
International Telephone and Telegraph (I.T.T.), 266
Interpretive model, 138
Intervention, humanitarian, 406
Interviews, in ethnological research, 135–37
Inuit society. *See* Eskimo society
Involution, agricultural, 346
Iran
  economic development in, 349

European division of, 343–44
expansionist policies of, 299
revolutions in, 299, 362–64
Iraq, 27, 349
Iroquois tribe
  cultural change in, 295–96
  language of, 99
  social structure of, 120, 194, 197, 200
  subsistence patterns of, 187
  technology of, 189
Irrigation systems, 237, 238
Isaac, Barr, 295
Islam
  medical traditions of, 398, 400–401
  pig taboo in, 49, 50
  revitalization of, 156, 362–66
  sexism in, 245
  spread of, 346
Islamic societies
  dress codes in, 45, 48, 79, 354–55
  greeting behaviors of, 112, 113
  social structure in, 351–55
Ismail, Shah, 362
Israel
  collectives in, 77–78
  elder roles in, 202
  lineages in, 204
  pig taboo of, 49–50

J

Jackson, Andrew, 296
Jajmani economy, 245, 355–57
Jamaica, 50–51
Japan
  economy of, 263, 385–86
  feudalism in, 239, 287
  field studies in, 399
  group model in, 276–77
  language of, 101, 111
  legal system in, 278
  population growth in, 373
  religion in, 281
  social stratification in, 273–74, 275
  social structure in, 71–72, 268, 269, 271, 272
  values in, 44
Japanese Consumer Behavior (McCreery), 399
Jati relationships, 355
Java (island), 25
Jehovah's Witnesses, 42
Jewish people
  annihilation of, 53
  collectives of, 77–78
  greeting behaviors of, 112
  resettlement of, 344
  time perception of, 81–82

Jihad (holy war), 366
Jivaro Indians, 100, 189, 208
Jobs, creation of, 380–81
Johanson, Donald, 24, 25
John Paul II, Pope, 43
Johnson, Allen, 135
Jones, Sir William, 108
Judaism, 49–50, 151, 245
Ju/'hoansi society. *See* !Kung San society

K

Kafr El-Elow village, 351–52
Kaluli society, 9, 72–73
Kamehameha (Hawaiian chief), 300
Kanzi (chimpanzee), 93
Karma (destiny), 347, 357
Katchina dolls, 210
Kaupuku tribe, 190
Kay, Paul, 99–100
Keddie, Nikki, 354
Keesing, Roger, 198
Kennedy, John F., 33
Kenya, 322
Kenyatta, Jomo, 322
Kephart, Ronald, 105–6
Key informants, 135, 139, 140
Khatami, Mohammad, 364
Khomeini, Ayatollah, 299, 363, 364
Kibbutzim (collectives), 77–78
Kicking Bear (Sioux leader), 301
Kikuyu tribe, 322
Kimoto Kazuhiko, 399
Kindreds, 193, 242
Kinesics, 113, 116
Kin-ordered production, 240
Kin selection, 128–29
Kinship
  in agricultural states, 242–43
  among foragers, 171–73
  Chinese, 358–59
  emotional ties of, 78
  fictive, 329
  in industrial states, 267
  in political systems, 152
  prehistoric, 30
  principal unit in, 148
  sodalities and, 202
  terms for, 99
  theories of, 120
  tribal, 191
Kirghiz tribe, 202
Klein, Laura, 228
Kluckhohn, Clyde, 58, 209
Knauft, Bruce, 177
Knowledge
  diffusion of, 28, 121, 257–58
  intelligence and, 53

Knowledge (*cont.*)
  Native American, 306
  objective vs. subjective, 14
  in postindustrial economy, 261
  sources of, 12–13
Koko (gorilla), 92
Koran. *See* Qur'an
Korean language, 111
Kpelle chiefdom, 220
Kula exchange, 221–22
Kulturkreise (culture circles), 121
Kultur-System, Dutch, 345
!Kung San society
  cultural change in, 292–93
  economy of, 168–69
  history of, 162–63
  language of, 97
  political organization of, 177, 178
  population control in, 166
  social structure of, 171–76
  studies of, 136, 139
  subsistence in, 163, 169–70
  technology of, 167
Kurds, 360
Kuwait, 349
Kwakiutl chiefdom, 68, 222–23, 231

L

Labor, 240, 260, 262, 267–68
Labor, division of, 146
  age and, 150
  in agricultural states, 239
  among foragers, 164, 165, 173–74
  gender and, 149, 269–71
  global changes in, 386
  in industrialized states, 260–61, 270
Ladino, 331
Laitman, Jeffrey, 96
Lakota Sioux tribe, 301–2
Lana (chimpanzee), 92
Land
  grant system for, 316, 345
  marketing of, 262
  Native American, 296
  ownership systems for, 239–40
Land bridge, 32
Language, 91. *See also* communication
  acquisition of, 82, 100–101, 104–6
  characteristics of, 94–97
  dialects in, 110–11
  ethnicity and, 56, 57
  evolution of, 26, 110
  honorifics in, 111
  preserving, 102–3
  Sapir-Whorf hypothesis for, 106–8
  structure of, 97–100
  study of, 8–10, 115–16

Language Socialization across Cultures
  (Schieffelin, Ochs), 9
Lapp tribe, 187
Larynx, 96
Lascaux Caves, 31
Latah (hysteria), 85
Latin America
  colonialism in, 312
  cultural diversity in, 311
  demographic change in, 315–16, 336–37
  economic change in, 316–17, 325–27
  ethnic groups in, 46, 328, 331–32
  map of, 313
  political movements in, 322, 324–25
  religious change in, 317–18
  social structure in, 329–30
Latinos. *See* Hispanic Americans
Lauer, Carol J., 7
Law
  in agricultural states, 246–47
  in chiefdoms, 229–30, 232
  in industrial states, 278
  Islamic, 353–54
  norms and sanctions in, 153–54
  social control and, 153
  tribal, 205–8
Leach, Edmund, 155
Leadership, 176–77, 201–3, 224
Leaf, Murray, 378
Learning, types of, 39, 59
Lee, Richard, 136, 163, 166, 168, 169, 170,
  174, 177, 293
Legitimacy, political, 224–25
Lenin, Vladimir, 265
Leopard skin chief, 204, 205, 206
Leopold, King of Belgium, 314
Lepcha society, 78–79
Levirate rule, 196–97
Levi-Strauss, Claude, 77, 80, 87, 176, 177,
  195
Lewis, Oscar, 336–37, 355
Lexigrams, 93
Lieberman, Philip, 96
Life cycle, human, 150–51
Life expectancy, 144, 169, 236, 372, 376
Lifestyle, depictions of, 6
Liholiho (Hawaiian chief), 300
Lindenbaum, Shirley, 209
Lineage. *See also* matrilineage; patrilineage
  in chiefdoms, 226, 227
  defined, 192
  segmentary, 203–4
  totems depicting, 209
Linguistic anthropology, 3, 5, 8–10, 13, 15
Linguistic postulates, 108
Linguistic relativism, 99, 100
Linguistics, 8, 10, 99–100, 105, 108–10
Linnaeus, Carolus, 52
Literacy studies, 9
Little Dragons of Asia, 386

Locke, John, 100
Logic-of-growth model, 376–77
Lorenz, Konrad, 206
Lowell textile mill, 267
lower class, 274
Lower Paleolithic period, 25, 29
Lucy, John, 107
Lucy (*A. afarensis*), 24–25
Lugbara tribe, 209

M

McClelland, David, 286
McCreery, John, 399
McCreery, Ruth, 399
McDonald's restaurants, 382, 383
Machiguenga Indians, 135
Machismo, 329–30
Magic, 123–24, 229–30, 398
Makahiki festival, 230, 300
Malaysia, 85, 344
Malinowski, Bronislaw, 75, 77, 78,
  123–24, 131, 138, 221–22
Malotki, Ekkehart, 106–8
Malthus, Thomas Robert, 372, 376
Mammoth Cave, 8
Mammoths, 29, 30
Mana (cosmic forces), 229–30
Mandarin Chinese language, 107
Mandarin class, 245
Mandela, Nelson, 324
Mangu, in witchcraft, 208–9
Manifest Destiny, 296
Man's Most Dangerous Myth (Montagu), 7
Mao Zedong, 348, 350, 367, 374
Maquiladoras, 326–27
Marcus, George, 138
Margaret Mead and Samoa (Freeman), 69
Margaret Mead and the Heretic (Free-
  man), 69
Marginal environments, 161, 162, 181,
  292, 293
Marital exchange, 171, 172–73, 195, 243
Market economies, 261–62
Marketplaces, 241–42, 245
Marley, Bob, 50, 51
Marriage
  in agricultural states, 242–44
  among foragers, 171–73
  Asian, 357, 358–59
  in chiefdoms, 227, 232
  incest in, 77–78
  Indian, 406–7
  in industrial societies, 268–69
  Middle Eastern, 352–53
  patterns of, 148
  tribal, 194–98, 211
Marriott, McKim, 355

Martin, Kay, 195, 242, 244
Marx, Karl, 262, 275–76, 324, 390
Marxism, 127–28, 288, 348, 364–66
Material culture, 44, 59, 130
Materialism, 127, 130. *See also* cultural
    materialism
Matriarchy, 120, 199
Matrilineage
    in agricultural states, 242
    divorce in, 198
    female status in, 200
    tribal, 192, 193, 194, 197
Matrilocal residence, 172, 197, 227–28
Mau Mau uprisings, 322
Mauss, Marcel, 74–75
Maximal lineage, 203
Mayan Indians, 107, 238, 332, 337
Maybury-Lewis, David, 306, 398
Mbeki, Thabo, 324
Mbuti Pygmies
    cultural change among, 293–94
    economy of, 168
    music of, 180
    social organization of, 173, 174, 175,
        176
    subsistence pattern of, 163–64, 170
    technology of, 167
Mead, Margaret, 67–70, 83, 87, 123,
    198–99
Means, Russell, 302
Mediation, 206, 229, 247, 278, 396
Medical anthropology, 398, 400–402
Medicine, 306, 398, 400–401
Medicine man/woman, 156
Medieval period, 52, 74–75
Meggitt, Mervyn, 204
Meiji emperor, 263
Mein Kampf (Hitler), 53
Melanesia, 302–4
Menarche, 166, 172
Mendel, Gregor, 23
Mental illness, 84–86
Mercantilism, 257–58, 288, 312–14, 344
Merchants, 241
Mesoamerica, 248, 312
Messenger, John, 79
Mestizos, 43, 331
Metaculture, 408
Metallurgy, 237, 238
Metaphors, interpreting, 129–30
Metropole societies, 288
Mexican Revolution (1910–1920), 325
Mexico
    agricultural in, 378
    economy of, 326–27
    language in, 103
    population growth in, 316, 336, 373
    religion in, 42–43, 318, 320–21
Mezhirich site, 29
Middens, 6

Middle class
    emergence of, 267
    Japanese, 273
    power of, 275
    U.S., 263, 273, 274
Middle East
    archaeological sites in, 25
    colonialism in, 342–44
    demographic change in, 345–46
    economic development in, 346, 349–50
    ethnicity in, 46, 359–60
    political movements in, 347–48
    regions of, 341, 342
    religion in, 49–50, 346–47, 362–66
    social structure in, 351–55
Middle Paleolithic, 29
Migration patterns
    of foragers, 165–66, 170
    global, 388–90
    of horticulturalists, 186
    measuring, 142, 144
    of pastoralists, 187–88, 189, 190
    prehistoric, 26, 27, 31
    rural-to-urban, 336, 337
Millenarian movements, 303–4, 402
Minangkabau society, 83–84
Minimal lineage, 203
Mining, 316, 317
Ministry of International Trade and Indus-
    try (M.I.T.I.), 386
Minority groups, 45, 46, 246. *See also*
    ethnic groups
Minor marriage, 77
Mir (peasant commune), 264
Missionaries, 297, 317–18, 320–22, 347
Mississippi region, 217
Mixtecan Indians, 71
Moai figures, 231
Moche kingdom, 250–51
Modernization, 258, 285–88
Modules, innate, 82–83, 101, 104
Moieties, tribal, 193–94
Moksha (spiritual enlightenment), 347
Monarchy, British, 272
Monetary exchange, 190, 241–42, 262
Mongolia, 85, 190
Monkalun (arbiter), 207
Monk's Mound, 231
Monogamy, 148, 171, 243, 353
Monolingualism, 103
Monopolies, trade, 257
Monopoly capitalism, 266
Montagnais-Naskapi Indians, 85
Montagu, Ashley, 7, 206–7
Montazeri, Hussein Ali, 364
Montezuma, 312
Moral economy, 317, 346, 362
Morality, 153, 179, 405
Mores, 48. *See also* folkways; norms;
    values

Morgan, Lewis Henry, 120–21, 127, 130,
    145, 150, 169
Morocco, 342–43
Morphemes, 98, 101
Morphology, 98
Mortality rates. *See also* infant mortality
    rates
    in agricultural states, 236
    in colonized societies, 316, 345
    in industrial states, 259
    measuring, 142, 144
    in peripheral societies, 374
    trends in, 371–72
Moses and Civilization (Paul), 76
Mothers of Six Cultures, 71
Mounds, of chiefdoms, 218, 231
Mousterian technology, 27
Movius, Hallam L., 6
Mujahidin (holy warriors), 366
Muhammad, the Prophet, 362, 364
Mulattos, 331, 335
Multiculturalism, 46–47
Multidimensional approach, 140
Multiethnic societies, 56, 58
Multilingualism, 103
Multinational corporations. *See also*
    corporations
    in Africa, 335
    evolution of, 266–67
    expansion of, 380–82
    in Mexico, 326
    of NICs, 387
    oil production by, 349
    relocation of, 386
Multiple borrowings, 110
Multiregional evolutionary model, 28
Mundugumor tribe, 198
Mundurucu tribe, 205
Munson, Henry, 362
Murdock, George P., 58, 59, 148, 156, 189
Al-Murrah tribe, 298–99
Murray, Charles, 53–54
Murray, Gerald, 379
Music, 15, 179–80, 210, 231–32
Myths, 21–22, 154–55. *See also*
    cosmologies

N

Nagasaki, 279
Nakane, Chia, 276–77
Nakoda (matchmaker), 269
Nambikuara foragers, 176
Nanda, Serena, 79
Nasser, Gamal, 367
Natchez chiefdom, 225–26, 227, 228, 230
Natema (hallucinogen), 208

National Brazilian Indian Foundation (FUNAI), 298
National Environmental Policy Act (1969), 403
National Historic Preservation Act (1966), 403
Nationalism, 275
Nationalist movements, 322–25, 347–48
Nation-states, 256–57
Native American Church (NAC), 302
Native Americans
  blood quanta rules for, 55
  burial site of, 403–4
  chiefdoms among, 217–18
  colonization of, 295–96
  demographic changes among, 47
  homosexuality among, 79
  knowledge of, 306
  languages of, 102, 103
  origins of, 32
  relocation of, 296–97
  revitalization movements among, 301–2
  subsistence patterns of, 187
  20th-century, 297
Natural growth rate, 144
Naturalists, 22
Natural resources, 216–18, 251–52, 403
Natural selection, 22–23, 35, 128
Nature vs. nurture, 82
Navajo Indians
  marriage patterns of, 197
  religion of, 21–22, 302
  witchcraft among, 209
  worldview of, 12, 13, 44
Nayar society, 242–43
Nazi ideology, 53, 405
Neanderthals, 6, 26–27, 96
Needham, Rodney, 180
Negative reciprocity, 168, 190
Neocolonialism, 381
Neoevolutionism, 124–27
Neoimperialism, 288
Neolithic period, 235, 252, 370
Neo-Malthusians, 376, 377
Nepotism, 129
Net migration, 144
Neurosis, 84
New Apostolic Church (NAC), 303–4
Newly industrializing economies (NICs), 386–87
New York Stock Exchange, 261
New York Times, 8
Ngo Dinh Diem, 349
Nicaraguan Revolution, 325
Niche, environmental, 141
Nigeria, 327, 332–34
Nihondo (Japanese way), 281
El Niño events, 250–51
Nirvana (spiritual enlightenment), 347

Nkrumah, Kwame, 322
Nobility, British, 272
Nomads of the Long Bow (Holmberg), 295
Nonmaterial culture, 44, 48, 59, 130
Norget, Kristin, 320–21
Normalcy, standards of, 84–85
Norms, 38. *See also* folkways; values
  in agricultural states, 240–41, 244
  among foragers, 178
  double standard for, 404–6
  enforcement of, 153
  fluidity of, 86
  formalized, 153–54
  ideal, 268
  tribal, 197–98
  types of, 45, 48
North America, 32, 102
Northern Ireland, 55
Northwest Coast chiefdoms
  location of, 219
  potlatch feasts of, 222–23
  religion of, 230
  slavery in, 228
  subsistence in, 217–18, 220
  totems of, 231
Nuclear family, 148, 170–71, 267, 268, 352
Nuer tribe
  social structure of, 198, 203, 204
  subsistence pattern of, 188
  technology of, 190
  warfare in, 207
Nyakyusa tribe, 201
Nyerere, Julius, 322

O

Oaths, 207–8, 247
Objective knowledge, 14, 15
Objective scientist model, 138
Obligation, in law, 154
Observation, 14, 135. *See also* participant observation
Occupation, status and, 272
Ochs, Elinor, 9
O'Connell, James, 165
Oedipus complex, 73, 75, 76
Office, defined, 224
Oil, global consumption of, 375
Oil industry, 326, 327, 349–50, 362, 363
Oldowan technology, 25, 26
Old Stone Age, 25, 28
Oligopolies, 266
Oliver, Douglas, 203
Oman society, 79
On Aggression (Lorenz), 206
One-child policy, China's, 358–59, 374–75
One-drop rule, 55
On the Origin of Species (Darwin), 23

Open peasant community, 328
Opium Wars (1839–1842), 344
Optimal foraging theory, 165
Oracles, 207–8, 247
Orchard Town, 71
Ordeals, 206–7, 247
Origin myths, 21–22
Orr, Julian, 264
Ortner, Sherry, 199–200
Oswald, Lee Harvey, 33
Otterbein, Keith, 247
Ottoman Empire, 343
Ozone layer, 371

P

Pacific Islanders
  chiefdoms among, 216, 217, 226
  honorifics of, 111
  housing of, 219
  languages of, 102
  money of, 190
  technology of, 189
Paganism, 319–20
Pahlavi, Mohammad Reza, 299, 350, 363
Paintings, 31, 179, 180
Paiute Indians, 169
Paleoanthropology, 4, 34–35
Paleolithic period
  brain evolution during, 82, 83
  cultures of, 28–32
  diseases of, 236
  population of, 166, 372, 373
  subsistence during, 161
  technology of, 167
Palestine, 344
Papua New Guinea, 72–73, 187, 302–3
Paradigms, 14–15, 405
Parallel-cousin marriage, 195
Parry, Jonathan, 357
Participant observation, 10, 17
  in corporate studies, 264, 265
  criticism of, 138
  ethics in, 140
  in ethnological research, 135, 157
  first use of, 122
Party of the Institutionalized Revolution (PRI), 326
Pastoralism, 142
Pastoralist societies, 187–88, 189, 201, 203–4, 298–99. *See also* tribal societies
Patriarchy
  African, 330–31
  in agricultural states, 244–45
  among foragers, 174
  Asian, 357–58, 359
  in chiefdoms, 228

cultural legacy of, 270, 271
evolution of, 120
in Middle East, 352–55
tribal, 199–200, 211
Patrilineage
in agricultural states, 242
in chiefdoms, 226
Middle Eastern, 352
tribal, 192–93, 194, 197, 199
Patrilocal residence, 171, 172, 197, 199,
227–28, 269
Patrimony, 242
Patron-client ties, 329
Patterns of Culture (Benedict), 67, 84
Patterson, Francine, 92
Paul, Benjamin, 337
Paul, Robert, 76
Peasantry
African, 328–29
in agricultural states, 240–41
in cash economies, 346
communities of, 328
Egyptian, 351–52
Indian, 355
Japanese, 273
revolt by, 324–25
Russian, 264–65, 273
social relations of, 243, 329–31
studies of, 291
values among, 268
Peasant Wars of the Twentieth Century
(Wolf), 291
"Penny capitalists," 146
Perestroika, 382–84
Perez, Carlos Andres, 298
Peripheral societies
defined, 289
dependency in, 381
economies of, 325–26
energy consumption in, 375
location of, 290
population growth in, 374
Perry, William J., 121
Persia. *See* Iran
Personality development, 67–70, 70–73,
73–74
Pesticides, 371
Peyote cult, 302
Pharynx, 96
Phillipines, the, 345
Philosophy, 8
Phonemes/phones, 95, 97, 101
Phonology, 97–98
Photography, 137
phratries, 193–94, 204
physical anthropology, 3, 4–6, 13
physical traits, 23, 32, 34, 51
Piaget, Jean, 80–82, 87
Pibloktoq (Arctic hysteria), 85
Picasso, Pablo, 279

Pidgin languages, 104, 105
Pig taboo, 49–50
Pine Ridge Indian reservation, 302
Pioneer Fund, 53
Pizarro, Francisco, 312
Plains Indians, 67–68, 302
Planned change, 395–98
Plantation system
African, 317
Caribbean, 315
Hawaiian, 300, 301
Latin American, 312, 325–26
slave labor in, 313
Plants, 30, 375, 376
Plato, 51, 251
Pleistocene period, 26, 31–32
Plow, advent of, 237–38
Plural societies, 56, 58
Poetry, 15
Pokot tribe, 12–13
Poland, 43, 384
Politboro, Soviet, 273
Political movements, 322–25
Political organization. *See also* govern-
ment
in agricultural states, 239–42, 252–53
among foragers, 176–78
Asian, 347–48, 384–85
British, 272
in chiefdoms, 220–25
components of, 151–54
global trends in, 387
in industrial states, 275–78
Middle Eastern, 347
socialist, 382–84
tribal, 202–8
Political power, 151, 176, 200, 229, 249.
See also power
Political science, 12
Pollution, 371, 376
Polyandry, 148, 196
Polygamy, 128, 148
Polygyny, 148
African, 330
in agricultural states, 243
among foragers, 171
in chiefdoms, 227
Middle Eastern, 352–53
tribal, 195–96, 199, 202
Polynesian chiefdoms
descent groups in, 226
law and religion in, 229–30
music of, 231–32
political authority in, 224, 225
regional symbiosis in, 221
technology of, 219
trade among, 223
Popé, prophet, 301
Popular sovereignty, 275
Population. *See* demographics

Population control. *See also* birth control
among foragers, 165–66
in China, 374–75
trends in, 371, 372
tribal methods of, 189
Population density, 166
Population growth
in agricultural states, 236–37
among foragers, 166
in chiefdoms, 218–19
cultural influences on, 145
environmental capacity for, 144–45
in industrial states, 259
Population growth
Mesoamerican, 248
in non-Western societies, 336, 345–46
optimistic view of, 376–77
trends in, 371–74
warfare due to, 204–5
Portugal, 312, 313
Pospisil, Leonard, 153–54
Postindustrial societies, 261, 386
Postmodernism, 138–39
Pot hunters, 402, 404
Pot irrigation, 238
Potlatch ceremonies, 222–23, 230
Potlatch Corp., 381–82
Poverty, culture of, 336–37
Power. *See also* political power
agricultural state, 239
chiefly, 224–25
coercive, 176, 202, 224
economic, 130, 229, 271, 275
legitimate, 151–52
tribal, 201–2
Practicing anthropology, 395
Predispositions, innate, 82–83, 86, 128,
129, 207
Prehistoric archaeologists, 5, 6
Preindustrial societies, 150–51, 370
Prejudice, ethnic, 34. *See also* racism
Preoperational stage, 81
Prestate societies, 292, 305–8
Priests/priestesses, 156, 249
"Primal Patricide," 76
Primary sector, 260–61
Primates, 5, 24
Primatology, 5
Primitive Culture (Tylor), 119
Primogeniture, 194, 224
Primordialist model, 57–58
Private property, 169, 262
Production, 146
among foragers, 169–70
factors of, 262
improving, 264
means of, 127, 131, 265
tributary vs. kin-ordered, 240
Productivity, linguistic, 94
Professional class, 273

Progress, 305, 306
Proletariat, 127, 275–76, 324–25
Property ownership
  in agricultural states, 239–40
  among foragers, 169, 178
  in chiefdoms, 220
  tribal, 191
Prophets, 301, 322
Prosimians, 24
Protein shortages, 204–5
Protestants, 281
Protolanguage, 108–10
Proxemics, 114, 116
Psychiatry, 84–85
Psychoanalytic anthropology, 73–76
Psychological anthropology, 63–64, 87
Psychology, 12, 85
Psychosis, 84
Puberty rituals, 175, 179, 180
Pueblo Indians, 67–68, 97, 210, 301, 302
Pueblos (towns), 345
Puerto Rico, 55, 337
Purdah (barrier) system, 244, 354–55,
  357–58
Puritanism, 80
Push-pull factors, 144
Pyramid of the Sun, 237
Pyramids, Moche, 250

Q

Qashqa'i tribe, 299
Qualitative data, 137
Quality control, 136
Quantitative data, 137
Quinn, Naomi, 41
Qur'an, 112, 346, 352–53, 354

R

Race
  classification by, 32, 51, 59–60
  intelligence and, 53–55
  study of, 7
  theories of, 34
  vs. ethnicity, 56, 246
Race Is A Four Letter Word (Brace), 7
Racial stratification, 246, 274–75, 322–24
Racism, 51. *See also* scientific racism
  among evolutionists, 121, 123
  basis for, 34
  in plantation system, 326–27
  prevalence of, 17
  in Western society, 51–53
Radcliffe-Brown, A. R., 123, 124, 131, 175
Raheja, Gloria, 357

Rahman, Abdul, 364
Railroads, 263
Rain forests, tropical
  characteristics of, 143
  controversy over, 379
  destruction of, 375
  industrial development in, 297–98, 306
  marketing products of, 307
  subsistence in, 163–64, 185–87
Rajahs (political rulers), 249
Rajput people, 71
Rameses II, temple of, 402, 403
Random sample, 136–37
Rank, sumptuary rules for, 225–26. *See
  also* status
Rappaport, Roy, 187
Rastafarian movement, 50–51
Rathje, William L., 7
Real culture, 48
Reality, 99, 106, 138
Reciprocal exchange, 167, 261. *See also*
  economic exchange; trade
  among chiefdoms, 221–22
  among foragers, 167–68, 170, 178
  dyadic contracts for, 329
  egalitarianism in, 223
  tribal, 190, 197
Recording media, 137
Redfield, Robert, 405
Red Flag Commune, 358–59
Red Guards, 350
Redistributional exchange, 222–24, 261
Reforestation, in Haiti, 378–79
Reformist movements, 347
Refugees, 365, 388–90
Reincarnation, 346–47, 357
Relative deprivation, 324–25
Relativism
  cultural, 49, 122, 404–6
  ethical, 404–6
  linguistic, 99, 100
Reliability, of research data, 136
Religion. *See also* spirituality; *specific
  religions*
  in agricultural states, 248, 249
  among foragers, 178–80
  in chiefdoms, 229–30
  common elements in, 154–56
  global trends in, 390–91
  in industrial states, 279–81
  knowledge derived from, 13
  in non-Western societies, 317–22, 346–47
  in prehistoric societies, 27, 31
  Rastafarian, 50
  symbols in, 42–43
  tribal, 208–9
Religious movements
  fundamentalist, 156, 362–66, 391
  Hawaiian, 299–300
  millenarian, 303–4

Religious specialists, 155–56
Renfrew, Colin, 108
Replacement model, 28
Representative role, 395–96, 397–98
Repression, 73
Research
  basic vs. applied, 13
  cross-cultural, 63, 156–57
  design for, 134–35
  ethnological roles in, 264–65
  interdisciplinary, 10–12
  scientific method for, 13–14
  undercover, 140
Reservations, Native American, 296–97
Resettlement, forced
  of foragers, 292, 293, 294
  of Native Americans, 296–97
Residence rules, 197, 227–28, 269
Restricted marital exchange, 195
Retribalization, 333
Reverse dominance, 176
Revitalization movements, 156, 301–2,
  362–66
Revival movements, religious, 362–66,
  391
Revolutionary movements
  Asian, 348–49
  Iranian, 299, 362–64
  Islamic, 362–66
  Latin American, 324–25
Rickford, John, 105
Riner, Reed, 266
Rio Declaration (1992), 379
Rising expectations, 324
Rites of legitimation, 249
Rites of passage
  Aborigine, 179
  American, 280
  among foragers, 174–75, 180
  stages in, 151
  tribal, 201
Rittenberg, William, 137
Rituals, 27, 155
Roles, 147
  gender-based, 149–50
Romance languages, 108
Roman Empire, 102, 241, 245
Romantic love, 268, 269
Romeo and Juliet (Shakespeare), 268
Roscoe, Paul, 78, 303
Rostow, Walt W., 286, 397
Royal incest, 76, 227, 242
Rozin, Paul, 82
Ruling classes, 257
Russia. *See also* Soviet Union, former
  colonialist expansion by, 343–44
  family in, 268
  feudalism in, 263–64
  language of, 274–75
Russian Revolution (1917), 265

S

Sackett, James, 29
Safa, Helen, 337
Sahlins, Marshall, 129, 168, 169–70, 206–7, 226
St. Luke the Evangelist, 43
Sambia people, 79
Samoa, 68–70, 381–82
Samurai (warrior-scholars), 263, 269
Sanctions, 153–54, 178, 205–6
Sanskrit, 108
Sapir, Edward, 106–8, 115–16
Sapir-Whorf hypothesis, 106–8, 115–16
Satellite societies, 288
Saudi Arabia, 79, 299–300, 349, 354
Savage Mind, The (Levi-Strauss), 80
Savage-Rumbaugh, Sue, 93
Savagery, vs. civilization, 120, 121, 130
Savanna, tropical, 143
Schaller, George, 93
Schemas (cultural models), 41
Schieffelin, Bambi B., 9, 72–73
Schizophrenia, 86
Schmidt, Father Wilhelm, 121
Science, 12–13, 14–15, 377
Scientific knowledge, 13
Scientific method, 13–14, 15, 16, 119, 258
Scientific racism, 52–53, 257. *See also* racism
    criticism of, 58, 258
Scientific revolution, 22–23, 256–58
Scudder, Thayer, 396
Sebei tribe, 201
Seclusion, female, 244, 354–55
Secondary sector, 260–61
Second World, 287, 288
Secularization, 279–81, 390–91
Segmentary lineage, 203–4
Segmentary states, 239
Selassie, Haile (Ras Tafari), 50
Self, concept of, 74–75
Self-help, 247
Semang foragers, 164, 167, 170, 174
Semantics, 99
Semiperipheral societies
    defined, 289
    economies of, 326–27, 386–87
    energy consumption in, 375
    location of, 290
Sensorimotor stage, 80, 82
Separatist movements, ethnic, 390, 392
Service, Elman, 202, 220, 252
Services, 145, 146, 260–62
Sesotho language, 107
Settlement, tribal, 188–89
Sex, vs. gender, 149
Sex and Temperament in Three Primitive Societies (Mead), 198

Sex drive, 78–80
Sexism, 199–200, 244–45
Sexual behavior
    among Eskimos, 172–73
    case study in, 128
    codes of, 78–79
    regulation of, 148
Sexuality
    double standard for, 128
    Freud's hypotheses on, 73
    Samoan attitudes toward, 70
Sexual reproduction
    cultural patterns in, 128–29
    strategies in, 195–96, 199–200
    warfare and, 205
Sexual revolution, 80
Shaduf device, 237
Shakespeare, William, 64, 268
Shamanism
    among foragers, 179, 180
    in chiefdoms, 230
    defined, 156
    Mayan, 249
    Thai, 400
    tribal, 208
Shanidar burial site, 27
Shankman, Paul, 381–82
Shantytowns, 336–37
Shariati, Ali, 364
Shelters, Upper Paleolithic, 29
Shepher, Joseph, 78
Shi'a Muslims, 362–63, 364
Shintoism, 281
Shoshone Indians, 125, 163, 169, 170, 171
Shostak, Marjorie, 139
Shweder, Richard, 84
Siane tribe, 190
Sibling marriages, 76, 227, 242
Sign language, 92–93
Signs, vs. symbols, 40–41
Sikhs, 359, 360–61
Simon, Julian, 376, 377
Singapore, 386
Singer, Milton, 355
Siriono foragers, 295
Situational learning, 39, 40, 59
Siuai tribe, 203
Six Cultures, 71
Six Cultures Project, 70–71
Skin color
    Caribbean classification by, 334–36
    mental capacity and, 35
    racial classification by, 32, 34, 51–53
Skinner, B. F., 100, 101
Slack Farm, 403–4
Slash-and-burn cultivation, 185–86
Slavery
    African system of, 312–14
    in agricultural states, 245–46
    in Caribbean, 315

    in chiefdoms, 228–29
    depopulation due to, 316
    forms of, 228, 246
    Jamaican, 50
    scientific promotion of, 52
Slaves, African, 104, 105
Slum dwellers, 336–37
Smith, Adam, 262
Smith, Eric, 169
Smith, G. Elliot, 121
Smith, M. G., 333
Smith, Margo L., 264–65
Smithsonian Institution, 120
Snow, Clyde, 33
Social control, 153–55, 178, 179, 229
Social-impact studies, 396
Socialism, 44, 263–66, 350–51
Socialist states
    development of, 127
    economies of, 266, 380, 382–85
    location of, 290
    political organization in, 275–77
    religion in, 280–81
Socialization, 9, 108. *See also* enculturation
Social learning, 39, 40, 59
Social mobility, 267, 273, 337
Social sciences, 11, 15
Social status. *See* status
Social stratification. *See also* caste system
    in agricultural states, 245–46
    in chiefdoms, 224, 225–26, 229–30
    defined, 147
    in industrial states, 272–75
Social structure
    African, 330–31
    in agricultural states, 242–45
    among foragers, 170–78
    Asian, 355–59
    in chiefdoms, 225–29, 232
    collapse of, 252
    components of, 147–51
    in industrial states, 267–72
    Latin American, 329–30
    Middle Eastern, 351–55
    tribal, 191–202, 211
    Upper Paleolithic, 29–30
Societies, 38–39. *See also specific societies*
    closed, 245, 272, 328
    egalitarian, 168, 293
    ethnographies of, 10
    evolution of, 127
    hierarchical, 224
    indigenous, 306–8
    kin-ordered, 152
    metropole, 288
    multiethnic, 56, 58
    open, 272, 328
    postindustrial, 261, 386
    preindustrial, 150–51, 370

Societies, 38–39. *See also specific societies (cont.)*
  prestate, 292, 305–8
  satellite, 288
  savage vs. civilized, 120, 121
  social structure of, 147–51
  symbols of, 40–41
  theoretical views of, 123–24
  underdeveloped, 287
Sociobiology, 128–29, 129
Sociocultural systems, 39, 126, 382
  Latin American, 312
  neoevolutionist view of, 124–25
  variables in, 134, 141
  warfare in, 126
Sociolinguistics, 5, 10, 110–13
Sodalities, 152, 202
Soil depletion, 186, 187, 335
Solidarity movement, 43, 384
Solutrean projectiles, 28
Somalia, 334–35
Song duel, Eskimo, 178
Sons of the Shaking Earth (Wolf), 291
Sorcery, 208–9
Sororate rule, 196–97
Soto (danger), 72
Soul loss, 179
South Africa, 293, 314, 322–24
Southall, Aidan, 239
Southeast Asia, 79, 85, 388–90
South Korea, 386
South-West African People's Organization (SWAPO), 293
Soviet Union, former. *See also* Russia
  Afghanistan and, 364, 366
  economic reform in, 382–84
  elderly status in, 272
  political organization in, 275–77
  religion in, 280–81
  socialism in, 263–66
  social stratification in, 273–75
Space, conceptualizing, 81, 106
Space, personal. *See* Proxemics
Spain, 312, 345
Spanish-American War (1898), 345
Spear points, Clovis, 32
Spear-thrower, 28
Species, 22, 306, 375–76
Speech, 94, 95–97, 110
Speech community, 110
Spencer, Frank, 7
Spencer, Herbert, 52
Sperber, Daniel, 82
Spirits, in religion, 210, 211
Spirituality. *See also* religion
  among Eskimos, 179
  Cro-Magnon, 31
  Neanderthal, 27
  in tribal music, 210
Spiro, Melford, 74–76

Sri Lanka, 361–62
Stalin, Josef, 276
Stanford-Binet test, 53
Starvation, 295
State, defined, 152, 235
State societies. *See* agricultural states; industrial states
Status
  age-based, 150–51
  in agricultural states, 240, 244–45
  in chiefdoms, 220, 225–26, 227
  competition for, 177
  of elderly, 175, 271–72
  female (*See* Women, status of)
  gender-based, 150
  in industrialized societies, 267, 272, 273
  IQ scores and, 54
  legal obligation and, 154
  reciprocity and, 168
  tribal, 191, 205
  types of, 147
Stereotypes
  cave-man, 27
  cross-cultural, 58
  ethnic, 47, 335–36
  exploitation based on, 326–27
  gender-role, 199
  Japanese, 71–72
  racist, 32, 51–53
Steven, Rob, 273
Steward, Julian, 125, 127, 131, 145
Strata, social, 225, 227
Structuralism, 80, 87
Structural linguistics, 5, 8, 10
Structural mobility, 273
Studying the Yanomamö (Chagnon), 11
Subjective knowledge, 14, 15
Subsistence patterns. *See also* agriculture; food production
  in agricultural states, 244–45
  among foragers, 162–65, 173–74
  in chiefdoms, 216–18
  environment and, 141–42
  tribal, 184, 185–88, 200
  types of, 142
  Upper Paleolithic, 29–30
Substance abuse, 401–2
substantive approach, 146
Sudan, 334–35
Sudarkasa, Niara, 330
Suez Canal, 342, 344
Sumptuary rules, 225–26
Sun Dance ritual, 302
Sunlight, adaptation to, 34, 35
Sunni Muslims, 362–63, 364
Sun Yat-sen, 348
Superego, 73, 74
Supply and demand, 261–62
Supreme Court, U. S., 42
Survival mechanisms, 58
Sustainability model, 380

Swadesh, Morris, 110
Swartz, Marc, 399
Symbiosis, regional, 218, 220, 221
Symbolic anthropology, 129–30
Symbolic learning, 39–41
Symbolism
  of dress, 50–51
  interpreting, 129–30, 138
  national, 42–43
  in nonmaterial culture, 48
  in origin myths, 21
  religious, 154, 155
Symons, Donald, 82
Syncretism, 304, 318–20, 322
Syntax, 92–93, 98

T

Taboos, 49–50, 76–78, 300
Tabu system, 229–30
Tagore, Debendranath, 347
Tahiti, 216, 224–25, 229–30
Tainter, Joseph, 250, 252
Taira people, 71
Taiwan, 77, 386
Taliban movement, 365, 366
Talmon, Yonina, 78
Tamayo, Rolando, 247
Tambiah, Stanley, 362
Tamil Hindus, 361–62
Tanganyika, 322
Taoism, 22
Tape recording, 137
Tarong people, 71
Tattooing, 221, 225–26
Tax, Sol, 146
Taxation, 224, 317
Tchambuli tribe, 198, 199
Technology. *See also* tools
  in agricultural states, 237–39
  assessment models for, 376–80
  in chiefdoms, 219–20
  concept of, 145–46
  diffusion of, 257–58, 285
  of foragers, 167, 181
  global trends in, 375–76, 382
  industrial, 260–61, 278–79
  military, 278, 279
  prehistoric, 25, 26, 27, 28–29, 30–31
  small-scale, 397
  sociocultural change through, 125, 126–27
  tribal, 189, 190
Terrace, Herbert, 92–93
Territorial rights, 169
Tertiary sector, 260–61
Testability, in scientific method, 14
Thailand
  colonialism and, 345

greeting behaviors in, 112–13
language of, 10, 111
medicine in, 398, 400–401
hai Ministry of Public Health, 401
hales of Miletus, 22
heater states, 239
heocracies, 229
heory, defined, 14
herapeutic pluralism, 400
hinking through Cultures (Shweder), 84
hird World, 287, 288
iananmen Square demonstrations, 384–85
ime, perception of, 81–82, 106–8
ime-allocation analysis, 135
io Se-lian, 399
iwi foragers, 174, 177
oda tribe, 196
okugawa period, 263
onantzin (Aztec goddess), 42, 43
onga chiefdoms, 229–30
ooby, John, 82
ools. *See also* Technology
  Acheulian, 26
  of agricultural states, 237–38
  of chiefdoms, 219
  chimpanzee, 40
  of foragers, 167
  H. habilis, 44
  horticulturalist, 189
  Neanderthal, 27
  Oldowan, 25
  Upper Paleolithic, 28–29
ordesillas, Treaty of, 312
otalitarianism, 276–77
otem and Taboo (Freud), 76
otems, 209, 231
ourist industry, Hawaiian, 304
rade
  in agricultural states, 239, 241–42
  caravan, 241, 298–99
  European-Asian, 344–45
  imbalances in, 385, 386
  networks for, 29
raditionalism, 286
rail of Tears, 296
raining the Body for China (Brownell), 361
ransformational rules, 101, 104
rial-and-error learning, 39
ribal societies
  art and music of, 210
  characteristics of, 184–85
  cultural change in, 295–99
  demographics of, 188–89
  economies of, 190–91
  political organization in, 152, 202–28
  religion in, 208–9
  social organization in, 191–202
  technology of, 189
ributary production, 240

Trobriand Islanders
  economy of, 220, 221–22
  magic of, 123–24
  political system of, 224
  social relations of, 75, 227
Tsembaga Maring tribe, 187
Tsimshian chiefdom, 227, 228
Tungus tribe, 188
Tooby, John, 82
Turkey, 343
Turnbull, Colin, 163–64, 174, 176, 293–95
Turner, Victor, 42, 399
Tutu, Desmond, 324
Tylor, Edward B., 38, 77, 119–21, 130, 145, 285, 404
Tzeltal language, 99

U

Ubelaker, Douglas, 297
Uchendu, Victor, 333
Uchi (safety), 72
Uganda, 397
Ukraine, the, 29
Ultimate Resource, The (Simon), 376
Ultimogeniture, 194
Unilineal descent groups, 192–93
Unilineal-evolutionary models, 120–23, 130, 404
United Fruit Co., 325–26
United Nations, 289, 308
United Nations Educational, Scientific, and Cultural Organization (UN-ESCO), 402
United Nations High Commissioner for Refugees (UNHCR), 390
United States
  adolescence in, 68, 69
  archaeological protection in, 403–4
  Asian relations of, 349, 358
  assimilation policies of, 56
  colonialist expansion by, 345
  economic structure of, 262–63, 385–86
  energy consumption in, 375
  individualism in, 45, 74–75
  political organization in, 275
  population growth in, 373
  religion in, 279–80
  slavery in, 314
  social structure of, 50, 55, 149, 273, 274
  values in, 44, 49, 80
Universalistic religions, 249, 253
"Universal People," 58
Universals
  behavioral, 58, 64
  cultural, 58–59, 81–82, 148
  emotional, 113–14
  linguistic, 99–100, 106–8
  religious, 154

Upper class, 257, 272–73, 274
Upper Paleolithic period, 28–32
Urban anthropology, 336–37
Urbanization, 259, 336–37, 346, 373
Use rights, 191

V

Validity, in research, 136
Value judgments, 49, 404–6
Values, 38, 44. *See also* folkways; mores; norms
  aggression and, 207
  Confucian, 272, 278, 358
  culture-of-poverty, 336–37
  double standard for, 404–6
  of foragers, 178
  interpreting, 129
  Japanese corporate, 276
Van Gennep, Arnold, 151
Van Willigen, John, 406, 407
Variable, research, 14
Variation, human
  behavioral, 86
  linguistic, 110
  physical, 32, 34
  study of, 4, 5
Varnas (social divisions), 355
Vasquez, Mario, 397
Veil, wearing of, 354–55
Venezuela, 298
Venus fertility goddesses, 31
Verdery, Katherine, 384
Verifiability, in scientific method, 14
Vicos Project, 397
Video recording, 137
Vietminh, 348
Vietnam, 112, 348, 350–51, 385, 389
Vietnam War, 42, 349, 388, 389
Violence
  among foragers, 177–78
  among !Kung, 293
  ethnic, 56, 361–62, 387, 390
  human instinct for, 204
  origins of, 206–7
Virgin Mary, 42, 43
Virgin of Guadalupe, 42–43
Visual anthropology, 137
Vocabulary, 107–8, 110
Vodoun (voodoo), 319–20
Voorhies, Barbara, 195, 242, 244

W

Walesa, Lech, 43, 384
Wallace, Alfred, 22, 23, 34
Wallace, Anthony, 85

Wallerstein, Immanuel, 289–91
Warfare
  in agricultural states, 247–48
  among chiefdoms, 225, 228
  among foragers, 177–78
  causes of, 126, 206, 207
  global, 278–79
  in industrial states, 278–79
  internal vs. external, 152
  tribal, 196, 197, 199, 204–5
  in Venezuela, 298
Warren Commission, 33
Washoe (chimpanzee), 92
Watson, James, 246
Watson, Patty Jo, 8
Watson, Richard, 8
Wealth, pursuit of, 195–96, 243, 257–58
Wealth of Nations, The (Smith), 262
Weatherford, Jack, 306
Weber, Max, 151, 285
Weiner, Annette, 222
Wernicke's area, 96
Western Europe, 102, 274, 373
Western societies, 51–53, 74, 75, 120
Whaling industry, 300
What Was Socialism and What Comes
    Next (Verdery), 384
White, Douglas, 196
White, Leslie, 41, 77, 124–25, 127, 131,
    145, 146, 258
White Revolution, 363
White supremacy, 322
Whorf, Benjamin, 106–8, 115–16
Wikan, Unni, 79
Williams, Holly Ann, 389, 390
Wilson, E. O., 375
Wilson, Godfrey, 328
Windigo psychosis, 85
Witchcraft, 208–9
Wok bilong Yali movement, 303

Wolf, Arthur, 77
Wolf, Eric, 152, 177, 239, 257, 291, 292, 328
Wolfe, Alvin, 266, 380
Women, status of. *See also* gender rela-
    tions
  in Africa, 330–31
  in agricultural states, 244–45
  in China, 358–59
  in foraging societies, 174
  human rights and, 406–7
  industrialization and, 269–71
  in Islamic societies, 45, 48, 79, 353–55
  in South Asia, 357–58
  in tribal societies, 200, 228
Women's rights movement, 270
Work, technology and, 260
Working class, 273, 274, 275–76
World Bank, 289, 380
World Council of Indigenous Peoples,
    307–8
World Health Organization, 86
World-systems theory, 289–91, 308
Worldview, 44, 106, 129
  of chiefdoms, 229
  of foragers, 169–70
  Hindu, 356–57
  Navajo, 12, 13, 44
  religious, 154–55
World War I, 278–279, 302, 303
World War II, 279, 302, 303, 405
Worsley, Peter, 304
Wounded Knee, Battle of, 301, 302
Wovoka, prophet, 301

X

Xaniths (transsexuals), 79
Xerox Corp., 264

Y

Yali (New Guinea leader), 303
Yaliwan (Yangoru religious figure), 303
Yangoru Boiken people, 303–4
Yanomamö tribe
  cultural change in, 11, 297–98
  political organization in, 202
  reciprocity in, 190
  religion in, 208
  social structure of, 194, 195, 196
  subsistence patterns in, 186
  technology of, 189
  warfare in, 204–5, 207
Yellen, John, 162
Yeltsin, Boris, 383
Yerkes Regional Primate Research Center
    92
Yin and *yang,* 22
Yoruban society, 317, 330, 332–34

Z

Zaibatsu families, 263, 386
Zaire (Congo), 294, 314, 322
Zambia, 396
Zapata, Emiliano, 325
Zapatista movement, 332
Zero population growth (ZPG), 373, 374
Zionist Church, 322
Zionist movement, 344
Zombification, 320
Zuni tribe, 198